INN By
SPOTS Rich

&

A guide to where to go, stay, eat and enjoy in 32 of the region's choicest areas.

SPECIAL
PLACES

IN NEW ENGLAND

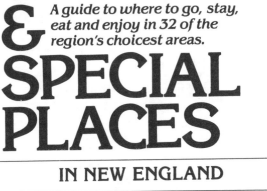

Wood Pond Press
West Hartford, Conn.

The authors have personally visited the places included in this book. They make their recommendations based upon their experiences and findings, and there is no solicitation or charge for inclusion.

Prices, hours and menu offerings at inns and restaurants change seasonally and with business conditions. Readers should call or write ahead to avoid disappointment. The prices and hours reported in this book were correct at presstime and are subject, of course, to change. They are offered as a relative guide to what to expect.

Rates quoted for inns are for peak periods; weekdays and off-season dates may be lower. They are for bed and breakfast, unless otherwise specified. MAP (Modified American Plan) includes breakfast and dinner; EP, European Plan, no meals.

The authors welcome readers' reactions and suggestions.

First Printing, April 1986.
Second Printing, March 1987.
Third Printing, May 1988.
Fourth Printing, April 1989.
Fifth Printing, May 1989.
Sixth Printing, May 1990.
Seventh Printing, March 1991.
Eighth Printing, June 1992.
Ninth Printing, May 1993.
Tenth Prining, April 1994.
Eleventh Printing, May 1995.

Cover Design by Bob Smith the Artsmith

Cover Photo: Porch at Mayflower Inn, Washington, Conn.

Copyright © 1995, 1992, 1989 and 1986 by Nancy and Richard Woodworth

Library of Congress Catalog No. 86-50203

ISBN No. 0-934260-77-X

Published in the United States of America.
Fourth Edition.

Contents

MAINE

MASSACHUSETTS

RHODE ISLAND

CONNECTICUT

Introduction

This is yet another inn book. But it's far more than that, too.

We enjoy reading all the others, but they rarely tell us what we *really* want to know, such as where to get a good meal and what there is to do. And the inns often are not grouped by location, so you don't get a feeling for what the area is like. We've found that out by talking with innkeepers, reading all the guidebooks and brochures, visiting tourist bureaus and Chambers of Commerce, and poring through the local newspapers.

That's what we now share with you. We start not with the inn but with the area (of course, the existence of inns or lack thereof helped determine the areas to be included). We sought out 32 extra-special areas, some of them New England's best-known and some not widely known at all.

Then we toured each area, visiting each inn, each restaurant and each attraction, as well as drawing on our experiences and memories of nearly 40 years of vacationing in and 25 years of living in New England. We *worked* these areas as roving journalists, always seeking out the best and most interesing. We also *lived* them – staying in, eating in, and experiencing as many places as time and budget would allow.

The result is this book, a comprehensive yet selective compendium of what we found to be the best and most interesting places to stay, eat and enjoy in these 32 special areas.

The book reflects our tastes. We want creature comforts like private bathrooms and comfortable reading areas in our rooms; we like to meet other inn guests, but we also value our privacy. We seek interesing and creative food and settings for our meals. We enjoy unusual, enlightening things to do and places to see. We expect to receive value for money and time spent.

While touring the past year to research this fourth edition of "Inn Spots," we were surprised again by how many innkeepers said we were among the few guidebook writers who ever visited their facility and did not simply expect them to fill out a form and forward it with a considerable fee.

We also were struck – as we have been while preparing our other books – by how times and places change. Many of the inns and restaurants that were "in" a decade or so ago have faded, their places taken by any number of newcomers not yet widely known. We're fortunate that our newspaper training and tight deadlines make this book as up-to-date as its 1995 publication date.

Yes, the schedule is hectic and we do keep busy on these, our working vacations that everyone thinks must be glamorous and nothing but fun. One of us says she never wants to inspect another inn bedroom (especially up on the third floor). The other doesn't care if he never eats another sundried tomato.

Nonetheless, it's rewarding to discover a little-known inn, to savor a great meal, to enjoy a choice musuem, to poke through an unusual store and to meet so many interesting people along the way.

That's what this book is all about. We hope that you will enjoy its findings as much as we did the finding.

Nancy and Richard Woodworth

About the Authors

Nancy Webster Woodworth began her dining experiences in her native Montreal and as a waitress in summer resorts across Canada during her McGill University years. She worked in London and hitchhiked through Europe on $3 a day before her marriage to Richard Woodworth, whom she met while skiing at Mont Tremblant. She started writing her "Roaming the Restaurants" column for the West Hartford (Conn.) News in 1972. That led to half of the book, *Daytripping & Dining in Southern New England,* written in collaboration with Betsy Wittemann in 1978. She since has co-authored *Weekending in New England, Getaways for Gourmets in the Northeast, The Restaurants of New England* and *Waterside Escapes in the Northeast* as well as a companion edition *of Inn Spots & Special Places/ Mid-Atlantic.* She and her husband have two grown sons and live in West Hartford.

Richard Woodworth has been an inveterate traveler since his youth in suburban Syracuse, N.Y., where his birthday outings often involved train trips with friends for the day to Utica or Rochester. After graduation from Middlebury College, he was a reporter for newspapers in Syracuse, Jamestown, Geneva and Rochester before moving to Connecticut to become editor of the West Hartford News and eventually executive editor of Imprint Newspapers. With wife Nancy Webster and their sons, he has traveled to the four corners of this country, Canada and portions of Europe, writing their findings for newspapers and magazines. He has co-authored four editions of *Getaways for Gourmets in the Northeast* as well as two editions of *Inn Spots & Special Places/Mid-Atlantic* and *The Restaurants of New England.* Between travels and duties as publisher of Wood Pond Press, he tries to find time to weed the garden in summer and ski in the winter.

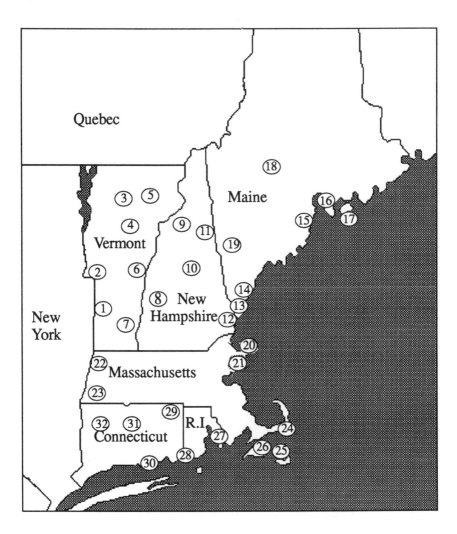

1. Dorset	12. Portsmouth	23. Lenox
2. Vermont Lakes	13. The Yorks	24. Chatham
3. Stowe	14. Kennebunkport	25. Nantucket
4. Waitsfield/Warren	15. Camden	26. Edgartown
5. Craftsbury	16. Blue Hill	27. Newport
6. Woodstock/Quechee	17. Mt. Desert Island	28. Watch Hill/Stonington
7. Newfane	18. Greenville/Moosehead	29. Northeast Connecticut
8. Sunapee Region	19. Oxford Hills & Lakes	30. Essex/Old Lyme
9. Franconia/Sugar Hill	20. Rockport	31. Farmington Valley
10. Squam Lakes	21. Marblehead	32. Litchfield and Lake
11. Jackson	22. Williamstown	Waramaug

Historical marker tells about Dorset outside Dovetail Inn.

Dorset, Vt.
The Town that Marble Built

There is marble almost everywhere in Dorset, a town that marble helped build and upon which it has long prospered.

You see it on the sidewalks all around the picturesque green, on the porch at the historic Dorset Inn and on the terrace at the newer Barrows House, on the side of the turreted United Church of Christ and on the pillars of the Marble West Inn. The sight of an entire mansion built of marble stuns passersby along Dorset West Road.

It seems as if all Dorset has been paved with marble – and with good intentions. Here is what residents and writers alike have called the perfect village. Merchant Jay Hathaway phrased it well in a Dorset Historical Society lecture: What could be better than running "a small country store nestled in the mountains of Vermont in a town that is as close to perfect as Dorset?"

A village of perhaps 1,800 (about two-thirds of its population during the height of its marble-producing days a century ago), it's a mix of charm and culture in perfect proportion.

Dorset is unspoiled, from its rustic Dorset Playhouse (the oldest summer playhouse in the state) to its handsomely restored inn (the oldest in the state) to its Dorset Field Club (the oldest nine-hole golf course in the state) to its lovely white, green-shuttered homes (many among the oldest in the state) to its two general stores, both of them curiously different relics of 19th-century life. Here is a peaceful place in which to cherish the past.

1

Barely six miles away is Manchester, one of the more sophisticated tourist destinations around. Many of its visitors, who come to shop until they drop, don't know about nor are they particularly interested in Dorset. But people in Dorset can take advantage of all Manchester's urbane attractions as desired.

So the Dorset visitor has the best of both worlds – a tranquil respite amid a myriad of activities and attractions. What could be more copacetic?

Inn Spots

Cornucopia of Dorset, Route 30, Dorset 05251. (802) 867-5751.

One of the more inviting and elegant B&Bs anywhere is offered by Bill and Linda Ley, who left Ipswich, Mass., to realize a goal of running a country inn. That they ultimately found Cornucopia of Dorset was as pleasing to them as it was to the guests who have been entertained there since. Their B&B lives up to its name, offering an abundance of warmth, comfort and personality.

Cornucopia has only four guest rooms and a cottage suite, but what accommodations they are! All air-conditioned and with large, modern baths, they contain poster or canopy beds ranging in size from king to twins, afluff with down comforters or colorful quilts and pillows. The front Scallop Room harbors a corner fireplace. Upholstered chairs flank three-way reading lamps. We found the Mother Myrick Room especially comfortable with a kingsize bed against a wall of shelves containing books and family photos, and a full bath with a double vanity. The rear cottage with a cathedral-ceilinged living room, fireplace, eat-in kitchen and a queensize loft bedroom comes with a stereo and a private sun deck.

The common rooms are more than an adjunct; they are the focal point of Cornucopia. Off a small, cozy library is an inviting living room with overstuffed sofas; both have fireplaces. Beyond is an enormous dining room opening into a sun room, a contemporary area that's cool and shaded in the summer, warm and bright in winter. It is here that we like to gravitate to study the leather scrapbooks of restaurant menus and area attractions, browse through a cornucopia of magazines or pore through a hardbound book called "At the Movies," listing all the video tapes the Leys offer on their VCR. But there's little inclination to read or watch, given the innkeepers' hospitality and propensity for lively conversation.

Outside are a marble patio and a covered porch. Enough bird feeders are attached to the sun room windows to accommodate a flock.

Breakfast is served at the formal table in the airy dining room. Our latest repast, detailed on a personalized card left in the room the night before, started with fresh orange juice and a colorful dish of honeydew melon, nicely pre-sliced into bite-size chunks and topped with fresh raspberries, strawberries, kiwi and banana slices, and French vanilla yogurt. The pièce de résistance was a baked croissant à l'orange with crème fraîche. Colombian coffee with a hint of cinnamon and Twining's English tea accompa-

Innkeepers Bill and Linda Ley welcome guests to Cornucopia of Dorset.

nied. The baked raspberry pancake served on another occasion was so good that we asked Linda for the recipe. Other specialties include bread pudding with warm berry sauce, quiche lorraine, baked ham and egg cup with Vermont cheddar cheese and petite croissants, and baked cinnamon french toast with sausage patties.

The goodies don't end there. Complimentary champagne is served at check-in (wines and champagnes are available for purchase as well), and help-yourself coffee, tea and hot chocolate are at hand 24 hours a day. Upon returning from dinner, you'll find your bedroom lights turned off, an oil lamp flickering, and candy – perhaps a slice of buttercrunch from our favorite Mother Myrick's confectionery store in Manchester – on the pillow of a bed turned down ever so artistically. In the room are stationery and stamped envelopes and postcards upon which we'd spread the word, "great place – you ought to be here."

Doubles, $110 to $135; cottage, $195. No smoking.

Marble West Inn, Dorset West Road, Dorset 05251. (802) 867-4155 or (800) 453-7629.

The thank-you note penned to June and Wayne Erla and displayed in the Marble West scrapbook says it well: "Every detail that could enhance your guests' comfort has been thought of: beautifully appointed rooms, superb cuisine, a comfortable sitting room, beautiful grounds,...wonderful hospitality." High praise, coming from a fellow innkeeper from Marblehead, Mass. And accurate. The Erlas took early retirement from their IBM positions in Burlington and started enhancing the historic Holley-West house two miles southwest of Dorset in 1993. The stately Greek Revival, built in the 1840s by the owner of a marble quarry, is graced with seven marble columns in front. A marble sign has identified its status as an inn since 1985.

The Erlas have redecorated and furnished with great style and taste. They retained the extraordinary stenciling (done by Honey West, one of the quarry owner's daughters) in the front entry and upstairs hall, and several other unusual decorative and architectural features, such as the low stairway banisters installed for a woman in the West family who was less than five feet tall. Swagged draperies, fine oriental rugs, a grand piano and furniture upholstered in Waverly fabrics and chintz welcome guests

3

into the main parlor. It's open to the dining room, where ten Queen Anne chairs flank a solid mahogany table. The adjacent library has a marble fireplace, comfortable furniture, a nifty window seat and a coffee table covered with the latest magazines vying for attention with shelves of century-old books.

The main floor also contains the West Suite with a working fireplace, a queensize bed topped with a Ralph Lauren comforter, a sitting room with sofa and wing chairs, and a small sun room just big enough for two. Off the library at the other end of the house is the Birch Suite with a kingsize bed, sitting area, a shower tucked into the small, ingenious bathroom space and a private patio. Upstairs off two stairways are six other attractive guest rooms with private baths. Each is amply furnished with oriental rugs and Laura Ashley or Ralph Lauren fabrics, and chocolates await on the night stands. We're partial to the rear-corner Dorset Room with a canopied queensize bed, lots of floral chintzes and windows on three sides. The windows were opened wide on a warm autumn evening for cross-ventilation, and we didn't hear a sound all night.

Breakfast was by candlelight in a serene dining room with gray walls, floral swags, colorful oriental rugs on a polished dark wood floor and a ficus tree in one corner. Wayne does the cooking. Our meal started with orange juice, a half grapefruit enhanced by just enough maple syrup and coconut to sweeten the tartness, and June's piping-hot morning glory muffins. The main course was walnut pancakes, half a dozen "medallions" garnished with cranberries and served with delicious mild sausages that Wayne imports by the case from Pennsylvania.

June played the piano during breakfast, as she does in the evening before dinner. Four-course dinners for $20 a person are available for house guests by reservation, nightly in summer and weekends the rest of the year. Guests bring their own wine.

Fed by a passing creek, a two-tiered pond out back provides skating in the winter and a home for 27-inch rainbow trout in summer. Around the grounds, Adirondack chairs face the pond as well as a croquet lawn.

Doubles, $90 to $135. No smoking.

Birch Hill Inn, West Road, Box 346, Manchester 05254. (802) 362-2761 or (800) 372-2761.

Just across the Dorset town line and closely allied with it in spirit if not address, this imposing hilltop house was built in the late 1700s and has been in innkeeper Pat Lee's family since 1917. It housed her grandfather and her father; she and husband Jim live here and capitalize on the home-like atmosphere, serving breakfast and often dinner and making their guests – many of them long-term and repeat – feel very much at home. The secluded location is a major asset, and all the rooms yield great views.

Guests dine family-style at two highly polished tables in the gracious dining room. They gather for games, reading or conversation in a cheery and comfortably furnished, 40-by-20-foot living room paneled in pine, or in a sun room pretty in wicker, pinks and blues. Outside is a marble terrace where Jim may barbecue cornish game hens or beefalo steak (the beefalo, providing meat that is low-fat and low-cholesterol, are raised on the Lees' farm next door). Large windows frame the grounds, where stone fences and cross-country trails abound. In back is a kidney-shaped swimming pool.

All five large guest rooms on the second floor have private baths, and each is decorated in country style with family furnishings. Every room contains a portable radio with a selection of interesting tapes. One has twin brass beds, another a queen bed with rose and green stenciling done by Pat, and one has a fireplace. Also available is a small cottage with bedroom, sitting room, bath and refrigerator. Art by local painters (many by the late Luigi Lucioni, a friend of Pat's late father) is everywhere.

At night, meals are the kind she'd serve at a dinner party (she was preparing a large

Expansive lawn and colorful gardens surround Birch Hill Inn.

salmon caught by a guest in British Columbia the night we first visited). Specialties are veal marsala, butterflied leg of lamb and chicken teriyaki. A soup (leek, tomato or zucchini-tarragon are some favorites) usually precedes. Green salad and vegetables from the couple's large garden accompany, as do Pat's homemade chutneys, mustard sauce and herb jellies. Lemon soufflé, rhubarb crunch, blueberry surprise or the Silver Palate's decadent chocolate cake might end the meal. The Lees have a beer and wine license, and serve hors d'oeuvre as guests gather for BYOB cocktails prior to dinner at 7:30. Dinners are offered on weekends for $18.

For breakfast, Pat serves fresh fruit, her popular homemade granola (in winter, hot cereal), and a choice of eggs or pancakes.

Doubles, $105 to $130; cottage, $115. Closed early April to late May and November to Christmas.

Barrows House, Main Street, Dorset 05251. (802) 867-4455 or (800) 639-1620.

We don't know what is more appealing about the Barrows House: the comfortable rooms and cottages amid eleven acres of park-like grounds with a swimming pool, two tennis courts and an intricate gazebo, or the meals in the smashing greenhouse addition that extends the dining room to the outdoors.

Black wicker rockers are at the ready behind the columns that front the 200-year-old main house, which has a fireplaced living room, the expansive dining room (see Dining Spots), six upstairs guest rooms and, beside a canopied outdoor patio, a charming tavern notable for its trompe-l'oeil walls of books so real you feel you're in a library.

The most popular rooms are 22 scattered in eight outbuildings converted into sophisticated lodging. All have private baths. Five suites have fireplaces and sitting rooms. Wallpapers, draperies and quilts are coordinated, and all are filled with nice touches like ruffled pillows and patchcraft hangings.

Innkeepers Jim and Linda McGinnis have enhanced the inn's services since taking over in 1993. They also sponsor the annual "Littlest Music Festival," a series of four free Sunday afternoon concerts on the inn's lawn each June. Attendees contribute food items and cash for the Manchester Area Food Cupboard.

Doubles, $140 to $190 B&B, $180 to $230, MAP.

5

The Dorset Inn, Route 30, Dorset 05251. (802) 867-5500.

Vermont's oldest continuously operated country inn, with a history dating back to 1796, was nicely renovated in 1984 and 1985 by what owners Sissy Hicks and Gretchen Schmidt bill as "the inspired revival of an historic site."

Overnight guests are greeted by a stunning collection of blue glass displayed in lighted cases at the top of the stairway on the second floor. All 35 rooms on the two upper floors have been redone with wall-to-wall carpeting, modern baths with wood washstands, print wallpapers and antique furnishings. Two of the nicest are the third-floor front corner rooms, one with twin sleigh beds, two rockers, Audubon prints and floral wallpaper, and the other with a canopy bed, marble table and wallpaper of exotic animals and birds.

Downstairs, stuffed bears in little chairs welcome guests in the reception area. The main sitting room is appealing with comfortable furniture around a fireplace, a collection of blue and white china on the mantel, scrubbed wide-plank floors and a small television set.

Beyond is a cheery breakfast room with Vermont-woven mats atop wood tables and green floral curtains against small-paned windows that extend to the floor. The inn serves a hearty breakfast (sourdough or fruit pancakes, all kinds of eggs, bacon, ham and sausage). Out back are an attractive, country-style dining room (see Dining Spots) and a pleasant tap room with a big oak bar.

Doubles, $130 to $175, MAP.

The Little Lodge at Dorset, Main Street, Box 673, Dorset 05251. (802) 867-4040.

"We have more places to sit per guest than any inn we've seen," says Allan Norris of the appealing, five-room B&B he and wife Nancy have run with TLC since 1981.

Guests in those five rooms have access to a formal dining room with oriental rugs, shining silver and bone china for breakfast service, a living room with wood stove and large hooked rug, a large and luxurious den with barnwood walls, blue leather sofa, fireplace and shelves of books and games, an attached five-sided gazebo that has black garden furniture cushioned with yellow and green pads, a wet bar with refrigerator and a hallway with separate entrance for stashing skis and boots. Outside are a rope hammock and a garden sitting area overlooking a trout pond, the verdant fairways of the Dorset Field Club and the mountainside beyond.

Given all these inviting public areas, one might expect the Norrises, transplanted Baltimoreans, to have skimped on their upstairs guest rooms. Not so. All have private baths and are furnished with twin beds usually made up as kings. They contain paintings by Nancy's great-uncle (one of the Boston School of Impressionists) and quilts made by Nancy or bedspreads crocheted by Allan's sister. They exude an air of lived-in comfort.

Breakfast is continental-plus, Nancy supplementing juices and cereals with her home-made strawberry-pecan, orange-coriander and pear-walnut breads or muffins. She and her guests are fond of exchanging recipes. Tea and coffee are available anytime, and Vermont cheese and crackers are put out in the late afternoon.

The grounds yield trails for cross-country skiing and hiking in the rear, a stocked trout pond (no fishing, but you can feed them) dug by the home's former owner who runs the Orvis sporting goods company in Manchester and a view of an oriental garden with colorful red bridges in front of the house next door. Enjoying all this with the guests is Columbine, an unusually friendly Doberman pinscher who nuzzles up to one and all. "More people write in our guest book about Columbine than anything else," Allan reports.

Doubles, $80 to $90.

Stone wall opens onto path to Little Lodge at Dorset.

Dovetail Inn, Main Street, Box 976, Dorset 05251. (802) 867-5747.

Nicely located facing the green in the heart of town just across from the Dorset Inn (in fact it was once an inn annex and housed chauffeurs and staff in the posh days) is the two-building Dovetail. Jim and Jean Kingston, he a marine engineer and now a local property manager, moved from Connecticut in 1984 and, as they say, picked a thriving area.

They have refurbished the eleven guest rooms, all with private baths, and added a sitting room with a TV in one structure. The other houses their quarters, a cheery "keeping room" for guests' use and a small gift shop in which are sold model wooden trucks that Jim makes. Rooms vary in size and have double, king, queen or twin beds. Most have a couple of easy chairs (ours had a sofa) and pretty new wallpaper and curtains. The Hearthside room in back offers a fireplace and kitchenette-wet bar, a queen bed, sofa, a private deck and easy access to the gardens. On the second floor landing is a nook with a window seat and many books for borrowing.

In the back yard, the Kingstons tired of the upkeep of the 20-by-40-foot swimming pool they inherited from the Dorset Inn and in 1995 filled it in with gardens "so we finally have a back yard," Jean said. The Kingstons have a beer and wine license and serve outside or in the keeping room. They also offer tea and cookies in the afternoon.

Breakfast consists of juice, muffins (the orange ones were delicious) and coffee or tea. You may have it brought to your room in a basket, if you wish.

Why the name Dovetail? "I like quality building and furniture," says Jim, "and a cutesy name didn't fit Dorset."

Doubles, $75 to $100.

Inn at West View Farm, Main Street, Dorset 05251. (802) 867-5715.

The accommodations have been upgraded, the bar and waiting area expanded, and a comfy parlor and sun porch added since Helmut and Dorothy Stein took over the Village Auberge. The dining room, made famous by former chef-owner Alex Koks, remains familiar to guests who predate the Steins' arrival, and the food is said to have improved lately after a few years of ups and downs.

The inn's addition has created a new entry and reception area and a welcoming

7

common area that was lacking earlier. No longer must arriving overnight guests share a small parlor with waiting dining patrons. Everyone can enjoy the expanded lounge, a large sitting room with a fireplace and two sofas, and an exceptionally nice enclosed porch full of white wicker sofas and chairs.

The four original guest rooms upstairs have been redecorated, and six more tidy rooms with full baths have been added. All but one have queensize beds. They are furnished with country antiques.

Breakfast is served to inn guests in the cheery, plant-filled bay-window end of the dining room. Eggs any style, pancakes, croissants and pain perdu with various fillings are among the offerings.

Doubles, $92 to $106. Closed early November and April.

Dining Spots

Chantecleer, Route 7A, East Dorset. (802) 362-1616.

As far as area residents are concerned, there's a surprising unanimity as to the best restaurant around: the Chantecleer in East Dorset, just north of the Manchester line. The food is consistent, the service professional and the atmosphere rustically elegant.

Swiss chef Michel Baumann acquired the contemporary-style restaurant fashioned from a dairy barn in 1981. His menu features Swiss and French provincial cuisine.

Our party of four sampled a number of the offerings, starting with a classic baked onion soup, penne with smoked salmon, potato pancakes with sautéed crabmeat and a heavenly lime butter sauce, and bundnerfleisch fanned out in little coronets with pearl onions, cornichons and melba rounds.

Appetizers are priced from $6.50 to $7.95, while entrées range from $17.95 to $25. We savored the rack of lamb, veal sweetbreads morel, sautéed quail stuffed with mushroom duxelle and the night's special of boneless pheasant from a local farm, served with smoked bacon and grapes, among other things. Fabulous roesti potatoes upstaged the other accompaniments, puree of winter squash, snow peas and strands of celery.

Bananas foster, grand marnier layer cake, crème brûlée and trifle were worthy endings for a rich, expensive meal. A number of Swiss wines are included on the reasonably priced wine list, and Swiss yodeling music may be heard on tape as background music.

In 1994, Chantecleer opened a neat little offshoot, **The Little Rooster Cafe,** an innovative (albeit pricey) place for breakfast and lunch in Manchester Center.

Dinner by reservation, nightly except Tuesday from 6.

Barrows House, Main Street, Dorset. (802) 867-4455.

Innkeepers Jim and Linda McGinnis preside over a dining operation that's long been known for good food in pleasant surroundings. The focal point for many is the sunken greenhouse on the side, where you almost feel you're dining under the stars. The main dining room has been made darker and more intimate with the introduction of dimmer switches, Pierre Deux wallpaper, swag curtains and white woven mats over rust and white patterned cloths. The cozy tavern, with its trompe-l'oeil walls of books, also is a pleasant spot for dining.

Chef Gary Walker, who had been sous chef here, assumed responsibility for the kitchen in 1994 and oversees the preparation of contemporary New England cuisine. The main menu is priced from $14.95 for grilled pork chops with sundried cranberry and orange sauce to $18.75 for grilled sirloin with batter-fried leeks and a four-peppercorn sauce. Or you can order light entrées ($9.75 to $11.95) like Maine crab cakes or sautéed lamb medallions.

Chantecleer restaurant occupies interior of old dairy barn.

At one visit, we started with smoked tuna with caper and red onion crème fraîche and a tartlet of smoked scallops and mussels with scallions and red peppers, both excellent. A small loaf of bread and a garden salad with a honey-mustard dressing came next. Main courses were pan-roasted chicken breast with roasted peppers, shiitake mushrooms and artichoke hearts and calves liver with Canadian bacon and scallions. They were accompanied by a platter of vegetables served family style, on this night spaghetti squash creole, lemon-scented broccoli, carrot puree with maple syrup, and risotto with fennel and red peppers. Vegetables have always been a Barrows House strong point; one summer dinner brought carrots glazed with raisins and ginger, asparagus with hollandaise, squash and spinach with dill, and warm potato salad.

A huckleberry tart and cappuccino ice cream appealed from the dessert list.

Dinner nightly, 6 to 9.

The Dorset Inn, Church and Main Streets, Dorset. (802) 867-5500.

Interesting, creative food has been emanating from the kitchen of this venerable inn since Sissy Hicks took over the chef's chores as co-innkeeper with Gretchen Schmidt in 1984.

The main dining room has been redecorated in hunter green with white trim and wainscoting. A focal point is a spotlit glass cabinet displaying cups and horse figurines along one wall. Out back is a tavern with dining tables and a large oak bar.

A practitioner of the new American cuisine, Sissy Hicks changes her menu seasonally. She also has changed the previously separate tavern and dining room menus into one that serves both areas. Now you'll find a classic burger ($7.50) on the same menu as loin lamb chops with roasted shallots and garlic confit ($17.50). Not to mention the spicy chicken wings and crisp potato skins alongside the "original warm chicken tenderloin salad." Five vegetarian items – including grilled wild mushroom sandwich, baked eggplant crêpes and garbanzo croquettes – also are offered.

Among appetizers, we found the crabmeat mousse with a cucumber-mustard dill sauce and a few slices of melba toast enough for two to share. Crusty French bread with sweet butter and green salads with excellent stilton or basil-vinaigrette dressings accompanied. Having been advised that the calves liver was the best anywhere, we had to try it. Served rare as requested with crisp bacon and slightly underdone slices of onion, it was superb. The fresh trout, deboned but served with its skin still on, was laden with sautéed leeks and mushrooms. These came with an assemblage of vegetables, including red-skin potatoes with a dollop of sour cream, and crisp cauliflower, broccoli and yellow squash. A Wente chardonnay, golden and oaky, was a good choice from the reasonably priced wine list.

Pies, bread pudding with whiskey sauce and chocolate terrine with raspberry sauce are on the dessert menu. We chose a kiwi sorbet, wonderfully deep flavored and with the consistency of ice cream, accompanied by a big sugar cookie. One of the favorite fall desserts is Sissy's cider sorbet with spiced wine sauce.

Lunch daily in summer and fall, 11:30 to 2; dinner nightly, 5:30 to 9.

The Inn at West View Farm, Route 30, Dorset. (802) 867-5715.

Former chef-owner Alex Koks was a tough act to follow, and a procession of chefs has had varying degrees of success since. The handsome Auberge dining room with its striking built-in china cabinets and a large bay window at the far end is about the only vestige of its former life as the Village Auberge. An addition houses Clancy's Tavern, an attractive room with dark green wainscoting and beams, where the polished wooden tables are topped with English place mats.

A piping-hot cheese fritter is delivered to each diner with the menu. Among starters are a stellar black bean and ginger soup with curried crème fraîche, oysters rockefeller and venison pâté with brandy and maple-mustard sauce. Excellent sourdough bread and house salads with zesty roquefort or vinaigrette dressings precede the main course. We savored the veal medallions with wild mushrooms and the pan-roasted breast of duck with rhubarb, ginger and risotto cake, among eight choices priced from $17.25 to $23.95 (for grilled filet mignon spiced with five peppercorns and served with mushroom caps and chestnuts). Desserts included an apple spice cake and a refreshing assortment of ice creams and sorbets.

The tavern menu adds items like grilled bratwurst, crab cakes and garlic shrimp with red pepper linguini, $9.75 to $12.95.

Dinner, Tuesday-Sunday 6 to 9. Also closed Tuesday in winter and early November and April.

The Garden Cafe, Southern Vermont Art Center, Manchester. (802) 362-4220.

This nifty cafe, halfway up a mountain, has been run for years by people associated with noted area restaurateur Alex Koks, formerly of the Village Auberge in Dorset and now owner of the Four Chimneys in Bennington. A dining room and outdoor terrace at the back of the Art Center is the setting, with sculptures all around in the sloping gardens, and a view of distant mountains through the birch trees. On a nice day it could not be a more idyllic site for lunch or Sunday brunch.

Silk flowers in little baskets and Vermont woven mats decorate the tables; chairs are the ice-cream-parlor type with flowered seats. Everyone gets a small dish of celery and carrots with a savory dip.

The menu ($6.25 to $11.50) is identical to that at the Four Chimneys, since sous chef Paul Dolan preps at the inn and cooks at the cafe. Soups, sandwiches and salads, with a few daily specials, are the fare, but everything has special touches. The tomato-orange soup, served in a glass bowl with a slice of orange and a dollop of whipped cream on top, was wonderful, delicate yet tangy. Almost everyone we saw was ordering the chicken pot pie with croissant crust, but we tried a sandwich of chicken salad with snow peas and a pasta salad with parmesan cheese and mushrooms, both excellent. Homey desserts include fresh fruit tarts and apple crisp with vanilla ice cream.

Lunch, Tuesday-Sunday 11:30 to 3. Open June to mid-October. No credit cards.

10

Diversions

Dorset Playhouse, Cheney Road, 867-5777. Tucked away in the trees just off Church Street, the rustic, all-wood barn with the red and white awning on the side was the first summer theater in Vermont. For twenty years it has been home to the Dorset Theater Festival, a non-profit professional theater company committed to the revival of plays from the past and the development of new plays and playwrights. Its rediscovery of Cole Porter's 1938 musical "You Never Know" went on national tour; other new plays have gone on to New York and Washington. Performances are nightly except Monday, June-September.

Merck Forest & Farmland Center, 394-7836. These days it's rare to find so large and unspoiled an area so available for public use as this 2,820-acre preserve northwest of Dorset off Route 315 in Rupert. Twenty-six miles of roads and trails are accessible for hiking in the forests, meadows and mountains. Established by George Merck of chemical-company fame, it is a non-profit outdoor education center open to the public year-round. Scholars study the organic garden, the maple sugaring and forest management. Hikers, campers and cross-country skiers enjoy the trails to Birch and Beebe ponds and the vista of the Adirondacks from the Viewpoint. The forest is a New England treasure.

Marble. It's everywhere, and hard to miss around Dorset. Take a gander at the large marble mansion on Dorset West Road, set back in the trees south of Marble West Inn. Although none of the six quarries that once made Dorset the most extensive quarrying center in Vermont still operates, you can swim in an abandoned marble quarry on the east side of Route 30 opposite the Mountain Weavers.

Local Lore. During Vermont's Bicentennial, the **Dorset Historical Society** moved to a new house donated as its headquarters, open Saturday mornings and by appointment. Take a recorded village walking tour, learn about the local marble and cheese-making industries or trace the genealogy of a Vermont ancestor here. Another local gem is the **Dorset Village Public Library** with its McIntyre Art Gallery, located in the restored Gray's Tavern building at Church and Main Streets, open daily except Sunday.

General Stores. Peltier's General Store has been the center of Dorset life since 1816, the more so since it was acquired in 1976 by Jay Hathaway and his wife Terri, who have augmented its everyday goods with exotica like balsamic vinegars, cheddar cheese from Shelburne Farms, aromatic coffee beans and fine wines. Just back from New York with an array of new items, Jay said his store "is ever-changing because we don't want to be routine." Peltier's celebrated its 175th anniversary during Vermont's Bicentennial. It abounds with every need from champagne to regional travel guides to newspapers.

Equally historic but thoroughly unchanging is the **H.M. Williams Department Store,** two attached barns identified by a small sign at the south edge of town and an incredible jumble of merchandise placed helter-skelter (foodstuffs amidst the hardware, boxes of ladies' shoes identified with a cardboard sign: "With this quality and these prices, let the big boys compete"). Prices are marked by crayon and the cash register is a pouch worn around his waist by proprietor Dennis Brownlee. While we waited for 50 pounds of sunflower bird seed for a bargain $13.10, the woman ahead of us bought 50 pounds of rabbit pellets and was told where she could find a bale of hay.

A few other Dorset stores like **Ten Ladies Dancing,** an upscale crafts shop, and **Stonewalls Antiques** and **Green Gate Antiques** are of interest, and plans were in the works for a high-style antiques co-op on the green. South of town is the **J.K. Adams Co.** factory store, which stocks a large assortment of woodware and housewares made from native hardwoods. Butcher blocks, knife racks, bowls, cutlery and homespun tablecloths are for sale at substantial savings.

More Shopping. Since adjacent Manchester offers such fine shopping opportunities, we suggest a few favorites. Silk-screened greeting cards from the **Crockett Collection** are available at discount prices at the showroom on Route 7 north of Manchester; other cards and notes are stocked as well, and you can watch the cards being made. Fishermen gravitate to the **Orvis Retail Store** in Manchester Center, where fishing rods are produced (and can be tried out at the adjacent trout pond). **Northshire Bookstore** is one of the best of its genre. **The Jelly Mill,** a three-story barn, is crammed with gifts, cards, gourmet foods, kitchenware and much more; the **Buttery Restaurant** on the second floor serves lunch and snacks. **Anne Klein, Polo-Ralph Lauren, Brooks Brothers, Coach, Cole-Haan** and **Benetton** are among the growing number of fashionable outlet stores.

Southern Vermont Art Center, West Road, Manchester, 362-1405. High up a mountainside along the back road to Dorset is this special place not to be missed. The oldest cultural institution in Vermont, it was started in 1929 when five local artists banded together to display their works at the Dorset Town Hall. Inside the 28-room Georgian Colonial mansion are changing exhibits staged year-round, plus the Garden Cafe for lunch. Plays and concerts by such groups as the U.S. Military Academy Band, the New England Brass Consort and the Southern Vermont Chamber Orchestra are always well attended. The Manchester Garden Club restored and maintains the Boswell Botany Trail, a three-quarter-mile walk past hundreds of wildflowers and 67 varieties of Vermont ferns, all identified by club members. An hour's hike through the woods is another attraction, and the sculpture garden featuring a 250-year-old sugar maple is bordered by amazing vistas.

Back Roads. They're all around, but a few are special. Dorset West Road and adjacent West Road in Manchester take you past some interesting and impressive country homes. Dorset Hollow Road makes "an absolutely gorgeous circle that takes about ten minutes," in the words of innkeeper Bill Ley of Cornucopia. The Danby Mountain Road winds through secluded forests and, if you keep bearing right at every intersection, you eventually come to a dead-end with a spectacular wide-open view across the hillsides toward mountain peaks 50 miles away. The sight at fall foliage's height actually produced a few "wows" out of us and lived up to Dovetail innkeeper Jim Kingston's promise of one of the best foliage trips in Vermont.

Extra-Special

Mother Myrick's Confectionery & Ice Cream Parlor, Route 7A, Manchester Center. (802) 362-1560.

We can't ever seem to get through this area without stopping at Mother Myrick's, the ultimate ice-cream parlor and confectionery shop, but much, much more. One of the things that lures us is the fudge sauce – so good that a friend to whom we give it hides her jar in a cupboard and eats it with a spoon. Here you can buy the most extraordinary homemade chocolates, get a croissant and cappuccino in the morning, tea and a slice of Vermont maple cheesecake in the afternoon, or a piece of grand marnier truffle cake and espresso at night. Ice-cream sodas, milkshakes, floats, sundaes and pastries are served in a fantastic art-deco setting with etched-glass panels, bentwood cases, light columns and the like done by gifted Vermont craftsmen. Mother Myrick's also carries, appropriately, a line of greeting cards about diets. Open daily from 10 to 6, weekends and summer to 9 or later.

Adirondack chairs are ready for lounging in front of placid waters of Lake Bomoseen.

Vermont Lakes Region
The Way It Used to Be

Vermont isn't known particularly for its lakes, other than, perhaps, Lake Champlain. But there was a time when a kosher resort on Lake St. Catherine was fondly likened to those in the Catskills and large hotels along Lake Bomoseen near the New York state line west of Rutland received guests by the trainload.

"Bomoseen used to be surrounded by old hotels, dance halls and casinos," recalls Cindy Baird, a transplanted Long Islander who now runs one of the B&Bs emerging across the area. "It was almost the Las Vegas of the East."

The hotels disappeared with the trains after World War II, and the lakes and their surrounding towns languished in a time warp. Fair Haven, Poultney, Castleton and Middletown Springs harbor few of the embellishments of tourism that transformed nearby areas like Manchester, Woodstock and Killington.

Now the area's tourism cycle is starting over, and half a dozen inns and B&Bs have sprouted since 1985. Despite the Vermont Marble Exhibit's claim to being one of the state's premier tourist attractions since 1933, tourism is still in its infancy here. Other than inns, you'll find few restaurants, shops or points of interest (the first McDonald's opened in the area only in 1988). "What we like is that this is rural Vermont the way it used to be," says Priscilla Lane, who moved here to open Priscilla's Victorian Inn.

Social life centers around the general stores, the Sunday evening band concerts, the weekly farmers' markets. Green Mountain and Castleton State colleges provide some cultural activity. There are historic sites in East Poultney and Castleton, mineral waters in Middletown Springs (much of the town is listed on the National Register), and a hilltop battlefield in Hubbardtown, where Ethan Allen and the Green Mountain Boys fought the only Revolutionary War battle in Vermont.

Lake Bomoseen, Vermont's largest, and Lake St. Catherine offer two state parks, good fishing and boating among water diversions. Ice fishing, ice sailing and cross-country skiing prevail in winter.

Except for the new Route 4 expressway that seems out of place as it cuts through the area, the roads are rural and undulating. You'll be struck by all the cows – and goats and sheep – grazing on the hillsides, and by all the domed hillocks and mountains that distinguish the area's landscape.

But there are stirrings in these rural hinterlands. "We came up here in 1986 to make this a destination area," Bea Taube of the Vermont Marble Inn says assuredly. "And we will."

Inn Spots

Vermont Marble Inn, 12 West Park Place, Fair Haven 05743. (802) 265-8383 or (800) 535-2814.

They were strictly novices when they bought the mansion in 1986, but they have thrown themselves into it with such abandon, you'd think they'd been innkeepers all their lives. Some guests even call Bea Taube and Shirley Stein "aunt" and Richard Taube "uncle" by the time they leave. "They come as guests and leave as friends," Bea says. "And they return as family."

Such is the spell cast by the ebullient innkeepers and their Italianate Victorian mansion, built in 1867 of Vermont golden marble. It has appealed to those seeking culinary treats and Victoriana since it was restored with great TLC and money. Today, some people come simply to enjoy a bottle of Dom Perignon in the museum-like, formal drawing room with its incredible molding, crystal chandeliers, and soft rose walls (a slightly less formal library on the other side of the hall has a TV set, games and magazines). Others come for cocktails and dinner (see Dining Spots). Those in the know partake of it all – afternoon tea, dinner, overnight lodging, an elaborate breakfast and Victoriana all around.

Each of the innkeepers carries out his or her tasks with enthusiasm. Very visible as a team (at dinner they occupy a front table in the dining room, where they are part of the comings and goings), they welcome arriving guests with sherry. They serve an elaborate afternoon tea with cakes, pastries and cookies, crudités or crackers and cheese at cocktail hour, and a full breakfast by candlelight. We enjoyed fresh orange juice, currant and almond muffins, baked apple slices and feathery pancakes with premium maple syrup. You might find at your visit peaches and cream french toast, a fritatta incorporating bacon, onion, tomato and cheese or a croissant stuffed with scrambled eggs and smoked salmon. Shirley has packaged her granola for sale, and says it's "selling all over the world."

The twelve upstairs guest rooms with private baths are as opulent as the common rooms. Named for favorite writers, they come in many shapes and sizes, but all are furnished with period pieces and items from the innkeepers' endless collections of antique beds, miniature

Innkeepers Bea and Richard Taube and Shirley Stein in front of Vermont Marble Inn.

shoes, candlesticks, paperweights and such. We stayed in the Shakespeare Room at the head of the long staircase (a third longer than usual), which was most spacious and had its own dressing room and fireplace. The Elizabeth Barrett Browning room has another fireplace, a four-poster bed and an antique lace bedcover; the Oscar Wilde, twin four-poster beds. Whimsical touches abound. An art deco wing added in the '20s on the third floor must be seen to be believed. Even the stair railings remind one of Radio City Music Hall.

Doubles, $145 to $210, MAP. Closed mid-November to Dec. 1.

Maplewood Inn, Route 22A South, Fair Haven 05743. (802) 265-8039 or (800) 253-7729.

A mile south of town and denoted by a sign of colorful maple leaves, this restored Greek Revival is really three houses in one. Two were moved to the site to join the original 1850 structure, which accounts for its size and the number of public rooms.

Cindy Baird, who used to run a wine and cheese cafe near St. James, Long Island, acquired the former dairy farmhouse in 1985 and renovated it into an appealing B&B with two suites and three bedrooms, all with private baths, air-conditioning, telephones, color TV and clock radios, and all but one with queensize beds and new gel-fuel fireplaces. She and husband Doug pamper their guests with comfortable accommodations and so many extra touches that many write on the guest critique form: "Don't change a thing."

The inn's rambling main floor has an uncommon amount of common space: a keeping room with fireplace and TV, a large breakfast room that doubles as a BYOB tavern, a formal dining room (with no fewer than seven doors), a gathering room with a library, a formal parlor with a cache of complimentary cordials, and a country kitchen, plus a guest bedroom and the owners' quarters. Old milk bottles and cartons on a living room shelf testify to the property's heritage as the former Maplewood Dairy farm. On display here and there are Doug's remarkably intricate wooden spinning wheels that he makes by hand.

Up various staircases are the rest of the bedrooms and suites, nicely separated from each other and handsomely appointed with period furnishings, wing chairs, thick carpeting, wreaths, Victorian jackets, old costumes and abundant plants. We enjoyed the Hospitality Suite, with a pineapple motif, a comfy sitting room, a step-up queensize four-poster bed dressed with a colorful quilt, and plenty of room to spread out – except in the tiny shower. A half-bottle of soave and a plate of crackers and cheese were presented upon arrival. Decanters of cordials and assorted toiletries are among the amenities, and nightly turndown service brings hand-dipped chocolates bearing the inn's logo and a wish for "Sweet Dreams."

Breakfast is hearty continental, from fresh fruit, hot and cold cereal, granola and yogurts through breads, muffins and perhaps a ham and cheese platter. It's set out buffet style on the bar and an antique ironing board. Cindy, who champions the area, will send you on your way with ideas to keep you busy around here for many a day. Plus a couple of gifts to remember the inn by: a sachet and a bottle of maple syrup.

Doubles, $70 to $85; suites, $105.

Middletown Springs Inn, On the Green, Box 1068, Middletown Springs 05757. (802) 235-2531.

The pink and white inn with gingerbread trim faces the tiny green in the center of what once was a mineral-springs resort that was Vermont's answer to Saratoga. It was acquired in 1994 by New Jersey residents Jackie and Steven Mott, who operated weekends in their first winter and planned to run the inn fulltime starting in the summer of 1995.

The inn has five common rooms with twelve-foot-high ceilings on the first floor. Up a curving staircase are seven guest rooms with private baths, each identified with a brass plaque and named for a famous personage in the area. A rustic rear carriage house holds three more bedrooms, one with private bath and two sharing. Bright and cheerful, the rooms in the main house are notable for elaborate Victorian furniture, oriental rugs, interesting beds, books and neat touches like porcelain dolls, high-button shoes and other Victoriana "so they look like someone is living there from the era," Jackie advised. Steve is an accomplished woodworker and some of his violins and antique reproductions are on display here and there.

Steve also is known for his homemade breads that accompany the prix-fixe dinners, served by prior arrangement in the inn's two Victorian dining rooms (see Dining Spots). Breakfast is Jackie's favorite meal, so she goes all-out with things like nut and fruit breads, muffins, quiches, eggs and sausage, and blueberry pancakes.

Doubles, $60 to $85.

Maplewood Inn is really three houses joined as one.

16

Pillared veranda and cupola enhance facade of Priscilla's Victorian Inn.

Priscilla's Victorian Inn, South Street, Route 1, Box 711, Middletown Springs 05757. (802) 235-2299.

A grand Victorian home with parlors on either side of the large front hall has been converted into a small B&B of great character by Priscilla Lane, an Englishwoman from Yorkshire.

A Steinway player grand piano, melodeons, music boxes, wall clocks and other collector's items are shown to advantage in the parlors of the inn, which is listed on the National Register of Historic Places. More collections are evident in the dining room and in the library. A rear sun room with a turret window is where a full breakfast is served. Below is a recreation room of substantial size, outfitted with nickelodeons, a VCR and a piano, among other items.

Priscilla, who once owned a tea room in Hillsborough, N.C., serves a different breakfast every day, catering to her whims and those of her guests. She offers afternoon tea at 4, complete with cream cakes and scones, and will prepare four-course dinners for guests at $15 each upon advance request. The 7 o'clock meal starts with soup and salad. Roast beef with Yorkshire pudding, chicken or fish are favorite choices. Desserts can get flamboyant, Priscilla says. They might be trifle, banana pudding, chocolate torte or perhaps a pastry from daughter Alison's bakery, Mirabelle's, in Burlington. Sherry or beer are offered before dinner, and guests can bring their own wine to have with.

There are six large guest rooms with private baths, colorful furnishings, and pretty linens and towels. Out back is a porch overlooking rock gardens, lawn, fields and the hump mountains that characterize the area.

Doubles, $65.

The Stonebridge Inn, 3 Beaman St., Poultney 05764. (802) 287-9849.

Dating to 1808 and listed on the National Register, this handsome structure with a Greek Revival front and two wings once housed the first bank in Poultney. The bank

Stonebridge Inn occupies Greek Revival structure dating to 1808.

vault was in the cellar of the west wing, where the foundation walls are five feet thick. The house later became the home of the area's most prominent merchant, who installed the first tiled bathroom in Poultney in 1903.

Opened to the public as an inn in 1984, it has been upgraded by new innkeepers Linda and David Paul, she a school teacher and he a dairy consultant who was with Hershey Foods for twenty years. They offer five second-floor guest rooms, three with private baths, and a first-floor bedroom with sitting area and private bath. All have canopy beds (three queensize) with down comforters and are furnished with period pieces and antiques.

Many antiques grace the main-floor common rooms, decorated in bold colors. They include a drawing room with a fireplace and a baby grand piano, a library with large-screen TV and modern leather seating, and a service bar with an antique pool table in the center of the room.

The dining room is the setting for what Linda calls a three-course European breakfast served on imported china. It involves fresh fruit juice, fruits with Vermont cheese, and such baked goods as croissants, popovers, muffins and quiche. Dinners are served here to guests and the public by reservation (see Dining Spots).

Doubles, $60 to $80. No smoking.

Tower Hall Bed & Breakfast, 2 Bentley Ave., Poultney 05764. (802) 287-4004.

A three-story turret graces this good-looking, olive green Victorian charmer with mustard trim and a wicker porch facing the Green Mountain College campus. You'd hardly know it once served as a college dormitory and more recently as an office building for Ski Racing magazine. Parquet floors, stained glass, original woodwork and ornate mantels tell of a more elegant time.

Kathy and Ed Kann opened it in 1988 with three guest rooms, one with private bath and two that share. Each is decorated with period furniture. Guests enjoy a pink and blue Victorian parlor, and a second-floor sitting room with a fireplace is good for reading or watching TV.

Kathy makes and sells all the crafts that abound; the wooden items are particularly interesting. A hearty breakfast of fruit, homemade breads and muffins, eggs, bacon and such is served in the large dining room.

Doubles, $55 to $60.

Lake St. Catherine Inn, Cones Point Road, Box 129, Poultney 05764. (802) 287-9347 or (800) 626-5724.

A family-style inn like those you remember from the 1950s, this once was an exclusive kosher resort. Since taking over in 1984, Patricia and Raymond Endlich have made an informal, friendly inn out of the only commercial property along a dead-end road on a peninsula jutting into crystal-clear Lake St. Catherine.

Tucked between summer cottages are the two-story, weathered-wood main inn with sixteen simple, quaint guest rooms (all with private baths) and a motel-style annex with nineteen more deluxe units. Quilts and country items enhance these rooms and the main-floor living room and lounge, with cozy furniture and a feeling to match. A three-bedroom housekeeping cottage also is available for $825 a week.

Hearty meals are served to house guests and the public (reservations required by 2 p.m.) in the large gold and brown dining room where windows look onto the lake. The five-course dinner is priced from $14.95 to $16.95, depending on choice of entrée. A typical Saturday night's offerings are prime rib, glazed roast duckling and rainbow trout amandine. Black Forest cake, fruit pies and bread pudding are favored desserts.

Guests like to take drinks onto the large free-standing deck beside the water. There are rafts for swimming and numerous canoes, pedalboats, sailboats and rowboats in the inn's marina are free for guests' use.

Doubles, $148 to $168, MAP. No credit cards. Open mid-May to mid-October.

Dining Spots

Vermont Marble Inn, 12 West Park Place, Fair Haven. (802) 265-8383.

The ubiquitous innkeepers here are heavily involved in their dining operation. Bea Taube does the baking and desserts, Shirley Stein makes the breakfasts, Rich Taube serves the wine and the breakfasts. But they leave the dinner menu and cooking up to David Bofinger, a local chef who calls his cuisine "gourmet American."

Candlelight dinners are served in two high-ceilinged, pink and white dining rooms seating about 60. One is elegant and formal, and the other has big windows onto the back yard.

A former gift shop has been converted into a small dining room with a fireplace, for overflow and private parties.

The changing menu lists appetizers like clam fritters and shrimp-stuffed raviolis, $4.95 to $6.95. The mild country pâté with leeks and grain mustard served warm and the assorted smoked fish plate proved quite satisfying starters. Homemade rolls, a

Dining room at Vermont Marble Inn.

tossed salad and a small dish of sorbets – blueberry and seabreeze (grapefruit and vodka) – came next.

The six main courses ($15.95 to $19.95) could include a classic paella, salmon roasted on a cedar plank with smoked shrimp and dill butter, and mesquite-smoked chicken quesadillas. We liked the smoked grilled duck breast with wild blueberry-ginger sauce and a loin lamb chop grilled with garlic and served with onion-bell pepper salsa. Both were accompanied by snow peas and wild rice pilaf, with herbal and floral garnishes from the gardens out back.

The strawberry and cream roll with pecans and a very rich triple chocolate pâté on a hazelnut crème anglaise were delicious endings. Gourmet magazine has published the recipe for Bea's berries and cream tart. She also does exotic sorbets like melon with medori and piña colada, and garnishes them with pansies. Candies come with your bill, and if you are staying overnight, you will probably find chocolate-covered nuts and raisins in a chocolate cup on your pillow – this inn is definitely not for dieters.

A Davis-Bynum pinot noir ($18) was a hit from the well-chosen, extensive wine list, which goes up to $130 for a 1978 Château Lafite Rothschild.

Dinner nightly in season, 5:30 to 9; Friday and Saturday only, November-April.

Fair Haven Inn, 5 Adams St., Fair Haven. (802) 265-4907.

Thirteen Greek pillars line the facade of this low-slung structure, nicely rebuilt in 1994 after the original burned to the ground. The restaurant rose from the ashes better than ever, with a couple of dining rooms (one more intimate with paneled wainscoting, framed pictures of Greece and a large fieldstone fireplace and the other larger with windows onto the outdoors). Cream-colored tablecloths, octagonal black-rimmed service plates, black bud vases and burgundy fanned napkins enhance the setting.

The place is lovingly run by ex-Connecticut restaurateur John Lemnotis and his wife Faith, whose dinner business thrived over the years to the point that when they rebuilt, they added lunch service and stopped renting rooms. John, the executive chef, calls his cooking "American and continental with a Greek flair." Seafood is his specialty, and he has a wholesale business that supplies other restaurants. The lengthy menu offers shrimp à la grecque, Grecian baked haddock, seafood souvlaki and such rare-for-these-parts fish as red snapper and grouper under catch of the day. Prices range from $11.95 for Boston scrod to $16.95 for a couple of steaks and lamb chops "seasoned with gusto." Veal marsala, souvlaki and beef kabobs are among the choices.

Spanakopita, stuffed grape leaves and calamari sautéed in pure olive oil are appetizer options, $1.95 to $6.95. Greek soup and salads and homemade pastas also are offered. An enormous dessert cart, containing all the coffee cups as well, is laden with cakes and baklava. Ten Greek wines, $14 to $22 a bottle, are among the wines.

A pleasant rear bar with black faux marble tables and a jukebox adds bar specials like a burger with potatoes or rice, sirloin steak or Greek baked lamb with orzo, $4.95 to $7.95.

Lunch, Monday-Saturday 11:30 to 2; dinner, 5 to 9, Sunday noon to 8.

The Stonebridge Inn, Route 30, Poultney. (802) 287-9849.

The Poultney area acquired a badly needed dining option when this inn started serving weekend dinners to the public in 1994. Its small dining room is outfitted with mauve tablecloths, windsor chairs and oil lamps, and restaurant patrons can enjoy the main-floor common rooms and a small bar as they nurse their drinks.

Owners Linda and David Paul found the demand such that they started offering lunches in 1995, and planned to serve dinner nightly summer through foliage. They hire a chef in the summer, but she does the cooking in the off-season.

20

Country elegance prevails in dining room at Fair Haven Inn.

The menu generally lists six main courses priced from $8.95 for lasagna to $13.95 for scallops scampi or Delmonico steak with mushrooms and madeira. Other choices could be cornish game hen, baked cob-smoked ham, veal madeira and a vegetable pasta laced with garlic, peppered parmesan sauce and balsamic vinegar.

Meals come with salad, breads, potato or rice and vegetable. The only appetizers are soup of the day, a cheese and crackers plate and a fresh fruit plate with cottage cheese.

Lunch in season, 11 to 2; dinner nightly in summer, 5 to 9, Friday and Saturday rest of year.

Blossom's Corner, Routes 30 and 149, Wells. (802) 645-0058.

This rustic barn of a place is actually two restaurants, a casual pub in which bargains are the rule and a dining room featuring slightly more complex fare.

Chef-owner Bob Kapp makes little obvious use of his Culinary Institute of America training, although the homemade granola that he has been marketing to grocery stores has snowballed into quite a success. His homemade salad dressings also have been bottled to go.

The dining room menu answers the area's meat and potatoes tastes, from ground round ("the secret is in the mushroom gravy") to sirloin steak, $6.95 to $12.95. You also can get vegetarian dishes (eggplant parmigiana or pasta mangia), "heart-friendly" items like plain broiled chicken or broiled fillet of sole, grilled swordfish, fried clam strips and veal parmigiana, plus spaghetti in various combinations. Chocolate mousse, cheesecake and apple pie are dessert favorites. The pub menu offers some of the same appetizers served in the dining room plus sandwiches, burgers, pizzas and entrées from $6.95 for spaghetti and tomato sauce to $12.95 for chargrilled sirloin.

The decor is barn-typical, with tiny white lights, hanging dried herbs and flowers dressing up the dining room. Seating is at benches, booths and captain's chairs in the high-ceilinged pub. Handcrafted gifts are available in a gift shop.

Dinner nightly from 5. Closed Tuesday and Wednesday, November-Memorial Day.

Ringquist's Dining Room, Route 30, Bomoseen. (802) 468-5172.

An attractive small white house with black shutters has been home since 1976 to Gordon Ringquist's pleasant little Colonial dining room, a tavern where lunch is served, and a side deck with tables facing Lake Bomoseen across the road. "The early bird is never too late," advised a sign at the entrance at a recent visit, noting that a complete dinner was available all evening for $7.95.

The decor ranks among the fanciest in area restaurants. The main dining room is clad mostly in white, with pink and blue swag curtains for color. Oil lamps and blue and white china top the tables.

Dinner entrées start at $7.25 for roast turkey, roast loin of pork, beef liver and baked sole with mushroom and celery stuffing. Those prices hadn't risen in years, nor had most of the other, though a sticker covered up the old $13.95 price tag for filet mignon, now the costliest item at $16.95. Start with Gordon's special clam chowder, barbecued chicken wings, marinated herring or escargots ($1.25 to $4.95). Wines and desserts are priced accordingly. Traditionally, lunch has been offered in summer, but its status was in doubt in 1995.

Lunch (tentatively), Monday-Friday noon to 2; dinner, Monday-Saturday 5 to 9, Sunday noon to 8. Open fewer nights in winter.

Middletown Springs Inn, On the Green, Middletown Springs. (802) 235-2531.

By reservation, the public may join inn guests for dinner at individual tables in two high-ceilinged, Victorian dining rooms at this venerable inn. Innkeeper Jackie Mott handles the cooking chores in a large country kitchen and her husband Steve helps with the bread baking.

The prix-fixe dinner tab is $15. A three-course dinner starts with soup or salad. The main course might be turkey pot pie or pork tenderloin, herbed baked potatoes and green beans amandine. Dessert could be cheesecake with caramel glaze or homemade apple crumb pie with vanilla ice cream.

Dinner by reservation, nightly at 7.

Casa Bianca, 76 Grove St., Rutland. (802) 773-7401.

Area restaurant-goers looking for authentic Italian cuisine head the short distance east to Rutland. Joe and Sharon Valente, who owned the old Fairmont restaurant there, took over the legendary Casa Bianca. They totally renovated the turn-of-the-century duplex, quadrupling the dining space. Now they seat 70 in four candlelit dining rooms, two with fireplaces and notable for chandeliers and Waverly print wallpapers with matching draperies.

Chef Brad Pirkey, formerly of the Corners Inn & Restaurant in Bridgewater Corners, retained some of the traditional Corners touches, including a Sunday pasta night for $9.95, allowing diners to mix and match four pastas and four sauces as appetizers and entrées. The house mesclun salad and breadsticks with infused olive oil come with the meal.

The regular menu ($8.95 to $13.95) lists main dishes like pastas, shrimp scampi, cioppino, veal jarlsberg, chicken roulade and steak au poivre. Specials might be salmon en papillote, veal chops and a mixed grill of lamb, chicken and lobster tail. For starters ($3.95 to $6.95), try braciole, grilled polenta with calamari, clams giovanni, spicy grilled shrimp, crostini or focaccia. Desserts include flan, cannoli with chocolate ganache and double cappuccino torte.

The wine list is unusual in that all 32 Italian and California labels sell for $14.95 each. There's a pricier connoisseur list for those who prefer.

Dinner, Tuesday-Saturday 5 to 10, Sunday 3 to 10.

White gingerbread trim over pink enhances Middletown Springs Inn.

Diversions

The area offers few tourist trappings in the traditional sense. Instead, it has unspoiled scenery, rural hamlets and historic districts, and good fishing and boating. The attractions of Manchester, Rutland, Woodstock and Killington-Pico ski areas are nearby.

East Poultney. Although the college town of Poultney has a walking tour with a brochure detailing sixteen historic points of interest, the earlier settlement of East Poultney commands more attention. Editor Horace Greeley stayed at the town's Eagle Tavern while apprenticing in the 1820s at the National Spectator, where he was joined by George Jones, a founder of the New York Times. Here, time literally stands still. The hands on the clock of the United Baptist Church never move; they're painted on at 10 o'clock. The church in the center of the village green was organized in 1802 and reorganized in 1987, according to a sign. Across from the impressive green is St. John's Episcopal Church, left exactly as it was built in 1831, without heat and electricity. It's used one Sunday a year to retain its status as a church. The Baptist church, the 1895 schoolhouse where Horace Greeley gave his first talk, a melodeon factory and the 1791 Union Academy are opened by the Poultney Historical Society on Sunday afternoons from 1 to 5 June-August or by appointment. Band concerts are presented on the green at 7 p.m. Sundays in July. Just south of the green is a bridge over a beautiful gorge and waterfall.

Middletown Springs. The town center and 91 buildings are listed on the National Register of Historic Places as an example of an unchanged New England village. Blink your eyes and you almost could miss this remote hamlet, but tarry and you'll see remarkable architecture and get the flavor of old Vermont. Take away the blacktop and you'd find the village as it was about the turn of the century. The mineral springs that give the town its name (and inspired the construction of the large but short-lived Montvert Hotel in 1871) have been restored by the local historical society in a quaint park. Five springs are left, and each is supposed to be different, but the only one we could find tasted like ordinary spring water.

Castleton Historic District. The first college in Vermont was founded in 1787 in this lovely little town, whose Main Street lined with pillared Greek Revival houses and interesting churches comprises an historic district. A comprehensive state college since 1961, Castleton State has a pleasant campus. The Higley Homestead Museum, operated by the Castleton Historical Society, is open periodically, as are several historic homes. North of Castleton – seemingly in the back of beyond – is the hilltop **Hubbardton Battlefield,** where Ethan Allen and Seth Warner planned the capture of Ticonderoga and staved off British invaders in the only battle fought in Vermont during the Revolution. The small visitor center is free, and the panoramic view of the surrounding mountains is priceless.

Lakes and Parks. Lake St. Catherine State Park south of Poultney has nature trails, a good sandy beach, picnic tables, fishing and boat rentals. **Bomoseen State Park,** a bit harder to get to on the west side of Lake Bomoseen, offers the same facilities plus a wildlife refuge. Smaller but more accessible is **Crystal Beach,** a park operated by the town of Castleton on the east side of the state's largest lake.

Shopping. Shopping is not this area's strong suit; indeed, the largest business in downtown Fair Haven appears to be the Cleanarama. The best shopping is in Poultney, where the **Original Vermont Store** nearly corners the market. Nooks and crannies in its Thankful Mears House, an 1840 Greek Revival, offer up everything from specialty foods and maple syrup to books, bunnies, baskets, birdhouses and brass butterflies, including Original Vermont Design products made in Poultney; a new Christmas room displays nice cards, ornaments and such. Across the street in an old train station is **Kay's Corner,** a mishmash of antiques and odds 'n ends; beyond in a second depot is the **Craft Seller,** with many quilted items. The **Ginger Jar** offers antiques and interior accessories in a good-looking yellow house. In a Victorian cottage at 27 College St., **Heartstrings** is stocked to the rafters with a potpourri of country gifts. Near Middletown Springs, the **Sugarhouse Gallery at Moonridge Farm** shows owner Stan Achey's photos among the works of Vermont artists. The farm also produces maple syrup products for sale and breeds pure Lippitt Morgan horses.

Extra-Special

Vermont Marble Exhibit, 62 Main St., Proctor. (802) 459-3311.

The working-factory exterior belies the sophisticated wonders within. A truck loaded with raw marble arrived as we did, and from the second-floor overlook onto the vast production floor we could view all the steps needed to turn the slabs into walls, floors and works of art. A fifteen-minute film is a good introduction to the world's largest marble museum and one of only two marble-producing plants in the country. Then tour the Hall of Presidents, where the faces of 41 past presidents have been carved from pure white marble by a local sculptor. Another overlook allows a glimpse of the 120-foot waterfall that powers the factory, the town of Proctor, the Danby quarry and more. There are exhibits on the geology of marble, photos of quarries, and more examples of marble than one could imagine. You can watch a resident sculptor at work, and the sculptures in the entry lobby are worthy of a museum. The Boy and Girl on a Swing, circa 1900, was brought here in 1976 to be repaired; its owner never returned, so it's on display as "unquestionably the work of a master carver." An interesting gift shop purveys everything in marble, from picture frames to worry stones, lamps to vases, chess sets to earrings. Outside is a marble market for seconds, available at bargain prices – the trick is to be able to carry your purchase away. Open daily 9 to 5:30, mid-May through October; rest of year, Monday-Saturday 9 to 4. Adults, $3.50.

Village of Stowe nestles in valley beneath Mount Mansfield.

Stowe, Vt.
A Resort for All Seasons

When Olympic skier Phil Mahre first saw Stowe clad in summer's green rather than winter's white, he was struck by its beauty. So were many in the Eastern Ski Writers audience he addressed that August day.

Most downhill skiers haven't been to Stowe in what for them is the off-season. But the undisputed Ski Capital of the East is a year-round destination resort, more than its newer, less endowed competitors can hope to be.

For one thing, Stowe *is* Stowe, a legendary village unto itself about eight miles from Mount Mansfield, a legendary ski area unto itself. The twain meets all along the Mountain Road, which links village and mountain. Such a marriage between town and ski area is unrivaled in New England and rich in history – a history unequaled by any other ski town in the country, according to Mount Mansfield Company officials.

The ski resort was led for years by Sepp Ruschp, who left Austria in 1936 to be ski instructor for the fledgling Mount Mansfield Ski Club. The alpine mystique of the area was enhanced by Baroness Maria von Trapp and her family, whose story was immortalized by "The Sound of Music," when they founded the Trapp Family Lodge.

The rolling valley between broad Mount Mansfield on the west and the Worcester Mountains on the east lends an open feeling that is unusual for northern New England mountain regions. In Stowe's exhilarating air, recreation and cultural endeavors thrive.

Cross-country skiing complements downhill in winter. Other seasons bring golf, tennis, polo, horseback riding, hiking, performing arts, art exhibits and enough sights to see and things to do to make credible the area's claim to being a world-class resort.

Foremost a ski center, Stowe rather lacks inns of the classic New England variety. Instead, it has resorts, motels, ski dorms, condominiums and more Alpine/Bavarian chalets and lodges than you'll find just about anywhere this side of the Atlantic.

25

Still, Stowe is Stowe, a storybook New England ski town dominated by Vermont's highest peak. It's a place to be treasured, by skier and non-skier alike.

Inn Spots

Edson Hill Manor, 1500 Edson Hill Road, Stowe 05672. (802) 253-7371 or (800) 621-0284.

A French Provincial-style manor with old English charm, built in 1940 as a gentleman's estate, became a country inn in 1954. It obtained a new role in life in 1991 after it was purchased by Eric and Jane Lande, well-traveled ex-Montrealers of the fabled Bronfman family, who had set up a thriving maple-syrup business at their Vermont farm in nearby Johnson.

The Landes hired a talented chef and lured veteran local hotelier Billy O'Neill to be their fulltime manager. In 1993, they acquired one of Stowe's other best-known small inns, Ten Acres Lodge, and brought in a noted chef from the Shelburne House to enhance its already acclaimed dining room. Continually perfecting these two premier places to eat and stay, the Landes have a corner on the high-end market. Many of their ideas and aspirations came from having lived in France for ten years while Eric was working on a doctorate in economics. On subsequent trips overseas they preferred to stay in Relais & Chateaux establishments, which they said served as models for the new Edson Hill and Ten Acres.

A mile-long country lane leads from the white post gates to the manor, which a loyal following considers one of the few true country inns in the Stowe area. It retains its original private-home flavor except in the four new carriage houses with modern accommodations.

Set high amidst 225 secluded acres, it has a spectacular terrace beside a spring-fed, kidney-shaped swimming pool, a pond stocked for trout fishing, an upgraded cross-country ski center and stables for horseback riding.

The manor was a prime location in 1980 for the filming of winter scenes for Alan Alda's movie, "The Four Seasons." The famous Mercedes scene took place on the pond.

Inside the manor are ten guest rooms, a pine-paneled parlor with oriental rugs and Delft tiles around the fireplace, a library with more books and magazines than anyone could possibly read, a refurbished downstairs lounge, plus a renovated dining room

where meals are available to the public (see Dining Spots). The beams in the large parlor are said to have come from Ethan Allen's barn. Many of the striking artworks are by Canadian artist Lillian Freeman.

The Landes are gradually upgrading the accommodations, starting with handpainting some of the bathrooms with floral and bird scenes. One family suite has a fireplace, sofa and armchair, a large bathroom with tub and a second bedroom.

Each of four carriage houses, up a hill beyond the inn, has four spa-

Ten Acres Lodge is known for fine dining as well as lodging.

cious bedrooms done in the decor of the original manor with beamed ceilings, pine-paneled walls, brick fireplaces and private baths. Billed as the inn's luxury units, they accommodate two to four people.

All told, five rooms in the manor plus those in the carriage houses contain working fireplaces – a great attraction for winter visitors. We'd happily settle any time for the manor's large Studio, which has queensize bed, fireplace, skylight (this was formerly an artist's studio) and an exceptionally nice sitting area with picture windows overlooking the pool, pond and gardens.

Breakfasts are a treat. The buffet table contains several hot entrées – on one winter morning, scrambled eggs with spinach and goat cheese, blackberry waffles and polenta. Fresh juices, fruit platters, homemade breads and muffins, and maple syrup from the Landes' farm accompany.

Doubles, $100 to $160, B&B; $140 to $200, MAP.

Ten Acres Lodge, 14 Barrows Road, Stowe 05672. (802) 253-7638 or (800) 327-7357.

Built as a farmhouse in 1826 with several later additions, this rambling and picturesque red frame house with white trim on a quiet hillside is best known for its restaurant (see Dining Spots). New owners Eric and Jane Lande of Edson Hill Manor have upgraded the overnight accommodations as well.

The dining rooms and the small, slate-floored tavern are altogether appealing, and the plush parlor and front library could not be more comfortable. The striking wing chairs and couches piled with pillows in the parlor are popular with houseguests. Large bay windows look out onto ever-changing vistas of valley and mountains.

All eight guest rooms on two floors of the main lodge have private baths. One is rather small; the rest are quite spacious and more luxurious. One with kingsize bed has a bathroom in two parts, one containing the tub and the other the toilet and wash basin. The Landes have redecorated every room with a mix of country furniture and antiques.

Two renovated cottages offer two or three bedrooms, kitchens, working fireplaces and terraces with great views in every direction.

Worth the extra tab are eight luxury fireplaced suites in the relatively new Hill House.

Each has a large sitting area, private deck, cable TV and phone. Guests here share an outdoor hot tub open to the stars.

A buffet breakfast includes fresh fruit, granola, yogurt, an egg dish, ham and Vermont cheese.

The grounds contain a small pool, tennis court, and flower and herb gardens that beckon white rabbits. Beyond, cows graze on neighboring farmlands. Who could ask for a more tranquil setting?

Doubles, $70 to $130, B&B; $110 to $170, MAP.

Stowehof Inn, 434 Edson Hill Road, Box 1108, Stowe 05672. (802) 253-9722 or (800) 932-7136.

"Slow – Deer Crossing," warns the sign as you drive up the steep road to the Stowehof, whose soaring Alpine exterior is a hilltop landmark hereabouts. "No parking – sleigh only," reads the sign at the door.

Such touches reflect the character of this unusual, thoroughly charming place that grew from a private ski house into one of Stowe's larger inns.

At the front entrance, the trunks of two maple trees support the enormous porte cochere above the small purple door. More tree trunks are inside the huge living room, nicely broken up into intimate nooks and crannies, the two-level dining room, the downstairs game room and the Tyrolean Tap Room. The bell tower, the sod roof laced with field flowers and the architecture are reminiscent of the Tyrolean Alps. The upstairs library and game room is a replica of the interior of a Vermont covered bridge.

You'd never suspect that the owners are from Hawaii, but their decorating flair is apparent in most of the 46 guest rooms, some of them unusually large and sumptuous. Queen Anne chairs and Chippendale desks add elegance. Terrycloth robes and Godiva chocolates are put out at nightly turndown. All rooms have balconies or patios with views in summer of lovely clumps of birches, a swimming pool, a trout pond, lawns and the mountains. Three guest rooms are available in a farmhouse on the adjacent working farm within walking distance.

Three meals a day are served in the well-appointed **Seasons** dining room with beamed ceiling, fireplaces and windows looking onto pool and mountains. There's also dining in summer on the terrace, site of a popular Sunday buffet brunch. The regional American dinner menu changes several times weekly. Specialties on the dinner menu ($14.95 to $21.95) are wiener schnitzel and beef wellington. Lighter fare is available in the Tyrolean Tap Room.

Locals advise going to Stowehof just to see it. We think it's an equally appealing place in which to stay.

Doubles, $110 to $180, B&B; $150 to $220, MAP.

Ye Olde England Inn, 433 Mountain Road, Stowe 05672. (802) 253-7558 or (800) 477-3771.

Stowe seems an unlikely spot for an English coaching inn, but this restored and expanded inn is British all the way from the bright red phone booth out front to the menu in the pub.

All seventeen guest rooms have private baths and seven have jacuzzis. They are spacious, decorated in Laura Ashley style, contain Gilchrist & Soames amenities and, on the third floor, are notable for interesting shapes and views of the mountains. Three luxury two-bedroom English "cottages" in a building out back beside the swimming pool each contain a fireplace, jacuzzi, cable TV, lounge-dining area and kitchen facilities. In 1994, the inn started construction of ten "super-luxurious suites" in the Bluff House, perched atop a granite bluff with spectacular views of the Worcester Mountain

Tree trunks support porte cochere at entrance of Stowehof Inn.

range. Each has a queensize four-poster in the bedroom, a bath with jacuzzi and separate shower, a private deck and a "lounge" with fireplace, sofabed, wet bar, refrigerator and microwave.

English-style tea is served in the afternoon. Transplanted Brits Chris and Lyn Francis, skiers both, are more in evidence at their inn than are many area innkeepers. Chris and two friends also formed the Stowe Polo Club and got the community involved.

An English breakfast and fancy dinners are served in the beamed **Copperfields** dining room in season. Here the fare includes sautéed pheasant, broiled venison, beef wellington, salmon oscar and tournedos rossini, priced from $15.95 to $18.95. The all-Australian wine list has been cited by Wine Spectator as one of the world's best.

A pub-type menu is available all day in **Mr. Pickwick's Pub & Restaurant** with a hearthstone fireplace or on the expanded quarterdeck, lined with umbrellas advertising British ale and presenting a scene straight from the English countryside.

The pub menu offers mulligatawny, fish and chips, bangers and mash, and cornish pasties, along with some of the Copperfields specialties at lower prices, from $6.95 to $15.95, served from 11 a.m. to closing. A number of non-British items like chicken wings, nachos and chicken curry also are listed. We enjoyed a lunch of spinach salad in a tostada shell and a good steak and kidney pie served inexplicably with a side bowl of gravy (could it have been for dipping the french fries in?), all washed down with pints of Whitbread and Watneys ales, presented in proper pub glasses. The list of more than 150 foreign beers and ales is extraordinary, and one can even get ale by the yard. In the evening, live entertainment is enjoyed by the laid-back crowd.

Doubles, $116 to $158, B&B; cottages and Bluff House, $175 to $208.

Green Mountain Inn, Main Street, Box 60, Stowe 05672. (802) 253-7301 or (800) 445-6629.

Its deep red facade a landmark in the center of the village since 1833, this inn has been carefully restored and upgraded in the last few years.

The complex includes the formal Main Street Dining Room and the legendary Whip Bar & Grill downstairs (see Dining Spots). The latter is where the action is, in the cozy bar as well as in the cafeteria-style grill and on the outdoor deck by the pool. A couple of small parlors in front retain the New England inn charm.

Most of the 64 guest rooms and suites are behind the inn in a motel-type configuration, albeit with an antique look. The modern baths, color TVs and phones are combined with twin or queensize canopy beds, floral quilts, custom-designed reproduction furniture manufactured specially for the inn, period wallpapers and stenciling. Fifteen rooms in the annex were nicely renovated in 1994; many have balconies overlooking the outdoor pool, brook and gardens. Two new clubhouse suites come with kitchen, living room, dining area, fireplace, jacuzzi and queen canopy bed.

The health center in the clubhouse offers a spa program.

Doubles, $105, EP; suites, $120 to $150, EP.

Butternut Inn, 2309 Mountain Road, Stowe 05672. (802) 253-4277 or (800) 328-8837.

The doorbell plays "The Eyes of Texas Are Upon You," and that's just the start at this transformation of the old Skimore Lodge. Texan owners Jim and Deborah Wimberly advertise theirs as "an award-winning, non-smoking, exclusive inn – a romantic couples' retreat" and have a hallway wall of letters and thank-you notes to prove it.

The eighteen guest rooms, all with private baths and most air-conditioned, vary widely in size and remain true to their ski-lodge heritage, although each is furnished with antique dressers, country crafts, and black and white TVs. Most have king or queensize beds and one of the nicer on the third-floor corner has a balcony.

There's a small living room on the main floor, but most of the action is on the lower floor: a parlor with a piano handmade from one large walnut tree, a billiards room with a 1905 pool table, a small sitting area and a large-screen TV (the room's walls are covered with photos that Jim has taken of inn guests), a sun room with a bay window to show off the inn's flowers, and a large dining room. Christmas decor is on display all year, from the lights out front on the spruce tree to the sleigh filled with teddy bears to the twinkling Christmas village with a little train in the dining room.

Looking up toward Mount Mansfield, the eight-acre back yard is a showplace of flower and herb gardens, a terrace, a flagstone courtyard, a grape arbor, a gazebo by the swimming pool, a fountain and a little park area for picnics by the river. Folks sit in red Adirondack chairs and feed the goldfish and koi in the pond at the side. Depending on the season, they can walk or ski on illuminated trails through five acres of woods to a secret tree house. There's plenty of room for eighteen romantic couples to be alone or sociable, as they wish.

Breakfast is bountiful enough that most don't eat lunch, according to Jim. A favorite is eggs Butternut – poached eggs on pork chops with sautéed onions and cajun peppers. The inn makes its own corned beef hash. On summer afternoons, tea and homemade chocolate-chip cookies are served. In winter, there's an after-ski "grazing board" that might include soup of the day, pheasant pâté, barbecued ribs, sirloin-blackened roast with horseradish sauce, pork roast with barbecue sauce, and Deborah's chocolate desserts and cheesecake. With that for cocktail-party fare, it's no wonder that some guests decide against going out for dinner.

Doubles, $110 to $150. No smoking.

The Gables Inn, 1457 Mountain Road, Stowe 05672. (802) 253-7730 or (800) 422-5371.

What many consider to be the best breakfast in town is served at the Gables, either

Breakfast on the lawn is a tradition at The Gables Inn.

under yellow umbrellas on the front lawn (facing a spectacular view of Mount Mansfield), on the front porch or on picnic tables inside.

Thirteen guest rooms in the main inn and four in a renovated carriage house have charming country furniture, homemade wreaths and, an unusual touch, all rooms (and even a couple of bathrooms) are decorated with a few fine china plates from the extensive collection of owners Sol and Lynn Baumrind. All have private baths, most gleaming white and modern. Some are in what Sol laughingly calls a "toilet tower" he added just for the purpose. The inn's master room offers a queensize, lace-canopy four-poster bed, a sofa, TV and a modern bathroom with skylight. Much in demand are four spacious rooms in the air-conditioned Carriage House, which shows no trace of its motel-annex heritage. These come with cathedral ceilings, fireplaces, jacuzzis, queensize canopy beds and television. Top of the line are two Riverview Suites converted in 1994 from a neighboring homestead. Each has a kingsize bed made of cedar fence posts with a split-rail fence for a headboard, a dual wood-burning fireplace shared by bedroom and living room, a convenience center with refrigerator and microwave, and a double jacuzzi tub. The upstairs suite with cathedral ceiling has a balcony off the bedroom and a deck off the living room. The wraparound porch off the main-floor suite faces the inn's pool area.

A landscaped swimming pool and hot tub, a plant-filled solarium and a large, comfortably furnished den and living room with TV are other attractions in this homey place. In winter the downstairs den is used for après-ski; the owners put out crockpots full of steaming hot soup, hot hors d'oeuvre, and cheese and crackers after 4 p.m. for hungry skiers, who BYOB.

As for that breakfast, it's open to the public, and some days the Baumrinds serve as many as 300. Says Sol with a smile, "service is leisurely – that's a code word for slow." Aside from all the old standbys, one can feast on eggs Portuguese, kippers or chicken livers with onions and scrambled eggs, matzoh brei, and eggs in a basket, poached eggs in puff pastry with crumbled bacon, artichoke hearts and mornay sauce. Croissant benedict with smoked chicken, raspberry and nectarine stuffed french toast made with raisin bread, blueberry or banana pancakes and a lox and bagel plate are popular choices on the extensive menu priced from $4.75 to $6.75.

In ski season, dinner is served in the dining rooms amid a collection of Royal Copenhagen plates. The tables are covered with tablecloths, and candles glow.

Breakfast daily, 8 to noon, weekends and holidays to 12:30.

Doubles, $75 to 95; Carriage House and suites, $120 to $150. No smoking.

Timberhölm Inn, 452 Cottage Club Road, Stowe 05672. (802) 253-7603 or (800) 753-7603.

The rustic, weathered cedar facade trimmed in Wedgwood blue hints that this 1949 house along a quiet road is more than just another ski lodge. Inside, the Great Room confirms it. This really is a great room – a huge, sunny space containing lots of sofas in two comfy sitting areas, a fieldstone fireplace, TV, shelves of books and, at the near end, an open dining area. Beyond are two walls of picture windows onto a wide deck – perfect for relaxing in summer – and a tree-framed view of the golf course and the Worcester Mountain range. Downstairs is a game room with a guest refrigerator and TV/VCR, and outside is a whirlpool spa. We'd gladly curl up with a book in the Great Room or on the deck and spend the day.

Overnight accommodations are in a lodge-style wing with eight rooms and two suites. Four rooms are small and have bathrooms with showers. Four that are a bit larger add full baths. The largest bedrooms are part of two-bedroom suites with living rooms that seem superfluous, given all the public space.

Innkeepers Louise and Pete Hunter, the latest in a succession of owners, serve lemonade and banana bread on summer afternoons, changing to soup by the fire in winter. Breakfast is a buffet with fresh fruit, homemade granola, yogurt, banana-bran muffins and perhaps quiche, pancakes or eggs florentine.

Doubles, $60 to $100; suites, $120.

The Inn at the Brass Lantern, 717 Maple St. (Route 100), Stowe 05672. (802) 253-2229 or (800) 729-2980.

The old Charda restaurant building was in sad shape when it was acquired in 1988 by Andy Aldrich, a home builder. "I could look at the property and see the potential," he said. Doing most of the work himself, he undertook a total restoration, "doing all the things people think about doing when they're upgrading."

The result is a comfortable, air-conditioned B&B with a pleasant mix of old and new and an award from the Vermont Builders Association for restoration. The walls are stenciled and baskets hang from the beamed ceiling in the dining room. Modern baths, some with whirlpool tubs, adjoin the nine soundproofed bedrooms, three with fireplaces and queensize beds. Each has stenciled walls, planked floors, brass or canopy beds with handmade quilts, and one or two wing chairs.

Guests gather around the fireplace in the living room or on a large rear deck overlooking the mountains. A native Vermonter, Andy features Vermont products on his breakfast menu, which changes daily. Sourdough french toast was the entrée at our visit. Broccoli-mushroom quiche, vegetable omelets, apple crêpes, blueberry pancakes or scrambled eggs with Cabot cheese and bacon are other possibilities. Tea and baked goods are offered in the afternoon.

Doubles, $80 to $120. No smoking.

Stowe Inn & Tavern at Little River, 123 Mountain Road, Stowe 05672. (802) 253-4836 or (800) 227-1108.

The old Yodler Inn was sold to Linda and Bruce Watson, who renamed it the Stowe Inn at Little River in 1994 and added a restaurant out back. The Watsons, whose background is restaurant and resort development (they helped the owners rebuild the Okemo ski area), renovated the 43-room inn, which has 21 guest rooms in the original 1825 inn building and 22 in a nice-looking brick and shuttered motel strip called the Carriage House in back. The main inn also possesses a large country living room and a couple of small parlors that double as function rooms.

Most of the inn bedrooms, which vary in size and age, contain kingsize or two double beds, TV, blond oak furniture, an upholstered wing chair and a windsor armchair. They were gradually being enhanced with new wallpapers, comforters, quilts and the usual inn trappings. Some of the motel rooms come with fireplaces and jacuzzis. A new wing along the river was in the works to house an indoor pool, spa and health center, plus ten to fifteen deluxe guest rooms with jacuzzis and fireplaces.

A buffet breakfast of eggs, pancakes, fruits and muffins is complimentary on weekends and holidays; a continental breakfast is served on weekdays. In the afternoon, cheese and crackers, mushrooms, crudités and other bar food are served in the large tavern, through which inn guests and the public pass to reach the new tiered, three-level dining room. Bright and airy, it has three walls of open glass overlooking the river and the town. The menu offers what Linda calls "a lot of fun foods for mixing and matching" for lunch and dinner.

Doubles, $70 to $140.

Dining Spots

Blue Moon Cafe, 35 School St., Stowe. (802) 253-7006.

Well-known local chef Jack Pickett, whose food we enjoyed during his ten-year tenure at Ten Acres Lodge, finally got the chance to do his own thing, opening his own

restaurant along a side street in Stowe. It's amazingly small, a main room with a dining bar and five tables plus two enclosed front porches, each with three tables for two. A side patio nearly doubles the size in summer – one record night Jack served 95 dinners, which doesn't sound like much until you consider the size of the place.

He's in his element here, serving exciting food in a simple bistro atmosphere. We could not have been happier with our lunchtime choices: a grilled lamb sandwich with sautéed sweet peppers and onions ($6.50) and grilled flatbread with sundried tomato pesto, grilled onion, sardo cheese and chorizo ($5).

At night, the changing menu lists about seven starters and entrées (the latter, $12.75 to $16.25). The meal could begin with sweet potato-leek soup, Maine crab cakes

Porch table for two at Blue Moon Cafe.

with grilled fennel and sweet onion puree, Cape Neddick oysters with spicy tomatillo sauce or grilled Craftsbury quail with stir-fried vegetables and polenta. For main courses, how about grilled yellowfin tuna with winter greens and coriander-lime vinaigrette, pan-roasted Atlantic salmon with pine nut and sundried-tomato herb crust, braised rabbit with wild mushrooms and sweet onions, New York strip steak with cracked black pepper and horseradish cream, or braised lamb shanks with black salsify and assorted mushrooms? Often on the menu are butterflied leg of lamb with grilled leeks and rosemary and a chargrilled cornish game hen with tomato, basil and crème fraîche that we sampled at Ten Acres and found outstanding. Among desserts are an acclaimed crème brûlée, chocolate ganache with hot caramel sauce, a deep-fried cheesecake and a mascarpone tart drizzled with chocolate sauce and fresh fruit.

Although Jack has downscaled his cuisine a bit from his Ten Acres days, he's hardly lost his touch, nor has he lost his reverence for regional ingredients. He's been getting his produce from the same farmer for twelve years.

Lunch, 11:30 to 2; dinner nightly, 6 to 9:30; Sunday brunch, 11:30 to 2. Fewer days in winter and off-season. No smoking.

Edson Hill Manor, 1500 Edson Hill Road, Stowe. (802) 253-7371.
Another "in" spot for dining in Stowe is the reborn dining room at Edson Hill – reborn in both decor and cuisine.

New owners Eric and Jane Lande transformed the inn's formerly rustic dining room

into an airy, garden-like setting that's exceptionally pretty. Tables with wrought-iron bases and chairs with deep green seats are spaced about a multi-colored slate floor. Stunning Martstone china rests atop pale pink tablecloths. A local artist painted flowers and birds on the walls and ivy on the ceiling; the sky shows through handpainted lattices. Even the walk-out lounge downstairs is graced with handpainted quails and partridges on the walls and a squirrel at the bar. A handpainted cat with its tail draped across a shelf graces the ladies' room.

Highly acclaimed contemporary fare with a continental accent is offered by chef Matthew Delos, a Culinary Institute of America grad who was associated with noted chef Bradley Ogden in California. Here his short dinner menu might start with red lentil soup with homemade fennel sausage and pesto,

Window table at Edson Hill Manor.

steamed pork dumplings, scallop cakes with chipotle beurre blanc, and grilled Vermont quail with sweet potato-cheddar cheese turnover and cider-shallot sauce. For entrées ($15.50 to $23), how about one night's choices of salmon wellington with corn and red onion stew and lobster rémoulade, grilled tuna with andouille sausage and chile-roasted calamari, grilled pork chop with wilted spinach and dried apple glaze, grilled beef tenderloin with horseradish butter and grilled antelope medallions with sweet potato fries, beans and kiln-dried cranberry sauce?

Desserts could be banana fritters with tropical fruit coulis and vanilla yogurt, chocolate chestnut cake with bittersweet ganache and sour cherry sauce, apple cinnamon bread pudding with pear sorbet or gingerbread cake with cranberry-orange compote and cider ice cream. The 80 or so wines, starting at $18, are pricey but as well chosen as the rest of the fare.

Lunch on weekends, noon to 2:30; dinner nightly in season, 6 to 9:30; weekends only in off-season.

Tables are set elegantly for candlelight dining at Ten Acres Lodge.

Ten Acres Lodge, 14 Barrows Road, Stowe. (802) 253-7638.

After putting Edson Hill Manor on the list of Vermont's top culinary destinations, owners Eric and Jane Lande acquired the highly rated Ten Acres Lodge in 1994 and installed in its kitchen talented chef Matt Larson. Matt trained at La Varenne in France and had spent summers at the Shelburne House in Shelburne and winters at Snowbird ski resort in Utah. Now, with skiing close at hand, he can ply his culinary skills year-round in Stowe.

The dining room and airy summer porch where we've enjoyed a couple of meals are classically pretty: mint-linened tables are set with Villeroy & Boch service plates and classical music plays softly in the background. The changing menu might feature pan-seared salmon with shrimp and scallion dumplings and black bean-ginger vinaigrette, pan-roasted monkfish with roasted red pepper coulis, grilled Vermont rabbit with tart cherries and green peppercorns, and sautéed loin of lamb with aged cheddar and ale. Accompaniments change with the entrée, perhaps asparagus or three-lentil risotto, garlic flan, mashed sweet potatoes, garlic creamed potatoes or grilled new potatoes. Among winter starters are belgian endive soup with smoked chicken and crème fraîche, crispy duck confit with frisée and black currant chutney, scallop stew with leeks and fennel, and wild mushroom raviolis with nutmeg parmesan cream and spinach walnut risotto.

Great desserts include chocolate marquise, berry gratin in rum-flavored crème anglaise, fruit tarte tatin and a trio of homemade sorbets. The huge wine list has a page of old and rare vintages.

Dinner nightly, 6 to 9:30; weekends only in off-season. No smoking.

Isle de France, Mountain Road, Stowe. (802) 253-7751.

Next door to the long-popular Shed but miles removed in terms of tone and atmosphere, this lavish restaurant was opened in 1979 by chef-owner Jean Lavina, a Frenchman from the Lyons area by way of the French Shack in New York City.

Formerly the Crystal Palace, the place shows its heritage: cut-glass chandeliers, mirrors, gilt ornamental work around the ceilings, rose-bordered service plates with gold edges, heavy silver and a single red rose on each white-linened table. Three tables have sofas for two on one side. The cozy bar with apricot-colored sofas and medieval chandelier features a menu of assorted specialties for $9.25 to $11.50 – a great value.

35

Dinner in the two dining rooms with plush round-backed chairs is in the classical French style. For appetizers ($4.50 to $7), you might start with pork and veal country pâté or escargots bourguignonne. Upwards of twenty entrées are priced from $14 for roast capon to $21 for dover sole meunière. Also available are six to eight nightly specials like poached salmon in beurre blanc or venison with a foie gras sauce. Eight beef presentations vary from entrecôte béarnaise to châteaubriand for two; one is slices of tenderloin with a creamy bourbon sauce.

Desserts range from frozen meringues chantilly and crème caramel to bananas foster, cherries jubilee and crêpes suzette for two. The large wine list is priced upward from the high teens.

Dinner nightly except Monday, 6:30 to 10:30.

The Cliff House Restaurant, Atop Mount Mansfield, Stowe Mountain Resort, Stowe. (802) 253-3000, Ext. 2317.

For a change of pace, try this summit ski-lodge cafeteria gone fancy. Others have tried – in fact, Stowe experimented unsuccessfully with it for years – but this one seems to be succeeding. A former manager from Ten Acres Lodge, Bob Howd, committed himself to providing haute dining on high, even in winter. He and chef Robert Kuiper, originally from The Netherlands, have managed consistency in food and staff in a summit environment fraught with challenges.

You reach the restaurant via a ten-minute airborne ride in one of Stowe's new eight-passenger gondolas ($9 for sightseers, but a free ride for diners). At the summit, pause for a drink on the outdoor deck or proceed into the 70-seat dining room. The tables bear linens, fresh flowers and candles, and the view from windows on three sides speaks for itself. In winter, you can watch skiers on the Gondolier, Stowe's new lighted trail below.

The fare is as lofty as the elevation. The four-course, prix-fixe meal ($39) might start with a triple fish terrine served with cucumber-dill salad and maple-mustard vinaigrette, rabbit pâté with tomato-golden raisin chutney or pan-fried crab cake on Boston brown bread with light curry sauce. A mixed green or caesar salad precedes the main course. Look for choices like grilled yellowfin tuna with a tomatillo salsa, sautéed pork tenderloin with caramelized shallot sauce, roast duck with fruit chutney and grilled filet mignon with shiitake mushroom sauce. Dessert could be chocolate chip cheesecake, chocolate linzer torte or hazelnut torte.

A prix-fixe lunch for $13.95 brings soup, salad and entrée.

Open Wednesday-Sunday, lunch in winter, 11:30 to 2:30; dinner, 5:30 to 9. Closed spring and fall. No smoking.

Stubb's, Mountain Road at Edson Hill Road, Stowe. (802) 253-7110.

This highly regarded dining spot is the reincarnation of a building that once housed the esteemed Steen's restaurant. Chef-owner Jim Dynan's fare, which changes with the seasons, is served in a candlelit setting of brass lamps, white linens and ladderback chairs. Entrées range from $11.50 for grilled chicken with lemon and mushrooms to $17.75 for grilled sirloin with black peppercorns. Spicy shrimp satay with fried noodle pancake, prime rib with Yorkshire popover, sautéed Vermont calves liver and grilled leg of lamb with sweet roasted-pepper salad are menu staples.

Standouts among appetizers include spicy grilled lamb sausage with radicchio and lentil salad, duck and scallion dumplings laced with ginger, and grilled shrimp with spiced pecans on watercress and Boston lettuce. Homemade pastries and ice creams are the dessert fare.

An appealing bar menu, including portions of the dining-room menu, is served in

Cut-glass chandeliers reflect in mirrors in Isle de France dining room.

the lounge. We'd go there just for the lamb mixed grill – spicy sausage and grilled brochette, with garlic-roasted potatoes and pepper salad ($8.75).

Dinner nightly, 5:30 to 10.

The Whip Bar and Grill, Green Mountain Inn, Main Street, Stowe. (802) 253-7301.

The Whip is a casual and creative counterpoint to the country-pretty Main Street Dining Room, which operates only in peak seasons (which is to say, foliage and winter) in the Green Mountain Inn. It's downstairs, smartly decorated and striking for the antique buggy whips in the wall divider separating bar from dining room and over the fireplace. Just outside is a most attractive deck, where the garden furniture is navy and white and tables are shaded by white umbrellas.

The day's offerings are chalked on blackboards above cases where the food is displayed. Some of the dishes are calorie-counted for those who are there for the spa facilities. Country pâté on toast points, smoked salmon with capers, Mexican vegetable soup, salads with dressings devised by the Canyon Ranch in Arizona, crabmeat on a croissant with melted cheddar, open-face veggie melt – this is good grazing fare.

At lunchtime, you might find grilled marinated shark, black pepper fettuccine alfredo, lobster ravioli on greens with mint vinaigrette or a crabmeat croissant, priced from $4.95 to $7.95. Or try an overstuffed sandwich on thick slices of homemade oatmeal-honey bread, a trademark as well known as the Whip's riding paraphernalia.

Main dishes ($8.50 to $17.95) like yellowfin tuna with lo mein noodles, broiled mako with kiwi-ginger-mango salsa, grilled breast of duck with pinot noir sauce and sautéed veal with brandied apple cream are posted starting at 6 at night. Blueberry-apple crumb pie, raspberry bash, lemon cream carrot cake and a sac de bon bon for two are some of the ever-changing desserts.

Lunch and dinner daily, 11:30 to 9:30.

The Shed, Mountain Road, Stowe. (802) 253-4364.

An institution among skiers for years, the Shed has grown from its original shed to include a wraparound solarium filled with Caribbean-style furnishings, trees and plants, and a menu offering something for everyone at all three meals. Following a disastrous 1994 fire, owners Kathy and Ken Strong rebuilt it bigger and better than ever, and added a microbrewery and Brewery Pub featuring European-style ales brewed on the premises.

Rebuilt to look old, the expansive main dining room has bright red walls, a beamed ceiling, a stone fireplace in the center and green woven mats on wood tables flanked by high-back chairs. An outdoor deck brightened by petunias is popular in season.

The food is straightforward and with-it, from nachos to bruschetta to Thai chicken and vegetables to jerk chicken 'n ribs. You can get scallops florentine, salmon persille, seafood linguini, roast duck, lamb bourbon, steak teriyaki, prime rib and goodness knows what else at dinner prices ranging from $10.75 to $15.50. The omelet and belgian waffle buffet had people lined up outside for Sunday brunch on the holiday weekend we tried to get in.

Lunch daily, noon to 4:30; dinner, 5 to 10; Sunday brunch, 9 to 2.

The Olive Grove, Stowe Center Shops, Route 108, Stowe. (802) 253-2033.

A local artist painted the mural of a lady leaning outside the window over the entry to this new restaurant in a shopping complex. She also painted the colorful mural of an Italian vineyard (whimsically accented with Stowe landmarks and Vermont cows) at the back of the dining room. "It's a work in progress," advised owner Alan Handwerger, a former Florida restaurateur who launched this venture in 1994 with his wife Lorrie.

Italian and Mediterranean farmhouse cooking is offered. Pastas and pizzas are featured, but there are interesting specials as well: basque chicken served over spanish rice, scampi provençal over linguini, pork à la naranja with a sauce of spanish brandy and even spanakopita and stuffed grape leaves at our visit. Prices are easy on the pocketbook, generally $8.75 to $13.50. Ditto for the all-Italian wine list, which is particularly strong on reds. There's an outdoor patio for dining beside the Stowe Recreation Path in the summer.

Dinner nightly except Tuesday, 5 to 10.

Restaurant Swisspot, Main Street, Stowe. (802) 253-4622.

Skiers have always been partial to fondues, and they're the specialty at this small and enduring place, brought to Stowe in 1968 after its incarnation as the restaurant in the Swiss Pavilion at Expo 67 in Montreal.

The classic Swiss cheese fondue with a dash of kirsch, $22.95 for two, made a fun meal for our skiing family. Also good is the beef fondue oriental ($33 for two), served with four sauces. There are six quiches ($12.95 to $13.95) and a handful of entrées like bratwurst, chicken florentine and sirloin steak, $10.95 to $16.95.

Open daily, noon to 10 p.m. Closed spring and late fall.

Austrian Tea Room, Trapp Family Lodge, Luce Hill Road, Stowe. (802) 253-8511.

In summer or foliage season, we know of no more charming place for lunch or a snack than the rear deck of the Austrian Tea Room, with planters of geraniums and petunias enhancing the view across the countryside and horses grazing nearby. Surely you can feel the spirit of the late Maria von Trapp (who lived at the lodge until her death in 1987) and the Trapp Family Singers. It's a majestic setting where you feel on top of the world.

The fresh spinach salad looks great, as does the tomato stuffed with shrimp salad, and you can get broiled knockwurst served with sauerkraut and potato salad or liverwurst with onions. There are daily specials like chilled raspberry soup and shrimp and crab quiche as well as open-face sandwiches, fancy drinks, cafe Viennoise and Austrian wines by the glass or liter.

Those Austrian desserts we all know and love, sacher torte, linzer torte, apfelstrudel and the like, as well as Bavarian chocolate pie, peach torte and jailhouse pie, are in the $4 range. With a cup of cafe mocha, they make a delightful afternoon pick-me-up.

The trip up Luce Hill Road gives you a chance to see the rebuilt, exotic Trapp Family Lodge, which the locals consider the closest thing to Disneyland in Vermont. The tea room remains true to the lodge's heritage.

Open daily, 10:30 to 5:30. No smoking.

Diversions

Mount Mansfield. Skiing is what made Stowe famous, legions of skiers having been attracted to New England's most storied mountain since the East's first chairlift was installed in 1940 (the Mount Mansfield Company is its official name, but everyone from near and far calls the ski area simply Stowe). Today, Mount Mansfield has sleek new eight-passenger gondola cars among its seven lifts and vastly expanded snowmaking. Nearly one-third of its slopes are for expert skiers, including the awesome "Front Four" – the precipitous National, Goat, Starr and Liftline trails, so steep that on the Starr you cannot see the bottom from the ledge on top; they almost make the Nosedive seem tame. There's easier terrain, of course, and the related Spruce Peak ski area across the way has four more lifts, a sunny southeast exposure and a special section for new skiers. Combined with accommodations and nightlife, the total skiing experience ranks Stowe among the world's top ski resorts. Adult lift tickets are $43.

Summer at Mount Mansfield. The Stowe Gondola takes visitors 7,000 feet up to the Cliff House, just below Vermont's highest summit (adults $9, mid-June to mid-October). Cars can drive up the 4.5-mile **Stowe Auto Road,** known to skiers who ease down it in winter as the Toll Road (cars $10, daily late May to mid-October). The **Alpine Slide at Spruce Peak** appeals especially to children; you take a chairlift up and slide down (single rides, $4; open daily in summer, weekends in late spring and early fall).

Smugglers' Notch. Up the Mountain Road past the ski area you enter the Mount Mansfield State Park, passing picnic areas and the Long Trail. A couple of hairpin turns take you into Smugglers' Notch, a narrow pass with 1,000-foot cliffs looming on either side. The closest thing we've seen in the East to Yosemite, it's a quiet, awe-inspiring place to pause and gawk at such rock formations as Elephant Head, King Rock and the Hunter and His Dog. Stop at Smugglers' Cave and, farther on, hike into Bingham Falls. The road is not for the faint-hearted (it's closed in winter, for good reason). We drove back from Jeffersonville after a summer thunderstorm and found waterfalls that had been trickles on the way over suddenly gushing down the rocks beside the lonely road.

The Arts. The hills are alive with the sound of music as the Stowe Performing Arts series offers Sunday evening concerts in the concert meadow near the Trapp Family Lodge. The Vermont Mozart Festival also presents concerts there. More concerts are staged at the Stowe Mountain Performing Arts Center, a 12,000-seat amphitheater at the base of Spruce Peak. The **Stowe Stage Company** presents an ambitious schedule of summer plays and musicals at Stowe High School. The **Helen Day Art Center** hosts rotating exhibits in a restored 1863 Greek Revival structure that once was the high school on School Street.

The **Stowe Recreation Path** is the pride of the community. Opened in 1984 with an extension in 1989, the nationally recognized 5.3-mile walking and biking greenway starts in the village behind the Community Church and roughly parallels the Mountain Road up to Brook Road. Also in the recreation category is the **Stowe Polo Club,** another community-based effort, which stages polo events throughout the season.

The **Cold Hollow Cider Mill,** south of town along Route 100, is a large and intriguing red barn where you can watch cider made (and drink the sweet and delicious free samples). For more than twenty years the Chittenden family also have sold tart cider jelly, cider donuts and other apple products as well as cookbooks, wooden toys, gourmet foods and about every kind of Vermont jam, jelly or preserve imaginable.

Nearby, all kinds of cheeses and dips may be sampled (and purchased) at the large new **Cabot Creamery Annex Store.** Also part of the complex is a branch of famed pastry chef Albert Kumin's **Green Mountain Chocolate Company,** headquartered down Route 100 below Waterbury, which caters to Stowe's sweet tooth.

Shopping. Shops are concentrated in Stowe and scattered along Route 100 and the Mountain Road. Along Main Street in the village, **Shaw's General Store** considers itself 90 years young and carries most everything, especially sporting goods, sportswear, gifts and oddities. Nearby are the **Old Depot Shops,** an open, meandering mall of a place containing the **Green Mountain Pantry, Vermont Furniture Works, The Craft Sampler, Stuffed in Stowe** with thousands of stuffed animals and **Bear Pond Books.** For a different experience, head to **Everything Cows,** which speaks for itself. It's a bovine boutique where cows prevail in sox, mugs, stained glass and even Christmas decorations. Upstairs is **The Udder End,** a gallery of cow country collectibles including cow-famed Woody Jackson serigraphs and custom-made quilts.

Up the Mountain Road at 108 West is the **Stowe Kitchen Co.,** with practical cookware and gadgets. Also on the Mountain Road are **Stowe Pottery,** the **Stowe Craft Gallery** and **The Christmas Place;** the excellent **Stowe Mountain Sports** is at Stowe Center. The **West Branch Shops** include **Mountain Cheese and Wine** with an impressive selection and **Samara,** an unusually good shop featuring works of Vermont craftsmen. **The Yellow Turtle** offers "classy clothes for classy kids," the kind that well-heeled grandparents like to buy. Vermont artists show at **The Artists' Gallery.** We were impressed with all the sophisticated handicrafts, the MacKenzie-Childs pottery, the Claire Murray rugs and the whimsical, even wild furniture at Constance Rasmussen's suave **Emotional Outlet Gallery.** At **Exclusively Vermont** you'll find jams, pickled fiddlehead ferns, beeswax candles, potpourri in large jars, boiled wool mittens and jewelry.

Extra-Special

Ben & Jerry's Ice Cream Factory, Route 100, Waterbury. (802) 244-8687.

Just south of Stowe, this factory producing 130,000 pints daily of the ice cream that transplanted Vermont characters Ben Cohen and Jerry Greenfield made famous is one of Vermont's busiest tourist attractions. And with good reason. During half-hour guided tours ($1), you see a humorous slide show, watch the ice cream being made, learn some of the history of this intriguing outfit that donates one percent of its profits to peace and, of course, savor a tiny sample, obtained by lowering a bucket on a rope to the production area below. At busy times, the place is a madhouse – with live music outside, lineups of people waiting to buy cones, a gift shop filled with Vermont cow-related items, and every bit of publicity Ben and Jeryry ever got decorating the walls. If you can't get inside, at least buy a dish or cone of ice cream from the outdoor windows. Tours daily 9 to 4, Sunday 11 to 4.

Skiers enjoy fresh powder conditions on a sunny day at Sugarbush.

Waitsfield and Warren, Vt.
The Spirit of the Valley

Even more than most Vermont areas best known for skiing, the Mad River Valley is a year-round paradise for sports enthusiasts.

The focus, of course, is on skiing – at the venerable and spartan Mad River Glen, a challenging area for hardy, serious skiers, and at Sugarbush, the tony resort spawned by and for jet-setters. Both are very much "in" with skiers, for vastly differing reasons.

In the off-season, which extends from May into November, there are the conventional athletic pursuits associated with other destination ski resorts, such as golf and tennis. There also are the more unusual: mountaineering, polo, rugby, cricket, Icelandic horse trekking and soaring.

Off-mountain, activity centers along Route 100, which links the villages of Waitsfield and Warren. Ironically, Waitsfield (the home of Mad River Glen) is busier and more hip in the Sugarbush style. Warren (the address for Sugarbush) is in the Mad River Glen tradition, remote and seemingly bypassed by the times. The skiing spirit extends to the entrepreneurial. An uncommon number of crafts ventures thrive here, as do unusual businesses. Two unassuming enterprises that ship fresh or frozen pizzas to connoisseurs around the East have suddenly turned Waitsfield into the pizza capital of northern New England.

The spirit of the valley – considered unique by its adherents – emerges from its rugged terrain as well as from the contrasting mix attracted by its two skiing faces.

Unlike other ski resorts where one big mountain crowns a plateau, here mountains crowd the valley on all sides, forging several narrow valleys that leave some visitors feeling hemmed in. To understand, you have only to stay in summer in a remote chalet at Mad River Glen, the mountains rising in silence all around, or descend the back road from Roxbury Gap, one of Vermont's more heart-stopping drives, which rewards the persevering with awesome close-ups of some of the state's highest peaks.

41

The chic of Sugarbush joins with the rusticity of Mad River to present choices from racquetball to backpacking, from boutiques to country stores, from nightclubbing to roadhouses. For fine dining, the valley is in the vanguard among Eastern ski resorts.

Although the valley is at its best and busiest in the winter, its spirit spans all seasons.

Inn Spots

The Inn at the Round Barn Farm, East Warren Road, RR 1, Box 247, Waitsfield 05673. (802) 496-2276.

The Joslin Round Barn – a National Historic Landmark and one of the last remaining of its kind in Vermont – is a focal point of this deluxe and animated B&B. Its three vast floors have been renovated into a cultural center, a theater, a space for meetings and weddings, and the headquarters of the new Round Barn Farm Cross-Country Ski Center. There's even a 60-foot-long lap pool on the lower level.

The inn is not in the Round Barn as one might think, however. Rather, it occupies a gracious farmhouse and connecting carriage house next door, has seven comfortable bedrooms and four extravagant suites, luxurious common rooms and a terraced, 85-acre back yard that rolls down a hill to a couple of ponds and meanders uphill past cows grazing in the distance. It's an idyllic setting, and an exciting B&B.

Innkeepers Jack and Doreen Simko, longtime skiers in the valley, retired from the family floral business in New Jersey to open the inn with daughter AnneMarie in 1987. So expect to see flowers and greenery throughout the house, pots of flowering hibiscus on the terrace, and flowers sprouting from piles of rocks beneath a giant apple tree.

Relaxing on the back terraces is a treat, what with animals grazing, a few barns scattered up the hill, whimsical things like a cow made out of iron and, at our first visit, a pen with Jack's three pet pigs – gifts for his 50th birthday. There's only one pig now, and a new attraction is an undulating, fourteen-foot-deep spring-fed pond for swimming, canoeing and fishing.

Our original stay coming at the end of one of the hottest summers ever, we passed up the two largest rooms with jacuzzi tubs in the main house in favor of the breezy Palmer Room at the rear corner. It had a highback Victorian queen bed sporting a crazy quilt made in 1915, lovely lace curtains and a framed fan on the wall.

The draperies match the canopy on the kingsize bed in the Joslin Room, notable for

cranberry walls and a heart-shaped lace pillow. Three people can sleep comfortably in the spacious, ground-level Terrace Room, with its queensize bed and sitting area with sofabed.

The best accommodations are now in four mini-suites with queen or kingsize beds, steam showers, gas fireplaces and separate sitting areas beneath twenty-foot beamed ceilings in the rear loft area of the original carriage house. The top-of-the-line Richardson suite contains a sunken bathroom with an over-size jacuzzi (you can watch the farm animals outside the window as you

Joslin Round Barn and landscaped lawns are focal points of the Inn at the Round Barn Farm.

soak), a separate shower, and his and her vanities. Relax on the chintz loveseat or chaise lounge beside the marble fireplace and you may never leave.

Striking fabrics on canopies and window treatments provide colorful accents against the barnwood walls in each suite; even the custom-designed Kleenex boxes match the decor. Although not as splashy as some, the pristinely white Dana Room at the end is favored by honeymooners for its Schumacher wall coverings and its crown-canopied black iron queensize bed draped in chiffon. Besides fine oriental and Claire Murray rugs, burgundy terrycloth robes, stenciling and other interesting decorative touches, the inn has nightly turndown service with chocolates as well as toiletries like Neutrogena bath conditioners and moisturizers.

The main floor offers a large, elegant library with walls of books, a fireplace and a fancy stereo system issuing forth perhaps Mozart or Vivaldi. A less formal game room downstairs contains a pool table, TV and VCR.

At cocktail time, AnneMarie gets creative with canapés, usually putting out something like guacamole or a hot shrimp dip.

Breakfast is served in a large sun porch with skylights, wicker and chintz, and teal blue swags across the top of the windows. Here we feasted on raspberries and bananas in cream, followed by a fantastic omelet blending bacon, cottage cheese, onions, red peppers and basil from the garden. AnneMarie's cinnamon-raisin belgian waffles with maple cream is another favorite, and her pumpkin soufflés are a hit in foliage season.

Upon guests' requests, the Simkos began bottling the raspberry sauce they serve with their cottage-cheese pancakes. Said a California friend who was enjoying a reunion with the Simkos and joined us all at the breakfast table: "These are high-energy people with 85 irons in the fire. Staying with them is like being part of the family."

Doubles, $100 to $140; suites, $155 and $185.

Hamilton House, German Flats Road, RR 1, Box 74, Warren 05674. (802) 583-1066.

There are those who would think Joyce and James Plumpton have it all: an aristocratic British background, a successful business career, world travels, three grown sons, a huge retirement home in the midst of 25 forested acres between golf course and ski mountain. So why would they want to open their home as a B&B? "We like to entertain," say the Plumptons, whose house lends itself to entertaining and is frequently the site of large parties for local groups and causes with which they are affiliated. "We love people, looking after them and making them feel good."

That they do to perfection, with great taste and jolly good British humor. The Plumptons first started thinking of doing a B&B when they were living in a substantial stone manor house in northern England in the 1970s. But James's business took them to New Jersey, and they also acquired a ski house at Sugarbush. In 1988, they purchased the 30-year-old home of the man who developed the Sugarbush Inn and golf course. They transformed the 8,000-square-foot structure from a ski lodge into an English manor house to accommodate friends and family gatherings. They named it Hamilton House in memory of Florence Hamilton, Joyce's mother, a member of one of Scotland's leading families and related by marriage to the Royal Family. "The crest we use is that of the Duke of Hamilton," advises the inn's detailed and informative welcome letter.

Some might think staying here would be intimidating – "I'm very pickity," Joyce said as she showed us the Maiden Cross Rooms, a suite named for their last home in England. "I won't put the twin beds together because I think a kingsize bed would spoil the effect of the room." And only one suite, the College Rooms, has a TV because Joyce could not fathom people "coming to Vermont to watch TV." But the Plumptons' welcome is down-to-earth and heartfelt. We selected the Garden Room for its kingsize bed, and quietly repaired after dinner to the empty College Rooms' living room to catch up on the evening news on TV.

Two spacious bedrooms and two suites are available for guests on the second floor. All have full private baths. Largest is the College Rooms, a living room and queensize bedroom with paraphernalia from the hosts' college days in England, including a stash of tennis and squash racquets displayed ever so smartly in a basket. The family's chappals (similar to sandals) are lined up beneath a side table in the India Room, which is dressed in rich fabrics and rattans reminiscent of the family's residence in India. The Garden Room overlooking a clump of rhododendrons and azaleas reflects the "great pleasure" that the Plumptons have derived from creating gardens in different parts of the world. Floral fabrics on the headboard matched the swagged curtains and wallpaper border along the top of the pale yellow walls. Three rows of framed floral prints traced the months of the year, two garden books were on a side table and a cement turtle served as the door stop. A basket of apples and grapes was in the room upon our arrival; a small gold box of chocolates was presented at turndown.

On the main floor, guests enjoy their own large drawing room, full of comfortable seating and shelves of books (but few conveniently positioned lights with which to read at night); a long, plant-filled conservatory that's a joy year-round, and a magnificent formal dining room centered by an oval mahogany table for eight. "Obviously my furniture came with me from England," Joyce points out. Off the long front hall are a wet bar, stocked with wines to which guests may help themselves, beers and James's favorite Long Trail ales, and a laundry room where skis and boots may be stashed and where the family cats Riley and Ophelia sleep in baskets atop the washer and dryer.

The conservatory was the setting for a "proper English breakfast," as described by Joyce and cooked by James. Orange juice and a glass dish rimmed with sugar and bearing raspberries, grapes and melon balls with mint and a sour cream sauce began the repast. Next came a plate of small harvest muffins and croissants. The main event was scrambled eggs, served with mushroom caps, link sausages and delicious grilled tomatoes on toasted bread rounds spread with a zesty pesto sauce.

Grounds of Hamilton House are blanketed in winter's white.

This is "very much our home and we intend to keep it that way," says James. They designed the house so it could remain as a family home if the B&B didn't work out. Eventually they may hire help, but meanwhile they do all the innkeeping work themselves – to determine whether they like it, and to know what to demand of any staff. In their first year, they were thoroughly enjoying their roles.

Doubles, $125 and $150; suites, $165 and $175. No smoking.

The Featherbed Inn, Route 100, RD 1, Box 19, Waitsfield 05673. (802) 496-7151.

There are plump featherbeds on the beds, naturally, and featherbed eggs are the breakfast specialty at this historic and stylish B&B opened in 1993 by New Jersey transplants Clive and Tracey Coutts. After three years of painstaking renovations, the place bears faint resemblance to its background as the area's first B&B/ski lodge in the 1950s. The result is the more remarkable in that the couple did most of the work themselves. He handled the construction end, even putting 3,000 of the original bricks into the foundation and the living-room fireplace. She did the decorating, window treatments and some spectacular stenciling.

Two pleasant guest rooms on the first floor share a large bath and a private den with television. Upstairs are three more bedrooms and two suites, all with private baths. The Ilse Suite at the north end has a skylit, beamed cathedral ceiling with a loveseat in the corner, a hooked rug on the original softwood flooring and an antique quilt on the queensize sleigh bed. The prized Beatrice Suite in the middle of the house holds a queensize canopy bed whose quilt coordinates with the floral swags draped across three windows and the fabric on the rare spindle bench beneath. The suite is also notable for fancy stenciling along the chair rails, a wet bar with refrigerator, and a small bedroom equipped with a day bed and trundle bed. The new Alexandra Room at the south end has a queensize iron bed and two wing chairs. The sprinkling of antiques and period memorabilia produces a simple but cheery look, one in keeping with the early 19th-century origin of the house.

Tracey's stenciling, evident in most rooms, reaches its zenith in the informal, main-floor lodge room. Here, beneath a beamed ceiling, stenciled geese and ducks fly up and around the windows and french doors in random procession. The room is sunny in wicker, the doors open onto an outdoor deck and an open fireplace is ablaze in winter. Guests also enjoy a handsome living room, where Clive may play for singalongs around the grand piano. Teal wainscoting and a lace-covered table enhance the formal dining room. Tracey often serves featherbed eggs in individual ramekins, eirkuchen (German pancakes stuffed with apples or peaches), or french toast stuffed with creamed cottage cheese sweetened with maple syrup and fruit. These treats follow a fancy fruit course (perhaps baked pineapple or grapefruit) and homemade apricot or strawberry breads. Fruit and cheese, cookies, tea and hot cider are put out in the afternoon.

Doubles, $80 to $110; suites, $110 to $120.

Beaver Pond Farm Inn, Golf Course Road, RD Box 306, Warren 05674. (802) 583-2861.

A farmhouse this may be, but an elegant one it is indeed. Located off a quiet country road overlooking several beaver ponds and the Sugarbush Golf Club fairways, the light green house with green roof has candles lighted in the windows even on a summer afternoon. The back yard has a driving range with two tees, such is the interest of owners Betty and Bob Hansen (she's been golf club champion and president of the Vermont Women's Golf Association).

They share their gorgeous property and home with guests, who enjoy a stylish fireplaced living room done in rusts and navy, a small bar where setups and hors d'oeuvre are provided in the late afternoon, a beamed dining room with a long harvest table on an oriental rug and decanters of brandy and sherry at the ready, and a small library with TV and telephone, furnished in contemporary style in red and gray. Best of all, perhaps, is a fabulous rear deck that runs the length of the house, where the Hansens and guests like to have cocktails and watch the beavers in the pond.

Betty, a French-trained chef and onetime New Jersey caterer, is considered the best cook in the valley by fellow innkeepers. Her full country breakfast starts with fresh juice, fruit and cereal. Orders are taken for choices among four main courses, always a special egg dish (eggs florentine at our last visit), eggs any way, grand marnier french toast and perhaps apple-walnut pancakes. The Hansens offer dinners in winter on Tuesday, Thursday and Saturday for $20 to $22. She cooks and he serves the meal, which starts at 7:30. A typical dinner could be soup or smoked trout mousse topped with caviar, salad, butterflied lamb and floating island. French wines accompany.

Upstairs are five well furnished guest rooms, three with private baths and two sharing. Three have queensize beds and two are twins. Those in the older section dating to 1840 have sloping "coffin windows;" explains Bob: "everything slopes, there are no straight angles in a Vermont farmhouse." The Hansens now offer a sixth queensize bedroom with private bath adjoining the rear deck downstairs. Cheery in pink and yellow, it became available when they moved to a new apartment in the barn.

Doubles, $86 to $96.

The Sugartree, Sugarbush Access Road, Warren 05674. (802) 583-3211 or (800) 666-8907.

Energetic new owners are leaving their mark on the Sugartree, an inviting inn transformed from what essentially had been a ski chalet for 30 years. Frank and Kathy Partsch traded corporate life in Boston for new roles as jack-of-all-trades innkeepers. Besides their hospitality roles, Frank has put his handyman/carpentry talents to good use and Kathy has taken up sewing. Her new job description lists cook, decorator, part-time work at Mad River Canoe and volunteer stints at the local Chamber of Commerce.

Guests arriving at the homey, nine-bedroom inn see evidence of Frank's talents

Rear deck is favorite gathering spot for guests at Beaver Pond Farm Inn.

immediately. He renovated the office/reception area at the entry to make it seem less like an office. It opens into a new fireplaced suite he created with a small wicker sitting room, a queensize bedroom and a renovated bath with a vanity he made himself in a workshop rapidly taking over the garage.

More of Frank's handiwork is evident in the spacious living room. He built the tall clock as well as the wood-carved folk art Santa Clauses lined up along the fireplace mantel. The figures often reflect local activities, from skiing Santas to one with a tennis racquet. Kathy's new-found sewing talent has revealed itself in the quilts she is making for the guest bedrooms. "I couldn't sew before I got here," she confessed. Now she has dressed up a couple of bedrooms with quilts, one made of 800 pieces. She made curtains for the sitting room in the suite, and found an antique pump organ for the living room. The bedrooms, all with private baths, are furnished in country style with puffy curtains, shams, dust ruffles, crocheted bed canopies, samplers, needlework wall hangings and wreaths on the doors. The bathrooms have glycerin soaps, herbal bath grains and built-in hair dryers.

Kathy serves a full country breakfast in the dining room. The menu, posted on a blackboard, included juices, apple crisp, bacon and french toast with orange sauce or maple syrup at our latest visit. Baked eggs with three cheeses and assorted berry pancakes are other specialties. In the afternoon, she's apt to put out cookies and perhaps chocolate fondue.

Outside, summer's trees, incredible gardens and window boxes envelop the inn in its own delightful island of color and greenery. There's a gazebo, and Frank has put in a rock garden and planned to add an herb garden. In winter, when the trees are bare, the landscape opens onto the mountains and guests can see skiers at Sugarbush across the way.

Doubles, $90; suite, $100.

The Lareau Farm Country Inn, Route 100, Box 563, Waitsfield 05673. (802) 496-4949 or (800) 833-0766.

This really is a farm with gardens, four dogs, four cats, seven horses and occasionally chickens and pigs, the whole menagerie dubbed the Lareau Zoo and the name delightfully emblazoned on sweatshirts, aprons, T-shirts and the like. The 1852 farmhouse with a barn, woodshed and appropriate 67-acre country setting on flatlands that were farmed until a few years ago by the Lareau family was converted into an inn in 1984 by Pennsylvanians Sue and Dan Easley, who have been expanding and upgrading it ever since. In the Mad River on the property, a ten-foot-deep swimming hole is flanked by rocks. You can dive into "water so clear you can see the brown trout," according to Sue. Actually, there are three swimming holes: one for the public and families, one for house guests and one for skinny-dipping ("we send one couple at a time," advises Dan). The flora and fauna on the property are so interesting that Sue has published a detailed walking trail guide for guests.

Since she pieced together the squares for ten bed quilts in their first summer, the Easleys have added bathrooms and expanded to thirteen guest rooms. In the former woodshed, the dirt floors have given way to carpeting, but the four rooms retain some of the original posts and beams amid such modern conveniences as private baths. Brass bedsteads and rockers are mixed with a profusion of hanging plants.

An addition to the rear of the main house holds four guest rooms, all with full baths and queensize beds, a vastly enlarged dining room and a sitting room around the fireplace in the former kitchen. A new jacuzzi suite is among the other five rooms, two of which share baths, in the oldest part of the house, built in the 1700s. The main structure was added to it, and has a parlor full of Victorian furniture and stuffed animals. Guests like to laze on the assortment of porches that wrap around the house.

The main gathering place has turned out to be the huge rear dining room and back porch with six columns obtained at auction. Pretty in beige and blue, the dining room has four big tables, oriental rugs and windows on three sides. "It's changed our orientation," says Sue, "bringing the focus out back." Adirondack chairs are gathered on the back lawn for gazing across the farmlands up against the mountains.

Dan is the breakfast chef, whipping up homemade muffins or breads and perhaps an egg soufflé casserole and blueberry or banana-oatbran pancakes. The inn has a beer and wine license, and provides hors d'oeuvre and setups for guests in the winter.

The old slaughterhouse has been turned into the home of the locally famous American Flatbread business and restaurant (see below).

The Easleys offer sleigh rides and cider parties. They donate their food leftovers to Meals on Wheels and give a percentage of the room rates to the Nature Conservancy ("our way of trying to protect Vermont's future," says Dan). One year every guest received a cookie cutter in the shape of a maple leaf for use as a napkin ring. It symbolized their theme to be "a cut above."

Doubles, $70 to $100.

West Hill House, West Hill Road, RR 1, Box 292, Warren 05674. (802) 496-7162.

A wonderfully secluded setting on fifteen acres next to the Sugarbush Golf Course and Ski Touring Center, a quaint Vermont farmhouse dating to 1862 and welcoming hosts commend this six-room B&B. Not to be overlooked are gourmet breakfasts, occasional dinners and charming common rooms.

The place reflects the talents of owners Dotty Kyle and Eric Brattstrom, both from Maplewood, N.J. Dotty, an artist and accomplished cook, hand-painted the beautiful border of flowers that winds around the living room, stairway and cathedral ceiling. She also painted the floral borders that match the spread on a queen bed in an upstairs bedroom. Her husband Eric, who commutes to New York for his latest assignment as a construction project manager, built the wall of shelves in the living room to house part of their huge book collection. He remodeled a shared bath upstairs to make private

Back porch at Lareau Farm Country Inn overlooks fields and mountains.

baths for two bedrooms. At our 1994 visit, he had broken ground for a rear wing to provide a skiers' entry, powder room and a second guest living room with french doors onto a big screened porch, plus new owners' quarters.

The dormer windows and sloping ceilings in the main house yield lots of nooks and crannies, which the artist in Dotty has turned to good advantage. She sponge-painted the walls light green in one bedroom and added a king/twin bed configuration to a second bedroom, which now has a new sitting room with a day bed. Arrangements of fresh or dried flowers and bowls of seasonal candies are placed about. Thick towels, down pillows and comforters, attractive quilts and assorted toiletries are the norm.

Guests relax on the wicker-filled front porch facing bird feeders, tiny red squirrels and prolific gardens or in the barnwood-paneled living room with its treasury of books, vaulted ceiling, wide-board floors and a large recessed fireplace at one end. A pantry holds a refrigerator and wet bar, where guests help themselves to cookies, soft drinks, cider and wine. A new picture window in the beamed dining room opens up views of the surrounding countryside. Breakfast begins with a fresh fruit bowl ("we have a blueberry patch that won't quit," Dotty advised), yogurt, homemade granola, muffins or coffee cake and "the best sticky buns in the world – I've always loved them and worked very hard to get them the way I want them." The other half of the dough for the sticky buns becomes rich cinnamon-raisin bread, often used for french toast. Other main courses could be baked apple pancakes, banana-nut waffles, vegetable soufflés and omelets with cheddar cheese and herbs.

On Saturday nights by reservation, Dotty prepares four-course dinners with soup, salad and dessert. The price varies from $18 to $30, depending on entrée. Favorites include roast chicken basted with maple syrup over roasted vegetables, braised pork chops with onions and apples, and steak diane.

Doubles, $95 to $105. Two-night minimum on weekends. No smoking.

1824 House Inn, Route 100, Box 159, Waitsfield 05673. (802) 496-7555 or (800) 426-3986.

Susan and Lawrence McKay moved back East from Washington state in December 1994 to take over Newtons' 1824 House Inn. Moving from Vashon Island and high-level careers, she said, there was only one other state in which they would choose to raise their young children and that was Vermont. They purchased a going operation but set about spiffing up the inn. They replaced dark curtains with sheers, took up the carpets to show the oak flooring, eliminated some clutter and added antiques from the West Coast. The result is a clean, fresh and elegant look in keeping with the house's designation on the National Register of Historic Places.

These versatile ex-Pennsylvanians took to innkeeping with enthusiasm. Lawrence, a film and TV writer who had just published a children's book "for children of all ages," is a gourmet cook. His talents are showcased at breakfast, when fresh blueberries and raspberries (even in winter) are the rule. The fruit course could be Texas grapefruit or raspberries with crème fraîche. Next might come blueberry or raspberry muffins. The main event could be yellow cornmeal pancakes with blueberries, a chile rellenos soufflé or waffles with raspberries and a fruit coulis. Espresso or latte accompany. In the afternoon, blue cheese and crackers might accompany sherry or port. You might get the host, a folk music buff, to play a banjo given him by Pete Seeger after he heard Lawrence perform.

Susan, an educator and psychologist, went to work with a decorator's eye in the common rooms and seven guest rooms, all with private baths. Enter the house through a foyer/parlor with a baby grand piano. On one side is a full-length living room with a fireplace, game table and a couple of spectacular Larson chairs. On the other side is the dining room with two tables and some of the McKay's newer Scandinavian pieces. The walls are enhanced by artworks given by an artist-friend, the late Russell Twiggs. Bedrooms contain king, queen or double beds. The biggest room we saw, pretty in blue and brown, has a queensize bed, armoire, an antique wing chair and a simple wood chair.

Susan is also a dressage rider, and is stabling her Morgan horse in the barn. She planned to create a dressage arena with white fencing facing the road. The 22-acre property includes trails, an organic garden that the McKays couldn't wait to get their hands on, and a swimming hole in the Mad River.

Doubles, $85 to $125. No smoking.

Tucker Hill Lodge, Route 17, RD 1, Box 147, Waitsfield 05673. (802) 496-3983 or (800) 543-7841.

Since it was acquired by the Baron Group in 1987, this inn of wide fame has had its ups and downs. New owners Susan Francheschini Noaro and her husband Giorgio moved from Ottawa in 1992, hoping to restore the place to its former glory and trying to find a niche that balances simple guest rooms with a reputation for high-end dining.

This has always been one of the more lavishly landscaped inns we have seen. In summer, the spectacular flower gardens contain hanging clematis, flowering kale and decorative mullen.

The 22 guest rooms vary in size and decor; fourteen have private baths. They are homey and rustic, with handmade quilts, bouquets of flowers and what the inn's brochure calls "a mountain cabin feeling." One of the nicest is the Innkeepers' Suite (home of the former innkeepers) with a fireplace, kingsize feather bed and connecting twin-bedded room. Also popular is the Catamount Suite in the former cross-country building across the way.

In the main inn, a paneled living room has TV and a fieldstone fireplace. The main dining room and a barnwood cafe/lounge downstairs are known as Giorgio's Cafe (see Dining Spots); the downstairs section is where the renowned American Flatbread country pizzas got their start. Tennis courts, the pool and a large outdoor deck ringed with cedar trees are attractions.

Breakfasts are hearty: seasonal fresh fruit, followed perhaps by cottage-cheese pancakes with fresh peaches, a broccoli, tomato and mushroom omelet, or Vermont toast, which is french toast with shredded cheddar cheese between the layers.

The Noaros recommend hiking the local trails (the Long Trail is not far away). You'll need to after one of their breakfasts or dinners.

Doubles, $60 to $90 B&B; $120 to $155 MAP; suites, $115 or $175.

Dining Spots

Sam Rupert's, Sugarbush Access Road, Warren. (802) 583-2421.

Skiers heading for Sugarbush once stopped at the Sugarbush Sugarhouse for pancakes and homemade syrup. Today, they stop at a vastly expanded dining establish-

ment with a smashing greenhouse room for superior food offered by Sandy Taber and JoAnna Jenkins, owners who took over in 1989. From the outdoor table set for a couple of lifelike characters at our fall visit at the access road entrance, to a look at the wine list cited with a Wine Spectator award of excellence, you can tell that this pair know their food. They have imbued Sam Rupert's with culinary adventure and elevated its status to tops in the valley, winning Taste of Vermont honors along the way.

White tablecloths with pink napkins set the color scheme for the large dining room with a greenhouse full of massed flowers at one end, flowered lamps on tables spaced well apart, a wood stove and hanging plants all around. The windows in the greenhouse addition bring the outside in, and in summer the fabulous gardens and trees are illuminated at night.

Outdoor 'dinner' at Sam Rupert's.

JoAnna, the chef, changes her ambitious menu nightly. At our October visit, you could start with Southeast Asian-style lamb and mushroom soup, Jamaican jerk mussels steamed with onions and peppers, Southwest fettuccine with sundried tomatoes and cilantro pesto, sautéed bay scallops served with a creamy Vermont goat cheese and corn polenta, and salads of Vietnamese warm chicken and oriental vegetables or grilled beef tenderloin with belgian endive, arugula and radicchio.

Entrées are priced from $12.50 for ravioli with shiitake mushrooms, duck and Vermont goat cheese to $26 for rack of lamb with chipotle, honey and mint glaze and green peppercorn sauce. Other tempters could be spicy grilled Thai tuna with cucumber-shrimp relish and sautéed beef tenderloin with crab sofrito sauce and mango relish. On a summer visit, we liked the pan-roasted salmon with smoked salmon purses, chive sour cream and caviar and a fine roasted Vermont pork tenderloin au poivre with a brandy sauce.

51

Desserts here are anything but afterthoughts. We would have settled for any, but particularly the watermelon ice with fresh pineapple, melon, apples and kiwi; the tropical lime mousse pie with papaya and kiwi; the creamy chocolate and sundried cherry mousse napoleon with tart raspberry sauce, and the chef's favorite four-nut tart with a bittersweet chocolate-cognac sauce.

Many of the night's appetizers and salads turn up on the lounge menu, along with such creations as angus steak quesadilla or venison sausage and smoked mozzarella sandwich. They're priced mostly in the $5 to $7 range and available Sunday-Friday.

Dinner nightly, 6 to 9, lounge to 9:30. Closed Tuesday except in winter; also early November and late April.

The Common Man, German Flats Road, Warren. (802) 583-2800.

Here is the ultimate incongruity: a soaring, century-old timbered barn with floral carpets on the walls to cut down the noise and keep out wintry drafts. Crystal chandeliers hang from beamed ceilings over bare wood tables set simply with red napkins and pewter candlesticks. A table headed by a regal Henry VIII chair occupies a prime position in front of a massive, open fieldstone fireplace.

Needless to say, the whole mix works, and thrivingly so since its establishment in 1972 in the site we first knew as Orsini's. Destroyed by fire in 1987, it was replaced by a barn dismantled in Moretown and rebuilt here by English-born owner Mike Ware. He operates one of the more popular places in the valley with an air of elegance but without pretension.

The extensive wine list comes in two picture frames, hinged together to open like a book, and contains good values. "The saddest part of the fire was losing some of our finest wines," Mike recalls. The ingenious, custom-made brackets holding wine buckets at the edge of the tables were among the few possessions saved from the fire.

The escargots maison "served with our famous (and secret) garlic butter sauce" leads off the French/continental menu. Other appetizers ($4.25 to $5.50) include a daily charcuterie, gravlax and ricotta-filled spinach tortellini. We can vouch for the Vietnamese shrimp with chilled oriental noodles and a peanut sesame sauce, and a classic caesar salad.

Main courses start at $10 and top off at $18.50 for rack of New Zealand lamb. With dishes like monkfish grenobloise, roast duck with a sauce of belgian cherries and cherry heering liqueur, and sautéed Vermont veal with local mushrooms all under $15, this is uncommon fare – not to mention value – for common folk. At one visit, the fresh Vermont rabbit braised with marjoram and rosemary was distinctive, and the Vermont sweetbreads normande with apples and apple brandy were some of the best we've tasted. Our latest dinner produced a stellar special of penne with smoked chicken and asparagus and a plump cornish game hen glazed with mustard and honey.

Desserts include kirschen strudel, marquise au chocolat and meringue glacé. The mandarin orange sherbet bearing slivers of rind and a kirsch parfait were refreshing endings to an uncommon meal.

Dinner nightly from 6 or 6:30 (from 5:30 or 6 on Saturdays and holidays). Closed Monday, Easter through Christmas.

Millbrook Lodge, Route 17, Waitsfield. (802) 496-2405 or (800) 477-2809.

"Apple brown betty is the dumbest dessert we make, but we have to make it every night," says Thom Gorman, innkeeper with his wife Joan and chef at this small inn on the road to Mad River Glen. Such is the demand of regular patrons and houseguests in the popular dining room. Indeed, we were told everywhere we went that Millbrook was one of the better places to dine in the Valley.

MAP guests at the inn eat here, of course, in one of the two small dining rooms (one with a fireplace) at tables covered with paisley cloths. But the restaurant can seat 40, and people come in from all over. Anadama bread, a specialty, is made in house, as are pastas and desserts, from scratch. Start with mushrooms a la Millbrook, filled with a secret blend of ground veal and herbs, if it's offered. Entrées ($10.95 to $16.95) include a daily roast, shrimp scampi, five-peppercorn beef, garden vegetarian lasagna, cheese cannelloni made with Vermont cheddar and fresh basil, and three-cheese fettuccine tossed with Cabot cheddar, parmesan, Vermont mascarpone and sundried tomatoes. There are also four dishes from the Bombay region, where Thom lived for two years. The badami rogan josh, local lamb simmered in all kinds of spices and yogurt and served with homemade tomato chutney, is a longtime favorite.

The Gormans have a wine and beer license. As for those desserts, ice creams like chocolate chip and brickle candy are made here, as is a coffee-crunch pie filled with coffee mousse in a nut crust. In summer, open berry pies (maybe a raspberry and blackberry combination) are gobbled up.

Upstairs are seven bedrooms, four with private baths, decorated with stenciling and interesting handmade quilts and comforters. A full breakfast with choice of menu is served. Doubles are $96 to $120, MAP.

Dinner nightly, 6 to 9. Closed Tuesday in summer and month of May. No smoking.

China Moon, Sugarbush Village, Warren. (802) 583-6666.

The much esteemed Phoenix restaurant closed in 1991, chef-owner Peter Sussman leaving to produce Green Mountain mousses in Boston. His longtime maître-d' and sommelier, Haddon Blair, bought the place and turned it into this upscale Oriental restaurant upstairs. Haddon's wife Jodie oversees Bella Luna, an all-day pizzeria-trattoria, downstairs in what had been the Phoenix-owned Odyssey.

Like the setting, the menu is rather sophisticated for a Chinese restaurant. The food, which covers an enormous range, is highly regarded and considered very good value. Some 75 items represent a mix of Szechuan, Mandarin, Cantonese and Hunan cuisines. Chef Steven Bogart, for whom Chinese cooking has been a passion for more than 25 years, marks his dishes with one, two or three red peppers to indicate hotness. The only three-pepper dish, yan jian rou, is sliced pork sautéed with jalapeño peppers, Szechuan peppercorns, ground red chilies, garlic and soy on a bed of watercress for $12.95. You could start with scallion pancakes, boiled dumplings with hot sesame sauce, steak kew or beijing spicy cabbage. Main dishes ($9.50 to $16.95) include kung pao chicken, red crispy duck, shredded pork with garlic sauce, Hunan orange peel beef, shrimp with sweet walnuts and broccoli, Taiwanese crispy shrimp and Cantonese ginger lobster. Among meatless dishes are dry fried green beans, mu shi vegetables with bean cake and braised eggplant in garlic sauce.

Fruits and fortune cookies are about it for desserts. But you could go downstairs for crème caramel, fruit tarts, gelato or tirami su. Bella Luna also features New York-style pizzas and pastas at earthy prices.

Dinner nightly, 5:45 to 10.

Chez Henri, Sugarbush Village, Warren. (802) 583-2600.

The longest-running of the valley's long runners, Chez Henri is into its fourth decade as a French bistro and an after-dinner disco. It's tiny, intimate and very French, as you might expect from a former food executive for Air France.

Henri Borel offers lunch, brunch, apres-ski, early dinner, dinner and dancing, inside in winter by a warming stone fireplace and a marble bar and outside in summer on a small terrace bordered by a babbling mountain brook.

The dinner menu, served from 4 p.m., starts with changing soups and pâtés "as made in a French country kitchen," a classic French onion soup or fish broth, and perhaps mussels marinière, smoked trout with capers or steak tartare "knived to order" ($3.75 to $8.75).

Entrées range from $9.75 to $18.50. Served with good French bread and seasonal vegetables, they often include frog's legs, calves liver and onions, bouillabaisse, veal kidneys, chicken breast in garlic sauce, rabbit in red wine sauce, sweetbreads normande and filet au poivre. A shorter bistro menu is available as well at peak periods.

Crème caramel, coupe marron and chocolate mousse are among the dessert standbys. The wines are all French.

Open from noon to 2 a.m. in winter; weekends in summer, hours vary.

Giorgio's Cafe at Tucker Hill Lodge, Route 17, Waitsfield. (802) 496-3983.

A brief fling with a seafood theme and restaurant didn't work, so innkeepers Susan and Giorgio Noaro went with what did – their popular Giorgio's Cafe, which had been ensconced in the basement lounge. In 1995, the cafe menu was expanded into what Susan called an amalgamation of northern Italian fare from Giorgio's and specialties of the more traditional main dining room. The same menu is used in both locales. The upstairs "used to be pretty plain and formal," Susan said. Now it's warmer and more colorful, with red tablecloths and a Mediterranean theme. The inner dining room is paneled and beamed; the outer addition is greenhouse-style, with skylights and brick floors.

Stone-oven pizzas ($9.50) are baked in an outdoor beehive oven like that in which the famed American Flatbreads got their start here. An outdoor wood grill is used to prepare such entrées ($7.75 to $14.95) as yellowfin tuna with a tomato-garlic relish and chicken with oyster mushrooms and a white wine cream sauce. Stone-seared scallops in a raisin-pine nut sauce reflects a recipe from Giorgio's mother in Italy. The night's specials could be Idaho trout with wild mushrooms, caramelized onions and sundried tomatoes; pork stew served over polenta; seafood fricassee with fettuccine, and changing pastas.

Desserts change as well: perhaps chocolate-almond crackle cake, blueberry trifle, maple crème brûlée, amaretto cheesecake and an orange genoise layered with apples, maple syrup and blueberry butter cream (deceptively called Vermont apple pie torte). A good finale is flaming grolla – a grappa-laced coffee that is the Italian version of a peace pipe, says Susan. It's passed around the table amid much toasting and fanfare.

Dinner nightly, 5 or 5:30 to 9:30; Sunday brunch in summer, 11-2.

John Egan's Big World Pub & Grill, Route 100, Warren. (802) 496-3033.

Newly ensconced at the front of the Madbush Falls Country Motel is this casual, 50-seat place with a mouthful of a name and a skier's spirit. It was opened in December 1994 by two well-known local restaurateurs who met at Tucker Hill Lodge and the Sugarbush Inn. Chef Jerry Nooney teamed here with maître-d' Bernie Isabelle in their first solo venture. They named it for John Egan, a world-renowned "extreme team" skier from Sugarbush who is a local contractor (he built Jerry's house) when he's not jumping off cliffs for moviemaker Warren Miller. The "big world" refers to Egan's worldwide connections and the theme is carried out on the restaurant's wallpaper.

Jerry mans the wood grill in the semi-open kitchen, from which he can chat with patrons. George Schenk of the nearby American Flatbreads, with whom Jerry started at Tucker Hill, built a dome-shaped bread oven outside the restaurant in which to bake the small flatbreads he furnishes.

The menu is simple but with-it. The corn and crab stew comes in a mug. Appetiizers

Founder George Schenk bakes pizzas in earthen oven at Flatbread Kitchen.

include big world nachos, roasted garlic and hummus, beer-battered shrimp with sweet and spicy pineapple dip, and "dog bones," a revival of Tucker Hill days: Polish sausage in puff pastry with kraut and mustard on the side. There are a few burgers and sandwiches, salads (one of fancy greens with lots of roasted garlic cloves, grated asiago cheese and croutons) and pastas (perhaps grilled shrimp and asiago over fettuccine).

Main courses run from $9.25 to $16.95, but most are in the $10 range. They come with a small salad, fresh bread, veggies and starch. Among the entrées are grilled chicken with cider and ginger, Hungarian goulash, grilled leg of lamb, eggplant steaks, sea scallops with sundried tomato pesto, New York sirloin and fish of the day.

The full bar features Egan's Extreme Ale from Catamount Brewery in White River Junction.

Breakfast on weekends, 7 to 10; dinner, Tuesday-Sunday 4 to 10.

Flatbread Kitchen, Lareau Farm Country Inn, Route 100, Waitsfield. (802) 496-8856.

The American Flatbread pizzas that got their start in the outdoor wood-burning oven at Tucker Hill Lodge are now produced for the gourmet trade in the old slaughterhouse at Lareau Farm. Here, in an 800-degree wood-fired earthen oven with a clay dome, founder George Schenk and staff create the remarkable pizzas that are frozen and sold at the rate of more than 2,000 a week to grocery stores as far south as Florida and west to Chicago in a phenomenon that is making Waitsfield the pizza capital of Vermont, if not New England.

We were among their first on-site customers the first time we stopped by for a tour and a snack. They since have opened a wildly popular weekend restaurant, serving pizzas, great little salads dressed with homemade ginger-tamari vinaigrette, wine and beer to upwards of 250 people a night at tables set up around the production facility's oven room and kitchens and outside on the inn's west lawn. The delicious flatbreads with asiago and mozzarella cheese and sundried tomatoes ($9.25 to $13.50 and generally enough for two people) have made many a convert of pizza skeptics. The bakers use organically grown flour with restored wheat germ, "good Vermont mountain water" and as many Vermont products as they can. Each night's dinner is dedicated to an employee, a friend or maybe the people of Bosnia. George's heart-felt "dedications," posted around the facility, make for mighty interesting reading.

Dinner, Friday and Saturday 5:30 to 9:30; Fridays only in off-season.

R.S.V.P., Bridge Street, Waitsfield. (802) 496-7787.

The initials stand for Richard's Special Vermont Pizza in this mega-funky place near the covered bridge. Its old chrome, naugahyde chairs and strange lamps transport one back to the '50s, as does the loud music. The oblong, thin-crust pizza is indeed special. It's made with unbleached white and stone-ground whole wheat flours and topped with exotica like cob-smoked bacon, roasted garlic, hot salsa, Basque chorizo and cilantro pesto. Thirteen flavors of fresh pizzas (which they market to fine stores across the East to the tune of 2,500 a week) are available here for takeout or mail order (overnight by Federal Express).

We lunched on a couple of sensational focaccia sandwiches ($5.95 to $6.95) – a Vermont classic club and a summer sandwich (with all kinds of veggies) – and each was enough for about four people. The next time we'll know to order half sandwiches. Addictive garlic fennel pita chips come on the side.

The salad bar, decorated with autumn leaves and green onions at our October visit, is filled with goodies – some from owner Richard Denby's garden. Among its treats were roasted red peppers with goat cheese and fresh rosemary, three-cheese tortellini, marinated cucumbers and poached pears. Over it is a sign saying "do not steal food off the salad bar – public humiliation will result. If you are hungry and have no money, we will feed you at no charge." Have a beer, a glass of wine or maybe some Cold Hollow apple cider. Dessert consists of ice cream.

Open daily from 11:30 to 9, 10 or 11.

The Warren Store Deli, Warren. (802) 496-3864.

At the rear of the Warren Store is a delightful place for breakfast or lunch. You can get a three-egg omelet or breakfast burrito for $2 to $3. For lunch, how about turkey a la king on buttered linguini with tossed salad and french bread ($3.95), or any number of possibilities from the gorgeous array of gourmet salads and sandwiches? Finish with a huge chocolate-chip cookie or one of the treats from the ice-cream stand. Take it all outside to tables on a deck under a green striped canopy beside the roaring falls of the Mad River, where our tomato-dill soup and a pesto-provolone sandwich tasted extra good on a summer day. The store also has a fine selection of rare wines.

Open daily, 8 to 7, Sunday to 6.

Diversions

Downhill skiing reigns supreme and gives the valley its character.

Mad River Glen, Waitsfield. Billed as a serious place for serious skiers, Mad River has been challenging hardy types since 1947 ("ski it if you can," is its motto). There are no frills here: little snowmaking, a few lifts including the original single chairlift (with blanket wraps provided to ward off the chill) to the summit, hair-raising trails like Paradise and the Fall Line, plenty of moguls and not much grooming, and a "Practice Slope" steep enough to scare the daylights out of beginners. The Birdland area is fine for intermediates. There's a Mad River mystique (blue jeans and milk runs) that you sense immediately and attracts you back. Owner Betsey Pratt, who bought the area in 1972 with her late husband, still skis it every day. Adult lift tickets: $26 daily, $30 weekends and holidays.

Sugarbush, Warren. Founded in 1958 and among the first of Vermont's destination ski resorts, Sugarbush with its own "village" at its base appealed immediately to the jet set and fashion models and became known as "Mascara Mountain." From its original gondola lift to its expert Castle Rock area, from its clusters of condos and boutiques to its indoor Sports Center, Sugarbush draws those who appreciate their creature comforts – and good skiing as well (we think the Glades offer the best glade skiing in the East). Recently the fastest-growing destination ski resort in New England, Sugarbush was acquired in late 1994 by LBO Holdings (Sunday River and Attitash) and the prospects were even more upbeat. The home of famed extreme skiing brothers John and Dan Egan, Sugarbush offers the first guided backcountry skiing in the East. A bus shuttles skiers back and forth between Sugarbush and neighboring Sugarbush North (which has the valley's greatest vertical drop, 2,600 feet). Adult lift tickets: $42 daily.

Other Sports. This is a four-season sports area with a difference. Yes, there is golf, at the Robert Trent Jones-designed **Sugarbush Golf Club** par-72 course with water hazards (pond or brook) affecting eight consecutive holes. Yes, the **Sugarbush Sports Center** has indoor and outdoor tennis courts, racquetball and squash courts, indoor and outdoor pools, whirlpools and an exercise facility.

But there's much more: this is something of an equestrian center with a number of stables offering trail rides. Among them are the **Vermont Icelandic Horse Farm,** which specializes in horse trekking on one of the oldest and purest breeds in the world – anything from half-day rides to four-day inn-to-inn rides to six-day mountain expeditions. The **Sugarbush Polo Club,** started in 1962 by skiers using ski poles and a volleyball, now has four polo fields for games and tournaments, staged Thursday, Saturday and Sunday afternoons June through September. Also for horse fanciers are the annual Valley Classic and Sugarbush horse shows in late July and early August.

The **Mad River Valley Cricket Club** sprang out of a chance conversation in 1991 between two resident Brits, innkeeper James Plumpton and restaurateur Mike Ware. Now 100 members strong, it stages weekend cricket matches, an annual cricket festival and a summer garden party with a cherry-pit spitting contest and a cow pat frisbee contest (BYOCP). James Plumpton is president, player, newsletter editor and frequent party host. He says his club is the only one with a choir master and a poet laureate. It's so much fun that other innkeepers are taking up the sport.

Soaring via gliders and sailplanes is at its best from the Warren-Sugarbush Airport, where instruction and rentals are available. Biplane rides for one or two persons also go from the airport, which hosts an annual air show early in late June.

For hiking and backpacking, the Long Trail is just overhead; innumerable mountain peaks and guided tours beckon. The Mad River and Blueberry Lake are ready for swimming, canoeing and fishing. The Mad River rugby team plays throughout the summer and fall at the Waitsfield Recreation Field. Finally, a round-robin English croquet tournament is staged in mid-summer.

Clearwater Sports, Route 100, Waitsfield, offers canoes, kayaks, mountain bikes, snowboards and such for rent, and leads day trips for canoeing, biking and hiking.

Scenic Drives. The Lincoln Gap Road, the McCullogh Turnpike (Route 17) beyond Mad River Glen and the steep Roxbury Gap Road each have their rewards. For the most open vistas and overall feeling for the area, traverse Brook Road and Waitsfield Common Road out of Warren, past the landmark Joslin Round Barn and Blueberry Lake, Sugarloaf Airport and come the back way into Waitsfield.

Shopping. Waitsfield has three shopping complexes, each worthy of exploration: the Mad River Green and the Village Square along Route 100 and the Bridge Street Marketplace beside Vermont's second oldest covered bridge. Our first stop at every visit is **The Store** in the red 1834 Methodist Meeting House along Route 100. Owner

Jackie Rose, dean of the area's merchants (hers was the first store at Sugarbush Village), has an exceptional and vast array of Vermont foods, books, accessories, gifts, Christmas things, and a lovely collection of handmade quilts and pillows. A rear children's room resembles a giant toy box, while the second floor is stocked with antique furniture. The well-known **Green Mountain Coffee Roasters,** founded in Waitsfield with a retail store in Mad River Green, roasts 30 varieties of coffees and decafs, including founder Jamie Balne's special blend, and offers teas, coffee grinders and accessories, plus a cafe and espresso bar that's good for breakfast and lunch. **The Collection** features high-quality American arts and crafts, antiques and accessories. In Village Square, the **Blue Toad** gift shop specializes in particularly nice, inexpensive baskets from twenty countries and good greeting cards, as well as English tin boxes and jelly beans. **Tulip Tree** shows Vermont crafts and art, including lots of cows and many of the prints by Sabra Field, our favorite Vermont artist.

The **Bridge Street Bakery** offers great Portuguese breads, baked goods and snacks (cranberry buns with orange crème, gorgeous fresh fruit Danish pastries, ham and Vermont cheddar croissants, and maybe even a hearty sausage stew with French bread ($3). Gargoyles are everywhere at the offbeat **Gargoyle Shop,** where you can select from a fantastic array of angels, statues and concrete animals for the garden. **Baked Beads** is a factory outlet store for some of its jewelry – dig through the bead bird bath to create your own. Upstairs, Elisabeth von Trapp sells the custom clothing she designs.

Along Route 100 are Luminosity stained glass and **Cabin Fever Quilts,** stocking a wondrous array of handmade quilts in the Old Church. **Waitsfield Pottery** sells nice lamps and vases, mostly in greens and blues, made in the basement of an 1845 house. South of town next to Fiddler's Green at the Black Sheep Farm is **Three Bags Full** with "ewe-nique" things, featuring wool, handmade sweaters, blankets, sheepskins and, of course, lots of grazing black sheep for the watching.

In tiny Warren, everything you need and a lot you don't expect is found at the **Warren Store,** an old-fashioned general store with provisions, fine wines and a deli (see Dining Spots), plus upstairs, the **More Store,** with handicrafts from around the world, kitchenware, jewelry, apparel and cards. Lots of the things here are from India. Owner Carol Lippincott's criterion is "products with integrity." Up the street, blue and white stoneware made on the premises is displayed on the lawn in front of the **Warren Village Pottery. The Bradley House** shows some whimsical crafts and furnishings among its sophisticated stock. We were struck by the pretty pillows and "Memories of Skiing," a box of old skis for a cool $500.

The **von Trapp Greenhouse,** run by Maria von Trapp's grandson Toby, off a dirt road east of Waitsfield Common, is worth a visit (limited hours). Beautiful flower gardens surround the family's alpine-style house. There's a retail shop in front of one of the two greenhouses, which furnish lavish floral displays and produce for the valley's inns and restaurants.

Extra-Special

All Things Bright and Beautiful. Bridge Street, Waitsfield. (802) 496-3997.

In a shop next to the covered bridge is the ultimate collection of stuffed animals, mainly bears, outfitted in everything from a London bobby's uniform or a wedding dress to ski vests that proclaim "Save the Bear." The Victorian house has twelve rooms and porches presided over by two sisters and Malcolm the cat, perched atop the cash register. It's a bit overwhelming, but not to be missed.

United Church is on view from gazebo on Craftsbury Common.

Craftsbury, Vt.
The Look and Lifestyle of a Century Ago

Picture the picture-perfect Vermont town: a white-spired church and public buildings facing the village green, pristine clapboard houses on shady lawns, cows grazing against a hilly landscape, youngsters picking wildflowers along the road.

The town is Craftsbury, population 1,000. And the picture is of Craftsbury Common, a hilltop village of perhaps 200 souls in the middle of nowhere – the west-central section of Vermont's most remote region, the Northeast Kingdom.

Craftsbury Common indeed has a common, which is nearly as big as the rest of the village. It's a serene two acres or so flanked by a few houses (one turns out to be an annex of an inn) and institutional buildings. Among them are the nation's smallest accredited college, the state's smallest public high school, a rickety post office, a wonderful little library and a funeral home, the village's only commercial enterprise besides the inn. North of the village is a sports/education center believed to be unique in the world.

A few miles downhill from Craftsbury Common's perch astride a ridge is the village of Craftsbury, site of the town hall, the Catholic church, two general stores and another inn. From here an unnumbered road leads to East Craftsbury, home of a British woolens store and an English-style B&B.

That's about it for Craftsbury, the most prosperous part of a Northeast Kingdom that reflects the Vermont of old, uncondoed and uncutesied. Nearby is Greensboro, a lakeside summer colony of academics and the "metropolis" of the immediate area, the place where the flatlanders go to pick up the New York Times. There are also East Hardwick and Hardwick, the latter perhaps a place you've heard of – perhaps. It's the metropolis for a somewhat broader area.

A bit farther afield but worth the trip are Peacham, Cabot and Lake Willoughby.

The lapel buttons that proclaim "I love Peacham" don't mention Vermont because, we're told, there's no other Peacham in the world. Cabot's fame has been spread by the Cabot Creamery, the East's largest maker of cheddar cheese. Lake Willoughby, the "Lucerne of America," is a sight to behold from a couple of inns on its sharply rising shores.

Vermont's most rural region is an area of tranquility, scenic beauty, little-traveled byways, country stores and, somewhat unexpectedly, considerable summer music and exotic garden enterprises. Time spent here celebrates the look, the landscape and the lifestyle of a century ago.

Inn Spots

The Inn on the Common, Craftsbury Common 05827. (802) 586-9619 or (800) 521-2233.

Greensboro summer cottagers Penny and Michael Schmitt chucked their New York corporate jobs in 1973 and, on a whim, bought a house in Craftsbury that they proceeded to turn into a small inn. "We started with four small bedrooms with shared baths and were too naive to know better," Penny recalls. "As we traveled more and became more demanding, we became more demanding of ourselves." In the next eight years, they turned two more houses into inn annexes, created a dining room of renown, added a pool and a tennis court, upgraded the gardens, helped found a sports center and, in effect, turned tiny Craftsbury Common into a destination area. They have spent the last fourteen years at the inn upgrading everything in sight, fussing over details to make everything as perfect as possible.

Theirs is a class act, far classier than one would expect in out-of-the-way Craftsbury and more intimate than its size would suggest. Spread out in three houses, the sixteen guest rooms with private baths are the ultimate in comfort. All have sitting areas made for relaxing instead of show and are stylishly furnished with vivid, color-coordinated prints and fine wallpapers, good artworks and antiques. We're partial to the South Annex across from the main inn. Here, besides an office and a lounge with TV/VCR and a video library of 300 cassettes, is our favorite Room 12, main floor rear. It contains a kingsize bed, a sofa, a reclining chair custom-designed for a frequent guest, an enormous bathroom that doubles as a dressing area and plenty of room to spread out. Many like the upstairs Room 10 with its wood stove, a queensize canopy bed covered

with a blue-starred quilt, a sofa and two side chairs, and an old butter churn in the bathroom. Another favorite is Room 3, The Porch, upstairs and rear in the main inn with a great view of the spectacular specimen rose garden and the perennial gardens and mountains to the rear. For what once was a porch it has what Penny calls serious furniture (meaning antiques), plus two leather chairs that are so soft you think you'll never get up.

These are three of the eight deluxe rooms, which cost $20 more than the others but are worth it. Every room is a treasury of caring

Picket fence surrounds main building at The Inn on the Common

touches, however. Penny is partial to those in the North Annex, the Schmitts' latest acquisition, where they were able to do everything they wanted to. It's a couple of blocks removed from the main inn and the only one actually facing the serene, expansive common. The main inn has a parlor, a library and a gorgeous dining room looking onto the rose garden. Its five guest rooms are up a steep, tightly curved staircase.

Meals are an integral part of the inn experience here, although the Schmitts – blessed with a talented young staff – no longer preside at the dinner hour as they used to. The meal is served in a dinner-party atmosphere at the civilized hour of 8, following cocktails and hors d'oeuvre in the library. Talented young chef Yves Morrissette, a French-Canadian from the Vermont border town of Troy, explains the night's choices posted on a blackboard. Our table of ten sampled the entire menu and was impressed with both the food and service.

Superior appetizers were rabbit pâté and homemade fettuccine with mushrooms stuffed with sausage and leeks. Homemade bread and a spicy cucumber-dill soup with slivered carrots followed. Main courses were chicken with creamy thyme sauce, grilled local partridge with pommery mustard glaze and swordfish with herbed aioli, accompanied by small yellow beans, broccoli and baked potatoes. A green salad with a cracked peppercorn dressing preceded desserts, an ethereal pear strudel with homemade buttermilk sorbet and a light chocolate pecan torte with vanilla ice cream. Michael Schmidt's carefully chosen wine list is pricey, but a low markup produces great values.

Breakfast the next morning followed suit. An extensive menu offered many choices. Juice, a platter of fresh fruit and cranberry-lemon muffins came first. The herbed-cheddar quiche with Canadian bacon was a succulent special. Shirred eggs and Vermont-made sausage were accompanied by thick toasted bread.

Play English croquet on the course laid out between perennial gardens behind the main inn or tennis on the clay court beyond the perennial gardens behind the main inn. Swim in the natural-looking, free-form gunite pool sequestered behind the South Annex. Read a book in your room or watch a movie in the lounge. Almost every creature comfort you could want is at the uncommon Inn on the Common, and all the area's rural pleasures are close at hand.

Doubles, $210 to $230, MAP.

The Craftsbury Inn, Craftsbury 05826. (802) 586-2848 or (800) 336-2848.

A white-columned building across from the general store houses ten guest rooms and a restaurant of note (see Dining Spots). Blake Gleason, a young chef with Sheraton experience, and his wife Rebecca have been the innkeepers since 1988.

The long front parlor offers a small fireplace (from the original post office in Montpelier) and a piano beneath an embossed pressed-tin ceiling. Adjacent is a game room with a TV. Guests also enjoy wraparound verandas on two floors.

Six of the upstairs guest rooms have private baths. One called the honeymoon room possesses a canopied double bed and the inn's only combination bath-shower. Two front bedrooms are summery in wicker. One room has a 1750 Quaker bed so high that the occupants may need a ladder to climb into it. Four rooms in the oldest section of the house share a large hall bath. Mini-print wallpapers, sheer curtains, pretty quilts made by Rebecca's great-grandmother and the inn's own toiletries are the rule.

The Gleasons offer a full breakfast in the sunny dining room overlooking the garden and a rear yard bordered by the Black River, which winds around the property. The choice might be eggs any style, a mushroom or cheese omelet, or french toast.

Doubles, $64 to $92, B&B; $110 to $140, MAP. Closed mid-October through November and April through mid-May.

Finchingfield Farm Bed & Breakfast, East Craftsbury Road, RR 1, Box 1195, East Craftsbury 05826. (802) 586-7763.

An English flavor pervades this turn-of-the-century house, converted into a B&B in 1988. Owners Janet and Bob Meyer used to run a B&B in the picturesque British town of Finchingfield; hence the name and the theme.

Here they offer four guest rooms, two with private baths. All are outfitted with down duvets and pillows, English sheets and English antiques, and most still bear the original wallpaper hung in the house in 1904. Lots of things made of straw are in the Corn Dolly Room on the main floor. Upstairs is the Blue Goose Room, the largest, with twin beds that can be joined as a king, pine furniture imported from England, floral wallpaper and a painted armoire. Janet makes the interesting bolster-type pillows that serve as headboards in each room. One room is decorated totally in blue, down to the blue painted floor.

There's a cozy upstairs sitting room with TV and lots of books and magazines, many of them British. The main downstairs room is used for breakfast. Off it is a library overlooking part of the seven acres where the Meyers keep sheep and horses.

Janet serves a full breakfast, perhaps poached eggs or waffles topped with cooked fruit and local syrup. Above the bigger of two tables is a striking brass and maple chandelier bearing twelve candles in hurricane lamps. Classical music plays throughout, and you may see a herd of cows leaving the barn just across the street.

Doubles, $60 to $80. No smoking.

Highland Lodge, RR1, Box 1290, Greensboro 05841. (802) 533-2647.

On a hillside across the East Craftsbury Road from Caspian Lake is a country inn of the old school. "A real refuge from the busyness of modern life" is how its brochure describes it. Families comprise the bulk of the devoted clientele. Built in the 1860s as a farmhouse, it was converted into an inn in the 1920s, and is now run by David and Wilhelmina Smith, the second generation of an innkeeping family.

Accommodations are basic in eleven guest rooms, reached by three separate staircases from the main floor. Each has private bath, an assortment of beds with white Bates spreads, Ethan Allen furniture and sheer white curtains. Amenities consist of a small bar of Ivory soap and a box of Kleenex. The rooms are clean, but not the kind in which to linger.

That's okay, because much of the downstairs is given over to three side-by-side common rooms. One is a cozy library with a corner fireplace, another has a TV and a wood stove, and one in the middle contains a grand piano with a sign regulating the hours of play. Out back, behind the gift shop and office, is a children's library and game room where the ping-pong table was getting a good workout the rainy day we visited. On summer mornings, youngsters aged 4 to 9 link up with the "Play Lady," who devises crafts programs and nature hikes.

Across the street are a clay tennis court and, down a path, the lodge's private beach and "bathhouse," which looked to us like a boathouse. Rowboats, paddleboats and canoes may be borrowed to explore Caspian Lake, which the Smiths say is Vermont's cleanest. Along its shores are Victorian cottages favored by academics and writers.

Three meals a day are served in the restaurant, which is open to the public (see Dining Spots), except on summer Mondays when lunch is a picnic at the beach. Just behind the lodge is a lineup of eleven white cottages, each with one to three bedrooms. Four are winterized and some have kitchenettes.

Doubles, $170 to $210, MAP; cottages, $200 to $210, MAP; service charges included. Closed mid-October to Christmas and mid-March to Memorial Day.

The Village House Inn, Route 14, Box 212, Albany 05820. (802) 755-6722.

A glider and tall rockers on the wraparound veranda greet visitors at this new in-town inn fashioned from a big white extended house that is typical of Vermont. Jerry and Mary Peters renovated an old house and added a new section behind, with bedrooms above the new dining room and kitchen. They offer eight cozy guest rooms with private baths, appointed in Victorian florals and crisp country curtains. Bed configurations vary from twins to queen.

Guests share a homey but spare living room outfitted with a TV and rocking chairs. Breakfast and dinner are served at sturdy wood tables in the dining room, or on the back porch where three white tables overlook the fields. The dining room, pretty in cream and Wedgwood blue, has frilly curtains on the windows and print wallpaper above the wainscoting.

Mary prepares an optional four-course dinner for inn guests ($13.50 per person). The meal might start with cream of mushroom soup and garden salad. She generally offers a choice of four main courses, breast of chicken, grilled salmon, filet mignon and a vegetarian selection, perhaps tomato-herb-cheese tart or eggplant lasagna. Cheesecake and pies are favored desserts. The inn has a beer and wine license.

Doubles, $70 B&B, $97 MAP. No smoking.

WilloughVale Inn & Restaurant, Route 5A, Westmore 05860. (802) 525-4123 or (800) 541-0588.

Overlooking the length of beautiful Lake Willoughby from its more built-up, less picturesque north end, this is a restaurant (see Dining Spots), a new inn with lodging facilities and – the prize, we think – four cottages across the road and right on the lake. Frank and Joan Symcak from North Haven, Conn., who have a farm in Burke Hollow, bought the old WilloughVale Inn, razed it and put up a new, weathered-gray clapboard building with front and side verandas in 1988.

The seven upstairs rooms with private baths in the main inn vary in size and layout.

We liked Room 1, fairly large with a table and chair against the wall, a sofa, a queensize bed with a woven coverlet, pictures of birds on the walls and two windows overlooking the lake. Room 3 is a deluxe room with a queensize four-poster, sofa and upholstered chair, and a bathroom with a double jacuzzi, a separate shower and a double sink. But we'd splurge for one of the four cottages, especially No. 2 with a queen bed, a sunken living room, kitchen, a screened porch and a deck with lounge chairs, right at lake's edge and renting for $130 a night or $630 a week. Each of the other cottages has two bedrooms and either a dining area or eat-in kitchen.

There are gathering spots on the front porches and in the inn's library, which has antique books and games but no TV. Joan Symcak recently moved into the inn to become fulltime innkeeper (her husband is here from Connecticut on weekends). She stresses that the continental-plus breakfast is "quite substantial and good for you." Expect fresh orange juice, fresh fruit, homemade granola, Vermont cheddar cheese, muffins or sweet breads (peach and raspberry muffins and banana bread at our visit).

Doubles, $90 to $110; cottages, $130 to $170.

Fox Hall, Barton-Lake Willoughby Road, Barton 05822. (802) 525-6930 or (800) 566-6930.

This early Colonial Revival mansion with two turrets and a great front porch on a hill above the west shore of Lake Willoughby is listed on the National Register of Historic Places. But for the lineup of little cabins in front and the huge Camp Westmore safe in a corner of the dining room, you'd hardly guess that it used to be a girls' camp.

Ken and Sherry Pyden from Detroit took one look at the place and fell in love with it. They started in 1988 with one room and have worked their way around the house, to the point where they now offer eight guest rooms, four with private baths and four sharing two. The moose-crossing sign in the driveway gives fair notice of Sherry's passion for moose. They're everywhere inside. In the common room, one is made out of grapevines, a big moose resides in a sleigh, three stuffed varieties are on the couch, a real moose head is surrounded by a wreath atop the fireplace, and an intense little moose is perched on the bench in the turret, playing the piano. There's plenty of space to spread out in a reading room in the other main-floor turret, a large dining room and the curving front porch full of Adirondack chairs.

Impressive woodwork flanks the stairway, which is topped by a skylight. The spacious second floor has summery-looking guest rooms, most with white walls, white frilly curtains and a queensize bed plus a twin bed for singles, a popular combination with the cycling tours that visit the inn. The turret rooms are the most interesting and spacious. The moose motif gives way to horses in the Carousel Room.

A full breakfast is served at four tables in the dining room. Raisin-oatmeal muffins, a cup of fresh fruit with yogurt and blueberry-banana pancakes was the fare the day we were there. Lemonade and date squares greet guests in the afternoon. Guests enjoy a private beach and use of canoes, paddleboat and windsurfers.

The camp's former open-air dining hall behind the inn has been rechristened the Pavilion at Fox Hall in honor of the musical events staged there. A concert grand piano was being delivered from White River Junction in the back of a pickup truck for the second annual July chamber music festival at our latest visit. Sherry Pyden said they had "high hopes of becoming the next Marlboro."

Doubles, $70 to $90. No smoking.

Heermansmith Farm Inn, Heermansmith Farm Road, Coventry 05825. (802) 754-8866.

A bit hard to find along a dirt road west of Coventry, this is the family home of Jack

Turrets are on either side of early Colonial Revival mansion that is now Fox Hall.

and Louise Smith, part of the Heerman family who have been dairy farmers here for five generations. The Smiths began serving ice cream to people who came to pick the strawberries in their fields. When someone suggested they should offer cross-country skiing in winter, they found that skiers wanted something to eat. So in 1982 the Smiths opened their 1860 home to guests in a homey yet elegant dining room (see Dining Spots) and then began putting up guests overnight.

Upstairs are six guest rooms, all with private baths, in the old farmhouse and a new addition above a private dining room. The newer ones contain beds with colorful quilts and interesting built-in sinks with wood all around. Except for an end room with a sofa, rooms here are smaller than in the older section.

Jack cooks a hearty breakfast, served in the main dining room. Guests might have scrambled eggs with bacon and muffins or pancakes with strawberries and maple syrup.

The Black River skirts the surrounding strawberry fields and pasture lands, providing a place for wildlife, fishing, canoeing and swimming at the base of a waterfall.

Doubles, $60.

Ha'Penny Gourmet, Peacham 05862. (802) 592-3310.

Desi and Kati Kegl-Bognar, who both fled Hungary after the 1956 revolution and met in New York, moved in 1985 to Peacham, a quaint hamlet they had visited while their children were at summer camp. "We've got a little United Nations here," Desi said of his gourmet food shop, his general store and gallery, and the B&B they run upstairs. "Peacham is a very cosmopolitan place."

Four guest rooms above the Peacham Store share baths, one of them downstairs. The rear Peach Room, furnished with antiques, has a kingsize bed. The "big Gray Room," named for the color of its floor, contains two twin beds and two chairs. The little Ivory Room offers a double bed beneath a sloping ceiling. "This is the 'Wow' Room," Desi said as he noted our awe in the skylit upstairs gallery off the bedrooms, an international potpourri of African and oriental rugs, Nigerian batiks, Hungarian pillows and Portuguese towels.

Guests get to enjoy (and purchase from) the gallery, as well as the downstairs dining room, where the Bognars serve a continental breakfast with wonderful homemade baguettes, croissants and French rolls. "The game is to find out what the jams are," says Kati, noting she serves at least four kinds every day.

We were intrigued by the dandelion jelly, the dried pastas and the local pottery in the store, and picked up a jar of curried butternut squash soup from the small but interesting takeout selection to enjoy with dinner that night.

Doubles, $60 to $65. Closed in winter.

Dining Spots

The Craftsbury Inn, Craftsbury. (802) 586-2848.

A pretty little dining room overlooking spotlit gardens and a talented young chef commend this restaurant that's open to the public by reservation. Dining is at round tables set with white linens, candles and fresh flowers in a cheery room with yellow floral wallpaper above white wainscoting and big windows onto the back yard.

Dinner is à la carte, with entrées priced from $10.25 for cheese-filled tri-colored tortellini to $18 for sautéed scallops with brandy cream sauce. Chef-owner Blake Gleason changes his four-course menu seasonally. You might start with gazpacho, cream of asparagus soup or steamed mussels with a marinara sauce and a house salad with a choice of dressings. Entrées could be cajun catfish, poached salmon with cucumber-caper sauce, sautéed pork medallions with an apricot-brandy sauce, sautéed antelope with chasseur sauce or rack of lamb with roquefort sauce. Plates are garnished with edible nasturtiums and fresh herbs, and three or four vegetables accompany.

Dessert choices could be raspberry mousse, blueberry pie and chocolate truffle torte. There's a short but serviceable wine list. A small bar contains a couple of high round tables and chairs.

Dinner by reservation, Wednesday-Sunday, 6:30 to 8.

Highland Lodge, Greensboro. (802) 533-2647.

Lunch on the front porch with a distant view of Caspian Lake is a summertime treat here, but we were surprised how many were enjoying it on a raw, dank day. The menu covers the basics, but the daily specials can get interesting: a warm spinach salad with grilled duck breast and a rabbit and ham stew with buttermilk biscuits and rainbow cole slaw at our visit. The problem was they'd run out of the spinach-duck salad and one special was sort of lacking: the borscht with Ma Smith's beets didn't seem like the real thing and its accompaniment, half a beer cheese and tomato sandwich on wheat bread, was rather strange-tasting. The sautéed sea scallops with snow peas on rice ($6.25) was much more successful.

Nightly specials are the heart of the dinner menu as well. Grilled blank angus sirloin steak is a staple, but other entrées could be coho salmon with mushrooms and white wine, grilled mustard-glazed chicken breast and maple-cured Vermont ham with apple chutney ($14.25 to $16.75).

Starters could be corn and green chile soup, grilled mushroom salad, herbed Vermont chèvre or fresh fruit cup. For dessert, try the blueberry-lemon cream cake or chocolate cream pie.

Some people come here just for the lodge's special dessert hour, starting nightly at 7:30. In addition to the specials, they go for things like chocolate mousse parfait, ishkabibble (brownie à la mode with hot fudge sauce) and something called forgotten dessert, a meringue with ice cream and strawberries. The lodge also has a short menu

Side porch at The WilloughVale Inn yields full-length view of Lake Willoughby.

of lighter dinner fare, $8 to $8.75. The L-shaped dining room with a wood stove is rustic and pretty in pink, but we'd choose the porch any time we could.

Lunch, Tuesday-Sunday noon to 2; dinner nightly by reservation, 6 to 8.

WilloughVale Inn & Restaurant, Route 5A, Westmore. (802) 525-4123.

The dining room is the star here, thanks to the striking view down Lake Willoughby and the cuisine of noted area chef Michael La Croix, who gained quite a reputation at Michael's in Derby Line and at restaurants in Burlington before we lost track of him for a few years.

He has resurfaced at the WilloughVale, where he oversees two dining rooms and a taproom menu in the lounge. Windows onto the water, shiny wood tables with fanned moss green napkins and matching mats, heavy cutlery, windsor chairs and oriental rugs on the floors create a crisp country setting. The ceiling of the smaller dining room is painted like a quilt, and there's quite a display of antique fly rods in a glass case in the main dining room.

The fare has been toned down since the heady early days, when the menu changed daily. We heard an elderly gent complaining to the waiter that the chef had put too much pepper in the spicy clam and red pepper chowder that began one dinner. Now the menu is changed seasonally, and the soups are a safe New England clam chowder or chilled blueberry. Those with more adventurous palates can start with mascarpone torta with basil and pine nuts, Vermont chèvre with bruschetta and strawberry vinaigrette, or smoked salmon with buckwheat pancakes, capers and sour cream.

Main courses run from $14.50 for grilled chicken with spinach and Vermont chèvre to $21 for rack of lamb "roasted to a crisp" and served with a concasse of tomatoes and mint. Baked blue cod with lemon garnish is a signature dish, as is the shrimp tossed with linguini, garlic and herbs.

Desserts include Maine wild blueberry crisp, maple crème brûlée, vanilla and lemon cheesecake with fruit soaked in cointreau, and a Shaker cream biscuit with strawberries and cream. There's a surprisingly strong (for the area) wine list to go with, plus a

67

nice selection of dessert wines, cognacs and single-malt scotches at half the usual prices.

Some of the dinner items are incorporated on the short lunch and tap room menu that changes monthly.

Lunch daily in summer, noon to 3; dinner, 6 to 9; Friday-Sunday in off-season.

Heermansmith Farm Inn, Heermansmith Farm Road, Coventry. (802) 754-8866.
There is something immensely appealing about the dining experience at Heermansmith Farm. Perhaps it is the setting: glamorous, white-linened tables scattered about an open living room and dining room centered by a huge slate fireplace amid antiques and the glow of candles and kerosene lamps. Perhaps it is the food served up by young local chef John Fletcher, whom innkeepers Jack and Louise Smith wooed back after he left for a year to build himself a home in Coventry and try making a living at carpentry. Perhaps it is the good little wine list, amazingly priced from yesteryear.

Probably it is everything put together. The food is certainly the match for the stylish living-room setting. The short menu might start with haddock chowder or cream of leek soup with jalapeño cheese, sherried mushrooms in puff pastry, smoked salmon with egg garnish or escargots with roasted sweet red peppers and garlic.

For main courses ($15.95 to $17.50), how about the house specialty, roast duck with a strawberry and chambord sauce, or oriental grilled swordfish, poached Atlantic salmon with lime butter sauce, grilled pork loin with madeira mushroom sauce or fettuccine tossed with shrimp and salmon in a dijon-wine cream sauce with julienned vegetables?

Desserts could be blueberry buckle, amaretto cheesecake with hazelnuts, french bread pudding with whiskey sauce, and puff pastry with lemon cream and fresh raspberries.

Dinner nightly, 5 to 9. Closed Tuesday in off-season.

The Creamery, Hill Street, Danville. (802) 684-3616.
Run by the Beattie family with five generations in the dairy business, this restaurant is the favorite of many area residents. Upscaled a bit lately, it has tables in a high, beamed-ceiling dining room and on an enclosed, two-level rear porch. A mezzanine at the front of the dining room overlooks the whole scene. Windsor chairs are at tables draped in white linen.

The blackboard menu is short and to the point. Entrées ($12 to $16) at our latest visit were chicken and artichokes, broiled haddock, broiled swordfish, scallops mornay, broiled salmon and grilled sirloin. Shrimp or crab cocktail, fish chowder and smoked salmon usually comprise the appetizer list.

Marion Beattie, the lady of the house who is known for her chicken pie ("never add vegetables"), also puts out a great maple cream pie. Raspberry shortcake and black raspberry pie are summer favorites. The short wine list is priced in the teens and twenties.

Lunch, Tuesday-Friday 11:30 to 2; dinner, Tuesday-Saturday 5 to 8.

Diversions

There's a lot to see and do – or nothing to see and do – in the Northeast Kingdom, depending on your point of view. The scenery varies from low-key to spectacular. This remains an essentially rural, old-fashioned area where folks meet at the general stores, and church suppers and band concerts are the social gatherings of importance. All kinds of sports and educational pursuits are offered on the property and under the auspices of the **Craftsbury Center Sports Resort** in Craftsbury Common, 586-7767.

Open living/dining room is popular with guests at Heermansmith Farm Inn.

Walking, running, hiking, cycling, sculling, cross-country skiing, horseback riding – you name it, they've got it. There's also a new, state-of-the-art fitness center, **The Wellness Barn at CoachWorks Farm,** Page Pond Road, Albany, 755-6342. Owners Bill and Judy Bevans offer an indoor swiming pool, spa, sauna, steam bath, massage, weight machines, aerobics and more.

Craftsbury Common is a wonderful hilltop town with a serene common and an institutional presence lent by Craftsbury Academy, the state's smallest public high school and one of the town's drawing cards for newcomers, and Sterling College, the nation's smallest degree-granting, accredited college with 70 students involved in environmental studies.

Music. The Craftsbury Chamber Players are in such demand that they cross the state on a pre-season tour and share their talents with audiences in Burlington each summer. But they're in residence at the Town House in Hardwick from mid-July to mid-August, playing Thursday evenings at 8. They also give free Thursday afternoon mini-concerts at 2 "for children and their friends" in Hardwick, at the Craftsbury Town Hall and at the Greensboro Fellowship Hall. The annual **Summer Music from Greensboro** series takes place in the Church of Christ sanctuary and the Greensboro Fellowship Hall. The Greensboro Association has sponsored concerts on a dock at Caspian Lake every summer Sunday at 7:30 for nearly 50 years. The signature scene in Craftsbury Common is the summer band concerts in the bandshell on the common, four Sunday nights at 7. Those who remain in their vehicles honk their horns if they like what they hear.

Gardens. Gardeners in the know flock to **Perennial Pleasures Nursery** in East Hardwick, where two acres of perennial and herb gardens are on display and English cream tea is served by reservation on the lawns outside the Brick House, a quirky Victorian B&B (four rooms, $50 to $65), Tuesday-Sunday from noon to 4:30. Old-fashioned, hardy perennial flowers and herbs from the 17th to 19th centuries are the specialties. Gardeners also seek out places like **Stone's Throw Gardens** in East Craftsbury for hardy perennials, including heritage roses and lilies, displayed on several levels around a restored 1795 farmhouse, against stone walls and in fields strewn with flowers. Other favorites for rare varieties are **Vermont Day Lilies** on Barr Hill in

North Greensboro, where retired Colgate University administrator David Perham and his wife Andrea also run the Greensboro House, a homey B&B (two bedrooms with shared bath, $50) and a collectibles and sports card business, and **Dooryard Lilacs** in Greensboro.

Shopping. There's not much of it, but what there is is interesting. **Willey's** in the center of Greensboro is a general store to end all general stores. Celebrating its 95th birthday in 1995, this local institution is a ramble of rooms, with three levels of hardware and housewares, a rear meat market and grocery and an upstairs for clothing. It's the kind of place where you'll find an open box of dog biscuits sandwiched between a display case of Timex watches and a crate of fresh peaches. Across the aisle are shelves of chewing tobacco. Bulletin boards on either side of the entry dispense fascinating information. One poster announced a public forum on the future of Greensboro, "Condos or Cupolas?" Across the street is **The Miller's Thumb,** two levels of gifts built around a chute opening onto the basement mill and waterfall. **The Old Forge** in East Craftsbury has Scottish and Irish woolens, including tams, deerstalkers and perfectly beautiful sweaters from $100 to $200-plus. Arts and crafts by Vermont artisans are featured at the **South Albany Store** on the East Craftsbury Road. Want Vermont game birds? Visit the **Wylie Hill Farm** in Craftsbury Common, where pheasant, partridge, quail, turkeys and more are raised naturally and sold by mail-order.

Cabot Creamery, Main Street, Cabot. (802) 563-2231. If this area has a real, live tourist attraction, this is it. Upwards of 350 people on busy days visit the Cabot Farmers' Cooperative Creamery, begun in 1919 when 94 dairy farmers founded the original creamery plant to churn butter. Today, nearly 500 Vermont farmers sell milk to the creamery, which produces twenty to thirty tons of cheese daily. Its sharp Vermont cheddar won top honors in the 1990 U.S. Championship Cheese Contest in Wisconsin, which considers itself the home of American cheddar, and it is sold at Harrods in London. Following a video presentation, visitors leave on guided tours of the manufacturing plant. Through windows into the production areas you can watch many of the 250 employees as they separate the curds from the whey, mold the cheese into 42-pound blocks and package it for aging in the huge uphill warehouse. The half-hour tour tells you all you want to know about cheese. At tour's end, you get to sample low-fat, jalapeño, sharp and extra-sharp varieties to spur sales in the gift shop. The visitor center, opened in 1987, is dedicated to the unheralded role of farm women everywhere. Open Monday-Saturday 9 to 5, Sunday in summer, 11 to 4; no cheese production on Sunday and one day at midweek. Admission, $1.

Extra-Special

The Old Stone House Museum, Brownington, 754-2022. This charming place is part of the out-of-the-way Brownington Village Historic District, a time warp listed on the National Register. The impressive structure lives up to its billing as "the rarest kind of museum: a building as fascinating as the collection it houses." The four-story structure was built stone by stone in the 1830s by the Rev. Alexander Twilight, who is believed to have been America's first black college graduate (Middlebury) and its first black legislator, and his neighbors. The school in which he taught the region's school children for two decades is history, but the 30-room monument still instructs and inspires. It's filled with antiques and memorabilia displayed by the Orleans County Historical Society. You can see Alexander Twilight's desk and Bible there. Open daily in summer, 11 to 5; Friday-Tuesday in off-season; closed mid-October to mid-May. Adults, $3.

Wintertime scene along the green in Woodstock.

Woodstock-Quechee, Vt.
A Chic Blend of Old and New

Picture the perfect Vermont place and you're likely to picture Woodstock, the historic shire town portrayed by the media as the picture-perfect New England village.

Picture an old river town with handsome 19th-century houses, red brick mill, waterfall and covered bridge and you have Quechee, the emerging hamlet being restored to reflect Vermont as it used to be.

Join them with Rockefellers, Billingses, Pearces and other old names and new entrepreneurs, and you have an unusual combination for a chic, changing dynamic.

Carefully preserved and protected, Woodstock has such an impressive concentration of architecture from the late 17th and 18th centuries that National Geographic magazine termed it one of the most beautiful villages in America. That it is, thanks to its role as a prosperous county seat following its settlement in 1765 and to early popularity as both a summer and winter resort. Vermont's first golf course was established south of town around the turn of the century and the nation's first ski tow was installed on a cow pasture north of town in 1934.

That also was the year when Laurance S. Rockefeller married localite Mary Billings French, granddaughter of railroad magnate Frederick Billings. The Rockefeller interests now are Woodstock's largest landowner and employer. They buried the utility poles underground, provided a home and much of the stimulus for the Woodstock Historical Society, bought and rebuilt the Woodstock Inn, acquired and redesigned the golf course, bought and upgraded the Suicide Six ski area, opened the Billings Farm Museum, and built a multi-million-dollar indoor sports and fitness center.

Entrepreneur Simon Pearce, the Irish glass blower, has provided some of the same impetus for neighboring Quechee. He purchased an abandoned mill as a site for his

71

glass-blowing enterprise, powered it with a 50-year-old turbine using water from the river outside, added more craftspeople and a restaurant, and sparked a crafts and business revival that has enlivened a sleepy hamlet heretofore known mainly for its scenic gorge.

In this inspirational setting of old and new, entrepreneurs are supported, and arts and crafts are appreciated.

Inn Spots

Twin Farms, Barnard 05031. (802) 234-9999 or (800) 894-6327.

A dozen miles north of Woodstock at the edge of the unlikely hamlet of Barnard lies the ultimate in small, luxury country resorts, one attracting jet-setters from across the world. The secluded farm once owned by writers Sinclair Lewis and Dorothy Thompson was converted to the tune of $11 million into the East's most sumptuous inn in 1993. One of a kind, it offers thirteen-going-on-sixteen rooms and cottages, superb dining and a full-time staff of 27 to pamper up to 36 guests. The rates – $700 to $1,500 a night for two – includes meals, drinks and recreational activities, but not the tax and fifteen percent service charge.

Twin Farms is deluxe, of course, but understated and not at all ostentatious – not nearly as drop-dead showy as one might expect. "The idea is you're a guest at somebody's country estate for the weekend," says Beverley Matthews, innkeeper with her husband Shaun, both of whom are British and who come with impeccable resort-management credentials. "For our guests, money is not an object. Time is."

The idea evolved after the Twigg-Smith family of Honolulu acquired the estate's main Sonnenberg Haus and ski area as a vacation home in 1974 when chef Sepp Schenker left to open his nearby Barnard Inn. In 1989, Laila and Thurston Twigg-Smith acquired the other half of Twin Farms from Sinclair Lewis's grandchildren, returning the estate to its original 235 acres. Son Thurston (Koke) Twigg-Smith Jr. and his wife Andrea, twenty-year residents of Barnard, managed the development phase of Twin Farms.

Their resources and taste show throughout the property, from the electronically operated gates at the entrance to the fully equipped fitness center and separate Japanese furo soaking tubs beneath a creekside pub reached by a covered bridge. In the main house, three living rooms, each bigger than the last, unfold as the innkeepers welcome

their guests. One with a vaulted ceiling opens onto a library loft and soaring windows gazing onto a 30-mile view toward Mount Ascutney. Decor is elegantly rustic and utterly comfortable.

Upstairs are four bedrooms bearing some of the Twin Farms trademarks: plump kingsize feather beds, tiled fireplaces, comfortable sitting areas, fabulous folk art and contemporary paintings, TV/VCR/ stereos, tea trays with a coffee press and Kona coffees from the family-owned corporation, twin sinks in the bathrooms, baskets of all-natural toiletries, terrycloth robes,

South porch and terrace of main house at Twin Farms are decorated for autumn.

and unbleached and undyed cotton towels. They impart a feeling of elegant antiquity, but come with every convenience of the ultimate home away from home.

Less antiquity and even more convenience are found in the newly built stone and wood guest cottages, each with at least one fireplace, a screened porch or terrace, and its own private place in the landscape. The Perch, for instance, is situated above a small stream and beaver pond. It harbors luxuriant seating around the fireplace, a desk, a dining area, a refrigerator with ice maker, a bed recessed in an alcove and shielded by a hand-carved arch of wooden roping, a wicker-filled porch where a wood sculpture of a shark hangs overhead, and a bathroom with a copper tub the size of a small pool and a separate shower stall, both with windows to the outdoors. The Treehouse is furnished in Adirondack twig. The Studio, with a two-story window, fulfills an artist's dream. Four new cottages were to open in mid-1995 and the last three were scheduled for completion in 1996.

Good food and drink (from help-yourself bars) are among Twin Farms strong points. Guests meet at 7 o'clock for cocktails in a changing venue – perhaps the wine cellar, one of the living rooms or, the night before our visit, in the Studio, the largest cottage. A set, four-course dinner is served at 8 in a baronial dining hall. Chestnut tables are flanked by Indiana hickory chairs with leather cane seats and seem strangely dwarfed by the vaulted ceilings and the fieldstone fireplaces at either end. Although the hefty 32-page, four-color book that serves as the inn's brochure says guests "are often inspired to dress for dinner," the reality is that more casual attire is encouraged.

Talented chef Neil Wigglesworth came here from The Point on Saranac Lake in the Adirondacks, a smaller but similarly grand inn. A typical dinner might start with medallions of lobster with avocado relish and angel-hair pasta, followed by warm red-cabbage salad with slices of smoked chicken. The main course could be veal mignon with timbales of wild rice and xeres sauce. For dessert? Perhaps fresh figs with beummes de venese ice cream and peach-caramel sauce. Coffee, cheeses and a glass of aged port might round out the evening.

Breakfast is continental if taken in the guest rooms and cooked to order in the dining room from a small menu – raspberry pancakes or eggs benedict with lobster the day we visited.

Lunch is a movable feast, depending on the day and guests' inclinations. It could be a sit-down meal in the dining room, a picnic anywhere, or a barbecue beside the inn's seven-acre Copper Pond or at its own ski area, where there's never a lineup for the pomalift. Afternoon tea is a presentation worthy of the Ritz, complete, perhaps, with little gold leaves on one of the five kinds of tea pastries.

The creekside pub, incidentally, is nearly a museum piece with its collection of beer bottles from around the world. Beer-bottle caps cover the light shades over the billiards table, outline the mirror and sconces above the fireplace, and cover the candlesticks on the mantel. Even a pub chair is dressed in beer caps – a dramatic piece of pop art from the Twigg-Smiths' renowned art collection. Such are some of the delights and surprises encountered by guests at Twin Farms.

Doubles, $700 and $850; cottages, $850, $1,050 and $1,500. All-inclusive, except for 15 percent service charge and 8 percent state tax. Two-night minimum on weekends, three nights on holidays.

The Jackson House, Route 4 West, Woodstock 05091. (802) 457-2065.

If ever almost every room in a small country inn were worthy of coverage in an antiques or decorator magazine, it would be these. All nine guest rooms and three suites are different and eclectically furnished with such things as antique brass lamps on either side of the bathroom mirror, a marble-topped bedside table, an 1860 sleigh bed, a prized Casablanca ceiling fan, Chinese carved rugs, old steam radiators painted gold, handmade afghans coordinated to each room's colors, bamboo and cane furniture, a blanket box made of tiger maple, a 300-year-old grandfather clock made by Henry Merriman and so much more.

Suffice to say that the rooms vary from French Empire to British Oriental to old New England and bear such names as Gloria Swanson, who once stayed here when it was a guest house, and Mary Todd Lincoln, with furniture of the period. The floors in each room are of different woods because the house was built in 1890 by a sawmill owner. A lovely celadon collection is housed in a lighted stand at the top of the staircase with a highly polished banister of cherry wood.

Each bathroom has a glassed-in shower and hair dryers, but those are about the only modern touches beyond the idea of luxury espoused by the innkeepers: elegant guest rooms, a parlor in which champagne and wine are poured and an elaborate buffet of hors d'oeuvre is set out at 6 p.m., an adjacent library where you can shut the door, turn on the 1937 Zenith radio and curl up with a classic, and a formal dining room in which extravagant breakfasts are served.

Innkeepers Jack Foster and Bruce McIlveen give you fuzzy brown slippers in the winter so your shoes won't mar the floors and take you to a bedroom that – with a couple of small exceptions – would do justice to a museum. Most choice are two third-floor beauties, considered suites because they're about twice the size of most other rooms. Both have queensize cherry sleigh beds, Italian marble baths and french doors onto a rear deck overlooking an English garden. We found plenty of room in the Francesca suite to spread out on an upholstered sofa, a wing chair and, on the deck beyond, two lounge chairs. The mirrored bathroom was so sparkling it looked as if we were the first ever to use it. Upon our return from dinner, a couple of Godiva chocolates were on our pillows.

At breakfast, guests gather around an 18th-century mahogany table from England for quite a feast. The first course might be a plate of honeydew, cantaloupe and kiwi,

Two front porches beckon guests at The Jackson House.

bananas in cream or, in winter, baked apple with mincemeat in rum and wine. Juices, croissants and muffins come next. Poached eggs on dill biscuits with poached salmon and hollandaise sauce highlighted one of the best breakfasts we've had. Jack and Bruce are always creating new treats, however. At our latest visit, they served a spectacular dish incorporating a braised teriyaki chicken thigh, braised asparagus spears, a poached egg and a cone of polenta, sprinkled with minced red and green peppers, carrots and zucchini amidst a swirl of port wine sauce. The next day produced a plate of fresh fettuccine with homemade pesto and a poached egg with béarnaise sauce in the center, teamed with salmon poached in court bouillon with a sprig of dill and a stuffed mushroom cap. After all this, settle into a deep wing chair in the library or retire to a lounge chair in the back yard for a morning nap.

Doubles, $135 to $165; suites, $195 and $250. No smoking.

Woodstock Inn and Resort, 14 The Green, Woodstock 05091. (802) 457-1100 or (800) 448-7900.

The biggest institution in town, the Woodstock Inn is solid. Solid, as in the 1823 Paul Revere bell weighing 1,463 pounds standing guard outside its newish 18th-century-style wing or the expanses of rich hardwoods comprising floor, walls and ceiling of the elegant Richardson's Tavern.

The inn sits majestically back from the green, its front facing a covered bridge and mountains, the rear looking across the pool and putting green and down the valley toward its golf course and ski touring center. The resort's other leisure facilities include the Suicide Six ski area, ten tennis courts and two lighted paddle tennis courts, an indoor sports and fitness center, and such attractions as sleigh rides, dogsledding and horseback riding.

The interior of the inn is impressive as well. Built by Rockresorts in 1969 after Laurance Rockefeller found the original Woodstock Inn beyond salvation, it contains a lobby warmed by a ten-foot-high stone fireplace around which people always seem to be gathered, a large and glamorous dining room, a cafe, a wicker sun room and lounge where afternoon tea is served, an always-busy gift shop and a smashing barnwood library outfitted with books and the day's Boston and New York newspapers.

The main inn has three stories in front and four in the rear, the lowest downstairs from the lobby. The 146 guest rooms are among the more luxurious in which we've stayed, with handmade quilts on the beds, upholstered chairs, three-way reading lights, television, telephones, and large bathrooms and closets. Walls are hung with paintings and photographs of local scenes.

The most prized rooms now seem to be 34 in the newer rear brick wing, many with fireplaces and three with sitting-room porches overlooking the putting green. They are notable for graceful reading alcoves, dark blue and burgundy bed coverings matching the carpets, TVs on wheels hidden in cupboards, mini-refrigerators, and double marble vanities in the bathrooms. Interestingly, they seem smaller and more intimate than many of the rooms in the main inn. Covered parking is provided in a garage below.

The long main dining room, lately doubled in size, has large windows onto a spacious outdoor terrace overlooking the pool, putting green and gardens. It offers dinner nightly (see Dining Spots).

Doubles, $139 to $265, EP; $231 to $357, MAP.

The Maple Leaf Inn, Route 12, Box 273, Barnard 05031. (802) 234-5342 or (800) 516-2753.

The would-be innkeepers from Texas could not find the perfect old New England inn in their search among existing buildings. So they built it – a brand new, meant-to-look-old Victorian structure with the requisite gingerbread and gazebo – in a clearing amid sixteen acres of maples and birches at the end of a long driveway in tiny Barnard.

For their September 1994 opening, Gary and Janet Robison from Houston engraved their names and the date – as they would for a cornerstone – at the beginning of the sidewalk leading to their impressive Victorian manse. "We couldn't resist," said Gary. "It's the child in all of us."

Up the long sidewalk guests head to the wraparound front porch with its corner gazebo and authentic Tennessee oak rockers. Enter the front door, its window engraved with a maple leaf. On the right is an intimate library, full of foreign travel books and artifacts from the days when the Robisons lived abroad. On the left is a parlor with a corner fireplace, one of seven woodburning fireplaces in the house and all topped with different antique mantelpieces. The traditional furniture here blends nicely with the occasional antique. Beyond and still farther out in this undulating house that seems to have a surfeit of windows everywhere is a fireplaced dining room, its five tables for two set for breakfasts by candlelight. "We cater to the getaway couples market," explains Gary.

Couples get away in five comfortable bedrooms, most positioned so as to have windows on three sides. All have modern baths (four with whirlpool tubs), kingsize beds, fireplaces, sitting areas, TV/VCRs secreted in the armoires, ceiling fans and closets. An unusual picket fence affair replaces the usual headboard behind the kingsize bed in the main-floor Country Garden Room because the Robisons preferred not to block the window against which the bed rests. The pickets also continue the theme of the fences and gardens just outside. This room is typical with its swivel club chair/rockers, colorful bed quilt, gray carpeting and walls, and sheer lace curtains. Each mantelpiece holds what Gary calls an antique doodad. Stenciling and oriental rugs add color. The four

Maple Leaf Inn is new, built-to-look-old Victorian structure.

upstairs corner rooms are named and decorated for each season. The Winter Haven with an oak Victorian roll-top panel bed and whirlpool tub for two is the largest. The unfinished attic contains space for two more guest rooms.

The Robisons serve a full breakfast with juice, a fresh fruit dish such as poached pears, muffins and fruit breads, and a main dish, perhaps pancakes, waffles, omelets or frittatas. In the afternoon, they offer tea and wine with crackers and cheese. They planned eventually to serve guests dinner by reservation.

Doubles, $100 to $150. No smoking.

The Charleston House, 2l Pleasant St., Woodstock 05091. (802) 457-3843.

When we first saw the Charleston House, it was festooned for Christmas, inside and out, and looked like a spread for House Beautiful.

But the red brick 1835 Greek revival house is gorgeous at any time of year. Named for the hometown of the original innkeeper, it remains the epitome of Southern charm and hospitality under owners Barbara and Bill Hough from Maryland, who retired in 1994 and turned it over to their son and daughter-in-law, John and Marie Hough.

John had run the nearby Canterbury House for four years for his parents, who used to own it. As Marie tells it, she was a corporate banker in New York who "checked into the Canterbury House and never checked out." They got married, headed west for a couple of years and returned in 1994 to Woodstock, where they planned to become ski instructors at Suicide Six.

The Charleston House, listed on the National Register of Historic Places, is furnished with period antiques, eclectic art and oriental rugs. All seven comfortable bedrooms have private baths and most have queensize four-poster beds. The rear Gables room, which contains Barbara's childhood furniture, is the most popular, although honeymooners favor the Summer Kitchen room, downstairs in back with its own entrance. The most expensive room, Pomfret Hills, has a TV set.

Stunning floral arrangements and needlepoint pillows grace the dining room and comfortable living room, where a fire is usually going in the fireplace.

John is the breakfast cook, preparing such treats as eggs in puff pastry, oven-baked french toast and puff pancakes.

In 1995, the younger Houghs were looking to add two deluxe rooms with fireplaces and kingsize beds in an extension behind the inn.

Doubles, $110 to $150. No smoking.

The Canterbury House, 43 Pleasant St., Woodstock 05091. (802) 437-3077.

The British flag flies in front of this 1880 Victorian house. It's appropriate, for the daughter of new innkeepers Fred and Celeste Holden married a Brit and presented them a granddaughter on July 4. And moving here from Timonium, Md., they took over an inviting boarding house-turned-B&B with eight bedrooms, each with a link to that hallmark of English literature, Chaucer's *Canterbury Tales.*

The rooms, while smaller than many others in town, are cheerfully decorated with period furnishings from the 1880s – "a combination of good antiques and comfortable reproductions, so guests don't feel they're in a museum," says Fred. All the bedrooms come with private baths and six have queensize beds. On the main floor, the Reeve's Tale, with a pretty quilt and matching pillows on its white wicker bed, is the only handicapped-accessible room at any B&B in town. A stuffed duck graces the Canadian pine bed in the Squire's Tale. The spacious Chaucer's Garret on the third floor holds a double bed and two twins. The most coveted accommodations are in the rear Monk's Tale with a private entrance, fireplace, clawfoot tub, stereo and TV. Its queen bed is dressed with an antique mahogany headboard, the spread matches the poof curtains, and wicker rockers await on the porch. All rooms are equipped with bottles of Vermont pure water, chocolates and Gilbert & Soames toiletries.

Guests congregate in a comfortable, family-style living room with a fireplace. In the morning the action is at two side-by-side tables for eight in the spacious dining room. Here, Fred draws on his 30 years' experience as a developer of food products to prepare gourmet breakfasts. A house specialty is eggs lasagna layered with potatoes, ham, sliced tomatoes and four kinds of cheese. Other favorites are eggnog french toast, puff pancakes with berries and cheese (described as like a blintz in flavor) and puffed omelets that look like popovers. A plate of six to eight fruits precedes. Lemon-poppyseed muffins and croissants accompany, but, Fred laments, few guests have enough appetite left to eat them.

Doubles, $85 to $135. No smoking.

Ardmore Inn, 23 Pleasant St., Woodstock 05091. (802) 457-3887.

A structure that looks like a covered bridge stands beside this white Georgian Greek Revival house that for years was the home of the well-known F.H. Gillingham family. The look was created by opening the rear of what had been a garage – it was the only way for cars to get through to park in the back yard, explained owner Bill Gallagher.

Father Bill, as he's known to Woodstockers, bought the impressive house with distinguished palladian windows as "a nice place for my aunts and me" when he retires as parish priest at Our Lady of Snows church across the street. Meanwhile, he and resident innkeeper Giorgio Ortiz restored the original woodwork, added new bathrooms, brought in family furnishings and opened it in 1994 as a B&B. They named it Ardmore, which means "Great House" in the Irish tradition.

In his booming baritone voice, the ebullient priest likes to show prized features of the house, such as the etched glass in the solid mahogany front door, the circular moldings around the original light fixtures on the ceilings and the recessed pocket windows screened with Irish lace curtains in the living room, The five bedrooms, all with small private baths, are painted in light pastel colors. "That's my grandmother's bed," says Bill of the carved black walnut headboard in the mint-green front bedroom, which is accented with Waverly fabrics and hand-hooked area rugs. "My father was in

Ardmore Inn wears its Christmas finery.

the marble business," so the bathroom floors are enhanced with marble. The biggest bedroom is in the rear. Called Tarma, Irish for sanctuary, it lives up to its name with a kingsize bed, a loveseat facing a marble coffee tablet and guardian angels as night lights. The inn's own toiletries are placed in little white baskets.

Breakfast is served for ten at an English mahogany banquet table inlaid with rosewood. Giorgio, the chef, gets creative with things like pumpkin pancakes, stuffed french toast and vegetable frittatas. His masterpiece is the "Woodstock Sunrise," Vermont flatbread bearing baked spiced eggs, Vermont cheddar, smoked apple sausage and asparagus with béarnaise sauce and designed to look like a sunrise. Tea biscuits and cheesecake are offered with tea and cider on the rear screened veranda on summer afternoons.

Doubles, $110 to $150. No smoking.

The Carriage House of Woodstock, 15 Route 4 West, Woodstock 05091. (802) 457-4322.

Mike and Shirley Wagner traded their jobs in medicine in Baltimore for a new lifestyle. "We were in businesses where people always were sick and we wanted to be where people were happy," explains Shirley. They took over a bankrupt B&B with a wraparound veranda up against the highway, did a total renovation, put on a rear addition and became one of three area B&Bs to open just in time to catch the foliage season in 1994.

The Wagners offer seven carpeted bedrooms on the second and third floors, all with private baths (one with a whirlpool tub) and queensize beds. They're furnished in a fresh, flouncy style that Shirley calls "relaxed Victorian."

Shirley's prized antique glass collection is housed in custom-made glass cases separating the living room and dining room. From her spectacular new, cathedral-ceilinged kitchen come daily breakfasts involving a choice of eggs any style with bacon or sausage, pancakes, waffles or french toast. Fruit cup, juice and homemade muffins accompany. Cookies and tea or hot cider are offered in the afternoon.

At our visit, the Wagners were turning a walkout basement in the rear carriage house into a game room and a little antiques shop.

Doubles, $95 to $110.

Quechee Bed & Breakfast, 753 Woodstock Road (Route 4), Quechee 05059. (802) 295-1776.

The waters of the Ottauquechee River can be seen from the back yard and rear upstairs guest rooms of this large 1795 house perched on a cliff not far from Quechee Gorge. It was converted into a luxury B&B by Susan and Ken Kaduboski, transplanted Boston accountants, who have restored eight spacious, air-conditioned bedrooms with private baths.

Guests enter a large living-dining area with comfortable sofas gathered around a huge fireplace. A large cactus stands in one corner, and an interesting art collection is on display.

A smaller parlor has been converted into a breakfast area with four tables for two. It leads through heavy doors into the original house and the guest quarters, nicely secluded and private with a separate entry hall and staircase. Three rooms are on the first floor and five on the second, including two with beamed, half-cathedral ceilings. Each is suavely furnished with king or queensize beds (four of them rice-carved four-posters) or, in one case, twin mahogany sleigh beds that can be joined as a king, antique dressers, two wing chairs, sprightly wallpapers and decorative touches like swags and stenciled lamp shades, and large bathrooms with beige towels. Sheets and pillow cases are beige and cream and lavishly trimmed with lace. One new bathroom is all in pink and pretty as can be.

The Kaduboskis serve a full breakfast of juices, broiled grapefruit or apple-cinnamon custard, homemade breads with different jams, and such main dishes as herbed scrambled eggs, apple pancakes, buttermilk waffles with fresh fruit or french toast stuffed with cream cheese and walnuts.

Doubles, $85 to $135.

The Quechee Inn at Marshland Farm, Clubhouse Road, Quechee 05059. (802) 295-3133 or (800) 235-3133.

This venerable establishment – a beautifully restored 1793 farmstead built by Vermont's first lieutenant governor – is every Hollywood set designer's idea of what a New England country inn should look like: a pure white rambling Vermont farmhouse, red barns out back against a backdrop of green mountains, and across the quiet road the Ottauquechee River heading into Quechee Gorge.

The interior lives up to expectation as well: a welcoming beamed and barnwood living room, lately expanded and so carefully integrated with the older section that many don't notice the change.

In addition to a rustic, stenciled dining room (see Dining Spots), there are 24 comfortable guest rooms, all with private baths, Queen Anne-style furnishings, brass and four-poster canopy beds, wing chairs, braided and Chinese rugs on wide-plank floors and, a surprise for the purists, cable TV.

With fourteen rooms in the original farmhouse and ten more on the second floor of a wing that houses the expanded common rooms and dining room, the inn is large enough to be a focal point for activity – a Christmas Eve open house for inn guests, cocktails before a crackling fire in the lounge, summer get-togethers on the canopied patio, the Wilderness Trails Nordic Ski School in a small barn. The Vermont Fly Fishing

School is based here, and guests have golf, tennis, swimming and skiing privileges at the private Quechee Club.

A full breakfast buffet – from fruits and yogurts to scrambled eggs and sausages – is served in the main dining room. Coffee, tea and fruit breads are offered in the afternoon.

Doubles, $148 to $178, MAP; suites, $188 to $198.

Parker House Inn, 16 Main St., Quechee 05059. (802) 295-6077.

Guests have filled the room diaries with comments about the food and hospitality since Walt and Barbara Forrester left Chicago with their teenaged sons to become innkeepers here. The lively couple look at their inn as a continuing house party. "Schmoozing is my calling," says Walt, and cooking is his new profession.

Walt was selling medical equipment for Toshiba when he decided to enroll in the Culinary Institute of America with the idea of buying an inn in the East. Barbara had been a pastry chef and the couple had operated a pub near Wrigley Field. It was love at first sight when they came across the Parker House, an elegant red brick and white frame Victorian mansion with a steep mansard roof crowned with an ornamental wrought-iron railing.

A Vermont state senator and mill owner, Joseph C. Parker, built the mansion in 1857 next to his mill on the Ottauquechee River. It was converted into an inn by Frank Parker, no relation to the original owner but – by amazing coincidence – Walt's one-time boss at Toshiba. The two had lost track of each other; in the interim, Frank had started and sold the Parker House and Walt had come along unknowingly eight years later.

Long known for its restaurant (see Dining Spots), the accommodations have been upgraded with three cheery and fresh guest rooms with queensize beds and modern baths on the third floor and a second floor TV/sitting room. The new rooms join four large, high-ceilinged guest rooms with private baths on the second floor. Emily's huge room in front, named for the original Mrs. Parker, has twin white enamel and brass poster bedsteads joined by a kingsize mattress, a dressing room with an enormous modern bathroom and an antique desk that Walt calls an early Murphy bed – it opens up, the sides go down and voilà, a futon. Even larger is another kingbedded room running along most of the back of the house with a fine view of the river. We chose Joseph's Room in the rear corner with a queen brass bed, chest, armoire and writing desk and a large bathroom with double vanity, real as opposed to plastic glasses, liquid soap and thick towels. The only drawbacks were only one chair and a lack of reading lights, but we simply adjourned to the small sitting/TV room across the hall.

Breakfast the next morning was a treat in the sunny bar area (it's served outside on an awninged deck in the summer). Juice and half a grapefruit preceded an ample platter of bagels with smoked salmon, cream cheese and all the fixings. On other occasions you might have scrambled eggs with cream cheese and dill and homemade sausage, pancakes with maple syrup or frittata.

Doubles, $90 to $125. Smoking restricted.

Dining Spots

Simon Pearce Restaurant, The Mill, Quechee. (802) 295-1470.

The restaurant beside the Ottauquechee River has as much integrity as the rest of Irish glass blower Simon Pearce's mill complex. The chefs all train at Ballymaloe in Ireland, and they import flour from Ireland to make Irish soda and Ballymaloe brown breads.

You sit on sturdy ash chairs at bare wood tables (dressed with white linens at night).

Simon Pearce Restaurant features brick walls and soaring windows.

The heavy Simon Pearce glassware and the deep brown china are made at the mill. Irish or classical music plays in the background. Through large windows you have a view of the river, hills rising beyond. A large dining addition looks through a hand-some arched window out onto the falls and, in season, an enclosed deck that can be opened to the outside is almost over the falls. (Indeed, a couple of interior tables could give one vertigo, being right over the falls).

Several wines from the Wine Spectator award-winning list are available by the glass. At lunches we've tried both the house white and red ($4 a glass) as well as spicy bloody marys with a real kick, while nibbling the sensational Ballymaloe bread.

The menu changes frequently but there are always specialties like beef and Guinness stew (which is delicious – for $9.50 a generous lunch serving of fork-tender beef and vegetables, plus a small side salad of julienned vegetables). Soups at one visit were hearty split pea with ham and creamy broccoli with cheese ($3.50). Entrées ($7.25 to $11.50) included lamb and rosemary pie, warm goat cheese salad, sesame seared salmon with wasabi and pickled ginger, and brochettes of beef tenderloin with crispy sweet potatoes. The pasta salad, a huge heap of spirals, featured many vegetables and a splendid dressing of oil, vinegar, basil and parmesan cheese. Hickory-smoked coho salmon with potato salad and a skewer of grilled chicken with a spicy peanut sauce and a green salad with vinaigrette also were extra-good.

The walnut meringue cake with strawberry sauce, a menu fixture, is crisp and crunchy and melts in the mouth. Cappuccino cheesecake also is super, as are bittersweet choco-late tart with an espresso sauce, white chocolate mousse cake with raspberry sauce and homemade sorbets. Chocolate rum cake, Irish apple cake and pecan pie are other pos-sibilities, but when we go back, which we seem to do often, nothing but the walnut meringue will do.

At night, a candlelight dinner might start with some of the luncheon entrées as appe-tizers ($5.50 to $7.75), like that grilled chicken with spicy peanut sauce or grilled Cavendish quail with apple cider glaze and cranberry compote. Main courses ($15.25 to $23) could be grilled swordfish with lime hollandaise, poached salmon with white wine sauce, crisp roast duck with mango chutney sauce, scallops of veal with sundried tomatoes and black angus sirloin flamed with Irish whiskey and served with caramelized onions. Desserts are more of the delectable luncheon choices, and the coffee tastes like espresso.

The wine list ranges widely, with plenty of good vintages, charmingly pictured in Simon Pearce glass settings. Naturally, you can get beers and ales from the British Isles. You also can buy loaves of bread and the restaurant's flavored vinaigrettes.

Here's a restaurant that's so unpretentious but so appealing that we're not surprised that several of the traveling friends we've directed there for lunch liked it so much they have returned for an encore the next day.

Lunch daily, 11.30 to 2:45; dinner nightly, 6 to 9. No smoking.

Barnard Inn, Route 12, Barnard. (802) 234-9961.

Ever since Swiss chef Sepp Schenker left the old Sonnenberg Haus (now part of Twin Farms) to open the Barnard Inn, this serene, sophisticated restaurant has been considered one of the best in Vermont. Marie-France and Philip Filipovic from Que-

bec knew they had a lot to live up to when they purchased the restaurant in 1994. They also came with impeccable credentials. Self-taught Yugoslav chef Philip, who started as a waiter in Montreal's Ritz-Carlton Hotel, and his wife owned a four-star restaurant called simply Marie Philip in the Laurentian resort town of St. Sauveur. It had been rated the best in the province by the Quebec government in its annual awards competition.

Moving to Vermont for "quality of life," Marie said, they took over a going concern and began adding their imprimatur. They hung their favorite paintings, added more French wines, and planned to add oriental rugs and upholstered chairs. They also started smoking their own salmon. We, who enjoyed several great meals here previously, were pleased to hear from local innkeepers that the new Barnard Inn was equal to, if not better than, the old.

Fireside dining at Barnard Inn.

A fire blazes in the hearth in the biggest of four small dining rooms in the elegant, late-Colonial inn. Dusky rose cloths, gold-rimmed china, candles in hurricane chimneys and sparkling wine globes dress the well-spaced tables, and the only lighting is from the candles and the wall sconces. It's an altogether charming backdrop for leisurely dining – the meal takes up to the three hours, says Marie, who oversees the front of the house.

From the kitchen comes the inn's longtime specialty, roast crisp duck, done as in the past and teamed with the inn's trademark potatoes, shaped and coated to look like a pear with a clove at the bottom and a pear stem on top. Philip has added more chicken dishes (one is stuffed with small vegetables and served with pickled ginger and turmeric sauce). He considers lamb his trademark – the noisettes of Green Mountain lamb are laced with herbs and served with a tarragon sauce. The fish of the day could be a strudel of three fish – salmon, tuna and swordfish, mixed with braised leeks and spinach and wrapped in phyllo, Other main courses ($20 to $28) include grilled tenderloin of venison with a raspberry vinegar and bitter chocolate sauce, and veal chop with a sauce of green peppercorns, cognac and crème fraîche.

The signature appetizer ($6.50) is the house-smoked salmon shaped like a rose and garnished with cucumber fettuccine and dill mayonnaise. Other possibilities could be ragout of escargot and smoked seafood sausages on a bed of sauerkraut with cilantro-cream sauce. Dessert could be a potpourri of the night's cakes or a palette of sorbets – six different flavors brushed with sesame seeds and looking like an artist's palette.

Dinner from 6, nightly except Monday.

The Prince and the Pauper, 34 Elm St., Woodstock. (802) 457-1818.

A newish cocktail lounge with the shiniest wood bar you ever saw has freed up space for more tables in what many consider to be Woodstock's best restaurant. Tables in the expanded yet intimate L-shaped dining room (many flanked by dark wood booths) are covered with linens, oil lamps and flowers in small carafes. The lamps cast flickering shadows on dark beamed ceilings, and old prints adorn the white walls, one of which has a shelf of old books.

Chef-owner Chris J. Balcer refers to his cuisine as "creative continental." His soup of the day could be billi-bi or Moroccan lentil, the pasta perhaps basil fettuccine with a concasse of tomatoes and garnished with goat cheese, and his pâté a mixture of venison, pork and port wine, served with toasted croutons and apple-cranberry chutney.

Meals are prix-fixe for $30, not including dessert. There's a choice of six entrées, perhaps the signature dish of boneless rack of lamb in puff pastry, medallions of veal sautéed with forest mushrooms, pan-seared duckling with mango-rum sauce, grilled ahi tuna with a coulis of roasted sweet bell peppers, and fillet of Atlantic halibut baked in parchment paper with julienned vegetables.

Homemade bread, house salad and seasonal vegetables accompany. The interesting wine list, honored by Wine Spectator magazine, is heavy on Californias.

Desserts include a fabulous raspberry tart with white chocolate mousse served with raspberry cabernet wine sauce, strawberry sabayon with triple sec, pumpkin cheesecake with pecan topping or homemade Jack Daniels chocolate-chip sorbet. Top them off with espresso, cappuccino or an international coffee.

A bistro menu is available for $11.95 to $14.95 in the bar. Grilled Maine salmon with garlic butter, Indonesian lamb curry, crab cakes with tomato mayonnaise and sautéed chicken with calvados are among the offerings. Besides a pasta of the day, there are five hearth-baked pizzas, all $9.95.

Dinner nightly, 6 to 9 or 9:30; bistro to 10 or 11.

Parker House Inn, 16 Main St., Quechee. (802) 295-6077.

After fourteen years in sales in Chicago, Walt Forrester decided to attend the Culinary Institute of America and team up with his wife Barbara, a sometime pastry chef, in the hospitality business. The Parker House Inn is the fortuitous result. Moving here with their teenagers, who sometimes help in the dining room, they have changed the restaurant's focus from haute French to what Barbara calls "American comfort food," presented with style. One look at the choice wine list harboring five prized pinot noirs from Oregon hints of treats to come.

The atmosphere is elegant in two dining rooms and a rear cocktail lounge opening onto a balcony overlooking the Ottauquechee River. Dinner begins with an amuse-gueule, in our case roasted eggplant, red peppers and garlic pickled with fennel. A sampler of three appetizers ($6.95) produced a stellar grilled portobello mushroom

Walt and Barbara Forrester create house party atmosphere at Parker House Inn.

with warm Vermont goat cheese on a spinach salad, a mushroom cap stuffed with escargot and a country pâté. An extraordinary house salad of California mesclun with mustard vinaigrette and goat cheese followed.

Among main courses ($16.50 to $20.95), the pork normandy sauced with apples, leeks, cider and applejack, and roasted Hudson Valley moulard duck breast marinated with soy sauce, garlic and ginger lived up to advance billing. Other possibilities ranged from pan-seared scallops accented with lemon grass and sundried tomatoes to rack of lamb with a rosemary-wine sauce. After a couple of Barbara's desserts, apple crisp with vanilla ice cream and chocolate-almond torte, we lingered over cappuccino and savored the memory of an unforgettable meal.

Dinner nightly except Tuesday, 5:30 to 9.

Itas'ca, 2 North Main St., White River Junction. (802) 295-1025.
The artworks are of fruits and vegetables, and the salt shakers are in the form of ceramic vegetables. Over the front door are the Latin words Veritas Caput, meaning true source, and the odd name is a combination of the last four letters of veritas and the first two of caput. "We chose the name because we strive to know the true source of the foods we use," explained Marilyn Ashley-Sack, one of the principals.

But this new-world style cafe that's taken the Upper Valley by storm is far different from the traditional health foods restaurant. It's exceptionally stylish, the chefs are Culinary Institute of America grads and the menu is cutting-edge. This place could be in Manhattan or California, but instead it turned up in 1994 in White River Junction.

Marilyn and her husband, Brad Sack, an architect, retired from Boston to this area, where they had a second home. They sensed a need for a health foods restaurant, but had "gourmet tastes," said Brad, who had grown up on meat and potatoes. After searching far and wide for a chef who could combine healthful cooking with new world cuisine, they found Ravi Scher in Miami and Jeff Rotondi in the Carolinas. Head chef Ravi, who had cooked in the Keys and the Caribbean, uses new world spices and does wonderful things with vegetables, fish and poultry.

He showed his culinary prowess in a couple of masterful dinner appetizers, a roasted vegetable napoleon with a trio of caviars and blood oranges, and a tuna sashimi on a hot and spicy red pepper sauce. Both came on oversize white plates and were visual

85

knockouts as well as triumphs in taste. We'd happily return to sample the other starters ($4.95 to $9.25), perhaps Creole fish soup with Haitian pickled slaw, Vermont chèvre rolled in toasted cumin seeds and served with a purple potato salad and red pepper compote, or a chilled crab spring roll with seaweed salad and mustard miso dipping sauce.

Tables are set for dinner at Itas'ca.

Main dishes ($9.75 to $18.25) continue the culinary excitement. Expect exotica like pasta pomodoro and eggplant, wok-seared soba noodles with crispy Asian vegetables, spice-rubbed and fire-grilled Atlantic salmon with ancho honey, seafood risotto and plantation chicken marinated in molasses sugar cane, grilled and served with Cuban black beans and tropical salsa.

The pastry chef's desserts are spectacular, as in maple-pumpkin tofu cheesecake, chocolate nouveau torte or apple-berry crisp with ice cream. They looked so good we'd recommend trying the dessert sampler for $7.95. The wine list is well chosen, with a couple of organic wines and priced from the low teens to $45.

The storefront setting at the prime corner in downtown White River is chic with high ceilings, brick walls, white linens, votive candles and fresh flowers. The locals proved so receptive that Itas'ca was planning to expand into the next storefront and open a juice bar.

Lunch seasonally, Tuesday-Saturday 11 to 2:30; dinner, Tuesday-Saturday 6 to 9.

Woodstock Inn and Resort, 14 The Green, Woodstock. (802) 457-1100.

A more glamorous restaurant setting than the Woodstock Inn's curved, pillared Dining Room is difficult to imagine in Vermont. Tables on two levels look out onto gardens and putting green. Lavish flower arrangements, wine glasses and the inn's own monogrammed, green-rimmed china sparkle on crisp white linens. Smaller, more intimate dining rooms go off each side of the main room.

It's a lovely backdrop for the Sunday brunch, which is popular with townspeople. It's also a serene setting for dinner, when entrées are priced from $21.75 for wood-grilled provimi veal chops with creamy pearl onion sauce to $24 for wood-smoked prime rib of beef with crisp onions, balsamic fries and fresh tomato ketchup. Roasted salmon with lobster homefries and oven-roasted Cavendish pheasant are other possibilities. Billings Farm ice creams and sherbets are among the desserts.

Quite reasonably priced and serving meals all day is the **Eagle Cafe,** transformed from the old coffee shop and attractive in both decor and fare. At lunch, we've enjoyed fine salads – chef's, chilled bouillabaisse and seared tuna with wild rice, among them.

Lunch, 11:30 to 2; dinner, 6 to 9; Sunday brunch, 11 to 1:30.

Bentleys Restaurant, 3 Elm St., Woodstock. (802) 457-3232.

Entrepreneurs David Creech and Bill Deckelbaum Jr. started with a greenhouse and plant store in 1974, installed a soda fountain, expanded with a restaurant catering to every taste at every hour, added a specialty-foods shop, and then developed the colorful Waterman Place with retail stores and a Mexican restaurant called Rosalita's in a 100-year-old house along Route 4 in Quechee.

The flagship of it all is the original Bentleys, a casual, engaging and often noisy spot at the prime corner in Woodstock. On several levels, close-together tables are set with small cane mats, Perrier bottles filled with flowers, and small lamps or tall candles in holders. Old floor lamps sport fringed shades, windows are framed by lace curtains, the plants are large potted palms, and walls are covered with English prints and an enormous bas-relief.

The menu is interesting as well. For lunch, we enjoyed a house specialty, French tart ($6.75), a hot puff pastry filled with vegetables in an egg and cheese custard, and a fluffy quiche ($5.95) with turkey, mushrooms and snow peas, both accompanied by side salads. From the dessert tray came a delicate chocolate mousse cake with layers of meringue, like a torte, served with the good Green Mountain coffee in clear glass cups.

Appetizers, salads, sandwiches and light entrées such as saucisson, chicken caesar salad and cold sliced flank steak make up half the dinner menu. The other side offers entrées from $14.95 for maple mustard chicken to $18.50 for Jack Daniels steak. With options like these, it's no wonder that Bentleys is always crowded and bustling.

Lunch, daily 11:30 to 2:30; dinner, 5:30 to 9:30 or 10; Sunday brunch, noon to 3.

Quechee Inn at Marshland Farm, Clubhouse Road, Quechee. (802) 295-3133.

Most people enjoy a drink by the fire in the living room-lounge before adjourning for dinner in the antiques-filled dining room. Beamed ceilings, wide-plank floors and lovely pink and blue stenciled borders on the walls provide the setting for some interesting cuisine.

The short dinner menu changes seasonally. Winter offerings might start with chicken and cheddar turnovers with wine sauce incorporating diced tomatoes and thyme or house-smoked Eastern brook trout with maple-horseradish mustard.

Entrées run from $16.50 for pan-seared tuna topped with cucumber and pickled ginger to $20 for West Texas antelope with a smoked chile barbecue sauce. Others include sautéed gulf shrimp in a sauce of oranges and fennel, grilled pork loin wrapped in pancetta with a warm maple-apple puree, and sautéed breast of duck with a sauce of pears and lingonberries. Homemade desserts could be french silk pie, tirami su, bitter-sweet chocolate terrine, frozen fruit soufflé and puff pastries with fresh raspberries.

Dinner nightly, 6 to 9.

The Caffe Mill, 47 Central St., Woodstock. (802) 457-3204.

Need a coffee fix? Pop in to this new cafe for a Vermont latte, flavored with maple syrup and topped with whipped cream and crystallized maple sugar. Owner Tina Sheridan Palmer offers exotic coffees by the pound, as well as teas and light lunches (and some delicious looking scones, popovers, cookies and the like). You might find carrot soup with ginger and orange, or panini (an Italian sandwich) with fried egg-plant, fontina and tomato sauce. "We're an alternative to the bar scene," says Tina. The attractive high-ceilinged, brick-walled cafe beside a creek extends its hours to be open at night on summer weekends.

Open daily, 7 or 8 to 6, to 10 p.m. Friday and Saturday in season.

Diversions

The sportsman and the sightseer have plenty to do in the Woodstock-Quechee area. You can ski at Suicide Six, not far from Gilbert's farm where Woodstockers installed the nation's first rope tow in 1934, or you can ski at nearby Killington, the East's largest ski area. You can golf at the historic Woodstock Country Club, site of Vermont's first golf course and home also of the fine Woodstock Ski Touring Center, or at a newer golf course in Quechee. You can hike through the Quechee Gorge area or the hundreds of acres of forests maintained by the Woodstock Inn. You can climb a switchback trail up Mount Tom for a bird's-eye view of the area. You can walk around the village green and center, marveling in the architectural variety and browsing through the Dana House Museum of the Woodstock Historical Society. But it is arts, crafts and shopping that make Woodstock so appealing for many.

Billings Farm & Museum, Route 12 north of Woodstock, 457-2355. This is an artfully presented display of life-like exhibits portraying the Vermont farm year of 1890. Housed in four interconnected 19th-century buildings on the working Billings Farm, it shows how crops were planted and harvested. Farm life also meant making butter and cider, cutting ice and firewood, sugaring and darning socks, as well as going to school and the general store and participating in community life; such activities are imaginatively shown. Down a path the modern farm is evident: visitors can see the Jersey herd, calves, sheep, oxen and two teams of Belgian horses, and the milking barn is open. Special events include a 19th-century crafts day and a cow-milking contest. Open daily 10 to 5, early May to late October, and 10 to 4 in November and December. Adults, $6.

Shopping. The Vermont Workshop, 73 Central St., is said to be the oldest gallery in Woodstock, having evolved from a summer workshop established in 1949. Everything from woven mats and interesting lamp shades to wall hangings and cookware is for sale in room after room of great appeal. Nearby on Central Street is one of the two locations of **Gallery 2;** the gallery has paintings, sculpture and art glass pieces. The print room around the corner at 6 Elm St. holds lots of Woody Jackson cows and woodcuts of Sabra Johnson Field, whose studio in nearby East Pomfret, Tontine Press, is worth a visit (by appointment).

The Looking Glass has sweet clothing for the little ones, and the **Christmas Treasures** shop everything you might need to decorate. Check out the pottery depicting fish by Giovanni DeSimone, a student of Picasso, at **Aubergine,** a kitchenware shop, where you might find a thermos full of chocolate-raspberry coffee to sample and some dips to spread on crackers. **Log Cabin Quilts** has everything for the quilter plus the finished products. Lately, it seems to be going in more for T-shirts. Next door is the **Unicorn,** a gift shop with jewelry and woodcrafts by New England artisans and some clever games and toys. **North Wind Artisans Gallery** is rather avant garde – we were struck by a papier-mâché flamingo, a mirror shaped like a face with hair on top and big earrings, and a torso of a nude male made of mesh.

A sculpture of a man walking five dogs, taken out to the sidewalk every morning, attracts visitors into the spectacular **Stephen Huneck Gallery** at 49 Central St.,

Display outside Stephen Huneck Gallery.

where the sign says "dogs welcome" on the door. Animals (especially dogs and cats) are the theme of Vermont resident Huneck, one of America's hottest artists, who's known for playful hand-carved furniture, jewelry and sculpture. His flying dalmatian and angel-face cat pins and Christmas tree ornaments are affordable "mini-sculptures." The smallest pins start at $10 but you could spend up to $30,000. You'll come out of here chuckling and feeling that the world isn't such a bad place, after all.

F.H. Gillingham & Co. at 16 Elm St. is the most versatile store of all. Run by the Billings family for 100 years, it's a general store, but a highly sophisticated one – offering everything from specialty foods and wines to hardware – and so popular that it does a land-office mail-order business. Here you'll probably find every Vermont-made dressing, candy, condiment and more. Owner Jireh Swift Billings's young son represents the ninth generation of the Swift family, dating to the 1600s. Next door is the **Village Butcher** where you can get a good sandwich, or maybe a bowl of lobster bisque or chili. There's a table full of maple sugar and maple syrup products.

In Quechee, the **Upper Valley Collection** across from Simon Pearce offers beautiful quilts. We coveted a queen-size in deep burgundies and blues for $450. We also liked the dolls in country clothes, especially the black sheep. Beside it is **Chumley's Bakery,** where you can get light lunch if you are not in the mood for Simon Pearce. At our visit, cheddar, mushroom and spinach soup sounded good, as did a California sandwich of avocado, cream cheese, tomato and sprouts on a croissant, baked in house. Raspberry bear claws and peanut-butter cookies were among the baked goodies. Shops seem to come and go on the three levels of **Waterman Place,** a 100-year-old restored house with a glass atrium above Quechee village off Route 4.

Extra-Special

Simon Pearce, The Mill at Quechee. (802) 295-2711.

Every time we're in the area, we stop at Simon Pearce's magnificent mill, partly because it's all so fascinating and partly because there's always something new. Simon Pearce is the glass blower who left Ireland in 1981 to set up business in the abandoned flannel mill beside the Ottauquechee. The site is inspiring: thundering waterfalls, covered bridge, beautifully restored mill and classic white Vermont houses all around. The interior has a fine restaurant (see Dining Spots) and a handsome shop offering glass, pottery and Irish woolens, all beautifully displayed, plus a second floor with seconds at 30 to 40 percent off, although even then, everything is expensive. Downstairs is a glass-blowing area where you can watch Simon Pearce and eight associates turn out 120 pieces a day, a working pottery, the hydro station with enormous pipes from the river and a steam turbine that provides enough power to light the town of Quechee as well as serve the mill's energy needs (melting sand into glass, firing clay into porcelain and stoneware). "The whole idea was to become self-sufficient and provide an economic model for small business in Vermont," says Simon. The mill is zoned utility in the sub-basement, manufacturing in the basement, retail in the restaurant and shop, office-retail on the second floor and residential on the third, where Simon lived with his family for a while. The enterprise is growing all the time, opening retail stores (two locations in New York and one in Boston), expanding its production capability with a new facility in nearby Windsor and adding ventures (furniture, wooden bowls and brother Stephen Pearce's Irish pottery). We defy anyone not to enjoy, learn – and probably buy. Beautiful clear glass balls, $15 each, are marvelous ornaments for a Christmas tree.

Open daily, 9 a.m. to 9 p.m.; glass-blowers work weekdays.

Newfane/West River Valley, Vt.

The Essence of Vermont

There's not much to do in Newfane and Vermont's surrounding West River Valley. And that's the way the inhabitants like it.

The interstates, the ski areas, the tony four-season destination resorts are some distance away. This is the essence of old Vermont, unspoiled by tourism and contemporary commercial trappings.

The meandering West River creates a narrow valley between the mountains as it descends toward Brattleboro. Along the way are covered bridges (one is the longest in Vermont), country stores, flea markets and a couple of picture-book villages.

The heart of the valley is Newfane, the shire town of Windham County, without so much as a brochure to publicize it. In 1824, Newfane "moved" to the valley from its original site two miles up Newfane hill and now has fewer residents than it had then. The Newfane green is said to be Vermont's most-photographed. Clustered around the green are the white-columned courthouse, the matching Congregational church, the town hall, two famed inns, two country stores and, nearby, some houses – and that's about it.

Upriver is Townshend ("Historic Townshend," one of the area's few tourist brochures calls it), with a larger green and more business activity, though that's relative. Beyond is Jamaica, an up-and-coming hamlet with some good art galleries and gift shops.

There are back roads and country stores to explore, but for many visitors this quiet area's chief blessing is its collection of fine inns and restaurants amidst a setting of Vermont as it used to be.

Inn Spots

The Four Columns Inn, 230 West St., Box 278, Newfane 05345. (802) 365-7713 or (800) 787-6633.

Ever since French chef René Chardain left the Old Newfane Inn to open the Four Columns, this spot has been widely known for outstanding cuisine (see Dining Spots). Under the auspices of subsequent innkeeper Jacques Allembert and his wife Pamela, it

has become known for comfortable overnight accommodations as well.

Five guest rooms and four suites, all with private baths and most with king or queensize beds, are located in the main columned inn, built in 1830 by General Pardon Kimball for his Southern-born wife as a replica of her girlhood home. Another five rooms and a suite are in the main restaurant building.

All rooms are colorfully decorated with antiques, hooked rugs, handmade afghans and quilts. An 84-year-old craftsman made the canopied four-poster bed in one. We're especially fond of the

Guest rooms are in front and restaurant at rear of Four Columns Inn.

third-floor hideaway suite in the front building. Centered by an exposed chimney that divides the room into unusual spaces, it has a canopied bed set into an alcove, a sitting room with a private front porch overlooking the Newfane green, thick beige carpeting and Laura Ashley fabrics.

Several common rooms are good for relaxing or watching television, and the pewter-topped bar in the tavern to the rear of the dining room is a popular gathering spot. Beyond is a cozy little plant-filled sun room with a TV/VCR atop an old iron stove.

Pam prepares a healthy country breakfast buffet, which includes fresh fruits, homemade granola, yogurt, hot oatmeal in winter, apple brown betty, scones and corn muffins. "Nobody leaves the table hungry," says Jacques.

The spacious and attractive grounds include a landscaped swimming pool, rock gardens and a trout pond beloved by ducks. Beyond are a trout stream and hiking trails up the inn's own little mountain.

Doubles, $100 to $125; suites, $140 to $175. No smoking.

The Inn at South Newfane, Dover Road, South Newfane 05351. (802) 348-7191.

What better way to approach a country inn than through a covered bridge? The one we have in mind is in Williamsville, the town next to South Newfane, where the handsome Inn at South Newfane, with its olive green trim and masses of pink impatiens surrounding the porte cochere, opened in 1984.

A private turn-of-the century estate on 100 acres, it was purchased by Connie and Herb Borst of Westchester County. They had traveled extensively in Europe, always enjoying small inns more than hotels, so decided to open one of their own.

Herb Borst does the baking for breakfast, when dishes like Alsatian kugelhofs, fruit pancakes and french toast made from three slices of different homemade breads are served in a sunny morning room. His tiny Scandinavian pancakes with whipped honey butter and Vermont maple syrup were about the best we've had.

An expansive, well-furnished living room with fireplace and the "Great Room" that is just inside the front door, in shades of gold and with shelves of books, are available for guests' use.

The porch in back is set with garden furniture and beyond are extensive grounds, embracing grand gardens and a fair-size pond for swimming in summer and skating in winter. Hiking and cross-country trails abound, some on the mountain that rises behind the inn.

The six bedrooms, of different sizes, have queen or twin beds and all have been totally redone by the Borsts, who added private baths. Quilts made by "the ladies in the church across the street," floral wallpapers, frilly curtains, and stuffed animals or quilted cat pillows on the beds add to the charm. One room contains a reproduction of an old Colonial bed, so high you must use a stool to climb up, and another has twin cannonball beds. The windowed back room has a bathtub in which, says Connie, you can soak and look out at birds and trees. Flowers and bowls of fruit are in the rooms.

In the big hall upstairs is a reading and writing alcove, where a chest holds all kinds of good books and magazines, and old glass bottles of many colors are displayed by the window.

Quiet and tranquil, the Inn at South Newfane is a good place to relax and read that book you haven't had time for. Although the Borsts had been trying to sell for some time and were about to close a deal in 1995, they pledged that it would remain so.

Doubles, $120 B&B. Closed November and April. No credit cards.

Windham Hill Inn, West Townshend 05359. (802) 874-4080 or (800) 944-4080.

Up a steep hill so far off the main road that we had to stop to ask if we were on the right track is this gem of an inn, a speckled brick and white wood structure built in 1825 and distinguished by a suave oval sign and a commanding view of the West River Valley. Grigs and Pat Markham from Connecticut took over a going concern in 1993 and, with skilled decorating touches and hospitable nuances like small decanters of Harvey's Bristol Cream in each room, have enhanced it as a destination unto itself. "There's not much to do but relax, admire our 160 acres of trees and hills, and enjoy two good meals a day," says Grigs.

Since their arrival, the Markhams have been remodeling bathrooms, adding fireplaces in rooms, and upgrading beds so that all but one room have king or queensize. All fifteen rooms have private baths and, Pat says, come with "pets" from the Mary Meyer Stuffed Toys factory store in Townshend. But don't be misled. They're furnished with a panache that merited a six-page photo spread in Country Decorating magazine. One rear room is nicknamed the tree house because, Pat says, "when you wake up in the morning you feel as if you're in the trees." It has a queen canopy bed, a sofa, a corner window seat afluff with pillows and a private balcony.

Among the most popular are the five rooms fashioned from nooks and alcoves in the White Barn annex, particularly the two sharing a large deck overlooking the mountains. The Markhams took the smallest room there and gave it a total new look with a queensize bed, fireplace and skylights. In 1995, they planned to create three more accommodations with fireplaces in the main inn from space vacated when they moved into a new house on the property. The largest was designed as the premium room with a kingsize bed, sitting area and a soaking tub in the room with a view of the fireplace, and a second is a suite with a small sitting room.

Food is taken seriously at Windham Hill. The Markhams were planning in 1995 to enlarge the dining room to make more room for the public for dinner (see Dining Spots). The couple take turns manning the bar in the bar area, which they opened up into the living room, where cheese and crackers and hors d'oeuvre are available with cocktails from 5:30 to 7 each night. Besides the evening meal, guests also enjoy a full breakfast served amid a background of taped chamber music, antique silver and crystal: fresh orange juice in champagne flutes, breakfast breads and fresh fruits, and a main dish like waffles, eggs mornay or griddle cakes shaped like little doughnuts, made of winter wheat and cornmeal.

92

Other rooms at guests' disposal are a sitting room off the living room, and a large and sunny back room with oriental rugs, a television set and game table.

Doubles, $180 to $195, MAP; suites, $215. No smoking.

Three Mountain Inn, Route 30, Jamaica 05343. (802) 874-4140.

The aromas of dinner emanating from the kitchen and a wood-paneled living room with a fireplace welcome guests to this charming inn, now encompassing three buildings and offering sixteen guest rooms, a two-room suite with woodburning stove, a honeymoon cottage beside the pool, a small conference center and good meals (see Dining Spots).

Charles and Elaine Murray took over the old Jamaica Inn with eight rooms in 1978, and have been adding rooms and private baths ever since. Accommodations in the main house vary from a corner room with private balcony and kingsize four-poster bed in shades of green and rose in the new "Wing Up" above a stable to a couple of simple rooms sharing a bath on the first floor. Architect Rodney Williams of the nearby Inn at Sawmill Farm designed the new wing with his trademark barnwood and beamed-ceiling touches, as well as the new rear cottage with a queensize bed and a fireplace, perfect for honeymooners.

Next door in the Robinson House are six more guest rooms, one notable for a square bathtub and another that Elaine decorated around a lovely patterned rug. A small living room with a wood stove connects with a bedroom to make a suite. Guests enjoy a large deck out back. Across the street is the Sage House, a once-primitive place that the Murrays upgraded with a redecorated living room, two bedrooms, a kitchen and a whirlpool tub.

An inviting swimming pool is a favorite backyard gathering spot in the summer.

Pecan waffles, french toast, local sausage and eggs, homemade biscuits and blueberry muffins are typical fare at breakfast, served in two fireplaced dining rooms.

Doubles, $130 to $190, MAP; suite and cottage, $230. Closed November and April.

The Old Newfane Inn, Route 30, Newfane 05345. (802) 365-4427.

Built in 1787, this classic New England inn along the green proclaims itself "virtually unchanged for more than 200 years" and proud of it. Even the spectacular banks of vivid phlox outside the entrance have stood the test of time.

For more than twenty years, German chef Eric Weindl and his wife Gundy have run the place in the continental style, with an emphasis on their restaurant (see Dining Spots). Theirs is one of the few inns we know of requiring a two-night stay anytime.

The ten old-fashioned (the Gundys call them quaint) guest rooms upstairs are meticulously clean. Most are furnished with twin beds, pretty floral wallpapers, samplers and wall hangings, wing chairs and rockers. Eight have private baths and one is a suite. Several rooms, which once were part of the ballroom, have gently curved ceilings and access to a side balcony looking onto the green.

Guests enter via a front porch with a lineup of rocking chairs into a lobby whose walls are hung with faded magazine articles touting the inn. Off the entry on one side is a parlor with fireplace, upholstered chairs and sofa. On the other side is a narrow and dark beamed dining room.

Doubles, $105 to $155, including continental breakfast. Closed November to mid-December and April to mid-May.

Boardman House B&B, On the Green, Box 112, Jamaica 05343. (802) 365-4086.

Breakfast is a big deal at this casual, low-key B&B facing the village green, and innkeeper Sarah Messenger has "a lot of clippings to prove it." It's not "the usual stuff," says she. She prepares a fancy strata, pear pancakes or egg casseroles, accompanied by warm fruit compote or a dish of mixed fruit and homemade muffins. "Nobody goes away hungry."

Besides being well fed, her guests are well taken care of in five bedrooms with private baths. One connects to a smaller bedroom with twin beds and a TV to form a family suite. They're simply furnished in a Shaker motif, with white walls, red duvet bed covers and Shaker pegs or benches. Guests share a living room with TV, the breakfast room and an unheated barn with a pool table and sauna.

The B&B is geared to weekend and summer operation, since Sarah works a flexible schedule during the week as a caseworker in Brattleboro and her husband, Paul Weber, teaches at the local high school.

Doubles, $70 to $75; suite, $90. No credit cards.

Green Valley Farm B&B, Auger Hole Road, Box 70, South Newfane 05351. (802) 348-7913.

White Adirondack chairs facing the big side yard await guests at this 200-year-old working farm. Lois and Harold Kvitek share their white, dormered farmhouse with overnight guests in two bedrooms, both with private baths.

One room with twin beds, off an entrance/breezeway, is designed for privacy at one end of the structure. The other bedroom, upstairs in the main house, has a queen bed and a twin bed. The rooms are furnished in what Lois calls country style. "We're very casual," she says. "We try to make people feel at home."

She serves a continental breakfast of juice, fruit and homemade breads and coffee cake. Regular guests – of which this B&B seems to have many – may get treated to more substantial fare that would call for some of the maple syrup produced on the farm. Guests enjoy the animals and barns, walk the logging trails on the 56-acre property and wander down the street to Olallie Daylily Gardens.

Doubles, $55. No credit cards. Smoking restricted.

Dining Spots

The Four Columns Inn, 250 West St., Newfane. (802) 365-7713.

Beamed timbers from the original barn, a huge fireplace, antiques on shelves and walls, and tiny white lights aflickering make the dining area at the rear of the inn a charming setting. Add pink and white linens and an inventive menu that changes seasonally and you have one of the premier dining experiences in southern Vermont.

The culinary tradition launched here by René Chardain has been enhanced by Jacques Allembert and his head chef, Gregory Parks, who was sous chef under Chardain.

The dinner menu is supplemented with specials so that chef Parks can take advantage of local seasonal products. Appetizers ($6 to $7) seem to get more interesting with every visit: the last time, they included assorted pan-seared mushrooms with garlic, pumpkin seeds, swiss chard and roquefort; course country pâté with pistachios, apricots and cognac, and a soup of fennel, spinach and acorn squash.

For entrées ($21 to $25), it would be hard to choose among such dishes as broiled salmon with ancho chile pepper sauce, grilled swordfish with black olive and caper vinaigrette, grilled pheasant with ginger-raspberry sauce, sautéed sweetbreads with artichoke bottoms and swiss chard, and venison chops with juniper demi-glace.

Pam Allembert's desserts change nightly. She's known for her chocolate pâté, but you also might be enticed by her tirami su, apple-spice cake with cappuccino ice cream and caramel sauce, hazelnut layer cake with mocha cream, and seasonal sorbets.

Dinner nightly except Tuesday, 6 to 9. No smoking.

Adirondack chairs on side lawn await guests at Green Valley Farm B&B.

Three Mountain Inn, Route 30, Jamaica. (802) 874-4140.

When they opened initially as a B&B, Elaine and Charles Murray never considered serving meals since there were good restaurants in the area. But some of the restaurants have vanished and "guests would come back and find that we were eating better than they were," Elaine reported, "so we started offering dinner." Now, more than fifteen years later, Elaine is still in the kitchen, cooking straightforward meals for inn guests and the public in two fireplaced dining rooms dressed with pink and white linens, dainty curtains and ladderback or bow chairs.

The handwritten menu changes nightly but retains signature dishes. Favorites among the four appetizers ($3 to $5.50) are tomato-dill soup, country pâté and smoked trout.

Folks rave about the seafood or beef kabobs, trout amandine, chicken paprikash and pork tenderloin with red onion confit among the five or six changing entrées, priced from $12.50 for baked ham to $18.50 for filet mignon.

Kahlua-mocha fudge pie, butter-pecan ice-cream pie with caramel topping, apple-cranberry crisp with Vermont apple ice cream and a French gâteau made without flour are in Elaine's dessert repertoire. A small but good wine list contains such bargains as Firestone cabernet and Beringer fumé blanc in the mid teens.

Dinner nightly by reservation, 6 to 9.

Windham Hill Inn, West Townshend 05359. (802) 874-4080 or (800) 944-4080.

Five-course dinners are served nightly to guests and, increasingly, the public, as innkeepers Grigs and Pat Markham expand their dining operation with a new addition in 1995. Diners gather for hors d'oeuvre and drinks with the innkeepers around the franklin stove in the living room. Then they adjourn to the main dining room or the adjacent Frog Pond Room looking onto the pond and lawns.

Chef Cameron Howard, whom we first met at the Pilgrim's Inn in Deer Isle, Me., changes her menu nightly. The meal is prix-fixe ($35), with three choices for most courses.

Dinner at our latest visit began with chèvre-apple-sage fritters, pear-leek soup and a salad of mesclun greens with French nut bread. An orange sorbet over raspberry sauce cleansed the palate for the main course, a choice of fillet of salmon with roasted red pepper-rosemary butter, boneless breast of duck with a currant-wine sauce, and rack of lamb with port wine-mushroom sauce. Dessert was a bittersweet chocolate tart.

Dinner by reservation, nightly 6:30 to 8:30. No smoking.

Townshend Country Inn, Route 30, Box 3100, Townshend. (802) 365-4141.

Down-home country cooking and good values are enjoyed by patrons of this farm-house-turned-restaurant with three upstairs guest rooms.

Joseph Peters, formerly manager of the Yankee Pedlar Inn in Holyoke, Mass., picked up his culinary skills while observing the kitchen there. Assisted by wife Donna and three of their children, he presents an extensive menu at both lunch and dinner, an old-fashioned Vermont Sunday buffet brunch with more than twenty items for $9.95, and a series of enticing gourmet wine-tasting dinners for $35 a head.

Donna's festive seasonal decorations enhance the main dining room with bare pine floors, white-linened tables, windsor chairs and a fireplace mantel topped with striking German chocolate pots. A smaller dining room has tables with white woven mats, and there's a lounge at the entrance.

The dinner menu offers something for everyone, from vegetarian platter ($12.75) to $16.95 for sirloin steak. Pasta dishes, baked scrod, pork gruyère, veal piccata and roast duck are among the offerings.

Joseph is proud of his homemade sherbets, pies and Indian pudding. Most of the 70 wines are bargain-priced in the teens.

Yankee pot roast, chicken pot pie, sautéed calves liver, fish and chips, seafood cannelloni and sandwiches are among the lunchtime offerings. The Friday night all-you-can-eat prime rib dinner for $12.95 packs in the locals.

Upstairs are three guest rooms with shared baths, $65 to $85 double.

Lunch, daily except Wednesday 11:30 to 2:30, July-October; dinner, nightly except Wednesday 5 to 9; Sunday, brunch 11 to 2:30, dinner 5 to 9. Closed in April.

The Old Newfane Inn, Route 30, Newfane. (802) 365-4427.

Chef-owner Eric Weindl, who trained in a Swiss hotel, cooks in what he calls the classic French and continental style at this classic New England inn dating to 1787. The food is as predictable as when we first went out of our way to dine here more than two decades ago during a ski trip to Mount Snow – that is to say good, but not exciting.

A few daily specials spark up the enormous printed menu, which remains virtually unchanged over the years and lists most of the standards, starting with a slice of melon for $3.95 through marinated herring and escargots bourguignonne to Nova Scotia salmon for $7.95. Capon florentine, duckling à l'orange or with peppercorns, veal marsala, brochette of beef bordelaise, frog's legs provençal, shrimp scampi and pepper steak flamed in brandy are a few of the entrées, priced from $14.75 to $25.95 and accompanied by seasonal vegetables and salad. Châteaubriand "served the proper way" and rack of lamb bouquetière are available for two. Featured desserts include peach melba, Bavarian chocolate cream pie, cherries jubilee and pear hélène.

The decor matches the vision of what tourists think an old New England inn dining room should look like. Narrow and beamed with a wall of windows onto the green, it has white lace curtains, pink and white linens, lamps on the window tables, shiny dark wood floors, floral wallpaper and a massive fireplace.

Dinner nightly, 6 to 9:30, Sunday 5 to 8:30. Closed November to mid-December and April to mid-May.

Casa del Sol, Main Street, Putney. (802) 387-5318.

For a change of pace and one of the better Mexican meals of your life, try this pure place with refined food and prices from the past. It's run with great charm by Susana Ramsay, the cook from Mexico City, and her husband Richard, an anthropologist from Georgia, whom she met in Peru.

Working in a tiny kitchen, Susana turns out some great dishes, from her tortilla soup

Table is set for dinner at Windham Hill Inn.

to her flan de leche. The tostada sampler, five small tostadas with toppings of tinga, mole, picadillo, cochinita pibil and refried beans, makes a superb lunch for $4.95. The suizas ($5.95), a chicken casserole with green tomatillo sauce, sour cream and cheese, served with refried beans, would satisfy the heartiest of eaters, as it did one of us. At another visit, we ordered dinner plates ($9.95) of pork tenderloin in salsa verde and pollo en mole rojo and savored every bite. A third time, Susana outdid herself with a fantastic chile en nogada. End with one of Richard's plates of pecan balls, chocolate walnut squares and lemon curd or, if you've indulged in the mixiotes (barbecued lamb in a very hot chile guajillo), you might like some non-fat frozen yogurt with fresh berries.

The small dining room with a few tables beneath a cathedral ceiling is decorated with fine Mexican crafts (some are for sale in a little gift shop). More seats are at picnic tables in a garden outside. A lazy susan on the table holds five of Susana's homemade salsas, pickled jalapeños, serrano chiles and marinated onions. Bring your own beer or have a bottle of Penafiel, Mexican mineral water.

Lunch, Tuesday-Friday 11:30 to 2; dinner, Tuesday-Friday 4 to 8, Saturday and Sunday, 11:30 to 8.

Diversions

There aren't many diversions – at least of the traditional tourist variety. For those, head for Brattleboro, Wilmington, Weston or Manchester, all within less than an hour's drive. In the West River Valley, you simply relax, hike or drive scenic back roads, and browse through flea markets, crafts shops and country stores.

Shopping for some begins and ends at the **Newfane Country Store.** One of the best selections of custom-made quilts in New England is carried in a store chock full of "country things for country folks." Some of the quilts, which represent a local cottage industry, hang outside and beckon passersby in for herbs, jams and jellies, penny candy, maple syrup, sweaters, Christmas ornaments and such.

Other general stores are the **Newfane General Store, a** family-operated grocery store and deli on its way up under new owners with a food background in New York, the **South Newfane General Store** ("experience nostalgia in a working general store and post office"), the **Townshend Corner Store** with a 1949 vintage soda fountain and the **West Townshend Country Store,** a fixture since 1848 with foods, gifts, cookware, old pickle and cracker barrels (would you believe pickled limes?), spruce gum and two-cent penny candy; there's an entire wall of beer steins with family crests in the $10 range.

Newfane's off-the-beaten-path West Street also is home to a couple of unusual, part-time enterprises. New and used books with a New England theme are represented seasonally at **Old and New New England Books,** located in a barn behind the first frame house (1769) in Newfane. Just beyond, the British flag on the side door of a stark white house identifies **The British Clockmaker,** where antique clocks and music boxes are restored and sold.

Along Route 30 in Townshend, **Lawrence's Smoke Shop** carries maple products and corn-cob smoked bacon, ham and other meat products as well as jellies, honey and fudge, and they'll make up sandwiches. The factory outlet for **Mary Meyer** stuffed toys on Route 30 in Townshend is where doting grandmothers and the objects of their affections can go wild. The **Townshend Furniture Co.** factory has an outlet store with Colonial, country and contemporary pine furniture, plus English country antiques and used furniture in the Back Store. The **A. Richter Gallery** offers vintage posters, etchings, Japanese woodblock prints, antique advertising artifacts and original period art.

Jamaica is abloom with nifty little shops of late. **American Country Designs** offers contemporary accessories and gifts; we acquired a piece of striking sponge pottery. **Butter Up** is a homey kitchen gift store. We liked the eclectic collection of contemporary art at **Elaine Beckwith Gallery.**

Flea markets seem to pop up all along Route 30. The original Newfane flea market, Vermont's largest now in its 28th year, operates every Saturday and Sunday from May through October one mile north of the Newfane common. The Old Newfane Barn advertises an auction every Saturday at 6:30. The Townshend flea market, beginning at the ungodly hour of 6 a.m. every Sunday, is considered a bit schlocky.

Swimming is extra-special in the Rock River, just off Route 30 up the road to South Newfane. Cars and pickup trucks in a parking area identify the path, a long descent to a series of swimming holes called locally "Indian Love Call," with sections for skinny-dippers, the half-clothed and the clothed. More conventional swimming is available in the West River reservoir behind the Townshend Dam off Route 30 in West Townshend.

Extra-Special _____

Jamaica State Park, off Route 30, Jamaica. This 772-acre park with three hiking trails is considered a godsend for visitors to the area. From the parking area at the park entrance just north of town, an old railroad bed meanders along the bank of the West River for several miles and provides easy walking, jogging or biking. Near the start of the trail is Salmon Hole, with a beach for swimming. Near the end of the trail, an old switch road branches off along Cobb Brook for another mile. It leads to Hamilton Falls, a 125-foot-long stretch of three pools cascading into each other, so perfect that you'd think it was manmade. Park admission, $1.50.

Lake Sunapee is quiet in early morning in this view from Scenic Three Mile Loop.

Sunapee Region, N.H.
The Lure of the Lakes

The fortuitous combination of lakes, mountains and meadows makes the Sunapee Region a choice year-round attraction, especially for the sportsman and those who are drawn to the water.

Lake Sunapee, New Hampshire's third largest, and its neighbors, Little Sunapee and Pleasant Lake, provide all kinds of water pleasures within view of Mount Kearsarge, central New Hampshire's highest peak, and Mount Sunapee, a state park and ski area. In between on the rolling flatlands are four golf courses and two tennis clubs.

So it comes as no surprise that historic New London, the largest village in the region (year-round population, 3,180, but swelled by second-home residents, tourists and students at Colby-Sawyer College), is a mecca for the affluent. Its hilltop setting with posh contemporary homes, country clubs and trendy shops casts an unmistakable aura of prosperity. Legend has it that the song made famous by Kate Smith, "When the Moon Comes Over the Mountain," was written by a Colby-Sawyer student as she watched it rise above Mount Kearsarge.

Little Sunapee and Pleasant lakes, hidden from the tourists' path, are happily unspoiled. Some of the Lake Sunapee shoreline is surprisingly undeveloped as well, and old Sunapee Harbor – the heart of the lakes resort region – looks not unlike a cove transplanted from the coast of upper Maine.

The area's inns, many of which have been around a while, reflect the solitude and variety of the region.

Inn Spots

Dexter's Inn & Tennis Club, 150 Stagecoach Road, Sunapee 03782. (603) 763-5571 or (800) 232-5571.

Its facilities and location a mile or so up a country lane, high above Lake Sunapee, make this a retreat for sports enthusiasts as well as for those seeking peace and quiet.

The main house, painted a pale yellow, was built in 1801, extensively remodeled in 1930 and converted into an inn in 1948. Longtime innkeeper Frank Simpson has turned over the reins to his son-in-law and daughter, Michael and Holly Simpson Durfor, but still lives next door and retains the title of innkeeper emeritus. It was he who added "Tennis Club" to the name in 1973. Tennis buffs have use of three all-weather courts, with a tennis pro and tennis shop at hand, "and we've never heard of anyone who didn't get enough court time," Frank says proudly. Lately, the tennis operation has been managed by a Sanibel Island firm that runs Jimmy Connors tennis camps – "a real boost for a small property," adds Mike.

Tennis players – and others, for this is by no means exclusively a tennis resort – can cool off in the attractive swimming pool. The twenty-acre property offers shuffleboard, croquet and a horseshoe pit. The sports theme continues inside the large barn recreation room, with bumper pool and ping-pong tables.

The main inn has a living room full of chintz and walls of books, a pine-paneled lounge with games, fireplace and an alcove for TV, and a small gift shop. Particularly appealing is the screened porch with more chintz and wicker, a ceiling painted with red and white stripes, and tables covered with blue cloths.

All ten guest rooms in the main inn and seven in the annex have private baths. Each is decorated in vivid colors coordinated with the striking wallpapers. The front rooms afford glimpses of the lake in the distance. Rooms in the annex and barn have high ceilings; two have queensize canopy beds, another has sliding doors leading to a patio, and all are bright and cheery.

The newest lodging is in the Holly House Cottage, a two-bedroom, two-bath house that belonged to a grandmother in the family and contains a living room, kitchen and porch. It's available for up to six people for $1,200 weekly without meals.

Coffee and juice are served in the bedrooms (and you could have your whole breakfast there), but most guests gather near the bay window in the dining room for a view of the lake and order, perhaps, eggs benedict or Michael's innovation, Dex-Mex omelets with salsa and cheese. Dinner is served to the public by reservation (see Dining Spots).

Doubles, $105 to $145, B&B; $130 to $170, MAP. Open May-October.

Seven Hearths, 26 Seven Hearths Lane, Sunapee 03782. (603) 763-5657 or (800) 237-2464.

There really are seven hearths in this farmhouse dating to 1801, and five of them are in the bedrooms. David and Georgia Petrasko from Cotuit, Mass., who purchased the inn in late 1994, expected to cater to skiers. Instead, they found the fireplaced bedrooms so popular with "romantic couples" that they planned to add canopied beds in those rooms.

They have also added cross-country ski trails in the woods behind the inn and installed a hot tub and exercise equipment in a small back room off the dining room. They offer massages by a registered nurse by appointment, an activity that "really took off."

Although the Petraskos took over

Dexter's Inn & Tennis Club occupies house dating to 1801.

a turnkey operation, they changed the huge living room dominated by an enormous fieldstone fireplace from Victorian to Colonial decor. "We've been told it's a more relaxed atmosphere," George advised. Here they have sofas and a couple of game tables, one of them a glass coffee table for board games.

An aquarium in an old-fashioned dry sink next to the stairway attracts a good deal of attention. Upstairs are ten guest rooms, all with private baths and air-conditioning.

Rooms vary in size from very large to fairly small; some have king beds, but most are queensize. They are fresh and pristine and quite elegant, with sofas or upholstered chairs in sitting areas, interesting area rugs and period furnishings. Mini-refrigerators have been added in a few.

The spacious grounds contain flower gardens and, in back, a swimming pool up a slope landscaped with rocks and flowers.

David, who got a taste for the business years ago at his uncle's old inn on Cape Cod, is the breakfast chef. Eggs any style, blueberry pancakes and french toast are the choices.

Under previous owners, Seven Hearths offered public dining and was well known for its food. The new owners were thinking of reopening the dining room to the public. Meanwhile, they offer dinner to house guests on weekends. The four-course, prix-fixe meal costs $18.50 to $22, depending upon the night's entrée. Typical offerings are shrimp scampi, chicken marsala and veal française.

Doubles, $120 to $140.

The Rosewood Country Inn, Pleasant View Road, Bradford 03221. (603) 938-5253.

Electric candles are lighted in the windows of this expansive, rose-trimmed beige building that comes as a beacon for visitors arriving after a roundabout ride on back roads west of Bradford. The inviting facade is a sign of things to come. Inside this new B&B fashioned from an old summer resort is a stylish, comfortable place that's quite unexpected out here, seemingly in the middle of nowhere.

Youngish Rhode Island transplants Lesley and Dick Marquis opened in 1992 after a year's worth of renovations to the abandoned Pleasant View Farm, once a summer resort accommodating 100 guests, including the likes of Jack London, Mary Pickford,

Abandoned resort gets new look as The Rosewood Country Inn.

Charlie Chaplin and the Gish sisters. "This was a nightmare," recalled Lesley, showing photos of the neglected interior.

You'd never guess today. The Marquises and their contractor transformed the center section of the structure from head to toe, creating five spacious, handsomely appointed common rooms on the main floor and seven bedrooms with private baths upstairs. Lesley stenciled the intricate rose design that flows atop the walls from room to room, coordinating with changing fabrics and styles of window treatments along the way. The decor is handsome in rose colors in the formal living room and its arched annex. The side tavern room with TV and potbelly stove is bright and airy in the California style. In the center of the structure is an enormous dining room, big enough for a restaurant, with seven tables set for the inn's "candlelight and crystal" breakfast. Beyond the dining room is an open guest kitchen, family room and gift shop, all opening onto a broad deck overlooking the inn's twelve rolling acres of woods and fields.

Upstairs, the comfortable bedrooms are nicely decorated in a range of styles with painted walls, stenciling and coordinated fabrics. Roses and grapevines twine around the canopy above the queensize bed in the bridal suite, where a wicker loveseat is cosseted in a corner turret. Ivy paisley fabrics are featured in an adjacent, more masculine room with queensize bed. An angled double bed is dressed in gold and black in a Victorian-style room in back. Sturbridge and Williamsburg are the respective themes of two third-floor Colonial rooms. Whimsical accents abound, from a little white dress hanging in the bridal suite to gloves resting on a table in the Victorian room to a bed warmer perched on the bed in the Williamsburg room.

Breakfast is served in the dining room, on the porches or the rear deck. A fruit course (at our visit, peaches with raspberries and vanilla yogurt) and pastries (perhaps cinnamon swirl muffins) come first. The main event could be a breakfast quiche or french toast with strawberry-maple syrup (made by a neighbor from maple trees on the inn's property). The signature dish is oven-baked apple pancakes with cider sauce.

Their first phase a success, the Marquises were about to renovate one side of the building into a function room. They planned to add seven more rooms with king and queensize beds above it in the near future.

Doubles, $69 to $85; suites, $89 and $110.

New London Inn, 140 Main St., Box 8, New London 03257. (603) 526-2791 or (800) 526-2791.

This village inn next to the Colby-Sawyer College campus has been around since 1792, but never more spiffily than since it was taken over and nicely refurbished in 1986 by Maureen and John Follansbee, whose grandfather started the Follansbee Inn. A focal point in the community, it is now a full-service inn worthy of its landmark status, and its restaurant is receiving acclaim for regional cuisine (see Dining Spots).

The Follansbees remodeled and redecorated 30 guest rooms on three floors, replacing many a carpet, 28 beds and 101 windows ("we found windows that hadn't been washed in 195 years," recalls Maureen). Mini-print and sprigged wallpapers, brass and spool beds, decoys, tin wall sconces and sitting areas enhance many of the rooms, which come in various sizes and configurations. All have private baths. Choicest are the larger corner rooms (one of which accommodated Ronald Reagan when he campaigned in the New Hampshire primary), furnished in blue and white with two double beds, a sofa and two wicker chairs. From a front porch stretching the width of the second floor, guests can view the passing scene and get a bird's-eye view of some of the award-winning gardens below.

Returning Colby-Sawyer and Dartmouth types are surprised by the refurbished main floor, with a new entrance lobby, graceful parlors and a relocated tavern. John tells how they redid the kitchen to allow for a bigger dining area near the fireplace, only to open up the fireplace and discover it was fake. Undaunted, they built one with 200-year-old bricks from the foundation.

Breakfast from a full menu is included in the room rates. Red flannel hash with poached eggs is one of the specialties that attract the public as well. Fruit and cheese are put out in the parlor in the afternoons.

The Follansbees lately have turned innkeeping duties over to their son Jeffrey, who had been the chef and still oversees the dining room, and his wife Rosemary.

Doubles, $65 to $100. Two-night minimum in summer, fall and college weekends.

Follansbee Inn, Route 114, Box 92, North Sutton 03260. (603) 927-4221 or (800) 626-4221.

"Welcome to the Follansbee Inn – a great place to relax and enjoy a slower pace of living," greeted the sign at the porch entry to this rambling old inn fronting on Kezar Lake. And on a blackboard underneath: "Today's saying: Swallowing your pride occasionally will never give you indigestion."

Such are the distinctive touches that imbue the Follansbee with plenty of personality. A big place with a hotel-style main floor and 23 guest rooms, it seems smaller and is much more friendly than a hotel, thanks to innkeepers Sandy and Dick Reilein. Thus it is not unrealistic for Sandy to say that theirs is "like the country home you've always wanted to have – with none of the work." They do it, seemingly effortlessly, for you.

Outgoing hosts who are apt to join arriving guests for a late-afternoon swim, they share the work with teen-aged son Matthew. He checks in guests, helps with luggage and tends to the waterfront with his lively English springer spaniel Samantha. Between dinner preparations and making small talk during cocktails in the living room, the Reileins can be counted on to bring out a tray of munchies to those seeking solitude on the porch.

Off a second-floor hall full of antiques are eleven guest rooms with private baths, all spruced up with Eisenhart Vintage wallpapers, new mattresses, carpeting, large towels and bayberry soap made specially for the inn. Our corner room overlooking the lake had good cross-ventilation, a must on a sultry night. The third floor has twelve more bedrooms with shared baths.

Where the Follansbee once thrived on numbers, the Reileins stress intimacy and conviviality. They downsized the operation, closed the restaurant to the public and made the inn totally non-smoking. That last move has increased business, says Dick, a former IBM executive. "In our own small way, we feel we are helping people to live a healthier life style."

The homey main floor has a cozy sitting room paneled in barnwood and furnished with patchwork cushions, baskets and all kinds of games, and a large front parlor, a bit more formal but most comfortable. It opens onto a dining room, where breakfast starts with fresh fruit and Sandy's homemade granola and features an entrée such as french toast, puffed apple pancake, egg soufflé or a choice of omelets. Guests are encouraged to sit at tables of six or eight to get acquainted.

At night, Sandy occasionally cooks an optional, all-you-can eat dinner for house guests. Peaches and cream soup, salad, homemade bread and baked Alaska pie surrounded the main course, stuffed shrimp, the night we were there. The price is $16 to $22, depending on the entrée. Dick, who helps serve, oversees an interesting stock of beer and wine.

Besides partaking of the Reileins' hospitality, guests enjoy peaceful Kezar Lake, where Matthew's armada now includes a sailboard, rowboat, canoe and paddle boat, and 500 wooded acres for hiking and cross-country skiing.

Doubles, $75 to $95. No smoking. Closed part of April and November.

The English House, Route 4 & 11, Box 162, Andover 03216. (603) 735-5987.

Gillian Smith, a talented craftswoman, and her husband Ken moved from Surrey, England, in 1986 to open a B&B with an English name and tradition next to the Proctor Academy campus. "The house looked derelict from the outside, like a brown tooth in a jaw," recalls Ken. "I first saw it two months after Gillian bought it and was horrified."

Hard work, arty touches and good taste have transformed seven bedrooms on three floors into accommodations of distinction. There's afternoon tea, of course, served with cakes or orange shortbread.

An attractive dining room with windsor chairs at a long table is the setting for a full breakfast: fruit salad, a choice of five juices, homemade yogurt, granola with twelve ingredients, and scrambled eggs with bacon or pancakes. Sometimes there's kedgeree made with haddock or smoked cod from Canada. Swiss eggs, eggs benedict, quiche and oyster frittata are other possibilities.

All seven guest rooms have private baths. Decorated in bright colors, most are spacious and accented by wicker, plants, dhurrie rugs, Gillian's striking quilts and landscape paintings done by a relative who is a watercolorist of some repute, Ken says. We were intrigued by one room with a niche above the bed containing a painting framed by plants.

Guests enjoy a common room with comfortable sofas, TV and VCR overlooking a deck beside showy rock gardens. They may get a peek at Gillian's studio, where she teaches classes in needlecrafts, makes quilts and clothing for exhibits and lately has started jewelry production.

Doubles, $80. No smoking.

The Inn at Sunapee, Burkehaven Hill Road, Box 336, Sunapee 03782. (603) 763-4444 or (800) 327-2466.

Ted and Susan Harriman returned after 29 years of living in Southeast Asia to take over this folksy inn, which now reflects their world travels. She was originally from New Hampshire and he from Needham, Mass., and they met at Colby College in Maine, so New England remained in their blood.

104

Lake Sunapee is on view in distance from The Inn at Sunapee.

Perched high on a hill, with a distant view of Lake Sunapee and the surrounding mountains from the wraparound porch, the inn has spacious grounds with a swimming pool and tennis court, and there's a decidedly "out-in-the-country" feel to it. Beyond the pool are four motel-like units and a honeymoon cottage for use in summer.

The rest of the sixteen rooms are on two floors of the main inn. All have private baths and five are family suites. The hallways of the rambling structure are hung with interesting artworks from across the world. Filipino brass instruments hang on one wall of a favorite rear corner room with a double and twin bed and wicker rockers.

Chairs from China and a bench from the southern Philippines grace the reception area, where an enormous brass tray, also from the Philippines, hangs on one wall. Guests gather in a small TV room upstairs or in a large bar-lounge transformed from a barn, complete with fieldstone fireplace.

Ted cooks breakfast to order and Susan does most of the serving – anything from omelets to french toast. It's taken on the back deck or in the country dining room, where meals are available nightly for house guests and often for the public (see Dining Spots).

Doubles, $80. Smoking restricted.

Pleasant Lake Inn, 125 Pleasant St., Box 1030, New London 03257. (603) 526-6271 or (800) 626-4907.

Down a long hill north out of New London at the end of Pleasant Lake is the area's oldest operating inn, built in 1790 as a Cape farmhouse and converted in 1878 into a summer resort.

"The view from our front window is the most spectacular in the area," claim inn-keepers Grant and Margaret Rich, and they could be right. From a beach across the road, you look down the lake toward Mount Kearsarge at the far end.

All eleven guest rooms on the second and third floors have private baths. "We've been adding baths left and right since we took over with one private bath in 1983," says Marilyn. She's particularly proud of the second-floor rooms that have been completely refurbished in what she calls country antiques style. Her favorite is No. 7 with a brass bed, an armoire with an old marble sink, and blue floral Laura Ashley wallpaper that she hung herself.

For years, the handsome dining room was the main attraction, although that has changed with the upgrading of rooms and the downscaling of the restaurant (now open only to houseguests). The wraparound flagstone patio room that originally served as the restaurant is now a wicker sun porch and a family room with TV, piano and games.

Dinner is served at 6:30 amid white and pink linens at heavy pine tables in a small front room with bare wood floor, oriental carpet and a lake view. The tariff varies with the changing, no-choice menu. One night it was $17.50 for salad, breast of chicken with cranberry glaze and apple pie. The next it was $22 for fresh fruit salad, prime rib and French lemon bars.

For breakfast, guests have a choice of eggs, pancakes, french toast and "Whatchamacallit" – scrambled eggs on an English muffin with cheese and sausage.

Doubles, $75 to $95. Smoking restricted.

Colonial Farm Inn, Route 11, Box 1053, New London 03257. (603) 526-6121 or (800) 805-8504.

Bob and Kathryn Joseph got their feet wet at a small B&B in Sutton Mills before deciding to open a larger, full-service country inn. They took over a handsome, 1836 center-chimney Colonial residence, of which they are only the fourth owners, and spent five months renovating prior to opening in 1993. They now offer a choice little restaurant (see Dining Spots), four bedrooms with private baths and a growing antiques business.

Up a pulpit staircase and leading off rambling halls are the well-spaced bedrooms, handsomely decorated by Kathryn, who had been in the window design business. Everything in the guest rooms is carefully color-coordinated, from dust ruffles to pillows to balloon shades on the windows. She used picture framing to outline the head of the double bed in the Cabbage Patch Room. The rear Southport Room is decked out in white and blue Laura Ashley prints. The largest room is the Wauwinet, with a queensize poster bed – it's named after Nantucket, "where we were married," Kathryn advises. It comes with a handsome leather reading chair and a wicker rocker, and a pedestal sink in the modern bath.

Guests share a cozy front parlor with outside guests arriving for dinner. A full breakfast includes fruit, muffins and a main dish, perhaps frittata, eggs or pancakes flavored with orange juice, blueberries or toasted walnuts.

In the carriage house beside the main house is Colonial Farm Antiques, where twelve dealers show their wares.

Doubles, $85 to $95.

Hide-Away Inn, Twin Lake Villa Road, Box 1249, New London 03257. (603) 526-4861 or (800) 457-0589.

This establishment gained a wide reputation as a restaurant under former owner Wolf and Lilli Heinberg. Subsequent owners tried to continue the restaurant and then closed it to focus on the accommodations. The B&B operation is being continued by Theresa and Ken DeWitt from New York, who arrived on the scene in 1992. They keep busy with other jobs as well as raising a five-year-old daughter.

The DeWitts added a few antiques and sturdy maple furniture to the lodge-style structure, whose walls are paneled in Oregon fir. Upstairs are seven guest rooms with private baths. One with a queen bed and windows on three sides is particularly popular. All the rooms are homey and retain their lodgey look and feeling.

Wine and cheese are served in the afternoons in the spacious entry parlor, where chocolates and a decanter of sherry also await beside a great stone fireplace. An informal parlor next door was full of toys at our visit. The main gathering spot is the downstairs Pipedream Lounge, with a BYOB bar, game tables, a dart board and plenty of sofas and chairs for lounging around a TV/VCR. The wine cellar off the lounge has been the site of many wine tastings, both lately and in the lodge's previous incarnation.

Ken prepares a full breakfast, served in a breakfast nook with an inviting window seat. Fruit, cereal, yogurt and homemade muffins accompany eggs any style, pancakes or french toast. He proudly shows an autographed copy of *Collected Poems* by Grace Litchfield, which turned up in nearby Potter Place. Signed "Hide-Away, New London," it is one of the prized works of the poet-author for whom the lodge was built as a hideaway in the 1930s.

Doubles, $75 to $90.

Highland Lake Inn, Maple Street, Box 1044, East Andover 03231. (603) 735-6426.

Taking over an old inn with seven bedrooms and shared baths, an extended family of Greek heritage poured big bucks into a total renovation and reopened in 1994 with ten bedrooms, all with private baths.

"There's not one piece of the original plaster left of the old Patchwork Inn," said Mary Petras, innkeeper with her husband Chrys, her parents and son Peter. The place was fashioned from a 1767 Colonial farmhouse that had been enlarged, and looks and smells quite new. A window was left open in the stairway to show the old bricks and post and beam construction that the renovators had to deal with.

The inn, not fully furnished at our visit, was in transition. The bedrooms on three floors looked crisp and clean. Two on the main floor have fireplaces and one, the Highland Room, has a window seat yielding a glimpse of the channel leading into Highland Lake. Each is decorated in a different style – "some country, some early American, some English – whatever I felt like," said Mary. They come with twin, queen or kingsize beds. Some on the third floor have extra beds for families.

The Petrases offer an extra-large breakfast "because we've never gotten enough to eat at B&Bs," according to Mary. She compensates with fruit salad, three kinds of cereal, pastries and a main dish, perhaps pancakes or french toast, omelets with feta and ham, or baked eggs with cheese. Breakfast is served in a light and airy great room with stained-glass windows or in a sun room.

Doubles, $85 to $100. No smoking.

Dining Spots

New London Inn, Main Street, New London. (603) 526-2791.

This inn's serene dining room, with its windows yielding full-length views of the colorful gardens outside, offered a couple of the best meals of our travels in years past. It's the domain of Jeffrey Follansbee, son of the owners, who recently became innkeeper and has turned kitchen duties over to a chef and also oversees a new seasonal restaurant at Sunapee. Either Jeff or his wife Rosemary are at one property or the other every night, they stress.

The menu changes seasonally, but some dishes are basically the same as we've enjoyed in years past. One was roasted garlic puree served with crostini and tiny niçoise olives – really zippy, and a favorite to this day. Other appetizers ($4 to $6.95) could be coconut fried shrimp with a pear-pimento compote, chicken satay with a spicy Indonesian peanut sauce, a salad of sautéed kale with goat cheese, pancetta and wal-

Colorful gardens mark entrance to New London Inn.

nuts, and risotto cakes with sopresseta sausage, tomato, goat cheese and roasted pepper aioli.

Sourdough, zucchini and corn breads are accompanied by swirls of butter. Perfect green salads, dressed with a mellow raspberry and walnut vinaigrette, were dotted with raspberries and garnished with edible nasturtiums on a summer evening.

Main courses begin at $15.95 for chicken breast topped with gorgonzola cheese and sundried tomatoes and served with charred tomato sauce and gaufrette potatoes. They top off at $19.95 for pan-seared filet mignon with roasted garlic sauce and a potato basket of fresh vegetables. One of ours was grilled lamb medallions with a smoked tomato coulis sauce and roasted eggplant. The other was grilled Maine rabbit with a spicy mole sauce and cornflower pasta. Vegetables came family-style: green beans with bacon and potatoes with balsamic vinegar, served at room temperature.

Desserts included a marvelous peach clafouti with vanilla-bean ice cream, bittersweet chocolate torte with brandied raspberries and crème fraîche, and homemade peach and coconut sorbet with sugar straws and blueberry coulis. Pumpkin cheesecake with warm cranberry sauce and Swedish hazelnut torte with raspberry puree were desserts at another visit.

The flawless service included a complete change of silver with each course and provision of real wine globes for our bottle of Tyrell's Long Flat Red, a zesty Australian from the well-chosen cellar. Wines are nicely priced in the teens and twenties.

The airy room is a match for the meal: pale green wallpaper flecked with white peacocks and well-spaced tables flanked by windsor chairs and set with burgundy over white cloths, white china, hurricane lamps and vases of alstroemeria.

Dinner nightly, 6 to 8:30; Sunday brunch, 11 to 1.

La Meridiana, Route 11 at Old Winslow Road, Wilmot. (603) 526-2033.

You can tell there's a culinary master in the kitchen of this old, rambling farmhouse, its dining room entered via a long corridor running the length of the building. A collection of Italian cookbooks is on display in the hall, and the wine list bears many interesting Italian vintages at prices mainly in the teens. You may hear chef-owner Piero Canuto singing arias in the kitchen; when he makes his rounds after dinner he'll show you pictures of his home town in northern Italy.

Peter makes most of his own pastas and encourages sharing of dishes at no extra cost. "Our menu is designed for you to choose as much or as little as your appetite allows." Prices are so low as not to be believed.

Start with crostini with chicken livers ($2.50), squid salad, hot or cold antipasto or, the highest-priced appetizer, carpaccio ($4.50). Soups are $1.50 and pastas $4.25 to $5.50 (for manicotti with three cheeses).

Most of the fifteen entrées are in the $8 to $10 range. Chicken cacciatore is $6.25 and veal chop baked with mushrooms and cheese tops the price list at $13.95. When did you last see sautéed trout, grilled sole or calves liver for $8.95 in a top restaurant? Entrées come with fresh vegetable and potato of the day.

The menu is supplemented by many specials, among them osso buco and lamb casserole at our visit. People come especially for the rack of lamb, we were advised.

Among desserts might be pumpkin pudding with mascarpone cheese, chocolate mousse cake, frozen chocolate soufflé and tirami su.

The candlelit dining room is country Italian with posts and hand-hewn beams, attractive hanging lights, handsome oak chairs with round backs at white linened tables, fresh flowers and a fieldstone fireplace.

Dinner nightly, 5 to 9, Sunday 3 to 8.

Dexter's Inn & Tennis Club, 150 Stagecoach Road, Sunapee. (603) 763-5571.

Dining here has become so popular that house guests no longer are required to take the evening meal, such is the clamor for reservations from the public. Lake Sunapee may be glimpsed in the distance from the main dining room or the popular screened porch.

When Mike and Holly Simpson Durfor took over innkeeping duties from her father, they upgraded the dinner operation and Mike often found himself assisting in the kitchen. Dinners are table d'hôte, the price depending on the choice of entrée – $14.95 for the evening special to $18.25 for salmon or filet mignon. A soup like chilled melon or the clam chowder that won first prize in the King Ridge Chowder Fest in 1993 starts the meal, followed by a salad of tossed greens or kidney beans. Menu entrées like swordfish steak, chicken piccata, veal marsala, filet mignon and lamb chops are supplemented by such specials as poached salmon with dilled hollandaise, scallops in cheddar cheese and white wine, rosemary haddock and brandied chicken with sauté of apples and walnuts.

Desserts could be Mike's killer kahlua mousse (so named because it nearly killed him, making so many during one foliage season when his pastry chef left), chilled butterscotch pecan pie, lemon meringue pie, Wellesley chocolate cake and apple pie.

Dinner by reservation, nightly except Tuesday 6:30 to 8:30. Closed November-April.

Colonial Farm Inn, Route 11, New London. (603) 526-6121.

Bob and Kathryn Joseph learned to cook at a small B&B in Sutton Mills before opening this small inn and restaurant in 1993. Their impressive center-chimney Colonial holds two fireplaced dining rooms seating a total of 30. The candlelit rooms have the requisite beamed ceilings and wide-plank floors, and are done in warm salmon and platinum colors, from the walls to the table linens to the china.

Bob, who does the lion's share of the cooking, offers four starters: on one autumn night, wild mushroom soup, cajun crab cakes with a scallion-horseradish sauce, roasted red and green peppers with goat cheese, and the signature house salad, a mix of red and green leaf lettuces tossed with dijon mustard and sprinkled with toasted walnuts and blue cheese. The house specialty is tenderloin of beef sautéed with burgundy-shallot sauce. Other main courses ($12.75 to $15.50) could be chicken stuffed with homemade boursin cheese and walnuts, poached sole with garlic-parsley sauce and grilled swordfish with a compound butter of basil, ginger and lime. Potatoes au gratin and carrots glazed with honey and brandy might accompany.

Desserts include apple-raspberry pie, homemade profiteroles with vanilla ice cream and bittersweet chocolate sauce, and chocolate pâté with ground almonds and strawberry puree. Port and stilton are offered after dinner. The inn has a full liquor license.

Dinner by reservation, Wednesday-Saturday 6 to 8:30 or 9.

The Inn at Sunapee, Burkehaven Hill Road, Sunapee. (603) 763-4444.

The dining room at the Inn at Sunapee is cheery, affording wondrous views of the distant lake and mountains through bay windows. White tablecloths, green fanned napkins, green and white plates, vases of fresh flowers and the original wood floors effect a country look. Cat figurines in a corner cupboard supplement the inn's six pet cats.

Innkeeper Susan Harriman does the cooking, which hints of her well-traveled background. She offers a curry of the week to soothe those who miss her Indonesian rijsttafel, an early hallmark that gradually found too few takers. Otherwise, her short menu might feature shrimp santorini, chicken piccata, medallions of pork singapore, duck à l'orange and veal marsala, priced from $13 to $17. Start with tortellini with venison sausage madeira, Chinese spring rolls or tyropitakia with lemon-mint coulis. Finish with chocolate mousse amaretto, cheesecake with butterscotch sauce, Indian pudding with ice cream or frozen maple mousse.

The wine list has been expanded with the help of consultant Wolf Heinberg, former owner of the Hide-Away Lodge.

Dinner nightly except Tuesday, 6 to 9; weekends only in winter. No smoking.

Woodbine Cottage, River Road, Sunapee Harbor. (603) 763-2222.

This is an outgrowth of the seasonal restaurant that Eleanor and Bob Hill began 65 years ago in their home. They had a small screened porch that they built around and, said Eleanor, it just grew from there. Now a thriving enterprise, the vine-covered cottage incorporates two pine-paneled inner dining rooms and a garden porch beyond, as well as a large gift shop. Next door is the Holly Shop, chock full of everything for Christmas.

Breakfast, lunch, tea and weekend dinners are served, although the hours were scaled back in 1994 as Mrs. Hill's health began to fail. The atmosphere is endearingly tea-roomish, with lacy paper mats on the tables. An arrangement of mums and berries is over the mantel of the fireplace (which is lit on cool days), and gorgeous flower gardens, spotlit at night, are outside. Each table sports a different colored candle and flowers to coordinate.

"Full-course luncheons" (meaning with soup or juice, muffin, relish tray, salad wagon, vegetable, potato, dessert and beverage) are priced from $10.75 for turkey pie or grilled sandwich to $15.50 for lobster salad or newburg. Ordered à la carte, sandwiches and salads are in the $3 to $6 range. At teatime you may have tea sandwiches and cake or a fruit salad, with tea in a proper pot.

Full dinners run from $16.25 for chicken and mushroom casserole to $19.95 for steak, lobster salad or newburg. This is good solid New England fare – broiled halibut, salmon or Cape scallops, roasts and chops.

Desserts get the most raves at Woodbine. Among the goodies are strawberry

Candlelight dinners as well as guest rooms are offered at Colonial Farm Inn.

shortcake, pecan, date macaroon and chiffon pies, tortes, cheesecakes, homemade sherbets and ice creams, served with a choice of six sauces including French apricot and ginger, and frozen cake balls (choose your own flavor of ice cream and sauce). Fresh fruit in season, meringue glacé and Dixie crunch ice-cream ball are more.

A little cookbook, *Our Favorite Recipes,* is for sale in the gift shops, as are jars of the house caesar salad dressing.

Lunch, noon to 2:30; dinner on weekends, 6 to 8; Sunday brunch, 10 to 2. Closed Monday and mid-October to May.

Murphy's Grille, 1407 Route 103, Sunapee. (603) 763-3113.

An offshoot of a restaurant group based in Manchester, this large new establishment beside the even larger and newer Best Western/Sunapee Lake Lodge found a receptive clientele. You can dine casually on front and side decks outdoors or inside at a mix of booths and tables around the perimeter of a skylit bar in the center.

The extensive menu has something for everyone, from California garlic bread topped with sundried tomatoes and fresh garlic to smoked trout fritters, from baby back ribs to peel-and-eat shrimp. There are California and "mighty caesar" salads, burgers and hefty sandwiches (Mexican BLT and lobster-shrimp salad croissant). Can't decide? Consider the "ribs, wings, rings and things" (the things being a choice of steak fries, cole slaw or pasta salad), a full meal for $10.75.

At night, the menu adds entrées from $10.95 for pecan chicken dijon to $14.50 for lazy lobster or chargrilled shrimp and andouille sausage on rice with creole mustard sauce. Blackened sirloin topped with crumbled bacon, blue cheese and scallions is a specialty. For dessert, how about key lime pie or peach-blueberry crisp?

Lunch and dinner daily , 11:30 to 9 or 10; Sunday "brunchfast" in summer, 11 to 3.

The Anchorage at Sunapee Harbor, Sunapee Harbor. (603) 763-3334.

Jaunty window treatments and artworks lit by track lighting give a fresh look to the old Anchorage. They are highlights of a total renovation undertaken in 1994 by new owners Jeffrey and Rose Follansbee, who have made the New London Inn a mecca for

111

gourmet dining. Here they have a total of 140 seats in a couple of dining rooms, the rear bar and outside on an expansive deck right beside the water.

Besides sprucing up the long and narrow main room with deep green booths and yellow walls, they've upscaled the menu from its traditional beer and sandwich days. Jeff oversees the cooking, featuring soups, salads, specialty sandwiches, fresh seafood and steaks – "pretty basic stuff and accessible to a broad clientele." Dinner entrées ($7.95 to $13.95) include linguini with pesto, rainbow trout amandine, broiled halibut with garlic butter, fried shrimp or scallops, chicken teriyaki, Yankee pot roast and broiled sirloin with onion rings.

Lunch daily, 11:30 to 4; dinner, 4 to 9 or 10; closed Monday and Tuesday in off-season. Open Memorial Day to Columbus Day.

Millstone Restaurant, Newport Road, New London. (603) 526-4201.

A lofty cathedral ceiling with skylights lends an airy feel to this casually elegant place that is popular with the Colby-Sawyer College crowd. Owned by Tom Mills, who branched out with the casual Four Corners Grille at the other end of town, it has a pleasant, canopied brick terrace for dining in the summer. Inside are well-spaced tables, covered with beige linen and blue napkins.

Entrées ($10.50 to $18.95) on the large and varied dinner menu run the gamut from quite a variety of pasta dishes and Bavarian schnitzel to roast duckling, lamb chops with mint jelly, Kansas City sirloin steak with brandy-peppercorn cream sauce and New Zealand venison with juniper-coriander sauce.

Among appetizers ($4.50 to $6.95) are baked brie with almond herb crust, stuffed mushrooms gratinée and hummus served with Syrian bread points. Desserts include profiteroles au chocolat, marble cheesecake, Belgian chocolate mousse pie and maple crème caramel.

Lunch daily, 11:30 to 2:30; dinner nightly, from 5:30; Sunday brunch, 11 to 2:30.

Gourmet Garden, 127 Main St., New London. (603) 526-6656.

A specialty-foods shop par excellence ("give a gift of good taste with a local flavor"), this establishment run by Sarah and Michael Cave also puts up great salads and sandwiches to eat in or take out.

Curried chicken with water chestnuts and tortellini with artichoke hearts and turkey are two of the salad favorites. Smoked turkey or ham, tuna or chicken salad and pâté sandwiches are in the $4 to $5 range. Great bargains are the stews: venison, beef or chicken ($4.25, with a French roll).

This is the place for a real continental breakfast: espresso, cappuccino or latte with a choice of pastries from the full bakery. The cafe seats 225 inside, plus more outside in season on a garden patio.

Gift boxes contain all kinds of New Hampshire goodies.

Open Monday-Saturday, 7 to 5.

Baynham's Country Store and Cafe, 180 Main St., New London. (603) 526-8070.

Trompe-l'oeil drawings of turtles and a very real looking $1 bill grace the cafe floor at this upscale country store and kitchen shop. Dining takes place on two levels: a bright, sunny area known as the upper cafe near the 1950s soda fountain, and the cozier, lower cafe with a fireplace and tables dressed with checkered cloths.

Besides sandwiches and ice creams, you'll find such entrées ($8.95 to $11.95) as broiled or baked haddock with sherried crumbs, beef and chicken brochette, baked stuffed chicken breast with apricot sauce, charbroiled sirloin steak with herbed butter and Baynham's version of surf and turf: haddock or scallops with sirloin. Dessert

Busy Sunapee Harbor provides entertainment for outdoor patrons at The Anchorage.

specials supplement the standbys, among them chocolate-peanut butter pie, flavored cheesecakes, carrot cake and apple pie.

Breakfast daily, 8 to 11; lunch, 11 to 3; dinner, 5 to 8:30 in summer and fall; Sunday brunch, 10 to 4:30.

Diversions

Cultural Offerings. For 61 years, the **New London Barn Players,** New Hampshire's longest operating summer theater, have presented matinee and nightly performances of musicals and comedies from mid-June to Labor Day. Six Thursday evening concerts are staged in a pops atmosphere during the **Music at King Ridge** series at the King Ridge ski lodge. Despite its generally low-key flavor, the area bustles during the League of New Hampshire Craftsmen's annual crafts fair, the nation's oldest, which attracts 1,500 craftsmen and 50,000 visitors for a week in early August to Mount Sunapee State Park.

Mount Sunapee State Park. A 700-foot-long beach is great for swimming in the crystal-clear waters of Lake Sunapee. Across the road is the 2,700-foot high Mount Sunapee, criss-crossed with hiking and ski trails and its summit lodge accessible in summer and winter by a 6,800-foot-long gondola lift. The park is also the site of such special events as a gem and mineral festival, the Great American Milk Bicycle Race and the New England championship Lake Sunapee Bike Race.

Sports. All the usual are available, plus some in abundance. Golfers have their choice of four semi-public country clubs and smaller courses: the venerable Lake Sunapee Country Club and Inn, the hilly and challenging Eastman Golf Links in Grantham, picturesque Twin Lake Villa beside Little Sunapee, and the Country Club of New Hampshire, rated one of the nation's top 75 public courses by Golf Digest. Downhill skiers get their fill at Mount Sunapee or King Ridge ski areas, and cross-country skiers take over the fairways at the area's golf clubs in winter.

Lake Excursions. From Sunapee Harbor, the 150-passenger M.V. Mt. Sunapee II gives 90-minute narrated tours the length of Lake Sunapee at 10 a.m. and 2:30 p.m. daily from mid-June to Labor Day, and 2:30 weekends in spring and fall. The steamer

M.V. Kearsarge offers buffet-supper cruises at 5:30 and 7:45 nightly in summer. Another way to view the lake is to drive the Scenic Three-Mile Loop around Sunapee Harbor; you'll find striking new houses interspersed with older traditional cottages.

Shopping. For a town its size, New London has more than its share of good shopping – spread out along much of the length of Main Street and clustered in shopping centers and a mall along Route 11 on the southwest edge of town. Along Main Street are excellent crafts stores like **Artisan's Workshop** (which also has a new branch in Sunapee Harbor) and the **Crafty Goose,** the **Spring Ledge Farm** flower and produce stand, and the kind of clothing stores one finds in college towns like the **College Sport Shop** and **Pine Creek. C.B. Coburn** has "unique gifts for home and palate."

In Guild, to the southwest of Sunapee, is the **Dorr Mill Store,** a large and attractive shop specializing in woolens. Despite its location at the mill, this is no mill outlet and the prices are what you'd expect to pay back home.

Plan some extra time for a visit to the new **Baynham's Country Store and Cafe** at 180 Main St., New London. The upscale country store and kitchen shop (a.k.a. New England Mercantile Inc.) is a sprawling emporium of varied merchandise, some of it shown in room-style settings. It still has traces of its heritage as a hardware and garden shop, but now you'll find china, lingerie, high-tech electronic gadgetry, country apparel and nautical brass memorabilia. There's an air of whimsy here, from the stuffed gent relaxing out front to the lineup of three bathrooms designated for men, women and politicians. The enterprise, co-owned by an Englishman who has an inn there and a summer home here, is viewed as a prototype for several around this country.

Worth a side trip is **Nunsuch,** Route 114, South Sutton, the picturesque wooden home and farm of Rita and Courtney Haase, producers of Udderly Delicious goat cheese. Not your ordinary cheesemakers, Courtney is a former cloistered nun and Rita, her proper New Orleans mother, has five offspring scattered around the world. Their 21 milking goats, all but one named for nuns Courtney has lived with (to the amusement and consternation of some), yield about 70 pounds of cheese a day, which the Haases sell herbed or plain from their kitchen or by mail-order. We bought some of the herbed variety to take home and it was delicious. At our latest visit, Courtney had acquired a smoker and was starting to smoke some of her cheese. She also was running day-long workshops on cheese-making "for the serious dairy person."

Extra-Special _____

The Fells at the John Hay Estate, Route 103-A, Newbury. (603) 763-4789.

Three generations of diplomat John Hay's family have enjoyed the rugged landscape and cultivated gardens they developed along nearly 1,000 hillside acres above Lake Sunapee since 1891. Now the public also can enjoy a rare combination of nature preserve, botanical garden, library, historic house and landscape in a single location. The Fells Estate is maintained as a state historic site, and the gardens were replanted in 1994 by the national Garden Conservancy as a regional center for horticultural education. The property includes the 163-acre John Hay National Wildlife Refuge. Depending on season, masses of mountain laurel, rhododendron, azaleas, blueberries, perennial borders, a rose terrace, a rock garden, an old walled garden and more can be seen. Noted nature writer John Hay, son of the late horticulturist and archeologist Clarence Hay, and his sister Adele frequent a private cottage reserved for their use. Visitors park in a lot off Route 103-A and walk a quarter of a mile to the main house and gardens. Guided house tours on weekends and holidays; grounds open daily, 10 to 6, late May through Columbus Day. Free.

Robert Frost worked at this desk in Franconia with a view of Cannon Mountain.

Franconia-Sugar Hill, N.H.

The Road Less Traveled

The lines are from Robert Frost: "Two roads diverged in a wood, and I – I took the one less traveled by, and that has made all the difference."

They were written when the poet lived in Franconia beneath Cannon Mountain, and the road less traveled has made a difference historically in maintaining the Franconia area as an island of serenity just beyond the crowds.

Even the opening of the beautiful Franconia Notch Parkway connecting completed portions of Interstate 93 on either side of the notch has failed to bring in the hordes. Many people don't know about the area's history and beauty, said one innkeeper. "They think that beyond the Old Man of the Mountains, there are just woods and Canada."

Indeed, Franconia and its upcountry neighbor, Sugar Hill, are remote and relatively untouched by the usual trappings of tourism. They retain much of the look and the flavor of the late 19th century when they were noted mountain resort areas. In the 1930s, Austrian Sig Buchmayer established the country's first ski school at Peckett's-on-Sugar Hill (now designated by a primitive historic marker) and Cannon Mountain dedicated skiing's first aerial tramway.

But for the mystique of the name, one might not be aware of the area's storied past. Gone are the large hotels and, as ski areas go, Cannon keeps a low profile. Today, the crowds and the condos halt below Franconia Notch to the south, leaving Cannon Moun-

115

tain, Franconia, Sugar Hill, Bethlehem and even the "city" of Littleton for those who appreciate them as vestiges of the past.

For those who want action, the magnificent Franconia Notch State Park stretching eight miles through the notch offers some of the Northeast's most spectacular sights and activities.

But the road less traveled takes one beyond. There are few better places for fall foliage viewing than from Sunset Hill or the ridge leading up to Sugar Hill above Franconia. The heights afford sweeping vistas of the towering White Mountains on three sides and toward Vermont's Green Mountains on the fourth.

In winter, downhill skiers revel in the challenges of Cannon Mountain, the venerable World Cup area so full of skiing history that the New England Ski Museum is located at its base.

In spring and summer, the quiet pleasures of an area rich in history and character suffice. The Frost Place, the Sugar Hill Historical Museum and the Sugar Hill Sampler are classics of their genre.

Don't expect trendy inns, fancy restaurants or tony shops. Immerse yourself instead in the beauty and the tranquility of New England as it used to be.

It's little wonder that long after he left, poet Frost wrote, "I am sitting here thinking of the view from our house in Franconia." It's unforgettable.

Inn Spots

Rabbit Hill Inn, off Route 18, Lower Waterford, Vt. 05848. (802) 748-5168 or (800) 762-8669.

If you have an iota of romance in your soul, you'll love this white-columned "inn for romantics" in a tiny hillside hamlet just across the Connecticut River from New Hampshire. Where else would you find, upon retiring to your room after a candlelight dinner, the bed turned down, the radio playing soft music, the lights turned off, a candle flickering in a hurricane chimney, and a small stuffed and decorated heart on the bed to use as a "do not disturb" sign and yours to take home?

That's just a sample of the care and concern that innkeeper icons Maureen and John Magee, who bought the venerable Rabbit Hill inn in 1987, show for their guests. "We set the stage," says Maureen, who has an air for the theatrical, "and our guests are the players." Upon arrival, John is apt to greet you with a "welcome to our home." In your

room is a personal note of welcome from Maureen. Depending on the season you'll find hot or iced tea, perhaps flavored with red clover, and delicious chocolate-chip cookies in the afternoon in the cozy parlor. Next to it is a pub, the Snooty Fox, with comfortable sofas and upholstered chairs in one section and a newer section with game tables, an authentic 18th-century barn decor and handcrafted Vermont furniture. Across the road are hammocks, side-by-side swings and a small gazebo near a pond for swimming and fishing, a covered bridge and nature trails.

Aptly named Canopy Chamber awaits guests at Rabbit Hill Inn.

The 21 guest rooms, all with private baths and some with air-conditioning, are in the 1825 main inn, a carriage wing and the 1795 tavern building next door. The basement of the last has been converted into a video room with a TV and VCR and a microwave for popping popcorn.

The Magees have decorated with loving care. Each room has a theme and seven have working fireplaces with andirons in the shape of rabbits. In Caroline's Chamber, the bed is draped with blue curtains. The Samuel Hodby suite (named after the original owner in the late 18th century) has a Georgian fireplace and a king bed covered with lacy pillows. Even in the carriage wing, where the rooms are in a motel-like configuration, they are done in a most unmotel-like way. Three rooms on the lower floor here have been gutted and turned into two deluxe suites with corner fireplaces and sitting areas, and one has a soaking tub for two. Our room, Clara's Chamber, was named for Maureen's grandmother and contained many mementos of her life as well as the standard room diary in which guests describe their feelings and rave about the innkeepers. On a tape to be used in the cassette player in each room are the voices of staff members telling the story of the inn and the particular room.

Among the more prized accommodations is the Tavern's Secret, transformed from two existing rooms and a bath at the rear of the building next door. The Magees call it their "fantasy suite" and that it is. The secret? Pull up what appears to be a floor-to-ceiling bookcase opposite the fireplace and you find a gleaming bathroom with brass fixtures and a double jacuzzi. Romantics can enjoy the fireplace from either the kingsize canopy bed or the jacuzzi.

No sooner was this completed than the Magees set about creating the Nest, converting an office and private quarters upstairs into a fireplaced bedroom with custom-made king canopy bed, a Victorian dressing room with a soaking tub for two and a private sun deck. The Loft and the Turnabout raise the total of "fantasy chambers" to four.

Two front porches, one on the second floor awash with wicker, are where guests like to sit and watch the distant mountains. Downstairs in the parlor, Maureen keeps adding to a collection of books written by guests. Everywhere are rabbit items, many of them gifts sent by people who have stayed here.

Breakfast is an event at Rabbit Hill; it is served in the dining room after 8:15 but you can find coffee in the pub earlier. To the accompaniment of the soundtrack from "The Sound of Music," we helped ourselves to a buffet spread of orange juice, a chilled fruit soup, a cup of melon pieces and tiny blueberries, homemade granola and assorted pastries. Two changing main dishes are prepared to order: at our visit, a poached egg on a croissant with cheese sauce, homefries and bacon as well as pancakes with bananas and strawberries. You might hit the day they offer a breakfast banana split with yogurt. And the granola is so good that guests buy packages to take home. The treats continue in the afternoon, when a table in the living room is stocked with quite an array of beverages and goodies. The inn's restaurant is the finest in the area (see Dining Spots).

At our latest visit, Maureen was scheduling events like a Victorian fashion show, a dance festival and an ice-cream social for 1995, the inn's bicentennial year. She pronounced that "the gap between our vision for the inn and what it is" had finally been narrowed. "We'll never get bigger," she said. "Just better."

Doubles, $179, MAP; fireplaced rooms and chambers, $209 to $249. No smoking.

Adair, Old Littleton Road, Bethlehem 03574. (603) 444-2600 or (800) 441-2606.

A "welcome slate," bearing the names of arriving guests and the fare for the next morning's breakfast, is posted in the wide entry hall of this country inn of uncommon charm. It's the first of many thoughtful touches guests will find at Adair. The hilltop mansion was built in 1929 as a wedding gift for Dorothy Adair Hogan from her father, nationally famous Washington trial lawyer Frank Hogan. The early guest list included Presidents, governors, senators, judges, sports figures and actors. Helen Hayes visited each summer for many years.

Adair was restored in 1992 to AAA four-diamond status by Hardy Banfield, a former Portland (Me.) contractor, who sold his construction business to return to college for a degree in hospitality management, and his wife Patricia, former owner of a knitting and needlework store in the Old Port Exchange section of Portland. They are joined here by their daughter Nancy, who is the fulltime inn manager.

The Banfields opened with eight large bedrooms, all with private baths, and planned an addition with eight more guest rooms eventually. They also leased their dining operation to Tim and Biruta Carr, owners of our favorite Tim-Bir Alley restaurant in nearby Littleton, who moved their business lock, stock and barrel to the main floor of Adair in 1994.

Adair's country-estate-style rooms on the second and third floors are named after nearby mountains, which is fitting considering their scenic setting. Rooms are tastefully decorated and comfortable, and all have private baths and king, queen or twin beds. We particularly enjoyed the front Lafayette Suite, a commodious affair including a sitting room with a gas fireplace and a bedroom with feather pillows atop the kingsize bed. A stash of thick towels was wrapped and tied with green string. Also notable were an assortment of the inn's own toiletries and a gift basket bearing an Adair bookmark and a crock of the inn's maple syrup.

Assorted hats that the Banfields found in the attic now rest atop a shelf on the land-

Carriage at side is trademark of Sugar Hill Inn.

ing of the main staircase, which is lined with a library's worth of books. Guests also enjoy a grand, fireplaced living room with several sitting areas and a remarkable, all-granite (from walls to ceiling) basement recreation room with TV/VCR, a billiards table and a bar with setups. Out back is a large flagstone patio, terraced gardens and a rear lawn sloping down to a tennis court and a water garden beside a gazebo. There's not a sign of civilization in sight (or within earshot).

The Banfields serve an elegant breakfast in the dining room, a potpourri of stunning black oriental fabric walls, pale yellow curtains, large Chinese figurines, mirrored sconces and a growing collection of teapots. It might start with juice, fresh berries, granola and popovers and end up with eggs florentine or french toast. Cinnamon-raisin french toast with Vermont cob-smoked bacon was the delicious fare at our latest visit. Fruits and homemade cookies accompany afternoon tea.

Doubles, $125 to $145; suite, $175. No smoking.

Sugar Hill Inn, Route 117, Franconia 03580. (603) 823-5621 or (800) 548-4748.

Nestled into the side of Sugar Hill is this old white inn, built as a farmhouse in 1789, its wraparound porch sporting colorfully padded white wicker furniture and a tele-scope for viewing Cannon Mountain.

When Barbara and Jim Quinn of Rhode Island took over the inn in 1986, they ex-pected to see deer but were quite unprepared for the bear that "pitched his camp at our dumpster for the summer," Barbara recalls. The bear has departed, but the deer remain.

The Quinns have been hard at work redecorating the ten inn rooms, all with private baths. They exude country charm with hand-stenciling, rocking chairs, quilts, eyelet curtains and even a teeny pillow shaped like a duck on most beds. Among the neat touches are a lamp on an old sewing machine pedestal and a hooked rug in the shape of a heart. We found stenciling on the wood rim of the mirror in our bathroom. All rooms are different, with choice of twin, double, queen and king beds.

In 1994, the Quinns winterized four cottage units in back with new windows and doors, free-standing gas fireplaces and king or queen beds. They come with front porches, plush carpeting, television sets and Barbara's trademark stenciling.

Two living rooms in the inn are available for guests. One next to the dining room has a wood stove and the other embraces the reception desk and gift shop. A pub contains a small service bar and a TV set.

The effort that went into the decorating extends into the kitchen. Jim Quinn does the cooking, a talent harkening back to his days in the grocery business in Westerly, R.I. "I do it my style, the way I want to do it," says he. Available to guests and the public is a four-course dinner for $25, served in a country-pretty dining room.

The menu allows four choices among entrées, perhaps poached salmon with dill sauce, baked stuffed shrimp, beef wellington and, our choice, sautéed veal with champagne sauce, followed by chocolate kahlua mousse and bread pudding with warm whiskey sauce.

Jim's breakfasts are treats as well. We started with orange juice laced with strawberries, followed by blueberry muffins. Then came a choice of cinnamon french toast or swiss and cheddar cheese omelet, both excellent.

Doubles, $159 to $179, MAP. No smoking.

Bungay Jar Bed & Breakfast, Easton Valley Road, Box 15, Franconia 03580. (603) 823-7775.

Here is one exceptional B&B, tucked away in an 18th-century barn on eight acres without a neighbor in sight. The mountains of the Kinsman Range loom behind, providing an awesome backdrop for some rather awesome rooms and balconies on three floors.

The house – which looks like a small, two-story cottage in the woods in front – expands into a large, four-story structure overlooking gardens and mountains in back. The hayloft of the old barn became the two-story living room, where the fireplace is lit from fall to spring. Here are many sitting areas, a reading corner, an antique Steinway piano and Adirondack stick furniture. Some beams are draped with dried flowers and others bear a collection of birch-bark canoes. "It's a rustic setting, but the rooms are elegant," says Kate Kerivan, host with her lawyer-husband, Lee Strimbeck, and their young son, Kyle.

That's an understatement. You work your way upward through six rooms, two on each floor and varying in size. The higher you go, the more incredible the room and the more stunning the vista. The four on the top two floors have private baths.

Start with the main floor, where two "modest" rooms full of antiques share a bath. They might be the ones of choice elsewhere, but here, move up to the second floor. The Rose Suite offers a kingsize pencil-post canopy bed, a full bath, a day bed and armchair in a sitting area, and a private reading balcony overlooking the common room and fireplace. Just outside the suite is a two-person sauna available to all. On the other side, the Cinnamon Suite has a quilted queen bed, french doors to a private balcony and a six-foot soaking tub that belonged to Benny Goodman. Kate acquired it at an auction, keeps a Benny Goodman record nearby and, at our visit, was looking for a clarinet to serve as a towel rack.

Keep going. Banister rails made of lightning rods line the staircase to the third floor. Here is the Stargazer Suite, where a telescope is aimed on the Kinsman Range or the tramway atop Cannon Mt. It has a kingsize bed beneath four skylights, a clawfoot tub under antique leaded-glass windows, a toilet behind a cloister table, and a twig loveseat and armchairs. Lovely in beige and brown, it's remarkable to the last detail. But wait. There's still the Hobbitt Room, with a double bed beneath a skylight – "like being in a treehouse," says Kate. This has the best view, "Mount Kinsman staring you in the eyeball." The bed faces a tiled shower underneath another skylight.

That's not all. Along the way you've noticed the outside balconies, one off the

Sloping lawn yields verdant setting for guests at Foxglove.

common room big enough for all and notable for a barrel full of water lilies and a goldfish. The view will entice you to get up, eventually, to tour the gardens (Kate is a landscape architect who practices on her property) or walk the wooded path to the hidden Ham Branch River.

Kate and her innkeepers will feed you well. Afternoon treats are minted iced tea or lemonade in summer and hot mulled cider in winter with zucchini bread and cookies. In the morning, breakfast in the dining room or on the balcony brings local fruits, popovers and a treat like zucchini quiche, salmon pâté, blueberry pancakes or french toast with melted ice cream, accompanied by meats from Gould's Smokehouse nearby.

Oh, the name? The Bungay Jar is a legendary wind that funnels from Mount Kinsman through the Easton Valley past this property. Kate has incorporated the name into a T-shirt, which she sells along with country antiques and other items. Take a look at the B&B's brochure: it's one of the most artistic and informative we've seen.

Doubles, $65 to $130. No smoking.

Foxglove, Route 117, Sugar Hill 03585. (603) 823-8840.
A watercolor of foxgloves on the enclosed front porch welcomes guests to this inviting new B&B, named for owner Janet Boyd's favorite flower. She "fell in love with the house" and all the prolific blueberry and raspberry bushes in back and decided to turn it into a small country inn.

A former recording studio manager and decorator for musicians in New York, Janet had a good eye for the both the potential and the execution of the rambling, three-section country house dating to the turn of the century. The original pantry is now a foyer and shop. The dining room opens onto a rear glassed-in porch and three acres of park-like gardens and woods, dotted with hideaway terraces, trickling fountains and quiet glades. The dainty living room, decorated to the max, is housed in a front turret.

Each of five bedrooms with private baths has its own personality and comes with interesting decorative knickknacks. One on the main floor has a black tiled bath and a deluxe queen sofabed dressed in black leopard sheets. Prints of old shoes along a wall adorn a lacy bedroom with English paisley wallpaper, an antique white bed cover and

121

hat boxes on the radiator. Upstairs in the turret is a queen bedroom, while a summery bedroom up and to the rear has lots of wicker and lace and a kingsize bed.

Breakfast turns out to be quite a feast. You might start with blueberry or orange juice and move on to a quiche of smoked salmon with asparagus and tomato slices, buttermilk banana-pecan pancakes garnished with blueberries and raspberries, and creamy scrambled eggs with three kinds of fried apples. The fine linens, china and silver are coordinated to the day's fare.

Janet serves afternoon tea, plus champagne or wine with smoked salmon and hors d'oeuvre before dinner. A silver tray bears chambord or cream sherry for after dinner. And occasionally she cooks romantic candlelight dinners by reservation for guests. Pampering service and attention to detail are considered her hallmarks.

Doubles, $85 to $125.

The Inn at Forest Hills, Route 142, Box 783, Franconia 03580. (603) 823-9550 or (800) 280-9550.

A basket full of thank-you cards from guests in the sun room indicates that new owner-innkeepers Joanne and Gordon Haym are on the right track. Taking over a deteriorating property from absentee investors, they reopened in 1993 after a year's worth of renovations. The eighteen-room, English Tudor-style mansion, which had mildly piqued our interest in its earlier B&B days, has benefited from the Hayms' brand of TLC. "This is our home, our business, our future," acknowledges Joanne.

The inn is pleasantly situated off by itself on a knoll, hidden behind a clump of trees and enormous boulders with a grassy expanse on three sides. Off to the side is the Forest Hills residential association, successor to the old Forest Hills Hotel and later the short-lived Franconia College campus. The inn had been built as a private house to accommodate family groups and social functions for the hotel.

Now, inn guests are accommodated in five bedrooms with private baths and a three-bedroom family suite, which also can be rented individually sharing one bathroom, on the third floor. The kingsize Franklin Pierce Suite on the second floor offers a queen sofabed, full bath and one of the many walk-in closets with which the house abounds. The other main bedrooms have queensize beds and new or updated bathrooms. They are colorfully decorated with quilts on the bed and walls of one, a floral cover and matching pillows in another. Reading lamps are placed over the beds.

Most of the main floor is given over to common rooms. The focal point is an open, lodge-style living room with a wood stove in the corner fireplace. Beyond is a fireplaced dining room, where the day's breakfast menu is posted (at our visit, orange juice, homemade granola with wild blueberry yogurt and fresh strawberries, poached bananas, coffee spice cake and sour-cream belgian waffles with raspberry sauce or New Hampshire maple syrup). At the rear of the inn is the timbered Alpine Room with vaulted ceiling, oversize fireplace and deep lounge chairs for reading or watching TV. A refrigerator is close by for guests' use. Along the side of the house is a cheery sun room, another inviting spot with a TV/VCR.

Hummingbirds are attracted to feeders beside the long, open front porch. The Hayms have printed directions for guests to follow to favorite restaurants. They also offer a simple, three-course dinner of soup, entrée and dessert for guests by reservation.

Doubles, $80 to $95; $65 (shared bath). No smoking.

Sunset Hill House, Sunset Hill Road, Sugar Hill 03585. (603) 823-5522 or (800) 786-4455.

Big bucks and a cast of thousands, according to local hyperbole, have transformed this historic hotel into much more than a shadow of its former self. Michael Coyle, a

Enormous boulders at side identify The Inn at Forest Hills.

youngish wheeler-dealer from Boston who liked to play golf here and had "a little house up the street," told friends that someday he would buy the landmark annex building that was all that was left of the famous hotel straddling the ridge of Sugar Hill. As he tells it, the opportunity came in 1993 when he and Dr. Gloria Korta, "my lady friend and partner," bought the hotel at a foreclosure auction after it had been closed for fire-code violations. They kept the physical structure but renovated the interior from top to bottom. Gloria did the decorating, and Michael's parents — Frank and Retsy Coyle from Boston — came on board as fulltime innkeepers. "We're here for three years to help Michael get going," advised Retsy, who has warmed to the task of innkeeping. "But this has turned out so nice our plans might change."

The public spaces are beauties. Along the front is a succession of three open, airy living rooms with fireplaces and splashy floral arrangements. Strung along the rear are four elegant dining rooms (see Dining Spots) with windows onto the mountain panorama and one of the best fall foliage views in New England. On the other side of the reception desk is Rose McGee's tavern (named after Michael's 90-year-old great aunt), which is fun for drinks or light fare.

The upstairs guest rooms were in transition at our visit. We toured some of the first eighteen to be finished; six more were under construction, and four were yet to be started. Some have a couple of chairs in bow windows, some have fireplaces and four suites have jacuzzis. All have new private baths (some with fiberglass showers or clawfoot tubs) with the inn's own toiletries. All are simply but attractively furnished in Waverly prints and coordinated colors, with draperies that Gloria made during breaks from her medical practice.

Michael, a self-styled entrepreneur and originator and operator of start-up businesses, augments his weekday business by holding computer training sessions here "for some of my companies." He has maintained the inn's tradition of "work weekends" and has added cooking school weekends and special events such as a Victorian garden party with a five-piece brass band and a lupine festival celebrating "the incredible fields of lupine around here."

The shady back yard harbors a most attractive rock-rimmed swimming pool – an all-new heated pool within a pool because the old one was deemed beyond repair. In

1995, the Coyles cleared twenty kilometers of trails for cross-country skiing on their nine-hole golf course and through the woods. The trails also are used for sleigh rides.

Rates include a full breakfast with juice, fresh fruit, yogurt, homemade granola and homemade blueberry or cranberry muffins. Several choices are offered for the main course – at our visit, eggs benedict, banana-nut french toast, two kinds of omelets and eggs any style with homefries, bacon or sausage.

Doubles, $75 to $125; suites, $145. No smoking.

Franconia Inn, Easton Road, Franconia 03580. (603) 823-5542 or (800) 473-5299.

Situated by a meadow with Cannon Mountain as a backdrop, this rambling white structure looks the way you think a country inn should look and is the area's largest and busiest. "We have a reputation for lots of activities," says Alec Morris, innkeeper with his brother Richard for their parents, who run a resort in the Ozarks.

Thirty-two rooms and suites on two floors have been gradually upgraded since the Morrises took over the vacant inn in 1980. Most of the changes were cosmetic, but every guest room now claims a private bath and carpeting.

Rooms vary in size and beds; some connect to become family suites. The Morrises have added matching window cornices and bedspreads and larger beds. We like pine-paneled Room 27 with a canopied queensize bed, a duck bedspread, matching curtains and a lamp base in the shape of a duck. A suite includes a bedroom with queen bed, a living room with fireplace and sofabed, a kitchenette and a balcony. A honeymoon suite holds a whirlpool tub. The corner rooms are best in terms of size and view.

The main floor has an attractive dining room (see Dining Spots), living room and oak-paneled library with fireplaces, a pool room, a game room with pinball machines, and a screened porch with wicker furniture overlooking a large swimming pool. Downstairs is the spacious **Rathskeller Lounge** with entertainment at night and, beyond, a hot tub in a large room paneled in redwood.

Outside there is swimming in a pool or in a secluded swimming hole in the Ham Branch River. Four clay tennis courts and a glider/biplane facility are across the street ("soaring lets you see the mountains from the ultimate vantage point – the sky," says Alec). The stables next door house horses for trail rides in what the inn touts as a western adventure. In the winter, the barn turns into a cross-country ski center; sleigh rides and snowshoeing are other activities. Movies are shown at night.

Doubles, B&B, $90 to $110; suites, $130; MAP, $145 to $165; suites, $185. Closed in April.

Lovett's Inn By Lafayette Brook, Profile Road (Route 18), Franconia 03580. (603) 823-7761 or (800) 356-3802.

Although this inn, a fixture for two generations, added a swimming pool a few years ago for its summer clientele, it's at its best in the winter – and we'll always remember it that way. We were lucky enough to stumble onto one of its fireplaced cottages during a snowstorm more than twenty years ago and liked it so well we stayed for two nights.

Many of the patrons have been coming here for years, such was the spell that long-time innkeeper Charles H. Lovett Jr. and family cast on his inn and dining room. New owners JoAnna and Lee Wogulis from California, who bought the inn in 1994, were maintaining the reputation and upgrading the facilities and decor. Their son, René LaBerge, took over as chef and totally revamped the menu.

The main house, dating from 1784, contains three guest rooms with private baths, six twin-bedded rooms with shared baths, an acclaimed dining room (see Dining Spots), a lounge with mooseheads perched over a curved marble bar and a sunken sun porch with TV. The carriage house has a recreation room as well as six guest rooms with shared baths, good for budget-minded groups.

Summer or winter, we'd choose one of the sixteen cottages in duplex chalets scattered beside the pool and around the lawns. Each offers a small patio with chairs for gazing upon Cannon Mountain in summer. The nine with fireplaces are idyllic on chilly nights. All have sitting areas and small television sets. The elongated narrow bathrooms at the rear are ingenious as well as serviceable.

A full breakfast could include shirred eggs with mushrooms and herbed tomatoes or one of several renditions of pancakes.

Doubles, $120 to $150, MAP. Closed in April. No smoking.

The Hilltop Inn, Main Street (Route 117), Sugar Hill 03585. (603) 823-5695 or (800) 770-5695.

Prolific hanging baskets of fuschias on the front porch greet summertime visitors to the Hilltop Inn. Baskets of dried flowers or wreaths on the doors welcome them to their rooms.

Mike and Meri Hern have upgraded the 1895 Victorian home they acquired in 1984, adding private baths for every room in 1991 and restoring the dining room to serve dinners during foliage season. The six homey guest rooms lack pretension. Handmade quilts, English cotton flannel sheets, a decorating motif of bunnies, and bedside mints are among special touches. One two-room suite includes a queensize brass bed and a day bed.

The fancy hand stenciling on the walls of the Victorian living room matches the inn's china pattern of pink morning glories. Also striking is the Tiffany-era lamp against a backdrop of draped lace curtains.

A full country breakfast buffet is set out mornings from 8:30 to 9:30. Overnight guests help themselves to baked goods, cob-smoked meats and perhaps cheese soufflé, quiche or golden raspberry and blueberry pancakes, made with berries picked by the innkeepers.

Doubles, $70 to $85; suite, $95.

Dining Spots

Tim-Bir Alley, Old Littleton Road, Bethlehem. (603) 444-6142.

For ten years, this little establishment named for its owners, Tim and Biruta Carr, was a culinary landmark in the basement of a building really down an alley in downtown Littleton. In mid-1984, it moved from the alley to a 200-acre rural estate and the main floor of an inn called Adair. Inn owners Hardy and Patricia Banfield took advantage of the opportunity to provide a full-service inn without having to cook dinner themselves. The Carrs acquired a new commercial kitchen and twenty seats in Adair's main dining room plus fourteen more in a room converted from the inn's office.

Stunning oriental wallpaper of black and mustard yellow sets the decorative theme for new linens and china in the main dining room, which is warmed by a fireplace and lit by antique wall sconces. It's an elegant setting in which the Carrs continue to serve some of the most sophisticated and inventive food in the area.

After optional BYOB cocktails with snacks served in the inn's basement Granite Tavern or outside on the flagstone terrace, inn guests and the public adjourn to the dining room for a meal to remember. Our latest began with fabulous chicken-almond wontons with coconut-curry sauce, in one case, and delicate salmon pancakes on a roasted red pepper coulis for the other. The house salad was an interesting mix of greens, mushrooms, red peppers and Swiss cheese, served on glass plates with piquant vinaigrette or blue cheese dressings. From the selection of six main courses ($13.75 to $16.95) on a menu that changes weekly, we enjoyed the breast of chicken with maple-balsamic glaze and plum-ginger puree and the pork tenderloin sauced with red wine, grilled leeks and smoked bacon.

At an earlier visit, we sampled an outstanding scallop mousse with fresh dill and dijon vinaigrette, more than enough for two to share. This preceded an unusual mixed grill of lamb chop with rosemary and feta, veal scaloppine with banana, rum and cream (rather sweet for our tastes) and tournedos of beef with choron sauce. It was beautifully presented around asparagus spears, red caviar on sour cream over roast potatoes, and bits of asparagus and zucchini in the middle. A smoky flavor pervaded the linguini with duck, scallions, tomato and smoked Swiss cheese, also an unusual and memorable combination.

Desserts are to groan over: at our latest visit, white-chocolate strawberry tart with mango puree, peach ricotta strudel with caramel sauce, chocolate-hazelnut pâté with kahlua cream and pecan-cinnamon cake with warm maple-banana sauce. The well-chosen wine list is affordably priced.

Dinner by reservation, Wednesday-Sunday 5:30 to 9 or 9:30. No smoking. No credit cards.

Rabbit Hill Inn, Lower Waterford, Vt. (802) 748-5168.

Innkeeper Maureen Magee keeps the doors to her dining room closed until dinner begins at 6, so that if it's your first visit, you will appreciate the drama of a candlelit room, silver gleaming on burgundy mats on polished wood tables and napkins folded into pewter rings shaped like rabbits. Even the electrified lanterns and chandeliers look like candles; elimination of the former free-standing candles was a requirement for the dining room's four-diamond AAA rating. Fresh flowers and porcelain bunnies on each table add to the charm, and a spinning wheel stands in the middle of the room. A second dining room has been added behind the original to accommodate a growing clientele attracted by the food and the magical atmosphere.

Chef Russell Stannard, who trained with Boston culinary whiz Frank McClelland when both were at the late Country Inn at Princeton, offers a changing, interesting prix-fixe menu with a choice of appetizer or soup, seven entrées, salad and dessert. The cost to the public is a bargain $31. We feasted on cream of celery soup with pimento and chives and a great dish of scallops and three-pepper seviche with mint, papaya and toasted pine nuts, delicate salads with a creamy dressing, and a small loaf of piping-hot whole wheat bread served with the butter pat shaped like a bunny, with a sprig of parsley for its curly tail. Citrus sorbet drenched in champagne cleared the palate quite nicely. Main courses were a very spicy red snapper dish and sautéed chicken with bananas, almonds and plums, served with an asparagus-leek tart and garnished with baby greens. Sautéed potatoes shaped like mushrooms were a novel touch. A Beringer fumé blanc ($16) went well with all this. With desserts of homemade peanut-brittle ice cream in an edible cookie cup and double chocolate-almond pâté with crème anglaise came brewed decaf coffee with chocolate shells filled with whipped cream to dunk in – a great idea!

Other nights might bring steamed Atlantic salmon with a sunflower-macadamia nut crust, served with a kiwi-coconut sauce and saffron linguini and garnished with a black bean and green onion relish and a medley of caviars, or roasted beef tenderloin with a peppercorn-ginger jus and a gratin of smoked gouda, potato and zucchini, garnished with sautéed garden greens and a red radish relish.

Guitarist Chuck Morrison plays gentle jazz and classical music during dinner. Maureen, a classical flutist, often joins in, but in the parlor so as not, she says, to

Tim-Bir Alley restaurant occupies dining room of Adair, an elegant country inn.

upstage her guitarist or the guests. "I'm playing more than ever," she says, "which makes me happy." This is a serene dining room, where no detail has been overlooked and service is well paced. Plan on at least two hours for a fulfilling meal and evening.

Dinner nightly by reservation, 6 to 8:45. Closed early November and month of April. No smoking.

Sunset Hill House, Sunset Hill Road, Sugar Hill. (603) 823-5522.

Perhaps no restaurant in northern New Hampshire presents a finer mountain panorama than the Sunset Hill House. Four dining rooms seating a total of 100 are strung along the rear of the hotel, their tall windows opening onto the Franconia, Kinsman and Presidential ranges. The rooms are handsome with yellow Schumacher bird-print wallpapers, oriental print carpets and well spaced tables set with white linens and china, candles in hurricane chimneys and vases of alstroemeria.

Co-owner Michael Coyle, who managed a restaurant after graduating from college, wanted to get back in the restaurant business as owner and hoped to make the hotel the focal point of the community.

The contemporary international menu offers seven main courses ($16 to $21.50), perhaps shrimp sautéed with wild mushrooms and sundried tomatoes over angel-hair pasta with fruit salsa, sesame-crusted chicken with crispy peanut noodles and a fruit tonkatsu, or beef tenderloin served on a crouton of goose liver pâté with mushroom-cognac sauce. Expect starters like a Thai salad or a trio of pâtés with lentil relish. Sweet endings could be apple strudel, English trifle or bananas foster.

A tavern menu offers most of the dining-room appetizers and light fare, from nachos to baked Cuban pork sandwich and a couple of chicken dishes, in the $5.75 to $10 range. A poolside lunch is offered in the summer.

Lunch in summer, Thursday-Sunday noon to 3; dinner nightly, 5:30 to 9. Closed Monday-Wednesday in off-season.

Lovett's Inn By Lafayette Brook, Profile Road, Franconia. (603) 823-7761.

Under founding innkeeper Charlie Lovett, the restaurant here was a bastion of tradition. Chef René LaBerge, son of the new innkeepers, has totally revamped the menu and given it a more contemporary flair with what he calls California nouvelle cuisine.

Before dinner, guests usually gather around the curved marble bar (obtained from a Newport mansion) in the lounge for socializing. Then they're seated in one of the three beamed-ceilinged dining rooms for five-course dinners priced at $29 for the public.

A mixed green salad comes first, followed by choice of soup or stuffed mushrooms, a plate of gyoza and pierogi, or pâté stuffed with crostini and roasted garlic. Black raspberry Italian ice precedes the main course. The six choices range from prawns provençal over eggplant ravioli to blackened duck with mango salsa to porterhouse steak with peppercorn sauce.

Desserts include orange crème caramel and chocolate-almond-espresso torte. The signature is called chocolate bleeding heart: two layers of chocolate-almond cheese-cake shaped like a heart, with raspberry sauce dribbled over the top.

René spent ten years cooking in San Luis Obispo but is proudest of his summer stint as personal chef for actress Julie Andrews and her husband Blake Edwards aboard their yacht.

Dinner nightly, 6 to 8:30. Reservations required.

The Franconia Inn, Easton Road, Franconia. (603) 823-5542.

The large dining room with well-spaced tables and small-paned windows looking out toward the mountains rather resembles a ballroom. It's quite handsome with peach and white linens, a floral carpet, peach walls and chairs with curved cane backs. The limited menu changes frequently and is considered locally a bit pricey.

A typical dinner might begin with escargots in puff pastry, mussels in pesto or fettuccine carbonara. Entrées are priced from $16.95 for chicken florentine to $21.95 for rack of lamb dijonnaise. Veal is featured: with apple-mustard or champagne sauces, cordon bleu or saltimbocca. Even the filet mignon might be paired with smoked veal breast. Other possibilities could be shrimp and scallops saffron, brandied scallops, breast of duck with leek sauce and steak diane.

"We're not all that elaborate with our desserts," says innkeeper Richard Morris. Cakes, pies and fruit melbas make up most of them. The many fancy after-dinner drinks and coffees compensate.

Richard and his brother Alec also run **Hillwinds,** a restaurant and motel in Franconia village. They scaled back the bar operation and expanded the menu, featuring an open grill for steaks, shish kabobs, seafood, chicken and ribs, priced from $7.95 to $16.95.

Dinner nightly, 6 to 9. Closed in April.

Polly's Pancake Parlor, Hildex Maple Sugar Farm, Route 117, Sugar Hill. (603) 823-5575.

Polly and Wilfred "Sugar Hill" Dexter opened their pancake parlor in 1938, when they charged 50 cents for all you could eat, mainly to have a way to use up their maple syrup. Their daughter, Nancy Dexter Aldrich, her husband Roger and their daughter and son-in-law operate the farm and restaurant now. They charge considerably more than 50 cents, but it's still a bargain and a fun place to go for breakfast, lunch or early dinner and a slice of local life.

Bare tables sport red mats shaped like maple leaves, topped with wooden plates handpainted with maple leaves by Nancy Aldrich, who, in her red skirt and red bow, greets and seats diners, many of whom seem to be on a first-name basis. Red kitchen chairs and sheet music pasted to the ceiling add color to this 1820 building, once a carriage shed. Big louvered windows afford a stunning view of the Mount Lafayette range beyond.

You can watch the pancakes being made in the open kitchen. The batter is poured from a contraption that ensures they measure exactly three inches.

Pancakes are served with maple syrup, granulated maple sugar and maple spread; an order of six costs $4.40 for plain pancakes made with white flour, buckwheat, whole wheat or cornmeal. All are available with blueberries, walnuts or coconut for $5.60. The Aldriches grind their own organically grown grains and make their own breads, sausage and baked beans (with maple syrup, of course). Waffles, seven inches wide, are available in all the pancake versions.

If, like us, you don't really crave pancakes in the middle of the day, try the home-made soups (lentil is especially good), quiche of the day (our ham and cheddar melted in the mouth) or a super-good BLT made with cob-smoked bacon. Cereals, eggs, muffins made with pancake batter, salads and sandwiches like grilled cheese and cob-smoked ham, croque monsieur and even peanut butter with a maple spread are available.

The homemade pies are outstanding. Hurricane sauce, made from apples, butter and maple syrup, is served over ice cream. The back of the menu lists, for extra-hearty eaters, all-you-can-eat prices.

No liquor is served, but the coffee, made with spring water, is great and, as a matter of fact, a glass of the spring water really hits the spot. In the shop you pass through to get to the dining room, you may purchase pancake packs, maple syrup and sugar, jams and jellies and even the maple-leaf painted plates.

Open daily, Monday-Friday 7 to 3, Saturday and Sunday 7 to 7, mid-May through mid-October; weekends only, 7 to 2, April, early May and late October. No smoking.

Village House Restaurant, 651 Main St., Franconia. (603) 823-5405.

Casual dining by a culinary family that know their stuff is featured in this restaurant of the old school. Pine-paneled walls covered with old signs and artifacts mark the front room with a counter and two large, dark dining rooms in back.

It was taken over in 1994 by Carol and Phil Fullerton (she a former Montreal caterer), who previously owned the Mountain Lake Inn in Bradford, N.H. The chef is their son Rob, who had trained in Boston and Newport, R.I. They keep busy serving three meals a day, and attract the locals with a daily breakfast buffet for $7.95, specials like Wednesday night pasta nights (all you can eat, $7.99) and even Thai dinners every other Tuesday.

The regular menu is a mixed bag of the tried and true plus a few surprises, say a cajun chicken sandwich with habañero mayonnaise or a vegetable stir-fry with ginger and soy at lunch time. For dinner, expect main dishes ($10.95 to $15.95) like grilled swordfish with homemade tomato salsa, baked chicken cacciatore, barbecued pork spare ribs, grilled New York strip steak with béarnaise or raisin-peppercorn sauce, and grilled leg of lamb with a fresh mint sauce. There's a vegetarian entrée of the week.

Breakfast, 7:30 to 10:30; lunch, 11:30 to 2; dinner, 5 to 9 or 10; lounge food, 3 to 11.

Diversions

Franconia Notch State Park, south of Franconia. The wonders of one of the nation's most spectacular parks are well known. Thousands visit the Flume, a 700-foot-long gorge with cascades and pools (adults, $6), and the Basin and gaze at the rock outcroppings, most notably the Old Man of the Mountains. Echo Lake at the foot of Cannon Mountain is fine for swimming. Cannon Mountain has retired its original 1938 aerial tramway but a modern replacement carries tourists to the summit for the views that skiers cherish – and gets them back down without the challenges that hardy skiers take for granted. New in summer are summit barbecues, scheduled Thursday-

Sunday from noon to 7 for $6 (plus $8 for the tram ride). In the large visitor center at the southern entrance to the park, a good fifteen-minute movie chronicles years of change in the area and advises, "when you see Franconia Notch today, remember it will never be quite the same again."

Cannon Mountain. In an era of plasticized, free-wheeling skiing, the serious ski areas with character are few and far between. One of the last and best is Cannon, which considers itself the first major ski mountain in the Northeast (1937). Operated as a state park, it remains virginal and free of commercialism. The setting is reminiscent of the Alps, when you view the sheer cliffs and avalanche country across Franconia Notch on Lafayette Mountain and the majestic peaks of the Presidential Range beyond. From the summit, much of the skiing varies from tough to frightening, as befits the site of America's first racing trail and the first World Cup competition. But there is plenty of intermediate and novice skiing as well. Lift prices are relative bargains: $38 on weekends, $31 on weekdays.

New England Ski Museum, next to the tram station at Cannon Mountain, Franconia, 823-7177. Skiers in particular enjoy this small museum that opened in 1982 and houses the most extensive collection of historic ski equipment, clothing and photography in the Northeast. The maroon parka belonging to the founder of the National Ski Patrol is shown, as is a photo of him taken at Peckett's-on-Sugar-Hill. One of the more fascinating exhibits traces the evolution of ski equipment. "Ski Tracks" is an informative and impressive thirteen-minute audio-visual show with 450 slides tracing the history of New England skiing. Open daily except Wednesday, noon to 5, Memorial Day-Columbus Day and late December through March. Free.

Sugar Hill Historical Museum, Sugar Hill, 823-8142. Sugar Hill people say not to miss this choice small place, and they're right. Established as a Bicentennial project by proud descendants of Sugar Hill founders, it displays an excellent collection in a modern, uncluttered setting and gives a feel for the uncommon history of this small hilltop town, named for the sugar maples that still produce maple syrup ("everyone who can, taps the trees," reports museum director Mitchell Vincent). The life of the community is thoroughly chronicled in photographs and artifacts. The Cobleigh Room recreates a stagecoach tavern kitchen from nearby Lisbon, and the Carriage Barn contains mountain wagons and horse-drawn sleighs, including one from the Butternut estate that used to belong to Bette Davis. Open July to mid-October, Thursday, Saturday and Sunday 1 to 4. Adults, $1.

Sugar Hill Sampler, Route 117, Sugar Hill. A horse was grazing out front on our last visit to this store behind the Homestead Inn, where commercialism gives way to personality and history. The large dairy barn, with nooks and crannies full of New England items for souvenir shoppers, is literally a working museum of Sugar Hill history. Owner Barbara Serafini is the sixth-generation descendant of one of Sugar Hill's founders and takes great pride in sharing her thoughts and possessions, even giving handwritten descriptions on the beams. In one rear section full of family memorabilia, she displays her grandmother's wedding gown, which she wore in a pageant written by her father and presented for President Eisenhower on the occasion of the Old Man of the Mountain's birthday in 1955. Amid all the memorabilia is an interesting selection of quaint and unusual merchandise, including maple syrup made by the Stewart family on Sugar Hill, and a special spiced tea mixture called Heavenly Tea. Many New Hampshire foods are featured, and you can taste samples of several. Toys and Christmas decorations are displayed in nooks off the main barn. Open daily, 9:30 to 5, mid-June through October.

Shopping. In Sugar Hill, **Harman's Cheese and Country Store,** a tiny place with a large mail-order business, proclaims "the world's greatest cheddar cheese." Many of its food and local items are one of a kind, according to owner Maxine Aldrich, who is carrying on the late Harman family tradition. In Franconia, the **Garnet Hill** catalog store shows fine bedclothes (English flannel sheets, comforters and the like), as well as pricey children's clothing, all in natural fibers, although you cannot buy anything here. Its main retail outlet is on Newbury Street in Boston – enough said. At the Quality Bakery (home of **Grateful Bread**), you can pick up a loaf of soy-sesame bread for $2. Two dozen varieties of breads and rolls are made; "we mill our own flour and our sourdough starter came from Germany 40 years ago," said owner Mike Valocourt. The Studio, a cooperative open Thursday-Saturday, offers an interesting selection of pottery, intricate birdhouses, painted furniture and jewelry. We were struck by the incredible jewelry boxes that artist Sara Foss painted to look like houses. She'll also do a painting of your house atop a stool. A collection of frogs is featured amid the country gifts at the **Green Frog.** We liked the local handcrafts displayed by volunteers at **Noah's Ark,** a shop run by the Church of Christ.

Two other places are of interest near Bethlehem:

Bethlehem Flower Farm, on Route 302 east toward Twin Mountain, specializes in day lilies. Owners Joan and Bob Schafer grow more than 100 varieties, with names like Precious One, Christmas Carol and Venetian Sun, which Joan will dig for purchasers straight out of the fields. Also on the premises are a woodland walk that takes about twenty minutes, The Gift Barn and Abigail's Antiques for gifts and collectibles, and Lily's Cafe where you may get a light lunch or ice cream. Bob says "we have the world's best chili," served with a corn muffin for $3.95. Open daily 10 to 6, mid-May to mid-October.

At **Gepetto's Barn,** retired writer and editor Win Brebner, a.k.a. Gepetto, joyfully follows his hobby of woodworking. In his big red barn he crafts puzzles, toys, dollhouses, furniture (some Shaker style) and much more. The barn is at the end of bumpy Blaney Road, off Brook Road, off Route 302, and is open daily from Memorial Day to Columbus Day. We had a bit of trouble finding it, and when we got there Gepetto was away. Thanks to a workman on the property, we got to see the inside of the barn and admired the imaginative craftsmanship of the furniture and toys.

Extra-Special

The Frost Place, Ridge Road off Route 116, Franconia. (603) 823-5510.

The farmhouse in which the poet lived from 1915 to 1920 and in which he summered through 1938 is a low-key attraction not to be missed. It was here he wrote most of his best-known works, a spokesman said of the property opened by the town of Franconia as a Bicentennial project in 1976. The house remains essentially unchanged from the 1920s. Each summer a different visiting poet occupies most of it, but the front room and a rear barn are open with displays of Frost memorabilia, including his handwritten "Stopping by Woods on a Snowy Evening" and a rare, large photo of Frost at age 40 working at his desk in the room. Out back, a half-mile nature trail has plaques with Frost's poems appropriate to the site; in two cases, the poems are on the locations where he wrote them. As if the poetry and setting weren't awesome enough, the stand of woods happens to contain every variety of wildflower indigenous to Northern New England. Open daily except Tuesday 1 to 5, July to Columbus Day; also weekends, Memorial Day through June. Adults, $3.

Squam Lake is visible through porte cochere at The Manor.

Squam Lakes, N.H.
Midas Touches Golden Pond

The movie "On Golden Pond" cast the largest private lake in the country quietly into the public eye.

"Before the movie, not that many people knew the lake was here," said Pierre Havre, who with his wife Jan restored a rundown resort into The Manor, shortly after the movie debuted. Since retired, they started something of a boom in year-round innkeeping in an area that long has been a low-key haven for homeowner-members of the influential Squam Lakes Association, whose membership reads like a Yankee who's who.

Now, the Holderness area between Squam and Little Squam lakes has two inns and the surrounding area has at least five bed-and-breakfast establishments. Meredith, just east of the Squam Lakes at the closest section of better-known Lake Winnipesaukee, is the site of a large inn of more recent vintage.

"All of a sudden," notes Bill Webb of the Inn on Golden Pond, "the Squams have more than 50 beds and, with skiing close by, we're making this a destination area year-round."

Passersby see the striking sign in front of his inn and "stop just to ask if this is the place where the movie was filmed," he says. It isn't, but like most of the Squams' entrepreneurs, he takes full advantage of the association.

Pierre Havre boards visitors on his 28-foot pontoon craft for daily cruises along the 50-mile shoreline of Squam Lake. Its water is so pure that the 1,000 or so homeowners drink straight from the lake and its setting is so quiet that it's a nesting place for loons, which are the lake's trademark. Other than by private boat, Havre's Lady of the Manor and Capt. Joe Nassar's newer pontoon-boat excursion are the only ways visitors can see the sights that Katharine Hepburn and Henry Fonda made famous (the Thayer house, Purgatory Cove) and sample the changing moods of a very special lake.

Besides the lake, quaint downtown Holderness is undergoing something of a rebirth as merchant Deborah Holland and colleagues impart what she calls "a breath of fresh air." Nearby, the historic town of Center Sandwich – a picturesque crafts colony that is everybody's idea of what an old New England village should be – and the upscale pleasures of Meredith also beckon visitors.

Thanks to the continuing emergence of some good inns, they have a home base from which to enjoy the charms of Golden Pond.

Inn Spots

The Manor, Route 3, Box T, Holderness 03245. (603) 968-3348 or (800) 545-2141.

Sometimes called the Manor on Golden Pond, this is the largest and most luxurious of Squam Lake inns. It is also the only one with lake frontage and access, which is a major plus.

Built in 1903 by an Englishman who had made a fortune as a Florida land developer, the mansion with its leaded windows, gigantic fireplaces and oak and mahogany paneling is a gem. High on Shepard Hill, commanding a panoramic view of mountains and glimpses of Squam Lake, the honey-colored stucco structure has a porte cochere for an entrance and thirteen acres for a yard. A large swimming pool off to one side, a clay tennis court in the pines and a broad lawn set up for croquet complete the picture. Down at the beach and boathouse, a raft, canoes and paddleboats are available.

Enthusiastic owners David and Bambi Arnold, transplanted Californians, grandly upgraded almost all aspects of the inn in their first two years. The new look begins in the expansive living room, where the old brown carpet was removed and the original floors restored. A custom-made area rug, comfortable new furnishings and fine English antiques show taste and flair. Beyond is a cozy library opening through french doors onto a walled front patio with dark green molded chairs at marble tables – a delightful spot to which we repaired after helping ourselves to the afternoon tea spread set out in the library. A handsome piano bar called the Three Cocks Pub, paneled in rich woods and ever so elegant with copper tables and a copper bar, is a convivial setting for cocktails or after-dinner drinks.

Upstairs is a small library/common room with a telephone for guests and a "squire's basket" stocked with necessities that a traveler might have forgotten. All seventeen guest rooms have private baths and ten have wood-burning fireplaces. Most have been

redecorated by the Arnolds, who added jacuzzi tubs in three bathrooms in 1995. Handsome in coordinated Laura Ashley fabrics and fancy window treatments, they are outfitted with both antiques and remote-control TVs. We were happily ensconced in the front Windsor room, with a fireplace and big windows facing the lake. It was pretty in deep pink, white and hunter green, with the comforter on the queensize poster bed matching the balloon curtains and the cover on the night stand. A large antique armoire and a writing desk bearing an unusual desk lamp with a silver teapot as a base were other attributes. Another favorite is the Buckingham, a huge corner room with a marble fireplace and kingsize tester bed upon which the elegant blue and white checked canopy matched the draperies. A small box of Godiva chocolates is presented on arrival, and gold-wrapped chocolate medallions on your pillow bid sweet dreams in the evening.

Four bedrooms with private baths and a couple of two-room suites are available in the nearby Carriage House, and four more rustic efficiency cottages are rented by the week. Smack beside the lake is our favorite Dover Cottage, which has two bedrooms and a kitchen/living room with fireplace.

A full breakfast is served in the side Van Horne Room, which is also used for dinner overflow on busy nights. An elegant room with french doors opening onto a side deck, it proved a cheerful spot for an ample breakfast of orange juice, lemon-poppyseed bread, unusually good coffee and a main dish, in our case shirred eggs and a quiche of tasso ham and shiitake mushrooms. Both came with potatoes sautéed with onions and peppers, and sausage or bacon.

The inn's elegant restaurant (see Dining Spots) is known for special-occasion dining.

Doubles, $155 to $285, MAP; cottages by the week, $825 to $1,500 with continental breakfast basket. No smoking.

Red Hill Inn, Route 25B, RD 1, Box 99M, Center Harbor 03226. (603) 279-7001 or (800) 573-3445.

The red brick summer estate that served as the administration building for the short-lived Belknap College is now a full-fledged inn and restaurant atop a rural hillside with a view of Squam Lake.

"From your room you can see where they filmed 'On Golden Pond,'" the inn's publicity proclaims. All ten guest rooms on the second and third floors of the mansion have private baths. They vary from double rooms with twin beds to four suites with sitting rooms and working fireplaces, two with private balconies and pleasant views. A separate stone cottage contains another suite, and a second cottage has two guest rooms with franklin fireplaces and jacuzzis. Co-owners Rick Miller, a Meredith native who returned to the area after ten years of innkeeping in the Bahamas, and Don Leavitt added eight more guest rooms (three with jacuzzis, franklin fireplaces and queensize beds) in an 1850 farmhouse near a pond at the foot of the property. Surprisingly, given the fact there's plenty of space, only the five jacuzzi rooms have beds as large as queensize. Thirteen offer fireplaces, however, and the inn goes through some twenty cords of wood a year.

Room rates include a full country breakfast, with a choice of cereal, eggs, toast, muffins and such, served buffet style in a front dining room.

Dinner is served nightly in four dining rooms (see Dining Spots), two of them airy sun porches with large windows capitalizing on glimpses of Squam Lake. In the spacious Runabout Lounge in the rear woodshed, an old mahogany runabout was cut in half lengthwise to become a bar and the walls are lined with Don's old auto license plates.

Guests relax in the many lawn chairs and stroll along the labeled herb path, where hardy varieties are grown for the kitchen. In winter, the paths through the inn's 60 acres of fields and forests are used for cross-country skiing.

In 1995, Rick and Don acquired and started renovating the abandoned Kimball's Castle, built a century earlier by a railroad baron as a private home on Lake Winnipesaukee. Commanding a 360-degree view of the lake from its hilltop perch on a point, the new **Kimball's Castle Inn & Restaurant** was being anticipated as the jewel of the Lakes Region. Rick said it would have twenty deluxe bedrooms with jacuzzis and fireplaces, a 125-seat restaurant specializing in upscale regional New

Snow blankets grounds of Red Hill Inn during holiday season.

England cuisine, a cocktail lounge and a small pool. Left to the Nature Conservancy, the property ended up in the hands of the Town of Gilford, which sold the buildings to fund a 200-acre nature preserve around the castle. Rick said the property, listed on the National Register of Historic Places, would be restored to National Park Service standards for opening in late 1995. Rooms were to be priced in the $130 to $180 range. Rick and Don planned to divide oversight duties between their two establishments.

Doubles at Red Hill, $85 to $150; suites, $85 to $125.

The Inn on Golden Pond, Route 3, Box 680, Holderness 03245. (603) 968-7269.

Franconia native Bonnie Webb and her Massachusetts-born husband Bill returned from three years in California to open this bed-and-breakfast inn in a 110-year-old residence with a rear section dating back 200 years.

No, the inn is not on Golden Pond (it's across the road from Little Squam, which is hidden by trees in summer) and "other than the fact that Jane Fonda once used the upstairs bathroom, we have no connection with the movie," the inn's fact sheet tells guests.

The Webbs have spruced up the place considerably. All nine guest rooms with private baths are handsomely appointed with queen or twin beds, pretty curtains with matching cushions, hooked rugs and needlepoint handwork done by Bonnie. Each room, named for an animal (Bear's Den, Raccoon's Retreat), has its needlepointed sign with the appropriate animal thereon. Bonnie also makes the mints that are put on the pillows when the beds are turned down at night. The latest additions are an upstairs suite with a kingsize bed and a rather spare sitting room. More deluxe is Chipmunk's Corner, a new rear suite with a kitchen area, a big living room with sofa bed and two velvet arm chairs, and a skylit loft with a kingsize bed.

The spacious, comfortably furnished living room, with a fireplace and numerous books and magazines, is particularly inviting for reading and quiet conversations. The large rear window looks onto a treed lawn with garden chairs and a hillside of 55 acres for cross-country skiing. A smaller room offers cable TV and, almost covering one wall, a fascinating map with colored pins locating "our guests' other homes." A 60-foot-long front porch is a relaxing spot in summer.

A full breakfast is served at individual tables in the attractive pine dining room, expanded when the Webbs added a second floor to the attached rear shed. Bacon and eggs as well as another hot dish like baked french toast or baked apple pancakes are among the daily choices. Bonnie sells a little cookbook of her breakfast specialties for $4 and, at the edge of their property, recently opened the nearby Yankee Kitchen Sampler, featuring New England foods and gifts.

Doubles, $105; suites, $130. No smoking.

The Glynn House Inn, 43 Highland St., Box 719, Ashland 03217. (603) 968-3775 or (800) 637-9599.

The crowning jewel on a residential side street in Ashland, this blends Victoriana and romance. Betsy Paterman and her Polish husband Karol, a chef of note, acquired the grand turn-of-the-century home in 1989 and redid everything but the wallpaper in the dining room to achieve what she calls "a Victorian love affair." They offer four guest rooms and three suites with private baths, gourmet breakfasts and much TLC for guests.

The exterior of the house is lit all year with tiny Christmas lights, a disarming yet charming sight in summer. The parlor is decorated to the hilt in mauves and purples. Off it is the front veranda, a fine spot for relaxing with iced tea and cookies.

A basket in the upstairs hall contains every conceivable toilet article and necessity that you might have forgotten to bring along. Two of the four guest rooms on this floor have queensize beds and two have full baths. Our room in front, quiet as could be since this is a residential street with little traffic, contained a fishnet canopy queen bed with a Victorian loveseat at the end, a huge armoire, and a sink and a jacuzzi open to the room. A doll was ensconced on the mahogany bed in the corner facing the fireplace in the room next door, quite frilly with floral curtains and a little lace-covered table between two side chairs.

The third floor now contains a family suite with a sitting room and two bedrooms, each with a queensize and single bed.

At the side of the main floor is a honeymoon suite with a double jacuzzi beside the fireplace, a very lacy canopy queen bed angled from the corner beneath a ceiling bearing gold embossed wallpaper, and a bathroom with a stall shower and pedestal sink. New at the rear of the house is another honeymoon suite that was the owners' quarters until they moved out back. Reached by a separate entrance, it has a living room with TV, fireplace and queensize sofabed and a kingsize bedroom and whirlpool bath upstairs.

Breakfast, prepared by Karol, is a treat. Early risers enjoy a pot of coffee before they sit down in a candlelit dining room at a lace-covered table expandable to seat sixteen. When we were there, a wooden goose with grapes wrapped around its neck was a striking centerpiece, and upwards of 50 dolls were looking on. Classical music played as Betsy served a fresh fruit cup, orange juice and a delicate cheese strudel with raspberry jam. The main course involved a choice of french toast or eggs benedict, the latter really special and served with hash browns. When he's not cooking breakfast or innkeeping (his wife often is on the road for her food marketing job), Karol collects and restores antiques for the inn.

Doubles, $85 to $95; suites, $125 and $150. No smoking.

Strathaven, Route 113A, North Sandwich 03259. (603) 284-7785.

There is artistry as well as hospitality here. Betsy Leiper, an embroidery teacher from suburban Philadelphia, and her husband Tony bought this rural manse as a summer home for their family of seven in 1978; upon his retirement from Bell Telephone in 1981, they decided to live here year-round. When the Corner House asked if the Leipers would take their overflow, Strathaven became a low-key B&B. "We found it an inexpensive way to entertain, which is what we like to do," says Tony.

136

Winter scene at The Inn on Golden Pond.

And entertain they do, in a grand, beamed living room beneath a cathedral ceiling, amid bookshelves, an upright piano and sectional seating facing picture windows overlooking rear gardens and pond. Or in a front solarium facing more gardens – just the spot for soup and a sandwich between cross-country expeditions in the winter. Or in the fireplaced dining room with a twelve-foot-long table and a wonderful glass cabinet full of china. The sideboard here was carved by Betsy's father, who also fashioned the mantelpiece displayed over a bay window and painted the watercolors that grace the house. Betsy's maternal grandfather did the oil portraits throughout.

Betsy's embroidery shows up here and there, perhaps as crewelwork on the valances in a pretty blue downstairs bedroom with private bath and two double beds. A second downstairs room in gold also has two double beds and a private bath. Upstairs in the older section of the house (1830 to 1840) are two more double rooms plus a single that share a bath with the host and hostess. The Quimby Room bears the maiden name and portrait of Betsy's mother, a musician who played with the Boston Conservatory. The Victorian Room contains a shelf of cottages and castles from England, acquired during her annual group tours for embroiderers. There's a canopied twin bed in the single room.

Guests enter the house through the kitchen, which says something about the hospitality of the place. Tony prepares a full breakfast: juice, cereal, homemade breads, omelets, three pancakes and sausages and coffee cake – "any or all of the above." Between meals, he serves as town treasurer and leads cross-country ski expeditions, videotaping guests' exploits and recording their pratfalls. In summer he joins guests on the front or side porches where, he quips, it's so quiet that "we sit and count cars."

Doubles, $55 to $60.

Curmudg-Inn, Shepard Hill Road, Box 684, Holderness 03245. (603) 968-4417.

"Turn off – tune out – drop in" is the slogan for this attractive, newly renovated establishment across the side road from The Manor. Richard "Doc" Martens, a retired physician, bills himself as innkeeper and resident curmudgeon.

Doc did all the renovations himself to a house that we once knew as Cafe Normandie.

137

He furnished it in eclectic style – the open living room and adjoining dining room, for instance, combining Victorian and Oriental elements (he lived in the Orient for four years).

The eight guest rooms, all with private baths and six with queensize beds, are painted in different colors. A tour of the property is like walking through a rainbow. Bedrooms come in a variety of shapes and sizes, some with corner cupboards like you'd expect in a dining room. The beds, covered with white spreads and down pillows, bear damask linen sheets. Two rooms have sitting areas, and all rooms come with luxuriant towels, robes and Crabtree & Evelyn toiletries.

Accents of Asian art stand out amid the decor that ranges from high Victorian and Eastlake to American country and oriental.

A self-taught cook, Doc prepares elaborate four-course breakfasts for guests. A typical meal includes a bread course, a fruit course, a breakfast soufflé of grits or oatmeal, and a main dish, perhaps stuffed crêpes, poached eggs with smoked salmon, caviar-leek cream sauce and asparagus, or polenta sticks stuffed with scallops and parmesan cheese.

With a commercial kitchen in the works, he planned to open a 24-seat restaurant in the dining room, serving dinner five or six nights a week in season.

Doc, originally from Michigan, prefers New Hampshire because it has fewer rules and regulations. He's really a curmudgeon, an assistant allowed, but "he doesn't crab at guests."

Doubles, $85 to $110. No smoking.

The Inn at Mill Falls, Mill Falls Marketplace, Route 3, Meredith 03253. (603) 279-7006 or (800) 622-6455.

This 54-room luxury hotel was erected in five months by a crew of 150 in what its manager called "a minor miracle."

With two Bostonians as partners, local real estate broker Edward "Rusty" McLear developed the $2.5 million inn as the last phase of an ambitious shopping and restaurant complex fashioned from an old mill site at the western end of Lake Winnipesaukee, about eight miles southeast of Holderness. "We couldn't understand why a beautiful resort area like this had nothing more than a couple of cottages in which to stay," Rusty explained.

A white frame structure on five levels, the inn has rooms of varying size and color schemes, decorated in contemporary French country style with matching draperies and bedspreads, plush chairs, television sets and spacious baths, each with a basket of amenities. Old samplers on the walls, framed pictures of 19th-century Meredith, plants in an old sleigh and antique headboards lend a bit of history.

The inn has a small indoor swimming pool, jacuzzi and sauna. A bridge over the waterfall that gives the project its name connects it to the busy marketplace, in which inn guests and the public can dine at the Millworks restaurant or pick up a gourmet pizza at Giuseppe's.

In 1994, Rusty acquired a lakefront property and office structure that previously housed a bank across the street. He undertook a total renovation to turn it into **The Inn at Bay Point.** Plans called for 24 deluxe guest rooms facing Lake Winnipesaukee. Eighteen have balconies directly onto the lake and some come with jacuzzis and fireplaces. Rates upon opening in mid-1995 were to be in the $139 to $235 range.

He leased main-floor space to Alex Ray of the Common Man restaurants. Alex planned to open the **Common Man Steak House** with an open kitchen, an antique boat and nautical theme, and a 100-foot deck right beside the lake. Three meals a day would be served.

Doubles, $79 to $159.

Cooking instructor Barbara Lauterbach prepares breakfast in kitchen at Watch Hill B&B.

Watch Hill Bed & Breakfast, Old Meredith Road, Box 1605, Center Harbor 03226. (603) 253-4334.

The third oldest house in Center Harbor was built in 1772 by the brother of the village's founder. Barbara Lauterbach, who used to raise champion bullmastiffs from the Watch Hill kennel in Cincinnati, has imbued it with a dog motif and "dog sense." Also great food (she's a longtime cooking instructor). And personality-plus.

The personality reflects Barbara, who we knew as a fellow ski club member when we all lived in Rochester, N.Y., more years ago than we care to remember. Since then she has lived around the world, ran a cooking school in the Lazarus department store in Cincinnati, does culinary programs and TV shows for King Arthur Flour and teaches part time at the Culinary Institute of New England in Montpelier, Vt. So you'd expect her breakfasts to be good: perhaps maple-batter french toast with homemade sausage, belgian wafflers or chunky apple and maple-syrup stuffed crêpes with maple butter (the maple syrup comes from a retired pilot of Air Force I in the Kennedy days, who lives in Center Harbor). Local melons and blueberry buckle are other treats. It's taken on the front porch with a view of Lake Winnipesaukee or at a long table in the dining room, so full of depictions of dogs she calls it her "doggie room." Her champion bullmastiff certificates decorate the paneled walls.

Dogs play second fiddle to a huge leather hippo in the beamed living room, comfy with magazines, TV and VCR.

Four pleasant guest rooms upstairs share two baths. Each has a doggie touch, but you're more likely to notice that each has a little library and a basket of toiletries collected by friends who travel. They are furnished with American and English antiques.

Barbara sells her own delicious jams, which vary from peach to tomato. She gives cooking lessons in her kitchen (where her Amazon parrot can do a pretty good imitation of a Cuisinart), and was dreaming about opening a restaurant in the area.

Doubles, $65. No smoking. No credit cards.

139

Dining Spots

The Manor, Route 3, Holderness. (603) 968-3348.

The main dining room here is a picture of elegance, from its leaded windows and tiled double-sided fireplace to the crystal chandelier hanging from the beamed ceiling covered with rich floral wallpaper. Owners David and Bambi Arnold have added new draperies and window treatments to match the wallpaper. Exotic lilies and burgundy napkins fanned in crystal wine glasses accent the candlelit tables dressed in cream and burgundy linens.

They also hired talented chef John Rindge, a Johnson & Wales culinary grad who previously had his own four-star restaurant, Rembrandt, in Philadelphia. Highly visible in culinary circles through TV appearances and contest awards, he was invited in 1995 to prepare dinner for a meeting of the James Beard Foundation in New York City.

He changes his contemporary American menu nightly. Dinner is prix-fixe, $40 for five courses. The meal begins with a tasting of the house fruit ice – a huge, decorated plate with crème fraîche, striped with a reduction of balsamic vinegar. At our visit, the five appetizer choices included scallop wontons with a wonderful tobiko beurre blanc sauce and Thai-cured salmon flavored with tequila, chiles and olive oil and served with wafers. Salads were lump crabmeat on baby field greens with balsamic vinaigrette in one case, chicory with warm black pepper and garlic dressing in the other.

Main courses were pistachio-crusted lamb loin with a dried cherry and juniper sauce with calvados and pan-seared filet mignon with black truffle and cognac sauce. These were nicely presented with julienned carrots and very thin asparagus, garbanzo and black beans. An $18 bottle of Conn Creek zinfandel accompanied from a choice but affordable wine list.

Dessert was John's rich, award-winning Remy-Martin chocolate torte and a chocolate pâté with homemade vanilla ice cream, two of the more decadent choices from a selection that also included cheesecake with blueberries and the inn's award-winning apple pie.

Service by a formally clad waitress was pleasant if a tad errant (she forgot to bring the bread and mistakenly served the main course ahead of the salad) – a typical hazard in an up-country resort area. The New Age background music, flickering candlelight and exceptional food more than compensated.

Dinner by reservation, nightly from 5:30; winter, single seating at 7.

The Corner House Inn, Center Sandwich. (603) 284-6219.

Over eleven years, innkeeper Jane Brown and her chef-husband, Don have created one of the area's more popular restaurants in this delightful Victorian house in the center of town. They also teamed up with fellow restaurateur Alex Ray of the Common Man to open a restaurant and catering service at Glove Hollow, upcountry toward Plymouth a bit.

Dinner is by candlelight in a rustic, beamed dining room with blue and white tablecloths and red napkins, or in three smaller rooms off the other side of the entry. The striking quilted pieces on the walls are for sale by Anne Made; the same for the artworks from Surroundings gallery.

Lunches are bountiful and bargains; we saw some patrons sending half of theirs back for doggy bags. We, however, enjoyed every bite of the Downeaster ($6.95), two halves of an English muffin laden with fresh lobster salad (more than you'd ever get in a Maine lobster roll costing far more), sprouts and melted Swiss cheese. We also tried a refreshing cold fruit soup (peach, melon and yogurt, sparked with citrus rinds) and the crêpe of the day ($4.50), a Corner House tradition and this time filled with ground

Windowed alcove offers view from small dining room at Corner House Inn.

beef and veggies. Sesame chicken, Maine crab cakes and broiled scallops were among the entrées ($7.95 to $9.95). Most people seemed sated with soup and half a sandwich ($3.95), and possibly a dessert of cappuccino cheesecake, frozen chocolate kahlua pie or piña colada sherbet.

For dinner, you might start with a cup of the inn's famous lobster and mushroom bisque, mushroom caps stuffed with spinach and cheese, crab cake with cajun tartar sauce or sesame chicken with honey dip. Entrées run from $12.95 for chicken piccata or cordon bleu or a single lamb chop "for those who like to clean their plate" to $17.95 for double two-inch-thick lamb chops. One diner said the last, a house specialty, were the best she'd ever had. Shellfish sauté, seafood mixed grill, brandied peach duckling, pork zurich, five pasta dishes and filet mignon are among the choices; grilled swordfish, venison au poivre and New Zealand rack of lamb were specials at our latest visit. The wine list is affordably priced. "Sandwich was a dry town when we came here and they finally granted us a beer and wine license," Jane said, "so they must think we're all right."

Upstairs, she is gradually redecorating three guest rooms – one up a separate steep staircase – each with a private bath. A handstitched teddybear sits atop each bed, surrounded by plants, antiques and handmade quilts. Doubles are $80 and include a full breakfast.

Lunch, Monday-Saturday 11:30 to 2; dinner nightly, 5:30 to 9. Closed Monday and Tuesday in winter.

The Common Man, Ashland Common, Ashland. (603) 968-7030.

Founded in 1971 by Alex Ray and hailed for food that is the some of the most consistent in the area, the Common Man attracts enormous crowds – we faced a half-hour wait at 8:30 one Wednesday evening. It also has spawned many other restaurateurs, Jane and Don Brown of the Corner House among them, as well as other restaurants in the area.

A jigsaw puzzle is at the ready on a table near the entrance. Inside, old records, sheet music and Saturday Evening Post covers are for sale. Upstairs is a vast bar and grill with buckets and lobster traps hanging from the ceiling, a long pine counter set for Chinese checkers and chess, plush sofas in intimate groupings and an outside porch overlooking the shops of Ashland Common. Pizzas, nachos, burgers and an uncommon number of snack foods are offered here nightly till 11.

The rustic, beamed main dining room, separated into sections by a divider topped with books, is crowded with tables sporting a variety of linens and mats, chairs and banquettes.

The dinner menu is plain but priced right, from $10.95 for Yankee pot roast, grilled pork tenderloin or three chicken dishes to $16.95 for filet mignon. Planked "grate steak" serving "from one ridiculously hungry person to three very hungry people," complemented with a medley of vegetables, is one of the best bargains around for $26.95. We can vouch for the prime rib and the "uncommon steak," served with potatoes and excellent tossed romaine salads. A bottle of the house cabernet, specially blended by a California winery and something of a precedent among New Hampshire restaurants, was a fine accompaniment. Another innovation at our table was a box of menu recipes, marked "please don't steal" (they're meant to tempt the palate, rather than be specific).

Desserts ($2.95) vary from hot Indian pudding to a creamy cheesecake and white chocolate mousse. As you leave, a sign at the reception desk invites you to "take home a bar of our uncommon white chocolate," $3 to $9.95.

Lunch, Monday-Saturday 11:30 to 2; dinner nightly, 5:30 to 9.

Red Hill Inn, Route 25B, Center Harbor. (603) 279-7001.
Colorful china with a pattern of morning glories, fresh flowers and oil lamps accent the pink-linened tables in the two dining rooms and two airy sun porches of the Red Hill. The front dining room and the ends of the porches offer a view of Squam Lake. A warming fireplace compensates for the lack of view in the inner room.

The kitchen is the special preserve of Elmer Davis, a chef of the old school who worked in long-gone American Plan hotels and never takes a day off. "From scratch" cooking is his motto, and he even makes all ten dressings for the house salads. The extensive menu ranges from old-fashioned (marinated herring) to contemporary (corn-cob smoked gouda cheese with sliced apples and crackers) for appetizers, shrimp scampi to roast Long Island duckling and roasted rabbit for entrées. Prices run from $8.95 for breast of chicken natural ("for the purist") to $26.95 for filet mignon with escargot-stuffed mushrooms. There is a good selection of dishes for the vegetarian.

Chef Elmer's signature dessert is Kentucky high pie, a concoction of chocolate, pecans, bourbon and more chocolate. Others include vinegar pie, which is sweeter and better tasting than it sounds, amaretto cheesecake and windswept fudge cake supreme. The wine list is extensive by New Hampshire standards and offers some half bottles.

Lunch daily in summer and fall, noon to 2; dinner nightly, 5 to 10; Sunday buffet brunch, 11 to 2.

Squam Seafood Company, Route 3 at Route 175, Holderness. (603) 968-3474.
Area restaurant impressario Alex Ray got his start in 1971 at the old Pine Shore restaurant beside Squam Lake. In 1994, he returned to his roots, as it were, offering "a new take on the old familiar seafood restaurant" in a former filling station-turned-restaurant.

And it's quite a place, from the small cocktail lounge on a lobster boat out front to the sign on the canopy over the doorway that shouts in capital letters "Get in here!" The inside is a vast sprawl with another cocktail lounge, catering hall and summery

142

dining areas with crayons and white paper on the booths and tables and a salad bar ensconced in a boat. It seems bigger than its 120 seats, and the manager said it served an average of 300 people nightly in its first summer – a lot for the area, and more than any of the owner's seven other dining establishments.

The fare is seafood, from raw bar to lobster bake. Any number of usual and not so usual fish dishes can be baked, fried or baked stuffed, priced from $6.95 to $9.95. The seacoast sauté yields scallops, shrimp and fresh fish over linguini. There are sand-wiches and a few meats for those who prefer. Prices top off at $10.95 for broiled sirloin steak and $12.95 for "yuppie stew," described as bouillabaisse with the addition of half a lobster.

Dinner nightly in season, from 5.

Mame's, Plymouth Street, Meredith. (603) 279-4631.

Owner John Cook takes pride in the fine restoration of the brick house and barn once owned by a 19th-century physician. A meandering series of small dining rooms on the main floor is topped by a large lounge on the second.

The menu is traditional steak and seafood with a continental flair, from seafood diane and lobster-scallop divan to prime rib and veal sautéed with crabmeat and scallops. Artichokes and shrimp tossed with pasta, blackened salmon and sliced london broil are other favorites. The prices are gentle (generally $10.95 to $15.95), and the atmosphere intimate and romantic. New England mud pie, chocolate silk pie, orange decadence and liqueur parfaits are among desserts.

A tavern menu is available all day and evening.

Lunch daily, 11:30 to 3; dinner, 5 to 9 or 9:30; Sunday brunch, 11:30 to 2.

The Millworks, Mill Falls Marketplace, Meredith. (603) 279-4116.

The outdoor Fallside Patio and an upstairs greenhouse overlook the town docks and Lake Winnipesaukee at this popular, multi-level restaurant in the middle of the Mill Falls Marketplace. In the Grill Room are intimate fieldstone alcoves, booths, tables with woven green mats and white napkins, an abundance of hanging greenery, ex-posed pipes on the ceilings, mill artifacts and local paintings on the arched brick walls.

Also owned by John Cook of Mame's, this restaurant offers something for everyone, from nachos to steak au poivre. For dinner, we sampled baked stuffed shrimp and veal marsala among choices from $10.95 for chicken and broccoli alfredo, fried scallops or herbed haddock jardinière to $18.95 for Texas T-bone. Salads with poppyseed or but-termilk dill dressings came on clear glass plates; a bread board with two big Pepperidge Farms-style rolls was accompanied by pads of butter in foil.

The Millfalls Magic dessert of vanilla ice cream, Irish cream, crème de cacao, chocolate cookie crust, hot fudge sauce and whipped cream is really good, our earnest waitress said. Too decadent, said we. We stopped for black raspberry ice cream in a homemade waffle cone at an ice-cream parlor outside.

Breakfast daily, 7:30 to 10:30; lunch, 11 to 3; dinner, 5 to 9 or 10.

Diversions

Squam Lake. The lake made famous in the movie "On Golden Pond" is so screened from public view that passersby get to see it only from a distance or up close at pre-cious few points. But you can – and should – experience it in one of two tour boats. The newest is Capt. Joe Nassar's Squam Lakes Tour. He gives two-hour excursions on a 28-foot pontoon boat daily at 10 and 4 from his residence off Route 3 half a mile south of Holderness; adults, $10.

We're partial to Pierre Havre's **Lady of the Manor,** a 28-foot covered pontoon boat with a 90-horsepower motor, docked in the boathouse at the Manor, which he used to own. Former airline pilot Pierre is a knowledgeable and talkative guide as he conducts two-hour tours of the lake, leaving from the Route 3 bridge in Holderness three times daily at 10, 2 and 4 from Memorial Day through foliage season (adults, $10). He tells the history, relates vignettes, stops to watch nesting loons and visits the places made

famous in the movie. "That's the Thayer cottage," he says from a distant vantage point before discreetly passing the house loaned for the summer's filming and so remote that many locals have yet to find it. Purgatory Cove with Norman's famous rock was as foreboding the stormy day we visited as it was during the dramatic scene in the film. "Even on a sunny day," he relates, "you'll generally see no more than a dozen boats on the second biggest lake in New Hampshire."

Chocorua Island, also called Church Island, is a favorite stop on both boat tours. The site of the first boys' camp in America, it now has an inspiring outdoor chapel in which summer worship services, complete with crank organ, have been conducted continuously by area churches since 1903. On Sunday morning, the dock area is said to resemble the approach of the Spanish armada as upwards of 250 churchgoers arrive in a variety of boats.

Holderness. Huddled around the little Squam River channel that joins Big Squam and Little Squam lakes, the small downtown area of Holderness is on its way up. A key mover in the rebirth is Deborah Holland, proprietor of the nifty **Loon's Nest Gift Shop,** situated in an 1812 farmhouse at Curry Place and purveyor of loon-related gifts, decorative accessories, jewelry, specialty foods and more. She and her husband, Willis, chairman of the town selectmen and operator of a local guide service for hikers, are instrumental in developing a meandering "reflection path" with benches upon which to sit and reflect along the downtown waterfront. Deborah also has been anointed by the locally based Maxfield Parrish Family Trust to operate its first licensed museum store in the country. Parrish, a New Hampshire native son who lived and worked from an estate near Plainfield, was ranked with Cezanne and van Gogh among the world's most popular artists in the 1920s. Deborah's first **Maxfield Parrish Museum Store** in a front section of her shop is authorized to sell Parrish prints and derivative art products such as calendars, note cards and posters. Her second-floor museum has a permanent exhibition of 60 Parrish pieces made from transparencies of the original works. Several are in frames made for the original works by Parrish himself.

Center Sandwich, an historic district, still looks much as it did two generations ago when Mary Hill Coolidge and the Sandwich Historical Society organized a display of hooked and braided rugs that led to the opening of a crafts shop. Known as **Sandwich Home Industries,** the shop became the first home for the League of New Hampshire Craftsmen. It is open daily from mid-May through mid-October with myriad craft and gift items, from carved birds to cribbage boards, handmade clothes to silver jewelry. We could spend hours (and a small fortune) here. Free crafts demonstrations are given several days a week in summer, and an outdoor art exhibit is staged during Sandwich Old Home Week in mid-August. The Sandwich Fair, one of New England's outstanding country fairs, has been held annually in mid-October since 1910. Summer residents might go home after Labor Day, but they often return for the Fair.

144

The main roads and byways of this picturesque village lead to any number of interesting crafts and antiques shops. Surroundings, long a favorite gallery in the center of town, moved in 1994 to expanded quarters next to owner Jessie Barrett's home a mile south on Holderness Road. Now called **Surroundings at Red Gate,** its four rooms display fine and country art. We were intrigued by the handweaving (vests, pillows, jumpers and much more) done by Roberta and Robert Ayotte, on display and for sale at **Ayotte's Designery,** their fascinating shop and studio in the former high school, open Thursday-Saturday 10 to 5. We also admired the wonderful pillows, especially those with cat portraits, done by Anne Perkins of **Anne Made** at **Country Hill Antiques.** Her wall hangings, quilts and pillows decorate the walls of the nearby Corner House Inn and are snapped up by purchasers almost as fast as she puts them up.

Shopping. Other than the antiques shops and galleries of Center Sandwich, the best place for shopping is the **Mills Falls Marketplace** in Meredith, which contains twenty enterprises from **The Country Carriage** with country gifts and accessories to the **Catalog Outlet Store** carrying women's apparel overstock from the Nicole Summers, The Very Thing and J.Jill Ltd. catalogs. We liked the birdhouses, garden benches and the cans labeled "Grow Your Own Forest" at **Upcountry Pastimes.** Absent are the souvenir shops indigenous to much of the Lakes Region. We overheard one customer ask if a shop had any T-shirts with "Meredith" printed on the front. No, was the reply – you have to go to Weirs Beach to find that kind of thing. Lamented the customer: "But then it won't say 'Meredith.'" Similarly, the loon items at the Science Center's Nature Store and Gift Shop in Holderness signify, but do not say, Squam Lakes.

Annalee Dolls, Reservoir Road, Meredith, is a gift shop, a museum, a Factory in the Woods and more, attracting sightseers by the carload. From humble beginnings, Annalee Thorndike has built quite an operation in her Meredith complex. Although we personally are not crazy about these dolls, we must be in the minority because the Annalee Doll Society has more than 23,000 members. There are dolls for all occasions and seasons, especially Christmas, with Santas and Mrs. Santas and elves galore. Mice are dressed as Pilgrims for Thanksgiving, bunnies for Easter and kids in costume for Halloween. Little frogs surround a pond in one corner of the shop. Although commercial, it's fun – especially for collectors and youngsters. Open daily, Memorial Day to Halloween.

Extra-Special

Science Center of New Hampshire, Junction of Routes 3 and 113, Holderness. (603) 968-7194.

This 200-acre wildlife sanctuary has a nearly mile-long exhibit trail featuring native New Hampshire animals in natural enclosures. Trailside buildings are full of hands-on exhibits, games and puzzles of particular appeal to the young and young at heart, and daily programs are offered in summer. The new Children's Activity Center is an entire barn full of fun and adventure; youngsters can climb a giant spider web or plunge into a groundhog hole. The visitor center contains an excellent **Nature Store and Gift Shop,** where we admired a tile-top table bearing loons for $195. Displayed outside at one visit was a Maine woodsman's weather stick, a rustic weather predictor. "They really work," said a sign, noting that when the stick bends down, it portends bad weather. It was bending down, and a hurricane brushed by the next day. Upstairs in the **Favner Gallery** was a fascinating exhibit of stuffed birds and mammals, part of a collection on permanent loan. Trail and exhibits open daily 9:30 to 4:30, May-October; adults, $6 in summer, $4 spring and fall.

Sleigh rides and skating are featured on "Victorian Afternoon" at Nestlenook Farm.

Jackson, N.H.
A Rugged Mountain World

Drive through the old red covered bridge into Jackson and you enter another world.

It's a world isolated from the hubbub of the lower Mount Washington Valley and enveloped by mountains of the Presidential Range, tiptoeing toward the East's highest peak (6,288 feet). It's a highland valley of pristine air, scenic beauty, and peace and quiet. It's a European-style mountainside village of 600 residents and often a greater number of visitors.

Jackson is one of the nation's earliest year-round destination resorts, dating to pre-Civil War days (and not much changed since its heyday around the turn of the century). It's a village of spirited tradition and pride, from the local book based on recipes used in Jackson's early lodges to the Jackson Resort Association's claim that "nowhere else in the world will you find a more concentrated area of diverse recreational opportunities."

Today, skiing is the big draw in Jackson and its sister hamlets of Glen and Intervale. There are two downhill ski areas, Wildcat and Black Mountain; a world-class cross-country center in the Jackson Ski Touring Foundation, and fabled Tuckerman Ravine, where the diehards climb to the headwall of Mount Washington for one last run in June.

The two worlds of skiing – alpine and nordic – co-exist in friendly tension. Explained Betty Whitney, who was staffing the village information center when we stopped: "The foundation wanted to advertise `Ski Tour Jackson' and I wanted to stress alpine, so we ended up simply `Ski Jackson.'" Betty Whitney and her husband came to Jackson in 1936 to establish Black Mountain and the Whitneys' Inn.

There are modern-day amenities, two golf courses among them. But this is a rugged area, better epitomized by the Appalachian Mountain Club hiking camp at Pinkham Notch than the Mount Washington Auto Road (its bumper stickers boasting "This Car

Climbed Mount Washington"), better experienced from a secluded mountain inn than from one of the chock-a-block motels down the valley in North Conway.

Inn Spots

The Inn at Thorn Hill, Thorn Hill Road, Box A, Jackson 03846. (603) 383-4242 or (800) 289-8990.

Probably Jackson's best view of the Presidential Range is from the front porch of this pretty yellow building, built as a private residence in 1895 and converted into an inn in 1955. All the mountains are labeled for identification purposes on the painting at one end.

An even broader view, wide enough to encompass the weather station atop Mount Washington, opens through the picture windows in the living room. Dressed in antiques, velvet upholstered furniture and fine oriental rugs, the room is Victorian to the hilt and contains a soapstone wood stove and a baby grand piano. Between the living room and the entry hall is a more casual Victorian parlor with the inn's only television and VCR.

Some of the valley's best meals are served in an attractive dining room at the rear (see Dining Spots). Next to it is a cozy pub with a fireplace.

Innkeepers Jim and Ibby Cooper came here from Florida, where he was in food and beverage management for the Four Seasons hotel chain. They have added queensize beds in all but one of the inn's rooms, and expanded the menu and wine list in the dining room.

In 1994, they upgraded two cottages with gas fireplaces and jacuzzis, and gave one cottage a deck and a kingsize bed beneath a skylight. They also added an outdoor hot tub at the carriage house.

Until the cottage upgrades, the most choice rooms were the ten on the second and third floors of the main inn. They are richly furnished with Victorian antiques, colorful floral wallpapers and oriental rugs. Sachet pillows are scattered about the large antique beds, and there are many special touches. The Ramsey Suite is stunning with a queensize canopy bed, ruffled curtains and a gorgeous patterned rug over wall-to-wall carpeting.

A deck has been added to the carriage house, which is losing its former ski-chalet appearance. It has six large carpeted bedrooms with modern baths off a pine-paneled great room done with plump sofas near the raised fireplace. The East Room adheres to

an all-lamb motif: lambs on the quilt, rugs, lampstand, wallpaper and pictures, and there's even a big stuffed lamb.

We enjoyed our quarters in the nicely furnished, two-room Forest View cottage, where the front porch caught the evening breeze. The two renovated cottages are close by, and a pleasant swimming pool is screened from view by a hedge.

Breakfast, served formally on white china, lives up to the inn's culinary reputation. It starts with five kinds of juices, homemade breads and muffins, and granola and cereals. The main course could be

147

the inn's spicy chicken hash with poached eggs and peppered hollandaise sauce or grand marnier french toast with peach conserve, both excellent.

Doubles, $140 to $200, MAP. No smoking.

Christmas Farm Inn, Route 16B, Box CC, Jackson 03846. (603) 383-4313 or (800) 443-5837.

A basket of bright red buttons proclaiming "We Make Memories" is beside an arrangement of garden flowers inside the entrance to this ever-expanding property where Christmas is reflected, if not celebrated, all year long. The buttons are part of Sydna and Bill Zeliff's promotion effort for their lively inn (he was in marketing with du Pont and handled this venture accordingly before turning day-to-day operations over to his wife and son Will when he was elected to Congress). The flowers are from the well-landscaped grounds, which are frequent winners in the valley's annual garden competition.

Few inns have such a fragmented history: part jail, part church, part inn, part farmhouse, part sugarhouse. The property was given by a Philadelphian as a Christmas present in the 1940s to his daughter, who tried and failed at farming on the rocky hillside before the place was revived as an inn. Hence the name, and whence all nicely detailed on the back of the dinner menu (see Dining Spots).

Located off by itself above Jackson Village, the inn posts a guest list beside the reception desk naming and welcoming the day's arrivals. The Zeliffs aim to bring people together for an inn-family experience, putting on everything from rum swizzle parties in summer to cross-country trail lunches in winter. They publish the North Pole Ledger, a fancy newsletter for guests, and keep a scrapbook for every year in the cozy Mistletoe Lounge "so that the guest experience becomes part of the memory," says Bill. Patrons reciprocate; many of the wreaths, samplers and such on the walls are gifts from guests.

A brick fireplace is the focal point of the 200-year-old inn's living room, which is done appropriately in red and green with plaid loveseats, a big red velvet duck and holly on the pillows. Bingo, games and movies on the VCR are nightly features of the adjacent TV-game room. The rear barn has a huge game room with ping-pong, bumper pool, large-screen TV, an enormous fireplace and a sauna. Across the road are a swimming pool with a cabana where lunch is available, a putting green, shuffleboard and volleyball court. Everywhere you look are paths, brick walls and gardens with flowers identified by labels.

Oh yes, about the guest rooms, of which there are 35, all with private baths. Ten in the main inn have Christmasy names like Three Wise Men and those of Santa's reindeer, and are decorated in sprightly Laura Ashley style; the spacious Blitzen and Vixen have jacuzzis as well. The red and green 1777 Salt Box out back has nine deluxe rooms, and most luxurious of all are the four suites in the barn, each with a sitting area with sofa and velvet chair, television, high sloped ceilings, large baths and loft bedrooms. Three cottages, each with two bedrooms and private baths, large sun decks, TV and fireplace, are first to be rented in the winter. Other accommodations are in the Log Cabin and the Sugar House.

Doubles, $150 to $190, MAP.

Dana Place Inn, Pinkham Notch, Route 16, Jackson 03846. (603) 383-6822 or (800) 537-9276.

Harris and Mary Lou Levine never expected to own an inn, but they went to lunch with a broker and somehow got talked into buying Dana Place in 1985. They've been busy upgrading the inn ever since, except for a brief hiatus when they sold to an absentee

Lush flowers greet summer guests at Christmas Farm Inn.

owner who doubled the inn's size within a couple of years and nearly ran it into the ground. "We felt we had left the job unfinished," said the Levines, who reacquired the inn in 1989 and returned it to stability.

Following its expansion, the historic Dana Place is an unusual mix. It's at once a rural country inn with a few quaint rooms sharing baths, juxtaposed against luxury suites in three new additions. Its elegant, high-ceilinged Lodge Room with a fireplace, a huge sectional, oriental rugs and quite a library is New England traditional; the airy new addition with an indoor free-form swimming pool and a jacuzzi is anything but. The lobby and entry have been expanded and the side patio enclosed to make a bar and cocktail lounge with a dance floor. An addition nearly doubled the size of the dining room (see Dining Spots). Two clay tennis courts were installed.

The out-of-the-way location of the inn, which still carries the name of the original owners of the Colonial farmhouse/inn from which all these additions have sprung, is special. It's up in the mountains some 2,000 feet above North Conway, just before you reach Pinkham Notch in the midst of the White Mountain National Forest, and right beside the Ellis River.

The Ellis River cross-country ski trail, one of the most skied trails in the country, ends at the inn, and skiers often come inside for lunches of hearty soups and chili in the lounge. In summer, inn guests cool off in a scenic swimming hole in the rushing river.

The 35 guest rooms vary in size and decor from rustic to deluxe. Six rooms with shared baths are used as two-room family suites. All have been redone with pretty floral wallpapers, period furnishings and wreaths or straw flowers on the doors. The large room with sitting area in which we first stayed in the original inn has a view over the gardens toward Mount Washington, a kingsize platform bed and a large modern bathroom with tub and shower. At our latest visit, we enjoyed one of the ten large "porch rooms" in a rear addition, with decks or balconies overlooking the Ellis River and mountains. Our corner room had not one but two decks (on the rear and on the side), and the sound of the rippling river lulled us to sleep at night.

Restored Wentworth Resort Hotel retains style of its turn-of-the-century beginnings.

Six more rooms are available in two new guest houses with contemporary cedar facades and more modern furnishings beside the river. One is called the Tree House for the tree growing through two of its porches. Its third floor contains a family suite for six, and the five bedrooms in the building can be private or inter-connected, making it good for groups.

A country breakfast is served (and available to the public from a menu). We liked the eggs benedict and the omelet of the day (green peppers and cheese), the latter a huge plate bearing garlicky hash browns and honeydew melon. Afternoon tea and complimentary mimosas accompany a changing array of goodies, perhaps spice cake, peanut-butter squares and nut breads, served in the pleasant Pinkham Notch Pub. Aprés-ski nibbles are put out in winter.

Doubles, $95 to $110, B&B; $135 to $155, MAP.

The Wentworth Resort Hotel, Route 16A, Jackson 03846. (603) 383-9700 or (800) 637-0013.

Built in 1869, the Wentworth was the grand hotel of Jackson at the turn of the century when Jackson had 24 lodging establishments. Abandoned for a time, it was restored in 1983 into a luxury resort with modern conveniences but retaining much of the style and charm from its golden era. It really came into its own after its acquisition in 1991 by Fritz and Diana Koeppel, he a Swiss-born hotelier who had been with the Ritz and Four Seasons chains and was general manager of the Banff Springs Hotel in the Canadian Rockies.

Their move East was a homecoming of sorts for Diana, a native of East Conway. A wide search for a three-season resort of their own near skiing, golf and the water led the couple to The Wentworth, where they have ambitious plans for upgrading and designs on eventual five-diamond awards.

The eighteen-hole golf course behind the hotel is part of the Jackson Ski Touring Center layout in the winter. Other facilities include clay tennis courts, swimming pool, cocktail lounge and an elegant restaurant (see Dining Spots).

150

The turreted, yellow and green Victorian structure plus annexes and outbuildings (some with great views of the golf course) contain a total of 62 guest rooms.

Plushly carpeted halls lead to twenty spacious guest rooms on the second and third floors of the main inn. All are beautifully restored in different shapes and sizes, with private baths (most have refinished, old-fashioned Victorian clawfoot tubs with showers), French Provincial furnishings, an upholstered chair under a reading lamp and color television. Beige patterned draperies and bedspreads are coordinated with restful cream walls and rust carpeting. Fritz warmed up the rooms with inn touches like dried flowers and stenciling.

Fireplaces were added in nine rooms, three of them with new jacuzzi tubs. Top of the line is the new ground-floor Thornycroft Suite with a king canopy bed, a Victorian settee in front of the fireplace, polished floors of white and flaming birch, an armoire holding a TV/VCR, and a three-room bath area with marble floors, a vanity with wet bar and a jacuzzi beside a fireplace.

The Koeppels also rebuilt the fireplace in the large, formal lobby and added Victorian antiques to cozy seating areas. At our latest visit, they were converting a function room along a rear sun porch into a swish pool room and library. Beyond is a dining deck with tables topped with Samuel Adams umbrellas. The dining room was up-graded, and antique couches and small tables were envisioned for the lounge. A health club with a pool was in the planning stage.

Doubles, $89 to $119, EP; suites, $119 to $149. Add $56 for MAP.

Nestlenook Farm, Dinsmore Road, Box Q, Jackson 03846. (603) 383-9443 or (800) 659-9443.

The plaque out front understates: "A new romance, Nov. 1, 1989, Robert and Nancy Cyr." Local condominium developer Robert Cyr invested big bucks and grand ideas into the transformation of a rustic B&B specializing in horseback riding into a deluxe fantasyland built around the oldest house in Jackson.

The Cyrs sought romance and a gingerbread look and ended up with an abundance of both. Such is their appeal to passersby along Route 16 that tours of the property are given daily at 2 p.m. Behind the locked front doors of beveled glass lie a lovely living room with beamed ceiling and fireplace, a tin-ceilinged dining room that earlier was home to an acclaimed but short-lived restaurant and now serves breakfast for guests only, an intimate tap room and a bird cage full of finches in the lobby.

Upstairs are five bedrooms and two suites, each named for the Jackson artist whose paintings hang in the room. All have two-person therapy spa tubs and 19th-century parlor stoves or fireplaces and are decorated to the hilt. Everything is pink and mint green and ever-so-coordinated in the prized William Paskell Room, which has a handcarved four-poster kingsize bed with a crocheted canopy, cherry and mahogany furnishings and french doors opening onto a small balcony. The Horace Burdick Suite includes a queensize bed and a small sitting room with a ruffly day bed for a third guest. The penthouse master suite takes up the entire third floor and accommodates four guests in three rooms, including a separate jacuzzi room with wet bar.

A low-fat country breakfast is served in the dining room at seven tables set with high-back chairs and fine English china. It includes fresh oranges and grapefruit, cereals, homemade muffins and perhaps the house specialty, an omelet stuffed with vegetables.

Gingerbread and romance continue outside onto landscaped grounds outfitted with statuary, gardens and even a big pond into which a waterfall trickles beneath a curving bridge. Music is piped into a huge gazebo, complete with a fireplace, park benches, a ceiling fan and a red sleigh in the middle. Horses, deer, sheep, llamas and donkeys from Nestlenook's new petting farm graze in a nearby pasture.

A riverside chapel (for making or renewing marriage vows), a heated pool, sleigh or horse-drawn trolley rides and daily massages are among the offerings. Such amenities don't come cheap; Nestlenook charges the valley's highest prices in an effort to recoup some of its enormous investment. Innkeeper Lionel Tetreault has warmed up the B&B part of the expanding 65-acre "Victorian estate" resort that justifies its billing as "fantasyland."

Doubles, $145 to $195; suites, $195 to $215. Two-night minimum stay. No smoking.

Paisley and Parsley, Route 16B, Box 572, Jackson 03846. (603) 383-0859.

The name reflects two of the many interests of energetic hosts Bea and Chuck Stone: paisley for the textiles, folk art and early antiques, and parsley for the gardening and cooking. Put them together and you have one fine B&B in a dramatic contemporary house on a hillside overlooking Mount Washington.

The house is oriented so "I can stand behind the kitchen sink and see Mount Washington," says Bea from her open kitchen, looking across the dining room and out tall windows onto an awesome view. The mountain also is on view through the "sky window" of the living room, where a brick wall encloses the fireplace.

The Stones offer three guest rooms with private baths. Most in demand is one on the main floor off the dining room. It contains a kingsize bed and two wicker chairs and a private porch with lounger and wrought-iron chairs. Its large, pale yellow bathroom is sensational: a cathedral ceiling, picture window, a two-person jacuzzi tub surrounded by a collection of small boats, a separate shower stall, a row of books on the back of the commode, and bottles of Perrier and Poland Spring water.

Upstairs on what amounts to a balcony overlooking the downstairs are a teddy bear's tea party in the hall and a sitting area with TV, spinning wheel, books and games. One guest room here has two double beds, decorated in white, red and deep green. The other, all in blues, has a crocheted canopy four-poster bed, many botanical prints and a huge window with a view of the mountains. Antique clothing is hung in both rooms.

The dining room or the rear deck beside the herb gardens are the settings for elaborate breakfasts served on English bone china. "I have never offered blueberry pancakes," avers Bea. Her preference is for the exotic: perhaps eggs benedict, belgian waffles, crêpes aux duxelles, eggs baked with shrimp, curried eggs, potato pancakes or frittatas. These treats look as good as they taste, accompanied by garnishes from Chuck's gardens – "we always serve the fruit on ferns," says Bea.

The Stones offer afternoon tea with cookies, have jacks for TV and telephones in the rooms, and take pictures of every guest to add to an album. Lately they added a little covered bridge on the side yard for decorative purposes and for guests to sit in.

Doubles, $65 to $95. No smoking.

Harmony House, Tin Mine Road, Box 92, Jackson 06386. (603) 383-4110 or (800) 383-4110.

When Ruth and James McFarland built their dream home here in 1991, the builder said he could save them money if he reduced the size of the windows. Ruth said, "No way. Windows are my thing. I want to bring the outdoors in." Friends agreed, feeling the house was in tune with nature. So when their neighbors, the Stones of Paisley and Parsley, suggested they open a B&B in 1994, they called it Harmony House.

Theirs is a large, contemporary Cape Cod-style house on a three-acre, birch-studded knoll overlooking the mountains. Like the Stones' house, it's also a very open house but decorated more formally. Guest quarters include a large master bedroom on the second floor with queensize bed, bath, sitting area with TV and a private balcony with mountain view. The main floor holds a second bedroom with queen bed, sitting area,

Big windows, deck and balcony yield mountain views at Harmony House.

full bath and one of the palladian windows of which Ruth is so fond. It can be rented alone, or as part of an upstairs-downstairs suite; the spacious loft above has a kingsize bed and a half bath. All three guest quarters reflect Ruth's decorating talents and window treatments.

Guests gather in the living room, a game room, a solarium, a rear hot tub and a gazebo out front. They also enjoy Ruth's large and open country kitchen as she prepares a hearty country breakfast, which is served in the dining room. French toast, pancakes and strata could be the fare. Jim has a professional photography studio in Massachusetts during the week, but is home on weekends to help with the B&B venture.

Doubles, $95 to $115; suite, $170.

Whitneys' Inn, Route 16B, Jackson 03846. (603) 383-8916 or (800) 677-5737.

A somewhat Bavarian feeling pervades this self-contained resort – a rambling complex of inn, outbuilding, barn and cottages totaling 29 guest rooms – at the foot of Black Mountain. It has been granted new life after falling upon hard times and being closed for a spell. Bob and Barbara Bowman, who have a condo nearby for the winter, added it to their growing list of resort properties, which include Henry Farm Inn in Chester, Vt., and the Folger Hotel in Nantucket, Mass. They painted the Whitneys' facade blue in honor of their Nantucket connections, where they began with the old Wauwinet House. They also hired as manager Kevin Martin, who had been with the inn for eight years and knows its strengths and foibles.

Although primarily a winter place (with the family-oriented ski area out back, a lighted skating rink, sledding and tobogganing), summer fun is not overlooked. Tucked away in the trees across the street, the skating rink turns out to be a lovely spring-fed pond for swimming and lazing. The inn has a tennis court and volleyball, croquet and other lawn games. Once you're here, you're away from everything but nature. No wonder it's popular for an old-fashioned country vacation.

All with private baths, guest rooms vary from standard to deluxe with sitting areas and family suites with living rooms. Cottages come with two bedrooms, living room and fireplace.

Breakfast and dinner are served in a country-pretty dining room. Dinner entrées are priced from $12.50 for grilled orange sesame chicken or london broil to $16.50 for

New York sirloin steak. A dining feature is the children's dinner table, since the inn's niche remains its family clientele.

The new owners planned to add an indoor pool behind the Shovel Handle Pub, and cut the Betty Whitney Cross-Country Trail from the inn's pond to link up with the Jackson Ski Touring complex.

Doubles, $90 to $110 B&B, $130 to $150 MAP; cottages, $150 B&B.

Wildcat Inn & Tavern, Route 16A, Box T, Jackson 03846. (603) 383-4245 or (800) 228-4245.

Long known for its restaurant (see Dining Spots) and award-winning gardens, the Wildcat has come up in the lodging world as well. "We wanted to upgrade our rooms to match our food service," innkeeper Marty Sweeney said of the extensive renovations to the accommodations on the second and third floors a few years back.

Now all but two of the fourteen air-conditioned guest rooms have private baths. Most are billed as suites and contain sitting areas, sofabeds and reclining chairs. Soft pastel colors, subdued floral prints and primitive antiques bestow country charm. New mattresses and plush carpeting add comfort, but "we draw the line at electronic annoyances such as ringing phones and noisy televisions," says Marty.

With two fireplaces and a large-screen TV, the huge Tavern is a popular gathering place for aprés-skiers and others. Folksingers perform on weekends.

A full breakfast featuring pastries baked on the premises is served guests. Marty and his wife Pam are proud of their muesli, a Swiss dish of chilled oatmeal mixed with fruit and nuts and topped with fresh whipped cream, and sometimes spike their hot chocolate with schnapps. In summer, breakfast may be taken on the rear terrace surrounded by Pam's colorful English-style gardens, which often win top honors in the valley's annual garden contest.

Doubles, $82; suites, $96.

The Bernerhof, Route 302, Box 240, Glen 03838. (603) 383-4414 or (800) 548-8007.

Long known for its European food, the Bernerhof has become a good place to stay. "Food had provided 85 percent of our revenues, but I want to get lodging up to 50-50," says Ted Wroblewski, owner with his wife Sharon. Their goal was to create the ambiance of a small, elegant European country hotel.

To do that, they expanded with a three-room addition featuring private baths, kingsize brass beds and, the crowning touches, jacuzzi tubs in window alcoves, where you can gaze at the stars as you soak. Since then, they have turned four rooms sharing baths into a couple of two-room suites with sofabeds in the sitting rooms and jacuzzis. All nine accommodations now have private baths, six with jacuzzis. One suite includes a sauna.

Guests have use of a second-floor sitting room with cable TV and VCR, and can walk to a secluded swimming hole in summer.

The main floor is devoted to things culinary, including the restaurant, the European-style lounge called the Zumstein Room (after the original owners), and the Taste of the Mountains Cooking School. A full breakfast is included in the rates, and a complimentary champagne breakfast with eggs benedict is served in bed on the third morning of one's stay.

Doubles, $89 to $119; suites, $139. Add $50 for MAP.

Riverside, Route 16A, Intervale 03845. (603) 356-9060.

Located beside the east branch of the Saco River on the Intervale loop between

North Conway and Glen, this is a homey country inn with a gourmet restaurant that serves dinners on weekends (see Dining Spots).

Geoff and Anne Carter, who had several restaurants in her career, moved from Portsmouth to the turn-of-the-century summer house built by his grandfather, an industrialist from Lynn, Mass. It's a warm and summery place, steeped in family history.

Three of the seven guest rooms have private baths and two used as suites share adjoining baths. Our favorite is Esther's Room (all are named for members of the family, down to the chauffeur and governess). Formerly the master bedroom, it has a brass bed, a pink chaise lounge and a great bathroom. A painting by Anne's mother adorns Lolly's Room, pretty in chintz and the deep-green carpeting that runs through all the bedrooms. Rooms are as comfortable as they were when this was a lived-in home. "People feel as if they're coming to Grandma's house," says Anne.

Common areas include a fireplaced parlor with a jigsaw puzzle in progress, a front porch, the dining room and "Auntie's Bar," the enclosed side porch where Geoff presides over cocktails and liqueurs.

Breakfasts are sumptuous. There's a choice of three fruits, followed by perhaps English toast (as opposed to french toast, it's English muffins in an egg batter), scrambled eggs with croutons and cheddar, or corned-beef hash. "We always have a sweet dish and an omelet," says Anne. Eggs from local chickens and blueberries grown by the county extension agent are used.

Doubles, $55 to $95.

The Village House, Route 16A, Box 359, Jackson 03846. (603) 383-6666 or (800) 972-8343.

A greenhouse-style porch for breakfast, a tennis court and a small swimming pool and a year-round jacuzzi out front are attractions at this cheery yellow and white B&B on seven peaceful acres in the valley at the edge of Jackson Village. A small gazebo atop a hill and a wicker-filled front porch provide fine views of the mountains.

A cozy parlor contains rustic furniture, TV, a wood stove and a guest refrigerator. In summer, innkeeper Robin Crocker serves a continental-plus breakfast of fruit salad, cereal, homemade granola, muffins and fruit breads. A full breakfast is offered in winter.

Eight of the ten guest rooms on three floors of the main house have private baths. Each is named for a New England resort village the innkeeper likes, and books from the particular area are displayed in each room. The Sturbridge is done up in peaches and greens, while Kennebunkport is all violet and white. Snacks are served to guests in the afternoon.

Five new rooms with kitchenettes are offered in a renovated barn out back. They have TV and air-conditioning and are particularly good for families.

Doubles, $55 to $75; kitchenette units, $75 to $95.

Dining Spots

The Bernerhof, Route 302, Glen. (603) 383-4414.

A turreted Victorian inn with sloping greenhouse addition is home for Swiss cuisine in an old-world setting, plus the noted cooking school, A Taste of the Mountains. Here is where visiting chefs Richard Spencer and Scott Willard teach five-day and weekend cooking courses periodically through the year. "Our kitchen and cooking school set us apart," says innkeeper Ted Wroblewski, who has created a culinary dynamic that pervades the establishment.

We can vouch for lunch, when we enjoyed the pâté platter ($5.25) and the day's raw plate of gravlax and vegetable salad ($4.75), both appetizers but plenty for a meal after a hearty breakfast. The three pâtés of duck, trout and seafood-vegetable were memorable, and the smoked salmon was a generous serving around a salad in the middle, much enhanced by the melba toast that, upon request, the chef prepared from good French bread.

At dinner, the specialty is fresh Delft blue provimi veal, deboned by the chef and used in wiener schnitzel, emince de veau zurichoise and veal cordon bleu. Other entrées ($15.50 to $21.95) include a melt-in-your-mouth salmon and lobster sauté in a caper crème fraîche sauce, chicken wallbanger layered with ham and smoked gouda and finished with orange galliano glaze, roast duckling with a mandarin orange sauce and grilled tenderloin with a sundried tomato and smoked jalapeño sauce. Cheese fondue with an array of fresh vegetables and bread cubes is $25 for two.

Traditional délices de gruyère and escargots compete with more contemporary appetizers like smoked duck breast and mushroom rice cakes (shiitakes and basmati with a roasted corn and bell pepper relish) on chef Mark Prince's changing menu. A delectable array of desserts includes a concoction of vanilla ice cream and kirsch in a meringue topped with bing cherries and whipped cream, profiteroles aux chocolat and chocolate fondue for two.

Meals are served in three dining rooms amidst pine paneling, beamed ceilings, crisp white linens, a piano and a Swiss stove. The Black Bear Pub has an oak-paneled bar and a good pub menu.

The wine list, large by New Hampshire standards, includes a few Austrian, German and Swiss vintages along with the predominantly French.

Lunch daily in season, 11:30 to 3:30; dinner nightly, 5:30 to 9:30.

The Inn at Thorn Hill, Thorn Hill Road, Jackson. (603) 383-4242.

The pretty dining room here is long and narrow with pressed-oak, high-back chairs at well-spaced tables set with pink damask linens and fanned napkins, white china, antique oil lamps and baskets of flowers from the gardens. New owner Jim Cooper, whose background was in food and beverage management for the Four Seasons chain, has overseen the expansion of both menu and wine list.

Chef Ken Beaudoin brings vegetables and herbs from his home gardens to update the seasonal dinner menu, which is prix-fixe for the public, $32 for four courses.

Our dinner started with a sensational cucumber soup with red bell peppers, diced tomato and mint and an appetizer of grilled shrimp on a bed of julienned cucumber and tomatoes with coriander. A basket of herbed sourdough bread accompanied; then came salads bursting with croutons, scallions, carrots, tomatoes, sprouts, mushrooms and impeccable greens, served with mini-carafes of poppyseed or honey dijon dressings. Mesclun salad tossed with prosciutto and shaved parmesan in a warm balsamic vinaigrette was a recent option. The sautéed pork medallions served with roasted red pepper puree and coated with a blend of cumin and other spices and sautéed hominy lived up to advance billing, as did the broiled beef tenderloin with a whiskey sauce and shiitake mushrooms. The trio of fish (house-smoked salmon, spicy red snapper and rare tuna with pancetta and sage, served over lemon linguini with tomato vinaigrette and parsley pesto) also sounded interesting.

There was no letdown at dessert: frozen grand marnier soufflé, warm ginger-pear pie with cranberry swirl ice cream, profiteroles and Louisiana bread pudding with lemon sauce and chantilly cream.

Jim Cooper has expanded the wine list, emphasizing California chardonnays and cabernets and French bordeaux and burgundies, with particular value on the high end. He also added single-malt scotches and grappas.

Dinner nightly, 6 to 9. No smoking.

Elegant country look prevails in dining room at The Inn at Thorn Hill.

Wildcat Inn and Tavern, Route 16A, Jackson. (603) 383-4245.

Food is what the Wildcat Inn is known for. The old front porch had to be converted into dining space to handle the overflow from the original two dining rooms, as cozy and homey as can be. There's also patio dining at tables scattered around the prize-winning gardens.

Sitting beneath a portrait of Abraham Lincoln, we enjoyed an autumn lunch in a small, dark inner room with bare floors, windsor chairs, woven tablecloths and blue and white china. A superb cream of vegetable soup was chock full of fresh vegetables; that and half a reuben sandwich made a hearty meal for $5.75. We also liked the delicate spinach and onion quiche, served with a garden salad tossed with creamy dill.

Dinner entrées run from $12.95 for lasagna to $20.95 for beef oscar. Wildcat chicken is served like cordon bleu but wrapped in puff pastry and topped with mustard sauce; lobster lorenzo is the tavern's version of lobster fettuccine. You also can get mondo chicken with Italian sausage and apricot brandy, shrimp and scallop scampi and "the extravaganza" – shrimp, lobster and scallops sautéed with vegetables and served with linguini or wild rice.

The desserts slathered with whipped cream are memorable. Chocolate silk pie, mocha ice cream pie, blueberry cheesecake, frozen lemon pie and the Mount Washington brownie topped with vanilla ice cream, hot fudge sauce, whipped cream and crème de menthe are tempters.

In summer, you can dine out back at white, umbrella-covered tables in the attractive tavern gardens. In winter, the historic tavern is a popular watering hole for skiers, and the tavern supper menu appeals both in price and content.

Breakfast daily, 7:30 to 9:30; lunch, 11:30 to 3; dinner, 6 to 9 or 10.

Dana Place Inn, Route 16, Jackson. (603) 383-6822.

The three dining rooms here are country elegant with an accent of Danish contemporary. There's a cozy room with Scandinavian teak chairs. The skylit and airy lower level has large windows for viewing the spotlit gardens, crabapple trees and bird feeders outside, and a large addition offers round tables at bay windows with views of the river. White cloths, pink napkins and oil lamps provide a romantic atmosphere.

Hungarian chef Bali Szabo's menu ranges widely. Entrées ($15.95 to $18.95) include braised Atlantic salmon with cucumber-dill sauce, spicy haddock casablanca, roast duckling stuffed with a curry-pear dressing, a signature veal chasseur and prime rib. We shared an appetizer of blackened carpaccio, served over an extra-spicy mustard sauce, before digging into excellent house salads so abundant they were nearly falling off their plates, and main dishes of brandied apple chicken (a menu fixture, featured in Bon Appétit magazine) and tournedos choron, which came with broccoli and pesto pilaf. Among desserts were a good strawberry tart, a refreshing lemon mousse with chambord sauce, cappuccino cheesecake and original sin chocolate cake, the last described by our server as "just fudge."

Wintertime lunches ($5.25 to $7.25) are popular. Up to 300 people a day come in for sustenance off the Ellis River Cross-Country Trail that ends here.

Lunch in winter, 11 to 3; dinner nightly, 6 to 9.

The Plum Room, Wentworth Resort Hotel, Jackson Village. (603) 383-9700.

Continental cuisine with American flair is the theme of the elegant restaurant here, its decor enhanced with sponge-painted walls, upholstered French Provincial chairs and skirted tables with floral prints.

Owner Fritz Koeppel has elevated the dining experience by hiring as executive chef Greg Basner, who trained with the Four Seasons and Ritz-Carlton chains. Fritz keeps him happy by sending him in fall and spring to work with former colleagues at great hotels around the world.

Dinner entrées at our latest visit ranged from $15.50 for grilled Caribbean chicken on a bed of mango chutney to $18 for sautéed loin of veal madeira. Other possibilities included herb-crusted salmon with a mango beurre blanc, grilled pork tenderloin with a honey-mustard vinaigrette, citrus-marinated duck breast with a raspberry coulis and honey-roasted New Zealand rack of lamb.

The day's starters included chilled blueberry soup, homemade seafood sausage, tequila lime shrimp, and New England cheese pie served with baby greens and marinated beets. Among desserts that evening were peaches and cream pie, Maine raspberry-chocolate cake and blueberry napoleons served on vanilla anglaise.

Dinner nightly, 6 to 10. Closed in April.

Christmas Farm Inn, Route 16B, Jackson. (603) 383-4313.

The former Christmas theme has been toned down in the large, candlelit country dining room here. The year-round decor now sports fanned napkins on mint green cloths with white overlays, delicate stemware, cushioned wood chairs, pretty floral window treatments and lots of plants all around. There are three comfy booths for two along one wall.

Little white lights twinkle and classical music plays as diners enjoy a choice of nearly twenty entrées ($12.95 to $17.25). They run the gamut from shrimp scampi with linguini and grilled salmon with tarragon beurre blanc to sautéed pheasant breast with grand marnier and dried cranberry sauce, veal with wild mushrooms and grilled lamb chops marinated in ginger and garlic. Heart-healthy items and a handful of lighter entrées also are offered.

Warm duck salad, fried wonton bundles, and turkey and bacon terrine are choice appetizers. The pastry chef is known for decorated tortes and gorgeous cakes, among them a strawberry cream cake. The huge wine list is heavily into Californias.

Dinner nightly, 5:30 to 9. No smoking.

158

Dana Place Inn offers dining and lodging against a backdrop of river and mountains.

Thompson House Eatery (T.H.E.), Route 16A at 16, Jackson. (603) 383-9341.

An old red farmhouse dating from the early 1800s holds an expanded restaurant renowned for salads, sandwiches and original dishes plus a soda fountain.

In the eighteen years since he opened, chef-owner Larry Baima has created many unusual dishes, some of them vegetarian. Sandwiches have flair: turkey with asparagus spears, red onions, melted Swiss and Russian dressing; knockwurst marinated in beer and grilled with tomatoes, bacon, cheese and mustard. Salads are creative: cheese tortellini and rotini tossed with a sundried tomato and basil vinaigrette, served atop greens with artichoke hearts; a spicy vegetable salsa piled on greens with kidney and garbanzo beans, shredded cheddar, sweet peppers, sprouts and nacho chips, and curried chicken, almonds and raisins atop greens and garnishes. At both lunch and dinner, such items are in the $6 to $9 range.

Dinner entrées ($13.95 to $16.95) often include "Baked Popeye," a notable spinach casserole with fresh mushrooms, bacon and cheese, with an option of adding scallops. Other artful combinations are chicken and sausage parmigiana, shrimp and scallops flavored with ginger and cinnamon, and seafood francesca over linguini. The pork tenderloin piccata and a special of scallops with spinach, plum tomato sauce and ziti made a fine dinner by candlelight on one of the flower-bedecked rear patios flanked by huge pots of tomatoes and basil at one visit.

Swiss chocolate truffle, Dutch mocha ice creams and wild berry crumble are great desserts. Kona coffee and black raspberry are among the flavors of ice cream available at the soda fountain. There's a full liquor license as well.

Patrons eat in several small, rustic rooms and alcoves at tables covered with pastel floral cloths, in a glamorous new skylit room (made by enclosing a former deck) with slate floors, chandeliers and hanging plants, or outside on canopied patios.

Lunch daily, 11:30 to 4; dinner, 5:30 to 10. Closed November to Memorial Day.

Red Parka Pub, Route 302, Glen. (603) 383-4344.

This is the perfect place for aprés-ski, from the "wild and crazy bar" with a wall of license plates from across the country (the more outrageous the better) to the "Skiboose,"

159

a 1914 flanger car that pushed snow off the railroad tracks and now is a cozy dining area for private parties. Somehow the rest of this vast place remains dark and intimate, done up in red and blue colors, red candles and ice-cream-parlor chairs. A canopied patio for outdoor dining was added in 1994 to provide another 70 seats in summer.

The menu, which comes inside the Red Parka Pub Tonight newspaper, features hearty steaks, barbecued ribs, teriyakis and combinations thereof ($8.95 to $18.95, including a salad bar with 30 items and breads), and homemade desserts like mud pie and Indian pudding.

You can start with nachos, Buffalo wings, spudskins or spareribs (or an assortment platter, $12.95 to share). Snack on soup and salad bar ($8.95) or the "hardly humble hamburger" with spicy fries and salad bar for $7.95. Or go all out on prime rib or sirloin steak.

Dinner nightly, 4:30 to 10, weekends 4 to 10; pub open daily from 3:30.

Riverside, Route 16A, Intervale. (603) 356-9060.

Although dinner is served only on weekends, it's worth mentioning for the ambiance (a turn-of-the-century country summer home) and the food (innkeeper Anne Cotter, a former restaurateur, is in the kitchen). "Creative country cooking – hearty, neighborly and abundant" is what it's all about, according to the chef.

An inventive cook who decides her menu by whim, Anne is likely to offer a handful of entrées ($11 to $17.50), perhaps crab and scallop tuscany, stuffed flounder with vodka sauce, plum rum pork, chicken diablo with sweet mustard butter and veal with tomatoes and oregano. Beef tenderloin salad and stuffed lobster tails could be on the menu as well. Entrées come with crisp mixed green or tomato-cucumber salad and changing accompaniments like creamy tomato penne and squash with snow peas or green beans. Mushroom crostini, chilled scallop bisque and smoked sausage are possible starters. Desserts could be homemade ginger-pumpkin ice cream, pear-cranberry crisp with brandy sauce, raspberry shortcake and lemon ice cream spiked with vodka.

Pink cloths and pale green napkins dress the dining area, which runs the width of the house behind a front parlor and adjacent to the pleasant side porch bar, a great place for cocktails or cordials.

Dinner, Friday and Saturday 6 to 9.

Yesterday's, Route 16B, Jackson. (603) 383-4457.

Yellow striped awnings and pretty flower boxes identify the exterior of this unassuming little restaurant, billed as the "home of the all-day breakfast."

The countryman's special of two eggs, pancakes or french toast, breakfast meat, homefries and coffee goes for $5.25, and everything else but the omelet prima donna ("the works") is considerably less.

For lunch, burgers, sandwiches and salads start at $1.50 for a hot dog. Grilled chicken salad and Monte Cristo and chicken teriyaki sandwiches are the most expensive items at $5.25. No wonder we couldn't even get in for a weekday lunch without a long wait. Proprietor Will Zeliff, son of the owners of Christmas Farm Inn, is onto a good thing – so good that in the winter of 1995 he started offering weekend dinners, with nothing priced higher than $10.95.

Breakfast daily, 6:15 to 3; lunch, 11:30 to 3; dinner, Friday and Saturday from 5.

Diversions

Downhill Skiing. Wildcat, looming across Pinkham Notch from Mount Washington, is a big mountain with plenty of challenge, a 2,100-foot vertical drop from its 4,100-

foot summit, top-to-bottom snowmaking, five chairlifts and a gondola (adult lift tickets, $36 on weekends and holidays, $19 midweek). **Black Mountain** is half its height and far smaller in scope, but its sunny southerly exposure and low-key, self-contained nature make it particularly good for families. Nearby are **Attitash** in Bartlett and **Mount Cranmore** in North Conway. **Tuckerman Ravine** on Mount Washington is where the hardy ski when the snows elsewhere have long since melted, if they're up to the climb (a 1,500-foot vertical rise for a half-mile run down).

Hikes and Drives. The Jackson Resort Association publishes a handy guide to nine walks and hikes, from the "Village Mile" stroll to Thorn Mountain trails. A good overview is offered by the Five-Mile Circuit Drive up Route 16B into the mountains east of Jackson, a loop worth driving both directions for different perspectives. Look for spectacular glimpses of Mount Washington, and stop for a picnic, a swim or a stroll through the cascades called Jackson Falls, part of the Wildcat River just above the village. The Appalachian Mountain Club has a guide for tougher hikes in the White Mountains.

Shopping. It's no surprise that Jackson's biggest store is the Jack Frost Shop, a distinctive landmark that's a serious ski shop as well as a fine apparel store with a few gift items plus a Nordic rental shop and ski school. A promising newcomer is the **Jackson Trading Company,** located next to the Thompson House Eatery, which is owned by one of the store's owners. Here you'll find sweatshirts, Christmas blankets, pottery, jewelry, collectibles and much more, artfully displayed in a rustic setting. Other than a couple of small galleries and antiques shops, "downtown" Jackson consists of a post office, a town hall, the Jackson Community Church and the tiny red 1901 Jackson Library, open Tuesdays from 10 to 4 and Thursdays from 10 to 4 and 7 to 9. For a more rigorous shopping foray, head down the valley to the stores of North Conway and its ever-expanding factory outlet centers and shopping complexes like the upscale Settlers' Green.

Other Attractions. Heritage-New Hampshire and **Storyland** are side-by-side destinations, suitable particularly for families. The former lets visitors walk through stage sets in which dioramas, costumed guides and talking figures depict 30 events in state history. Storyland is a fairytale village with buildings, fourteen themed rides and performances for children. Nearby is the **Grand Manor,** a museum of antique automobiles. Children and non-skiers also enjoy riding the Wildcat gondola, a 25-minute round trip to the summit looking across to Mount Washington. You can look down on Wildcat and the rest of New England from the top of the Mount Washington Auto Road, a 90-minute round-trip drive.

Extra-Special _____

Cross-Country Skiing. Jackson was rated by Esquire magazine as one of the four best places in the world for ski touring. That's due in large part to the efforts of the non-profit Jackson Ski Touring Foundation, founded in 1972 and now with 91 miles of well-groomed and marked trails starting in the village of Jackson and heading across public and private lands into the White Mountain National Forest. They interlace the village and link restaurants and inns, as well as connecting with 40 miles of Appalachian Mountain Club trails in Pinkham Notch. It's possible for cross-country skiers to take the gondola to the summit of Wildcat and tour downhill via a twelve-mile trail to the village of Jackson 3,200 feet below.

Sherburne House (circa 1695) is one of the oldest structures at Strawbery Banke.

Portsmouth, N.H.
A Lively Past and Present

Settled in 1623, the Portsmouth area ranks as the third oldest in the country after Jamestown and Plymouth. In many ways it looks it, the early Colonial houses hugging the narrow streets and the busy riverfront conceding little to modernity.

This is no Jamestown or Plymouth, nor is it a Newport, a similarly sized and situated community with which it occasionally is compared. The city has only one large hotel, its downtown blessedly few chain stores or trendy boutiques, its residents little sense of elitism. What it does have is a patina of living and working history, a pride in its past and present, and a noticeable joie de vivre.

The sense of history is everywhere, from the famed restoration called Strawbery Banke to the ancient structures dating back to the 17th century tucked here and there all across town. Named for the profusion of wild berries found on the shores by the English settlers, Strawbery Banke after 35 years of restoration efforts is a living museum of more than 40 historic buildings at the edge of downtown.

Portsmouth's pride in past and present evidences itself in the six museum homes of the Historic Portsmouth Trail and the creative reuse of old buildings around Market Square and on the Hill.

You can sense Portsmouth's joie de vivre in its flourishing restaurants (good new ones pop up every year). Their number and scope are far beyond the resources of most cities of 26,000 and give it claim to the title, "Restaurant Capital of New England." You can see it in its lively Seacoast Repertory Theater. You can feel it in its Prescott Park Arts Festival, the Ceres Street Crafts Fair, the Seacoast Jazz Festival. The people on the streets and in the shops exude friendliness.

Happily, Portsmouth retains its historic sense of scale. It is an enclave of antiquity along the tidal Piscataqua River, four miles inland from the Atlantic. The Portsmouth Navy Yard is across the river in Kittery, Me. The Pease Air Force Base is west toward Dover. The shopping centers and fast-food strips are out in Newington. The beach action is down in Rye and Hampton. Many tourists stay at motels near the Portsmouth Circle.

While travelers pass by on the New Hampshire Turnpike, Air Force jets stream overhead, and tugboats and ocean vessels ply the river to and from the sea, Portsmouth goes its merry, historic way.

Inn Spots

Martin Hill Inn, 404 Islington St., Portsmouth 03801. (603) 436-2287.

The first B&B in Portsmouth (1978), the Martin Hill was acquired in 1983 by Jane and Paul Harnden, who with another couple were visiting their favorite town from Nashua, where they lived. "We had hardly heard of bed and breakfast," says Jane, "but during breakfast at the inn the owners said they would like to sell in about three years and, I thought, this is me."

It turned out that medical problems forced the owners to sell that summer, and since then the Harndens have been the friendly innkeepers who dispense gobs of information about the many restaurants in town, historic attractions and whatnot, as well as cooking delicious breakfasts and dispatching every innkeeping task themselves, without staff. "We still air-dry our sheets and iron the pillowcases while watching the TV news," says Jane. As innkeepers go, the Harndens are among the most welcoming and dedicated we know.

Their handsome yellow house, built in 1820, is within a long walk of downtown. Although it is on a commercial street, it's quiet because of air-conditioning and one can retreat in summer to a deep and nicely landscaped back yard where 400 plants thrive and where tea is served about 4 p.m. The yard was featured in the Unitarian Church's annual pocket garden tour in 1991. The Harndens since have installed cedar fencing around the property and converted a courtyard into an illuminated water garden.

Although the inn lacks a common room inside, guests have plenty of room to spread out in the three spacious guest rooms in the main inn and four suites in the Guest House. The downstairs front room, called the Library, is in shades of rose and holds a twin and a double pineapple poster bed. Upstairs, the Master Bedroom, in white and

Wedgwood blue, has a queensize canopy bed and oriental rugs on the wide-board floors. The Greenhouse Suite in the spiffy side annex contains a small solarium furnished in wicker looking onto the water garden, rattan furniture in an inside sitting room and a queensize bedroom with full bath. Balloon curtains frame the windows in the Green Room, which has a small sitting room, an antique tub with a hand-held shower, and a queensize iron and brass bed that's so frilly it reminds Jane of a big crib. All rooms have modern baths, loveseats or comfortable chairs, good read-

Martin Hill Inn is decked out for Christmas season.

ing lamps, writing desks, armoires, and nice touches like potpourri in china teacups and the inn's own wildflower glycerin soaps.

Breakfast is served on a gleaming mahogany table in the antiques-filled dining room, whose walls display three coordinated English wallpapers and paints. Orange juice might be followed by Jane's scrumptious baked apple, the core filled with brown sugar. Paul makes dynamite french toast with Italian sourdough bread, slathered with almonds and accompanied by Canadian bacon and homemade cranberry relish. Our scrambled eggs with cheese and chervil were served with cranberry bread, and the coffee pot was bottomless. It's a great time for guests to compare notes on the restaurants they visited the night before and to plan the day with the help of Paul, who can even plot you out a trip up to Canada and back. Clearly, the Harndens relish their role as innkeepers and go out of their way to be helpful and accommodating.

Doubles, $83 to $98.

Sise Inn, 40 Court St., Portsmouth 03801. (603) 433-1200.

The first United States branch of a twenty-inn Canadian chain called Someplace(s) Different Ltd., this is a fine operation. The company took the original Queen Anne home built in 1881 for the John E. Sise family, remodeled it with great taste and put on a large rear addition that blends in very well. Walk in the front door past the stained-glass windows on either side, gaze at the rich and abundant butternut and oak throughout, marvel at the graceful staircase and three-story-high foyer, peek into the sumptuous living room and you're apt to say, as its marketing director did upon first seeing it, "this is the real Portsmouth."

The 34 rooms and suites on three floors vary in bed configuration, size and decor. All are elegantly furnished in antiques and period reproductions with striking window treatments and vivid wallpapers. Geared to the business traveler, they have vanities outside the bathrooms (some of which contain whirlpool baths), writing desks, clock radios, room phones, and remote-control television and VCRs often hidden in armoires. Some have sitting areas. Businessmen must like to watch TV in bed, for in many of the rooms we saw the TV wasn't visible from the chairs or, as is so often the case, the single chair. Windows that open, English herbal toiletries and mints on the pillow may compensate for the occasional lack of places to sit.

Or you can sit in the stylish main-floor living room, very much like an English library with several conversation areas and fresh flowers all around. Innkeeper Carl Jensen is the usually visible host.

A help-yourself breakfast of fruits, juices, yogurt, cheese, cereals, granola, croissants, bagels and all kinds of preserves and honey is available amidst much ornate wood in the dining room.

The lower floor, notable for an antique English phone booth in the hallway, contains three function rooms. A modern elevator shuttles guests between floors of this deluxe inn.

Doubles, $99 to $125; suites, $150 to $175.

Governor's House, 32 Miller Ave., Portsmouth 03801. (603) 431-6546.

There is artistry here, from the stunning wall mural in the living room to the mermaid handpainted on the tiles of a shower and the arty little floral displays all around. There are personal notes from governors, convivial breakfasts staged in the biggest room in the house, a romantic bedroom where the tiles around the jacuzzi are inscribed in French love words, surprise touches of nostalgia awaiting discovery – and even a tennis court.

This stately 1917 white Georgian Colonial is the home of John and Nancy Grossman, who retired here from Southern California. The Governor's House is their "retirement project."

The stage is set in the cozy living room, where the tiles around the fireplace have been handpainted by Nancy, a professional tile painter and artist whose house is her showroom. The focal point here is the mural covering one wall, a Peaceable Kingdom concept varying from Colonial landmarks to jungle animals. The Grossmans commissioned a New York artist-friend to do the mural. Other artists have come along and added to the work in progress. The scrolls unfurled by two town criers bear the names of at least 40 people involved in the structure's lengthy restoration, which won the Portsmouth Advocates' preservation award for 1993.

More artistic touches unfold, primarily in the bathrooms. The main-floor powder room harbors a remarkable strip of handpainted tile patterned after the Stetson hat boxes of old. A lifesize mermaid on the shower wall carries out the nautical theme in the Captain's Room. Around the double jacuzzi in the Prescott Room are what Nancy calls distelfinks, the Pennsylvania Dutch double-headed symbols of love, here bearing romantic endearments in French – with a French dictionary at hand for translation.

The Prescott is the largest and fanciest of the four guest rooms, each with private bath and antique queensize bed. It's billed as "a romance of flowers, history, lace and mahogany" and has a wicker sitting area. Each room contains a stash of old postcards and copies of Ladies' Home Journal editions from the 1940s. Nancy has hidden more such surprises here and there for discovery "by nosy guests," according to John. The nicest surprise of all, we thought, was the framed collection of personal notes and photographs from more than 30 of the nation's sitting governors in 1994, displayed on a wall in the namesake Governor's Room. Nancy sent cards to governors asking each to pen a few lines, and her fascinating wall exhibit is the result.

Breakfast is a particular treat, served beside the fireplace at a table for eight in what obviously had been the living room. "We like to have everybody sit together for breakfast," said John in explaining why they had reversed the functions of the original living and dining rooms. Fresh fruit and John's baked goods accompany Nancy's main dishes, perhaps popover pancakes topped with sautéed fruits, country onion and potato quiche, omelets with vegetables and feta cheese, or potato pancakes with smoked salmon and caviar. Nancy incorporates California touches in her cooking and tries "to keep it creative, because I don't want to get bored." Afternoon tea is put out on the sideboard alongside a "bottomless" cookie jar.

Guests help themselves to morning coffee in the second-floor library, full of interesting books and equipped with a small TV. They also enjoy a side porch, and a tennis court in the spacious back yard. Available for overflow is a fifth guest room, the Attic Suite.

Doubles, $95 to $140. No smoking.

The Inn at Christian Shore, 335 Maplewood Ave., Portsmouth 03801. (603) 431-6770.

An abundance of antiques, an inviting dining room with a fireplace, and quite lavishly decorated, air-conditioned guest rooms with television are attractions in this 1800 Federal house, located in the historic Christian Shore area.

Across from the Jackson House, Portsmouth's oldest, the structure was renovated and redecorated in 1978 by three antiques dealers, Charles Litchfield, Louis Sochia and Tom Towey. "It was a neighborhood eyesore," Tom says, but you'd never know it today.

In the main entry hall is a desk with baskets of candies and nuts, a grandfather clock and an etched-glass light. The richly furnished sitting room crammed with antiques is used as a sixth guest room in summer.

Upstairs are five guest rooms, three with queensize beds and one a tiny single available for $35 a night. Four rooms have private baths (including one with peach towels resting on a leather settee). All contain handsome furnishings, antiques and crocheted afghans.

A harvest table dominates the beamed breakfast room, with its large brick fireplace and an organ in the corner. Three

Breakfast table at Inn at Christian Shore.

smaller dining tables with upholstered wing chairs are beside windows on the sides. Covering every shelf in the room is the innkeepers' growing collection of rabbits – some ceramic, some cement, some in a 1900 lacquered Japanese cabinet, some on the floor. "New ones arrive all the time," says Charles.

A full breakfast including ham or perhaps steak is cooked by any of the three innkeepers, with the other two waiting on tables. They served a dish of bananas with blueberries, orange-nut muffins, scrambled eggs with ham and homefries at our visit.

Though the partners were tiring of the pace and have had the inn for sale, they continue to upgrade the facilities and make enthusiastic hosts.

Doubles, $79.

Handpainted mural is focal point of living room at Governor's House.

Gundalow Inn, 6 Water St., Kittery, Me. 03904. (207) 439-4040.

The nicest of the B&Bs popping up across the Piscataqua River in Kittery is this appealing establishment facing the Portsmouth waterfront, which is within walking distance across the Memorial Bridge.

George and Cevia Rosol acquired the 1889 Italianate New England structure, formerly a two-family house, in an estate sale. They spent two years restoring the building, taking out the only two bathrooms and putting in seven new ones. They offer six guest rooms, each with private bath and several with views of the river. All are named after gundalows (a corruption of the word gondolas), the 250-year-old flat-bottom boats with sails that plied the Piscataqua and are believed to have transported the bricks for the house downriver from the Berwicks in Maine.

Vivid Victorian wallpapers and ten- and twelve-foot-high ceilings are the rule in the second-floor rooms, one of which has windows on three sides. The bathroom in the Minx room is big enough to include both a chair and a closet. A curved stairway beneath a skylight leads past a plant-filled shelf to a new third floor, where two guest rooms afford the best views of the river and of Portsmouth. We're partial to the Royal George, which has a wicker loveseat beneath a skylight, a queensize bed with a sturdy Colonial bedstead, an armoire, blue carpeting and walls with a yellow floral print. Thick white towels are in abundance in baskets and on towel racks. The Rosols added stained-glass interior windows to enhance those bathrooms without outside windows.

Guests gather in a large, comfortable parlor furnished in a mix of Colonial and Victorian styles. Focal points are a grand piano and an enormous table displaying half a dozen newspapers and some of the magazines and books that abound throughout the house. Tea, wine and sherry are offered here in the afternoons to the accompaniment of classical music.

A full breakfast is served on the side patio or in a sunny garden room converted from a former passageway to the connecting barn, which the Rosols have transformed into their quarters. The room has a corner fireplace, three tables and windows on two sides onto colorful gardens. Breakfast starts with a fruit course, perhaps blueberry-lemon soup or baked apples with granola, and scones. Then come creamy scrambled eggs, pecan pancakes, zucchini fritters or bread pudding. Next is a meat or fish course – smoked salmon, fish cakes, homemade sausage or corned-beef hash. There might be a "dessert" of concord grape pie when the grapes are in season.

Doubles, $95. No smoking.

The Inn at Strawbery Banke, 314 Court St., Portsmouth 03801. (603) 436-7242 or (800) 428-3933.

You can't stay much closer to Strawbery Banke than this 1800 ship captain's house situated right up against the street, as so many in Portsmouth are. It also shows its age, but it's gradually getting improvements over the years.

All seven guest rooms come with private baths, although one is in the hall (and one in the attic suite is open to the room). Two rooms on the main floor share a common room. Strawberry stenciling, strawberry comforters and strawberry candies on the pillows accent the prevailing green and white color scheme here. More rooms go off an upstairs common room. One, done up in blues, has inside shutters, two rattan chairs and pineapple stenciling. Another with windows on three sides contains a double and a single bed and three ice-cream-parlor chairs around a glass table. The aforementioned attic suite, with the open toilet and shower added in the corner, must be for young, short people. It's up steep stairs and we had to duck to avoid the roof as we entered the sleeping alcove.

Innkeeper Sally Glover O'Donnell, who grew up in the family that ran the Colby Hill Inn in Henniker, serves a full breakfast in a skylit breakfast room with an abundance of hanging plants. The main course at our visit was sourdough blueberry pancakes with sausages, supplemented by oatmeal, cold cereals and homemade pastries. The room looks onto a strawberry patch, bird feeders and the trellised rose garden of the historic Governor Langdon House just behind. Sally keeps cookie jars stocked for afternoon or evening snacks in the two small common rooms, both with TV sets.

Doubles, $80 to $90. No smoking.

The Bow Street Inn, 121 Bow St., Portsmouth 03801. (603) 431-7760.

A succession of owners continues to improve this downtown riverfront establishment, which really is a cross between a motel and a small hotel. It occupies the second floor of a restored four-story building that also houses condominiums, a theater and a cafe.

Access to the inn is by buzzer and then up an elevator. Nine guest rooms with private baths go off either side of a center hallway. The views are of rooftops or the street, except for two that look onto the river. Unexpectedly small, the rooms are furnished simply but attractively in light pastel colors with brass queensize beds, thick carpeting, cable TV, telephones and a single chair. A mini-suite with a pullout couch and a harbor view accommodates four.

Juice, cereal, muffins, bagels and breads for toasting are put out in a pleasant brick dining room with three tables and a small refrigerator for guests' use. The owners "try to make people feel at home," said the assistant on duty at our visit. There's no specific parking area, but the inn supposedly pays if guests are ticketed for parking illegally.

Doubles, $99 to $115; mini-suite, $130. No smoking.

Facing Portsmouth waterfront is brick structure housing Gundalow Inn.

Dining Spots

Blue Mermaid World Grill, The Hill, Portsmouth. (603) 427-2583.

Two restaurateurs and a chef from Boston took over the old Codfish restaurant here in 1994 and found Portsmouth receptive to their idea of new world grill cuisine. They installed the town's first wood grill, gave the restaurant an arty and whimsical decor, and started dispensing spicy foods of the Caribbean, South America, California and the Southwest.

"We want to make it fun and festive," said Jim Smith, a native Mainer who had been food and beverage director at Boston's Colonnade Hotel. Here he's in partnership with Scott Logan, formerly of the Parker House in Boston and the Charles Hotel in Cambridge. They hired as chef Tom Tenuta, whom we first encountered at Mirabelle on Boston's Newbury Street. They removed some walls for a more open feeling on two floors, added embellishments like a fascinating abstract mural of the Portsmouth Farmers' Market and iron animals atop some chandeliers, and identified the rest rooms with mermaids and mermen. These were the ingredients for instant success.

One lunch was enough to tell. As we sat down, tortilla strips with fire-roasted vegetables and salsa arrived in what otherwise might be a candle holder. These piqued the tastebuds for a cup of tasty black bean soup, a sandwich of grilled Jamaica jerk chicken with sunsplash salsa ($4.95, available mild, medium or hot) and a sandwich of grilled vegetables with jarlsberg cheese on walnut bread ($4.95). These came with sweet-potato chips and the house sambal, and we also sampled a side order of thick grilled vidalia onion rings with mango ketchup. A generous portion of ginger cheesecake, garnished with the hard candy-like topping of crème brûlée, was a sensational ending.

We'd return for one of the pizzas and pastas (perhaps the hotter than hell pizza with yucatan sausage and habañero peppers), the herb-marinated chicken with smashed sweet potatoes and swiss chard, the Caribbean lamb stew or the shrimp and scallop skewers with watermelon salsa, most priced in the $6 to $9 range at lunch.

Prices rise a bit at night, starting at $9.25 for zuni vegetable stew with cilantro pesto and topping off at $16.95 for grilled lobster with mango butter. Among the treats are marinated skirt steak with sweet red pepper relish, Cuban-spiced pork, whole fire-roasted bass served flaming with spicy green beans and roasted new potatoes, and a skewer of marinated lamb with couscous. Bottles of incendiary Inner Beauty sauces from the East Coast Grill in Cambridge are on the tables to add fuel to the fire. Cool off with desserts like homemade caramel ice cream, tia maria flan or chocolate-banana bread pudding.

The drink list details ten kinds of margaritas and a good selection of beers and wines, very affordably priced.

Open daily, 11:30 to 10 or 11.

Cafe Mirabelle, 64 Bridge St., Portsmouth. (603) 430-9301.

French chef Stephan Mayeux and his wife Chris opened this casual gourmet restaurant in the former Fish Shanty in 1991. Now very un-shantyish, it's crisp and contemporary on two floors. There are a few tables for dining downstairs near the bar. Upstairs is a cathedral-ceilinged room with beams and interesting angles, mission-style chairs at burgundy-linened tables up against tall windows, shelves of country artifacts along sand-colored walls and twinkling lights on ficus trees.

Stephan served five years as sous chef at the late and acclaimed Strawbery Court, and that tradition continues here. He offers an interesting cafe-style menu and a five-course prix-fixe dinner for $19.95 that allows a full choice from the menu. Otherwise, dinner entrées are priced from $8.50 to $18.50. Bouillabaisse and frog's legs are menu fixtures. Also expect things like salmon epernay with scallops in a champagne and shallot basil cream sauce, veal paupiette stuffed with prosciutto and spinach, beef tenderloin au poivre and roasted lamb loin with rosemary and horseradish sauce.

Start with baked brie with walnuts and thyme in puff pastry, wild mushroom raviolis or grilled shrimp and scallops on a coulis of tomato, garlic and olive oil. Finish with lemon-bourbon cheesecake with a pecan crust, chocolate charlotte with raspberry coulis, homemade sorbet or tarte tatin.

Some of the dinner entrées, a crêpe, quiche, salads and interesting sandwiches are offered at lunch, which is a available in season on a new side courtyard.

Lunch, Monday-Friday 11:30 to 2:15; dinner nightly, 5:15 to 8:30 or 9; Sunday brunch, 10 to 2.

Porto Bello, 67 Bow St., Portsmouth. (603) 431-2989.

Yolanda Desario and her mother took over the well-regarded but hidden-away Guido's Upstairs Trattoria, where Yolanda had worked as a waitress. She hung out a handsome sign to announce the change, lowered the prices and started cooking northern Italian meals that had local diners-out abuzz.

She prepares authentic and traditional Italian food from scratch, "cooked simply," says she, but sounding rather complex to anyone else. Creative specials supplement the short dinner menu, which offers main dishes ($9.95 to $13.95) like grilled albacore tuna steak with a sauce of plum tomatoes and balsamic vinegar, organically fed chicken stuffed with prosciutto and porcini mushrooms, butcher-made sausages roasted with garlic and served with roasted peppers and potatoes, and loin lamb chops roasted with garlic and rosemary. Friends who sampled the mozzarella appetizer with slices of parma prosciutto, plum tomatoes and basil said they never knew mozzarella could be so good. They also said the delicate homemade lasagna layered with five cheeses in ragu sauce is out of this world. Eight other pasta dishes are priced up to $13.95 for farfalle tossed with Maine crabmeat and parmigiano reggiano. Desserts include profiteroles, cannolis, poached pears and zuppa inglese.

Mural of farmers' market graces wall at Blue Mermaid World Grill.

Some of the eighteen white-clothed tables, set amid a beamed ceiling and brick walls, are flanked by windows onto the harbor.

Lunch, Wednesday-Saturday 11 to 2:30; dinner, Tuesday-Saturday 4:30 to 9:30.

The Blue Strawbery, 29 Ceres St., Portsmouth. (603) 431-6420.

Portsmouth's restaurant renaissance was inspired by chef James Haller and the Blue Strawbery, which opened in a narrow 1797 restored ship's chandlery across from the waterfront in 1970. It's known far and wide, better regarded nationally than locally, although lately it's risen in the esteem of hometowners.

Buddy Haller has long since left, and Gene Brown, the last of the original partners, decided to retire. The place was for sale in 1995.

Prix-fixe dinners of six courses ($42) are offered at two seatings nightly. Waiters serve the meals family style from huge platters in a small brick and beamed dining room oozing antiquity.

A typical menu might start with a soup of champagne, pickled thyme, artichoke hearts and cream, followed by a choice of two appetizers, phyllo pastry stuffed with spiced pork or snails baked in garlic. A "relief course" of mixed greens with saga blue cheese caesar dressing precedes the main course, perhaps seafood baked in a duxelle with pernod lime butter, roast duck or tenderloin of beef wellington with a gingered madeira sauce. Vegetables like sugar snap peas sautéed in grape seed oil and black pepper fettuccine with a sundried tomato pesto might accompany. The signature dessert is fresh strawberries with brown sugar and sour cream.

Dinner by confirmed reservation, Monday-Saturday 6 and 9, Sunday 3 and 6. Single seatings, Thursday-Saturday at 7:30 and Sunday at 6, Labor Day to Memorial Day. No credit cards.

The Library Restaurant at the Rockingham House, 401 State St., Portsmouth. (603) 431-5202.

The old Rockingham Hotel has been converted to apartments, but part of the ground floor was restored into an extravagant restaurant in 1975. Its ornate carved-wood ceiling, mahogany paneling, fireplaces, huge mirrors and bright blue napkins set the stage for books, books and more books on shelves in three rooms. Some bookshelves enclose booths for intimate dining.

The appealing menu is reasonably priced and the specials varied (sweet and sour chicken, veal amandine, tournedos oscar and cream of eggplant soup one time we were there).

For lunch, we tried a fennel and gruyère quiche ($5.75) that was as tasty as it was generous, accompanied by a super-good spinach salad with a mustard dressing and homemade croutons. The mussels marinière ($6.75) arrived in a large glass bowl abrim with garlicky broth in which to dip chunks of the homemade rolls. The strawberry cheesecake for dessert was at least three inches high.

Dinner entrées run from $13.95 for pan-fried chicken with sundried tomato sauce to $18.95 for sirloin steak with cracked peppercorns. Possibilities include baked stuffed shrimp, roast duckling with raspberry glaze and New Zealand rack of lamb roasted in garlic and rosemary. Start with pesto-fried calamari, coconut shrimp or baba ghanoush. Finish with pecan pie, Indian pudding or a platter of biscotti.

Lunch, Monday-Saturday 11:30 to 3; dinner, 5 to 10 or 11; Sunday brunch, 11:30 to 4.

The Dolphin Striker, 15 Bow St., Portsmouth. (603) 431-5222.

Closed in a tax foreclosure in 1991, this riverfront landmark was reopened by new owners and quickly garnered a surprising number of culinary awards, including a tie with the late Strawbery Court for most elegant in the annual Seacoast Sunday reader poll.

Here the atmosphere is strictly historic, with bare sloping floors, beamed ceilings, flickering oil lamps and a sense of Colonial times in three dining rooms and the cozy, stone-walled tavern beneath. The white napkins on each table are folded to look like schooners.

Seafood is foremost, from baked fillet of haddock to salmon en papillote. Swordfish stuffed with leeks and mozzarella and lobster and scallop tortellinis topped with matchstick vegetables show that chef Ray Guerin knows what he's doing. Dinner entrées are priced from $11.95 for grilled chicken to $19.95 for grilled tenderloin glazed with goat cheese.

Haddock chowder and crabmeat-stuffed mushroom caps are popular starters, as is a smaller portion of the acclaimed lobster and scallop tortellinis. Desserts could be chocolate mousse en croûte, key lime pie, grand marnier soufflé or Irish whiskey cake.

A separate, light menu ($5.95 to $9.50) is served downstairs in the **Spring Hill Tavern.**

Lunch daily, 11:30 to 2; dinner, 5 to 9 or 10; Sunday brunch, noon to 4.

The Grotto, 75 Pleasant St., Portsmouth. (603) 436-1373.

This handsome, Mediterranean-style restaurant was opened in 1991 by the owners of the popular State Street Saloon. Known there for good Italian and Greek food at affordable prices in a crowded and casual atmosphere, Eli and Sharon Sokorelis moved across the street into vastly nicer quarters. They took their extensive menu with them, converting the saloon into a seafood bar and grill.

Stucco walls, a skylit ceiling with plants hanging from the beams, Mediterranean-style murals and sleek black chairs with upholstered seats at nicely spaced marble tables give a warm, inviting look. No reservations are taken and, arriving at 8 on a weeknight, we had to wait nearly half an hour for a table; some others opted to eat at the bar.

Dinner entrées run from $8.95 to $14.95, with nearly half under $10. One of us tried

Murals evoke warm Mediterranean feeling at The Grotto.

the State Street chicken ($9.95), a house specialty from the other restaurant. It was sautéed with artichoke hearts, prosciutto and pesto and smothered beneath a parmesan cheese sauce – very tasty but too heavily sauced and too much to eat; we also would have preferred it with rice instead of the side of spaghetti and tomato sauce. An excellent caesar salad ($3.25) preceded. Our other entrée was the Greek sampler ($11.95), which yielded a fine sausage, lamb and chicken kabob with a great marinade, a stuffed grape leaf and stuffed cabbage. The rice, potato, peas and lima beans in a tangy tomato sauce were a bit of overkill. A good Greek salad ($3.75) came first. Pleasant Frank Sinatra songs and a carafe of Folonari pinot grigio ($13) from a short wine list accompanied. With delicious chocolate grand marnier mousse and a lemon walnut tart, our bill was about half the cost of a regular dinner out.

Dinner nightly, 5 to 10.

The Metro, 20 High St., Portsmouth. (603) 436-0521.

Very popular locally is this art nouveau bar and cafe, decked out with brass rails, stained glass, old gas lights, mirrors and dark wood, leather banquettes, bentwood chairs and nifty Vanity Fair posters.

The Metro's award-winning clam chowder (which won first prize in a New England competition at Newport) is a popular starter among the appetizers, which have been updated lately from their traditional continental bent to include wild mushroom ravioli with herbs and roasted garlic and smoked brook trout with whole wheat toast points. Salads, sandwiches, fettuccine alfredo and such entrées as baked haddock with brandied pecans are offered at lunch.

Dinners start at $13.50 for baked lemon sole stuffed with mushroom duxelle or tomato-basil fettuccine tossed with grilled chicken and sundried tomatoes. Prices top off at $21.50 for rack of lamb. In between are items like seared Canadian salmon with lemon-caper beurre blanc, roast Long Island duckling with raspberry-port wine sauce and medallions of pork tenderloin with caramelized apples and bermuda onions, served over sweet potato ravioli. Desserts, attractively displayed on a fancy old baker's rack, include cappuccino crème caramel, pecan fudge pie and walnut cake.

Lunch, Monday-Friday 11:30 to 2:30; dinner, Monday-Saturday 5:30 to 9:30 or 10.

Anthony Alberto's, 59 Penhallow St., Portsmouth. (603) 436-4000.

New owners took over the old Anthony's Al Dente, a local institution hidden away in the Custom House Cellar. Tod Alberto and Massimo Morgia, who had been associated with the posh Ponte Vecchio in nearby Newcastle, renovated and reopened the space in late 1994 and named it after Tod's father.

The place is elegant, dark and grotto-like with stone and brick walls, arches, exposed beams on the ceiling and oriental rugs on the slate floors. Aqua upholstered chairs, mauve fanned napkins and white tablecloths add a Mediterranean look.

The menu (entrées, $14.95 to $21.95) is high Italian, as in grilled salmon with lentils, mushrooms and spinach served in a barbera wine sauce or grilled breast of duck in a raspberry and port wine demi-glace, served with a medley of spinach, roasted green apples and toasted pine nuts. Red snapper and vegetables might be baked in parchment paper and the veal sautéed with fontina, sundried tomatoes and artichokes. Eight pastas and risottos are available as appetizers or main dishes.

Expect such starters as grilled polenta with ragout of white mushrooms, grilled calamari stuffed with crabmeat and pistachio cream sauce, and a sampler of crostini misti. Desserts include bananas flambé, tirami su and crème caramel.

Dinner, Monday-Saturday 5 to 9:30 or 10:30, Sunday 4 to 8:30.

Karen's, 105 Daniel St., Portsmouth. (603) 431-1948.

Some of the most interesting dinners (to say nothing of breakfasts and lunches) in town are served by Karen Weiss and staff in this unassuming little place with bare floors, stenciled walls and a dozen or so tables flanked by windsor chairs.

The weekend dinners are exciting. How about this October menu that started with spicy crab cakes with mango mayonnaise or goat cheese rolled in black sesame seeds and served warm with crudités and french bread ($4.50 to $5.95)? Main courses included grilled swordfish with lime-ginger sauce, grilled Caribbean-spiced chicken with peanut sauce over pasta and lamb provençal baked in parchment. Prices start at $6.95 for three vegetarian dishes and top off at $10.95.

If you can't get in for dinner, settle for lunch, perhaps a hummus and vegetable salad plate, crab cakes, chicken fajitas, vegetarian burrito or blackened swordfish sandwich, $4.50 to $6.50. Karen's desserts are renowned; a strawberry-rhubarb pie was featured at one of our spring visits.

Breakfasts are memorable: five versions of scrambled eggs (the southwest scramble includes peppers, onion, cheddar cheese, sour cream, salsa and avocado), eggs sardou, buttermilk pancakes, french toast with Karen's cinnamon-raisin bread and homemade granola with fruit and yogurt. Splurge for eggs benedict ($5.95) or steak and eggs ($6.95).

Breakfast and lunch, Monday-Friday, 8 to 2; dinner, Thursday-Saturday 5:30 to 9:30 (also Wednesday in summer); weekend brunch, 8 to 2. Beer and wine license. No credit cards.

BG's Boat House Restaurant, 191 Wentworth Road, Portsmouth. (603) 431-1074.

If you're hankering for lobster and down-home surroundings, head for this popular little restaurant with outdoor decks and a marina out past the old Wentworth resort in Newcastle. Windows look onto what longtime owners Bruce and Joanne Graves say is Sagamore Creek; to us it looks more like an ocean inlet.

174

Statuary shimmers in dining room of Anthony Alberto's.

The walls are pine paneled, the floors bare and tables have captain's chairs and paper mats, the better for gorging oneself on a lobster dinner ($9.95), a lobster roll with french fries ($7.25), fried oysters ($12.95) or a seafood platter ($13.95). The lobsters are delivered to the back door by boat by BG's own lobstermen. The Graveses accommodate other tastes with BLT sandwiches, hamburgers, potato skins and mozzarella sticks, but most people go here for lobster and seafood, plain and simple.

Lunch, Monday-Friday 11 to 4; dinner nightly, 5 to 9. Closed Monday and Tuesday in spring and fall and December-February.

The Portsmouth Brewery, 56 Market St., Portsmouth. (603) 431-1115.

An award-winning restoration in 1991 turned this downtown building into a brewery with a bar and restaurant that packs in the locals day and night.

Sitting at booths or tables on one of several levels of a deep, high-ceilinged room full of brick, glass and mirrors, you can watch workmen pouring from 200-gallon tanks in the glass-walled brewery. You also can contemplate the incredible large wall collages designed by a friend of the owner. And you can sip some mighty good golden lager and pale ale from a choice of six brewed and sold on site for $2.75 a pint, $2.25 a glass. With them we enjoyed a chicken salad Santa Fe ($6.95), served in a tortilla shell, and an oversize sourdough sandwich of feta cheese, vegetables and black olive garlic spread ($5.50), served with corn chips and salsa. The extensive menu pairs American with Mexican, anything from a cajun swordfish sandwich to chicken fajitas. Dinner entrées run from $8.95 for vegetable stir-fry to $14.95 for tuna au poivre.

Although beer is the raison d'être, the food and ambiance receive high marks from a hip, young crowd. Owner Peter Egelston also runs the Northampton Brewery.

Lunch daily, 11:30 to 5; dinner, 5 to 11.

Cafe Brioche, 14 Market Square, Portsmouth. (603) 430-9225.

Lately expanded into an old stationery store and now twice its original size, Portsmouth's only sidewalk cafe in summer is a good place to stop anytime for a light breakfast like a ham and cheese croissant with cappuccino. It's also popular for lunch, with several kinds of quiche (ham and tomato, spinach and mushroom, $2.25 a slice), salads and great soups (caldo verde and curried crab bisque at our last visit). Sandwiches ($3.50 to $4) range from hummus to country pâté.

The cafe will put up box lunches (perhaps to take out to Newcastle?) for $6.50 to $9.50. The latter is for a rather elaborate one of brie in puff pastry, chilled chicken jardinière on spinach, Mediterranean rice salad, a baguette, fruit and sacher torte. Open daily 8 to 5 or 6, Friday to 9.

A few other good places for a snack: **Ceres Bakery** at 51 Penhallow St. offers wonderful breads and pastries. On a recent visit we saw a mushroom, havarti and dill quiche, tomato, mozzarella and green pepper quiche; mushroom and barley soup; pesto, onion and black olive pizza, and several sandwiches in the $4 range. Hermits go for 50 cents, and you can get cafe au lait and cappuccino. **Moe's Sandwich Shop** at 22 Daniel St. is famous for grinders; a regular half is $2, a super whole $3.75, and extras are 30 to 50 cents. **Izzy's** at 33 Bow St. is the place for frozen yogurt and specialty coffees. **Belle Peppers** at 41 Congress St. is a good deli-gourmet store with three little tables where you may eat in. Soups, salads, sandwiches, Jamaican patties and spring rolls are among the goodies, and you can get a picnic lunch here. We were intrigued by the boxes of chocolate-covered potato chips. Expected to open in 1995 was **Dunfey's Tugboat Restaurant** at Harbour Place Marina, on the Piscataqua River beneath the State Street bridge. Walter Dunfey of the Hampton-based Dunfey chain purchased the old John Wanamaker tugboat in Quincy and was planning a fine dining menu plus a snacky deck menu.

Diversions

Portsmouth offers much for anyone with an interest in history. The Greater Portsmouth Chamber of Commerce publishes a "Walking Tour of Downtown Portsmouth's Waterfront," which also can be driven (although directions get confusing because of one-way streets). The 2.3-mile tour takes in most of the city's attractions, including some we had passed for years unknowingly. Such is the charm of an area crammed with discoveries at every turn. A new way to tour is by horse and carriage with **Portsmouth Livery.** Talkative Ray Parker, in beard and top hat, adds dimension to the city's history as he gives sightseeing tours for $15 to $25, leaving from the Market Square carriage stand from noon into the evening, daily May-October.

Strawbery Banke, Marcy Street, Portsmouth, 433-1100. Billed as "an American original," this walk-through museum is the careful restoration of one of the nation's oldest neighborhoods. Its more than 40 structures date from 1695 to 1945 and depict four centuries of cultural and architectural change. Some have simply been preserved; some are used by working artisans (independent of the museum, they are earning their living as well as re-enacting history); others are used for educational exhibits including archaeology, architectural styles and construction techniques and, on the outside, historic gardens. Strawbery Banke's collection of local arts and furniture is shown in six historic houses. Significantly, these are not all homes of the rich or famous, but rather of ordinary people. As the museum's 25th anniversary program noted, "This is the real story of history – the dreams and aspirations, the disappointments and frustrations of common people." That is the glory of Strawbery Banke, and of much of Portsmouth. Open daily 10 to 5, May-October; also evening candlelight stroll, first two weekends in December. Adults, $10.

The Portsmouth Trail. Six of Portsmouth's finest house museums are open individually and linked by a walking tour. Considered the one not to miss is the 1763 **Moffatt-Ladd House,** a replica of an English manor house located just above Ceres Street restaurants and shops. The yellow 1758 **John Paul Jones House** and the imposing **Governor John Langdon House** (1784) are others.

Shopping. Most of the traditional tourist shopping attractions have passed Portsmouth by, heading for the upscale outlet strip along Route 1 north of Kittery or the shopping malls of Newington. But downtown Portsmouth has plenty of interesting shops concentrated around Market Square.

In one of its five stores, the expanding **Macro Polo Inc.** has inventive children's toys; we were transported back to our childhood while gazing at the assortment of marbles in the window. Next door, **Macro World** is full of ecologically correct gifts; **Wholly Macro!** stocks handmade Texas boots among its wares. **Macroscopic** struck us as rather New Agey. Everything at **City & Country** is good looking, from glassware and cutlery to furniture and things to streamline your closet and make one better organized. **Not Just Mud! Craft Gallery** stocks great hand-blown art glass, kaleidoscopes, pottery, jewelry and titanium clocks among its contemporary crafts. **Gallery 33** at Ceres and Bow streets has some of the wildest jewelry we've seen. The **Paper Patch** is the shop for cards. **Bow Street Candle and Mug** is room after room of – you guessed it – but also has a section called **Southwest Passage** where you'll find things with the Santa Fe look. We liked the spoon wind chimes and the quilts at **Tulips. Worldly Goods** purveys birdhouses, oil lamps, interesting baskets and adorable cat pins, and **Portsmouth Candle Co.** has great mugs with animal handles, as well as pretty candles. **Treehouse Toys** had a neat stuffed giraffe in the window. **Jus' Lookin** carries darling children's clothes, as does **G. Willikers!**

Among its treasures, **Les Cadeaux** stocks exotic bath salts, fancy stationery, boxes of decorated sugar cubes from Kentucky, chocolate spoons to dip in hot chocolate, lovely china casseroles with different fruits on top for handles, and preserves and mustards from Le Cordon Bleu in France. You'd have to see them to believe the high-heeled shoes made of papier-mâché and trimmed with jewelry at **Gallery 33;** we also liked the hand-carved whimsical animals here. The **Little Timber Nature Store** is a fun place to browse: the bonsai is incredible and we liked the T-shirts and baseball caps adorned with fireflies. The **Ceres Trunk Shop** is known for antique jewelry as well as refinished trunks. Wearing a T-shirt urging "squeeze me, crush me, make me wine," jovial proprietor David Campbell brings a sense of fun along with expertise to his wines, specialty foods and gift baskets at the **Ceres Street Wine Merchants.** We did some Christmas shopping at the **N.W. Barrett Gallery**, which has some of Sabra Field's woodcuts and fantastic jewelry. Strawbery **Banke's Museum Shop** at the Dunaway Store on Marcy Street is a classy gift shop. **Strawbery Banke's** working crafts shops offer the wares of potters, a cabinetmaker, a weaver, and dories made in the boat shed.

Extra-Special _____

Newcastle. Drive or bicycle out Newcastle Avenue (Route 1B) through the quaint islands of Newcastle, the original settlement in 1623, dotted with prosperous homes. The meandering roads and treed residential properties, many with water views, mix contemporary-style houses with those of days gone by. You can view Fort Constitution with one of several towers built during the War of 1812 and visit the new seacoast park at **Great Island Common,** where there are a playground, waterfront picnic tables and views of the Isles of Shoals. Take a gander at the old Wentworth-by-the-Sea, a majestic resort hotel if ever there was one; its golf course has been sold to make way for expensive houses. Another rewarding drive is out Maine Route 103 past the Naval Yards in Kittery to Kittery Point, where attractive houses large and small seem to be surrounded by water on all sides.

The ocean lies just beyond guest rooms at Stage Neck Inn in York Harbor.

The Yorks

Great Gateway to Maine

The visitor quickly agrees with what the Chamber of Commerce directory proudly proclaims: "The Yorks are a perfect introduction to Maine. They have everything for which the Great State is famous: rocky coast, sandy beaches, a lighthouse, a mountain, rivers,...lobsters, folks who really do say 'ayuh.'"

The focal point of the Yorks is, of course, the water – specifically, the harbor where the river confronts the sea. From fashionable York Harbor, whose waters are as protected as its seaside homes, it's barely a mile inland along the York River to historic York Village, the oldest surviving English settlement in Maine. From the harbor, it's also barely a mile along the shore to York Beach. Abruptly, the rocky coast yields to sand. Trailer parks symbolize the transition from tree-shaded affluence to honky-tonk strand.

Beyond are Nubble Light, one of America's most photographed lighthouses, and Cape Neddick Harbor, a quieter and quainter fishing site. Sand gives way again to rocks as Bald Head Cliff rises off the forested Shore Road near the Ogunquit town line.

Yes, the Yorks provide a good introduction to Maine, from the Cape Neddick fishermen to the amusement areas at crowded York Beach.

But much of the appeal of the Yorks lies elsewhere. It's in York Village, where a national historic district embraces both private structures and eight house museums and inspires the slogan, "Where Maine's History Begins." It's in York Harbor, a verdant enclave of Colonial homesteads and gracious estates whose occupants in 1892 formed the York Harbor Reading Room men's club, an offshoot of which was the York Harbor Village Corporation. It established the first zoning laws in Maine and prevented the hordes and development of York Beach from spilling into York Harbor.

Growing numbers of inns are concentrated in York Village and York Harbor, allowing visitors to partake of private places in which past melds into present.

178

Inn Spots

Stage Neck Inn, Off Route 1A, Box 97, York Harbor 03911. (207) 363-3850 or (800) 222-3238.

Once an island and now a promontory where the York River becomes a harbor, Stage Neck was the site of the Marshall House, the first of the area's resort hotels. It was razed and rebuilt in 1973 as the Stage Neck Inn, a low-profile contemporary resort whose understated luxury fits the setting.

Disproportionate numbers of Cadillacs are in the parking lot, hinting of the clientele for whom Stage Neck is designed. There are tennis courts, a swimming pool and private beach, an indoor pool and jacuzzi, golf privileges, posh public rooms with water views, and a gorgeous dining room in which the traditional jacket requirement has given way to "proper dress" for dinner.

There also are water views from the private patios or balconies of 60 guest rooms on three floors. The building was designed into the landscape and opens on three sides to ocean, river and beach. Guest rooms are comfortably furnished in restful shades of deep rose and moss green, with twins, two doubles or kingsize beds, two comfortable chairs and a table, color TV and phone. Rates vary with the view. The most choice are corner rooms with wraparound porches and views of the water in two directions.

Three meals a day are served in the grill or the main dining room (see Dining Spots). The inn is now open year-round, and offers good package plans in the winter.

Doubles, $150 to $205, EP. No smoking.

Wooden Goose Inn, Route 1, Cape Neddick 03902. (207) 363-5673.

Tantalizing aromas and spirited classical music greet visitors to the Wooden Goose Inn. The aromas come from the kitchen, where innkeepers Jerry Rippletoe and Tony Sienicki take turns baking their specialties, perhaps a flourless chocolate torte for afternoon tea or date bread for breakfast. The music comes from myriad speakers, which send Mozart and Vivaldi across the house.

This is one decorated inn, from its Terrace Room breakfast area and two comfy parlors to the six guest rooms. All would do any house and garden magazine proud. Jerry was a decorator in New York and New Jersey before he and Tony acquired the derelict house in 1984; he still commutes to the metropolitan area for consulting jobs. Lately they bought 750 yards of fabric to redo three bedrooms and learned to use a sewing machine when they found it would cost $11,000 to have done what they wanted. Their do-it-yourself window treatments, billowing canopies and coordinated pillows

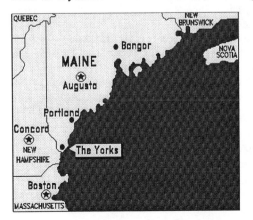

are remarkable. So are the decorative birdhouses that Tony builds and displays around the house. They're for sale at up to $350 each. Guests had purchased three the weekend before our latest visit.

As befits the inn's name, geese and ducks are everywhere – even on the white-lit Christmas tree during the holiday season. Many are gifts from guests.

The rooms have been sumptuously outfitted with Victorian country furnishings in a masculine style and the walls are hung with many

179

paintings. Each air-conditioned room has a queensize bed, private bath and a sitting area. Blinds are down and curtains drawn to screen out distractions from the road outside. There are bedside lights for reading, and the setting epitomizes escape and romance. "The room is the important part of the stay," contends Jerry. "We try to provide a tranquil, peaceful house." He keeps his charges well fed. Afternoon tea is taken in the rear Terrace Room or outside in lush gardens around a trickling pond bordered by rocks. Eleven varieties of tea are offered, and come with pâtés on toast rounds and a choice of desserts, perhaps a tart of Granny Smith apples and lemons, a butter pecan cheesecake or other fancy desserts prepared by Tony.

Breakfasts are sumptuous as well. The day begins with coffee on a silver tray outside your room at 8 o'clock. Fresh juice and homemade baked goods precede such fruit courses as strawberries romanoff or peach and cherry soup. Then comes the pièce de résistance: eggs oscar, hard-boiled eggs with shrimp and creamy dill sauce, or baked egg in puff pastry on smoked Canadian bacon with hollandaise sauce, garnished with pimento and black olives. Recent dishes have included shepherds pie made with chicken instead of lamb, topped with cheddar cheese and mashed potatoes, country French chicken with a poached egg encased in puff pastry, and haddock sautéed in brandy with honey and apples, served with thyme-roasted potatoes and garlic-fried broccoli. "People sometimes remark how nice it is to have dinner for breakfast," says Tony. After all this, he concedes, you might need to go back to your bedroom for a snooze.

Doubles, $110. Closed in January.

Dockside Guest Quarters, Harris Island, Box 205, York 03909. (207) 363-2868 or (800) 270-1977.

Just across the river from Stage Neck on a peninsula unto itself is the Dockside, which 40 years ago began taking in boaters in the handsome late 19th-century white homestead. Owners David and Harriette Lusty enjoyed innkeeping so much they added the Crow's Nest with an apartment and two studios on the water, then built the Quarterdeck cottages, and finally added the contemporary Lookout on the hill. They retain the name "guest quarters" (which is something of a misnomer), such is the tradition of this place.

The lovely grounds lead to water's edge and are dotted with lawn chairs, flower gardens and picket fences.

The day's tides are posted on the blackboard in the Maine House, where the dining room and parlor are furnished with antiques, marine paintings and models of ships, and the rambling wraparound porch opens to sea views. Scrapbooks full of pictures of inn guests are displayed on a coffee table. There's a TV set in the parlor, and a table holds tea bags and apples for afternoon snacks.

The house has five guest rooms, ranging from two twin rooms sharing a bath to a studio sleeping two to four. The front corner room is the choice of many, with its full-length porch from which to view the buoys bobbing in the harbor.

The three multi-unit cottage buildings scattered around the property hold twin or double bedrooms, studios, an efficiency and apartment suites for two to four. Each has a porch or deck with a view out the harbor entrance to the ocean. You can't get much closer to the water than the balconies in the Crow's Nest, but some prefer the wider decks of the Lookout, higher up on the lawn. All told, there are 22 units. We reveled in the waterside setting of a Crow's Nest studio, complete with kingsize bed with floral spread and matching pillows and shams, two chairs, good reading lights, a small color TV, light colors and french doors onto a balcony beside the water. Very private and comfortable, it was the kind of "guest quarters" we wish we could buy for our very own in coastal Maine.

Elegant furnishings enhance guest bedroom and parlor at Wooden Goose Inn.

Son Eric Lusty and his wife Carol have infused new enthusiasm and creature comforts into Dockside. They planned to add another building with four more rooms, two with fireplaces. They also have decided to keep the Maine House and Crow's Nest open weekends in winter.

A continental-plus breakfast buffet featuring fresh fruit and just-baked muffins is offered in the dining room for $3. Lunch and dinner are available next door at The Restaurant at Dockside Guest Quarters (see Dining Spots).

Doubles, $60 to $98.50; studios, $102 to $114; apartment suites, $143 to $147. Two-night minimum in season.

York Harbor Inn, Route 1A, Box 573, York Harbor 03911. (207) 363-5119 or (800) 343-3869.

A history dating back to 1637 and a family's labor of love. That's the story of this busy turn-of-the-century inn restored by twin brothers Joe and George Dominguez, their younger brother Garry and Joe's wife Jean.

Listed in the National Register of Historic Places and built around a 1637 post-and-beam sail loft that was moved to the site and now serves as a common room, the 32-room inn once was headquarters for the York Harbor Reading Club, which continues to this day. The Dominguez brothers, all graduates of Colgate University, spent a year and a half restoring the inn, and are still adding and upgrading. In 1994 they redid three larger rooms with solid cherry furniture, queensize four-poster beds, color TVs and jacuzzi tubs. Except for the fifteen newer rooms, this is an old-fashioned, full-service inn with a character you sense immediately when you enter the main Cabin Lounge, its pitched ceiling (the former sail loft) now covered with tiny white Christmas bulbs lit all year. The dark, English-style Wine Cellar Pub Grill with a long solid cherry bar and lots of sofas clustered around the corner fireplace offers frequent entertainment, and the dining rooms serve three meals a day (see Dining Spots).

All but five of the oldest rooms in the main inn have private baths, and all but the three newest and a suite have one or two double beds. Eaves and dormers contribute to interesting shapes, nooks and crannies in many rooms. They are nicely furnished with such touches as white wicker headboards and rocking chairs, pink puffy quilts, good-looking prints and perhaps a writing desk. One room has a four-poster bed, white frilly curtains, oriental rug and towels stashed in an antique crib. Seven have fireplaces. A deluxe suite includes a kingsize bed and a whirlpool tub.

In the newer Yorkshire House adjacent, a large front room has an oak bed, a working fireplace and a case full of books. From most rooms you can hear the ocean rolling up against the inn's beach beneath the Marginal Way across the street.

Guests are served a continental breakfast of fresh fruit, cereals, yogurt and homemade pastries and muffins.

Doubles, $89 to $129; suite, $149.

Edwards' Harborside Inn, Stage Neck Road, Box 866, York Harbor 03911. (207) 363-3037 or (800) 273-2686.

An inn with a grand location at the entrance to Stage Neck, "where harbor and ocean meet," this three-story, turn-of-the-century residence has been renovated by owner Jay Edwards. A Portsmouth auto dealer and third-generation innkeeper, he says he jumped at the chance of acquiring what he thinks is "the prettiest place in the world."

The property faces water on three sides, has its own long wharf (from which Jay has been known to take guests on his boat for whale-watching or moonlight cruises) and a crescent beach beyond the lawn.

All ten bedrooms have air-conditioning and television and most have queen or kingsize beds and a view of harbor or ocean – or both. Friends who stayed in the second-floor York Suite with water views on three sides felt as if they were on a yacht. The suite is a beauty: a queensize bed, a sofabed against one picture window, two Queen Anne chairs, blue carpeting, colorful floral wallpaper and an enormous blue bathroom with a tub, shower, double sink and what Jay says is "the only potted bidet on the East Coast" (a plant sprouts from inside). A tiled spa in the suite's entry overlooks the harbor. Other rooms are of different sizes and shapes. Eight have private baths.

The Bay View Room on the main floor is a living room in the off-season. It's richly furnished with a plush white sofa, chairs and red patterned rugs, and sherry is available for guests on the sideboard. In the summer it's rented as part of a suite connecting with the adjacent bedroom. A lobby area contains books and games. A continental breakfast buffet is put out on the sun porch. Expect several kinds of juice, fruits, cereals and homemade muffins, breads and bagels.

Doubles, $105 to $150; suites, $170 to $220. No smoking.

Hutchins House, 209 Organug Road, York 03909. (207) 363-3058.

This handsome manse in a quiet area of substantial homes beside the York River was converted into a B&B by Melinda Hutchins, whose six children had left the hearth.

The common areas are a delight. There's a long, airy sun porch full of wicker with wonderful views of the river at the rear of the house. It's decorated in blues and whites with a collection of willowware, a TV and VCR, and books and games. A sun deck off it has a jacuzzi underneath. A formal living room with a restored baby grand player piano resounds upon occasion with classical scores. The focal point of the dining room is a spectacular indoor water garden built around a collection of wooden bird carvings. The large back yard is a great place for lounging and watching the placid tidal river.

Upstairs are three guest rooms with private baths and river views. A favorite contains a queensize four-poster bed with mounds of down pillows and is decorated in Laura Ashley pinks and whites.

Edwards' Harborside Inn has own wharf where harbor meets ocean.

Melinda, an outgoing woman who loves to cook, serves a full breakfast on the sun porch. The fare includes fresh fruits, homemade breads and perhaps eggs benedict, blueberry pancakes or shirred eggs. The hostess, who has skippered and cooked on a 50-foot charter sailboat, offers canoes and rowboats for rent. Lately her interest has turned to kripalu massage, and she does massage therapy here by appointment.

Melinda is proud that hers is the only B&B in the historic district. "We're small enough to be family," she says, "but the house is so large there's a lot of peace and quiet." It's refined and formal, and the only one we've encountered where a sign advises: "Please ring doorbell and await your host. No unannounced entries, please."

Doubles, $85 to $89; suite, $130. Open weekends only, November-April. No smoking.

Riverbank On the Harbor, 11 Harmon Park Road, Box 1102, York Harbor 03911. (207) 363-8333.

Ice damage from the hard winter of 1994 was a blow to owner Marie Feuer after part of the second floor of her family's home of eight years collapsed onto the first floor. But she and her husband rebuilt and redecorated their century-old house, and guests in the five upstairs bedrooms are the beneficiaries of all new furnishings.

They are also the beneficiaries of some great water views, best enjoyed from the broad rear porch perched on a river bank above the harbor. Along with an abundance of chairs and loungers, the porch contains an ice chest that guests find handy during happy hour. The porch is reached from a wonderful, long living room/dining room with large windows onto the harbor scene. It's pleasantly furnished in contemporary style with oriental rugs, oriental prints and screens, and maritime paintings done by Marie's uncle. The dining end is the setting for a full breakfast buffet, which includes fruit, cereal, muffins, danish pastries and perhaps omelets or quiche, accompanied by a signature maple syrup sausage. Sherry and chocolates are put out at 4.

Upstairs are five guest rooms with kingsize beds. The only shortcoming is the bath configuration. The front Garden Room enjoys a private bath, and the Sunset Room with a water bed has its own marble bath in the hall. The other three bedrooms, including the prime waterfront Harbor and Balcony rooms, share a large bath and a half bath. Rooms are bright and cheery with thick carpeting and designer bedspreads or duvets.

You probably will not spend much time in your room here, given the common areas inside and out. All you need to do is to step off the back porch and descend the stairs to the shore to hook up with the Captain's Walk, a scenic path that runs along the harbor from Edwards' Harborside Inn to the Hutchins House.

Doubles, $100 to $150. No smoking.

RiverMere, 45 Varrell Lane, Box 141, York Harbor 03911. (207) 363-5470.

Gourmet breakfasts, harbor views, wondrous gardens and artistic floral arrangements are the hallmarks of this small new B&B, opened by Brian and Paulette Chernack after their second floor became vacant when their daughter went off to college.

The breakfasts are something else, prepared in a kitchen open to the living room and served on the side deck or in the sun room. The latter, a plant-filled aerie outfitted with a comfy sofa and lots of wicker, affords a head-on view of the harbor. Here you might enjoy fresh raspberries from the garden, baked eggs and homemade scones, as we did at a mid-October visit. Brian proved himself to be quite the breakfast cook, and we particularly liked his elder-plum jelly, one of the preserves he and Paulette make from six kinds of berries they grow in their exotic gardens. Other breakfast treats could be a clafouti filled with fruit, belgian waffles, omelets or french toast.

Upstairs on the second floor is a double-bedded room with private hall bath, a settee that folds into a single bed and a corner fireplace. The premier lodging takes up the entire third floor. On one side of the staircase is a library and sitting room with a single wing chair. The bedroom holds a queensize brass bed, wicker chairs, a settee and, as is the case throughout the house, a lot to look at (actress Jane Seymour wore the white dress displayed in the corner in a movie). You get a distant view of the ocean from the window above the bed, although most guests are content with the wide-angle view of the harbor through the side windows. A spice rack in the bathroom holds all manner of soaps and perfumes that the Chernacks have picked up on their travels.

Artistic touches abound, reflecting the talents of Paulette, who is cultural coordinator for the local school district. Splashy dried plants, wreaths and collections make the entry foyer look like a gift shop. Brian's artistic talents are evident in the front and side vegetable and flower gardens. We could spend hours here marveling at their varied output and getting ideas to try at home.

Doubles, $65 and $90. No smoking.

Inn at Harmon Park, 415 York St., York Harbor 03911. (207) 363-2031.

Maine artists and books are well represented in this homey inn run with TLC by energetic Sue Antal, a font of local lore. Her 1899 Victorian home at the corner of Harmon Park Road comes with a wide front porch, a fireplaced parlor, an open kitchen that seems to be the heart of the house and five guest rooms, three with private baths. The B&B is known for good value.

The second floor holds two large bedrooms with private baths and wicker furniture: the Georgeanna with a queen bed and a plush sofa facing the fireplace and the Blue Heron with a king bed and a clawfoot tub with sitdown hand-held shower. Two other small rooms with double beds, one with a glimpse of the harbor down the street, share a bath. The main floor also has a bedroom with a double bed and a private bath reached through the kitchen. All rooms are appointed with lovely quilts and comforters.

Sue compensates at breakfast for "not being on the water." Apple-blueberry crisp was the main course the morning of our visit; belgian waffles with blueberry sauce were on tap the next day. Other treats include apple torte, baked french toast, apple-cinnamon quiche and several potato dishes, since Sue doesn't serve breakfast meats. The meal is taken on a pleasant little sun porch.

184

Water is on view from back porch at Riverbank On the Harbor.

Sue, who has been innkeeping since 1983, obviously subscribes to the slogan we spotted in her kitchen: "Enjoy life – this is not a dress rehearsal."

Doubles, $59 to $79.

The Canterbury House, 432 York St., Box 881, York Harbor 03911. (207) 363-3505.

A compact, unassuming white house in the heart of York Harbor holds seven guest rooms with private and shared baths. It's owned by James Pappas, who ran the now-defunct York Harbor Chowder House and an adjacent market across the street.

The common rooms are beautifully decorated, the living room with bleached maple floors and chintz sofas in shades of pinks and blues, and a formal rear dining room with silver candelabra, a crystal chandelier and a cherry table set with Royal Albert china, silver and linen napkins. A charming breakfast room at the side of the house is where a complimentary continental breakfast is served; for an extra $10 a couple, you have a choice of things like eggs Canterbury (eggs benedict with the addition of spinach or asparagus), scrambled eggs with homefries and biscuits, or belgian waffles. Afternoon tea, with scones, clotted cream and black currant jelly or maybe quiche or cucumber sandwiches with nasturtium blossoms, is taken in the living room or on the wicker-filled front porch. Dinners are served as part of special packages on holiday weekends.

Up a stairwell of pecan wood are guest rooms on two floors in a variety of bed configurations. One room with a double bed has a new private bath; another new bath is private for a suite with queen bed and TV/VCR. The other five rooms share two baths. Among them is James's favorite Iris Room, with a double and single, light and airy with irises on the comforters and linens. All the rooms have striking colors and abundant plants.

Doubles, $65 to $85 with continental breakfast, $75 to $95 with full breakfast; suite, $110 or $120.

Dining Spots

Cape Neddick Inn, Route 1 at Route 1A, Cape Neddick. (207) 363-2899.

This interesting combination of restaurant and art gallery reflects one of the more artistic settings and one of the more creative menus for dining along the southern Maine coast. On two levels, the dining room has windsor chairs at nicely spaced tables covered with beige cloths, mismatched china, glass candlesticks, rose napkins and cobalt blue water glasses. Potted palms, flowers in vases, fancy screens, paintings and sculptures emphasize the feeling of dining in a gallery (the artworks are for sale).

A huge fieldstone fireplace, a collection of baskets, art books to read and a cherry bar enhance a smaller dining room, the perfect spot for enjoying the new "light side" menu ($9 to $12 for treats like chicken and vegetable pot pie or lobster ravioli on wilted greens with lemon butter and pine nuts). Owners Pamela Wallis and Glenn Gobeille change their menu every six weeks. Both the dinner and light side menus are available in either room and are perfect for devotees of mix and match.

Soups ($3) might be lamb broth with roasted vegetables, roasted garlic, cauliflower-fennel or cream of potato and leek. Appetizers ($5 to $8) at one visit included pâté de foie gras, grilled shrimp with jalapeño sauce, chilled smoked salmon with chèvre and an extraordinary macadamia-lobster tart served on mushroom duxelles.

Entrées are priced from $16 for pork tenderloin sautéed with apricots in maple sweet and sour glaze to $23 for châteaubriand on an herbed french toast crouton with roast garlic brown sauce. We passed up one of the night's specials of swordfish grilled with ginger and gin for a fantastic special of fettuccine with chicken breast and a Korean-style lamb kabob on rice with sesame sauce and a spicy vegetable relish. Served on large oval plates, the entrées came with glazed parsnips, broccoli and yellow beans. A complimentary plate of raw vegetables with dip accompanied drinks. It was followed by salads swathed in warm creamy bacon or cucumber-dill dressings.

"Don't forget dessert," the menu correctly urges. Choices range widely from tortes and tarts to chocolate confections from a repertoire of more than 500 developed over the years. We were too full to sample the chocolate grand marnier torte or the kahlua cheesecake and requested a doggy bag for our leftover pasta, which provided a delicious supper at home the next evening.

Dinner nightly in summer, 6 to 9, Wednesday-Sunday in winter; Sunday brunch, noon to 3, mid-October to May.

The Restaurant at Dockside Guest Quarters, Harris Island, York. (207) 363-2722.

Overlooking the harbor next to the Lusty family's Dockside Guest Quarters, this gray-shingled structure houses an airy dining room on two levels, several round tables on the porch screened from floor to ceiling and an outdoor dining deck from which you're apt to spot cormorants, blue herons and seals. The restaurant is run by Philip Lusty, who had been a catering director at the Crowne Plaza Hotel in White Plains, N.Y., and his wife Anne.

The Lusty family and staff made the striking tables inlaid with nautical charts and topped by blue mats. Nautical pieces on shelves and colored glassware in the windows provide accents for the decor, which is secondary to the water view.

It's an especially fine setting for lunch. For $5.95 to $10.50, you can get broiled scrod, fried scallops, English-style fish and chips, grilled chicken caesar salad, lobster croissant and seafood cobb salad. Most are accompanied by crudités and dip, mini-loaves of fresh bread and the "salad deck" – items from a salad bar set in an old boat.

The same appetizers are offered at lunch and dinner, among them onion soup gratinée, gravlax, a trio of raviolis, duck liver pâté and seafood tostada. Dinner entrées run from

Dining tables are right beside the water at Restaurant at Dockside Guest Quarters.

$10.95 for broiled scrod to $17.95 for a fisherman's platter. Favorites are the roast stuffed duckling with orange-sherry glaze, baked haddock with a crab soufflé, salmon fillet baked with basil and bacon, grilled swordfish served on a bed of fried spinach and finished with a strawberry salsa, chicken gai yang, braised lamb shanks and steak teriyaki. Anne Lusty is responsible for such desserts as bread pudding, apple crisp, key lime pie and a terrine of chocolate and pistachio ice cream with raspberry crème anglaise.

Lunch, 11:30 to 2; dinner, 5:30 to 9. Closed Mondays, also Columbus Day to Memorial Day.

York Harbor Inn, Route 1A, York Harbor. (207) 363-5119.

From their hilltop perch, three of the four charming dining rooms here look onto (and catch the salty breeze from) the ocean across the street. One room, the main Cabin Loft lobby with fireplace, is used in winter. Another is an enclosed porch, and a third beamed room looks like a pub.

Mismatched chairs, small paned windows, blue and white plates displayed below the beamed ceiling, rose-colored napkins shaped like swans, small oil lamps and sloping floors convey an old-fashioned feeling.

Veteran chef Gerry Bonsey's continental/New England menu is priced at dinner from $14.95 for medallions of turkey breast served with grilled red and green peppers to $23.95 for baked stuffed lobster. Angel-hair pasta with shrimp and scallops, baked stuffed haddock and chicken cordon bleu are signature dishes. The recipe for veal Swiss was requested by Gourmet magazine.

Among appetizers ($5.50 to $6.95) are mussels provençal, Maine crab cakes, grilled cilantro chicken and grilled brie with French bread. Brie cheese soup is another popular starter.

Special desserts include a chilled lemon-caramel soufflé, homemade maple-bread pudding and strawberry shortcake. The well-chosen wine list is fairly priced.

Soups, salads, sandwiches and a few entrées are listed on an extensive luncheon menu. A bar menu is offered in the cozy cellar pub.

Lunch, Monday-Friday 11:30 to 2:30; dinner nightly, 5:30 to 9:30; Sunday brunch, 10:30 to 2:30.

Stage Neck Inn, Off Route 1A, York Harbor. (207) 363-3850.

Meals in the elegant, chandeliered Fort Point dining room with floor-to-ceiling water views from windows on three sides are what some consider special-occasion deals. In shades of beige and peach, the spacious room is restful with upholstered high-back chairs and swagged balloon draperies.

The extensive dinner menu embraces American and continental fare. Appetizers are priced from $3.25 for fresh fruit medley with cottage cheese or sherbet to $6.95 for shrimp cocktail or blackened Maine crab cakes with spicy rémoulade sauce. Entrées ($14.95 to $18.95) run the gamut from boiled lobster to New York sirloin with sherried mushroom caps. Seafood fettuccine, grilled salmon with snap peas, sea scallops sautéed with sundried tomatoes, duckling with raspberry sauce, veal oscar and pepper-crusted pork with a course-grain mustard sauce are possibilities.

Locals are partial to dinner in the **Sandpiper Bar & Grille,** which is bright and cheery in raspberry colors, with upholstered chairs at well-spaced tables and views of the water, and on the canopied outdoor deck beside. The extensive all-day menu offers pizzas, sandwiches and entrées from $7.25 to $13.95.

Dinner nightly, 6 to 9 or 10; Sunday brunch, noon to 2. Grill open daily, noon to 9.

Fazio's, 38 Woodbridge Road, York. (207) 363-7019.

Started as a neighborhood storefront restaurant in a shopping plaza, Annette Fazio's expanding enterprise recently moved into a former lumber shed and it's quite a place. The main entrance is in the rear past an awninged courtyard that's popular for summer dining. Inside are a bar/lounge with Italian murals and an attractive dining room with booths and banquettes around the perimeter and tables covered with pinkish oilcloths. Not to mention the casual La Stalla Pizzeria at the side, or the function rooms upstairs.

The main dining room is immensely popular with the locals, although rather brighly illuminated for our tastes. We were well satisfied with the chicken française and the seafood tecchia, accompanied by good house salads with blue cheese or raspberry vinaigrette dressings and a $14 bottle of Murphy-Goode fumé blanc. The prices certainly are right: any number of "neighborhood favorites" for $7.95 and $8.95 and complete dinners for $12.50. Many items are available in light portions, and nobody goes away hungry. The pastas are homemade, and the kitchen knows what it's doing.

Besides the predictable Italian fare ($9.95 to $13.95), there are interesting specials – at our visit, grilled swordfish with red pepper vinaigrette and roasted garlic aioli, served with garlic-herb risotto and tomatoes provençal; grilled lamb medallions with a sweet red pepper sauce, teamed with mashed potatoes and broccoli with garlic, and grilled beef tenderloin with a horseradish-dijon demi-glace, served with oven-roasted herb potatoes and a mushroom-onion compote. Such treats hint of the special wine-tasting dinners that Fazio's stages periodically in the off-season.

La Stalla Pizzeria offers pizzas, subs and salads daily from 11 a.m.

Dinner nightly, 4 to 9 or 10.

Frankie & Johnny's, 1594 Route 1 North, Cape Neddick. (207) 363-1909.

"Food that loves you back" is the hallmark of this new gourmet natural-foods restaurant. It isn't much to look at – a manufactured home beside the highway, painted with colorful triangles and sporting a Haagen-Dazs sign in front. But stop and venture in for a healthful meal at unbelievably low prices, either inside in a whimsical dining room, outside at a couple of picnic tables or to go.

Personable Frank Rostad handles the front of the house while partner John Shaw cooks in a state-of-the-art kitchen. Everything here is made from scratch and almost all of it on site, say these purists (it took them fourteen months to find an all-natural cone to serve with their Haagen-Dazs ice cream). They even squeeze juices at their juice bar.

The soups could be vegetarian or vegan (dairy-free). Six salads ($4.75 to $6.75) range from tabbouleh and hummus to grilled or blackened chicken on assorted greens. Favorites among entrées ($7.75 to $9.75) are poached or blackened Atlantic salmon and blackened chicken served over sweet and sour cabbage with potatoes and feta cheese. Sweet endings could be fresh peach pie with a crunchy streusel topping or whole wheat honey cake.

The place is best known for its trademarked crustolis ($8.50), ten-inch-round French bread crusts made from unbleached flour and not unlike pizzas. For dinner, we ordered one with shrimp, pesto and goat cheese and another with capers, olives, red onions and feta cheese, split a house salad and had more than enough left over for lunch the next day.

Dinner is by candlelight and the food is fairly serious, but it's dispensed in a relaxed and playful environment. Decor in the pine-paneled room is nil except for a few abstract oils by Frank's sister at one end and a handful of rocks and perhaps a miniature dinosaur on each table. "It's hard to take yourself seriously with rocks and a little dinosaur in front of you," says Frank, whose aim is to help customers enjoy healthful food and have a good time.

Open in summer, Monday-Saturday noon to 9, Sunday 2 to 8; closed Monday-Wednesday in off-season and Dec. 21 through March. BYOB. No smoking.

Diversions

Beaches. Inn guests probably will be grateful for the peace and quiet of the inn grounds and sheltered beaches. Or you may be as lucky as we were and find a parking spot and place at Harbor Beach, next to a private club. But if you want surf, join the throngs on Long Sands Beach, one of Maine's sandiest and deservedly crowded. It was a refreshing oasis on one unforgettable 100-degree day when we and everyone else placed our sand chairs in the ocean and lounged in the water trying to keep cool. If there's not enough action on the beach, surely there is in the amusement area of downtown York Beach. On past Short Sands Beach at Cape Neddick Harbor is a sheltered beach good for children.

Nubble Light. Don't miss the landmark Cape Neddick Lighthouse on the nubble separating Long Sands and Short Sands beaches. From the bluffs you can see up and down the coast and out to Boon Island and the Isles of Shoals off Portsmouth. Along Nubble Road you'll pass tiny cottages and institutions like Fox's Lobster House and Brown's Old-Fashioned Ice Cream ("We make our own"). Another spectacular view is from Bald Head Cliff off Shore Road.

Not far inland is 673-foot-high **Mount Agamenticus,** a landmark for sailors and the highest spot on the southern Maine coast. You can drive up a paved road or hike a steep but pleasant, .8-mile trail to the top for a panoramic view of the area. The York recreation department operates a saddle horse livery stable offering scenic trail rides at the summit. You also can rent mountain bikes there.

Marginal Way. A three-mile walk along the ocean between shore and homes begins at Harbor Beach and extends to Nubble Light. It's more rugged than nearby Ogunquit's better known Marginal Way, but well worth the effort for the views and the natural landscaping (wild roses, bayberry, blueberries and ground juniper).

The York Historic District. The history of the first chartered English city in North America (a refuge for early Puritan settlers from Massachusetts) is on display in York Village. The Chamber of Commerce has an excellent brochure detailing walking and driving tours. The **Old York Historical Society** in the historic George Marshall Store at 140 Lindsay Road, 363-4974, offers guided tours of its six properties (Tuesday-Saturday 10 to 5, mid-June through September, $2 each, combination $6). The **Old Gaol,** once the King's Prison, is the oldest surviving public building of the British Colonies in this country; on view are the dungeon, cells, jailer's quarters and household effects. Also open are the **Emerson-Wilcox House** (1742) and the enormous **Elizabeth Perkins House** (1730) beside the river, **Jefferds Tavern** (1750), the 1745 **Old School House** and the **John Hancock Warehouse,** with old tools and antique ship models in a warehouse owned by a signer of the Declaration of Independence. Most are concentrated along Lindsay Road, which leads to **Sewall's Bridge,** a replica of the first pile drawbridge in America dating to 1761. Nearby, Route 103 passes an intriguing looking suspension bridge for pedestrians (called the "wiggly bridge," for good reason), which leads to a neat pathway along the river from York Harbor to Sewall's Bridge. The rambling **Sayward Wheeler House** (1718) at 79 Barrell Lane is opened Wednesday-Sunday noon to 4, June through mid-October, $4, by the Society for the Preservation of New England Antiquities. Out Route 91 is a small stone memorial next to the trickling **Maud Muller Spring,** which inspired John Greenleaf Whittier's poem.

Shopping. Located in an 18th-century house at 34 York St., **Accent & Design** is an interior design shop with exceptional gifts, paper products and accessories. We coveted the shell Christmas decorations and the pretty handpainted clay pots that were works of art. A landmark church built in 1834 in the center of York Village now houses **York Village Crafts & Antiques,** a cooperative featuring more than 100 area craftsmen and dealers. Also in the village is the **Williams Country Store,** which has evolved from a general store into an antiques shop.

The Goldenrod, which has been operated every summer since 1896 by the same family in York Beach, is where everyone stops for saltwater taffy kisses – choosing from dozens of flavors. It's also a restaurant with a nice old-fashioned menu, listing sandwiches like fried egg and bacon or cream cheese and olives, club sandwiches, toasted "frankfort" and lots of soda-fountain goodies. Also in York Beach is **Shelton's Gift Shop,** which offers attractive clothing, cards and jewelry.

Extra-Special

Factory Outlet Shopping. Anyone who rejoiced as we did when **Dansk** opened its first large factory outlet at Kittery is probably ecstatic about the several miles of outlets along Route 1 from Kittery to York. Although some are the same kinds of clothing outlets that you find in Freeport, the specialty here seems to be china, glass and kitchenware. We have found tremendous bargains at **Villeroy & Boch** (place settings and oversize dinner plates at up to 75 percent off), **Mikasa, Royal Doulton** and **Waterford-Aynsley.** You can admire the river view from benches outside the **Corning Designs** store at the Maine Gate Outlets, and pick up an assortment of bargains at **Reading China & Glass.** There are **Lenox** and **Oneida, Scandinavian Design** and **Georges Briard, Van Heusen** and **Samuel Roberts** (ultrasuede at 50 percent off) in various malls and small plazas on both sides of the highway. New ones pop up all the time (a **Brooks Brothers** factory store was there at our latest visit), and it takes policemen to untangle the bumper-to-bumper shopper traffic on summer weekends.

Harbor at Cape Porpoise is on view through rose trellis at The Inn at Harbor Head.

Kennebunkport, Me.
The Most and Best of Everything

For many, the small coastal area known as the Kennebunk Region has the most and best of everything in Maine: the best beaches, the most inns, the best shops, the most eating places, the best scenery, the most tourist attractions, the best galleries, the most diverse appeal.

It also has a starring role as the summer home of George Bush, a visible figure around town.

All have combined to produce what some old-timers see as overkill. Concerned over a gradual deterioration in the century-old traditions of one of Maine's earliest summer havens for the wealthy, local leaders have embarked on a campaign to preserve the town's character.

The Kennebunks offer a case study in town character. Actually, there are at least three Kennebunks. One is the town of Kennebunk and its inland commercial center, historic Kennebunk. The second is Kennebunkport, the changing coastal resort community that draws the tourists. A third represents Cape Arundel, Cape Porpoise and Goose Rocks Beach, whose rugged coastal aspects remain largely unchanged by development in recent years.

Even before George Bush's election as president, Kennebunkport and its Dock Square and Lower Village shopping areas had become so congested that a bus started shuttling visitors from vast parking areas on the edge of town. Although some of the luster faded after its favorite son left the White House, visitors still are drawn much as they are by the Kennedy name to Hyannis Port. The streets here teem on summer evenings with strollers who have spent the day at the beach.

And yet you can escape: walk along Parson's Way; drive out Ocean Avenue past Spouting Rock and the Bush estate at Walker Point and around Cape Arundel to Cape Porpoise, a fishing village; bicycle out Beach Avenue to Lord's Point or Strawberry

Island; visit the Rachel Carson Wildlife Preserve; savor times gone by among the historic homes of Summer Street in Kennebunk or along the beach at Goose Rocks.

One of the charms of the Kennebunks is that the crowded restaurants and galleries co-exist with events like the annual Unitarian Church blueberry festival and the Rotary chicken barbecue, and the solitude of Parson's Way.

Watercolorist Edgar Whitney proclaimed the Kennebunks "the best ten square miles of painting areas in the nation." Explore a bit and you'll see why.

Inn Spots

The White Barn Inn, Beach Street, Box 560 C, Kennebunkport 04046. (207) 967-2321.

Long known as one of the area's premier restaurants (see Dining Spots), the White Barn has become a top-rate inn under Australian owner Laurie Bongiorno and his wife, Laurie Cameron. Indeed, shortly after he took over, refurbished the facility and added deluxe suites, the inn became only the second in New England to be accepted into Relais & Châteaux, the international group of prestige hotels.

The inn's 24 rooms and suites vary considerably, as their prices indicate. Most sumptuous are the six in the Carriage House, the height of luxury with library-style sitting areas, dressing rooms, spacious marble bathrooms with jacuzzis and separate showers, Queen Anne kingsize four-poster beds and secretary desks, chintz-covered furniture and plush carpeting. The desk in the Blue Suite here contains a detailed book on everything about the inn and the area except how to fill the ice bucket (just phone, we were told after walking across the way to the bar area). The only other drawback was that the armoire containing the TV was positioned so that it was not comfortably visible from the sitting area in front of the fireplace. The fireplace was laid with real wood and we were wrapped in total luxury with a personal note of welcome from the innkeeper, a bowl of fresh fruit, Poland Spring water, no fewer than four three-way reading lights, much closet and drawer space in the bathroom, terry robes, Gilchrist & Soames toiletries and a couple of cookies when the bed was turned down.

Four large rooms in the Gatehouse, considered intermediate, have cathedral ceilings, whirlpool tubs, sitting areas with wing chairs, ceiling fans and queensize sleigh beds, chintz spreads and fine art on the walls. The Cottage incorporates a living room, bedroom and porch. Less regal are the thirteen smaller rooms upstairs in the inn, all refurbished in 1994 with modernized bathrooms and whimsical artistic touches to enhance what the owner calls their "basically quaint, country-style" nature. A local artist

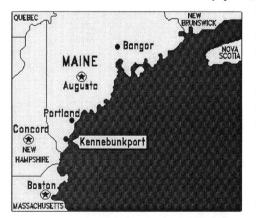

did the delightful trompe-l'oeil accents in each room – robin's eggs on a desk, car keys on a night stand, a shell book on a side table, a crane on an armoire, even a beach scene at the end of one bed and a lighthouse on the bureau. The inn's trademark straw bonnet is placed atop each bed, which come in double, queen or twin sizes.

The inn's handsome main floor contains a reception area, three sitting rooms with comfortable furniture and an inviting sun porch with a TV set. Flowers, mints, decanters

Fireplace warms Oriental guest room at The Captain Lord Mansion.

of brandy and port, newspapers and magazines are all around, and oriental rugs are scattered over the polished wood floors. Lush flowers and prolific herbs add color to the grounds.

Guests enjoy a substantial continental buffet breakfast in the quietly elegant Colonial dining room. Fresh orange juice and slices of cut-up fruits are brought to your table by a tuxedoed waiter, and you help yourself to assorted cereals, yogurts, and an array of muffins and pastries like we've seldom seen before – including a wonderful strawberry-bran muffin with a top the size of a grapefruit and a cool crème d'almond (at least that's how the waiter identified it after we inquired) with a sliced peach inside.

Doubles, $130 to $190; suites, $295. Two-night minimum most weekends.

The Captain Lord Mansion, Pleasant Street, Box 800, Kennebunkport 04046. (207) 967-3141 or (800) 522-3141.

For starters, consider the architectural features of this beautifully restored 1812 mansion: an octagonal cupola, a suspended elliptical staircase, blown-glass windows, trompe-l'oeil hand-painted doors, an eighteen-foot bay window, a hand-pulled working elevator.

The inn is so full of historic interest that public tours are given in summer for a nominal fee. You'd never guess that it was converted from a boarding house for senior citizens in 1978.

Guests can savor all the heritage that makes this a National Historic Register listing by staying overnight in any of the sixteen sumptuous guest rooms and enjoying hot cider or iced tea in the parlor or games beside the fire in the Gathering Room. Each of the guest rooms on three floors has been carefully decorated by Bev Davis and her husband Rick Litchfield, whose innkeeping energy and flair are considered models by their peers. Eleven rooms have working fireplaces, much in demand in the autumn and winter. All have private baths (though some created from closets are rather small), and the corner rooms are especially spacious. Nice touches like sewing kits, Poland Spring water, and trays with wine glasses and corkscrews abound.

Bev makes pin cushions and needlecraft "Do Not Disturb" signs for the rooms and oversees the gift shop on the main floor. Breakfast is served family-style at large tables in the kitchen. It includes fresh fruit, yogurt, whole-grain muesli, a changing entrée (perhaps quiche or apple-cinnamon pancakes), fresh-ground coffee with a flavor of the day, hot muffins and sticky buns. Bev's zucchini bread is renowned, as are some of the hors d'oeuvre she prepares for wine gatherings for guests at Halloween and New Year's.

Always on the move, Rick and Bev opened two annexes that add six ultra-deluxe rooms and suites. The first was the Captain's Hideaway, which has two honeymoon quarters three doors away in a house that Rick calls "our gourmet B&B" and bills as even more romantic than the mansion. The second-floor suite has to be seen to be believed: you enter through an enormous bathroom complete with fireplace, two-person whirlpool tub, an oversize shower and the commode hidden around the corner; beyond is a room with a massive kingsize four-poster bed and another fireplace. Chocolates come with turndown service at night. Hideaway guests enjoy breakfast by candlelight.

Phoebe's Fantasy, the latest addition, offers four guest rooms, all with king or queen beds and fireplaces. Guests here take breakfast at a seven-foot harvest table in a gathering room with a chintz sofa, fireplace and television. The large corner bedroom has windows on three sides, Indian shutters, a king bed, a Franklin stove and a jacuzzi.

The mansion's basement summer kitchen with large fireplace has become a second common room that doubles as a conference area.

Doubles, $135 to $199; suite, $249; two-night minimum weekends. No smoking.

Old Fort Inn, Old Fort Avenue, Box M, Kennebunkport 04046. (207) 967-5353 or (800) 828-3678.

The main lodge in a converted barn is the heart of the Old Fort Inn. You enter through the reception area and Sheila Aldrich's antiques shop. Beyond is a large rustic room with enormous beams, weathered pine walls and a massive brick fireplace, the perfect setting for some of Sheila's antiques.

That's where she and husband David, transplanted Californians, set out a buffet breakfast each morning. Guests pick up wicker trays with calico linings, help themselves to bowls of gorgeous fresh fruits and platters of pastries, and sit around the lodge or outside on the sun-dappled deck beside the large swimming pool. Sheila bakes the sweet breads (blueberry, zucchini, banana, oatmeal and pumpkin are some); the croissants are David's forte and there are sticky buns on Sundays. They added granola and yogurt to the spread, and went through twenty pounds of granola a week.

The stone and brick carriage house out back contains fourteen large and luxurious guest rooms and two suites, all newly air-conditioned. All are decorated in different colors, all have private bathrooms, wet bars with microwaves, plush carpeting and color television, plus such nice touches as velvet wing chairs, stenciling on the walls and handmade wreaths over the beds. "My wife agonizes over every intricate detail," says David. "I call her Ms. Mix and Match." Her decorating flair shows; even the towels are color-coordinated. In the hall, her framed shadow boxes containing Victorian outfits are conversation pieces.

In the most deluxe rooms, of which there seem to be more at every visit, the TV may be hidden in a handsome chest of drawers, the kingsize four-poster beds are topped with fishnet canopies, and the baths are outfitted with jacuzzis and Neutrogena amenities. The sitting room in the carriage house has two settees and a pine hutch; a small adjoining room has wicker furniture.

White fence surrounds spacious grounds at Captain Jefferds Inn.

The inn is a quiet retreat away from the tourist hubbub but within walking distance of the ocean; at night, David says, the silence is deafening. The inn offers a tennis court as well as the pool. Many guests are repeat customers, and it's easy to see why.

Doubles, $125 to $250; two-night minimum in summer and weekends. Closed mid-December to mid-April. No smoking.

The Captain Jefferds Inn, Pearl Street, Box 691, Kennebunkport 04046. (207) 967-2311.

If you like antiques and pets, you'll love the Captain Jefferds, which has an abundance of both. Tessie Fitzsimmons, the Maine coon cat, was snoozing on the porch chair when we came through the ornate white iron fence and up the brick walk.

Innkeeper Warren Fitzsimmons, an antiques dealer from Long Island, bought the inn in 1980 and moved his collection in. A decorator and antiquarian, he has made the 1804 sea captain's mansion into a stunningly colorful and comfortable spot, one that was once pictured on the cover of House Beautiful.

Warren cooks breakfast in the small but efficient kitchen; partner Don Kelly serves it formally in the handsome dining room, or outside on the delightful front porch or the flagstone terrace. Guests may eat at 8 or 9 o'clock seatings. Eggs benedict, blueberry crêpes, quiche, frittata with seasonal vegetables and New England "flannel" (hash with a poached egg) are in Warren's repertoire and he never repeats a breakfast in a week.

A living room with an amazing collection of majolica, a sunlit solarium, a rear brick terrace, the front terrace and an expansive lawn with comfortable loungers are places where guests can relax with a book or whatever. Afternoon tea with cookies and finger sandwiches is served in the cooler months.

All twelve guest rooms have private tiled baths and canopy beds. They are luxurious and perfectly decorated, with chaise lounges, Laura Ashley linens, firm mattresses, woolen blankets and four pillows on each bed. Warren collects antique white cotton spreads and quilts; he has such an extensive collection that he changes them around from time to time. Three large apartment suites with separate living rooms and kitchen areas are available in the adjacent carriage house.

Most of the rooms have Victorian wicker pieces. "I hate plastic," says the innkeeper. We defy anyone to find a bit of it in this enchanting place.

Doubles, $85 to $135; suites, $145 to $165. Two-night minimum, July-October. Closed November-March except weekends in November and December.

The Kennebunkport Inn, Dock Square, Box 111, Kennebunkport 04046. (207) 967-2621 or (800) 248-2621.

In a nicely landscaped setting just off busy Dock Square, with a view of the river, is the graceful, clapboard turn-of-the-century mansion housing The Kennebunkport Inn, plus a 1930 motel-style River House annex in the rear. A small octagonal swimming pool with a large wooden deck fits snugly in between.

Innkeepers Rick and Martha Griffin, both schooled in hotel management, knew what they wanted after apprenticing at inns elsewhere. They wanted an appealing location, spacious rooms, a large dining room, a bar and a swimming pool in a town with character. "We found everything we were looking for here," says Rick. They have decorated the twenty guest rooms in the annex with period pieces, chintz, Laura Ashley wallpapers and different stenciling everywhere. One of the larger rooms has a four-poster bed, sofa and velvet chair. All rooms have private baths and color TV.

Five more bedrooms are upstairs in the main inn. Nine deluxe rooms with four-poster beds have been added behind the restaurant in a wing that also provided the handsome piano bar and lounge, the last of the Griffins' requisites. A pianist entertains nightly in summer through foliage season.

The Griffins, who live with two daughters in an apartment attached to the inn, are hands-on innkeepers, assisted by a professional staff.

Excellent meals can be sampled in the inn's lovely dining rooms (see Dining Spots). Breakfast is extra, but includes such interesting dishes as custard french toast with pear-honey sauce and potato skins stuffed with scrambled eggs and mushrooms in a mornay sauce.

Doubles, $79.50 to $189, EP; $178 to $258, MAP. Three-night minimum on summer and holiday weekends.

The Inn at Harbor Head, 41 Pier Road, Cape Porpoise, RR 2, Box 1180, Kennebunkport 04046. (207) 967-5564.

The location of the rambling shingled home of David and Joan Sutter on a rocky knoll right above the picturesque Cape Porpoise harbor is one of the attractions at this small B&B. Out front are gorgeous gardens with a sundial. A rear terrace and lawns lead down to the shore for swimming from the floats or just relaxing in one of the oversize rope hammocks, watching the lobster boats go by.

Breakfast is another attraction. From Joan's country kitchen come such dishes as pineapple boats decorated with edible flowers, pears poached with lemon and vanilla and topped with a cointreau-laced custard sauce, and broiled grapefruit with nutmeg. The "Maine" course could be vegetable frittata, blueberry strata, mushroom omelet topped with salsa or "the bakery lady's special from Montana" – grated potatoes, scallions and sausages with monterey jack cheese and salsa – so named because her daughter got the recipe from a bakery lady in Montana. No one ever leaves a bite of the roast beef hash made from scratch with red and green peppers and a touch of garlic. Pecan sticky buns and fruit croissants might accompany this feast. The meal is served at 9 in the dining room at a long table where there is much camaraderie. Coffee for early risers is put out at 7 in the parlor or the library, where a telescope is at the ready.

The five bedrooms, three up and two down, have private baths and king or queensize canopy beds. They are decorated to the nth degree by Joan, who is a sculptor and artist. Her murals are exquisite. The Harbor Suite's murals are of Cape Porpoise on the walls, with clouds and sky on the ceiling, mirroring the view from the window. It boasts a new gas fireplace, tiled with ivy and birds crafted by local artist Lou Lipkin of Goose Rocks Pottery. The entrance to the Garden Room is paved with stones and a little fountain, and original drawings of peach and plum blossoms float on the wall. French

Graceful, turn-of-the-century mansion houses Kennebunkport Inn.

doors open onto a private, trellised deck overlooking the harbor. The Greenery in which we stayed has a handpainted, tiled jacuzzi and a queensize bed covered in white with tons of lacy pillows; a mural of lakes and mountains is above the beams. Next time we'd opt for the Summer Suite, with wraparound views of the water through windows screened by louvered shutters, a kingsize bed with a vivid floral-on-black spread, a wicker loveseat and chaise lounge, and a cathedral-ceilinged bath with bidet and double jacuzzi. The newly renovated Ocean Room is different from the rest, Joan says – "bold and masculine with a library of books about sailing, the sea and shipwrecks," plus a trompe-l'oeil window scene she painted in its skylit bathroom to simulate a window. Bottles of the inn's own-label Poland Spring water are in each room.

The innkeepers, who say they like to do things in the "poshest way possible," put out a decanter of wine with cheese and crackers in late afternoon and, after guests leave for dinner, turn down their beds, light soft lights and leave silver dishes of Godiva chocolates on the pillows. It's little wonder that some guests stay for a week or more, and that many are honeymooners.

Doubles, $150 to $180; suites, $185 to $225. Closed in winter. Two-night minimum on weekends. No smoking.

Bufflehead Cove, off Route 35, Box 499, Kennebunkport 04046. (207) 967-3879 or 967-5151.

Down a long dirt road and past a lily pond is this hidden treasure: a gray shingled, Dutch Colonial manse right beside a scenic bend of the Kennebunk River, the kind of summer home you've always dreamed of. Owners Harriet and Jim Gott hardly advertise and don't need to. Their six-room B&B is filled by word of mouth.

The public rooms and the setting are special here. A wide porch faces the tidal river, one of the lovelier spots around; there are porches along the side and a huge wraparound deck in back, too. A large and comfy living room contains window seats with views of the water, and the dining room, which is shaped like the back of a ship, has a dark beamed ceiling, paneling, stenciling and a carpet painted on the floor. There are a dock with boats and five acres of tranquility with which to surround oneself.

197

All bedrooms are bright and cheerful, but the Balcony Room is perhaps the most appealing of those in the main house. It has a fabulous, wicker-filled balcony overlooking the river, a queensize brass bed, a large antique armoire that the Gotts discovered in their attic ("we couldn't figure out how it ever got up there," Harriet noted), and a dramatic decor with splashes of black, including the striking glossy stenciling – green leaves on a black band. In the small Teal Room, the bathroom is stenciled like the bedroom with ribbons and bouquets of flowers. The walls and ceilings are handpainted with unusual designs in the Cove Suite, two rooms with lots of wicker and a private bath. The Garden Studio in back has its own entrance and patio, a wicker sitting area, a handcrafted queensize bed and grapevine stenciling that echoes the real vines outside the entry.

The crowning glory is the secluded Hideaway, newly fashioned from the Gotts' former quarters in the adjacent cottage. Mostly glass and windows, it holds a kingsize bed, a central fireplace open to both bedroom and living room, two couches, and a bathroom with a double jacuzzi tiled by a border of fish. Outside is a private deck.

Harriet serves a full breakfast on the porch or in the dining room. A typical repast might be fresh orange juice, ginger-poached pears in an English custard sauce, lobster quiche and a croissant. Soufflés, asparagus strata, Jim's green-apple stuffed french toast, waffles and popovers are other specialties. White wine and cheese are served in the afternoon, and there are decanters of sherry plus bottles of Bufflehead Cove sparkling water in each room..

Jim is a lobster fisherman. Guests may not see much of him unless they get up to join his fishing expedition at 4:30 a.m., but they know he's around by the lobster in the quiche and omelets.

Doubles, $95 to $150; Hideaway suite, $190. Smoking restricted.

Cape Arundel Inn, Ocean Avenue, Box 530A, Kennebunkport 04046. (207) 967-2125.

A choice location facing the open ocean and an excellent dining room commend this Maine-style inn containing seven oceanview rooms with private baths and seven motel units at the side.

Innkeeper Ann Fales has upgraded the rooms upstairs in the inn, which are spacious and pleasantly traditional. Master Bedrooms 2 and 3 are most coveted, the former with twin beds, a loveseat and chair by the picture window, and a private balcony. We liked ours on the far-front corner, where white organdy curtains fluttered in the breeze and a white chenille spread covered the kingsize bed. The walls were wood and the carpeting attractive, but the view was all: two chairs in the corner from which to take in the bird's-eye panorama of the George Bush compound and the ocean.

Also coveted are the motel rooms, each with a double and a twin bed, full bath and TV, and a little balcony with striped chairs and a front-on view of the ocean.

The spacious front porch of the inn is a super place to curl up with a good book, enjoy a cocktail or a nightcap, or the morning newspaper before breakfast. Breakfasts are extra but well worth it; we know people who drive miles for the Downeast sampler (sausage, blueberry pancake, scrambled egg and broiled tomato, $6.25) and the view. We can vouch for the fried codfish cakes served with baked beans and broiled tomato and the omelet of the day (sour cream, avocado, tomato and chives), accompanied by unlimited refills of coffee.

Doubles, $125 to $1435. Open mid-May to mid-October.

Harbor Inn, Ocean Avenue, Box 538A, Kennebunkport 04046. (207) 967-2074.
The large, wraparound front porch with river view is appropriate at the Harbor Inn.

Breakfast room at Captain Fairfield Inn. **Veranda awaits guests at Harbor Inn.**

Texans Charlotte and Bill Massmann find themselves right at home on the wicker rocking chairs on the Southern-style veranda of the 1903 Victorian summer house they converted into a B&B in 1985. A decanter of sherry awaits guests in the large front parlor. At one side is a small antiques shop stocking Waterford glass and old quilts, among other items.

To the rear is a lace-curtained dining room with wallpaper patterned with pretty iris, where Charlotte offers a buffet breakfast of seasonal fruits, cereals, bagels with cream cheese, blueberry pancakes or crêpes with ham and egg soufflé, all prepared in a Texas-size kitchen created from four downstairs rooms.

Two of the eight guest rooms on the second and third floors are suites and all have private baths. They are handsomely furnished with canopy or four-poster beds, comfortable chairs, antique coverlets and fresh flowers. An efficiency cottage in the rear has one bedroom and sliding glass doors onto a patio.

Doubles, $90 to $110; cottage, $120. Two-night minimum in summer and all weekends. Closed November to mid-May. No smoking.

The Captain Fairfield Inn, Pleasant and Green Streets, Box 1308, Kennebunkport 04046. (207) 967-4454 or (800) 322-1928.

A new lease on life has been given this Federal sea captain's mansion, listed on the National Register and overlooking the River Green. Bonnie and Dennis Tallagnon, formerly of the Red Clover Inn in Mendon, Vt., bought the inn after it was closed and in bankruptcy. "We failed at a normal life," Dennis quipped as to why they re-entered the hospitality business.

After serious upgrading, they now offer nine guest rooms, all with full new baths, queensize beds dressed with pretty linens and lots of pillows, and comfortable sitting areas. The one downstairs on the corner opposite the living room is a beauty. It has a fishnet canopy bed, two armchairs, a desk, a fireplace and its own porch with two rocking chairs. Three rooms lined up off a hall in the rear wing each offer four-poster beds draped with sheers and chintz, a day bed, and a wicker loveseat and chair. Bonnie has outfitted each room with fluffy towels, Gilchrist & Soames toiletries and night lights, and hung grapevine wreaths on the doors.

Beautiful woodwork and molding and fresh flowers are evident throughout. The formal living room is elegant and pretty, yet comfortable. French doors open from the library/TV room onto the garden and a large side lawn.

Breakfast, a highlight here, is served in a fireplaced dining room and a sun room. It's prepared by Dennis, the son of a chef in Switzerland, who was off demonstrating how to make blueberry crêpes at Filene's in Boston at our latest visit. That morning, he'd served fruit compote and juice, homemade muffins and croissants, and then a choice among three entrées: Spanish frittata topped with Vermont cheddar cheese and homemade toasted bread, apple pancakes, and granola with fruit, nuts and yogurt. Tea and treats are offered in the afternoon.

Doubles, $95 to $160. Two-night minimum on weekends. No smoking.

The Maine Stay Inn & Cottages, 34 Maine St., Box 500A, Kennebunkport 04046. (207) 967-2117 or (800) 950-2117.

A wraparound veranda and a cupola designate this 1860 house, listed on the National Register. It's been nicely upgraded by new innkeepers Lindsay and Carol Copeland, who live nearby with their two young children and welcome families in their suites and cottages out back.

The main house offers a stylish living room, dining room and six guest rooms with private baths. The largest is a fireplaced suite on the main floor, with a pullout sofa and two chairs and a queensize bed tucked into a corner of the bedroom, which also has a sitting area. Another main-floor room has a private deck onto the back yard. Up a suspended spiral staircase are four more rooms, one a suite with a canopied queen bed, a sink in the sitting room and the bathroom in a closet. All rooms here have TVs hidden away in armoires or credenzas; beds are queensize and bathrooms contain the inn's own brand of toiletries.

In back are eleven cottages, one with a queen bedroom and small living room with sofabed and fireplace. Three others have fireplaces, some have two double beds, and all have kitchenettes.

A spacious, shady back lawn between inn and cottages contains a multitude of lawn chairs and a play area with an elaborate climber-swing apparatus that was "supposed to take eight hours and took two of us sixteen hours to assemble," Lindsay recalls. Carol cooks breakfast and he serves: juice, fresh fruit, homemade granola, fresh breads and muffins, and such entrées as featherbed eggs, egg strata with sausage and cheese, baked french toast, apple bread pudding, fruit-filled blintzes and apricot or currant scones. Cottage guests may have a breakfast basket delivered or share breakfast in the inn. Complimentary afternoon tea and desserts are served to all.

Doubles, $125 to $150; fireplaced cottages, $125 to $170; suites and two-bedroom cottage, $165 to $195.

1802 House, 15 Locke St., Box 646-A, Kennebunkport 04046. (207) 967-5632 and (800) 932-5632.

A quiet location on an out-of-the-way residential street overlooking the 15th green of the Cape Arundel Golf Club is offered by Ron and Carol Perry in their attractive and updated old B&B. The Perrys have given it a new lease on life since taking over in 1992, updating all six guest rooms, each with private bath, and providing knockout gourmet breakfasts.

The Camden Room in which we stayed a decade ago in the downstairs corner now has a queensize poster bed and two arm chairs. A total makeover has been provided for the fireplaced Arundel Room across the hall. Two club chairs were reupholstered to match the comforters and shams that Carol made for its queensize poster bed. Carpeting, floral wallpaper above the wainscoting and a pedestal sink in the bathroom were added. The Windsor Room with a fireplace upstairs has become a honeymoon suite with the addition of a double whirlpool tub, carpeting and two armchairs. At our visit, Ron was planning to convert the Sebago Room into a suite with a private deck.

Guests gather in an open common room, where a cast-iron potbelly stove on a brick platform warms the air on chilly days, there are couches and lots of magazines for reading, and you're apt to find fresh chocolate-chip cookies in the afternoon. Adjacent is a tile-floored dining room with a dark beamed ceiling and three tables for four looking onto the side deck. Baskets on the wall and ceiling give a homey effect that belies the breakfast treats Ron prepares in the commercial kitchen that sold him on buying the house. At our visit, the fare included sautéed pears, baked eggs florentine with cheese and red peppers, and corn wheat muffins with chopped walnuts on top. Subsequent mornings yielded waffles with homemade blueberry-strawberry-raspberry sauce, eggs benedict, banana-apple pancakes and Carol's 1802 eggs, baked in a puff pastry shell with mushrooms and sour cream. Carol, who works in Portland by day, is the gardener responsible for the attractive grounds.

Doubles, $85 to $145.

Dining Spots

White Barn Inn, Beach Street, Kennebunkport. (207) 967-2321.

Soaring up to three stories, with a breathtaking backdrop of flowers rising on tiers outside its twenty-foot-high rear picture window and illuminated at night, the elegant White Barn is almost too atmospheric for words. A local florist designs the dramatic backdrops that change with the seasons (lush impatiens in summer, assorted mums in fall, and a Christmas scene that begins with potted red cabbage and escalates to full spruce trees dressed with velvet bows, golden bells and tiny white lights). Talented 30ish executive chef Gethin DuValle Thomas, who was nationally recognized at Adirondacks in Washington, D.C., comes from a family of artists. He chose cooking as his art, which changes every week here but keeps getting better and better. And owner Laurie Bongiorno, a personable but perfectionist Australian of Italian descent, is the host who ensures that the dining room runs flawlessly.

Little wonder that in 1994, the White Barn became the AAA's first five-diamond dining establishment in all New England. It's *that* good.

The food is in the vanguard of contemporary American regional cuisine. Dinner is prix-fixe in four courses, ($49 midweek and $56 on weekends), with

Seasonal floral backdrop at White Barn Inn.

Culinary staff has made White Barn Inn first five-diamond restaurant in New England.

eight to ten choices for most courses, and every bit as worthy as that at five-diamond citadels charging much more. It's prepared by a kitchen staff of sixteen and served with precision by a young wait staff who meet with the chef beforehand for 45 minutes each night. Guests at each table are served simultaneously, one waiter per plate.

Up to 120 diners can be seated at tables spaced well apart in the main barn and in an adjoining barn. They're filled with understated antiques and oil paintings dating to the 18th century, and the loft holds quite a collection of wildlife wood carvings. The tables are set with silver, Schottsweizel crystal and Villeroy & Boch china, white linens and white tapers in crystal candlesticks. A Russian pianist, here on a scholarship, plays seemingly by ear in the entry near the gleaming copper-topped bar.

Our latest dinner, the highlight of several over the years, began with a glass of Perrier-Jouët extra brut (complimentary for house guests) and the chef's "welcome amenity," an herbed goat cheese rosette, an onion tart and a tapenade of eggplant and kalamata olives. Really interesting olive bread and plain white and poppyseed rolls followed. We'd gladly have tried any of the appetizers, but settled on a lobster spring roll with daikon radish, savoy cabbage and hot and sweet glaze, and the seared Hudson Valley foie gras on an apple and celeriac tart with a calvados sauce. Both were sensational.

Champagne sorbet in a pool of Piper Heidsieck extra-dry cleared the palate with a flourish for the main courses. One was a duo of Maine rabbit: a grilled loin with roasted rosemary and pommery mustard and a braised leg in cabernet sauvignon, accompanied by wild mushrooms and pesto-accented risotto. The other was pan-seared tenderloin of beef topped with a horseradish gratin and port-glazed shallots on a pool of potato and Vermont cheddar cheese, with a fancy little side of asparagus (this in mid-autumn). A $29 bottle of Firestone cabernet accompanied from an excellent wine list priced upward from $22 and especially strong on American chardonnays and cabernets.

Dessert was anything but anti-climactic: a classic coeur à la crème with tropical fruits and sugared shortbread and a trio of pear, raspberry and mango sorbets, served artistically on a black plate with colored swirls matching the sorbets and decorated with squiggles of white and powdered sugar. A tray of petits-fours gilded the lily.

After an after-dinner brandy in the inn's living room, the little raisin cookies we found on the bed back in our room sent us happily into dreamland.

Dinner nightly, 6 to 9:30. Closed Monday and Tuesday in February and March. Jackets recommended.

Seascapes, On the Pier, Cape Porpoise, Kennebunkport. (207) 967-8500.

When President and Mrs. Bush first dined here, the First Lady exclaimed as they were seated, "my, what a pretty table." Owner Angela LeBlanc could not have been more pleased. The table settings, her pride and joy, won Restaurant Hospitality magazine's national table-top competition shortly after she and husband Arthur opened the restaurant. The table – pictured on the cover of our book, *The Restaurants of New England* – bears a teal cloth, a napkin ringed with fishes, handpainted Italian pottery in heavenly colors and fluted wine glasses. The setting is the match for the view of lobster boats in Cape Porpoise Harbor through large windows on three sides.

The chef handled the unexpected Bush visit with aplomb, as he does the lunch and dinner chores throughout the season. Waiters in Hawaiian shirts serve lunch from an interesting, extensive menu ($6.95 to $14.95). You can order anything from a grilled pizza to a Maine lobster tortilla with mixed greens and daikon sprouts, from a caesar salad with lobster to a risotto of wild mush-rooms, peas and artichokes.,

Excellent dark wheat rolls get dinner here off to a good start. For appetizers ($5.95 to $10.95), we've enjoyed a stellar bisque of lobster and crab with crème fraîche, crispy phyllo shrimp with a Thai mint melon salad and sweet chili sauce, and zesty mussels fra diavolo with lemon pep-per linguini, and thought the Maine crab cakes with crispy outsides and a tomato-rosemary sauce even better than the Chesa-peake Bay variety. A sorbet precedes the entrées ($17.95 to $24.95). At one dinner they were a classic Mediterranean bouilla-baisse with rouille and a roulade of chicken stuffed with ginger, shiitake mushrooms and baby bok choy; at another, a rich lob-ster tequila over linguini, a garlicky shrimp Christina with feta and saffron rice, and grilled salmon with a sesame-soy-sherry marinade and a trio of julienned vegetables.

Award-winning table setting at Seascapes.

We're usually too full after the main courses to order dessert, but you might succumb to an ethereal strawberry torte, blueberry cheesecake, chocolate decadence or polenta pound cake with berry sauce. The reasonably priced, primarily American wine list has been honored by The Wine Spectator.

Keeping a family tradition launched when the LeBlancs owned the nearby Kennebunk Inn, five entrées bear the first names of their grandchildren. The sale of the inn has allowed them to concentrate on Seascapes and to launch the **Lively Lobster,** a seafood shanty on the wharf next door. In the walkout basement beneath Seascapes they run the casual Cape Porpoise Pub. And in a corner off the entry to Seascapes is a new piano bar, where a pianist entertains on weekends.

Lunch daily, noon to 3, late June to late October; dinner nightly, 5:30 to 9 or 10,

Wednesday-Sunday in May and June. Closed late October to April. Lively Lobster open seasonally, daily 11 to sunset.

Cape Arundel Inn, Ocean Avenue, Kennebunkport. (207) 967-2125.

What could be more romantic than dining at a window table at the Cape Arundel, watching wispy clouds turn to mauve and violet as the sun sets, followed by a full golden moon rising over the darkened ocean? That the food is so good is a bonus.

The ocean and sky outside provide more than enough backdrop for a plain but attractive dining room with lots of windows and plants, dark wood and white linens. An excellent warm pheasant salad on radicchio with Thai dressing ($7.95) and cajun Maine crab cakes with avocado puree ($6.25) preceded our main courses, sweetbreads with a tart grapefruit sauce and roast loin of lamb, accompanied by rice pilaf, ratatouille, and julienned carrots and turnips. Other entrées ($16.50 to $22.95) included roast duck with wild rice pancakes and sundried cherry sauce, shrimp and scallops tossed with pesto over pasta, poached salmon with cucumber ribbons, dill crème fraîche and caviar, and roast veal chop with shiitake mushrooms, rosemary and madeira wine. The wine list offered a liter of River Oak red for $12.50.

The dessert tray harbored some interesting indulgences, a fruit shortcake and brandy pound cake among them.

Dinner, Monday-Saturday 5:30 to 8:30 or 9. Open mid-May to Columbus Day.

Kennebunkport Inn, Dock Square, Kennebunkport. (207) 967-2621.

The pristine dining rooms on either side of the inn's entry are extra pretty, with fringed valances, lace curtains, Laura Ashley wallpaper and stenciling, hurricane lamps, jars of fresh flowers on the fireplace mantels and tables with white over beige linens.

Innkeeper Martha Griffin, a graduate of La Varenne in Paris and the Elizabeth Pomeroy Cooking School in London, oversees the kitchen. She and husband Rick go to France frequently to learn new dishes with which to dazzle regular customers.

Seared carpaccio and salmon roulade stuffed with leeks are appetizer favorites ($4.95 to $6.95). Entrées are priced from $16.25 for sautéed breast of chicken on a bed of ratatouille to $22.95 for the signature bouillabaisse, served with a hot pepper sauce on the side. We remember an artfully presented grilled duck breast with raspberry sauce and an extraordinary mustard-ginger rack of lamb from past visits.

An ethereal key lime pie and a white chocolate mousse with strawberries in kirsch are good picks from the dessert cart ($5.25). The wine list offers 150 choices from an $11 pinot grigio to Château Lafite-Rothschild.

Dinner nightly, 6 to 9. Closed Sunday in off-season and November-April.

Salt Marsh Tavern, 46 Western Ave. (Route 9), Lower Village, Kennebunkport. (207) 967-4500.

If the makeover of the old Hennessy's restaurant reminds people of the old White Barn, that's the way its new owner planned it. Jack Nahil recreated the White Barn restaurant he used to know, before its elevation into the rarified realm of Relais & Châteaux. The focal point here, as in days gone by, is a piano bar in the center beneath a soaring barn ceiling.

After selling the White Barn he'd run since 1973, Jack ventured to Florida but "didn't like the market" and returned to Kennebunkport for "another restaurant challenge." He acknowledged: "There's a lot of déjà-vu here. Barns speak to me, I guess."

This barn speaks with oriental scatter rugs on the wide plank floors, the owner's oil paintings on the barnwood walls, farm implements and wood carvings on the lofts, and large rear windows onto a salt marsh stretching toward Kennebunk Beach. Tables

Loft floor and far dining room are on view from bar area at Salt Marsh Tavern.

dressed with white over forest green cloths and brass candlesticks are spaced throughout the open main floor and the upstairs loft. Up to 130 diners can be seated in "four different atmospheres under the same roof," Jack says.

The food, under chef Rich Lemoine, speaks with the authority of the old White Barn, blending the classic and the creative with equal flair. Among main courses ($16.95 to $22.95), the grilled salmon fillet is served with a julienne of basil and sundried tomatoes with cumin-scented spaetzle, the roast duckling with a raspberry honey demiglaze and gingered whipped potatoes, and the sliced medallions of lamb leg with a roasted garlic bread pudding and lemon-mint sauce. Steamed or stuffed lobster and pepper-coated sirloin of beef with a brandy dijon sauce revive memories of the former surf and turf years.

Among starters, roasted chicken and green chile soup with cilantro cream is a counterpoint to the traditional lobster, scallop and shrimp bisque, lately enlivened with Thai spices. Chilled oysters come on a bed of shredded radicchio and napa cabbage slaw, the grape leaves are stuffed with lobster and basmati rice, and the salmon pot stickers marry fried scallions with a hot and sour lobster sauce. Dessert could be profiteroles or fruit tartlets.

A pianist entertains nightly.

Dinner, Tuesday-Sunday 6 to 9 or 10. Closed January and February.

Arundel Wharf Restaurant, 43 Ocean Ave., Kennebunkport. (207) 967-3444.

This riverfront landmark had been plodding along for years until co-owner Bob Williamson got married. His wife Michelle gave the place a facelift, a new chef, a new menu and an extended season through mid-December. And voila! The locals responded in droves, joining tourists to pack the place at all hours.

The location, of course, has much to do with it. The blue-awninged deck (heated in fall) affords 125 patrons some of the best harbor views in town. Another 75 can be seated inside, at shiny nautical chart tables amidst wooden ship models, mahogany accents and a yacht club feel. Two half-circle tables extend out over the wharf for the most in-your-face waterfront dining we've encountered anywhere.

205

The food now earns accolades for its quality as well as its breadth. For dinner ($7.25 to $22.95), you can order a lobster roll, a hamburger, lobster stew or an avocado stuffed with lobster or crab at the low end; coastal paella or bouillabaisse at the high end. Most offerings are priced in the middle. Seafood reigns, from seven lobster dishes to charbroiled swordfish with corn-pepper relish, shrimp scampi and "bag of fish" (scallops and haddock steamed in parchment with orange, ginger and sesame). Other possibilities include pork negril, chicken diablo, sirloin steak and prime rib.

Start with a smoked seafood sampler. But save room. Bob says some people come here for the desserts alone. Consider the chocolate cake, the bread pudding with whiskey sauce, the mixed four-berry pie or the blueberry-apple crisp. Some stop in the afternoon for cappuccino and strawberry shortcake; others for the avocado stuffed with lobster. Clam chowder and a lobster roll make a fine lunch.

Open daily, 11:30 to 9. Closed in winter.

Windows on the Water, Chase Hill, Kennebunkport. (207) 967-3313.

The windows are architecturally interesting at this sleek, expansive restaurant of recent vintage on a hilltop above the water. So the name was a natural, as is the attractive two-level side deck, half enclosed and half remaining open, an attractive place for a summer lunch.

Lunch is the perfect opportunity to try the restaurant's highly touted lobster-stuffed potato, which has been featured in national magazines. Fresh lobster meat, scallions, jarlsberg cheese and sweet cream top a hot baked potato, and the $12.95 tab is probably more justifiable as a luncheon main course than as an appetizer at dinner. We were a bit disappointed in the diminutive size of the chef's salad ($7.50), mostly turkey and ham; for some reason the chilled seafood plate ($8.95) was much more ample. The poppyseed vinaigrette dressing was excellent, and the Whitbread's ale so cooling on a hot summer day that we lingered for two.

Chef-owner John Hughes, lately inducted into the Master Chefs Institute of America, has stamped his imprint on the extensive dinner menu, an ambitious and inventive collection of contemporary regional choices with occasional ethnic influences. We know people who think his award-winning lobster bisque is the world's best. Baked brie with warmed lobster salad and grilled brioche and a pizzetta of shrimp and pesto are other popular starters. Among entrées ($14.95 to $22.95), you might find lobster ravioli with pesto and drambuie cream sauce, baked crab and lobster cakes with cajun mustard, lobster Thai-style poached in coconut and ginger and seasoned with tamarind, and grilled lobster and avocado with tangy mango salsa. Though most of these dishes have won culinary awards, as listed on the menu, John is not a one-theme chef. His range incorporates jambalaya, fillet of halibut glazed with tequila and lime, shrimp in hot and sour broth with basmati rice, beef and chicken satay with Philippine dipping sauce, and roasted tenderloin with pinot noir demi-glaze. Among desserts are chocolate oblivion torte, lemon cheesecake and charlotte au chocolat.

The main dining room is attractive with a cathedral ceiling, track lighting, and a peach color scheme accented by vases of black-eyed susans. A smaller room beyond is even nicer with a bowed front window. Upstairs is a lounge with a cathedral ceiling and a palladian window overlooking the river.

Lunch daily, 11:45 to 2:30; dinner from 5:30; Sunday brunch, 11 to 2:30. No smoking.

Pizzoodles, Shipyard, Lower Village, Kennebunkport. (207) 967-0033.

Proprietor John Audley, an ex-Montrealer, figures there are ten trillion possible combinations in his food. Patrons choose the toppings for his brick-oven gourmet pizzas, perhaps caramelized onion, chèvre, sundried tomatoes, spam (yes, spam), wild mush-

Semi-circle table offers up-close water view at Arundel Wharf Restaurant.

rooms and more. He even offered a gator pizza in his first summer here. John makes his pastas the Italian way, and offers a variety of sauces, pasta salads, panini (Italian sandwiches – the toppings chosen from the pizza selections and spread on foccacia, $3.25), coffees, bagels and pastries. He was planning to install a brick oven in which to bake his pizzas and breads. There are tables inside or out upon which to enjoy.

Open daily, 11 a.m. to 9 or 10 p.m.

Diversions

Beaches. Gooch's, a curving half-mile crescent, and **Kennebunk** are two sandy strands with surf west of town (parking by permit, often provided by innkeepers). The fine silvery sand at Goose Rocks Beach looks almost tropical and the waters are protected. Beachcombers find starfish and sand-dollar shells here in early morning. More secluded is **Parson's Beach,** a natural sandy strand set among the tall grasses and undeveloped area next to the Rachel Carson Wildlife Refuge. The beaches are at their uncrowded best at non-peak periods and early or late in the day.

Parson's Way. A marker opposite the landmark Colony Hotel notes the land given to the people of Kennebunkport so that "everyone may enjoy its natural beauty." Sit on the benches, spread a blanket on a rock beside the ocean, or walk out to the serene little chapel of St. Ann's Episcopal Church by the sea.

Ocean Avenue. Continue past Parson's Way to Spouting Rock, where the incoming tide creates a spurting fountain as waves crash between two ragged cliffs, and Blowing Cave, another roaring phenomenon within view of Walker Point and the George Bush summer compound. Go on to Cape Porpoise, the closest thing to a fishing village hereabouts, with a working lobster pier and a picturesque harbor full of islands.

History. The Kennebunkport Historical Society has its attractions: the 1853 Greek Revival Nott House called **White Columns** and the 1899 **Town House School** with exhibits of local and maritime heritage. But inland Kennebunk is more obviously historic: There's a treasure behind every door on the block at the 1825 **Brick Store Museum,** which has an excellent collection of decorative and fine arts, Federal period

207

furniture, artifacts and textiles. It mounts a couple of major exhibits each year (photos of the great fire of 1947 were on at one visit) and offers walking tours of Kennebunk's historic district. Summer Street (Route 35) running south of downtown toward Kennebunkport is considered one of the architecturally outstanding residential streets in the nation; the 1803 **Taylor-Barry House** is open for tours, and the aptly named yellow-with-white-frosting Wedding Cake House (1826) is a sight to behold (though not open to the public).

Arts and Crafts. Its scenery has turned Kennebunkport into a mecca for artisans. The Art Guild of the Kennebunks numbers more than 50 resident professionals as members and claims the Kennebunks are the largest collective community of fine art on the East Coast. Art and galleries are everywhere, but are concentrated around Kennebunkport's Dock Square and the wharves to the southeast. In the Wharf Lane Shops are the **Priscilla Hartley Gallery,** in its 31st season and the oldest in Maine, and out over the water, Lou and Bob Lipkin's distinctive **Goose Rocks Pottery.** More than 80 artists show at **Mast Cove Galleries,** a lovely Greek Revival home and barn next to the library on Route 9. For a change of pace, visit the grounds of the **Franciscan Monastery** (where, as some savvy travelers know, spare and inexpensive bedrooms are available) and St. Anthony's Shrine. The shrines and sculpture include the towering piece that adorned the facade of the Vatican pavilion at the 1964 New York World's Fair.

Shopping. Dock Square and, increasingly, the Lower Village across the river are full of interesting stores, everything from the **Thurston House** country store to the **Port Canvas Co.,** with all kinds of handsome canvas products. Crowning the main corner of Dock Square is the decidedly upscale **Compliments,** "the gallery for your special lifestyle." It features lots of glass, including lamps and egg cups, trickling fountains and cute ceramic gulls, each with its own personality. Another extraordinary shop is **Punctilio,** stocking one-of-a-kind items from innovative designers. You might pick up a feather quill pen set or a beaded scarf that looks like a piece of jewelry. **Alano Ltd.** has super clothes, and we liked the contemporary crafts at **Kennebunkport Arts** and **Plum Dandy.** The splendid **Kennebunk Book Port, Paper Plus,** the **Haberdashery, Amicus,** the **Good Earth Pottery, Port Folio** ("paper with panache"), **The Whimsey Shop** and the shops at Union Square and Village Marketplace are other favorites.

Extra-Special ─────────────────────────

Rachel Carson National Wildlife Refuge, Route 9, Kennebunkport. (207) 646-9226.

A mile-long interpretive trail through saltwater marshes and adjacent grasslands leads one through an area rich in migratory and resident wildlife. The 5,000-acre reserve is named for the environmental pioneer who summered in Maine and conducted research in the area for several of her books. The trail, "paved" with small gravel, and boardwalks lead through tranquil woods until – just when you begin to wonder what all the fuss is about – the vista opens up at the sixth marker and a boardwalk takes you out over wetlands and marsh. Cormorants, herons and more are sighted here regularly, and benches allow you to relax as you take in the scene. An even better view of the ocean in the distance is at Marker 7, the Little River overlook. The widest, best view of all is near the end of the loop at Marker 11. If you don't have time for the entire trail, ignore the directional signs and go counter-clockwise. You'll get the best view first, though you may not see much wildlife. Open daily, dawn to dusk.

Fine view of Camden Harbor is offered from porch at Smiling Cow gift shop.

Camden, Me.
Where Mountains Meet Sea

From where she stood in 1910, all that native poet Edna St. Vincent Millay could see were "three long mountains and a wood" in one direction and "three islands in a bay" the other way. Her poem, written at age 18 and first recited publicly at Camden's Whitehall Inn, captures the physical beauty of this coastal area known as the place where the mountains meet the sea.

Today, the late poet might not recognize her beloved Camden, so changed is the town that now teems with tourists in summer. The scenery remains as gorgeous as ever, and perhaps no street in Maine is more majestic than High Street, its forested properties lined with the sparkling white homes that one associates with the Maine coast of a generation ago. Back then, when you finally reached Camden after the slow, tortuous drive up Route 1, you unofficially had arrived Down East.

Those were the days, and visitors in ever-increasing numbers still try to recapture them in a town undergoing a bed-and-breakfast inn boom and a proliferation of smart, distinctive shops. A sign in the window of Mariner's Restaurant, proclaiming itself

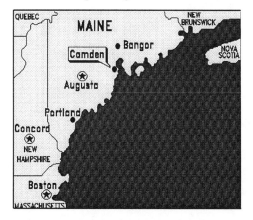

"the last local luncheonette," caught our eye: "Down Home, Down East; no ferns, no quiche."

A small-scale cultural life attracts some; others like the outdoors activities of Camden Hills State Park. But the focus for most is Camden Harbor, with its famed fleet of windjammers setting forth under full sail each Monday morning and returning to port each Saturday morning.

Camden has an almost mystical appeal that draws people back time and again.

209

Inn Spots

Norumbega, 61 High St., Camden 04843. (207) 236-4646.

Imagine having the run of a grand Victorian castle overlooking Penobscot Bay – a "castle to call home," in the words of businessman-turned-innkeeper Murray Keatinge.

It's possible, thanks to Murray, a Californian who summers in Camden and acquired Norumbega in 1987. "We're trying to build the best inn in the U.S.A.," he said on one of his not-infrequent trips back and forth from Pasadena, "and we're close to it." Even the harsh 1994 winter was a mere thorn along the path to paradise. Half a million dollars worth of ice damage forced the inn to close for four months, but Norumbega was rebuilt better than ever.

One of the great late-19th-century villas along the Maine coast, the 1886 cobblestone and slate-roofed mansion was built for Joseph B. Stearns, inventor of the duplex system of telegraphy, and for a few years was the summer home of journalist Hodding Carter. It has nine sumptuous guest rooms on the second and third floors, three more in the walk-out basement, a penthouse suite to end all suites and a main floor with public rooms like those in the finest estates.

Indeed, this is a mini-Newport-style mansion, from its graceful entry with oriental carpets and ornate staircase (complete with a cozy retreat for two beside a fireplace on the landing) to the smallest of guest rooms on the garden level, which rents for $145 with an ocean view and its own little deck. The once-smallest room now has become a sitting room for the Library Suite, a two-story affair with windows on three sides and a wraparound mezzanine to get at all the books.

The other rooms, all high-ceilinged and airy, are decorated in a fresh California style with lots of pastels and plush rugs. Each includes a kingsize bed, sitting area and a private bath. The Sandringham has a fireplace in the corner and a sofa and two chairs beneath balloon curtains in the turret window. The Canaervon, full of wicker, has its own little rear porch with deck chairs. A bay window and a private deck afford full bay views for guests in the Warwick Room. Even the basement rooms, with windows onto the garden, are cheery.

The ultimate is the penthouse suite, up a spiral staircase from the third floor. It harbors a regal bath with pillows around a circular whirlpool tub for two, a wet bar, a sitting room in pink and green, and a see-through, three-sided fireplace, plus a porch with two deck chairs and a fabulous ocean view.

The parlors, the conservatory, the downstairs lounge with pool table and TV, the flower-laden rear porches on all three floors and the expansive lawns are all available for guests' relaxation.

Murray's son Ken may greet guests and pour tea or wine in the afternoon. You also can help yourself to homemade soup, goodies from the cookie jar and a refrigerator stocked with mineral water and soft drinks.

In the morning, guests gather at the large table in the formal dining room, in the sunny conservatory or outside on the deck for a breakfast feast: platters of fresh fruits, homemade muffins and breads, breakfast meats and, the pièce de résistance, the main course – perhaps featherbed eggs with shrimp and hash-browns, lemon pancakes with blueberry sauce, raspberry crêpes or, in our case, french toast topped with a dollop of pink sherbet and sliced peaches, which all eight at our table agreed was about the best we'd ever had.

Being thrown together with strangers somehow works here – there's enough room for togetherness and also for escape, if you want. The price is steep, but most guests find it worth it.

Doubles, $145 to $270; suites, $295 to $425.

Norumbega is a grand Victorian manstion overlooking Penobscot Bay.

The Inn at Sunrise Point, Route 1, Box 1344, Camden 04843. (207) 236-7716 or (800) 435-6278.

Here's a switch: Travel writer visits more than 2,000 inns and decides to open his own on the coast of Maine. Finds old house within 100 feet of the ocean on four forested acres and 150 feet of waterfront near Lincolnville Beach. Doubles size of house, adds conservatory, builds new cottage and doubles size of another. Opens B&B in 1992 and awaits travel writers' reactions "with trepidation."

Jerry Levitin, a Californian who took over the late Norman Simpson's *Country Inns & Back Roads* guidebook for a time and ruffled the feathers of some longtime inn-keepers along the way, found out again what it's like to be on the receiving end of the pen (he opened the White Swan residential hotel on San Francisco's Nob Hill in 1979 before turning to travel writing).

"I built what I'd like to stay at," says Jerry with characteristic candor. Incorporating "the best of what I've seen," he and a succession of resident innkeepers have run what he calls a combination "English manor/country casual/seaside cottage." His goal was to join the ranks of Norumbega – which, he opines, is the only inn for the high-end market on the Camden coast, "and it isn't on the water."

The main house offers a living-dining room that's mostly windows onto Penobscot Bay, an English hunting-style library with cherrywood shelves and a stone fireplace, and a small conservatory with a breakfast table for two, a wicker couch and the sky visible above. Upstairs are three California-size (make that rather small) guest rooms with fireplaces, tiled showers, queensize beds with swing reading lamps, two swivel upholstered or wicker chairs in front of the window, built-in desks and honey-pine armoires holding TVs, VCRs, music systems and guests' clothing. They are decorated variously in yellow, raspberry and light blue.

Two fireplaced guest cottages next to the water are bigger and offer microwaves, wet bars and double jacuzzis with separate showers. The Winslow Homer Cottage that we occupied right beside the bay features a kingsize bed and an enormous bathroom almost as big as the bedroom. We were surprised there was no space to stash luggage other than in the bathroom, and the waterfront deck was so narrow as to be useless (the front porch of the main house compensated). New at bay's edge is the prized Fitz Hugh Lane Cottage, light and airy with a vaulted ceiling. Lie in one of its two queensize beds "and your feet are in the water," Jerry points out, with an understandable bit of hyperbole. There's a kitchenette as well as a jacuzzi and separate shower in the Edward Hopper Cottage in the old barn and carriage house.

Jerry or his innkeeper greets guests with tea, coffee, wine and hot and cold appetizers, served from 4 to 6 "and substantial enough so you won't need to eat dinner until 8 or 9." Although he prepares the appetizers, "you wouldn't want to eat my breakfast," so the innkeeper takes over. We feasted on fruit, pecan coffeecake, a terrific frittata with basil, bay shrimp and jack cheese, potatoes dusted with cayenne, crisp bacon and hazelnut coffee. Corn muffins, potatoes and crabmeat strata were on tap at a later visit.

Upon departure, we found a card under our windshield: "Our porter has cleaned your windscreen to allow you to get a clear picture of our Penobscot Bay."

Doubles, $150 to $200; cottages, $250 and $295. Open Memorial Day through October.

Windward House, 6 High St., Camden 04843. (207) 236-9656.

Guests enter this handsome B&B through the dining room, which is appropriate, for its gourmet breakfasts are well-known. A gleaming silver service, lace curtains, blue patterned rug and lots of plants immediately catch the eye. Innkeepers Mary and Jon Davis may greet you here and lead you to the nicely furnished parlor, or a pine-paneled TV room with all the current magazines, for orientation purposes before showing you to your room.

The house has five guest rooms, each with private bath, and a suite with queensize canopy poster bed and a sitting room. French doors open onto a private garden from the Wicker Room, pretty in pink and blue. The Rose Room has a queen canopy bed and lots of antiques, and the Camden Room comes with an eyelet cover and a doll on the bed. Special touches in each room include mints and Crabtree & Evelyn toiletries. A decanter of sherry awaits in the parlor.

Especially inviting is a new garden room in the rear. Here, light pours through three skylights in the cathedral ceiling to reveal a pink and green room with an 1850 crochet-canopy maple bed. Outside is a spotlit English garden, an ever-expanding showplace of annuals, perennials and herbs, carefully planned and tended for color all summer long.

About those breakfasts: Mary Davis, who was a caterer in Bernardsville, N.J., prepares things like peaches and cream french toast, apple-puff pancakes, waffles with blueberry-lemon nut sauce, crêpes, quiches, ham and cheese soufflés, and grand marnier-strawberry puffs. Fresh fruit comes first, followed by homemade muffins and rolls, then the entrée, accompanied by breakfast meats. After that, you may be temporarily immobilized. Take your coffee out onto the deck overlooking the long back yard and garden, and revel in the good life.

Doubles, $85 to $135. No smoking.

Edgecombe-Coles House, 64 High St., Camden 04843. (207) 236-2336.

On a hilltop almost across the street from Norumbega, this is another substantial summer home run by former Californians. Innkeepers Terry and Louise Price named it for their fathers and furnished it rather spectacularly with antiques, oriental rugs, original art, stenciling that Louise did herself (she also loves to wallpaper), and interesting touches like draperies around the showers and English soaps and herb shampoos for guests.

Each of the six guest rooms with private baths is different, but most have quilts and bedspreads made by Louise's mother. The most elegant is the huge front room with kingsize bed, fireplace and picture windows framing a grand ocean view for the occupant of the chaise lounge.

In the luxurious living room are a leather chesterfield, plush sofas and antique chairs angled around the fireplace, a baby grand piano, and many books and magazines. There's a TV in the book-filled den, which also has a fireplace.

A full breakfast is served in the pretty rear dining room or on the wraparound front porch, restored to its original look and furnished in wicker. Omelets, strawberry waffles, blueberry pancakes and dutch babies (giant sweet popovers) are among the specialties. The innkeepers will bring continental breakfast to your bedroom, if you wish. They also provide free bicycles, including a tandem bike, for guests to use.

Doubles, $120 to $175. No smoking.

A Little Dream, 66 High St., Camden 04843. (207) 236-8742.

This is a lacy valentine of a B&B, decorated with great flair by Joanne Fontana. She and her sculptor husband Billy (most of his time is spent in remodeling these days) bought the white Victorian turreted house in 1988. Former owners of toy stores in New York City and Boston, they seem to have brought their entire inventory with them. The collection of dolls and teddybears in their little dream world is not to be believed.

From the pretty wicker and chintz furnished parlor to the elaborately decorated dining room to the conservatory they added off the dining room, everything is accessorized to perfection. Lace pillows on a chaise, tea sets, old playing cards, tiny sentimental books tucked here and there – you know that Joanne, who says "I have the nicest guests in the whole world," loves to pamper them.

The choicest lodging in the main house is the master bedroom on the second floor. Done in greens and roses, it has its own bathroom and balcony, a four-poster bed entwined with pussy willows, a TV with a VCR and video library and a chaise lounge

Entrance to A Little Dream.

in a reading nook. When the leaves are off the trees, this room has a great view of Norumbega across the street and Penobscot Bay beyond. The newly expanded Yellow Room adds a bidet and an expansive deck and balcony. A large turret room is popular because it adjoins a sitting area in the turret. Every room has a private bath, a basket of hand towels and Crabtree & Evelyn amenities, everything is tied with ribbons, there are about eight pillows on each bed and Victorian clothing is displayed everywhere.

More lodging with wet bars and small refrigerators is available on two floors of the rear Carriage House. The upstairs unit is almost an apartment, with a separate sitting room, a balcony and a queen brass bed.

Breakfasts are gala happenings at A Little Dream. On lace cloths topped with flowered mats and heavy silver, you might find fresh orange juice in champagne flutes,

Kentucky butter cake with crème fraîche and local blueberries, a fruit platter with honeydew melon, black raspberries, kiwis, strawberries and grapefruit, and heart-shaped banana-pecan waffles with country sausage. Smoked salmon or apple-brie omelets, fruit crêpes, lemon-ricotta soufflé pancakes or baked featherbed eggs with pears, smoked ham and a raspberry puree sauce are other specialties. At check-in, the Fontanas will serve strawberry or peach herbal iced tea, with fresh mint from the garden, and at cocktail time, perhaps a tray of pâtés, including smoked trout, and olives.

Doubles, $95 to $139.

Victorian B&B, The Other Road, Box 258, Lincolnville 04849. (207) 236-3785 or (800) 382-9817.

New Yorkers Marie and Ray Donner moved with their almost-teenagers in 1993 to a Victorian house built in 1889, added 5,000 square feet and created a comfortable B&B. They offer six spacious bedrooms and suites with private baths and a superior location – 800 feet down a wooded hillside off Route 1, with views and a nature trail reaching to Penobscot Bay.

You can tell this place is special when you first see the substantial house – painted beige with lots of striking apricot-colored trim – and the broad, wraparound veranda that was part of the addition built by Ray, who was involved in heavy construction work in New York. The wicker-filled veranda is perfect for taking in the tranquil setting and the watery scene through a break in the trees. So is a shady gazebo over-looking gardens.

Also comfortable is the guest living room, a fireplaced dining room that opens onto an appealing eight-sided sun porch in a corner turret, and a large butler's pantry in which guests are free to use the microwave, refrigerator and such.

Little cloth dolls from their daughter's collection reside amid the pillows on the queensize beds in each room. Family heirlooms, quilts, window treatments and beds reflect the Victorian period, but without the clutter often associated with the era. A second-floor suite with a fireplaced sitting room in the turret is the most sought-after accommodation, although that may change as Ray was finishing a skylit suite on the third floor. It has a loft in the bedroom, a sitting room and an enormous bathroom in which Ray built wash basins into a library table.

Breakfast is served buffet style in the sun porch or dining room. At our visit the fare was juice, muffins, granola and blueberry pancakes. Other main dishes include stuffed french toast with cream cheese, chocolate belgian waffles with raspberries picked on the grounds, and crêpes filled with homemade jams.

The Donners serve afternoon tea and cookies or hot apple cider, depending on the season, to arriving guests. They offer dinners on Saturday nights in the off-season. Marie also runs a nice little Victorian gift shop in a section of the carriage house beside the inn.

Doubles, $85 to $100; suites, $125 and $135.

The Belmont, 6 Belmont Ave., Camden 04843. (207) 236-8053.

Camden's oldest inn, this cottage-style Victorian on a residential side street has sheltered guests first as the Green Gables and then, until 1988, as Aubergine. That's when David and Kerlin Grant, widely known for their French cuisine, sold to Gerald Clare and John Mancarella.

They changed the main-floor layout to enlarge a reception room/parlor, added a side porch and switched the cuisine from French nouvelle to regional American (see Dining Spots). All six upstairs guest rooms have private baths. They are nicely decorated with antique furnishings, floral wallpapers and a light, sunny quality in keeping with

Victorian B&B features turrets and wraparound veranda.

the yellow exterior. The two third-floor rooms we once occupied with our sons have been converted into one extra-large room. A suite offers a separate sitting room.

Wicker rockers on the side porch invite dalliance with a pre-dinner drink from the small bar off the parlor. The parlor, done up in rose and celadon with an oriental rug over the bleached wood floor, has a nifty window seat made from mattress ticking and small built-in benches beside the fireplace.

A full breakfast, perhaps with shirred eggs or dutch babies, is served in the country-pretty dining room or on the enclosed sun porch sparkling with white summer furniture.

Doubles, $95 to $125; suites, $145. Two-night minimum on weekends. Closed December-April.

Hartstone Inn, 41 Elm St., Camden 04843. (207) 236-4259.

Built in 1835 by a local merchant, this house on Camden's main street near the business district was renovated into an inviting inn in 1986 by Peter and Elaine Simmons.

They offer eight bedrooms, all with private baths and two with fireplaces, on three floors – from one on the third floor, you can glimpse the harbor. One bathroom has a marble sink, another an old wood-encased tub and all have trays of toiletries and thick, fluffy towels. Several beds have carved-oak headboards.

A restored carriage house in the rear offers two housekeeping suites, particularly good for families. Done in contemporary barn style, they have dark beams tempered with light walls and skylights, complete kitchens and futon beds.

A quiet parlor harbors a fireplace, and a common room is full of books, games and a TV. A pleasant dining room is where a complete breakfast is served; it could include baked eggs with smoked turkey and cheese, homemade corned beef hash, frittata, light sour-cream pancakes with blackberry sauce or french toast made with cornbread.

A four-course dinner is available for house guests by reservation in the off-season, priced from $17 to $22, depending on the entrée. A typical meal might involve curried asparagus soup, salad, chicken stuffed with goat cheese and herbs with souffléed potatoes, glazed carrots and parsnips, and chocolate truffle cake or frozen lemon pie. Guests may bring their own wine.

Doubles, $75 to $125; housekeeping suites, $700 a week.

Blue Harbor House, 67 Elm St., Camden 04843. (207) 236-3196 or (800) 248-3196.

Still more ex-Californians in Camden, Dennis Hayden and Jody Schmoll own this old-timer, nicely upgraded and expanded since their arrival in 1989. They offer ten guest rooms, all with private baths, ranging in size from tiny front Room 4, formerly occupied by a lady who lived in the house for 96 years, to two large suites converted from a rear apartment.

All the rooms are notable for attractive and varied stenciling, done by the former innkeeper who returns as Jody adds more rooms. It turns up in the most interesting motifs and places. Seagulls, tulips, pineapples – you name them, you may find them stenciled somewhere. Colorful quilts, period furnishings and treasured pieces from the couple's past abound. Traffic noise in rooms near the street has been reduced with the installation of thermopane windows and air-conditioning.

For privacy and comfort, we'd spring for one of the two rear suites, each with kingsize bed, circular whirlpool tub, TV and comfy sitting area. An antique posting board once used for stock prices adorns a wall in one.

Guests share a side porch, a small parlor, a sun porch/common room with TV where breakfast is served, and a second dining room for overflow. Dennis does the cooking. His favorite is blueberry pancakes, light and fluffy. He also does soufflés, rum-raisin french toast with rum-raisin ice cream, dutch babies filled with fruit, shirred eggs and lobster quiche – "I try to make every day a Sunday brunch," he says. Iced tea, cookies and sometimes homemade ice cream are served in the afternoon.

Candlelight dinners are available for house guests by reservation. The $50 tab for two might bring lobster stew, a green salad with basil vinaigrette, rack of lamb stuffed with spinach and hazelnuts, and chocolate brownie soufflé.. Dennis says he enjoys cooking better than his former executive job with the Korbel champagne company.

Doubles, $85 to $110; suites, $125.

Swan House, 49 Mountain St., Camden 04843. (207) 236-8275 or (800) 207-8275.

"Birds and gulls – not traffic – wake you up here in the morning," says Ken Kohl, formerly of Chicago, who with wife Lynn took over the Swan House from a consortium of local innkeepers in 1993 and began imbuing it with the renovations and TLC that energetic, on-site owners provide. Their location on a wooded double lot on a residential street away from busy Route 1 is an asset. So are the six comfortable, quiet guest rooms in the 1874 Victorian house built by the Swan family, on which the Kohls built an addition for their living quarters, and in a rear carriage house nestled in the trees.

Two guest parlors are full of interesting touches. Among them are a sleigh transformed into a coffee table and a game table made by Amish woodworkers; the latter has an astonishingly realistic Monopoly board made of needlepoint inlaid inside. Breakfast is served on butcher-block and glass tables in a front sun porch with a view of a hillside gazebo. Juice, strawberries in a pineapple half, homemade granola and pastries like almond coffeecake and apple crisp started the repast when we visited. Main dishes vary from pancakes to baked french toast to egg casserole.

Two bedrooms on the first floor of the main house and four more in the carriage house called the Cygnet Annex are each named for swans. All have private baths and all but two come with canopied queensize beds. Especially popular are the upstairs Swan Lake loft with skylights, two double beds and a day bed, a wicker loveseat and knotty pine walls hung with baskets, wreaths and artifacts. Also in demand are the quiet and cool Lohengren Suite with queensize sofabed in the sitting area, and, our choice, the Trumpeter Room in back with a vaulted ceiling and a deck in the trees.

Doubles, $85 to $95; suites, $95 to $120.

Fine dining is an attraction for guests and public at The Belmont.

Dining Spots

The Belmont, 6 Belmont Ave., Camden. (207) 236-8053.

The first fine restaurant in the Camden area (indeed, a pioneer in nouvelle cuisine on the Maine coast), Aubergine gave way to The Belmont and chef-owner Gerry Clare, who had a restaurant in Fort Lauderdale and a guest house in Nantucket. He changed the emphasis from French to American cuisine (lately with oriental accents), but otherwise repeat guests are hard-pressed to tell the difference.

The serene dining room is lovely with its white linens and aubergine carpet; the adjacent sun porch has pristine white tables and chairs, accented by new curtains. Floral china and flowers from the cutting garden provide color.

The menu changes every few days. Some of the fare is inspired, as in an appetizer of stir-fried mussels with fermented black beans and lemon grass or a white gazpacho with delicious homemade croutons. Pad Thai noodles with shrimp, chicken and peanuts, Maine crab and avocado salad, and duck and oriental vegetables in rice paper crêpes are other starters in the $6.50 to $8.50 range.

The eight entrées, one of them always vegetarian, are priced from $15 for calves liver with pancetta and onions to $24 for lobster sautéed with coconut-milk green curry, lemon grass, ginger and cilantro. We liked the grilled pork tenderloin with black beans and salsa and a special of poached salmon with citrus sauce.

Among desserts, always a strong point here, the sour-cream blueberry cheesecake is sensational. Other tempters are chocolate mascarpone dacquoise, warm plum tart, raspberry gratin and the trio of sorbets, perhaps piña colada, passion fruit and watermelon. "It could be anything," says Gerry; "when we run out of one kind, we make another."

The wine list is extensive and fairly priced.

Dinner nightly except Monday, 6 to 9:30. Closed December-April.

Cassoulet, 31 Elm St., Camden. (207) 236-6304.

Tiny, cute and very colorful is Cassoulet (the former Secret Garden). Now the garden in back has been enclosed. Reached via a winding path through the chef's herb garden at the side, the screened porch is summery as can be with pink deck chairs, dusty pink tablecloths, an abundance of hanging plants, fresh flowers and, overhead, stars visible through openings in the roof. It fairly exudes romance, making the small inside room seem a bit cramped, though it's an attractive riot of pinks, greens, purples and such amid moss green banquettes and chairs, cacti in the windows and striking pictures of flowers on the walls.

Chef-owner Robert Teague and his wife Sally, who had the place up for sale in 1994, featured "classic country cooking" with an Italian accent. The menu listed such appetizers as caponata with crostini and polenta with grilled mushrooms in the $4 to $10 range. We started with mozzarella galettes with sundried tomato pesto, excellent though we would have liked a bit more of the pesto, and a tossed salad with blue cheese dressing.

Heading the short list of entrées ($14 to $18) were bouillabaisse, cioppino and, of course, cassoulet – made with lamb, pork and garlic sausage. The night's specials ranged from tuna niçoise and scampi alla griglia to pesto chicken and lamb noisettes. Everyone seemed to be ordering the pasta of the day, fettuccine with scallops, and with good reason – it proved to be a masterpiece. The shrimp à la grecque, a house specialty, was good but could have used some rice or pasta to go with.

The hit of the evening was a frozen lemon mousse, intense and refreshing. Others of Sally's desserts could be a flourless chocolate-raspberry torte, strawberry shortcake with a citrus biscuit or zuccotto, a pound cake drizzled with grand marnier and layered with whipped cream.

Dinner, Monday-Saturday 6 to 9:30.

The Waterfront Restaurant, Harborside Square off Bay View Street, Camden. (207) 236-3747.

There's no better waterside setting in Camden than this appropriately named establishment with a breezy, nautical interior and a large outdoor deck shaded by a striking white canopy that resembles a boat's sails.

You can watch the busy harbor as you lunch on fried clams (with crab cakes, the most expensive entrée at $10.95, including a good salad and french fries), chicken dijon salad or a lobster roll. Other interesting selections include Tuscan bread soup, Thai shrimp and mussels, smoked salmon with toasted bagel, sandwich niçoise, mussels marinière and enchiladas.

Most of the interesting luncheon salads also are available as dinner entrées, and the homemade sweet and sour bacon, lemon-parmesan and blue cheese dressings are outstanding.

The accent is on seafood among main courses at night ($12.95 to $16.95). At various visits, we've enjoyed the Maine crab cakes with creamy mustard sauce, an assertive linguini with salmon and sundried tomatoes, shrimp with oriental black beans over angel-hair pasta and a special of swordfish grilled over applewood with rosemary, rich and succulent. Jerk chicken and sirloin dijon are the only non-seafood items.

There's a good little wine list, attractively priced. From 2:30 p.m. on, the **Oyster Bar** serves up fresh seafood from the raw bar and grilled items from hamburger to cajun shrimp to lobster roll, $5.95 to $9.95. A favorite is the sampler of locally smoked salmon, mussels and trout.

Lunch daily, 11:30 to 2:30; dinner, 5 to 10.

Peter Ott's, 16 Bay View St., Camden. (207) 236-4032.

We never could figure out why people would want to eat at a steakhouse on the coast, and those who did apparently diminished in number. In 1994, owner Keith May

Rear porch provides summery garden setting for diners at Cassoulet.

marked the 20th anniversary of Peter Ott's Tavern and Steakhouse with a considerable rehab and a change in name and menu.

The historic, high-ceilinged building with windows onto the waterfront area was lightened up with good art on yellow-sponged walls, different colored cloth napkins and fresh flowers accenting the shiny wood tables, Big lamps hang overhead.

It's a pleasant backdrop for a revised menu that adds pastas, seafood and light fare to the traditional steakhouse fare. One innkeeper says the pasta dishes are as good as they come in Camden. Look for starters like native shrimp and Thai curry soup, grilled eggplant provençal, cajun popcorn and grilled polenta with wild mushroom sauté. Among main courses ($13.50 to $19.50) are charbroiled tuna steak with ginger-sake sauce, blackened seafood sampler, Szechuan-style cashew chicken, grilled pork chops, assorted steaks and filet mignon. The action is on the nightly specials list: perhaps fresh lemon and black pepper fettuccine tossed with sea scallops, snow peas, mushrooms and garlic; pan-fried catfish with cilantro sauce; charbroiled swordfish with Thai pineapple curry; fillet of haddock with Cantonese mushroom and Maine lobster sauce, and grilled saddle of lamb loin chops.

A link with the past is the salad bar, billed as Camden's original. It's included in the price of all dinners, or you can make a meal of it along with fresh bread for $5.95.

Dinner nightly, 5:30 to 10.

O'Neil's, 21 Bay View St., Camden. (207) 236-3272.

Front and center on the main floor of this relative oldtimer in downtown Camden are trendy wood ovens and a wood grill. They're the latest focal point for a restaurant that seems to be continually renovating and changing culinary themes to find its niche. The consensus at recent visits was that O'Neil's had finally come into its own.

The walls of the main-floor lounge are mustard yellow, the pine tables are left bare and votive candles flicker. Upstairs is the dining room and, beyond and to the rear, a cozy outdoor deck that's popular with those who manage to snag its sixteen seats.

219

The theme now is grills, roasts and pizzas from the wood oven. The menu is subdivided into small plates, salads, pizzas and big plates. Among the last ($11.95 to $15.95) are spit-roasted garlic and herb chicken with panzanella, grilled salmon with braised fennel-tomato salad and fried leeks, changing pastas and grilled steak with gorgonzola-brandy cream sauce. Exotic pizzas ($6.95 to $10.95) are dressed with everything from shrimp and artichokes to duck sausage to lobster with tomatoes, basil and two cheeses. Grazers are content with the likes of fried calamari, black bean burritos, Mediterranean goat cheese salads and grilled fig, marsala and pine nut sausage with parmesan polenta.

Affordable wines are available by the bottle and liter. Lemon mousse is a favorite dessert.

Lunch daily, 11:30 to 2:30; dinner, from 5.

Cappy's Chowder House, 1 Main St., Camden. (207) 236-2254.

"The Maine you hope to meet" is one of the catchy slogans surrounding Cappy's, and local color is said to be its strong point. The scene is barroom nautical: lobster traps hang above the bar, and green billiards-room lamps light the bare wood tables. The upstairs Crow's Nest offers a view of the harbor. The something-for-everyone menu is Down East cutesy: Maine pigskins, burgers on the bounty, Camden curly fries, mussel beach pasta and desserted islands.

The place packs in the crowds for clam chowder ($3.50 a cup; by the pint or quart to go), a lobster salad croissant, crab cakes topped with salsa on a bed of spinach, seafood stir-fry, chicken cappenesca and the like. Main courses, accompanied by French bread from Cappy's Bakery below, rice pilaf and salad with a good house dressing, cost $9.95 to $15.95. Burgers, sandwiches, salads and lighter fare are in the $4.95 to $9.95 range.

Locals gather here for breakfast. The placemat is the menu, offering things like "pure eggstasy" and blueberry pancakes. For a snack, try a spinach and feta croissant or a Miss Plum's cookie sandwich from the bakery.

Oysters and shrimp by the bucket are served from the raw bar during happy hour in the Crow's Nest.

Open daily, 7:30 a.m. to midnight.

Mama & Leenie's, 27 Elm St., Camden. (207) 236-6300.

Stop at this little cafe and bakery for a cup of that good Green Mountain coffee and a breakfast of blintzes, french toast or the ever-so-good eggs in a frame – grilled in thick toast ($3.75 to $5.50).

At lunch you could order Mama's special beef stew, or a baconburger with blue cheese. Melted cheese and tomato on a bagel might hit the spot, or how about a pasta salad primavera?

Mama does a lot of the cooking. Daughter Leenie is a master baker as evidenced by the apricot strudel with coconut and walnuts, the double chocolate fudge brownies with orange zest, and the pure butter shortbread. The fresh berry pies with real whipped cream are masterpieces.

The decor is simple, with ladderback chairs and wild flowers in little jars. Leenie has painted flowers and ivy leaves all over the place, and "Vaya con Dios" is painted above the door. There's a nice little patio on one side.

You may bring your own wine for dinner, when you might find Indonesian marinated chicken on a skewer or a bowl of chili with homemade bread. The local Miss Plum's ice cream is offered, and nothing costs much more than $7.

Open 8 a.m. to 9:30 p.m., Sunday 8 to 4, fewer hours in off-season. BYOB.

Sea Dog Brewing Co., 43 Mechanic St., Camden. (207) 236-6863.

The Maine beers and ales are all the rage at this no-expense-spared micro-brewery cum restaurant run by the Camplin family in one of the former Knox Mill buildings. Most visitors gravitate to the fancy tavern – a mix of booths, beams, oriental runners and stone walls that's too atmospheric for words. The splashy waterfall outside the soaring windows adds to the effect. The large outside patio beside the Megunticook River is the icing on the mix.

The brewery's Penobscot Maine lager, Windjammer Maine ale, Owl's Head light and Old Gollywobbler Brown Ale are featured, along with a variety of snacks and sandwiches ($4.50 to $8.95). The food is surprisingly good, considering – anything from steamed mussels to crab cakes, welsh rarebit to a lobster roll. Sample the beer and ale soup, caesar salad and grilled chicken en brochette and you've made yourself a meal.

Tours of the downstairs brewery are given daily at 11 and 4 in summer, and Saturdays the rest of the year. There's a brewtique for bar ware and apparel. The brewery business blossomed beyond expectations, Peter Camplin said, and less than two years after opening, the Sea Dog expanded in 1995 with a large new plant and pub in Bangor.

Open daily, 11 a.m. to 1 a.m.

Diversions

Water pursuits. Any number of boat cruises on Penobscot Bay leave from the Camden landing, where there are benches for viewing the passing boat parade. Windjammers are a class apart, but lately the Appledore has been giving morning and afternoon cruises, there's a Sunday buffet lunch sail on the Timberwind and the Wendameen offers an overnight with dinner and breakfast. For more cruises or ferry rides to the islands, go to Rockland or Lincolnville Beach (a favorite excursion is the ferry trip to Islesboro). The Lincolnville Beach is popular for swimming. A more secluded, picturesque setting is the little-known Laite Memorial Beach with treed lawns sloping down to the water, a small beach, picnic tables and old-fashioned fireplaces off Bay View Street.

Inland pursuits. Some of the East Coast's most scenic hiking is available on trails in Camden Hills State Park. Mount Megunticook is the highest of the three mountains that make up the park and the second highest point on the Eastern Seaboard. If you're not up to hiking, be sure to drive the toll road up Mount Battie, an easy one-mile ride. The view is worth the $1-per-person toll. A scenic drive is out Route 52 to Megunticook Lake, an island-studded lake that emerged eerily from the clouds the first foggy afternoon we saw it. A walking tour of Camden and a bicycle or car tour of Camden and adjacent Rockport are available through the Camden-Rockport Historical Society.

Cultural pursuits. Summer entertainment, from band concerts to vaudeville, is provided periodically in the outdoor Bok Amphitheater next to the town library, just a few hundred feet from the harbor. The **Camden Civic Theatre** produces the occasional play at the Camden Opera House. Visitors can glimpse the future in the main-floor gallery of the **Center for Creative Imaging** at 51 Mechanic St. Founded jointly by Eastman Kodak and Apple Computer, the world's most advanced facility for electronic imaging experimentation has vaulted into the vanguard of digital imaging technology – in lay terms, the computerized manipulation of visual data. Guided tours of the four-story studio and think tank are given Wednesday-Sunday at noon. The **Old Conway House and Mary Meeker Cramer Museum,** a mile south of town along Route 1, includes a restored 18th-century farmhouse, a barn displaying antique carriages and sleighs, a blacksmith shop and an 1820 maple sugar house. The **Camden-Rockport**

Historical Society complex is open Tuesday-Friday 10 to 4 in July and August; admission, $2. The **Farnsworth Museum** in nearby Rockland ranks among the finer regional art museums in the nation. The collection focuses on American art from the 18th century to the present, with prized works by the Wyeth family. Included in the $5 museum admission is the adjacent **Farnsworth Homestead,** considered one of the most beautiful Victorian houses in the country.

Shopping pursuits. Camden is a mecca for sophisticated shopping, and all kinds of interesting specialty stores and boutiques pop up every year, particularly along Bay View Street. A major presence on Main Street is **Planet,** which started small in 1993 and expanded into an old department store across the street in 1994. It quickly became a department store in itself with a trendy selection of gifts, hip clothing, housewares, accessories, medicinal herbals, children's things and much more, many with a nature or planetary theme. **The Smiling Cow,** a large and venerable gift shop with a myriad of Maine items, has a great view from its rear porch over the Megunticook River, which ripples down the rocks toward the harbor; you can take in the picturesque scene while sipping complimentary coffee or tea between shopping forays. Along Bay View Street, **The Owl and the Turtle** is an excellent, many-roomed bookstore on two floors. Stylish picnic hampers in the window lured us inside **The Grasshopper Shop** to view its assortment of gifts and accessories. **Wild Birds Unlimited** has an amazing collection of bird feeders, carved birds, birdsong tapes and the like. **Heather Harland** is a large, sophisticated store offering interesting kitchen items, tableware, cookbooks, cards and linens – we especially liked the selection of placemats. A large carved gull wearing a windjammer tie drew us into the **Ducktrap Bay Trading Co.,** a gallery of wildlife from decoys to paintings. **The Admiral's Buttons** has preppy clothing and sailing attire. We bought a handcrafted Maine wooden bucket for use as a planter from **Once a Tree,** which also has great clocks, toys, bracelets and everything else made from wood. At **Touchstone,** we liked the stained-glass sailboats. The **Harbor Square Gallery,** which periodically opens the Blue Angel Cafe upstairs, displays some of the area's best and most expensive art. **Lily, Lupine & Fern** pairs a thriving floral business with wines, champagnes, chocolates and gourmet food items. **Unique 1** stocks a great selection of sweaters done by local knitters. Traditional favorites are the **House of Logan** and **Margo Moore,** for distinctive clothing and gifts.

Extra-Special

Camden Windjammers. Long known as the windjammer capital of the world, Camden Harbor is quite a sight when the windjammers are in. On Sunday evenings from June through September, people sit at the wharf to watch as passengers board the old-time sailing vessels for their week's cruise through Penobscot Bay. After breakfast on Monday, the eight windjammers set sail for who knows where; their routes depend on whim, wind and tides. Mates sleep and eat on board, helping the crew if they like but most relaxing and savoring a sail from yesteryear. Many beds are bunks, but at least one of the newer windjammers has double beds, and some have running water for showers. Generally, the captain handles the seagoing chores while his wife does the cooking – everything from chowders to roasts – on a wood stove. The evening lobster bake on a deserted island is usually the week's highlight. On Saturday afternoon, the watching resumes in earnest as the windjammers return to Camden. Passengers pay $400 to $700 each for the experience; landlubbers can watch the comings and goings for free.

Rowantree Pottery inspired others and put Blue Hill on the map.

Blue Hill, Me.
Treasure of Tranquility

Between the chic of Camden and the bustle of Bar Harbor lies a largely unspoiled area jutting into East Penobscot Bay. Its focal point is the tranquil treasure known as Blue Hill.

So small that the unknowing tourist almost could miss it, the village lies between the 940-foot-high hill from which it takes its name and an inlet of Blue Hill Bay. A few roads and streets converge from different directions and, suddenly, here it is: Blue Hill, Me., population 1,941.

This is the center of an area long known for fine handicrafts, especially pottery. Indeed, Rowantrees Pottery owner Sheila Varnum says it is the pottery that "put Blue Hill on the map." Founded more than 50 years ago, Rowantrees has inspired a number of smaller ventures by craftspeople who cherish the simplicity of the area. Another draw in summer is the Kneisel Hall Chamber Music Festival. Blue Hill also supports a volunteer radio station, WERU (We Are You), with a down-home cultural programming mix.

Not for water nor resort pursuits do most visitors come to Blue Hill. It's the kind of place where the sign at the outdoor phone booth warned, "This phone doesn't work the way you're used to. Dial your number, wait for the loud tone and after your party answers, deposit twenty cents." We managed to get through the second time around.

There are no town beaches or marinas, no shopping emporiums to

speak of, and only one motel. What there are, instead, are world-famous potteries and crafts cooperatives, a handful of exceptional inns and restaurants, rural byways that remain much the way they were a generation ago and invite aimless exploration, and a sense of serenity that draws the knowing few back time after time for the utter peace and quiet of it all.

Go, but don't tell too many others about your find.

Inn Spots

John Peters House, Peters Point, Box 916, Blue Hill 04614. (207) 374-2116.

Looking somewhat like a Southern plantation, this white pillared and red brick structure commands an idyllic hilltop location just outside Blue Hill, with water on two sides. Built in 1815, it's listed on the National Register of Historic Places.

Personable owners Barbara and Rick Seeger, who acquired the former Altenhofen House in 1986, rebuilt the kitchen, added a dining porch and moved all the guest rooms upstairs. The eight comfortable bedrooms have private baths and five have fireplaces. Everybody's favorite is the expansive Blue Hill Room, which has a kingsize bed, lovely carpets, a wet bar with refrigerator and a large private deck where we lazed away the early evening while gazing up at Blue Hill.

Six newer rooms are located in a rear carriage house. There you can stay in a room with a queensize brass bed and a loveseat looking onto a private deck, or in a larger room that's almost a studio apartment with queen bed, fireplace, kitchenette and private deck.

Now with fourteen guest quarters, the Seegers were eyeing the rear barn at our latest visit – possibly as the site for an antiques co-op. "No more rooms," stressed Barbara.

Nice touches include fresh fruit and flowers in the bedrooms, the morning newspaper, a living room with a grand piano (many musicians stay here) and cozy sofas and chairs for reading or socializing, an old-fashioned swimming pool, a canoe and a couple of sailboats.

The Seegers put out quite a spread for breakfast, served on the enclosed side porch amid fine china, silver and classical music. Our three-course repast began with cantaloupe with ice cream or fresh berries with champagne (extra champagne is poured in glasses for those who wish it; one couple finished off a bottle and retired to their room for an early nap, Barbara reported). Then came fresh orange juice with sliced and grilled blueberry and corn muffins. The main event was a lavish choice including eggs benedict, blueberry or banana waffles, cheese and eggs or, the pièce de résistance, a lobster and artichoke omelet – so colorful that it cried out to be photographed. Garnished with lobster claws, it was accompanied by bacon or ham and hash browns and was so good that one of us ordered it two mornings in a row.

Doubles, $95 to $150.

Blue Hill Inn, Union Street, Box 403, Blue Hill 04614. (207) 374-2844.

Its flag flying out front, this trim white Colonial inn with Wedgwood blue shutters – a landmark in the heart of Blue Hill for nearly 150 years – has been considerably spiffed up by Mary and Don Hartley.

The energetic Hartleys have enhanced the eleven guest rooms with plush carpeting, new wallpaper and modernized bathrooms. All come with private baths and three with fireplaces. Some have sitting areas. Our rear bedroom – occupied the previous night by Peter of Peter, Paul and Mary fame after a concert at the Blue Hill Fair Grounds – was comfortable with a kingsize bed, two blue velvet wing chairs, colorful bed linens, plump towels and windows on three sides to circulate cool air, which was welcome

John Peters House has the look of a Southern plantation.

after a heat wave. The other rooms we saw also were nicely furnished with 19th-century antiques and traditional pieces reflecting what Mary calls "a homey Down East style." Homemade chocolates come with nightly turndown service.

A small library-game room, where old Life magazines are prominent, is furnished in antiques. The larger main parlor with a fireplace is where the Hartleys serve hors d'oeuvre (perhaps smoked bluefish or local goat cheese) during a nightly innkeepers' reception at 6, preceding a five-course dinner (see Dining Spots). Wines and liquors are available.

Breakfast is a culinary event. Ours started with the usual juices, a plate of cut-up fresh fruit and a wedge of apple-custard pie that one of us thought was dessert. The main course involved a choice of eggs scrambled with garden chives in puff pastry, an omelet with chèvre or brie and Canadian bacon, waffles with strawberry topping or blueberry pancakes. Excellent french-roast coffee accompanied.

Outside, guests enjoy the Hartleys' perennial garden with lawn furniture, a gazebo and a profusion of huge yellow lilies. The innkeepers occasionally charter a schooner to take guests out on East Penobscot Bay for day trips. They also sponsor seasonal concert weekends, schooner day trips on Penobscot Bay and themed wine-tasting dinners in the off-season.

Doubles, $140 to $160, MAP. No smoking.

Eggemoggin Reach Bed & Breakfast, The Herrick Road, RR 1, Box 33A, Brooksville 04617. (207) 359-5073.

At the end of a long driveway lies this prize of a waterside B&B. It's the transformation of a summer/retirement home for an energetic Southern couple who decided they weren't ready for retirement.

Susie and Mike Canon built their summer home along a particularly picturesque section of Eggemoggin Reach, looking out past the Pumpkin Island lighthouse toward Penobscot Bay, with a view of the Camden Hills beyond. They liked it so much that he sold his business in Jacksonville, Fla., had the house winterized and they moved here in 1989 "without a plan." Mike started a brokerage business in the garage and, in 1993, Susie opened their home as a B&B.

The house lends itself perfectly for the purpose. The open main floor of post and beam construction has pine paneling and high ceilings. A large brick fireplace warms the living room, and a wood stove enhances the den. Comfortable period furnishings and oriental rugs make the place more than a summer home. Across the front of the house is a full-length porch, partly screened and partly open. As Susie served iced tea, we watched the resident osprey and cormorants and looked for the seals that cavort daily in Deadman's Cove.

Upstairs are three suites, all facing the water. On the second floor, the Crew's Quarters that formerly housed the Canons' three sons has a queen bedroom, a sitting room with twin bed and a large bath across the hall. The corner master suite known as the Captain's Quarters has a huge full bathroom, a kingsize bed and a sitting area with water views on two sides. The third floor holds the Wheelhouse suite with private bath, king bed and a large living room with a sofabed, chairs, a desk and two twin beds tucked beneath the eves.

New at the side of the house are two rustic-looking cottages facing Deadman's Cove. Paneled in pickled pine, both have cathedral ceilings, king or twin beds, efficiency kitchens and sitting areas with a sofabed and a franklin stove. Their private screened porches overlooking the water are idyllic.

Guests gather for breakfast on the large porch or in the open dining area of the main house. Susie, whose background is in catering, provides quite a spread: juice, fruit, cereal, and puffed apple pancakes with a rasher of bacon the day of our visit. Eggs benedict, Mexican eggs, chiles rellenos and Yankee hash are other favorites.

On Wednesdays and Saturdays when six or more guests are in accord, the Canons serve a "lobster on the rocks" feast at water's edge. Besides lobster, the $50-per-couple tab (BYOB) yields corn on the cob, salad, blueberry pie and much conviviality. Guests tell the hosts that being on the shore eating lobster fresh out of the Reach and watching the sunset provides some of their more memorable moments in Maine.

Suites, $130 to $145; cottages, $145. Closed November-April. No smoking.

Arcady Down East, South Street, Blue Hill 04614. (207) 374-5576.

A large, brown-shingled Victorian mansion on a hilltop south of town is run as a B&B by ex-Californians Bertha and Gene Wiseman, a saintly couple who moved to Maine for a better place to raise their three young grandchildren. They took over a going concern but added their own mark, from wallpaper throughout to tin ceilings in three rooms.

A century old and listed on the National Register, the structure offers on its main floor an enormous entry foyer, a parlor, a dark-paneled dining room with high-back chairs at three tables, and porches looking onto the distant bay. Busts of every American president line a shelf in a corner of the sun porch.

All the handmade dolls in evidence were fashioned by Gene's mother, who won about every award possible at the Blue Hill Fair before moving back to California.

A magnificent staircase from the foyer splits in two directions to the second-floor guest rooms. Bertha cherishes a wooden swan carved by Chris Murray of Castine, which occupies a special place on the landing. It was a gift of the famed wildfowl sculptor, whose son is a school classmate of one of her grandsons.

Of the eight bedrooms, five have private baths and three share. Ceiling fans, music boxes and rocking chairs are standard in each room. Not so standard are the old Navy trunk and chest and the handpainted porcelain balls on the eight posters of the open-toe wraparound bed in the wonderfully nautical Captain's Quarters, the bright red velvet spread on the kingsize bed beneath a tin ceiling in the Victorian Scarlet Room and the armoire, working fireplace and George Washington carved kingsize bed in the Celebration Suite, which includes a day bed in the sitting area. Two small rooms at the

Rocking chairs take in water view from front porch of Eggemoggin Reach B&B.

rear share a vast skylit bathroom containing what's said to be the oldest tub in Blue Hill.

The Wisemans offer a complete breakfast: juice, fruit, muffins and an entrée like a Mexican quiche with salsa or cinnamon french toast made with English toasting bread. In summer they add large plates of sliced tomatoes from the garden. Afternoons yield such treats as iced tea, lemonade or root-beer floats.

With their grandchildren much in evidence, the Wisemans welcome children as guests. An ice-skating pond is an attraction in winter.

Doubles, $85 to $110. No smoking.

Blue Hill Farm, Route 15, Box 437, Blue Hill 04614. (207) 374-5126.

Located out in the country north of Blue Hill, this B&B really has a farm feeling – from the barn exterior of a newer addition to the goats grazing outside to the garden, stone wall, trout pond and 48 acres of woods and brooks out back.

The barn, full of fanciful touches and furnishings, includes a spacious and lofty main floor where meals are served and where there are all kinds of sitting areas. Upstairs are seven modern, smallish guest rooms with private baths. Seven more guest rooms that share baths are in the original farmhouse to which the barn is attached. It offers a cozy, old-fashioned parlor for those who prefer more seclusion.

From an ample kitchen, innkeepers Marcia and Jim Schatz serve what they call a Maine continental breakfast: fresh orange juice, a plate of fruit and cheese, homemade granola, yogurt, cereals and, every third or fourth day, a treat of bagels and lox.

The table settings are charming: woven cloths and napkins, white china and dried flowers in baskets. Dinners are served by advance request. A typical meal might be seafood wellington or peasant bouillabaisse plus salad and a dessert of homemade ice cream for $20, BYOB.

Blue Hill Farm gives off good vibes. It's the kind of simple, homey place that many inn-goers look for.

Doubles, $70 to $85. No smoking.

Mountain Road House, Mountain Road, RR 1, Box 2040, Blue Hill 04614. (207) 374-2794.

Situated mid-way on the only road that traverses the face of Blue Hill is this 1890s Victorian farmhouse, converted into a B&B in 1993 by John McCulloch, a retired physician, and his wife Carol. They moved here from Spartanburg, S.C., renovated the main house and built an addition.

The addition holds a pleasant guest parlor and a large bedroom upstairs. The latter comes with a high queensize four-poster rice planter bed, a whirlpool tub and a sitting area with a loveseat, armchair and a view of Blue Hill Bay. Two smaller bedrooms in the main house, one with twin beds and a sitting area and the other with a double bed, also have private baths.

The McCullochs place after-dinner mints on the pillows and offer tea or wine and cheese in the late afternoon. The dining room is the setting for an elaborate breakfast, beginning with fresh fruit, juice, muffins and biscuits. The main course could be stuffed french toast (described as a sandwich with Italian bread, honey and cream cheese filling), three-cheese egg casserole topped with sausage, or eggs McCulloch (scrambled eggs and chunks of ham with curried butter and cheese on an English muffin).

Doubles, $55 to $75. No smoking.

The Pilgrim's Inn, Deer Isle 04627. (207) 348-6615.

A welcoming, tasteful Colonial inn run by Dud and Jean Hendrick beckons visitors to this 1793 house on a spit of land with harbor in front and mill pond in back. The inn exudes an aura of history, particularly in the main-floor library and parlor.

Eight of the thirteen guest rooms have private baths, and each has a wood stove. Jean has decorated the rooms in sprightly Laura Ashley style, mixing and matching artworks and plants. Oriental rugs and quilts lend elegance to the prevailing simplicity. Duvets and down pillows are typical of the Hendricks' caring touches.

Jean and chef Terry Foster serve a single-entrée dinner at 7 in the charming dining room (in a former goat barn), where ten outside doors open to let in the breeze. The meal, open to the public, is $28.50 and worth every penny. We'll never forget a Sunday night dinner: Jean's salad with goat cheese, homemade peasant bread, her heavenly paella topped with nasturtiums (such a pretty dish it should have been photographed for Gourmet magazine) and her sensational raspberry chocolate pie on a shortbread crust. Depending on the night, you might be served rainbow trout stuffed with lobster and crab or smoked boneless leg of lamb.

Homemade granola, scones, fresh melon and omelets are featured at breakfast.

Doubles, $136 to $160, MAP; cottage, $180. Closed mid-October to mid-May. No credit cards. No smoking.

Dining Spots

Firepond, Main Street, Blue Hill. (207) 374-2135.

It's hard to imagine a more enchanting setting than the dining porch beside the stream at Firepond, on the lower level of a mill complex that's been renovated to provide additional dining and kitchen space. The screened porch, which wraps around the small bar/waiting area and an interior dining room, is the place to be on a summer evening, with its garden-type glass tables lit by candles and topped by linens or woven mats, fresh flowers and Blue Hill pottery, the sounds of water rippling below and spotlights illuminating the gleaming rocks. It's almost magical, and usually must be booked well in advance.

The food is often magical as well, thanks to chef Craig Rodenheiser, who assumed

Porch dining beside the brook is magical at Fire Pond.

ownership in 1994 and launched a major expansion after a year-long shutdown in 1993. We like to start with the selection of terrines or pâtés ($6.95) – country pork, salmon mousse and vegetable on one visit – with croutons, cornichons, and interesting mustards and chutneys, or the warm spinach salad with bacon vinaigrette dressing ($4.50 and exceptionally good). Other recent choices included baked brie en croûte, smoked salmon ravioli with gruyère, escargots in puff pastry, smoked duck breast, wild mushroom ravioli, and hot or cold soups (cream of red bell pepper and gazpacho at one visit).

Entrées range from $14.95 for a sensational pork tenderloin with pancetta to $19.95 for medallions of lamb with brandy and wild mushrooms, tournedos of beef or black angus sirloin steak. Our party of four also enjoyed sea scallops paired with leeks and mushrooms in a vermouth cream sauce, a fabulous fettuccine with crabmeat and pine nuts, a zesty halibut espagnole topped with mussels and saffron beurre blanc, and roast duckling with raspberry-chambord sauce. These were accompanied by crisp snap peas, carrots and rice pilaf.

Among desserts are a superior lemon-raspberry cheesecake, chocolate-truffle dacquoise, fresh fruit tarts and homemade rum-pecan or ginger ice creams. The wine list includes expensive vintages along with a good variety starting in the teens.

The new owner has created two dining rooms on the main floor, one of them in a former gourmet shop. This now looks like a library, with shelves full of old books lining the walls and oriental carpets dotting the original wood floors. French doors look onto a flower-bedecked outdoor dining terrace facing Main Street. Craig also renovated the kitchen to handle the extra seats and the debut of lunch service, plus mid-morning pastries and espresso.

The lunch menu lists a few dinner appetizers and salads, plus five entrées from $8.95 for grilled chicken caesar salad to $14.95 for baked lobster and artichoke hearts.

Lunch daily in season, 11 to 2:30; dinner nightly, 5 to 9:30, fewer nights in off-season. Closed January to early May.

229

Jonathan's, Main Street, Blue Hill. (207) 374-5226.

How can one small town support two such good, full-service restaurants? Who knows, but Blue Hill does, and both get better and better.

Innovative cuisine and an award-winning wine list are the hallmarks of this cheery, informal spot run by Jonathan Chase. His latest claim to fame is the cookbook *Saltwater Seasonings,* written in collaboration with his sister, Sarah Leah Chase, the Nantucket caterer and cookbook author. He started here with somewhat close and intimate quarters in front, and expanded into an open and airy rear section with rough wood walls, pitched ceiling, bow windows and a bar.

The newer area is a welcoming and comforting place for an assertive summer meal. Our latest dinner started with a crostini with roasted elephant garlic and chèvre, served with ripe tomatoes, and a remarkable smoked mussel salad with goat cheese and pine nuts. Other choice starters are spanakopita, baja fish taco with fresh tomato salsa and minted yogurt, and some good soups.

Main courses run from $13.95 for caribbean grilled pork chop with jamaican jerk sauce and spicy jalapeño-pineapple salsa to $17.95 for grilled angus strip steak. The specials are really special: we've enjoyed scallops sautéed with mint and tomatoes, and grilled swordfish with tequila-lime mayonnaise, as well as Jonathan's signature dish, shrimp flamed in ouzo and served with feta on linguini. Pan-seared rainbow trout with scotch whiskey and scallions, rabbit braised with smoked bacon and sundried tomatoes, and braised lamb shank with beer-bourbon barbecue sauce were other recent choices.

Kahlua-mocha mousse, frangelico cheesecake, peach crisp and cantaloupe sorbet with macaroons are among the worthy endings. The exceptional and extensive wine list, honored by Wine Spectator, is reasonably priced.

Dinner nightly, 5 to 9. Closed Monday in winter.

Blue Hill Inn, Union Street, Blue Hill. (207) 374-2844.

"Dining is an integral part of our inn," says innkeeper Mary Hartman, who offers a five-course dinner for house guests (and for the public by reservation for $35, if there's room). Starting at 7 following cocktails at an innkeepers' reception in the large parlor or outside on the side lawn, a leisurely meal is served by candlelight at white-clothed tables in an intimate sun porch where classical music plays in the background.

Chef André Strong, an American whose mother came from France, changes the handwritten menu nightly. Braised shiitake mushrooms with saffron risotto was the appetizer at our latest dinner, which was artistically presented and exceptionally tasty throughout. A blueberry-campari ice cleansed the palate for the main course, a choice of ethereal paupiettes of trout with salmon mousseline and mint or tender noisettes of lamb with cob-smoked bacon, garlic and chèvre. A salad of local greens preceded the dessert, a remarkable frozen nougat with spiced orange rum – so good that we requested the recipe and quickly realized we could never duplicate it at home.

Other entrée choices could include sautéed lobster on a bed of garlic spinach, roast monkfish provençal, wolffish with tomato coulis and pesto, pork tenderloin with pancetta and rosemary, and filet of beef au poivre. The chef's French heritage also shows in such desserts as strawberry gratinée, chocolate mousse and crème caramel.

Dinner nightly at 7, June-October; weekends and holidays in off-season. Closed in winter.

Left Bank Bakery & Cafe, Ellsworth Road (Route 172), Blue Hill. (207) 374-2201.

This lively place has flowers on every table, a brick floor, shelves of books, a porch

Casual dining at Jonathan's.

Formal dining at Blue Hill Inn.

at the side, a large new addition and slate tables on pedestals for outside dining with a view of the huge garden. It offers three meals daily and some big-name entertainment.

The expanding enterprise was founded by Arnold Greenberg, who closed his Left Bank cafe along the Delaware River in Frenchtown, N.J., for a new life in Maine. Though without a river, the Left Bank retains its New Jersey motto, "a home away from home." It's obviously low-key and casual, with serious jazz, blues and folk music and occasional musicals on the concert stage.

Our favorite meal here is breakfast, which yields things like a spicy Left Bank omelet with jalapeño cheese and salsa, french toast made with homemade challah, homemade oatmeal and granola, at mix-and-match prices from 75 cents for a sticky bun or bagel to $5.95 for a Nova platter of lox, bagel with cream cheese, tomato and onion.

Salads, spinach pie, quiche and hefty sandwiches served on bagels, croissants or French bread are in the $3 to $5 range. For dinner there are stir-fries, pad thai, moussaka, enchilada romesco, Japanese dashi, paella, mussels milano over pasta, Brazilian pork tenderloin and more, $11.95 to $15.95.

European-style peasant breads are baked daily with flour imported from France and Germany, and no preservatives are used. The cafe serves Geary's Ale on tap and Bartlett wines by the glass or bottle.

Open daily, 7 a.m. to 10 p.m. No smoking.

Jean-Paul's Bistro, Main Street, Blue Hill. (207) 374-5852.

Gaelic charm and a great view of Blue Hill Bay emanate from this appealing bistro opened by Jean-Paul Lecomte, a former waiter at prestigious New York City restaurants, including the 21 Club. He moved into a classic white Maine home with green shutters and started serving lunch and tea with the best water view in town. Jean-Paul takes care of the front of the house and several relatives, like his mother, father, brother and sister-in-law, help out.

You can come in at 11 a.m. for a cup of cappuccino and a chocolate croissant. You may decide to stay for lunch. The simple menu ($3.95 to $6.95) yields things like salade niçoise, pasta salad, a "pizza" baguette, a smoked chicken sandwich and a roast beef sandwich with melted brie. We thoroughly enjoyed the croque monsieur with a side salad of mixed baby greens and the grilled chicken caesar salad, layered rather than tossed and served with a baguette. The side terrace with its custom-made square wooden tables topped with canvas umbrellas proved such a salubrious setting that we lingered over a strawberry tart and a slice of midnight chocolate cake that Jean-Paul insisted we taste, calling it a French-Japanese cake (why, we don't know).

You might even decide to stay on for tea and a snack, served from 3 to 5, amid prolific flowers and some Jud Hartmann sculptures on that great terrace.

All the atmosphere is not outside. Jean-Paul seats 80 inside in a couple of stylish dining rooms. The photogenic main room comes with cathedral ceilings, local art, white tablecloths, and blue and white spattered Bennington pottery for a simple and fresh yet sophisticated look. And it has big windows for enjoying the water view. Wines and beers are available (the house wine is Boucheron for $10 a liter).

Although Jean-Paul may eventually open for prix-fixe dinners, so far he is catering to private parties at night.

Coffee, lunch and tea, daily 11 to 5. Closed in winter.

Pie in the Sky Pizza, Mill Street, Blue Hill. (207) 347-5570.

New owners have expanded the space a bit and upgraded the food at this rustic, shingled building on an out-of-the-way street. It's funky but high-style for a pizza parlor, what with clouds painted on the high blue ceiling, a mélange of booths and tables with ladderback chairs, lots of paper balloon lamps and a good selection of herbal teas, beers and wines. We were pleased to have the breezy front porch to ourselves for dinner within earshot of the mill stream, away from the hubbub inside.

The Greek salad lived up to advance billing, fortunately lacking iceberg lettuce but, alas, they forgot the Greek olives. The pizza special with broccoli, walnuts and feta was delicious, as was the night's quiche of spinach and mushrooms. The pizzas, with homemade white or whole wheat crusts, are served by the slice or in assorted sizes. There's a choice of 21 toppings (the Hawaiian with ham, pineapple and mozzarella was a new one on us). Calzones, subs and sandwiches (grilled tempeh and hot falafel with salad are two for vegetarians), spaghetti, nachos and stuffed baked potatoes round out the menu.

Prices are in the $2.90 to $6.50 range. Even with an $11 bottle of quite decent wine and a shared dessert of Ben & Jerry's heath bar crunch, our dinner bill came to less than $30.

Open Monday-Saturday 11 to 9, Sunday noon to 9.

The Red Bag Deli, Water Street, Blue Hill. (207) 374-8800.

A local realtor said what the town really needed was a good deli. So Paula Briggs obliged, bringing in California caterer Stacey Mann as a partner. The pair opened a spiffy, upscale gourmet emporium in 1994, offering pâtés, sandwiches, salads, changing dinner items and desserts to eat in or to go.

A meat loaf sandwich with red onions and grainy mustard was a special when we stopped by. We liked the looks of the black bean soup, the zesty gazpacho, the curried chicken and nutted brown rice salads, the hefty sandwiches ($3 to $4) made on breads from Little Notch Bakery, the oversize cookies and the kahlua-brownie cake. You can even have your sandwiches dressed with pickled onions, marinated peppers or hummus. Everything leaves in shiny, bright red bags.

Open Monday-Saturday 9 to 5, Sunday 10 to 3.

Owner Jean-Paul Lecomte greets customers at entrance to Jean-Paul's Bistro.

Diversions

Crafts. Pottery and handcrafts abound in Blue Hill and, indeed, all across the East Penobscot Bay peninsula and onto Deer Isle and Stonington. The Brooklin Crafts Cooperative in Brooklin, the Eastern Bay Cooperative Gallery beside the water in Stonington, and North Country Textiles outlet store in South Penobscot are within driving distance.

The world-famous **Haystack Mountain School of Crafts** at Sunshine on Deer Isle, which sometimes has shows, is worth the drive simply for the breathtaking view from its unsurpassed setting on a steep, forested slope with stairs down to East Penobscot Bay. Public tours are offered Wednesdays at 1 p.m., June-August.

Rowantrees Pottery, the institution inspired in 1934 by Adelaide Pearson through her friend Mahatma Gandhi, is still going strong in a rambling house and barn reached by a pretty brick path through gardens at the edge of Blue Hill. Inside, you may be able to see potters at work; veteran employees like Grace Lymburner in the upstairs shop might recall for you the days when as children they joined the story hours and pottery classes run by Miss Pearson and her protégé, Laura Paddock. Sheila Varnum, who was associated with the founders since she was 3, has owned the pottery since 1976 and has continued its tradition. Named for the mountain ash trees above its green gate along Union Street, Rowantrees is known for its jam jar with a flat white lid covered with blueberries, as well as for unique glazes. Items are attractively displayed for sale.

Rackliffe Pottery at the other end of town is an offshoot of Rowantrees, Phil Rackliffe having worked there for twenty years. He and his family make all kinds of handsome and useful kitchenware in a work area next to their small shop on Route 172. The soup tureens with blueberry, strawberry or cranberry covers are especially nice.

Kneisel Hall Chamber Music Festival, Pleasant Street, Blue Hill, 374-2811. Concerts by well-known faculty members are given Friday evenings and Sunday afternoons from late June to early August in a rustic concert hall off upper Pleasant Street. The series is part of the summer session of the Kneisel Hall School of Music, founded by Dr. Franz Kneisel and called "the cradle of chamber music teaching in America." Innkeepers say a summer tradition for many of their guests is to arrive on Thursday and stay through Sunday, taking in two concerts, visiting the potteries and dining at Jonathan's and Firepond. Concert tickets, $15; unreserved veranda seats, $10.

Blue Hill Farmer's Market, Route 172 at the Blue Hill Fairgrounds. Each Saturday

233

in July and August from 9 to 11:30 a.m., local farmers and artisans gather here for a real down-home event. Horse-drawn wagons give the youngsters hayrides, while residents and visitors browse through a small but interesting display of everything from local produce to goat cheese, jellies, handmade gifts, lamb's wool and patterned ski sweaters. The well-known Blue Hill Fair, incidentally, celebrated its 100th anniversary in 1991.

Shopping. Along Main Street, big spenders are drawn to the famed Jud Hartmann Gallery. Here, sculptor Jud Hartmann shows quite spectacular paintings by artist-friends along with the exceptional bronze sculptures he crafts at his studio in nearby Brooklin (he also has a gallery in foliage season in Grafton, Vt.). Everything is artfully arranged at **The Handworks Gallery,** which shows contemporary crafts. Artist Judith Leighton's **Leighton Gallery** off Parker Point Road is considered one of the best galleries in Maine. Birdhouses, carved birds, hooked fish hangings, tables with driftwood bases and Victorian twig furniture appeal at **Belcher's Country Store,** an offshoot of the main store in Deer Isle. **North Country Textiles** has moved its main store here from South Penobscot, offering wonderful throws, rugs, table linens, wicker and wooden furniture, pottery and more. Even non-smokers are enticed by the aromas at **Blue Hill Tea & Tobacco Shop,** something of an anachronism modernized by a selection of fine wines. **Blue Hill Books** doubled its space by expanding into the basement of its historic building. **Blue Hill Pets** is a large gift store, where everything has a pet theme. The Emerson Antiques building houses **Sweet Myrtle,** which specializes in dried flowers and "everlasting creations." **Four Flags,** an offshoot of a favorite store in Castine, stocks nice gifts and accessories, many with a nautical theme.

Beside the causeway on Little Deer Isle is **Harbor Farm,** a new store and showroom in an 1850 schoolhouse and a wreath-production building moved there by barge. Starting by making wreaths of wicker, Dick McWilliams and company have expanded into an impressive mail-order and retail operation of fine crafts, down-home knickknacks, practical gadgets and Christmas items. Something of a cross between, say, Tiffany's and Brookstone, it features unique, made-to-order items from birch twig swan baskets, woven coverlets, and gold and silver jewelry to wooden hooks, folding stools, English bathracks and garden shears. Behind the country store is a Christmas shop with ornaments from around the world.

Extra-Special

Community Steel Bands. Spend any time in Blue Hill in the summer and you're sure to hear of the local steel-drum bands. The Blue Hill area now claims the largest steel band ensemble in the country, with hundreds of players in a variety of bands. The phenomenon started as a cooperative effort of Mary Cheyney Gould, director of the 80-member Bagaduce Chorale and the Bagaduce Music Lending Library, and Carl Chase, maker of steel drums and founder of the Atlantic Clarion Steel Band. An adult-education course was offered, one thing led to another and soon many folks hereabouts were playing steel drums. The Clarion band, which Carl started in Brooksville in 1974, is the most well known (it has played across the Northeast, including a concert at Lincoln Center, and came home to be featured at the fourth annual Blue Hill Pops benefit in 1994). Another of the ensemble's sub groups, called Flash in the Pans, gave a wildly popular series of Monday night concerts across the peninsula in the summer of 1994, culminating in an appearance at Kneisel Hall. "I do it for therapy," advised local innkeeper Barbara Seeger, one of the Flash in the Pans. "We have people dancing in the streets."

Lobsters and harbor view draw visitors to Thurston's Lobster Pound in Bernard.

Mount Desert Island, Me.
The Other Harbors

Mount Desert Island has long held a special appeal, first as a summer resort for society and later as the site of a national park beloved by campers and naturalists.

Its focus for us, as well as for increasing numbers of others, has always been Bar Harbor and the eastern part of Acadia National Park. Since our first vacation there more than 30 years ago, we've witnessed the changes – for better and worse – as tourism impacted relentlessly. And still Bar Harbor remains dear to our hearts.

Be advised, however, that there are other harbors and another side to Mount Desert Island. The other side is the quieter side, one that its devotees call "the right side" of this fabulously varied island. This side of the island celebrates its own identity in its annual Quietside Festival, three days of activities ranging from crab-picking demonstrations to the MDI Boat Show the last weekend in June.

Even the quiet side is wonderfully diverse. Northeast Harbor and Southwest Harbor are barely two miles across Somes Sound from each other, but far apart in spirit and character.

Northeast Harbor is the yachting harbor, a haven for Rockefellers and some of the world's great boats, a moneyed place where sailing is the seasonal preoccupation. Southwest Harbor is the working harbor, where fishing and boat-building are the year-round occupation. Here and in Bass Harbor, the oldtime flavor of coastal Maine remains.

Some of the choice portions of Acadia National Park are close at hand: Seawall, Wonderland, Beech Mountain, Echo Lake and Eagle Cliff. Thuya and Asticou gardens are special treats, and we know of few better views than those up and down Somes Sound, the only natural fjord in North America.

For a different perspective than most visitors get of Mount Desert, try the other harbors on the "right side" of the island.

Inn Spots

Asticou Inn, Route 3, Northeast Harbor 04662. (207) 276-3344 or (800) 258-3373.

Majestically situated at the head of Northeast Harbor on a hillside where the mountains slope to the sea, the Asticou has been a bastion of elegance since 1883.

The fireplace in the lobby is always ablaze – "to take the chill off foggy mornings or late afternoons," our friendly guide informed. The lobby with its huge oriental rug and wing chairs gives way to a parlor decorated in blues, beiges and a cheery rust. Beyond is a bright and breezy cocktail lounge with sliding doors onto the outdoor deck; amid white furniture, yellow umbrellas and petunias in planters, it's a great place from which to view the goings-on in the harbor. The enclosed east porch is used for games and television viewing. The spacious dining room (see Dining Spots) serves three meals a day and a Thursday evening buffet that draws people from all over the island.

A carpeted staircase and a 94-year-old elevator lead to 50 simple guest rooms on the second and third floors. Rooms vary from those with twin beds, rose carpeting and frilly white curtains framing views onto the harbor to a suite with a sofa, two peach chintz chairs and a desk in a sitting room plus two twins in the bedroom. Four have private balconies viewing the water. Seventeen more rooms are available in the Cranberry Lodge, Bird Bank and Blue Spruce guest houses and the Topsider cottages. Most striking are the contemporary, circular Topsiders with decks, full-length windows, attractive parlors and kitchenettes.

The perfectly landscaped grounds offer a swimming pool, tennis, gardens and, all the while, changing vistas of the harbor. Guests have privileges at the Northeast Harbor Golf Club.

Rates are MAP in season, EP with continental breakfast served in Cranberry Lodge in the off-season when only the guest houses and cottages are open.

Doubles, $218 to $271, MAP; shoulder season, $158 to $211, B&B; off-season, $75 to $135, EP. Two-night minimum in season. Closed January-April.

The Claremont Hotel, Clark Point Road, Box 137, Southwest Harbor 04679. (207) 244-5036.

The other grand dowager of Mount Desert, the Claremont marked its 100th anniversary in 1984, a year later than the Asticou. It's the island's oldest continuously operating inn, with only three owners in its first century.

Entered in the National Register of Historic Places in 1978 as a reminder of the "prosperous, relaxed and seasonal way of life" of Maine's early summer-resort era, the

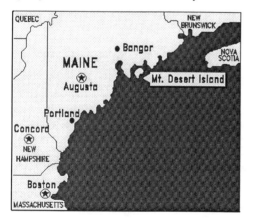

original light yellow structure has been considerably spiffed up of late and the name has been shortened from the Claremont Hotel and Cottages. But the inn's wraparound veranda and the heavy white Adirondack chairs lined up side by side on the rear lawn still provide a relaxing view of Somes Sound, and croquet remains the sport of choice. The annual Claremont Croquet Classic is known as the home of nine-wicket croquet.

The main hotel building contains a lobby and living rooms full of

Turn-of-the-century sea captain's house has been refurbished as Lindenwood Inn.

wicker chairs and sofas, a handsome restaurant (see Dining Spots) and twenty guest rooms (singles, doubles and suites) on the second and third floors, all with private baths. All were renovated for 1994 to include heat and full bath, and furnishings remain comfortable yet simple. Also available for longer stays are twelve housekeeping cottages with living rooms, Franklin or stone fireplaces and decks, and two guest houses. The Phillips House with five large rooms, a suite and a massive fieldstone fireplace in the parlor is particularly inviting.

Besides croquet, boating and tennis are offered, and the hardy can swim from the dock in chilly Somes Sound. The Boathouse is a favorite spot for a light lunch or cocktails.

Doubles, $115 to $185, MAP; cottages, $145 to $175, EP. Cottages and Clark House Suite available EP or MAP. Inn open mid-June to mid-October, cottages and guest houses Memorial Day to late October. No smoking.

Lindenwood Inn, 108 Clark Point Road, Box 1328, Southwest Harbor 04679. (207) 244-5335.

Towering linden trees shade this turn-of-the-century sea captain's home, now grandly refurbished by Jim King. Jim, who had opened the Kingsleigh Inn here, returned from traveling around the world in 1993 to purchase the Lindenwood, which is where area innpressario Don Johnson had started a decade earlier. After Don left to open the fabulously successful Inn at Canoe Point in Bar Harbor, the Lindenwood had fallen on lean times.

Enter Jim King, who has a decorator's eye, international tastes and an assortment of cosmopolitan possessions. He redid the entire place. You'll find palm trees on the front veranda, Italian chairs and glass tables in a breakfast room he dubs "tropical primitive – I got tired of the country look," a collection of shells and stones in each bedroom, sleek black modern lights, potted cactus plants on the tables, pottery from Mexico and Indonesia here, a contemporary mission bed there. He splashed around lots of color, from walls to down comforters to carpets. Call it different, call it eclectic, call it international. Jim calls it "a blend of old and new" and wants his inn to be "in the vanguard of the new look."

The two parlors are contemporary, accented with green and white striped uphol-stered chairs. Potted plants throughout the main floor bring the outdoors inside. Upstairs are nine guest rooms of varying sizes, all with private baths. Check out Room 6 with its six-foot-long clawfoot tub. It's one of six rooms with private decks or balconies affording views of the harbor.

At water's edge is our favorite cottage with kingsize bed, kitchen, TV and picture windows in the living room and a side deck. What Jim calls "my Winston Churchill cottage," newly renovated with a couple of bedrooms, kitchen and a patio bearing a table and barbecue grill, draws comments for its huge signed painting by Sarah Churchill of her father Winston overlooking the cathedral-ceilinged living room. In 1994, Jim leased an adjacent apartment building and two cottages, which he calls the **Lindenwood Annex.** Good for families, it includes six basic efficiency units with kitchenettes, fire-places and TVs.

Guests in the main inn are treated to elaborate breakfasts. Expect fresh fruit, home-made blueberry or orange blossom muffins, and a main course like french toast with homemade blueberry sauce, eggs Augustine with cream cheese and mild chile peppers, blueberry pancakes and omelets incorporating herbs from the backyard garden.

Doubles, $85 to $115; suites, $145; cottages and housekeeping apartments, $105 to $145. No smoking.

Harbourside Inn, Harbourside Road (Route 198), Northeast Harbor 04662. (207) 276-3272.

Built in 1888 in the style of the Seal Harbor Club, this shingled hilltop mansion is run very much their way by the Sweet family. "We're old-fashioned and intend to keep it that way," Geraldine Sweet explains. She and her husband, who formerly managed the Jordan Pond House, acquired the mansion in 1977 from a woman who would sell only to Maine residents who would maintain the heritage.

The heritage indeed remains, from the nasturtiums nurtured from the original seeds still brightening the entry circle and the blueberry plants along the entry path to the original carpets from China, repaired when they became worn because they were too prized to be discarded. Guests gather in a pleasant parlor with wing chairs in shades of blue or on the front sun porch, all done up with bright cushions and curtains in appropriate Northeast Harbor colors, preppy pink and green.

All but one of the ten guest rooms on the first and second floors have working fireplaces, and three have their own sun porches. Four more bedrooms on the third floor raise the total to fourteen. All have private baths and are furnished in 19th-century style. "We had great fun with the wallpapers," Geraldine said. One bathroom's paper has small red bears with big hearts on the borders, and one bedroom is papered with irises and another with fuschias. Room 1 with a wallpapered ceiling has a Wallace Nutting bed, a collector's item. The floral-papered honeymoon suite includes a kingsize bed and an enclosed porch with cathedral ceiling, wicker rockers, a glider and a teak deck chair from the liner Queen Elizabeth. A first-floor suite offers a sitting room with comfortable chairs grouped in front of the fireplace and a kitchenette in an alcove, a bedroom with a kingsize four-poster and a chaise lounge, and an old-fashioned tub in the bathroom. White organdy curtains in the windows frame the dark fir trees outside.

A continental breakfast with homemade blueberry muffins is served on the sun porch.

Lest the inn's name mislead, the Sweets stress that the once-sweeping view of the harbor from their hilltop is now obstructed by a century's growth of trees.

Lush plantings and hanging begonia grace entrance to Grey Rock Inn.

Doubles, $85 to $105; suites, $120 to $150. Open mid-June to mid-September. No smoking.

Grey Rock Inn, Harbourside Road, Northeast Harbor 04662. (207) 276-9360 or 276-5526.

Remarkable gardens and a prolific hanging begonia on the porch at the front door greet visitors to this little-publicized inn, said to have been a gathering place for Northeast Harbor socialites after it was built in the 1890s as a private residence.

Inside the inviting large fieldstone and shingled mansion with yellow trim is a veritable showcase for British innkeeper Janet Millet's decorating tastes: an array of wicker like you've never seen, fans and paintings from the Orient, fringed lamps, masses of exotic flowers – rather overwhelming, we found.

People who stay at Grey Rock must like eclectic elegance, for that's what they get. The two fireplaces in the living room and parlor are kept aglow, even in mid-summer, because the innkeeper finds her guests want it that way. Wicker serves as furniture and art, from table lamps to loveseats, from desk to plant stand.

The nine guest rooms are equally exotic. The huge main-floor corner room with canopied four-poster bed, oriental screen and private balcony could not be more romantic. The upstairs rooms are lacy, frilly and flowery, with much pale pink and green, all kinds of embroidered towels, and porches all around. Some have fireplaces, and all have views of the trees or gardens atop this wooded hilltop high above and back from the road.

The aptly named Tree House cottage holds two bedrooms, two baths and a full kitchen and adds a side deck.

Janet serves an exemplary continental-plus breakfast, including a fruit compote with eight to ten kinds of fresh fruit, assorted baked goods and bacon, occasionally eggs, and what she states is "a good cup of coffee for a British lady."

Doubles, $110 to $165; cottage, $175 for two, $200 for four. Open spring through October.

239

Southwest Harbor and islands are on view from on high at Island Watch.

The Kingsleigh Inn, 100 Main St., Box 1426, Southwest Harbor 04679. (207) 244-5302.

A wraparound veranda full of wicker, colorful pillows and flowers distinguishes this B&B with an unusual pebbledash stucco-stone exterior and the hospitality extended by innkeepers Nancy and Tom Cervelli.

Inside are inviting common rooms and eight comfortable guest rooms, all with private baths and ceiling fans. They are notable for Waverly wall coverings and fabrics, lace window treatments, plush carpeting and gleaming hardwood floors, and many have four-poster beds and wingback chairs. The Turret Suite, lately enhanced with a fireplace in the kingsize bedroom, offers a great view from a telescope placed between two cozy wicker chairs in the sitting room, which is equipped with TV. Sewing kits and hard candies are in each room, and the scent of potpourri is everywhere.

Pink and green china and deep-green tablecloths enhance the breakfast room. Breakfasts are bountiful. A tasty omelet with ham and cheese, broccoli, green peppers and mushrooms was served the day of our latest visit. Other favorites include blueberry pancakes, eggs benedict, spinach and mushroom quiche, sausage soufflé and cinnamon french toast. Fresh fruit, cereals, and homemade blueberry breads and jams accompany.

Guests may help themselves in the afternoon to coffee, tea or lemonade, They're available in the country kitchen, where Nancy holds forth and talks shop with visitors, a couple of whom volunteered that her breakfasts are "out of this world."

Doubles, $85 to $95; suite, $155. No smoking.

The Moorings, Shore Road, Southwest Harbor 04679. (207) 244-5523 or 244-3210.

Genial Downeasters Leslie and Betty King have run this delightfully informal, old-fashioned place for 35 years in a location they call the "Little Norway of America," and one we find the most scenic on the island, smack on the shore at the start of Somes Sound in Manset.

The rambling white house with dark shutters in the Maine style contains ten guest rooms, all with private baths. There also are three motel units (one with two exposures billed as having "probably the finest view on the coast") and six units in three trim white cottages with wicker porches and a garden apartment. The Kings have upgraded their rooms with cheery new wallpapers and furnishings, and the five on the inn's second floor now sport delightful decks and balconies to take advantage of the view. Peruvian lilies added color to each room at our latest visit.

We dubbed our corner bedroom the Agatha Christie Room because several of her paperbacks were on the bureau (Betty makes the rounds of all the lawn sales to pick up the books, son Storey volunteered). It's the only one without a water view but, as with the other rooms, the towels were large and fluffy, the beds had colorfully patterned sheets, and a candle was in a ceramic holder beside the bed. The Pilot House cottage with living room, fireplace, screened porch and television provided more expansive accommodations at a later visit.

The fireplace glows on cool mornings in the living room, which has a television set in a windowed alcove and enough books and magazines to start a library. The coffee pot is kept filled all day in the adjacent office, where complimentary orange juice and donuts are put out every morning.

Outside, two rowboats filled with geraniums brighten the path to the front door. In back are canoes, bicycles, a new pier and a stony shoreline for swimming (if you can stand the icy water), beachcombing, clamming and musseling. The Kings provide charcoal for the grills beside the shore, a memorable spot to barbecue a steak for dinner as you watch the sunset.

We're obviously fond of the Moorings. It's most unpretentious and the prices are, too.

Doubles, $60 to $75 (two small singles, $50); motel units, $75; cottages, $75 to $95.

Island Watch, Freeman Ridge Road, Box 1359, Southwest Harbor 04679. (207) 244-7229.

Little known but aptly named, this B&B in a contemporary ranch house occupies the top of a high ridge east of town. Floor-to-ceiling windows in the living room/dining room stretching across the rear of the house and an expansive deck take full advantage of the panoramic view of islands and water.

Maxine Clark, who says she's the only native-born hostess in the B&B business locally, grew up in the Bass Harbor Lighthouse as the daughter of the lighthouse keeper. Here, in a rather spectacular house, she offers six guest rooms (one a single) and an efficiency suite in a separate building. All have private baths, and three afford water views. One room with a private entrance on the ground floor has a double and single bed and built-in pine counters. An adjacent room offers a similar bed configuration plus a wood stove and a large bathroom with a clawfoot tub. Everything except the red carpet is white in Room 1 upstairs, a simple room with a kingsize bed and a glorious view. The efficiency in the outbuilding contains a queensize bed in back and a small living room with a TV and half a kitchen in front, plus a small private deck.

The living room in the main house has a huge stone fireplace and TV, VCR and stereo for guests' use. We settled down on the rear deck in the early evening and found it hard to leave for dinner (there's also a front deck that catches the late afternoon sun).

The next morning we were back on that great rear deck, but managed to arise long enough to enjoy Maxine's festive breakfast at a big round table in a dining room open to the country kitchen. Her french toast with ricotta stuffing and strawberry-raspberry sauce was the main event. Fresh fruit and cereal preceded. Belgian waffles and a ham and spinach quiche are other favorites.

For 1995, Maxine added a greenhouse at the end of the dining room so folks could enjoy breakfast amid the plants and with an island view.

Doubles, $75; efficiency, $85. No smoking.

The Maison Suisse Inn, Main Street, Box 1090, Northeast Harbor 04662. (207) 276-5223 or (800) 624-7668.

Pick a couple of blueberries along the entry path as you arrive at this inn, surrounded by gardens designed by a previous owner who trained as a landscape architect in Switzerland. Beth and David White took over in 1987, did a total renovation and ended up with six bedrooms and four suites, all with private baths.

Canopy beds, silkscreened wallpaper, feather pillows, down comforters, dust ruffles, antiques and Bar Harbor wicker comprise the decor. We like the upstairs suite, which has a small balcony with a wicker loveseat, and the Garden Room with a separate entrance and a charming little garden ringed by cedars to make it private.

The common rooms downstairs are nicely furnished. Beach stones form an unusual inset in the mantel of the brick fireplace in the main hall of the circa-1890 summer mansion, designed in the shingle style.

Room rates include a full breakfast with the inn's compliments at Colonel's Restaurant across the street.

Doubles, $105 to $155; suites, $175 to $215. Closed November-April. No smoking.

The Inn at Southwest, Main Street, Box 593, Southwest Harbor 04679. (207) 244-3835.

This inn has been taking in guests since 1884, first as a rooming house and lately as an attractive B&B, acquired in 1995 by Jill Lewis, a computer programmer from Michigan. She took over a going concern and planned to redecorate gradually. A mannequin in the hall, a baby grand piano, balloon curtains, stenciling and a living room with a big sofa, TV and stereo, a game table and an ornate fireplace mantel are features. Waverly and Schumacher wallpapers, old pictures and assorted costumes complete the downstairs decor.

All nine guest rooms upstairs have private baths, two down the hall. All are furnished with designer linens, down comforters, wicker or rattan tables and desks, potpourri, plants and the like. Jill was naming them after Maine lighthouses.

Full breakfast is served at three tables in a forest green dining room with cranberry accents or on a wraparound porch lined with geraniums and overlooking Victorian gardens. Quiches, blueberry pancakes and french toast were in Jill's early repertoire. In the afternoon, she serves blueberry tea and homemade pies.

Doubles, $90 to $125. Closed November to mid-April. No smoking.

Harbour Woods, Route 102, Box 1214, Southwest Harbor 04679. (207) 244-5388.

Enthusiastic new owners from Manhattan have upgraded the B&B portion of what essentially is a rental cottage complex at the edge of town. Joe and Christine Titka share their 19th-century farmhouse at the front of the property with overnight guests in three bedrooms, all with private baths.

Each bedroom contains a queensize bed piled with plump pillows. The colors of the linens coordinate with the decorator wallpapers and fabrics incorporated throughout. There's a cherry two-poster bed in the rear Garden Room with a fireplace, and a four-poster graces the large Princess Room, outfitted with a single armchair with an ottoman. Furnishings include restored antiques and family keepsakes, but artificial flowers were displayed here and there at our July visit.

Guests enjoy a rear living room with TV/VCR and videos, and an enclosed porch harboring an eight-person spa. Breakfast the day we were there included banana crunch, a bacon and onion quiche with home fries and hot cinnamon bread. Belgian waffles with whipped cream were on tap the next morning. Joe makes the cookies and perhaps white-chocolate cheesecake that the hosts serve after dinner.

Doubles, $95 to $105. No smoking.

Long Pond Inn, Route 102, Box 361, Mount Desert 04660. (207) 244-5854.

Swimming, canoeing and fishing are favorite pursuits at Long Pond, just across from this dark brown house blending in with the landscape beside National Park Canoe Rental in Somesville.

The house looks far older than its 1975 construction date, owners Bob and Pam

Mensink having wanted a rustic look and achieving it through the use of materials collected and stored for years from dismantled estates, summer cottages and hotels. The interior is barnwood, and the three guest rooms are in the walkout basement.

Each room comes with a queensize bed and a modern bath, one with a jacuzzi. Guests share a pretty little sun room outfitted with wicker and chintz. They also have access to a refrigerator and a washing machine, and enjoy the rear gardens and a greenhouse to which the Mensinks devote considerable time (he's also a registered Maine guide). A continental breakfast of fresh fruit, muffins and coffee cake is served.

Doubles, $75 to $95. No smoking. Closed Columbus Day to mid-May.

Dining Spots

Redfield's, Main Street, Northeast Harbor. (207) 276-5283.

This nifty commissary, restaurant and gourmet-to-go service is run by Scott and Maureen Redfield, two of the island's culinary stars. The Redfields, who made their name with dinners in the off-season at the Cranberry Lodge of Asticou Inn, said it was "time for us to open our own place."

Northeast Harbor proved highly receptive to their casually elegant, contemporary 30-seat establishment, which would be quite at home on Nantucket but for the prices and the refreshing lack of pretensions. The decor in two small dining rooms is simple yet sophisticated. Tiny lamps hanging from long cords over most tables illuminate some large and summery, impressionist-style paintings and make the rooms rather too bright for our tastes. But they do highlight the food, which is worth the spotlight here.

We staved off hunger with Maureen's fabulous French bread, exquisite house salads and a shared appetizer of venison carpaccio as we nursed the house La Veille Ferme wine. Lemon sorbet in a lotus dish cleansed the palate for the main dishes: sliced breast of duck with fresh chutney and marinated loin of lamb with goat cheese and black olives, both superb. Strawberry sorbet and a chocolate-almond mint tart ended a memorable meal.

Art is backdrop for dining at Redfield's.

Scott changes his short menu frequently. Recent choices ($16.95 to $18.95) were grilled tuna with wasabi vinaigrette, seared salmon with ginger-braised leeks, grilled loin of lamb with feta cheese and a compote of dried currants and mint, and duck breast with black cherry-mustard sauce. Starters ($5.95 to $7.95) were grilled quail with a caramelized onion-cranberry compote, chèvre with smoked salmon mousse and salmon caviar, and spinach pesto puffs with smoked chile-pepper sauce.

Lunch is equally appealing, perhaps crab cakes with sherried cajun mayonnaise and a house salad ($5.95) or smoked salmon mousse on a toasted bagel with the usual accompaniments ($4.95). Items from the commissary make for picnics of distinction.

Commissary open Tuesday-Sunday from 8:30 a.m.; dinner, 6:30 to 8:30.

The Burning Tree, Route 3, Otter Creek. (207) 288-9331.

It's a bit of a trek, but folks from Northeast Harbor are particularly fond of this simple restaurant in a rural setting along the road to Bar Harbor. There are tables on the long front porch, one section of which is a waiting area. Beyond are two small dining rooms, cheerfully outfitted in pinks and blues, their linened tables topped with tall, blue-edged water glasses. Colorful paintings by local artists adorn the walls.

The summer-cottage setting is the backdrop for inspired "gourmet seafood" offered by chef-owners Allison Martin and Elmer Beal Jr. A couple of chicken dishes are the only meats offered among entrées pleasantly priced from $12 (for veggie shish kabob with spicy peanut sauce) to $17.95 for cajun crab and lobster au gratin. Vegetarians hail offerings like a swiss chard, potato and artichoke pie and pan-fried polenta with sundried tomato-red pepper sauce and pesto vegetables.

Our party was quite delighted with such appetizers ($4.25 to $6.95) as mussels with mustard sauce, grilled scallops and an excellent vegetarian sushi. The cioppino for $15.50 came so highly touted that two of us ordered it, and the choice measured up. The others enjoyed grilled monkfish with a spicy tomato coulis, served with creamy potatoes with cheese and sautéed zucchini and peppers, and baked sole with crab and leek mousse. A couple of bottles of Chilean sauvignon blanc for $12 accompanied. Fresh strawberry pie, nectarine mousse cake and a rich chocolate kahlua cheesecake finished off an entirely satisfying meal.

Dinner nightly, 5 to 10. Open June to mid-October.

The Bistro at Seal Harbor, Route 3, Seal Harbor. (207) 276-3299.

Their kitchen isn't much bigger than that in a studio apartment, they grow their own herbs in wine casks on the back porch and they have only eight tables for dining. But Donna Fulton and Terri Clements, who teamed up in 1993 to open a bistro in the heart of old-money Seal Harbor, earned plaudits for their homespun endeavor. Formerly at the Fin Back in Bar Harbor, they offer a short and somewhat pricey (for the area) menu in a charming setting.

The storefront room is pristine with tables topped with white napkins, votive candles, fresh flowers and white china. Behind is a small service bar and aforementioned kitchen, snug with ten-burner stove. Donna handles the cooking chores, preparing half a dozen main courses ($16 to $21) like grilled salmon with champagne sauce and mashed potatoes, roasted swordfish with white beans and preserved lemon, sautéed pork tenderloin with mangos and shallots, and grilled loin lamb chops with garlic-rosemary butter. The Bistro salad comes with feta, apples and spiced pecans. Other starters range from Maine crab cakes with creole mustard sauce to smoked salmon with ginger-scallion pancake. Soup might be salmon chowder or lobster with jalapeño peppers and corn. Desserts could be crème brûlée, seasonal tarts and pies, plus intense ice creams (coffee-almond-praline or ginger) and orange-buttermilk sorbet served with biscotti. The choice, all-domestic wine list is priced mostly in the twenties.

This is obviously a pure place, where the owners make everything from scratch. They even pick their own berries for the blueberry pie and grate their own vanilla beans for the extract. A local blacksmith made the striking wine-glass rack that hangs over the copper bar. Donna and Terri crafted the interesting table pottery during their winter off-season in Arizona.

Dinner, Tuesday-Sunday from 6. Open Memorial Day to October. No smoking.

XYZ Restaurant & Gallery, Shore Road, Manset. (207) 244-5221.

The letters stand for Xalapa, Yucatan and Zacatecas, and the food represents the Mexican interior and coastal Maine. Chef Janet Strong had lived in Mexico and had

244

Gourmet seafood is the specialty in summery Burning Tree dining room.

the West Side Gallery here for a year before opening this enterprise to considerable acclaim in 1994. Part of the main floor of the Dockside Motel, it is attractive with white tablecloths, red and green napkins (the colors of the Mexican flag) and blond chairs. Also on premises is a small gallery showing original works of New England artists.

Here, lovers of Mexican food find the real thing. You want lobster? Try the lobster mole (bathed in a complex sauce of four types of chiles, fruit and nuts with a hint of Ibarra chocolate, served with flour tortillas), quite a steal for $12.50. Also at the high ($12.50) end is the tenderloin Zacatecas, grilled and served on a corn tortilla topped with mild cheese and chipotle sauce. Entrées start at $5 for black beans and white rice served with flour tortillas. The intrepid go for lengua (native Maine beef tongue stewed in a sauce of tomato and herbs and served with rice and flour tortillas), pollo pobol (Yucatan-style chicken breasts marinated in achiote and steamed in parchment) and cochinitas (Yucatan-style pork rubbed with achiote paste, marinated in citrus, baked and served with rice, black beans and flour tortillas). The timid settle for crab imperial, perhaps the only item familiar to gringoes, except for the "suggested children's meal:" cheese empanada and salad.

The treats begin with appetizers like mushrooms sautéed in chipotle sauce or tarascan soup. For dessert, the XYZ pie is not just another ice cream pie. It's two layers of mocha and maple-nut ice cream divided by a ridge of solid chocolate, served with a warm kahlua sauce and whipped cream. Yum.

Dinner nightly in summer, 5:30 to 9:30. Take-out lunches, Monday-Friday 11:30 to 1:30. Seasonal.

The Claremont, Clark Point Road, Southwest Harbor. (207) 244-5036.
The comparatively new dining-room addition with views on three sides, excellent service and consistently good food make this popular with residents on the quiet side of the island.

They like to have drinks at the **Boathouse** (which also serves sandwiches and salads for lunch) and then head into the high-ceilinged dining room, a picture of elegance with fancy china on white-over-pink linens, pink napkins, a moss green carpet and pink and green wallpaper. It's almost as pretty as the view across the lawns onto Somes Sound.

The short menu has shed some of its traditional, old-fashioned overtones. Now you might start with Maine shrimp sauté, cheese and herb raviolis with wild mushroom sauce or a salad of goat cheese and smoked shrimp with balsamic vinaigrette, priced in the $5 to $6 range.

Move on to such entrées ($15 to $17) as shellfish brioche, a ramekin of crabmeat and artichoke hearts, sole française, sautéed duck breast with onion confit and cracklings, grilled New York sirloin or lamb steak marinated in garlic and rosemary.

The produce comes from the inn's gardens and the baked goods from its bakery. The chef's homemade desserts include cheesecake, daily specials and either ice cream or lemon ice with Claremont cookies.

Lunch at the Boathouse, noon to 2, July and August; dinner nightly, 6 to 9, late June through Labor Day, jackets required. Cocktails at the Boathouse, 5 to 9.

Asticou Inn, Northeast Harbor. (207) 276-3344.

The $40 buffet every Thursday night draws up to 300 people in peak season to the posh dining room of the Asticou Inn. Thursday happens to be maid's night off hereabouts, so summer residents join inn guests for the extravagant spread, followed by live music and an evening of socializing.

The pillared dining room is restful with handpainted murals of trees and flowers on the deep yellow walls, a brass chandelier, oriental rugs, lovely flowered china and tiny plants in clay pots. Most coveted seating is in the adjacent enclosed porch, with great views through picture windows onto the harbor beyond.

Chef Lou Kiefer's changing fare is highly regarded. Look for main courses ($14.95 to $24) like lobster au poivre, seafood au gratin, grilled Atlantic salmon with lemon butter, broiled lamb chops and filet mignon with béarnaise sauce. You might start with lobster crêpe, smoked seafood antipasto, baked boursin with crabmeat or cranberry kissel, a chilled parfait of yogurt, cranberries and orange zest. Dessert possibilities are raspberry meringue glacé, chocolate-truffle torte and fresh fruit with cheeses.

On a sunny day, we lunched on the outdoor terrace high above the sparkling harbor. The buffet ($12) included a choice of chicken-vegetable soup or a most refreshing chilled lime-yogurt soup, cold meats and many salads, beverage and choice of five or six desserts like chocolate mousse and key lime pie.

Lunch daily, noon to 2:30; dinner, 6:30 to 9, mid-June to mid-September. Jackets required at dinner.

Seafood Ketch, On the Harbor, Bass Harbor. (207) 244-7463.

"For gosh sakes, come in quick before we both starve to death," urges the sign on this shanty beside the harbor. Here is the real thing, a delightfully down-home place run by Stuart and Lisa Branch, who took over from his parents, Ed and Eileen Branch, The seafood is fresh and everything's homemade, to the last loaf of crusty, piping-hot French bread served on a board with pads of butter at dinner.

Dining is by candlelight at white-linened tables in the rear room beside the water, each decorated with a bottle of wine. Thirty more seats are offered beneath Perrier umbrellas on an outdoor deck beside the water.

We've had fine meals here over the years, but were disappointed by both the food and the disinterested service at our latest dinner outing. The menu and the suave atmosphere are the same, as is the French bread that Ed still bakes daily. But what can you say for a mediocre salad of iceberg lettuce and a plate of broiled scallops and rice pilaf, both virtually tasteless? The lobster-seafood casserole was marginally better, but the steak fries were best left undescribed. The raspberry sherbet was a good dessert, and we enjoyed a bottle of Australian chardonnay for $11.95, selected from a wine list

Lawn chairs are lined up for visitors to take in view at The Claremont.

with several unusual, seldom-seen offerings at the low end. The extensive menu is nicely priced from $11.95 to $16.95. The menu also includes light or luncheon fare, from $3.50 for a toasted BLT to $8.95 for a lobster roll.

The Branches do have fun with their meals, as attested by their motto, "What foods these morsels be." We hope our latest dinner experience was an aberration.

Breakfast, lunch and dinner daily, 7 a.m. to 9:30 p.m. Closed November-April.

Jordan Pond House, Park Loop Road, Acadia National Park. (207) 276-3316.
Rebuilt following a disastrous fire, the Jordan Pond House is a large, strikingly contemporary complex with cathedral ceilings, two levels, outdoor porches and decks, huge windows and one of the good Acadia Gift Shops. The setting is majestic, with lawns sloping down to Jordan Pond and the landmark Bubbles mountains rising beyond.

Lobster stew or soup and a Jordan Pond popover served with strawberry preserves and butter are popular luncheon items. At one visit we enjoyed a fine seafood pasta and a curried chicken salad, garnished with red grapes and orange slices, and shared one of the famous popovers – good but a bit pricey at $2, considering it was mostly air.

The all-day menu starts at $7.50 for crab and havarti quiche. Dinners get more formal, featuring lobster (boiled, stuffed, sautéed, stew and salad), chicken, steak and seafood dishes, priced from $12.50 to $18. The fresh fruit ice creams are made here from original recipes dating to the late 19th century.

Even if you don't eat here, do stop for tea on the lawn, an island tradition. You sit on old-fashioned chairs and sip tea along with popovers and strawberry jam ($5).

Lunch, 11:30 to 2:30; tea on the lawn, 2:30 to 5:30; dinner, 5:30 to 8 or 9. Open mid-June to mid-October.

Cafe Drydock & Inn, 108 Main St., Southwest Harbor. (207) 244-3886.
Around-the-world cuisine is the billing for this popular corner cafe, lately doubled in size with a new bar and dining room bearing big kitchen-style chairs, Norman Rockwell prints on the walls and a profusion of plants hanging from the ceiling. Owner Marty Hanscomb has earmarked for non-smoking the 50 seats at booths and tables covered with floral runners in the older section.

The extensive menu is not nearly so international as the billing would have it, unless cajun and Mexican covers your world. It does touch many bases, from pastas, cajun and lobster to seafood (broiled haddock, crab mornay), chicken and beef, from $10.95 to $17.95. Appetizers include mushrooms boursin, crostini with feta and artichoke hearts wrapped in bacon. There's a full bar, a fairly good wine list and a large selection of beers. The dessert tray might bear raspberry torte, Kentucky Derby pie, cheesecakes, mousses and truffles.

For lunch or a light supper, try one of the burgers served on bulky rolls – the Maniac comes with cheddar and bacon – with home fries and cole slaw. There are plenty of salads, nachos, quesadillas, boboli pizzas and such.

Upstairs, Drydock offers two guest rooms and three larger units with kitchenettes, all with private baths and cable TV, for $60 to $85.

Lunch, 11:30 to 3:30; dinner, 5 to 10; shorter hours in off-season.

Thurston's Lobster Pound, Steamboat Wharf Road, Bernard. (207) 244-7600.

From the jaunty upstairs deck at this new lobster pound, you can look below and see where the lobstermen keep their traps. Thurston's is a real working lobster wharf. And if you couldn't tell from all the pickup trucks parked along the road, one taste of the lobster will convince you.

We loved our lobster dinner ($6.50 to $7 a pound, plus $3 for the extras, from corn to blueberry cake). Together we also sampled the lobster stew (bearing tons of lobster) for $4.50, a really good potato salad, steamers and two pounds of mussels (about one pound too much). Oh well, this *was* our first lobster feast of the summer. You wait in line for one of the twelve square tables for four on the covered deck, place your order at the counter and bring your own wine or beer. They provide the candles, and a little wash basin outside the kitchen so customers can wash the lobster debris off their hands.

This is a true place, opened in 1993 by Michael Radcliffe, great-grandson of the founder, and his wife Libby. A local couple, whose license plate said "Pies," was delivering the apple and rhubarb pies for the day the first time we stopped by.

Open daily in July and August, 7 a.m. to 8:30 p.m., 11 to 8, Memorial Day-June and September.

A sampling of other, more casual eating spots, particularly good for seafood or local atmosphere:

Head of the Harbor, Route 102, Southwest Harbor. A lobster dinner was $9.95 when we ate at Alan Hartling's rustic indoor-outdoor restaurant on a hill above Somes Sound. You see the lobsters steaming and place your order at the outdoor steamer and grill. Then a waitress delivers your order to the citronella-lit picnic tables on the expansive outdoor deck overlooking the water or on a screened porch adjacent. A fried clam platter with cole slaw and potato salad or french fries ($5.95) and chowder with a clam roll ($4.95) made a good lunch, washed down with a wine cooler and a Bud Lite. At our latest visit, we enjoyed a sunset dinner of stuffed shrimp with potato salad and sautéed scallops with french fries and three-bean salad (each $10.95), accompanied by a Napa Ridge chardonnay for $10.95 and followed by fresh raspberry pie. Open daily, noon to 10, Memorial Day to mid-October.

Beal's Lobster Pier, Clark Point Road, Southwest Harbor. Beside the Coast Guard Station, Beal's offers lobsters to go as well as to eat at picnic tables on the working dock. The last time we visited, they were priced at $6.85 to $7.85 a pound boiled (boiling from 9 a.m. to 8 p.m.) A lobster roll (all lobster meat with a dab of mayonnaise in a toasted hot dog bun, $6.95) makes a fine lunch, supplemented by great french fries, lemonade and ice cream from **The Captain's Galley** next door (open 8 a.m. to sunset).

The Docksider, Sea Street, Northeast Harbor. Strangely, the outdoor deck is on the

Expansive outdoor deck overlooks water at Head of the Harbor.

wrong side of the building (away from the harbor view), so many prefer to eat inside at booths with paper mats and paper plates. The fare runs the gamut from a fried haddock sandwich and fried clam roll to seafood linguini and lobster newburg, priced from $1.95 for a hot dog to $18.95 for a shore dinner. Wine and beer; open for lunch and dinner, Memorial Day to mid-October; breakfast in July and August.

Northeast Harbor Cafe and Ice Cream Parlor, Main Street, Northeast Harbor. Green checked cafe curtains and green marble-top tables identify this newcomer inspired by an heiress to the Godiva chocolate fortune who felt the town needed a good ice cream parlor. There's far more than ice cream, however: sandwiches, pizzas, stir-fries, quiches and entrées, at prices from $4.95 to $10.95 (for baked stuffed haddock or shrimp scampi). The cafe has a beer and wine license. Open daily in season, 11 to 8.

Maine-ly Delights, Ferry Road, Bass Harbor. From a van that dispensed hot dogs and crabmeat rolls opposite the Swans Island Ferry terminal, Karen Holmes Godbout has expanded over the years to the point where she now has a roof over her head, a room with an open kitchen and an outdoor deck. A hot dog costs $1.25 and a lobster roll $6.50; last we knew, you could get a complete lobster dinner with french fries and cole slaw for $6.95. Karen's fryolator is famous for her original O'Boy Doughboys, and she still picks the blueberries that go into her muffins and pies. Even with a beer and wine license, she stresses, "I am quaint, not fancy, Down East all the way." Open daily in summer, 8 a.m. to 9 p.m.

Jumpin' Java Espresso Bar & Bouncin' Buns Bakery, Main Street, Southwest Harbor. Relocated to a larger location in 1994, this is a bakery and an espresso bar with a Southwest theme. Ex-Californians Tom and Donna Wogan, who live on Swans Island, purvey croissants, cinnamon buns, baguettes, bagels and brownies to go with their cafe au lait and latte, among a host of coffees and beverages at their year-round storefront. There are a few stools and tables at which to partake.

Little Notch Bakery, The Shops at Hinckley Great Harbor Marina, Southwest Harbor. Founded as an adjunct of the West of Eden Whole Foods Cafe in Seal Cove, this exceptional bakery moved in 1994 to larger quarters here. Al Sabatini and Arthur Jacobs produce 4,500 loaves of bread weekly for a knowing clientele and some of Downeast Maine's finest inns and restaurants. Their specialties include Italian breads, focaccia, olive rolls and onion rolls. You can pick up some from the counter to munch on beside the water.

Diversions

Acadia National Park. The most famous sites are along Ocean Drive and the Park Loop Road out of Bar Harbor, but don't miss the park's other attractions on this side of the island. The Beech Mountain area offers Echo Lake with a fine beach, changing rooms and fresh water far warmer than the ocean. Hike up Beech Cliff for a great view of Echo Lake below (yes, you may hear your echo). Past Southwest Harbor and Manset are Seawall, created naturally by the sea, and the Wonderland and Ship's Harbor nature trails, both well worth taking.

Somes Sound and Somesville. Follow Sargent Drive out of Northeast Harbor along the fjord-like Somes Sound for some of the island's most spectacular views (it's the closest thing we know of to the more remote areas around California's Lake Tahoe). At the head of the sound is Somesville, a classic New England village and a joy to behold: the whites of the houses brightened patriotically by red geraniums, white petunias and morning glories in flowerboxes that line the street. Converted from a general store, the excellent **Port in the Storm Bookstore** stocks two floors with books and recordings. On the mezzanine, books are displayed the way they ought to be on slanted shelves around the atrium. Two resident cats and a pair of binoculars occupy a reading area in back beside Somes Sound, and you could not wish for a more beautiful spot for a bookstore. Also check out the old library with its new-fangled, wired-for-sound lounge chairs, and maybe an arts and crafts show outside. The entire town is listed on the National Register of Historic Places, and the **Mount Desert Historical Society** buildings chronicle the history of the island's earliest settlement. The Somesville Village Improvement Society conducts a bi-annual historical walking tour. The Masonic Hall in Somesville is home of the **Acadia Repertory Theater,** which has been staging five plays in two-week cycles each summer since 1973.

Museums. Southwest Harbor is widely known for its variety of birds (many consider it the warbler capital of the country), so fittingly this is the home of the **Wendell Gilley Museum,** a monument to the memory of one of the nation's outstanding bird carvers. Occupying a solar-heated building, it shows more than 200 of the late local wood carver's birds and decoys, ranging in size from a two-inch woodcock to a life-size bald eagle. The museum also has special exhibitions, and films and programs on woodcarving and natural history (admission, $3).

Also in Southwest Harbor is the main **Mount Desert Oceanarium,** a building full of sea life and lobster lore, with a touch tank, whale exhibit, fishing boats and more (adults, $4.95). Lately, the institution has branched out with a second oceanarium and a lobster hatchery, both in Bar Harbor.

New in Northeast Harbor is the **Great Harbor Collection Museum** in the old Town Hall/Fire Station. Artifacts from fire trucks to forks, toys to tools and sewing machines to sleighs reflect the heritage of Northeast, Southwest and Seal harbors. Adults, $1.

Boat cruises. Untold numbers of cruises – public, private and park-sponsored – leave from Northeast Harbor, Southwest Harbor and Bass Harbor. You can take a naturalist tour to Baker Island, a lobster boat or a ferry ride to Swans Island or the Cranberry Islands, and the park's cruises are particularly informative. If you'd rather observe than ride, poke around one of the ten or more boat-building yards in Southwest Harbor.

Shopping. The area's best shopping is in Northeast Harbor, although Southwest is catching up. In Northeast Harbor, **The Kimball Shop and Boutique** are two of the snazziest shops we've seen. The shop is a pageant of bright colors and room after room of pretty china, furniture, kitchenware and almost anything else that's in. A couple of doors away is the newer Boutique, filled with zippy clothes. **Beals Classics** is a branch of one of our favorite gift and clothing stores in Ellsworth. **Mrs. Pervear's Shop** is a nice hodgepodge of painted furniture (we loved the table with lupines painted on), handknit sweaters, yarn and more. Behind a wild awning, **Local Color** purveys marvelous handpainted clothing. **The Romantic Room** stocks a range from wicker and straw hats to brass beds. Try **Animal Crackers** for adorable clothes for children, **Sherman's** for books, and **Provisions** for suave groceries. There are several fine art galleries in which to browse, including **Smart Studio and Art Gallery,** with Wini Smart's wonderfully evocative paintings of Maine.

In Southwest Harbor, things are happening around the Hinckley Great Harbor Marina, a new state-of-the-art marina (it was the site of the international Wooden Boat Show in 1994) with a burgeoning complex of retail businesses. Check out the plants growing in all kinds of shoes, boots and sneakers outside **Hot Flash Anny's,** the hip showroom for Ann Seavey's stained-glass pieces. Almost everything is made of glass and is one of a kind; you could spend from $4 to $4,000 here. Next door is **Little Notch Bakery,** and across the way is **Black Ledge Lobster Pound.** In the downtown area, canvas tote bags of all colors are displayed at **Seafaring Crafts** and handmade crafts at **Calico Creations.** We liked the selection at **Wicker & Wool,** an artisans' gallery, and the nifty sweaters at **Periwinkles.** Great sweaters and skirts are for sale at **Common Threads.** A good selection of children's books is found at **Oz Books,** and toys and clothing for tots are offered at **Treasure Island. By Way Of Maine,** where everything for sale is made in the state, is fun to browse through; we admired the moose hatrack, the jewelry depicting loons, the capes and sweaters – even the pickled fiddlehead ferns. **Mrs. McVey's Ice Cream Shop** is where school teacher Judy McVey offers heath bar and cappuccino frozen yogurt, many flavors of ice cream and good sandwiches in summer. Little Notch Bakery products and Seal Cove goat cheese are hot numbers at **Sawyer's Market,** the local grocery with all the right stuff, including a rear deli case of fantastic looking salads, marinated cooked salmon and other gourmet items prepared exclusively for Sawyer's. You could fashion yourself a delightful picnic here. Anne Jones sells her much-in-demand paintings, as well as some jewelry, at the **A. Jones Gallery.** A few years ago, we acquired a small basket full of Maine shells and critters she had put together; it makes a great centerpiece for our dining room table, and brings back fond memories of Maine.

Extra-Special _____

Asticou Terrace and Thuya Gardens, Route 3, Northeast Harbor.

You can drive up, but we recommend the ten-minute hike nearly straight up a scenic, well-maintained switchback path and stairs to the prized gardens above Northeast Harbor. A plaque relates that landscape architect Joseph H. Curtis left this "for the quiet recreation of the people of this town and their summer guests." It is easy to enjoy the showy hilltop spread combining English flower beds with informal natural Japanese effects, some common and uncommon annuals plus hardy rhododendron and laurel that appear as a surprise so far north. As you might find on a private estate, which this once was, there are a gazebo, a free-form freshwater pond, and a shelter with pillowed seats and deck chairs for relaxing in the shade. Thuya Lodge, the former Curtis summer cottage, houses a rare botanical book library. Nearby are the **Asticou Azalea Gardens,** where twenty varieties of azaleas compete for attention with a Japanese sand garden and amazed us with their Southern-style lushness in late June. Open daily, 7 to 7. Free.

Moose-watching is a major pastime in Moosehead Lake region.

Peter Thibodeau Photo

Greenville/Moosehead Lake, Me.
The Maine You Remember

The drive through interior Maine on Route 6 and 15, the only road into the Moosehead Lake region, seems endless. But the intrepid traveler need not despair. Suddenly, the road crests atop a hill and now, before you in all its glory, unfolds the majesty of Moosehead, the Northeast's largest lake.

At the near end lies Greenville (population 2,200), the region's only town of note. On all sides are mountains – small ones, to be sure, but enough to alter the landscape of what to the south had been essentially rolling flatlands. The sky-blue glacier lake spreads

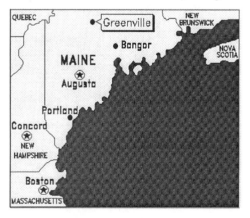

its tentacles like the antlers of a moose head around islands and into coves. Think of an inland sea stretching into a forest of green, rather like a freshwater version of Penobscot Bay.

The pristine lake, shaped vaguely like a moose head, is 40 miles long and 20 miles across at its widest. It's 300 feet deep at the base of the landmark Mount Kineo cliffs. Most of the 400 miles of shoreline, owned by paper companies more interested in raw lumber than in vacation condominiums, is undeveloped.

252

For visitors, the mystique of Moosehead has always been that of a sportsman's paradise in the North Woods wilderness. The area has long been a mecca for hunters and fishermen. Increasingly, its lure is broadening to embrace nature and wildlife lovers, hikers, rafters and canoeists in summer, and cross-country skiers, downhill skiers and snowmobilers in winter.

The area is poised for what one proponent calls "eco-travel, the tourism of the future," for those who like to pursue sports year-round in the great outdoors. Already the rough co-exists with the refined. Nationwide publicity has been accorded the Road Kill Cafe, a restaurant poking fun at the pretensions of some of its peers, and the Lodge at Moosehead Lake, an inn revising the standards for creature comforts and style in the Maine woods. New owners are improving the Squaw Mountain Resort, a troubled but promising ski area. True, much of the area remains raw and primeval. But its virgin veneer is leavened by a gentleness that the great lake gives to the mountains, by a subtle sophistication that escapes other north woods destinations.

Moose-watching is a mania, and few visitors leave without spotting at least a few, front and center during a moose cruise or safari or unexpectedly, simply feeding beside the road. The region has launched the annual Moosemania, a month of moose-related activities in late spring. At least three shops convey a moose theme.

This is the natural state of "the Maine you remember," as the Moosehead Lake Region Chamber of Commerce touts it. Just you and the moose, and a few others who like to get away from the crowds.

Inn Spots

The Lodge at Moosehead Lake, Lily Bay Road, Greenville 04441. (207) 695-4400.

High up Blair Hill overlooking Squaw Mountain and Moosehead Lake, this small new hostelry and restaurant sets a standard for low-key luxury in the wilds. Jennifer and Roger Cauchi, former resort and hotel managers in the Poconos, converted a Shingle-style summer home-turned-restaurant into a light and airy refuge of rustic

Elegant woodsy decor enhances living room at The Lodge at Moosehead Lake.

elegance. From the ultra-comfortable common rooms and guest quarters to some fairly exotic meals, guests are in for a treat.

Except for its view beyond, the unassuming exterior gives little hint of things inside. As you enter the foyer with its artful arrangement of fishing creels and other piscatory accessories, you know this is no ordinary inn. The foyer leads to a broad living room, its windows opening onto a full-length deck where you can look down on the lake activity in the distance and watch a sunset that's apt to be spectacular. Here and elsewhere, the high-style lodge decor is striking for flair employed with restraint. Adjoining the comfortable living room, filled with books and magazines, is a smaller parlor/library called the Toby Room. Its lineup of toby jugs reflects Roger's British heritage. Beyond is a summery dining room where breakfast and, in the off-season, dinner are served (see Dining Spots). Opening onto a patio on the lower level is the Moosehead Room, a large game room with English darts and a billiards table.

A neat little "Gone Fishing" sign, complete with a miniature rod and two tiny wooden fish, hangs gracefully on the door of each of the five bedrooms. The lodge's version of a "Do Not Disturb" sign, it flips over to say "In Camp." Utter comfort with a wildlife theme prevails within. Each room has a TV/VCR in a cabinet above the gas-lit fireplace, a private bath with jacuzzi for two, hand-carved four-poster queensize beds with fine linens, plush sitting areas and such amenities as toiletries, hair dryers, ironing boards, terrycloth robes and little Coleman ice chests.

Our quarters in the Bear Room came with plush carpeting, an assortment of loveseats and wing chairs richly upholstered in woodsy fabrics, and a private deck. Local wood sculptor Joe Bolf had carved small black climbing bears upon each post of the bed. The mirror in the bathroom, with a bear head on top, was carved to match. Whimsical bear accents (such as small needlepoint rugs depicting black bears, one on either side of the bed) enhanced the room at every turn. Jennifer repeated the sophisticated decorative scheme with other wildlife motifs in each room. There are loon books and a loon-patterned table in the Loon Room, sheets patterned with fish in the Trout Room, a buffalo rug in the Totem Room and antlers holding the valances in the Moose Room. Sculptor Bolf has carved the bed posts and mirrors in each to reflect the theme. Expect to find such decorative accents as a twig birdhouse in a corner, twig branches and pine cones outlining the hall windows, and full-length curtains draped smartly like an upside-down L in the bedrooms. These are the designs of which decorator magazines are made.

A deer bounded across the back lawn as we prepared for breakfast the next morning. Roger served a "wake-up cocktail," which turned out to be a small strawberry milkshake in a wine glass, and soufléed eggs in a crêpe garnished with cantaloupe, pineapple and wild blueberries. A choice of juices and toasting breads awaited on a side table. Other breakfast entrées include belgian waffles and stuffed french toast with cream cheese and fruits. You might also find Roger's eccles cakes, filled with chocolate and raspberry jam. The culinary treats resume in the afternoon, with complimentary hors d'oeuvre – in our case, smoked ham and mini-tortillas stuffed with parsnips and carrots.

Jennifer oversees a stylish little gift shop, Miss Elaine E. Moose, in the adjacent barn. She also has a larger Mainely Moose shop in downtown Greenville.

The innkeepers kept the lodge small so guests could be pampered in style. And style their lodge has in spades.

Doubles, $135 to $205, B&B; off-season, $135 to $175, MAP. No smoking.

Greenville Inn, Norris Street, Box 1194, Greenville 04441. (207) 695-2206.

Old money and solid furnishings prevail in this established inn, built as a summer home in 1895 by a wealthy lumber baron. Embossed lincrusta walls and gas lights

Greenville Inn occupies restored 1895 lumber baron's mansion

convey an air of antiquity in the halls, as does the old telephone fixture on the wall. A large spruce tree painted on a leaded glass window adorns the stairway landing. Carved mantels, mosaic and English tiles surround the fireplaces.

Foremost a restaurant of distinction run by Elfie Schnetzer and her two grown offspring, the inn is adding to its lodging business with four new cottages for 1995 and four more in 1996. These will be the deluxe accommodations: one-bedroom affairs with queen beds, sitting areas, front porches and TVs. Off to the side on a slope above the inn, the cottages are clustered around the site of two existing cottages, which were to be razed in 1996.

Nine more bedrooms, four with private baths, are available in the main inn. Here, the best glimpses of the water are obtained from two front bedrooms that share a bath with a deep tub and a separate needle-spray shower. The rooms are nicely furnished in uncluttered Victorian style and beds are covered with colorful quilts. Ours had one of the inn's two kingsize beds and one of its two fireplaces, but had only one chair and a clawfoot tub without a shower (which presented a problem when trying to wash one's hair). We found our stay in the inn somewhat confining, what with the only common room doubling as a pre-dinner gathering place and bar for restaurant-goers and the few chairs on the side porch being in full view and earshot of people eating in the dining rooms. We don't know who was more disconcerted – we, blocking their views, or they, spoiling our quiet reading time. (Next time we'll avoid the problem by staying in one of the new cottages.)

At breakfast the next morning, classical music muffled conversations echoing in the three small dining rooms. The innkeepers, nowhere in evidence, had put out a European buffet spread of fresh fruit, cereals, bagels, croissants, breads, ham and cheese. It was perfectly filling, but seemed rather impersonal.

The inn closed for the winter of 1994-95 for the first time. Daughter Susie Schnetzer said that decision could be reversed if new owners improve the skiing situation at Squaw Mountain as planned.

Doubles, $75 to $95; new cottages, $115. Closed November to April.

Evergreen Lodge, Route 15, HCR 76, Box 58, Greenville 04441. (207) 695-3241.
Five miles south of town is this attractive, all-cedar structure, built as a physician's home and set back from the road amid evergreens and birches on 30 acres. Nancy and

John Christman from Pennsylvania acquired the house and turned it into a comfortable B&B with six bedrooms, each with private bath. The rooms, paneled in varieties of cedar, are outfitted with an assortment of king, queen, double, twin and trundle beds to suit a clientele that varies from couples to groups to families with older children. Colorful quilts and Nancy's dried floral arrangements enhance each room. Especially appealing is the Deer Room, which comes with a private balcony and a skylit bathroom.

Guests gather in a cozy library, a large living and dining area with a free-standing wood stove or on the rear lawn beside prolific gardens. A cheery sun room is the site for breakfast, where juice, baked apples and sourdough blueberry pancakes were the fare at our visit. Plum-nectarine crumble was on the docket for the next day.

It's obvious that Nancy knows what makes for a good inn experience. In the off-season, she travels around the South and West as an evaluator and consultant for the American Bed & Breakfast Association, which inspects and rates member inns.

Doubles, $59 to $75. No smoking. Open mid-May to mid-October.

The Sawyer House, Lakeview Street, Box 521, Greenville 04441.(207) 695-2369.

A view of East Cove Harbor, a residential in-town location and comfortable accommodations commend this small B&B in an 1849 farmhouse long occupied by the Sawyer family, who were boat captains on Moosehead Lake and whose matriarch weathered 100 Maine winters. Pat Zieten, a former local newspaper reporter who seems to know everyone and everything going on in town, and her husband Hans, a plumber, offer three bedrooms and enthusiastic hospitality.

Our quarters in the main-floor Captain Fred Sawyer Suite could not have been more commodious. The large room contained a kingsize bed at one end, a sofabed in a sitting area at the other, light patterned wallpaper and fresh flowers. The bathroom held a collection of amenities, from shampoo to toothpaste to disposable razors. Two smaller rooms upstairs also have private baths, mini-print wallpapers, thick carpeting and beribboned bonnets hung on the walls here and there. "Hans wanted to panel but I'm partial to wallpaper," says Pat, who

Breakfast for two at The Sawyer House.

prevailed. Her light and airy decorating scheme complements the wallpaper, and vice-versa.

Guests spread out in a common room with dining area, a stylish side deck beside the woods and a front porch overlooking the harbor. The Zietens and their sons occupy a separate section of the house.

Popovers are Pat's trademark at breakfast, a treat that begins with orange juice and fresh fruit and ends with a choice of eggs, pancakes or french toast. We liked the scrambled eggs with chain-link sausages and thick homemade toast, accompanied by frequent insights and suggestions from the ebullient hostess.

Doubles, $55; suite, $65. No smoking.

The Whitman House, Pleasant Street, Box 524, Greenville 04441. (207) 695-3543.

A wicker-filled front porch welcomes guests to this handsome, 1910-vintage house for "bed and breakfast in the European tradition." Around here, "European" is a buzz word for shared baths, which the foreigners who make up a high proportion of the Whitman clientele don't seem to mind. Most Americans do mind, Concetta and Dick Edwards found after opening their seasonal three-room B&B in 1991. "We love the B&B business and want to expand," she said at our visit. "But we know now that we have to offer private baths."

When they did a major reconfiguration of their house and property in 1995, they decided to please both groups. They retained two bedrooms with shared baths for those who don't mind and want less expensive accommodations. Now they also offer three rooms with private baths. The extra space was gained from a couple of closets and two rooms vacated when they moved into the second floor of the rear garage, which has been redesigned to look like a carriage house.

The newly enlarged B&B is located on a quiet hillside east of town. The main floor holds a living room outfitted for communal activities: a puzzle in progress on a game table, a European writing table and a couple of chairs in front of a TV/VCR. Breakfast is served in a formal dining room amidst the home's original dark woodwork. The fare includes fresh fruits, cereals, Dick's coffeecake and blueberry muffins, and a main course like chocolate-chip pancakes, french toast or scrambled eggs with cheese.

Off the kitchen in the owners' former family room is a new guest room with a sitting area and a private bath.

Upstairs are four guest rooms, two with private shower-baths located in enlarged closets and two sharing the original hall bath. They're nicely decorated in traditional style with artworks and antiques. One room contains a sleigh bed and another has twins. Oriental rugs accent the hardwood floors and each room has a ceiling fan.

With the changes, the Edwardses extended their seasonal operation from two months in summer to six months. They hoped that improved ski business would allow them to remain open in the winter. And they were thinking of offering dinner for guests.

They also came up with a novel twist for a B&B. "We purchased a canoe and all the necessary equipment for each room," said Dick. The canoes are stashed in a rack along Moosehead Lake and are free for guests who stay two nights or more.

Doubles, $65 to $75. Closed November-April.

The Devlin House, Lily Bay Road, Greenville 04441. (207) 695-2229.

Ruth Devlin and her late husband, Jim, built this large contemporary ranch on Blair Hill specifically to run as a B&B. They'd become enamored with the setting during their tenure running the acclaimed Lakeview Manor restaurant next door in the building that is now the Lodge at Moosehead Lake.

"Isn't this peaceful, quiet and gentle?" Ruth asked rhetorically as we took in the stunning lake vista through the sliding doors and windows of her living room, while a hummingbird hovered outside at a feeder. The main floor is devoted to the owner's quarters (Ruth also runs a computerized bookkeeping business from a front room).

Upstairs are two large guest rooms with kingsize beds, full baths, thick carpeting, color TVs and comfortable sitting areas for reading or taking in the view. Downstairs in the walkout lower level is a suite with a double bed and two twins, a huge bath and a family room with two sturdy couches, three lounge rockers and a big TV.

Ruth serves a hearty breakfast between 6 and 9; "I'll feed people at 6 if they're going rafting," she says cheerily. Her repertoire includes bacon and eggs, muffins, cereal, raspberry pancakes and french toast.

Doubles, $60; suite, $80.

Manitou Cottage, Pritham Avenue, Box 1208, Greenville 04441. (207) 695-3082.

Former owners of the remote sporting camp Medawisla on Second Roach Pond, Russ and Mimi Whitten called on their experiences there when they opened a "village lake house" beside their retirement home at the edge of downtown Greenville in 1994. Their low-slung, Southern-looking, 19th-century cottage/house with wraparound veranda holds a paneled living room outfitted with TV and Texas willow furniture, and a country kitchen where continental breakfast is put out in the morning.

In back is a two-bedroom suite with a private bath. The main bedroom has a double and a twin joined together to form a kingsize Adirondack bed, the largest we've seen. Reproduction beacon blankets are used here and throughout the three upstairs bedrooms, which share a bath.

"This is a cottage, not an inn," cautions Mimi, who notes her breakfast spread involves "a nice fruit cup," homemade muffins, whole-grain bread and cereal. It's particularly good for families, groups and couples traveling together.

Russ is a Maine Guide and Mimi runs a small gift shop featuring Texas willow furniture, antiques and Indian blankets. From experience, they sing the praises of the area's new breed of wilderness camps where "mature" urban professionals enjoy indoor plumbing, three prepared meals a day and "sit on the porch with their martinis and watch the moose go by." But that's another story.

Doubles, $40 to $65.

Kineo House, Kineo Island, Box 397, Rockwood 04478. (207) 534-8812.

With the fabled old hotel of the same name long gone, this is the only public lodging and dining facility on idyllic Kineo Island. It occupies one of eight privately owned cottages left on the island, a sylvan retreat in the shadow of the famed Mount Kineo cliffs, and is a must visit – if not for overnight, at least for lunch or dinner.

Lynn and Marshall Peterson, mainlanders who used to camp nearby at Casey's at Spencer Bay, purchased the property in 1993 and set about its upgrading into what they call a casual island inn. Besides a popular restaurant (see Dining Spots), they offer six upstairs guest rooms, four with private baths. There's a water view from every room, this being located at the tip of a peninsula opposite Rockwood at the midpoint of Moosehead Lake, with water on three sides and Mount Kineo looming behind. The rooms are simple and rather cottagey, but sport good-looking floral prints on the walls. Some rooms connect to offer both double and bunk beds; new four-poster beds were in the works for others. A continental breakfast of cereal and bagels is included in the room rates.

On the main floor are a pub, a restaurant and a nifty little common room with windows right beside the water. Outside are lawn chairs and tables facing a nine-hole golf course, the abandoned Kineo House annex and a wildlife sanctuary. There's itinerant activity during the day, thanks to visiting boaters, golfers and sightseers. But the last scheduled shuttle leaves at 6, and overnighters have the island to themselves.

The Petersons are hands-on innkeepers, to put it mildly. "We wear nine hats each," says Lynn, who does the cooking and housekeeping. Her husband tends bar, greets guests and shuttles people back and forth to Rockwood on his pontoon boat. In winter, he picks up house guests by snowmobile or dog sled. Life here is simple, the Petersons say, but has its rewards.

Doubles, $65. Closed in April.

Northern Pride Lodge, HX 76, Box 588, Greenville 04441. (207) 695-2890.

Out in the semi-boondocks in Kokadjo, eighteen miles northeast of Greenville, this occupies prime waterfront property at the end of First Roach Pond at the headwaters of

Rich wood paneling enhances dining room at Greenville Inn.

the famed Roach River, a fisherman's mecca for salmon and trout. Jeff and Barb Lucas left careers as respiratory therapists in Ohio for a new life in the Maine wilds in 1993. In their first year, they managed to gain an avid following for some of the area's more creative meals (see Dining Spots) and they redid their guest quarters with considerable style. Only the basic necessities are lacking, since guests occupying the five bedrooms share two intimate bathrooms on the ground floor, one for men and the other for women but each seemingly big enough for only one at a time.

The Lucases make the best of the situation, however, as do their guests. The two most appealing rooms are on one side of the main floor, one with a queensize four-poster and the other with two double beds. Both have good-looking comforters and suave decorative touches. Upstairs are three rooms, two holding four twin beds each and the other a queen bed and a twin. Greenville wood carver Joe Bolf carved the striking wildlife scenes on the doors of each bedroom, as well as the lodge's new sign.

The common rooms in this lodge, built in 1896 by a logging baron as his summer home, are uncommonly attractive. A moose head in stained glass adorns the top of the french doors in the living room opposite a huge fieldstone fireplace. Meals are served in a summery dining area on an enclosed porch, part of a long screened porch that wraps around the front and sides. Guests also like to chat with Barb as she works in her large commercial kitchen. Breakfast the day of our visit included a choice of scrambled eggs or blueberry pancakes, fresh fruit (cantaloupe with kiwi), sausage and bacon.

The Lucases also offer 24 primitive campsites, which account for all the picnic tables scattered across the shady grounds beside the water.

Doubles, $80 B&B, $130 AP.

Dining Spots

Greenville Inn, Norris Street, Greenville. (207) 695-2206.

Among Greenville folk, this restaurant is "the toast of the town," in one innkeeper's words. Since 1988, the Schnetzer family has been serving some of northern Maine's fanciest fare in elegant surroundings. Three small dining rooms are clad in white linens amid rich wood paneling, ornate fireplaces, embossed Lincrusta walls and distant views of Moosehead Lake's East Cove Harbor. Austrian-born chef-innkeeper Elfie Schnetzer and daughter Susie are in the kitchen. Son Michael oversees the front of the house and the wine list, which with 132 entries is the best around.

Dining is taken seriously here, as is the solicitous service. Our leisurely meal began with a shared appetizer, a silken pâté of duck liver, truffles and port wine, served with the appropriate garnishes but with a homemade roll rather than the traditional melba toast. Next came simple green salads on glass shell-shaped dishes and huge, piping-hot popovers, with butter presented in a silver shell.

Among main courses ($15 to $17), we liked the breast of chicken in a very spicy peanut sauce and a trio of lamb chops with rosemary butter. Both were fairly unadorned and served with rice and a mix of yellow and green beans. Chocolate-coffee ice cream cake and plum strudel were refreshing endings among such exotic treats as Viennese chocolate cake, crème brûlée and citrus cheesecake with mango coulis.

Other favorites include crabmeat marsala au gratin and smoked venison with cumberland sauce for appetizers; shrimp with mustard-dill sauce, halibut fillet with fresh thyme and lemon, and chargrilled sirloin steak for main courses. Elfi says she has guests who come especially for her Atlantic salmon, which she marinates, broils and serves with sauce verte. She keeps the favorites from year to year, but rewrites her dinner menu seasonally.

A wood stove warms the inn's lounge-living room in which many diners choose to have cocktails or after-dinner drinks.

Dinner nightly, 6 to 9. Closed November to April.

Lakeview Restaurant, Lily Bay Road, Greenville. (207) 695-4400.

"We're the opposite of everyone else," avows chef-owner Roger Cauchi of the Lodge at Moosehead Lake. After two years of preparing dinners in summer, Roger canceled summer service for 1995 and instead served from mid-October to mid-June by reservation only. "We moved up here for an easier life," he said with tongue in cheek, "and being in the kitchen from 7 in the morning to 11 at night got to be too much."

Too bad, for we enjoyed one of our more interesting dinners in a lovely setting here in the summer of 1994. Similar treats now await those who are there during the off-season, when Roger has time to be in the kitchen and most area restaurants are closed. The night's menu is recited, and dinner is prix-fixe ($25).

Dining here is a paced experience that can best be described as romantic. Rush-seat chairs are at well-spaced, green-linened tables beneath a pitched ceiling in the airy dining room. The candles are in wrought-iron holders shaped like moose. The "flowers" on the tables may be pussy willows. Jazz, New Age and classical music plays in the background, interspersed occasionally with loon calls and sounds of the wild.

We started with a cup of the dynamite tomato-dill bisque, a house specialty, and the house salad, on this night described simply as broccoli. Presented nouvelle style, the small pieces of broccoli were tossed with onions, walnuts and raisins and carried a distinct bite. A dollop of lime sorbet, served in a champagne glass, cleared the palate for the main courses, sautéed chicken breast in a blueberry cream sauce and sherried seafood over moose-shaped puff pastry. Side plates produced samplings of the day's three vegetables: braised celery, sautéed carrots with cumin and sesame seeds, and green beans with walnuts. Desserts from the "moose cart" included raspberry pudding, rum cake and a novel chocolate mousse maximus with a surprise in the middle.

This is hardly your typical Maine Woods fare. The food is assertive, the service friendly and, as the sun sets across Moosehead Lake, the setting is spectacular.

Dinner by reservation, 5:30 to 7, mid-October to mid-June. Reservations required before 11 a.m. Restaurant closed in summer.

260

The Road Kill Cafe, Route 15, Greenville Junction. (207) 695-2230.

Only in Greenville, you think, could they get away with a place like this. Wrong. The concept debuted here, but proved such a success that the owners branched out to Rangeley Lake and Bartlett, N.H., and were planning to open in Burlington, Vt., and Southern Maine.

"Greenville is not your normal town," explains Leigh Turner, who launched the cafe to nationwide publicity in 1992. He had arrived here two years earlier to restore

the Kineo House resort after upgrading the Wolfeboro Inn on Lake Winnipesaukee, N.H. When the Kineo venture fell through, Leigh opened the cafe with partner Mariette Sinclair to lampoon what he calls "the pretensions of fine dining."

Here you'll find an irreverent menu ("Oh deer! The buck stopped here"), assorted roadside memorabilia, sassy servers and kitchen theatrics that defy description. Locals and tourists alike pack the close-together tables in the brightly lit front room, in the darker rear bar or on the umbrellaed rear deck overlooking an inlet into Moosehead Lake.

Heaping portions, affordable prices and fun, fun, fun are the Road Kill's hallmarks. Although there are a few nightly dinner specials ($7.95 to $13.95), this is basically sandwich and snack fare. "Never assume it's a raisin," warns the menu as "the most important advice for dining in the

Outdoor deck at Road Kill Cafe.

Moosehead area." The food is categorized as skidbits (starters like chicken knuckles, potato pelts and Canadian nachaux), mower clippings (salads), pot holes (soups, chili and chowder), bye-bye Bambi burgers, brake and scrape sandwiches, and ribs, fips, bucks and balls, served with nightcrawlers (french fries) and house mower clippings.

The cafe's theme is "where the food used to speak for itself," doled out with an audacious sense of humor (as in kitchen staff throwing handfuls of feathers through the kitchen door). If you're in the mood, it's lots of fun.

Open daily, 11:30 to 11:30.

Flatlander's, Pritham Avenue, Greenville. (207) 695-3373.

Billed as "a country place for food and drink," this small downtown emporium is a cut above the norm, thanks to its specialty of broasted chicken. Owners Red and Julie Springer decided in 1993 to feature the chicken and the concept took off. You can order a three-piece chicken dinner ($5.95), including french fries and cole slaw, to eat here or take out to a picnic table in the pocket-size town park facing the harbor across the street.

If broasted chicken is not your bag, there are plenty of other options, from appetizers to burgers, soups to salads. Among main courses ($4.75 to $12.95), expect a few things like beans and a long dog, spaghetti with meat sauce, shrimp with linguini, fish and chips, country ribs and ribeye steak.

Decor in the long, narrow room with a bar at the back is minimal, but the handsome bare wood tables are made of Maine pine – "you can hardly find trees like this any more," says Red.

Lunch and dinner daily in summer, 11 to 9; sharply reduced hours in off-season.

Northern Pride Lodge, Kokadjo. (207) 695-2890.

A small and pleasant dining porch and an inspired-for-the-area menu draw people for dinner at this small lodge in out-of-the-way Kokadjo (whose sign says Population; Not Many), just before the paved road ends on the back way to Baxter State Park and Mount Katahdin.

Ohio transplant Barb Lucas does the cooking. The short, à la carte menu starts with things like smoked trout or smoked salmon pâté, spicy Buffalo wings and, Barb's favorite, a baked brie cheese wheel with warm caramel sauce, seasonal fruit and french bread. Seasonal greens enhance the Mediterranean and smoked shrimp salads that come with the meal. Main courses always include filet mignon topped with sautéed mushrooms ($14.95). Two other choices are offered ($9.95 to $13.95), depending on the night: chicken teriyaki and pork normande on Thursday, prime rib and baked stuffed haddock on Friday, bacon-wrapped shrimp with maple-mustard cream sauce and spaghetti with meatballs on Saturday, and roast cornish game hen and beef stroganoff on Sunday. Dessert could be amaretto cheesecake, apple crêpes with maple sauce or carrot cake. The full bar offers a number of choice brands.

The Lucases pack interesting box lunches for house guests, who are granted the option of having three meals a day. "We'd never been in the food business before," says Barb, "so we're just winging it." Winging it rather well, we'd say.

Dinner by reservation, Thursday-Sunday 5 to 9.

Kineo House, Kineo Island. (207) 534-8812.

A pleasant summer outing involves a six-minute trip by shuttle boat or water taxi from Rockwood out to storied Kineo Island for a bit of sightseeing and lunch at the Kineo House. Lynn Peterson, who handles the cooking, has attracted quite a following, serving up to 50 people a day in her summery, Victorian-style dining room and outside on the front lawn facing a golf course.

Because of her location and the numbers of patrons, her lunch menu is rather basic. Prices range from $2.75 for a grilled hot dog to $4.75 for a cajun chicken sandwich. We ordered the chicken salad in a pita pocket, which turned out to be a half sandwich, good but small, and a burger with jalapeño cheese. Both were served on paper plates with potato chips and a bit of pasta salad. The iced tea came in plastic glasses.

Dinner gets a tad fancier in the old-fashioned dining room outfitted with floral-print tablecloths, captain's chairs and Victorian fluted lights. You might start with mushrooms stuffed with crabmeat, Mexican shrimp cocktail or the house pâté. Main courses ($8.95 to $12.95) include chicken stir-fry with vegetables, shrimp scampi on pasta, ribeye steak and catch of the day. Cheesecake with strawberries is a favorite dessert.

Marshall Peterson offers drinks in his convivial pub across the hall from the dining room. He also shuttles diners back to the mainland if they're out here for dinner.

Lunch daily, 11 to 3; dinner by reservation (before 4 p.m.), 5:30 to 8; reduced hours off-season. Closed in April.

Pittston Farm, West Branch Area, Moosehead Lake (Box 525, Rockwood). (207) 695-2821.

People fly in or drive 40 miles from Greenville to have one of the all-you-can-eat logger's dinners at this remote fishing camp at the point where the north and south

Northern Pride Lodge offers lodging and dining in former logging baron's summer home.

branches of the Penobscot River meet twenty miles above Rockwood. There's no phone (reservations are taken through Folsom's Air Service, with which it maintains radio contact) and the farm is primitive, as you might expect from its heritage as the main hub of Great Northern's lumber operations in the West Branch area and later as a Boy Scout camp.

Ken Twitchell took it over in 1993 and offers meals to house guests and the public. The dining room seats 60, but this is the kind of place where folks help themselves and are likely to take their plates outside to eat on the porch or on the front lawn. The farm features "lumber camp cooking," which means hearty, homemade fare and lots of it. Expect two main courses, vegetables, real mashed potatoes, homemade breads and rolls, half a dozen items from the salad bar, pies, cakes and desserts. The price: $7.95.

Ken remodeled nine upstairs guest rooms, which share four bathroom facilities on the main floor. They rent for a modest $35 a day per person, including three meals.

Dinner by reservation, seatings at 5 and 6:30. BYOB.

Diversions

Outdoor Sports. Fishing and hunting have traditionally been the leading activities here, although neither is quite as good in terms of take as in days gone by. "Overkill," explained a Maine Guide of our acquaintance. To compensate, some of the old sporting camps have altered their focus to appeal to nature lovers, wildlife watchers and photographers. White-water rafting is popular on the nearby Kennebec and Penobscot rivers. Hikers like the 75-minute hike up the 700-foot-high landmark Mount Kineo to a renovated fire tower, which yields a panoramic view of Moosehead Lake and environs. One of the prime waterfront spots is occupied by Lily Bay State Park, an uncrowded favorite of swimmers, picnickers and campers.

In winter, skiing at **Squaw Mountain Resort** is improving under new owners (from Florida, of all places), who took over in 1995. Just outside Greenville, Squaw has two chairlifts and a 1,700-foot vertical rise, facing Moosehead Lake. It offers plenty of

Shuttles leave state boat ramp in Rockwood for Kineo complex beneath Kineo cliffs.

skiing for $15 a day – especially with an increase in snowmaking coverage to the top of the mountain. Cross-country skiing also is popular, but tends to get overshadowed by the snowmobilers who make this their noisy base.

Moose Watching. Everyone looks for moose, and local promoters say more moose reside in the Moosehead area than anywhere in the East. You'll likely spot them feeding in ponds and rivers after dawn and before dusk. They're said to be at their most numerous around the roads and waterways near Rockwood and Kokadjo. A new brochure outlines "moose safari" packages by land, sea and air.

One of the best ways to see moose and understand their habitat is to take the two-hour moose cruise offered by the Birches Resort in Rockwood. Unexpectedly plush seats accommodate up to sixteen passengers on a 24-foot-long pontoon boat. Moose were spotted on 96 of 100 excursions in the previous summer, resort co-owner Bill Willard advised. We thought we were going to be among the four percent failure rate until, at the end of our two-hour cruise up and down a jungle-like river, a lone moose suddenly obliged up close. "Every trip is different," our laconic boat pilot-guide said. Two more moose were spotted from a distance on the return trip to the resort. We also encountered two moose along Route 15 on the drive back to Greenville after dinner. Our pilot pointed out one feeding in an inlet during a half-hour sightseeing flight the next morning. That was it for moose of the live variety on our four-day visit.

Airplane Adventures. Almost as much as moose, seaplanes define the Moosehead area, and their sheer numbers convey a different look and feel to this lake. Indeed, the lake is so favored by backwoods pilots that they converge every September on Greenville for the International Seaplane Fly-In, the largest of its kind in the Northeast. Since much of the Moosehead Lake shoreline and many sporting camps are not accessible by road, seaplanes get in quickly where motor vehicles and boats cannot.

Three commercial air services offer sightseeing excursions. We found a half-hour flight around the lower half of the lake with **Folsom's Air Service** ($30) the best way to appreciate the vastness of both lake and wilderness. Folsom's provides a canoe-and-fly service ($85) in which customers are flown to Penobscot Farm. There they board canoes for a leisurely three-hour paddle upstream to Lobster Lake, where they are met for the return flight to Greenville.

Other airplane sights may be of interest. Folsom's bases the last operating DC-3 seaplane, an ark of an Army Air Force plane fitted with pontoons, at Greenville's tiny municipal airport. The curious also may view remnants of the wreckage of a B-52, which crashed due to air turbulence against Elephant Mountain during the Cuban missile crisis in January 1963, killing seven crewmen. Access is via a logging road maintained by Scott Paper Co.

Boat Excursions. Another good way to see this area is by boat, and a variety of craft seems to be everywhere for rent or hire around Moosehead and its tributaries. Experience a bygone era with a cruise on the **Katahdin,** the last of 50 steamboats that plied the lake, ferrying cargo and people to resorts and sporting camps before cars and trucks reached the area. Now the star floating exhibit of the tiny Moosehead Marine Museum beside the lake at the municipal parking lot, the diesel-powered Katahdin gives three-hour cruises of the lower third of the lake daily at 12:30 in summer; adults, $12. A galley offers hot dogs, candy and the like. We didn't know this, so had picked up good sandwiches at Auntie M's (open for breakfast and lunch) across the street.

Shopping. Greenville's little downtown is of interest to browsers. Wonderful birdhouses (some made in the Smokies), fishing scenes painted on saws, twig furniture, moose mobiles and T-shirts are among the offerings at **Maine Street Station.** The name speaks for itself at **Mainely Moose,** an offshoot of innkeeper Jennifer Cauchi's **Miss Elaine E. Moose** shop at the Lodge at Moosehead Lake. She offers a variety of high-style gifts and accessories relating to moose and wildlife, from door stops to German beer steins to blankets. Replicas of some of the accessories at the lodge, among them the needlepoint bear rugs, are for sale here. Look for jams and jellies, cards, baskets, books, Hummel figurines, Christmas villages and more at **The Corner Shop**. Local crafts, including attractive pottery and Indian baskets, are on display at **Gabriel's.** Souvenirs of a more basic nature, as well as items from a rock shop, are offered at the **Indian Shop,** which appears to be the biggest store in Greenville. Rustic lamps with carved bears for the base, carved birds, prints and moose, of course, are available at **The Woodcarver's Shop.**

The original wood carver, **Joe Bolf,** has since moved on to his own quirky studio and shop across from the Municipal Building. Widely known for his wildlife carvings and signs, he lately spearheaded the National Institute for Hospital Art, launched in Greenville to provide artworks in hospitals. At our visit, he was about to provide its first gift, a large statue carved not by chisel but by chain saw. "After twenty years' making a living by carving wood," he volunteered, "I just discovered I can do it three times as quickly and just as well with a chain saw." We're believers.

Extra-Special _____

You want to get away from the "crowd?" A nostalgic place to visit on a sunny day is **Kineo Island,** actually a peninsula and site of the late Kineo House resort. For $10, you can play golf on a scenic nine-hole course (the midway point is almost at the foot of the sheer Kineo cliffs). Rent a golf cart ($10 an hour) to poke along three miles of bumpy roads on this island attached to the mainland by a 500-foot stone causeway on the far side of the lake. Swim at the secluded and picturesque Pebble Beach beside the causeway, where knowing boaters often tie up for the afternoon. Observe moose, deer, loons and eagles in the wildlife sanctuary. Hike up Mount Kineo or scale the rocky cliffs. Take a peak at the abandoned yacht club building known as the Breakers on the point, and dream of turning it into a restaurant or a B&B. Enjoy lunch or dinner or a drink at the Kineo House, the endearing little successor to the large resort of the same name. The island is reached by water taxi (The Francis C, on demand, from the state boat ramp in Rockwood, 534-8847, $5 round trip) or pontoon boat (Kineo Shuttle, every two hours from 8 a.m. to 6 p.m. from the state boat ramp in Rockwood, 534-8812, $4 round trip).

Oxford Hills and Lakes, Me.

Not Where It's At – Yet

The famous – some locals call it infamous – milepost sign out in the middle of nowhere giving distances to nearby places like Norway, Denmark, Mexico, Poland, Paris, Naples, China and Peru would deceive no one.

This is anything but the center of the universe. It's more like the name on the school bus we passed, "State of Maine, Unorganized Territory."

The Oxford Hills region is an unspoiled land of sparkling lakes, hills that back up to the mighty White Mountains and tiny hamlets with English-sounding names like Center Lovell and Lower Waterford. It's an area of great beauty – we hear that the National Geographic called Kezar Lake one of the nation's ten most beautiful (its other claim to fame is that Bridgton native Stephen King has a summer home along its forested shore). There's a fortuitous concentration of small country inns that epitomize the genre.

Unusual as a time capsule from the past, the area offers little in the way of formal activity or tourist trappings. "You are on your own," the Inn at Westways brochure advises.

More and more people seek the serenity of western Maine. "We're really out in the country," concedes Barbara Vanderzanden of the Waterford Inne. "But we have a central location not far from North Conway or the Maine coast."

The charms of this rural retreat have yet to be discovered by the crowds. But that may be only a matter of time. Says restaurateur Suzanne Uhl-Myers of the Lake House: "Western Maine is where it's going to be at."

Happily, it's not there yet. That remains its special joy.

Inn Spots

The Inn at Westways, Route 5, Box 175, Center Lovell 04016. (207) 928-2663.

Each of the inns in this area has its distinctive appeal. At Westways, it's the great location right on the east shore of upper Kezar Lake, plus its heritage as a small, private luxury lodge from the past.

Built in the 1920s by the owner of the Diamond Match Co. as a corporate retreat, it was opened to the public in 1975 with its original furnishings, from the books in the guest rooms to the 1925 billiards table and vintage bowling alley in the recreation hall. "We're unique as a time capsule," says one of the managers for the four owners from

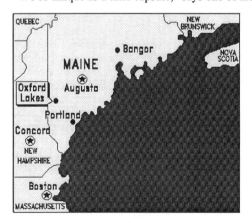

Boston. "It has been left as it was in the '20s."

The main floor contains a large kitchen and an immense living room, with many Italian antiques, a huge stone fireplace and, at either end, handcarved oak tables that each seat twelve for meals. Beyond is a long dining porch running the width of the lodge with windows right above the water, and a grand old boathouse where cocktails and nibbles are served on the screened porch as the sun sets over the White Mountains (see Dining Spots). A

266

Boat heads toward dock and boathouse at Westways on Kezar Lake.

small interior dining room, with many Japanese prints on the wall, is used for winter dining. The main floor also has a restroom with an ornate wraparound needle shower that invigorates the entire body and compensates for a lack of showers upstairs.

Four of the six guest rooms have private baths, one down the hall. The other two share a hall bath. Nicest is the Master Room with two double beds, handcarved furniture and windows on two sides. Many think the Horses Room, named for the series of foxhunt prints on the walls, has the best view in the house. All but one of the smaller rooms in the former servants' quarters has a water view.

Westways also rents out ten houses on the grounds (two quite new), accommodating six to fourteen people at weekly rates of $800 to $1,700.

Lodge guests are served full breakfasts, with choice of pancakes, french toast, eggs any style or omelets. They also have the run of the forested, 100-acre property, which includes a dock at the boathouse with a swimming area in the crystal-clear waters of the quiet, almost private lake and a sand beach a quarter-mile down the shore. If you're into handball, try the "fives" court in an outbuilding (tournaments are sometimes held here).

Across the lake, you can see the former estate of Rudy Vallee, who built a treehouse for one of his pianos and sometimes rowed his boat over to Westways, playing his ukulele and serenading guests during barbecues.

Doubles, $95 to $165. Closed April and November.

The Waterford Inne, Chadbourne Road, Box 149, Waterford 04088. (207) 583-4037.

This handsome inn and antiques shop really is out in the country – half a mile up a rural lane in East Waterford. The pale yellow and mustard structure commands a hilltop view and contains ten well-furnished guest rooms, a comfortable and charming living room full of folk art, a more formal parlor and a semi-public dining room of note.

Former New Jersey school teachers Rosalie and Barbara Vanderzanden, a mother and daughter team, carefully restored and furnished the 1825 farmhouse in 1978, even-

Waterford Inne occupies hilltop setting way out in the country.

tually augmenting the original five bedrooms with five more in the old woodshed leading to the red barn out back.

The common rooms and porch are unusually nice and ever so tasteful. Special touches abound in each bedroom, seven of which have private baths. Duck pillows, duck wallpaper and a duck lamp grace the deluxe Chesapeake Room, which has a kingsize bed, a working fireplace and a super second-story porch overlooking the farm pond and mountains. A quilted whale hangs behind the bed in the Nantucket Room, complete with a map of the island and a bathroom almost as large as the bedroom itself. The Strawberry Room in the woodshed has strawberries on the lamp, rug, quilts, pillow and sheets, and even strawberry-scented potpourri in a strawberry-shaped dish.

Fresh flowers decorate each room in summer. Electric blankets are provided in winter. And "you should see this place at Christmas," says Barbara. "Every nook and cranny is decorated and red bows are put on even the smallest folk-art lambs." In summer, the principal activity is watching the bullfrogs and birds, including a great blue heron, around the farm pond.

Full breakfasts, included in the rates, are served in the beamed dining room or in good weather on the porch. "We'll cook whatever you want," says Rosalie.

Prix-fixe dinners for $29 are served to guests and, by reservation, to the public in the dining room filled with the women's pewter collection. Up to twenty can be served when the front parlor and porch are used as well.

A typical dinner might start with cream of broccoli soup, go on to dilled scallops over angel-hair pasta with vegetables and salad not long out of the garden, and end with a fresh berry pie. Chilled cucumber soup and veal marsala might make up another dinner. Leg of lamb often appears, as do shrimp with pernod, game hens, duckling, sole, and pork or beef tenderloin. Grand marnier soufflé and pumpkin ice cream cake are frequent desserts, and guests may bring their own wine.

Doubles, $74 to $99, B&B. Closed April.

Admiral Peary House, 9 Elm St., Fryeburg 04037. (207) 935-3365 or (800) 237-8080.

Splendid gardens, a clay tennis court, an outdoor hot tub and four deluxe guest rooms commend this B&B run by Nancy and Ed Greenberg in a white clapboard house that once was the home of Arctic explorer Robert Edwin Peary. Not to mention a great rear porch, screened on three sides and full of wicker rockers and loungers, from which to view the back yard. Plus a rear deck and a side patio.

Avid tennis players, the Greenbergs run the tennis shop at Mount Cranmore Recreation Center in nearby North Conway, N.H., so their tennis court is a natural. So is the house they bought to convert into a B&B.

Each of their air-conditioned guest rooms contains a queen or kingsize bed, its own sitting area and a spacious bath with dressing table. All are spiffily decorated with an eye to flair and detail. Paintings by a local artist in some rooms are for sale. Slanted roof lines and odd nooks and crannies lend an air of coziness to the Jo, a kingbedded room named for Peary's wife. A spacious attic room called the North Pole has been transformed into everyone's favorite, with a great pink and teal quilt atop a kingsize brass bed and another quilt displayed on a rod. "I tried to decorate with a lack of clutter," says Nancy.

The public rooms are equally comfortable. Just inside the rear entrance is a billiards table on a raised floor, separated by a railing from a large rear living room. The latter has a barnwood wall behind the fireplace, a TV in an armoire, four wing chairs and two couches. Ten people can sit around the table in the open kitchen, all brick and barnwood and notable for stained glass and a chevron floor. Several smaller, more formal sitting rooms are available in the front of the house for guests who seek privacy.

Healthful breakfasts could include the Admiral Peary breakfast pie (like a quiche, says Nancy, with lots of cheese and meats but few eggs), french toast and blueberry pancakes. Fresh fruits and homemade breads and muffins accompany. The rhubarb and berries are obtained on the property.

Doubles, $89 to $98. No smoking.

The Noble House, Highland Road, Box 180, Bridgton 04009. (207) 647-3733.

Once a senator's home on four acres in a residential section overlooking Highland Lake, the Noble House is now a comfortable B&B with six bedrooms and three suites, run with much warmth and personality by Jane and Dick Starets with summertime assistance from their college-student offspring. Although they share a Victorian-antique theme, five rooms in the rear carriage house seem more modern – some with jacuzzi baths, large windows overlooking the grounds, a window seat and perhaps a private porch. They're decorated primarily in whites and mauves, furnished in wicker and have wall-to-wall carpeting, period antiques, floral quilts with matching draperies, and frilly touches like eyelet curtains and pillows, one in the shape of a heart.

Guests gather in the fireplaced parlor, which harbors lots of books and a grand piano outfitted with sheet music, or in the pine-paneled family room in back, with its huge mushroom-colored sectional and a grand fireplace.

Former home of Arctic explorer has been turned into Admiral Peary House, a deluxe B&B.

Breakfast is served on one of the porches or at a table for six in a Victorian dining room clad in blue and green. Tropical fruit salad, whole-grain cereal, raisin bran muffins and vegetable frittata were served the morning we were there.

Guests can swim, canoe or use the paddle boat from the inn's lakefront property across the road, where a hammock, barbecue grill and picnic table are available. Jane Starets has printed up several handy guides to restaurants and attractions in the area.

Doubles, $74 to $88; suites, $94 to $115. No smoking.

Center Lovell Inn, Route 5, Center Lovell 04016. (207) 925-1575.

The former owners who first saw this 1805 homestead bought it because of the view of Kezar Lake with the White Mountains beyond. They sat on the front porch, surveyed the scene "and that was it," Susie Mosca recalled, telling how she and her chef-husband Bill turned the abandoned farmhouse into an inn in 1974.

The new owners acquired the inn in a novel way. The Moscas had conceived the idea of a contest to sell the inn to the winning essayist. Some 5,000 entrants paid $100 each for the chance. The winners were Maryland restaurateurs Richard and Janice Cox, who had always wanted to own and operate an inn of their own. "Our dream came true when we won the contest," said Janice.

The Coxes arrived in 1993 and had three days in which to get ready for the summer season. They gradually renovated most of the ten guest rooms, five in the inn and five in an annex (all except two in each section with private baths). "There were a few problems," Richard conceded. "But what do you expect for $100?"

Janice's parents moved with the couple to make the inn a family operation (they ask guests to call them Mom and Pop.) The foursome had two houses full of antiques, which proved helpful in furnishing the place. Richard proudly showed "our room," the front bedroom in which they had stayed upon winning the contest. It now has a queen bed, an oriental rug and two chairs from which to absorb the lake view out the window.

The three-story structure has something of a Mississippi steamboat appearance, thanks to the Floridian who added a mansard roof topped by a cupola in the 1860s. The 1835 Norton House, a former barber shop, was moved to the site from Lovell to become a side annex. The Coxes have stripped the floors, put in some new baths and added queensize beds. Their main-floor common room has patterned rugs, a fireplace and an upright piano.

Breakfast the day of our visit included fresh fruit, hot baked grapefruit and eggs benedict. Other of Richard's specialties are eggs Chesapeake with Maryland crab, smoked salmon omelet and raspberry french toast. He's also the chef at dinner (see Dining Spots). Janice does the baking for the evening meal.

Doubles, $68 to $98 EP, $109 to $144 MAP.

Lake House, Routes 35 & 37, Waterford 04088. (207) 583-4182 or (800) 233-4182.

A landmark structure that had been Waterford's first inn (operating until the 1940s) was reopened in 1984 as the Lake House. A well-regarded restaurant (see Dining Spots) and a small parlor with a fireplace take top billing on the main floor, and owners Suzanne and Michael Uhl-Myers live with their daughter on the third floor. Two rooms and two suites with private baths are available on the second floor.

The Waterford Flat Suite had more than enough space in which we could spread out during a record hot spell, in spacious sleeping quarters with a ruffly queen bed and an adjoining reading room with a sofa, shelves lined with books and a coffee-maker. Two rooms are smaller, but like ours had a homey, lived-in feeling. Not at all home-like is the air-conditioned grand ballroom suite, which lives up to its name with a huge curved

Lake House offers accommodations and fine dining in Waterford.

ceiling, a queensize bed, seven windows, a sitting area and an open, carpeted platform for a bathroom. Lately, the inn has added the Dudley House, a bungalow with queensize bed, TV and screened porch.

A bottle of sparkling water is put out in each guest room, and a bowl of peanuts in the parlor staves off hunger. Breakfast, taken at 9 o'clock in the rear dining room or on the front porch, could be scrambled eggs, pancakes or waffles, accompanied by juice and a fresh fruit salad – in our case, bananas and blueberries with cream.

Doubles, $84; suites, $110 and $130; bungalow, $130. No smoking.

Kedarburn Inn, Route 35, Box 61, Waterford 04088. (207) 583-6182.

Built in 1858, this handsome white Colonial house with dark green shutters and broad lawns brightened with flower beds has been upgraded since its acquisition by Margaret and Derek Gibson, who had run a B&B in their native Bournemouth, England.

They added three guest rooms for a total of nine, including a two-bedroom suite, and put in more baths so most are private. Rooms come in a variety of configurations from kingsize to twins; one is a double-deck affair with stairs up to a single bed (the rear barn portion was Maine's first boys' camp, Margaret advised).

The bedrooms are enhanced by pleasant country touches, including antiques, quilts, arrangements of dried flowers and handsewn linens. Margaret sewed the curtains bearing ducks and learned upholstering "to redo the furniture myself." Mints, thick colorful towels and stuffed Paddington bears are extra touches.

The front guest parlor invites with a television set, comfortable sofas and books. An outdoor patio is within earshot of Kedar Brook.

Margaret's prime interest has turned to making quilts, wreaths, baskets and dolls, which she sells in the Kedar Craft shop that has taken over the dining room. "The quilts in gold frames sell as fast as I make them," Margaret advises.

The Gibsons no longer serve dinner but have a pub and serve four versions of English tea ($3 to $6) most afternoons from 3 to 4 o'clock. Their full breakfast offers a choice of eggs, omelets, pancakes or french toast.

Doubles, $69 to $88.

The Oxford House Inn, 105 Main St., Fryeburg 04037. (207) 935-3442.

Known primarily for its food (see Dining Spots), this inn run by John and Phyllis

Morris has five guest rooms with private baths as well. They're located upstairs in an attractive, pale yellow and green country house fronted with a wraparound piazza.

One front corner room has a bow window and two double beds. Velvet is draped behind the queensize bed in another room, and all the rooms are furnished with period furniture and antiques.

Guests share a parlor with waiting dinner patrons, but can retire as well to the large Granite Room Lounge downstairs pub with four small tables and a sitting area with a wood stove and a large TV. The wicker-filled wraparound porch is great for relaxing, and the back yard opens onto a super view of the Presidential Range.

The Morrises serve a complete breakfast. Eggs benedict, grand marnier french toast, berry pancakes and french toast with cream cheese and marmalade or raspberry jam are among the possibilities.

Doubles, $75 to $95.

Dining Spots

Lake House, Routes 35 & 37, Waterford. (207) 583-4182.

Almost since it reopened in 1984, the restaurant at Waterford's first inn has been making culinary waves in western Maine. A changing menu of creative regional cuisine, flaming desserts and a remarkable wine list are offered by proprietors Suzanne and Michael Uhl-Myers.

Each dining room is pretty as a picture. The small front room has burgundy wallpaper above pale green woodwork, burgundy carpeting, shelves of glass and china, a corkscrew collection and a picture of puffins over the fireplace. The larger rear, pine-paneled dining room has white and green linens, tables set with two large wine glasses at each setting and oriental rugs on the floor. Patrons enjoy the antics of birds at window feeders behind a couple of one-way mirrors.

The owners consider their award-winning wine list "the best in Maine." Notable more for depth than breadth, it reflects Suzanne's former career as a wine consultant. Prices are reasonable and each listing is accompanied by an intelligent description.

On a mild summer night, we chose to dine outside on the screened front porch. The Rhode Island squid sautéed with spinach ravioli and garlic sauce was an excellent starter. Other choices ($4.65 to $8.45) included a signature duck pâté seasoned with apples and grand marnier, ravioli agliata, Sicilian salad and an antipasti platter. The changing soups might be a creamy red onion with a shot of sherry on the side, curried carrot or smoked salmon.

A dollop of kiwi sorbet preceded the entrées, a generous portion of sliced lamb sauced with curry and vodka and a roast duckling in a sweet sauce of blackberries and raspberries. Sliced potatoes, cucumbers, tomatoes and pickled corn accompanied. Veal topped with ham and gruyère, chicken stuffed with goat cheese and served over a sauce of pine nuts, sundried tomatoes and prosciutto, filet mignon and fresh salmon filleted on site and served with tequila-lime butter were other main courses, priced from $15.85 to $18.95.

Served after the entrée, the salad of fresh fruit on a bed of lettuce was so refreshing we didn't need dessert, although one of us succumbed to a parfait pie. Cherries jubilee and bananas foster are flamed tableside for two, a duty that keeps Michael hopping on busy nights (he has increased his pace with his special homemade pizzelles, topped with coffee ice cream and an espresso-chocolate sauce and flambéed tableside with sambuca). Some people come just for the desserts, which are available separately with coffee and cordials after 8 p.m.

Dinner nightly from 5:30. Closed Monday-Wednesday in off-season. No smoking.

Oxford House Inn is known for good dining and lodging.

The Oxford House Inn, 105 Main St., Fryeburg. (207) 935-3442.

Opened in 1985, this 1913 country house is run personally by John and Phyllis Morris, formerly of North Conway, whose dinner fare commands a wide reputation.

Seventy-five people can be seated on white chairs (their tops hand-stenciled by Phyllis) on the rear porch with a stunning view of Mount Kearsarge North, in the former living room called the Parlor, and along the screened front piazza. Tables are set with delicate pink crystal, heavy silver and Sango Mystique peach china, with candles in clay pots and napkins tied like neckties. Green floral wallpaper, Phyllis's handmade curtains and draperies, and handsome paneling enhance the parlor.

The menu, which changes seasonally, comes inside sheet music from the 1920s. Dinner begins with complimentary homemade crackers and a cream cheese spread, a salad of fresh greens and fruits (blueberries and watermelon), perhaps with a tomato-tarragon dressing or a cranberry vinaigrette, and fresh nut and corn breads. Starters ($4 to $6.95) include Maine crab chowder, a house pâté, baked camembert in puff pastry with fruit and a smoked seafood plate. Crayfish bisque, cream of asparagus and chilled peach were among summer soups when we visited.

The ten entrées ($16 to $20) include poached salmon pommery, scallops in puff pastry, pork with pears and port, veal madeira, two steak dishes and rack of lamb. John does most of the cooking, but the desserts are Phyllis's: fruit trifles, cheesecake terrine, praline truffle, chocolate mousse, spumoni and frozen peach yogurt at one visit. Her bread pudding with peaches and blueberries is highly acclaimed.

We had a wonderful lunch here, but lunch service has since been discontinued. The wine list bears its share of bargains, the house offerings going for $3.50 a glass.

Dinner, 6 to 9, nightly in summer and fall, Thursday-Saturday rest of year.

Center Lovell Inn, Route 5, Center Lovell. (207) 925-1575.

Maryland restaurateurs Richard and Janice Cox won this venerable farmhouse-turned-inn in a much-publicized essay contest.

The chef is Richard, who started cooking with his Italian mother as a youngster and had been with the Loew's Hotel restaurant chain, most recently as chef in Annapolis. His wife was a restaurant manager at the well-known Busch's Chesapeake Inn there. Their experience stood them in good stead for taking over the small inn overlooking Kezar Lake and the Presidential Range. They redecorated the 40-seat Victorian dining rooms in muted peach and pink colors, and added colorful quilts and print cloths with burgundy napkins to the wraparound screened dining porch overlooking Kezar Lake and the Presidential Range.

The menu ($14.95 to $20.95) is short and to the point: perhaps swordfish florentine finished with a saffron clam sauce, pan-seared salmon with a tomato-basil coulis, shrimp fra diavolo with saffron rice, sautéed chicken with roasted red peppers and smoked onion relish, veal piccata and tournedos rossini. In season, Richard adds Maryland items, perhaps crab cakes or soft-shell crab with ginger, and game specials like rabbit and venison. He's known for his soups, especially the four-onion variety; the night's offering was scallop and artichoke soup at our visit. Other starters could be mussels provençal, smoked salmon, and brie baked with honey, toasted almonds and sliced apples.

Janice does the baking; house favorites proved to be strawberry-rhubarb and blueberry cream pies, strawberry shortcake and her mother's key lime pie. The short, select wine list is priced from the teens to $46.

Dinner nightly, 6 to 9, Sunday 5 to 8. Closed November and April.

The Inn at Westways, Route 5, Center Lovell. (207) 928-2663.

As the sun sets over Kezar Lake, the porch and the adjacent living room are a memorable setting for dinner at Westways. Meals begin with cocktails in the lounge above the boathouse, where raw vegetables with a curry dip and a plate of cheese, grapes and crackers might be served.

The menu opens with stuffed mushrooms, smoked trout, country pâté and shrimp cocktail. A new chef has added some novel twists to the entrées ($13.95 to $18.75), among them baked scallops served over a bed of peaches with a touch of brandy and raspberries, poached salmon with lemon-lime butter, pork loin rolled with a cranberry-sausage stuffing and served sliced on an artichoke sauce, and stuffed apple chicken with a grand marnier glaze. Fresh fruit tarts, raspberry bread pudding, New York cheesecake and grand marnier cake are dessert possibilities.

Tables are set with mauve linens, blue-gray napkins and interesting floral arrangements on the porch, where dinner is served with a water view on summer nights, inside the main room at hand-carved oak tables warmed by a fieldstone fireplace, or in the small winter dining room.

Dinner nightly, 5:30 to 9; reservations required by 4 p.m. Closed April and November.

Black Horse Tavern, Route 302, Bridgton. (207) 647-5300.

A big hit in the Bridgton area since its 1988 opening is this restaurant in a barn behind a gray house whose front porch looks as if it were straight out of Louisiana. The two structures are joined by a large bar. Most of the dining is in the rear portion, where all kinds of horsey artifacts hang from the walls and stalls have been converted into booths.

The Louisiana farmhouse look is appropriate. The chef, a Maine native, acquired a cajun flair while cooking in Texas and Louisiana.

The chicken and smoked sausage gumbo is a must starter for first-timers at lunch or dinner. Barbecued pork ribs, chicken fingers and macho nachos are other appetizers ($3.95 to $6.95).

Steaks, prime rib, pan-blackened sirloin and swordfish, chicken teriyaki, baked stuffed haddock and scallops au gratin are among the dinner entrées ($9.95 to $18.95). We liked the scallop pie and the night's special of mahi-mahi with shrimp and basil sauce. Hot rolls and good salads with pepper parmesan and vinaigrette dressings were served immediately upon ordering. The wine list was quite good and most affordable, a Fetzer fumé blanc selling for $12.95.

Deli sandwiches, burgers, salads and light entrées are available for lunch.

Open daily from 11 to 10 or 11.

Tut's General Store and Restaurant, Route 35, North Waterford. (207) 583-4447.

A general store of the old school, this is also a bakery, ice cream parlor and restaurant for today. Paul and Kay Legare run an expanding operation that retains the legacy of a former proprietor named Tuttle.

Their food operation and new bakery tend to overshadow the groceries and convenience items. In an area where lunch service is infrequent to non-existent, we were famished enough to order a couple of hot dogs ($1 each) and a buffalo burger ($2.99), made with locally raised bison. There are all kinds of sandwiches, subs and pizzas at distinctly non-urban prices. An extensive array of breakfast items is available morning, noon and night. Weekend suppers add dishes like chicken pie or lasagna, both with side salads, for $4.95 to $6.25. Finish with an oatmeal-raisin cookie, 45 cents each or two for 79 cents. Wash it down with an old-fashioned frappe There are assorted tables for enjoying it all at this place full of local color.

Open daily, 6 a.m. to 9 or 10 p.m.

Diversions

The area has many attributes, but they tend to be quiet and personal. As the Westways brochure states: "Whether you prefer browsing through local antique shops, visiting the country fairs, watching the sun rise over the misty lake as you fish from your canoe at dawn or spending a quiet evening around the fieldstone fireplace, you are on your own." Some ideas:

The Villages. General stores and the odd antiques or crafts shop are about the only merchandising in places like Waterford, North Waterford, Center Lovell and Lovell. But do not underestimate the villages' charms. As humorist Artemus Ward wrote of Waterford: "The village from which I write to you is small. It does not contain over forty houses, all told; but they are milk white, with the greenest of blinds, and for the most part are shaded with beautiful elms and willows. To the right of us is a mountain – to the left a lake. The village nestles between. Of course it does. I never read a novel in my life in which the villages didn't nestle. It is a kind of way they have." Waterford hasn't changed much since, nor have its surrounding towns. For action, you have to go north to Bethel, east to Bridgton or southwest to Fryeberg and North Conway.

The Lakes. Kezar, peaceful and quiet and somewhat inaccessible, lies beneath the mighty Presidential Range, its waters reflecting the changing seasons and spectacular sunsets. The lake is relatively undeveloped and private, with access only from the marina at the Narrows, the beach at the end of Pleasant Point Road and a point in North Lovell. The rest of the time you can rarely even see it (much to our dismay, for we got lost trying). Keoka Lake, at Waterford, has a small, pleasant and secluded beach just east of the village and an unexpectedly crowded village beach just to the south. Hidden lakes and ponds abound, and not far distant are more accessible Long Lake and Sebago Lake.

Antiques. The Bridgton area, in particular, is a center for antiquers; a special brochure described 23 antiques shops at last count. The **Oxford Common Antique Center**

on Route 26 south of Oxford is a collection of dealers and shops. Cynthia Hamilton's antiques and folk art in the **1836 Brick Schoolhouse** in Lovell and the **Kayserhof Alpine Village** with a country store and Christmas shop in North Waterford are shopping destinations.

Other Shopping. The handpainted gifts, crafts and furnishings of the talented Quisisana resort staff are featured at the interesting new **QuisiWorks** shop along the main highway at Center Lovell. We also liked all the pottery, jewelry, carved birds and the kitchen corner with themed cookbooks at the nearby **Kezar Lake Handcrafts.** The handthrown porcelain feeders for hummingbirds caught our eye at **Wiltjer Pottery,** Route 37, South Waterford. At **Craftworks,** ensconced in a refurbished church in Bridgton, we browsed through the baskets, rugs, candles, Maine wines and foods, and some interesting clothing. We also liked **Emphasis on Maine,** a gallery of gifts and handicrafts in Bridgton.

Bonnema Potters on lower Main Street in Bethel is a studio and showroom where Garret and Melody Bonnema craft and display their pottery in a barn beside their house. Seldom have we seen such appealing colors; according to the Bonnemas, their glazing is influenced by the colors in the mountains and valleys surrounding Bethel. Tankards, tiles, candelabras, casseroles, teapots and much more are their wares. We especially like their lamps and a couple of them help light up our home.

Extra-Special —————————————

Quisisana, Point Pleasant Road, Center Lovell. (207) 925-3500.

The chef prepares four-star dinners and then repairs to the music hall and sings his heart out at this music-oriented resort beside Kezar Lake. When Randy Braunberger received standing ovations after playing the leading roles in "Fiddler on the Roof" and "My Fair Lady," resort owner Jane Orans said, the audience was cheering both for his stage performances and his gastronomic prowess. The latter is not inconsiderable, prompting one well-traveled New Yorker to tip us off to what he called one of the finest restaurants in the land.

Magazine writers have long sung the praises of the venerable 75-room family resort that attracts a devoted following for music, Mozart and tranquil lakeside pleasures during mostly week-long stays. Two lodges totaling eleven rooms and 38 guest cottages with names like Sonata, Symphony and Pianissimo are strung along the beach or nestled deep in the woods (doubles, $192 to $276, full AP). Most of the 80 staffers are students at the nation's leading music schools, which gives the place a decided musical air – when the dining room staff sing as they dry the silver, Jane says, "it's an incredible sound." The sleeper in the publicity department has been chef Randy, something of a Renaissance man who studied cooking at the Ritz Hotel in Paris, has a master's degree in acting and paints incredible floral tapestries.

When space is available in the 150-seat, lodge-style dining room with screened windows on three sides, the public may join resort guests for an evening to remember. The prix-fixe menu ($25 to $30) changes daily. A typical dinner begins with a choice of steamed vegetable spring rolls or curried zucchini soup. After a house salad, the main course could be salmon-leek roulade with roasted yellow pepper sauce or saddle of lamb provençal with a black olive tapenade and confit of red peppers. Dessert could be a blueberry pie or frozen cappuccino mousse cake. Beer or wines from a good selection of reasonably priced Californias accompany.

After dinner, adjourn to the music hall and enjoy the chef's grand finale.

Dinner nightly by reservation, 6:30 to 7:30. Open mid-June through August.

Motif No. 1 is on view from rear dining room of The Greenery restaurant.

Rockport, Mass.
Bargains by the Sea

They certainly don't need more crowds, these habitués of Bearskin Neck, Pigeon Cove and Marmion Way. Nor do those who cater to them.

But bargain-conscious travelers can seldom do better than in Rockport, the seaside Cape Ann resort town where the costs of food and lodging consistently remain five years behind the times.

Last we knew, lobster dinners were going for $7.95 at Ellen's Harborside. Rooms in many of the finest inns and motels cost $60 to $100, about one-third less than they'd command in equivalent locations elsewhere.

Why such bargains? Because Rockport was developed earlier, when costs were lower, than many such coastal resorts.

"We were bed and breakfast long before the craze started," notes Leighton Saville of Seacrest Manor. Adds William Balzarini of the Old Farm Inn: "The inns here keep their prices down because they don't have new mortgages with high rates." Rockport's century-old ban on the sale of liquor has influenced prices, if only in lowering restaurant tabs when patrons BYOB.

The bargains help swell

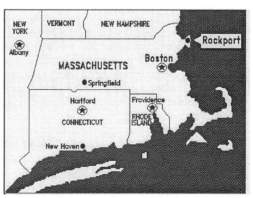

Rockport's year-round population of 7,500 to 35,000 in summer. Most folks, it seems, are on the streets near Dock Square and Bearskin Neck, the rocky promontory jutting into the harbor. Parking is usually a problem. Arrive early or expect to park on distant side streets and walk. Or take the Cape Ann Trolley.

Visitors are drawn by the rocky coast more typical of Maine, the atmosphere of an old fishing village crammed with shops, the quaintness of a "dry" town in which Sunday evening band concerts are the major entertainment, and the lively arts colony inspired by a harbor listed by Walt Disney Productions as one of the nation's most scenic. In fact, Motif No. 1, a fishing shack on the wharf, is outranked as an artist's image only by the Mona Lisa. When it collapsed in the Blizzard of 1978, villagers quickly rebuilt it – such is the place of art (and tourism) in Rockport.

All around Rockport are the varied assets of the rest of Cape Ann. They range from the English look of quiet Annisquam, which is New England at its quaintest, to the commercial fishing flavor of busy Gloucester.

The allure of Rockport is so strong that its devotées return time and again. Crowded it may be, but it's hard to beat the prices.

Inn Spots

Eden Pines Inn, 48 Eden Road, Rockport 01966. (508) 546-2505 or (508) 443-2604 (November-May).

You can't get much closer to the ocean than on the rear patio that hovers over the rocks – or, for that matter, in five of the upstairs guest rooms – at this delightfully secluded B&B by the sea.

The setting in what was formerly a summer home could not be more attractive. The lodge-like front parlor with fieldstone fireplace, the California-style side breakfast porch with white furniture and picture windows, the rear porch full of lounge chairs with neat brick patio below, even a couple of bathroom windows take full advantage of the water view across to Thatchers Island and its twin lighthouses. Although the shore here is rocky, the inn is within walking distance of two beaches.

The six upstairs guest rooms, all with private baths, are unusually spacious. Three have two double beds and two have king beds (Room 6 has striking white seersucker and lace curtains enclosing a canopied queen bed) and private balconies over the water. We'd choose Room 4, all beige and blue in decorator fabrics with thick carpeting, a comfortable sitting area and an enormous bathroom done in Italian marble with a bathtub, a separate shower and a large window onto the ocean next to the marble vanity.

Innkeeper Inge Sullivan, who is partial to marble and pastel fabrics, has redecorated all the rooms in California colors and style. She and her husband serve a continental breakfast that includes Scandinavian pastries, fruit salad and muffins, as well as mid-afternoon tea and setups for drinks. We know of few more picturesque places for the last than the lounge chairs on the rear patio smack beside the ocean.

The Sullivans also rent four bedrooms in their smashing, California-style **Eden Point House** down the street at 34 Eden Road, a corner lot with a sweeping ocean view. You can rent the entire house or it can be divided into two two-bedroom sections for $250 a night each.

Doubles, $100 to $130; two-night minimum. Open mid-May to mid-November.

Seacrest Manor, 131 Marmion Way, Rockport 01966. (508) 546-2211.

If Eden Pines has the ocean setting and decorator's flair, Seacrest has the lawns and gardens and a breakfast to remember. It also has a sweeping view of the ocean beyond the trees from its second-story deck above the living room.

Ocean lies just behind Eden Pines Inn.

Leighton T. Saville and Dwight B. MacCormack Jr. have run their inn since 1972, so personally that many of the repeat guests have left gifts – their own watercolors of the inn, crocheted pillows and countless knickknacks, including a collection of rabbits "which just keep multiplying, as rabbits are prone to do," according to Leighton.

The main-floor library displays so many British magazines that "our English guests tell us it feels like home," he adds. The elegant living room, where afternoon tea is served, has a masculine feel with leather chairs, dark colors and fine paintings, as well as exquisite stained glass and tiny bottles in the bow windows.

The formal dining room is decked out in fancy linens, Wedgwood china and crystal glasses at five tables for a breakfast that Town & Country magazine called one of the 50 best in America. It begins with fresh fruit cup and fresh orange juice, continues with spiced Irish oatmeal and bacon and eggs, and ends with a specialty like blueberry or apple pancakes, french toast or corn fritters.

Guests have the run of the two-acre property, which includes a remarkable, century-old red oak shading the entire front yard, prolific gardens, a couple of statues and a rope hammock strung between trees in a rear corner.

Six of the eight guest rooms have private baths. Rooms are comfortable and have been redecorated lately. Each has double, queen or twin/king beds, color television, a clock radio, a couple of chairs and a desk. The inn touch comes with mints on the bedside table with nightly turndown service, fine soaps and shampoos, overnight shoe shines and a complimentary Boston Globe at the door in the morning.

Seacrest Manor is a special place that measures up to its motto, "decidedly small, intentionally quiet."

Doubles, $88 to $120. Two-night minimum on weekends. Closed December to March. No credit cards. No smoking.

Yankee Clipper Inn, 96 Granite St., Box 2399, Rockport 01966. (508) 546-3407 or (800) 545-3699.

One of Rockport's larger and older inns, the Yankee Clipper continues to be upgraded by Barbara and Bob Ellis, daughter and son-in-law of its founders. It takes full advantage of a remarkable setting on a bluff, with beautifully landscaped lawns on a bit of a point jutting into the ocean.

Now with 27 rooms, all with private baths and telephones and fifteen with ocean views, the inn began with nine rooms in a Georgian mansion beside the ocean. More were added in the 1840 Bulfinch-designed neoclassic mansion across the road, and premium, somewhat contemporary rooms are in the Quarterdeck built in 1960 beside the water. The last has a knockout penthouse suite on the third floor with ruffled pillows on two double beds, a sofabed, and two velvet chairs facing floor-to-ceiling windows onto the ocean. Two ground-floor oceanfront lodgings that Barbara calls her "wow rooms" have been transformed lately with colorful chintz and wicker and look across new gardens to the open sea.

Another drawing card is the new Intrepid guest room in the Bulfinch House, created from two small rooms. It boasts a canopied, Queen Anne-style king bed beside a mirrored, in-room jacuzzi, an audio-visual center and, for those who cannot be without their electronic gadgetry, a modem outlet.

The main inn's rooms, all named after clipper ships, have been upgraded. Some offer spectacular close-up ocean views from sun porches or decks. We like the Sea Witch, with a queen canopy bed and an enclosed porch in rose and wicker, with a queen hideabed and a deck facing the ocean. The Red Jacket, favored by actress June Allyson during a filming stay here, offers a double and a twin bed plus a long porch with green wicker furniture that has been in the family for a century; we'd sink into the curved wicker sofa, the chaise or the rockers and never want to get up. Everyone shares a beauty of a deck off the third floor.

Also in the inn is a grandly furnished living room on the main floor. Downstairs is a function room, in which chairs are lined up in front of a huge VCR, with a bunch of videos at the ready.

The dining porch is leased to a couple who run it as **The Glass Verandah,** a restaurant open to the public (see Dining Spots). The inn's longtime cook continues to prepare breakfast for guests and the public, offering treats like poached eggs with spinach-basil sauce on a puff pastry nest for $6 to $8.

The heated saltwater pool is hidden from the public eye on the landscaped, terraced grounds beneath the road. Hurricane Bob felled three maple trees beside the pool in 1991, but their loss was not an unmitigated disaster – three rooms in the Bulfinch House across the street now have an ocean view, "though we never advertise that," says Barbara.

Doubles, $95 to $219 B&B; $149 to $273 MAP. No smoking.

Old Farm Inn, 291 Granite St. (Pigeon Cove), Rockport 01966. (508) 546-3237 or (800) 233-6828.

For years, this was tops on everyone's list of favorite eating spots on Cape Ann. Susan and Bill Balzarini, whose family ran the restaurant with tender loving care since 1964, closed it in 1986 to concentrate with equal TLC on their growing B&B operation.

The inn is housed in a red farmhouse with white trim and creaky floors, built in 1799 and once part of a dairy farm (the Balzarini grandchildren's ponies still graze in the meadow). One of the original dining rooms has been converted into a parlor; here, in something that resembles grandma's sitting room, sherry and cookies are available in the afternoon. Another of the former dining rooms is now part of the Garden Suite, which has a bedroom with queen bed, a sitting room with two twins and TV, and a private deck.

The main garden dining room with 80-year-old cast-iron stove and full-length

Century-old red oak shades front of Seacrest Manor.

windows looking out onto birch trees is where guests take breakfast in the morning. Colorful as can be, it's a tropical paradise of hanging plants and tables covered with floral cloths in vivid yellows, greens and reds. The fare includes fresh fruit and juice, cereals (and sometimes oatmeal in winter), yogurt, muffins and coffeecake.

Upstairs are three guest rooms with fireplaces, each with private bath and television, wide-plank floors and furnished in antiques. The barn out back has four guest rooms, all with private bath and TV and small refrigerators. They're recently upgraded, comfortable with country decor and rather motel-like. The Fieldside Cottage offers one to three bedrooms in various configurations. Secluded woodland paths lead through the inn's five acres to the rocky coastline and a scenic quarry at Halibut Point, Rockport's only oceanfront state park.

Doubles, $88 to $125. Closed December to mid-April.

Addison Choate Inn, 49 Broadway, Rockport 01966. (508) 546-7543 or (800) 245-7543.

An in-town location and a rear swimming pool draw guests to this attractive, flower-bedecked house built in 1851 and boasting Rockport's first bathtub – in the kitchen, no less.

That bathtub has been replaced, of course, but all six guest rooms and a two-room suite come with large and modern hand-tiled bathrooms with pewter faucets. New innkeepers Knox and Shirley Johnson have renovated and redecorated the inn from top to bottom. Shirley's touch as an interior designer shows in the main-floor Captain's Room, dressed in nautical navy and white with a fishnet-canopied, queensize mahogany poster, and the quiet Poet's Corner with private entrance, stained-glass window, antique wrought-iron queen bed and wicker chairs. The third-floor suite, furnished in white wicker with a canopy bed draped in lace, has a stained-glass skylight in the bathroom, television, refrigerator and a view of the ocean across the rooftops.

The comfortable living room, a small rear library with TV and a dining room with a beehive oven are cheery. Each contains a mix of antiques and modern furnishings and original art. A continental-plus breakfast buffet includes fresh fruits, cereal, granola, homemade breads and muffins, and house-ground coffee. It's taken in the dining room or at intimate tables for two on the narrow side porch facing showy perennial gardens across the driveway. Knox, a landscape architect, transplanted more than 60 potted beauties from the couple's previous home in nearby Lanesville.

The rear Stable House contains two housekeeping suites with loft bedrooms available by the day, week or month. One with a spiral staircase and skylights in the bathroom and bedroom has particular flair. Beyond is the tree-shaded pool area, a delightful refuge with chaise lounges and umbrella-topped tables away from the hustle and bustle of Rockport.

Doubles, $85; suites, $110. No smoking.

The Inn on Cove Hill, 37 Mount Pleasant St., Rockport 01966. (508) 546-2701.

Close to the heart of town and with a fine view of Motif No. 1 and the harbor from its rear third-floor deck is this Federal-style mansion built in 1791. It's surrounded by a white picket fence and lovingly tended gardens.

Innkeepers Marjorie and John Pratt have completed a lengthy restoration and re-decoration of the former guest house. Nine of the eleven bedrooms have private baths; two on the third floor share. Each is nicely decorated in Laura Ashley fabrics and wallpapers, and each has a small color television set. Most rooms sport handmade quilts and afghans and crocheted coverlets as well as oriental-style rugs.

The Pratts like to point out the structure's architectural features – such as the spiral staircase with thirteen steps in the entry hall – and the antique furnishings in the small common room. On the coffee table is a book called "Taster's Tattles and Titillations," written by guests who share their local dining experiences. It makes for lively reading.

A continental breakfast with muffins is served on English bone china at tables topped by yellow and white umbrellas in the side garden or on trays in the bedrooms.

Recipes for eight of the Pratts' popular muffins (oatmeal, orange-buttermilk and pumpkin, among them) have been printed for guests. A note is appended to the end: "If you find that your muffins are failing, we have conspired to leave out one essential ingredient from each of the recipes; that is umbrella tables in the summer and breakfast in bed in the winter. For access to both, come see us."

Doubles, $47 to $96. Two-night minimum in summer and most weekends. Closed late October to mid-April. No smoking. No credit cards.

Linden Tree Inn, 26 King St., Rockport 01966. (508) 546-2494.

Flowery and fragrant and about two centuries old, an enormous linden tree spreads its limbs beside this Victorian-style house dating to about 1850. Larry and Penny Olson offer stylish common rooms and eighteen bedrooms, all with private baths.

Guests enter through a pleasant side sun porch into a dining room and a formal living room with elegant Victorian furnishings and oriental rugs. Twelve bedrooms in the main inn are nicely appointed with period furniture, carpeting, fresh flowers and a mix of twin, double and king beds. The third-floor Room 34 with a double bed and a sitting area with a loveseat and chair has windows on two sides onto the distant ocean and the nearby Mill Pond, where the locals ice skate in the winter. For an even better view, Larry leads guests up to the cupola, lit by Christmas lights in the windows and visible from all around town.

The premium rooms are in a new carriage house the Olsons built behind the inn. Here you'll find four modern, year-round rooms, each with a double and twin bed, color TV, kitchenette and private rear deck.

Georgian mansion beside ocean houses Yankee Clipper Inn and Glass Verandah restaurant.

Penny is known far and wide for her baking. Some of her treats are served with afternoon tea and lemonade, and the aroma of her blueberry cake emanating from the kitchen nearly did us in upon arrival. The main event is breakfast around the large table or at smaller individual tables in the dining room. Expect all kinds of fresh fruits, juice and homemade coffeecakes and breads, from mango to apple-walnut. Rhubarb cake, fig-pineapple coffeecake and banana/chocolate-chip bread are other favorites.

Doubles, $85 to $90; carriage house, $98. Closed December-March except in carriage house.

Sally Webster Inn, 34 Mount Pleasant St., Rockport 01966. (508) 546-9251.

A good-looking gray house with red shutters and a lovely fan door, this 1832 structure contains six guest rooms and a suite, each named for one of its former occupants and each with private bath. The house has six fireplaces, original wide-plank pine floors, period door moldings, brick terraces and herb gardens.

The front parlor is known as "Sally's Share," because that is the part of the house that Sally Choate Webster inherited from her father, the local "housewright" who built it. Bearing a rather grim-faced portrait of her, the room contains family artifacts given to the inn by Sally's great-great-granddaughter, who has stayed here. Across the hall is Sally's Room, a bedroom with twin beds joined as a kingsize.

Double canopy, pencil-post four-poster and Jenny Lind beds are in the guest rooms. Each is attractively furnished to the period and outfitted with the inn's own toiletries. A new third-floor suite with two bedrooms accommodates up to five.

Young owners Tiffany and David Muhlenberg, newlyweds from New York's Westchester County, prepare a full breakfast. It's served with silver coffee pots and antique china in the dining room or, beyond through french doors, on a brick patio they added. The fare at our visit was a choice of eggs benedict or blueberry pancakes one day, a tomato quiche or cheesecake crêpes with strawberry sauce the next.

Doubles, $69 to $90. Closed in January.

Seaward Inn, Marmion Way, Rockport 01966. (508) 546-3471 or (800) 648-7733.

Across the street from the ocean in a residential area on attractive grounds full of gardens, lawn chairs, boulders and stone fences is this complex of inn, cottages and guest house, totaling 38 rooms with private baths.

Some guests prefer the oceanfront Breakers, a shingled house with a common room and nine homey guest rooms, each with two chairs and a telephone. Others like the accommodations in single or multi-unit cottages.

The main inn has ten rooms as well as a large front common room with flagstone floor, rattan furniture and windows onto the ocean. The beamed dining room is divided into several sections; one wall is strung with clothes pins that have held guests' napkins with their names over the last ten years.

Dinner, served nightly to guests, offers a choice of two entrées – roast beef and seafood newburg the night we were there.

"Gracious informality is the way of life at Seaward," according to longtime innkeepers Roger and Anne Cameron. Their information sheet asks men to wear jackets at dinner "and you ladies look lovely in dresses or pantsuits." At bedtime, the sheet advises, "yes, we too like our glass of milk. Come to the kitchen and let your wants be known."

Doubles, $98 to $138 B&B, $138 to $178, MAP. Open mid-May to mid-October.

The Captain's House, 109 Marmion Way, Rockport 01966. (508) 546-3825.

A fabulous location at water's edge commends this white stucco mansion, billed as "a comfortable and casual guest house" by owners Carole and George Dangerfield. Although they've owned it for 27 years, both the exterior and interior have been upgraded lately.

There's a wraparound porch, part of it open to the ocean and the rest enclosed for a library and TV. Inside are a huge parlor with beamed ceiling and fireplace, and a handsome dining room that catches a glimpse of the ocean.

Upstairs are five guest rooms with private baths. Two rooms are particularly large, and those in front yield the best views. Each is done in period wallpaper and has hand-creweled embroidery on the valances and reproduction Williamsburg furnishings.

Sour cream blueberry coffeecake, muffins and fruit breads are served for continental breakfast in the dining room or on the porches, where guests "feel closer to the water," Carole says. They really feel close to the water in the lounge chairs spread out on little cement patios nestled here and there among the rocks along the craggy shore.

Doubles, $85 to $105. Closed in January.

Dining Spots

Rockport's restaurants are dry, but most invite patrons to BYOB. Some of the more prominent restaurants and biggest advertisers are considered tourist traps; innkeepers and locals rarely recommend them. For fine dining, we offer a few nearby favorites where you also can get a drink and wine with your meal.

My Place By-the-Sea, 68 South Road, Rockport. (508) 546-9667.

You can't get much closer to the ocean than at this restaurant at the very end of Bearskin Neck. In fact, it's so close to the ocean that twice in recent years it has been damaged in storms. After the latest event, owners Charles Kreis and Annie Russell rebuilt the structure and reopened in mid-1994 with a crisp new summery look. A two-level outdoor porch wraps around the tiny interior, with an open lower level resting right above the rocky shore and a smaller side level covered by an awning and enclosed in roll-down plastic "windows" for use in inclement weather. Floral cloths cover the white molded tables and the atmosphere is romantic in rose and aqua.

Dining on canopied deck at water's edge is a drawing card at My Place.

Called "My Place" because a former owner couldn't think of anything else, chef Charles added "By-the-Sea" to its name when he took over. To complement the magical setting, he's built a reputation for the best food in town. Indeed, at our last visit the most recent entry in a local innkeeper's restaurant diary was by Californians who proclaimed My Place "the best over-all restaurant on our thirteen-state foliage tour. Excellent service, food and ambiance."

Dinner guests are welcomed with a complimentary "cocktail," a non-alcoholic blend of cranberry juice and lime sherbet. Dinners come with soup or salad, so you may not need an appetizer, unless you're into things like shrimp cocktail or the house specialty, poached mussels. The chef shines on such seafood items as fillet of sole stuffed with lobster, shrimp and scallops; tuna Mediterranean, and baked swordfish. Entrées are priced from $11 for baked scrod in lime butter to $18 for steak au poivre or shrimp and sirloin.

The restaurant's creative desserts are tantalizingly displayed in a glass case that diners pass on their way to their table. Favorites include an all-American pie plump with apples, raspberries and blueberries and a chocolate-pecan pie laced with bourbon. Aforementioned Californian raved about the Kentucky derby pie.

Lunch daily, noon to 4; dinner, 4 to 9:30 or 10. Fewer days in the off-season and closed in winter. BYOB.

The Glass Verandah, Yankee Clipper Inn, 96 Granite St., Rockport. (508) 546-3407.

The owners of the Yankee Clipper lease out their dining room to David Pierson, ex-chef and food and beverage manager at the Mountain Top Inn in Chittenden, Vt. He and his wife Amy moved to Rockport, where he quickly made a name for himself in the restaurant he christened The Glass Verandah. Amy takes charge of the front of the house, when not tending to their four young children.

The Glass Verandah is just that: a long and narrow enclosed porch running alongside the inn, with great views of the water off to the side. Navy and white linens dress up the wrought-iron furniture, and fresh flowers are at each table. It's a simple but effective setting for such specialties as shrimp sautéed with apple chutney and dijon mustard, poached salmon with sweet red pepper sauce, and swordfish medallions with artichoke hearts and mushrooms in basil cream sauce. Other entrées ($15.95 to $19.95) include baked haddock, seafood au gratin, chicken sautéed with artichoke hearts and sundried tomatoes, veal marsala and stir-fried beef tenderloin with cayenne pepper sauce.

Baked brie, seafood croquettes and lobster polenta with boursin cheese sauce are among starters. Salads come with the meal. For dessert, consider chocolate mousse pie, lime torte, chocolate-raspberry cake or blueberry pie.

Dinner nightly, 5:30 to 9:30, Memorial Day through mid-October. No smoking. BYOB.

The Greenery, 15 Dock Square, Rockport. (508) 546-9593.

The name bespeaks the theme of this casual and creative place, but hardly prepares one for the view of Motif No. 1 across the harbor from the butcherblock tables at the rear of the L-shaped dining room.

Seafood and salads ($5.95 to $11.95) are featured, as is a salad bar and an ice cream and pastry bar out front. Otherwise the fare runs from what owners Deborah Lyons and Midge Zarling call gourmet sandwiches to dinner entrées like grilled wolffish, poached salmon, seafood casserole, seafood linguini and chicken milano ($11.95 to $14.95). Dinners include the extensive salad bar, as do such lighter fare as pesto pizza and crab salad quiche.

At lunch time, we savored the crab salad quiche with a side caesar salad ($5.95) and the homemade chicken soup with a sproutwich ($4.95). The last was muenster and cheddar cheeses, mushrooms and sunflower seeds, crammed with sprouts and served with choice of dressing. We liked the sound of the crab and avocado sandwich special, and overheard diners at other tables raving about the lobster and crab roll.

Apple pie with streusel topping, key lime pie, tirami su and cheesecake with fresh strawberries are popular desserts. The chocolate chambord and amaretto cheesecakes are available to go.

Open daily, 10 to 9 weekdays, 9 to 10 weekends, mid-April through October.

Ellen's Harborside, T-Wharf, Rockport. (508) 546-2512.

Wholesome food, reasonably priced. That's the attraction at this plain-jane, local institution with a front counter and tables and a rear dining room overlooking the water. Crowds start lining up for supper at 4:30 for what other restaurateurs call "total value." Except for the fried seafood platter and prime rib, almost everything on the dinner menu is priced in the single digits.

The breakfast special could be eggs benedict for $3.95. You can get a clam roll or a cubano sandwich along with more mundane fare for lunch. Dinners run from $5.25 for fried squid to $12.95 for mixed grill or a full rack of barbecued ribs. Most desserts like cranberry-raspberry and orange-pineapple cream pies and pineapple-tapioca pudding are under $2. The exception was chocolate cake with strawberries, $2.25 at our visit.

Open daily in summer, 5:30 a.m. to 9 or 9:30. Closed mid-October to mid-spring.

Brackett's Ocean View, 27 Main St., Rockport. (508) 546-2797.

The old Oleana-By-the-Sea gave way in 1991 to this family restaurant that receives good reviews from residents. It's simple as can be, except for the sweeping view of the water on two sides of the main dining room tucked around to the rear and not visible from the entry. Windsor chairs are at bare tables topped by paper mats.

The all-day menu is priced right and contains some interesting fare, including cobb and cajun chicken salads and a hot veggie pocket sandwich with swiss cheese. Among lunch specials at our visit were homemade chicken pot pie with potato and broiled lemon-pepper bluefish. Old-time favorites ($6.25 to $7.95) include grilled liver and onions, baked scrod au gratin, codfish cakes and chicken parmigiana. Other entrées are baked shrimp casserole, broiled sea scallops and, the only item over $10, a deep-fried seafood platter for $11.95. Desserts of the day could be grapenut custard pudding, strawberry-rhubarb pie and french silk pie.

Lunch daily from 11; dinner from 4:30.

Ocean Cafe, 8 Wharf Road, Rockport. (508) 546-7172.

The restaurant at the Old Harbor Yacht Club has been leased to Ray and Carol Ferro, owners of the much-acclaimed new Square Cafe in Gloucester. Here, the billing is "a cafe in the rough" and the deck is open to the public for dining in summer.

Most of the menu is basic, from fried haddock sandwich to a quarter-pound hot dog. But there are interesting touches: gazpacho with shrimp and lobster, caesar salad with fried oysters, a fried catfish sandwich with jalapeño-lime mayonnaise, and mussels Moroccan style, heady with garlic and cilantro. From the "hot pot" come steamers and twin lobsters. A section of the menu designated "in a box" yields various fried seafood with fries and cole slaw.

Open daily in summer, from 11:30.

Helmut's Strudel, 49 Bearskin Neck, Rockport. (508) 546-2824.

This is not a restaurant as such, but you may share a small rear deck with a seagull or two on a few weathered captain's chairs, put your coffee on a rail and savor the view of the harbor. The small bakery makes a good stop for heavenly strudels (apple, cherry, cheese, almond and apricot, $1 a slice), blueberry croissants ($1.25), bagels, cinnamon buns, croissant sandwiches, coffee, tea and "the best hot chocolate in town." The strudel is real Austrian style with 81 layers of puff pastry. Helmut's is a good break from Bearskin Neck's prevailing seafood and ice cream.

Open daily in season, from 8 a.m.

Steep Hill Grill, 24 Essex Road (Route 133), Ipswich. (508) 356-0774.

Everyone in Rockport raves about this exciting, value-oriented restaurant, and we certainly found it worth the half-hour drive. Named for the landmark hill at Crane's Beach, it's run by Jan Addison in partnership with John Bruni in a corner of Bruni's Marketplace.

One guy was eating solo by candlelight at the bar as we were seated at a quiet table nearby, fortunately a bit removed and separated by a plant-topped pedestal divider from the happy hubbub in the main dining area, which was filled on a springtime Monday night. Wonderful sourdough bread staved off hanger as we deliberated over the menu. It's the kind upon which everything appeals, and the chef only makes the choice more difficult by adding a lengthy supplement of written daily specials.

Starters of shrimp pan roast served in a sauce of tomatoes, oregano and cream with two pieces of crostini, and a spinach salad with goat cheese wontons, wood ear mushrooms and a warm tomato-bacon vinaigrette were sensational. Not to be outdone were the main events: pan-roasted game hen with smoked bacon, yukon jack and pecan sauce and a grilled flank steak with spicy peanut sauce, an unlikely combination that worked. "Smashed potatoes" accompanied one dish and wonderful sweet potato sticks the other, all washed down with a Charles Krug cabernet sauvignon for a bargain $16. We were only sorry we had to pass up the signature items: an acclaimed corn chowder with scallops, basil and smoked bacon; caesar salad with gorgonzola and grilled portobello mushrooms, and sautéed breast of chicken with cashew crust and port wine sauce. Prices range from $9.95 for grilled jamaican jerk chicken to $15.95 for grilled veal chop with an herb chutney.

A warm berry strudel with ice cream and a lemon-strawberry tart ended one of our more enjoyable dinners out in a long time.

Lunch, Monday-Saturday 11:30 to 2:30; dinner, 5:30 to 9:30 or 10; Sunday brunch except in summer, 11 to 3. Closed Tuesday in winter.

Au Beaujolais, 284 Main St., Gloucester. (508) 283-5200.

The French flag flies in front of this gray and red brick storefront restaurant, one of three highly rated newcomers in Gloucester to which Rockport innkeepers steer guests who are so inclined. Stunning paintings on the yellow sponged walls and colorful fabric table cloths and seat cushions enliven the stylish cafe and wine bar inside.

Young chef Alec Maxon and partner David Amaral have put together a with-it establishment and menu. To begin the meal, dip the sweet sourdough bread and focaccia into the herb-infused olive oil provided on each table. The starters intrigue: roasted garlic and Ipswich goat cheese fritters with baby greens and sweet peppers, provençal-style tapas, beer-battered sweetbreads with tomato-bacon vinaigrette and greens, and wild mushroom and chèvre turnovers. How about a salad of grilled bitter greens with flatbread croutons and a cherry-port vinaigrette?

Main dishes are priced from $9.95 for roast chicken and blue cheese-stuffed ravioli with a pumpkin-sage sauce to $15.75 for broiled lamb chops with tapenade. Consider the savory chard pie with black olives and chèvre, the cassoulet, the grilled flank steak with port wine and pears, or the classic bouillabaisse with rouille crouton. A French pastry chef makes great desserts like chocolate-espresso pie, strawberry-mousseline layered genoise and crème caramel with figs on raspberry coulis.

Dinner nightly except Monday, 5:30 to 10 or 10:30, Sunday to 9.

Square Cafe, 197 East Main St., Gloucester. (508) 281-3951.

The walls and wainscoting are warm yellow and the ceiling is white in this new neighborhood bistro that occupies the space formerly known as the Raven. The colors are repeated in the outfits of the staff, who are clad in black pants, yellow shirts and floral neckties.

Owners Ray and Carol Ferro, who also run the seasonal little Ocean Cafe on Rockport's Bearskin Neck, have a winner of a place here. The dinner menu is nicely priced from $8.50 for penne with grilled chicken, plum tomatoes and escarole to $13.50 for Long Island duck roasted with fig-port wine sauce or grilled filet mignon served over a roasted vegetable sauce. Among the possibilities are fusion pork chops stuffed with oriental pesto and served over a sweet and sour plum sauce, pan-fried wolffish fillets with a hazelnut-crumb crust and steak au poivre. Tapenade is served with the house bread. You might start with pan-fried salmon cakes with cranberry rémoulade, wild mushroom torte with apricot-brandy sauce, or fried oysters with jalapeño-lime mayonnaise. Finish with the signature chocolate crème brûlée or walnut-fudge torte with chambord sauce.

Lunch, Monday-Saturday noon to 3; dinner nightly, 5 to 9:30 to 10.

Diversions

The Seashore. Rockport is aptly named – it has the rocky look of the Maine coast, in contrast with the sand dunes associated with the rest of the Massachusetts shore. Country lanes lined with wild flowers interspersed between interesting homes hug the rockbound coast and crisscross the headlands in the area south of town known as Land's End. We like the California look of Cape Hedge Beach from the heights at the end of South Street, the twin lighthouses on Thatchers Island as viewed from Marmion

Way, and the glimpses of yachts from the narrow waterfront streets in quaint Annisquam (stop for a lobster roll on the deck right over the water at the Lobster Cove).

Swimming is fine at Front and Back beaches in the center of town, the expansive Good Harbor Beach near the Gloucester line, the relatively unknown Cape Hedge and Pebble beaches at Land's End, and the Lanesville beach north of town. Parking can be a problem, but we've always lucked out.

Halibut Point State Park, Pigeon Cove, 546-2997. On a clear day, you can see Crane's Beach in Ipswich, the Isles of Shoals in New Hampshire and Mount Agamenticus in Maine from this 54-acre park along the rocky coast. In the middle of the park is an abandoned, water-filled quarry from which tons of granite made their way to some of the more notable buildings across the Northeast. Guided tours and demonstrations about the quarry are given Saturdays at 9:30. The park is popular with hikers and sunbathers. Parking, $2.

Bearskin Neck. The rocky peninsula that juts into the harbor was the original fishing and commercial center of the town. Today, most of the weather-beaten shacks have been converted into shops and eateries of every description. Glimpses of Sandy Bay and the Inner Harbor pop up like a changing slide show between buildings and through shop doors and windows; arty photo opportunities abound. The rocky point at the end of the neck provides a panoramic view, or you can rest on a couple of benches off T-Wharf and admire Motif No. 1 – the Rockport Rotary Club sign beckons, "This little park is just for you, come sit a while and enjoy the view."

Shopping. Most of Bearskin Neck's enterprises cater more to tourists than residents, and T-shirt shops abound. But we found some nice quilted handbags at **Mr. Bag Man,** and colorful pottery and fish mobiles at **Serendipity.** You could buy a lobster packed to take home at the **Roy Moore Lobster Co.,** or some baked stuffed clams, 75 cents each. Main Street and the Dock Square area generally have better stores. Colorful fused glass plates in the window drew us into **Square Circle,** where we marveled at incredible porcelain depictions of antipasto platters, fruit salad and the like, done by a woman from Virginia. **Sand Castles** sells colorful clothes for women and children. We liked the suncatchers and the trivets at **New England Goods.** Watch Claire Gehly make canvas and tapestry handbags, vests, log carriers and the like at **Bagcrafters;** things made from the print, "children of the world," are especially popular. **The Safari Connection** is a tiny shop where everything has an animal theme and there are many African designs. Interesting casual clothing and jewelry are offered at **Willoughby's;** owner Sharon McDonald also runs nearby **Confetti,** where bright colors are the theme of California designer Laurel Burch's cards, mugs, tote bags, jewelry and sweatshirts. Proceeds from the well-stocked **Toad Hall Bookstore** in the old Granite Savings Bank building further environmental causes; it carries a great selection of children's books.

If all this shopping makes you feel the need for a snack, stop for a pâté plate or cornish pasty at **Pâtisserie Élan** (suppers are served here Friday and Saturday nights), or a bagel and an espresso at **Dock Square Coffee and Tea House.** A tuna sandwich and cup of soup is $4.50; the raspberry crumble bar sounds delish.

The Art Galleries. For many, art is Rockport's compelling attraction, and by 1900 the town had become *the* place for artists to spend the summer painting. More than 200 artists make the town their home, and 31 galleries are listed in the Rockport Fine Arts Gallery Guide. The 73-year-old **Rockport Art Association,** with exhibitions and demonstrations in its large headquarters at 12 Main St., is a leader in its field. You could wander for hours through places like Paul Strisik's slick gallery next to the art association or Geraci Galleries in a 1725 complex of buildings at 6 South St.

Band Concerts. The summer Sunday evening concerts presented at 7:30 by the Rockport Legion Band at the outdoor bandstand near Back Beach have been a Cape Ann summer tradition since 1932. A few of the original members remain active today, providing stirring concert marches, overtures and selections from Broadway musicals under the stars. Other than these, the best entertainment in town may well be, as a couple of guests at Eden Pines Inn put it, "sitting on Dock Square and watching the world go by."

Museums. The Sandy Bay Historical Society and Museum shows early furnishings and exhibits on shipping, fishing, the local granite industry and Rockport history in the 1832 Sewall-Scripture House built of granite at 40 King St. and in the Old Castle, a 1715 saltbox on Granite Street (both open 2 to 5 daily in summer, $3). The **James Babson Cooperage Shop** (1658) on Route 127 just across the Gloucester line, a small one-story brick structure with early tools and furniture, may be the oldest building on Cape Ann (Tuesday-Sunday 2 to 5, free). In Pigeon Cove at 52 Pigeon Hill St. is the **Paper House,** built nearly 50 years ago of 215 thicknesses of specially treated newspapers; chairs, desks, tables, lamps and other furnishings also are made of paper (daily in summer, 10 to 5, $1).

Extra-Special

Like the rest of Rockport, its museums are low-key. But you only have to go next door to Gloucester to see two of New England's stellar showplaces.

Beauport, 75 Eastern Point Blvd., (508) 283-0800. Interior designer Henry David Sleeper started building his summer home in 1907 to house his collection of decorative arts and furnishings. Most of the 40 rooms are small, but each is decorated in a different style or period with a priceless collection of objects. Twenty-six are open to the public. Sleeper designed several rooms to house specific treasures: the round, two-story Tower Library was built to accommodate a set of carved wooden draperies from a hearse; the Octagon Room was built to match an eight-sided table. One of the breakfast tables in the Golden Step Room is right against a window that overlooks Gloucester Harbor; many visitors wish the place served lunch or tea. Guided tours Monday-Friday 10 to 4, mid-May to mid-October; also weekends 1 to 4 from mid-September to mid-October. Adults, $5.

Hammond Castle Museum, Hesperus Avenue, (508) 283-7673 or (800) 649-1930. Cross the drawbridge and stop for lunch or tea and castle-baked pastries at the Roof Top Cafe in this replica of a medieval castle, built in the late 1920s by inventor John Hays Hammond Jr. to house his collection of Roman, medieval and Renaissance art and objects. Concerts are given on the organ with 8,600 pipes rising eight stories above the cathedral-like Great Hall. Marbled columns and lush plantings watered by the castle's own rain system are on view in the Courtyard. Open daily June-August, 10 to 6; Thursday-Sunday 10 to 5 in May, September and October; weekends 10 to 5, rest of year. Adults, $5.50.

Winding residential street is typical of old Marblehead.

Marblehead, Mass.
Jewel of the North Shore

It's not difficult to understand why some call this beautiful town with so much cachet the jewel of the North Shore.

Poised on a rocky headland jutting into the Atlantic, Marblehead has a lot going for it. It is seventeen roundabout miles northeast of Boston, whose skyline can be seen on clear days across the water, much as San Francisco's can be seen from suburban Tiburon. Yet it's a world removed – from big-city Boston, and even from tourist-crazed Salem, its better-known neighbor on the mainland.

Founded in 1629 and apparently named for all the rocky (not marble) ledges upon which it grew without regard for 20th-century traffic needs, Marblehead was one of the earliest and richest settlements in America. Sea captains, merchant traders and cod fishermen erected houses and public buildings grand and small. Their edifices remain in use today, posted with discreet markers saying "Built for Ambrose Gale, Fisherman, 1663" and "Joseph Morse, Baker, 1715." The more than 300 pre-Revolutionary structures in the half-mile-square historic district have changed little since. A walking tour takes one past (and occasionally inside) the one-of-a-kind Jeremiah Lee Mansion, the art galleries in the King Hooper Mansion, the 1727 Old Town House that predates Boston's Faneuil Hall, the brick-towered Abbot Hall landmark (permanent home of the famous painting "The Spirit of '76"), the Lafayette House (whose corner was removed, legend has it, to let General Lafayette's carriage pass), the Fort Sewall harbor fortification and the second oldest Episcopal church still standing in this country.

As opposed to restored Colonial Williamsburg or relentlessly perfect Nantucket, Marblehead is a "real" historic town, lived in year-round and bearing well any foibles or blemishes. Its original character endures – and townspeople fight fiercely to keep it that way. Small treasures abound: glimpses of the harbor through vest-pocket side yards, lush impatiens in window boxes and cosmos blooms waving beside doorways, oversize benches in the many small parks, antique signs, friendly townspeople, winding and impossibly narrow streets whose one-way directional signs thwart unknowing motorists at every turn.

The fact that Marblehead is rather isolated and so difficult for visitors to navigate is both its bane and its charm. There are none of the tourist trappings that coax visitors to Salem, Gloucester or Portsmouth. It's at the end of the road, so you do not pass through town on your way to somewhere else. You may come here for a quick visit and leave perplexed as to what the fuss is about. Or you are smitten and stay a while.

Until recently, Marblehead – a bedroom suburb that seems far smaller than its official population of 20,000 – offered few overnight accommodations. The first inn of note emerged in 1986, and there has been a proliferation of small B&Bs only in the 1990s. The '90s have also brought trendy restaurants and tony shops catering as much to the resident gentry on Marblehead Neck as to visitors in Old Town.

Sailors have long been lured to Marblehead, which claims to be the birthplace of the American Navy and now the yachting capital of the nation. Some 2,500 pleasure craft bob at their moorings in Marblehead's harbor. Members and guests assemble at six yacht clubs, where cannons are fired in a sonic ritual at sunrise and sundown. The town is at its busiest in late July during its century-old Race Week.

Otherwise, as the world becomes homogenized, Marblehead retains a singular sense of place. As a local newspaper put it, "There is plenty of room for hollyhocks in 18th-century dooryards, but only grudging space made for automobiles. The arts flourish, public debate is often spirited, and Santa arrives by lobster boat."

Inn Spots

Harbor Light Inn, 58 Washington St., Marblehead 01945. (617) 631-2186.

Born and raised in Marblehead, Peter Conway had long wanted to operate an inn here but, like others, was stymied by the town's strict zoning regulations. Instead, he opened the Carlisle House in Nantucket, became immersed in the innkeeping business and bided his time. That time arrived in 1986, when he purchased a grand Federal mansion along the town's principal through street. He was able to win approvals from neighbors and four regulatory agencies, and opened a twelve-room B&B – "without a sign and without advertising."

Success was immediate, thanks to receptive townspeople (old-line residents were happy finally to have a quality place in town in which to put up relatives and friends) and a ready market (all the daytrippers who heretofore had had no place in which to

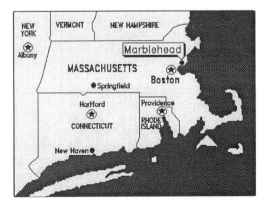

stay overnight). The fact that Peter was catering to the upscale market – "I wanted to have the best rooms on the North Shore" – didn't hurt. His rooms, constantly being upgraded, are handsomely furnished to the period, generally spacious and outfitted with private baths, TVs and telephones, fine antiques, oriental rugs, Crabtree & Evelyn toiletries, private-label sparkling water and local chocolates from Stowaway or Harbor Sweets – many

Breakfast is ready at Harbor Light Inn.

Federal mansion houses Harbor Light Inn.

of the modern-day comforts and amenities generally missing in Nantucket and other historic-house accommodations are found here.

Never content, Peter bought the Federal mansion next door in 1993, connected it to his existing building and added eight more guest rooms with modern baths. The result is, without doubt, the North Shore's most elegant inn. Five of the twenty bedrooms have whirlpool tubs, eleven have working fireplaces, most have sitting areas and several have private balconies and decks. A big (for Marblehead) back yard contains lounge chairs and a new swimming pool. Here, on a sloping lawn with a screen of thick trees, you'd almost think you were in the woods, except for the sounds of the harbor in the distance (a sight now visible only from the rooftop deck when the leaves are off the trees).

Peter and wife Suzanne, who has an eye for creative decor, continue to improve their inn. At our visit, they'd just installed a gas fireplace to warm the new formal dining room and were adding 300-count sheets in the deluxe bedrooms. Especially in demand are the front-corner Room 22, with hand-carved mahogany queensize bed, two wing chairs, a double vanity and a double jacuzzi beneath a skylight, with a mirrored wall beside, and the new Room 5, with deep-red walls above the wainscoting, built-in settees beside the fireplace, two wing chairs, a hand-carved four-poster queen bed and a double jacuzzi with glass brick wall. Smaller rooms have charms as well: the third-floor Room 34 has its own sun deck, Room 36 a beamed and vaulted ceiling, and Room 4, a summery-looking ground-floor room with a pine-poster bed, has a double jacuzzi and a private screened deck near the pool. There are no curtains in the inn, Peter points out – "just inside window shutters that are easily opened and closed." Elegant touches include fancy wallpapers, fine paintings and prints, brass or porcelain doorknobs, silver ice buckets and candy dishes, and votive candles beside the jacuzzis. The inn maintains a video library for the VCRs in the deluxe rooms.

An elaborate continental breakfast spread is put out in the dining room, which holds a table for eight and a tea table for two. Or the meal can be taken on trays to four tables beside the pool, or to one of the two elegant but cozy front parlors, where the day's newspapers await. The fare when we were there included orange juice, cut-up melon, lemon bread and especially good blueberry and cranberry-walnut muffins. Choices range from blueberry scones to Suzanne's no-fat bundt cake incorporating applesauce and yogurt. Tea is offered in the afternoon. On Saturdays in the off-season, the Conways serve hot hors d'oeuvre by candlelight for BYOB social gatherings.

Doubles, $85 to $150; luxury rooms, $160 to $195. Two-night minimum on weekends.

Spray Cliff on the Ocean, 25 Spray Ave., Marblehead 01945. (617) 631-6789 or (800) 626-1530.

The best waterfront location in town is enjoyed by guests at this substantial English Tudor home perched on a sea wall above the open Atlantic. After 35 years as corporate gypsies, Roger and Sally Plauché returned to the town in which they'd once resided to purchase Spray Cliff in November 1994. Although they inherited a turnkey B&B operation, they immediately undertook many enhancements and became hands-on innkeepers – which was viewed locally as an improvement, since the previous owners' priorities had rested with their larger inn in Salem. "We want to capitalize on a captivating place," said Sally.

The Plauchés offer seven large bedrooms with private baths. The spacious mainfloor common room has breakfast tables stretching along the oceanfront windows and a sitting area with comfy wicker furniture and huge pillows around the fireplace.

We'd gladly settle in the adjacent rear bedroom, summery and cheery with a queen bed, two wicker chairs dressed in chintz and doors onto a private patio facing the Atlantic. It was far more inviting than the much larger front bedroom, dark and masculine with fireplace and kingsize bed, which the Plauchés planned to convert into a conference room, a more appropriate use.

Sally, a professional decorator, had her eye on the second-floor bedrooms, named for places in which they'd lived (Lancaster and Winnetka, among them). "This house shouldn't be New England quaint," she advised. "It can be whimsical, fresher and freer, with a California feeling. The house lends itself to accessorizing." Expect dramatic upgrades to the summery rooms that back up to the ocean on the second and third floors. They are generally large and a couple have fireplaces. At our visit, Sally had already reconfigured the layouts of some of the beds and sitting areas to take better advantage of the ocean views. She upgraded the linens and towels, and added bottled waters in the bedrooms. A honeymoon suite was in the works for the third floor.

The Plauchés also enhanced the continental breakfast with the help of their daughter-in-law, a nearby resident and gourmet cook "who likes to experiment." Juice and exotic fresh fruit are supplemented by the likes of strawberry muffins, pumpkin biscuits, lemon-apple breads and homemade croissants. In the afternoon, they serve complimentary beverages, including tea and sherry.

Guests have access to a smashing garden terrace overlooking the ocean.

Doubles, $169 to $189. No smoking.

The Guest House at Lavender Gate, One Summer St., Marblehead 01945. (617) 631-3243 or (800) 800-6824.

Two lavender doors brighten the facade of what the owners call their raspberry-mocha colored house, built in 1714 in the heart of Old Marblehead. It faces a strip of lawn leading to historic St. Michael's Church, also built in 1714, the second oldest Episcopal church still standing in the country. Except for the Shakespearean garden nestled between the house and the ancient gravestones alongside the church, you'd never guess that this is actually a very English, very literary B&B.

Any doubts vanish the moment owners Cate Olson and Nash Robbins open the main lavender door. Inside is their home, a repository chock full of antiques and acces-

The Guest House at Lavender Gate is located at entrance to churchyard.

sories collected by these much-traveled anglophiles and bibliophiles, who own the nearby Much Ado Bookstore, which holds more than 35,000 volumes of old and out-of-print books. Their house is also full of books and literary accoutrements, of course.

Prepare to be overwhelmed in the living room, painted a lavender-blue color and draped with garlands of dried flowers from their gardens. Here a proper British tea is served in the afternoon amidst a clutter of books and bric-a-brac, unopened boxes of gifts from the couple's latest English buying trip and even a grand piano. That may pale beside the dining room, where a continental breakfast is set out buffet style on a table beside a framed pair of Eugene O'Neill's monogrammed boxer shorts, shelves of literary cookbooks and autographed pictures of authors, both famous and obscure.

Upstairs are two spacious suites with private baths. The second floor holds the airy Hogarth Suite, where a pastel patchwork quilt covers the queensize poster bed. There's space for a dinette table as well as a sitting room with a loveseat in a book-filled alcove in which we could get lost for hours. That is, if we weren't out on the suite's patio overlooking the garden, enjoying the flowers and a great birdhouse replicating the Globe Theater. On the third floor is the smaller Kelmscott Suite, furnished with William Morris wallpaper, a brass double bed and a clawfoot tub. A cushioned doorway (so that tall folks don't hit their heads) leads to a small alcove with a day bed, but the principal reading area is in the main room.

Breakfast is a festive affair, overseen by the chatty owner-occupants. Expect fresh orange juice, fruits, homemade coffeecake, fresh breads or croissants and cheeses.

"We're only the fifth family that has owned the house," says Cate, "so it's been well-loved." Now its guests can be well-read and well-fed.

Doubles, $80 and $90. Two-night minimum stay.

Stillpoint, 27 Gregory St., Marblehead 01945. (617) 631-1667 or (800) 882-3891.
Blessed with a fine location that catches a glimpse of Marblehead's harbor, this fine old house also is blessed with an innkeeper who cares. Sarah Lincoln-Harrison, who founded the local bed-and-breakfast association, is devoted to wholesome living, environmental innkeeping, healthful food and eco-tourism. She's an innkeeper with a mission, you might say.

"This B&B is a good teaching tool to show by experience how people can live more wholesome lives," says Sarah as she warms to her subject. If asked, she'll tell about the energy-saving compact fluorescent lights in the front parlor and the four varieties of plants that line a shelf above the bed in the front guest room, "which eat up bad toxins from the air." The tap water is all right, she advises, but you may be happier with the pitcher of purified water in the bathroom. She notes that she caters to chemically sensitive people at Lindsey's Garret, an efficiency apartment ($80, B&B) atop her other house at 38 High St.

This serene lady, a widow who was remarried to a widower in 1990 and moved into his home, is particularly proud of a new "edible landscape" – her former side lawn now transformed into a medley of herbs, vegetables, flowers and medicinals. We weren't the only guests to be fooled in mid-October by the still lush ripening "tomatoes," which turned out to be a rare variety of Turkish orange eggplant.

The accommodations are comfortable as well as comforting, simple yet refined. There are three bedrooms (one with a double bed, one with king bed, and one with twins and windows on three sides). They share two full hall baths, and the first taker gets a private bath. There are lots of local magazines and environmental literature, but no television "because that's not what we're about," says Sarah. She prefers restful atmosphere – which includes a side deck beneath a flowering crabapple tree, with a good view of the harbor below.

Breakfast includes an assortment of juices and organic cereals, homemade applesauce, muffins (perhaps morning glory) and no-fat bread for toasting, along with local preserves.

Proceeds from the small selection of environmental and crafts items for sale in the hallway go to local programs for the homeless and environmental causes. Stillpoint "welcomes guests from all cultures, races and lifestyles," says its brochure, which is printed on recycled paper. Guest-room diaries are full of praise and uplifting messages written by sensitive or sensitized guests. Wrote one Atlanta couple who stayed three weeks: "Sarah's serenity and sense of connectedness to the earth and people is a calming force in this retreat from the mainstream hubbub. Her edible landscape is both beautiful and delicious."

Doubles, $60 to $80. No smoking.

The Seagull Inn B&B, 106 Harbor Ave., Marblehead 01945. (617) 631-1893.

When Skip Sigler suddenly found himself "redundant in corporate America" at age 58, he opened his family home of 25 years as a B&B. It's about the only one on posh Marblehead Neck – and thus viewed skeptically by some of his neighbors, says Skip, although the property had been the site of a hotel, which burned down in 1940. He and his wife Ruth offer a bedroom and two suites, each with private bath and cable television. Bright and airy, their home up a hill from Marblehead Harbor is distinctly lived-in and laid-back.

Skip is a hands-on innkeeper (his wife works for an insurance company), from cooking breakfast to socializing with guests to housecleaning ("six years of college for this, but I love it"). His sideline is woodworking, and he made most of the furniture in the house. The gathering spot is the living room, with its cherry floor and door, homemade furniture and valances, and a remarkable carved wooden chess set on a table in the corner. The smallest suite is the Library, paneled in barnwood, with a double bed, bathtub and separate shower. Skip painted the sea scenes on a bedroom wall in a two-room suite with sitting room and queensize bed. The biggest accommodations are in the two-story apartment suite with its own side deck. It offers a living area with sofabed, daybed and kitchen and a bedroom with queensize bed. Climb one more flight of stairs

The Seagull Inn B&B occupies choice hilltop property on Marblehead Neck.

to the rooftop deck, from which the Boston skyline can be seen when the leaves are off the trees.

In his newfound profession, Skip is a convivial host, pouring wine for guests and sometimes cooking dinner. A breakfast burrito (eggs in a tortilla) is his morning specialty, accompanied by fresh fruit and lemon or banana-walnut bread. Guests also enjoy free use of the health and fitness club his son owns in Marblehead.

Doubles, $85; suites, $100 and $150. No smoking.

The Victorian Rose, 72 Prospect St., Marblehead 01945. (617) 631-4306 or (800) 225-4306.

Innkeeper Denise Campbell is into both Victoriana and roses, as the decorative theme of her turn-of-the-century B&B suggests. She's also into children, having three young ones of her own and providing lots of play space on the main floor and in the large back yard.

The functions of the various common rooms on the first floor seem to vary according to the whims of the owners and the nature of their guests. "We could have a living room in any of the rooms," says Denise. At our visit, the front room served as a dining room, notable for a long pine table and corner hutch made by husband Bob, who commutes to his engineering job in Boston. The dining room opens to a rear room centered by a billiards table and containing one leather chair and a fireplace. The adjacent rear living room was pressed into service as a playroom, full of toys stored in the butler's pantry.

The second floor holds three bedrooms that share a bath. Chintz and wallpaper with a rose theme decorate two of the rooms, one with twin beds and two wicker chairs and the other with a queensize brass bed, wicker sofa and a large cradle made by Bob and now filled with green plants. A small front bedroom with an antique mahogany double bed and a single chair is "perfect for a traveling grandmother," Denise says. There's also a small front-corner common room with a TV.

The Victorian and rose theme is conspicuously missing from a hidden side suite with its own entrance. Here, beneath a vaulted ceiling that once served as an artist's studio, is a high pineapple poster bed. The room is quite modern in white and blue, contains a little sitting area with refrigerator and TV, and has its own bath. The suite is so private and secluded that many a bride has honeymooned here, unbeknownst to her wedding party housed in the main inn, says Denise.

Guests enjoy a rear patio with barbecue grill and an enormous fenced-in back yard with a tree house, a fort, play equipment and some struggling perennial gardens. Continental breakfast includes fresh fruits, cereal, homemade breads, muffins and bagels.

In 1995, the Campbells had the place up for sale as a B&B. They had their eye on a waterfront house in which they hoped to open a five-room B&B.

Doubles, $65 to $70; suite, $95.

Brimblecomb Hill B&B, 33 Mechanic St., Marblehead 01945. (617) 631-3172 or 631-6366.

Built in 1721 by one of the first summer visitors to Marblehead, this house in the heart of Old Marblehead is run as a B&B by Gene Arnould, art gallery owner, organizer of jazz concerts and ex-Congregational minister who's considered one of the more interesting people in town. He lives on the second floor, and turns over the first floor to guests.

Everything here is properly historic. "Ben Franklin stopped by to visit," the B&B advertises. "You can spend the night." The Isaac Mansfield Room (named for the original owner) is the largest, an end room with private bath, queensize maple poster bed, cottage pine chest, shelves of books and wide pumpkin pine flooring. Two small rooms in the rear, reached by a separate entrance, share a full bath. Each has a double bed, basic furnishings, carpeting and a rocking chair.

Guests enjoy a small common room with fireplace, games table and a grand piano. A buffet breakfast of fruit, cereal, muffins and croissants is put out here in the morning.

Doubles, $60 to $75. No smoking.

The Golden Cod, 26 Pond St., Marblehead 01945. (617) 631-1846.

A bulletin board full of thank-you notes is a focal point in the small third-floor sitting room of this B&B, named for the town's early, lucrative codfish industry. The notes testify to the hospitality of gregarious hosts Jean and Rufus Titus, community leaders. Their late 19th-century house is located in a residential section a bit removed from Old Town. Besides the sitting room that's occasionally pressed into service as a third bedroom for a single, the third floor holds two skylit guest rooms with private baths. One has a queen bed and the other two twins that can be joined as a king. Both come with small black and white TVs.

Jean stenciled the borders that enhance the main-floor dining area opening into a large country kitchen. It's full of notable displays of gleaming silver and china. Here is where Jean serves a full breakfast, from juice and a bowl of cut-up fruit to blueberry pancakes or eggs benedict.

The Tituses sometimes share their comfortable living room with TV, if only to show their fine collection of framed, handpainted paintings of original Wallace Nutting photos. They also share their rear deck for lounging beside the gardens.

Doubles, $75. No smoking.

Dining Spots

Hawkes Street Cafe, 26 Hawkes St., Marblehead. (617) 631-4440.

Since its opening in 1994, this stylish cafe with a semi-open kitchen has been packing in those who appreciate assertive, sometimes daring food at reasonable prices. Chef-owner Peter Capalbo, who was executive chef at the late Union Grill in Beverly, found a receptive following and his wife Diane decorated with aplomb. Her color scheme is off-peach and forest green, and fabric is draped unexpectedly along the walls.

"Regional cuisine at the cutting edge" is the restaurant's hallmark, so much so that

Fabric draped along walls provides decorative motif at Hawkes Street Cafe.

it even presents Southern regional cooking on Sunday nights to the accompaniment of a live jazz saxophonist or guitarist. The midweek night we dined here, things were considerably quieter – except in the tastebud department. The meal started with a basket of the acclaimed house ciambatta bread for dipping into a bowl of herb-infused olive oil (we took a loaf home as they give unused bread away at the end of the night). The choice of appetizers ($2.95 to $7.95) was the most tantalizing section of the menu, from a Maine crab cake with a warm white bean salad to a grilled eggplant and goat cheese pizza with parsley pesto. We settled for a tasty shrimp tempura with prawn crackers and a house salad with three dressings (Thai curry, artichoke vinaigrette and buttermilk garlic) on the side.

The choice of main courses ($7.95 to $15.95) that autumn night was different, to say the least: things like sautéed chicken breast stuffed with chorizo sausage atop a chipotle pepper with toasted coriander, black and white ravioli stuffed with lobster and crabmeat, New England vegetable stew with roasted garlic and mashed potato crust, and mixed seafood grill with choice of exotic sauces. The scallion ravioli stuffed with pumpkin in a ginger-vegetable broth was a triumph, surrounding a dome of vegetables that included red and yellow peppers, celery, broccoli, snow peas and chives done up in a bow. Equally tasty was the rigatoni with a pancetta, garlic, wine and plum tomato sauce.

Among "finishing touches" ($3.95) were pumpkin flan, chocolate-raspberry velvet and a maple-walnut torte with cinnamon ice cream, offered with a selection of ports. The warm pear pancake with vanilla ice cream was stellar, a dainty crêpe on an oversize plate speckled with powdered sugar and a spring of mint. The interesting wine list is eminently affordable, and the service highly professional and knowledgeable.

Lunch, Tuesday-Friday 11:30 to 2:30; dinner, Tuesday-Saturday 5 to 9:30 or 10, Sunday 5 to 9.

Pellino's, 261 Washington St., Marblehead. (617) 631-3344.
Although it lacks some of the ambiance of its peers, this diminutive downtown hideaway is almost universally first on locals' lists of favorite restaurants. Naples-born chef-owner Francesco (Frank) Pellino's white-clothed tables as well as five booths

ensconced behind arches and fitted out with old church pews are much in demand. Twinkling white lights define the front windows above a colorful vest-pocket garden.

Whole roasted garlic cloves are served with olive oil for spreading on the crusty Italian bread that begins each meal. The dinner menu looks to be standard-issue Italian, but subtleties enhance the fare. Main courses ($12.95 to $16.95) come with house salads, which tend to be more mundane than the rest of the meal. Look for treats like salmon fillets pan-seared in a creamy saffron sauce and garnished with shrimp, whole brook trout roasted with lemon and sage in parchment, grilled chicken with arugula, fire-roasted peppers, wild mushrooms and aioli, and veal pellino sauced with port wine, shiitake mushrooms, sundried tomatoes and herbs.

Pasta dishes here may be the best in town, from shrimp diavolo tossed with linguini to fettuccine with roasted lamb, leeks and puree of vegetables. Starters could be carpaccio with wild mushrooms, Tuscan-style minestrone, grilled portobello mushrooms with fresh mozzarella and roasted garlic and chargrilled calamari with wild greens drizzled with a lemon-olive oil dressing.

Tirami su, chocolate mousse cake on strawberry coulis, cappuccino gelato and sorbets are among the homemade desserts ($4.50 to $4.95). Wine-tasting dinners and cooking classes are offered here in the winter.

Dinner nightly, 5 to 10.

Rosalie's, 10 Sewall St., Marblehead. (617) 631-5353.

For more than twenty years, this has been Marblehead's big-name restaurant. Lately it has been held in higher esteem elsewhere than locally, as some think Rosalie Harrington's enterprise here has slipped since she opened a second outpost in Sudbury.

Housed in an 1890 box factory, the restaurant on three floors is a family operation – that of Rosalie and her three children – and reflects the personality of its namesake, who also teaches cooking classes upstairs. The main-floor dining room is notable for its three cozy canopied booths in the bar area, a dogwood tree lit with white lights and striking balloon curtains on the windows.

The dinner menu lists ten entrées like baked salmon with a crust of pine nuts, spinach and wild mushrooms; scampi sautéed with red and green peppers and onions in a wine marinara sauce; chicken francesca sauced with grand marnier and mushrooms, veal stuffed with prosciutto, gruyère and caramelized onions, and steak au poivre.

Favorite appetizers include grilled portobello mushrooms, baked oysters on the half shell with prosciutto and garlic butter, and the house antipasti. Among pasta dishes are lobster and crab ravioli, grilled shrimp with linguini and wild mushroom alfredo.

Cappuccino or espresso are satisfying endings for what some consider the town's fanciest meals. Light fare, including pastas, pizzas, sandwiches and entrées like meat loaf and grilled pork ribs are available in the downstairs cafe.

Dinner, Tuesday-Saturday from 5:30, Sunday from 5; Sunday brunch, 11 to 2. Cafe, Tuesday-Sunday from 5.

The Landing, 81 Front St., Marblehead. (617) 631-1878.

This unassuming-looking place occupies a prime waterfront location, sandwiched between working fish docks and a little town park. Its reputation rises and falls according to who's in the kitchen, and at our 1994 visit a new chef was winning high marks.

The menu certainly is ambitious. We snagged a seat on the small outdoor deck at water's edge for a sunny autumn lunch, only to think we were being offered the dinner menu. Most lunchtime offerings were priced in the low teens and were the kinds of dishes you'd expect at night. One of us settled on a good chicken caesar salad ($7.95), augmented by a basket of bread. The other tried the thick, potatoey clam chowder and

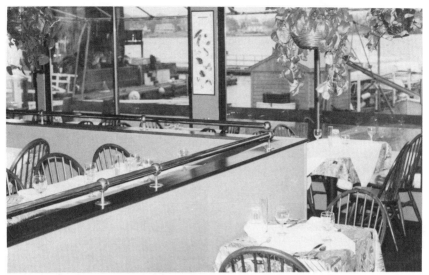
Two-level dining room at The Landing looks out onto Marblehead waterfront.

an imaginative appetizer, crab and boursin strudel on a bed of arugula ($6.95), which showed a creative hand in the kitchen. Service was somewhat disjointed, as often happens at a waterfront establishment whose fortunes ebb with the weather and seasons, and there was a fishy smell from the adjacent docks, but the setting beside the harbor more than compensated.

Dinner is served in a two-level dining room, mirrored to look larger and to reflect the water scene outside. White-linened tables, oil lamps and fresh flowers create a pleasant backdrop for such entrées ($14.25 to $19.95) as grilled yellowfin tuna over belgian endive, watercress and citrus sections; pan-roasted lobster served over pasta tossed with garlic and arugula; steamed salmon and artichokes with fennel and cherry tomatoes, pan-roasted duck breast fanned over sautéed raspberries and oranges with a pecan-ginger glaze, and twin filets of beef with grilled herb polenta. Blackened tuna carpaccio rolled in greens with wasabi dipping sauce and a lobster and papaya cocktail are tempting starters, as is the asparagus and crab soup. Dessert could be chocolate-raspberry mousse cake, chocolate bread pudding and white chocolate mousse cake.

Lunch, Monday-Saturday 11:30 to 4; dinner nightly, 5 to 9:30; Sunday brunch, 10:30 to 4.

Pleasant Street Cafe, 143 Pleasant St., Marblehead. (617) 631-8550.

A chef from Boston's well-known Meridien Hotel, Scott Robinson, and his wife Maureen opened this establishment in 1994. They upgraded what he called "a former dive" with white tablecloths, a mix of booths and tables, and a crisp if rather ersatz Colonial decor. A pianist enlivens the proceedings Thursday through Saturday evenings and at Sunday brunch.

The straightforward dinner menu titles barely hint at some of the complexities of the fare. For appetizers ($4.95 to $6.95), consider lobster stew laced with potatoes and brandy, warm shrimp salad with mixed greens and enoki mushrooms, chicken and wild mushroom raviolis served on a tomato coulis, or grilled duck breast tossed with greens and spiced walnuts.

Main courses run from $10.95 for chicken pot pie to $21.95 for rack of lamb. They are categorized according to New England (lobster pie and bouillabaisse), seafood and pasta (lobster and artichokes served over fresh corn pasta and shrimp sautéed with broccoli and plum tomatoes over linguini), and grills and roasts (swordfish served with fried oysters and tomato-corn relish and mixed grill of lamb chop, pork chop and duck sausage with merlot sauce).

Lunch, 11:30 to 2:30; dinner nightly, 4 to 10; Sunday brunch, 11 to 2.

The King's Rook, 12 State St., Marblehead. (617) 631-9838.

Every town should have a cafe and wine bar like this. Occupying the lower floor of a restored 1747 house in the historic section of Marblehead, it was established as a coffee house in 1959 – when a coffeehouse was radical and radical was a bad word, according to owner Frank Regan. "We've stayed with the concept for 36 years, but we express it in today's terms."

As the clientele has matured, so has the Rook. "We still have the same basic menu and the same cheesecake," says Frank, "but we keep looking for new items." Among the newest are gourmet pizzas, cafe latte and liqueurs. The wide-ranging, all-day menu is perfect for lunch, an afternoon drink, a casual supper or late-evening snack. House favorites are a frittata with salad of the day, a Middle Eastern plate, a pesto turkey sandwich on baguette or croissant, shrimp scampi pizza and a classic pâté platter or sandwich. Prices are reasonable – the only item over $5.95 is a chicken salad with grapes and almonds ($6.25).

Owner Frank Regan at The King's Rook.

Desserts here are special, particularly the creamy and rich cheesecake, the carrot cake and the Neopolitan mousse torte.

There are many coffees, teas, frappes and exotic beverages, and a fantastic selection of beers and wines by the glass. Frank often circulates through the beamed, low-ceiling rooms, and a casual, coffeehouse ambiance prevails. We know local folks who love to sip coffee or wine, listen to the classical music or jazz, read the newspapers or the Tatler from the magazine rack, and while away an afternoon.

Open Monday-Friday noon to 2:30; Tuesday-Friday 5:30 to 11:30; Saturday and Sunday, noon to 11:30.

Maddie's Sail Loft, 15 State St., Marblehead. (617) 631-9824.

This kind of local hangout (a fixture since 1946) is not our cup of tea, but we're obviously in the minority because it's generally packed at all hours and the bar is a favorite watering hole, known for wickedly potent drinks. Except for the mural of Marblehead and the harbor at the foot of the stairs, the scene and the setting could be anywhere, which is probably why we don't find it particularly alluring.

Nevertheless, for lunch you won't go wrong with the prize-winning clam chowder, a basic burger, grilled cheese or roast beef sandwich in the $2 to $4 range. You might be stunned to find a clam roll for $10.50, or Boston scrod for $13.95. The latter are also available at dinner, when prices go from $8.95 for fish and chips to $14.95 for a fried clam dinner, combination seafood platter, baked stuffed jumbo shrimp or

Marblehead seafood pie. Hearty portions and a convivial seafarer's atmosphere continue to draw the throngs.

Lunch, Monday-Saturday 11:45 to 2; dinner, 5 to 10; pub serves continuously from 11:45 to 11:30. Closed Sunday. No credit cards.

The Barnacle, Front Street, Marblehead. (617) 631-4236.

Considered on a par with Maddie's Sail Loft, this crowded, no-nonsense restaurant at least has a water view – one of the best in town. In fact, you can sit at a narrow counter running the width of the restaurant smack dab against the windows at the rear and feast on the panorama as you eat, or on a small outdoor deck during the summer.

The short menu lists New England seafood basics at fairly steep prices; for instance, a clam roll for $8.95 and a lobster roll for $10.50 – a bit stiff, we thought, for a weekday lunch. Featured at dinner ($10.95 to $15.95) are such standards as haddock au gratin, broiled scallops, baked stuffed shrimp, "jumbo shrimp scampi" and broiled sirloin. All entrées are served with salad, potatoes, rolls and butter – "no substitutions." The tables are almost on top of each other, the nondescript decor is vaguely nautical and the small, crowded bar in front also has a good view.

Lunch, daily 11:30 to 4; dinner, 5 to 10. Closed Tuesday in winter. No credit cards.

The Rockmore, Salem Harbor, Marblehead. (617) 639-0600.

This is a restaurant with a difference. It's located on a floating pontoon barge, and reachable only by boat. A free launch service from the Village Street Landing takes people to the barge moored in the harbor, where the dining experience is likened to that of eating on someone's yacht – a favorite Marblehead pastime.

The menu is surprisingly extensive, if unevenly executed. Expect salads and sandwiches in the $4 to $7 range, and grilled or fried seafood, chicken and steak dishes from $8 (for fried scrod) to $14.50 (for a fried seafood platter). Frozen drinks, regional beers and wines by the glass go with or on their own.

Open daily in summer, 11 to 8, weather permitting.

Diversions

On a presidential visit more than 150 years after it was founded, George Washington remarked that Marblehead had the look of antiquity. It still does (even more so, no doubt), particularly in the Old Town historic district near the harbor. It has so many ledges and glacial outcroppings that early settlers simply built where they could. Streets are winding and narrow, many seem to be one-way the wrong way, parking is limited and directional signs are few. A map of town from the seasonal Chamber of Commerce information booth at Pleasant and Essex streets is a must; even then, it takes most visitors several trips to get their bearings.

Driving Tour. With said map and a willingness for trial and error, orient yourself by driving along Pleasant Street (Route 114), the main drag from Salem through the uptown commercial center. It eventually intersects with **Washington Street,** the historic main street winding from uptown through Old Town, where the most notable landmarks are located. Get to the start of one-way **Front Street** to drive along the harbor and out to the views from **Fort Sewall,** the 1742 fortification at the mouth of the harbor. Another good view is from **Old Burial Hill** off Orne Street, one of the oldest graveyards (1638) in New England; a plaque notes that 600 Revolutionary heroes and several early pastors are interred at the top of the hill, the highest point in town. Return to Pleasant Street and head west to **Ocean Avenue,** the access route to Marblehead Neck. At the causeway is **Devereux Beach,** a sandy strand for sunning and swimming. The other side of the causeway overlooks Marblehead Harbor with all its moored pleasure craft and affords vistas of Old Town and **Marblehead Neck.** Turn left on Harbor Avenue and then Foster Avenue and pass the posh Eastern and Corinthian yacht clubs and lovely homes beside the harbor. At the tip of the neck is **Chandler Hovey Park,** where protected benches on the rocks are good vantage points for Marblehead Light and the passing boats. Continue around to Ocean Avenue with a stop at the alley leading to **Castle Rock** (one of the many public access points to the water throughout Marblehead). The rock may be of less interest than the multi-million-dollar castle residence beside. More palatial homes face the ocean on the way to the **Audubon Bird Sanctuary,** unmarked but reached off Risley Road. Head back to the causeway and where Ocean Avenue intersects with Harbor Avenue you'll be surprised by a stunning view of the Boston skyline across the water.

Walking Tour. Thus oriented, get out and walk – the best way to see and sense Marblehead. A Chamber of Commerce map outlines rewarding walking tours of one or two miles. We did our tour just after daybreak, when all was still and many Marbleheaders were out walking their dogs and taking their morning constitutional. Go slowly, so as to savor (and not miss) all the little treasures and to make your own discoveries. Here are some highlights, in addition to those itemized below. Colorful houses and gardens enliven winding **Lee Street,** including a residence marked by one of Marblehead's ubiquitous plaques, this one saying "Built in 1735 for Thomas Roads, innholder." (Others to be encountered were built for merchants, bakers, boat builders, blacksmiths, shoremen, fishermen and countless others, giving a fascinating who's who of early Marblehead.) Off Gregory Street, climb the steps of **Prospect Alley** to reach Boden's Lookout, a hilltop aerie above the harbor, next to a gray house built in 1710 for John Boden, shoreman. Pass the **Lafayette House,** with its cutout corner beside Union Street, and head down Water Street to the imposing **Boston Yacht Club,** one of the nation's first, where rockers are lined up on the long waterfront porch. Beyond is **Crocker Park,** a stony outcrop harbor blessed with long benches for viewing the harbor goings-on. A plaque, dedicated to George Washington's Navy, tells of "the first American vessels to engage in naval operations against an enemy...the forerunners of the U.S. Navy." They were manned by Marblehead sailors. Stop at the **Town Landing** at the foot of State Street to see working fishing boats. From the 1727 **Old Town House** area in the center of Old Town, take brief side trips to see Old North Church, the Unitarian-Universalist Church and St. Michael's Episcopal Church. None is quite as imposing as **Abbot Hall,** the 1877 town hall whose red brick tower is Marblehead's most visible landmark. The creaky main floor displays much Marblehead memorabilia; foremost is Archibald Willard's famed "Spirit of '76" painting, a larger-than-life piece made famous during the nation's centenary celebration and now framed permanently against a red velvet backdrop in the selectmen's meeting room here. The walking tour goes near or past many restaurants, B&Bs and shops detailed herein.

Jeremiah Lee Mansion, 161 Washington St., 631-1069. Step through the door of this impressive house and you're back in 1768. Almost every feature of this house, built by one of the richest traders in the local "codfish aristocracy," is original. Lee's residence was described by a Boston newspaper at the time as "the most elegant and costly home in the Bay State Colony." You're told that Lee emulated the houses of the British aristocracy, from the simulated cut-stone blocks of the Georgian wooden facade to the original rococo carving and architectural features inside. Guides point out the intricate carved spindles and newel posts (bearing spirals within spirals) of the unsupported Santo Domingan mahogany staircase with its free-standing landing, a focal point of the massive entry foyer. On either side of the landing are copies of portraits of Jeremiah and Martha Lee, among the few full-length portraits by John

Singleton Copley. Most unusual is the exotic, handpainted wallpaper created in England to exact specifications for the hallway and several grand chambers; the Lee is the only public house this old where you can see the original wallpaper on the same walls. The house is full of unique attributes and furnishings, from original fire backs and fireplace tiles to Colonial Revival gold draperies and "important" North Shore furniture – all gifts to the sponsoring Marblehead Historical Society from local families and Louise du Pont Crowninshield, an honorary director who summered in Marblehead and contributed much toward saving the house. The bedchambers and servants' quarters on the third floor have been turned into museum rooms to display local artifacts, including dolls, children's furniture, shoes, a wonderful sea captain's crib and a room full of paintings by local folk artist J.O.J. Frost. This mansion, billed as the most beautiful Colonial mansion in the country, is not to be missed. Open mid-May through Columbus Day, Monday-Saturday 10 to 4, Sunday 1 to 4. Adults, $4.

King Hooper Mansion, 8 Hooper St., 631-2608. Less awesome than the Jeremiah Lee Mansion around the corner, this is a much-used building that's headquarters of the

Marblehead Arts Association. It's actually two structures joined together: the original built in 1728 and a Georgian front added in 1745. There are fourteen fireplaces, original Delft tiles, pumpkin pine floors, double dentil moldings and formal British gardens in the rear, but the home of the wealthy merchant trader who was respectfully nicknamed King by his sailors is not overly daunting – except perhaps for the arched brick wine cellar off the basement kitchen or the enormous third-floor ballroom, now a handsome display space for changing art exhibitions. The oldest piece in the house is a blanket chest from the 1600s. Here you learn that the powder room was originally used by men to powder their wigs, and that the good-night bidding to "sleep tight" derived from the need to tighten the ropes beneath the mattress on the canopy bed. Open Monday-Saturday 10 to 4, Sunday 1 to 5. Free.

Shopping. Especially good specialty stores are concentrated around Washington Street in Old Town. They're also scattered along School Street, Atlantic Avenue and Pleasant Street in the newer uptown area. In the heart of Old Town is **Tyme,** featuring one-of-a-kind works of leading artisans from across the country. We coveted a floral-painted corner table, not to mention all the Christmas ornaments of Charles Dickens characters that owner Julia Bantly chose because of their connection with the local Jacob Marley's restaurant, or the fabulous pins that call out to women to purchase a few. It was here that we met Sushi, a neighborhood cat who stops in daily for a drink from the bird bath and then curls up for a nap in the shop's gift-wrap tissue paper.

A decorator friend at home tipped us off to the wonders at **Julie Keyes Designs & Ceramics,** 11 State St. We cherished everything here and so do the buyers from Henri Bendel, Neiman-Marcus and with-it shops across the country. In three years, Julie's operation has grown to fifteen young employees, all art school graduates. They keep four kilns fired every night to produce her incredibly colorful hand-painted creations: lamps, platters, trays, tables, urns, lobster vases, cat faces, even a dog cookie jar – all displayed in an expanding gallery that Julie calls "a work in progress." Prices generally range from $12 to $500, although we found a floral garden marker for $4.75.

Most unusual is Joan Wheeler's **Russian Gallery,** a trove of things Russian, including dozens of matrioshka nesting dolls, lacquered boxes, shawls, small colorful pens and eggs, even T-shirts. Downstairs are Russian watercolors and prints. **The Marblehead Kite Co.** carries everything that says Marblehead – T-shirts, coffee mugs, sweatshirts of sailboats on the harbor titled Marblehead Rush Hour and, yes, kites. Some of the cards here made us laugh out loud. Also specializing in Marblehead items is **Arnould Gallery,** with many local prints and some carved swans clad in straw hats. Nearby, **Remembrance** is full of wonderful gifts, **Much Ado** has two floors crammed with rare books and **O'Rama's,** which started selling antique lingerie and linens, expanded into a line of jewelry, frames, soaps, teapots and boxes, all very dainty and feminine. The **Marblehead Country Store** stocks more neat gifts, pottery, cards, handknit sweaters and toys. **Hector's Pup** is a great toy store, next door to the **Marblehead Doll Factory** and near **Cargo Unlimited.**

Uptown are **C'est la Vie** with imaginative gifts of the kind found in decorator showhouses, as well as unusual picture frames, china and glass, and exquisite baby things; **Accessories by Blass**, with unusual pins, pocketbooks and umbrellas, and the excellent **Spirit of '76 Bookstore,** the flagship of proprietor Robert Hugo's group of four. At 189 Pleasant St. is the **Garden Collection,** where proprietor Rebecca Ellis stocks all kinds of flowery gifts, botanical notecards, floral aprons and pottery with a floral or garden theme. We loved her T-shirts with cats or bird feeders.

For a break from shopping, stop at **Delphin's Gourmandise** at 258 Washington St., where you'll likely be overpowered by the most heavenly aromas of any bakery anywhere. This sensational French patisserie furnished the pastries when George Bush met French Premier Mitterand at Boston University. Master pastry chef Delphin Gomes creates delectables for eating in the cafe, on the side patio or to go. We can vouch for the plum tart, one of the best pastries we've ever eaten.

Marblehead excels in chocolate production. The well-known **Harbor Sweets** started in Marblehead but has moved its plant to Salem. Still a fixture is **Stowaway Sweets** in a quaint English country cottage at 154 Atlantic Ave. A candy maker from Somerville and four dippers, all in their 80s, produce chocolates as they have since 1929. The chocolates have been a tradition at Buckingham Palace and the White House since the days of Queen Mary and Franklin Roosevelt. Framed testimonials from Mrs. Calvin Coolidge and Cornelia Otis Skinner convey history, but sugar-free samples and piña colada truffles bespeak today. The signature mocha cream "meltaways" are to die for.

Extra Special

Hestia Handcrafts, 13 Hawkes St., Marblehead. (617) 639-2727.

Generally unknown by most visitors (not to mention residents), the little showroom here displays fine miniatures produced in the rear "factory" and sold to collectors across the country. Linda Macdonald, a Marblehead mother of four, turned her hobby of designing unique products in clays and porcelains into a lucrative business. Her original designs, which range from Christmas ornaments and miniature buildings ($8 to $15) to figurines and garden statues ($35 to $45), are first sculpted in clay. Latex molds are made for mass-producing air-dried plaster units, which then are individually handpainted and sealed by fifteen employees, many of whom work at home. We were struck by the AmeriScape ornaments devoted to different places, from Charleston to Cape May to Breckenridge to Natchez – not to mention Marblehead, for which a different design is produced each year. There are garden statues of cats, rabbits and dogs, as well as nativity scenes (to which collectors add characters over the years). We picked up a few finely sculpted and detailed woodland animals for Christmas gifts. Open Monday-Saturday, 9 to 5.

Renovated 1846 octagonal rotunda is a focal point of Williams College Museum of Art.

Williamstown, Mass.
Arts Town of the East

Blessed with an uncommonly scenic setting and the riches that prestigious Williams College attracts and returns, this small college town in the northern Berkshires is an arts center of national significance.

Newsweek called the annual Williamstown Theatre Festival "the best of all American summer theaters." Connoisseur magazine said its three leading museums make it "an unlikely but powerful little art capital." U.S. News and World Report revealed that educators consider Williams College tops among academic institutions in the country.

Williams, its associates and benefactors have inspired these superlatives. But they have geography and nature to thank for what some call "The Village Beautiful." Somewhat isolated in a verdant bowl, Williamstown dwells at the foot of Mount Greylock, the highest peak in Massachusetts, surrounded by Vermont's Green and New York's Taconic mountains. Not only do these provide great outdoor activities (in particular, golf, hiking and skiing). They also help Williamstown retain a charmed rural flavor that seems far more village-like than its population of 8,200 might suggest.

Williamstown is a sophisticated little town of great appeal, one that unfolds as you delve. The youthful dynamic of 2,000 college students is not readily apparent in the broader community. Besides natural and cultural attractions, there are good restaurants, selective shops and a handful of inns and B&Bs.

This is one place that has long been special. If you simply drive around town, you may not sense the subtle blend of sophistication and small town that is the real Williamstown. Here you must stop, stay awhile and explore.

Inn Spots

The Orchards, 222 Adams Road (Route 2), Williamstown 01267. (413) 458-9611 or (800) 225-1517.

Opened to the tune of many millions of dollars in 1985, the Orchards was designed to fill a conspicuous gap in terms of inn accommodations. It succeeds "along the lines of an English country hotel" (its words). But it's not the Berkshires' "most gracious country inn" nor "the finest inn in the Northeast," as its early publicity hoopla claimed (indeed, passersby along Route 2 might mistake its strange-looking, salmon-colored stucco facade for a condominium project). Its early status always rather tenuous, The Orchards was rescued from foreclosure in 1993 by Sayed M. Saleh, a hotel executive from Boston, who acquired the inn from the FDIC.

Despite its initial "newness," the now decade-old Orchards has aged surprisingly well. The 49-bedroom, three-story structure meanders around a small, open courtyard containing a free-form, rock-bordered pond with a fountain. Recently enlarged, the pond is surrounded by an outdoor dining area, lawns and flowers.

The interior layout separates the restaurant and lounge from the guest rooms. Winding corridors expand into a gracious drawing room, where intricate chandeliers hang from the cathedral ceiling and polished antique furniture of the Queen Anne style warms the space. Complimentary scones and English tea are served on fine china in the afternoon and, perhaps, dessert and coffee or liqueurs after dinner. Coffee and breakfast pastries are served there (gratis) before the dining room opens in the morning. Check out the inn's collection of antique silver teapots and the Victorian-era tin soldiers on display.

The guest rooms are large, comfortable and colorful in the Orchards' pink and green theme (the area was long an orchard, but lately has been commercialized). Amenities include telephones in bathrooms as well as bedrooms and TVs secreted in armoires, their remote controls at bedside. Each room is different within the prevailing theme: marble bathrooms with terrycloth robes and Lord & Mayfair bath oils and soaps, separate dressing area and small refrigerator. Some have working fireplaces, four-poster beds and bay windows. Cookies are served when the beds are turned down at night.

River Bend Farm occupies Georgian Colonial built in 1770 by a founder of Williamstown.

The Orchards is designed in the style of an English country hotel.

The inn has a sauna and jacuzzi, four function rooms, an antiques shop, a cocktail lounge with fireplace and a beautiful dining room (see Dining Spots).

Doubles, $150 to $215.

River Bend Farm, 643 Simonds Road (Route 7 North), Williamstown 01267. (413) 458-3121 or (800) 418-2057.

This inviting Georgian Colonial was built in 1770 by Col. Benjamin Simonds, one of Williamstown's thirteen founders, and the house exudes 18th-century authenticity.

Preservationists David and Judy Loomis acquired the house in 1977, spent years restoring it with great care and attention to detail, and slowly started sharing its treasures with B&B guests.

Guests enter the rear keeping room, where black kettles hang from the huge hearth, one of five fireplaces off the central stone chimney. The room is full of hooked rugs, antiques, dried flowers and grapevine wreaths. Here's where the hosts serve what they call a healthful continental breakfast of fruit, homemade granola, honey from their own beehives, muffins and breads.

All the lighting here and in the adjacent parlor comes from small bulbs in tin chandeliers and period lighting fixtures. The Loomises recently removed layers of flooring atop the original 1770 boards in the parlor. "Just to think that Ethan Allen stood here on the same floor is exciting," says Dave. The house contains what authorities consider to be the best examples of period woodwork in town.

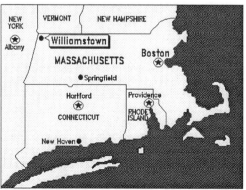

Five bedrooms share two baths, one upstairs with a tub and the other downstairs in the old pantry and harboring an ingenious corner shower with tiles that Dave fashioned from roof slate. Four rooms are upstairs off a hall containing a giant spinning wheel. We liked the front corner room with a crocheted coverlet over the four-poster bed and plenty of room for two wing chairs in a sitting area. A double bed nearly fills a cozy room in the rear. A downstairs bedroom in a former parlor is lovely, decorated in blues and whites with oriental rugs.

Lately, the Loomises leased the B&B temporarily to Jeff Miller, a good cook from New York City, who was serving full breakfasts, plus autumn dinners by the fireplace by special request.

Dave says the B&B proceeds help finance the ongoing restoration of this old home and tavern, which is listed on the National Register of Historic Places. Spending a night or two here is to immerse oneself in history.

Doubles, $90.

Field Farm Guest House, 554 Sloan Road, Williamstown 01267. (413) 458-3135.

When the 1948 American Modern-style home of arts patron Lawrence H. Boedel became available following the death of his widow in 1984, The Trustees of Reservations didn't quite know what to do with it. David and Judy Loomis of River Bend Farm proposed running it as a B&B and, true to their word, they ended up doing just that.

A stay in one of the five guest rooms in this rural hilltop home surrounded by 294 acres of conservation land is intriguing, given the home's history. The word "home" is used advisedly, for that's exactly what it is – looking much as the Bloedels left it, with the exception of some of the fabulous collection of paintings they donated to the Williams College Museum of Art and the Whitney Museum of Art in New York City. At our latest visit, eight of the original pieces were back on indefinite loan from the Williams Museum.

Guests have the run of a spacious living room, dining room, galley kitchen and grounds, which are striking for their sculptures, views and trails. Throughout the large house, most of the furniture was made by Mr. Bloedel, a 1923 Williams graduate and onetime college librarian. All five bedrooms retain their original baths and vary greatly in size. The huge main-floor Gallery Room, which the original owner used as a studio, has a double bed, two twins, a black walnut floor and a separate entrance.

Upstairs in this house that might be described as a mixture of art nouveau and Danish modern are four more guest rooms. In the North Room, tiles of butterflies flank the fireplace (fascinating tiles surround all the fireplaces). It has its own balcony, a dressing table with mirrored surface and a walk-in closet with sliding drawers. The master bedroom contains a built-in corner dressing unit, a fireplace with tiles of trees and birds, and an enormous private deck. The other rooms also are comfortable but considerably smaller. Continental breakfast includes fruit, granola, muffins and breads like banana and zucchini.

The architecturally interesting house, built of Western cedar and fronted by a mass of yellow creeping hydrangeas, was designed by architect Edward Goodell. Its 5,000 square feet of space include the quarters of innkeepers who have operated the place since the Loomises got it up and running, although the latter were occupying the house for three years while the Route 7 bridge in front of their River Bend Farm was under seemingly interminable repair.

Outside are a new swimming pool, a tennis court, picnic tables, woodlands, pastures, a pond, and trails for wildlife-watching or cross-country skiing. From the adjacent cornfield, Dave picked a few ears of sweet corn and sent them home with us for a farm-fresh dinner.

Field Farm Guest House backs up toward pond.

Don't be misled by the name. Field Farm is not a farm in the usual sense, but rather a home lived in by a wealthy and interesting man. You'll be charmed staying here among the furnishings of the period and enjoying the tranquil grounds.

Doubles, $90. Closed Thanksgiving to April.

The Williamstown Bed and Breakfast, 30 Cold Spring Road, Williamstown 01267. (413) 458-9202.

An attractive white Victorian house built in 1880 with room to spare, this was turned into a sparkling B&B in 1989 by young partners Kim Rozell and Lucinda Edmonds. "I cook and Lucinda cleans," quips Kim. Both perform their functions to perfection.

Kim's breakfasts are feasts, taken at a table for eight in the dining room. Start with fruit, cereals and homemade baked goods, but save room for her main course – perhaps blueberry pancakes, waffles, baked eggs or cheese blintzes.

Lucinda's "cleaning" is evident throughout the house. Besides the comfy living room outfitted in a crisp, almost contemporary style, there are five guest rooms with private bathrooms on the second floor. Two rooms have queensize poster beds and a third has a double bed. One with twin beds has a bath down the hall. A rear room with a queensize bed and two wing chairs has a new private bath. That room opens onto another guest room above the owners' quarters to form a two-bedroom suite. White cotton comforters top each bed.

Appointments are a blend of antiques and modern, with an emphasis on oak furniture and mini-print wallpapers with vivid borders. Typical of the caring touches are the bottles of Poland Spring water in each room.

Doubles, $70 to $80.

Le Jardin, 777 Cold Spring Road (Route 7), Williamstown 01267. (413) 458-8032.

A wooded hillside lush with pachysandra, a pond, a waterfall from the passing brook and, of course, colorful gardens welcome guests to this French-style restaurant and country inn converted from a 19th-century mansion two miles south of town.

311

Elegant dining room at The Orchards looks out onto courtyard.

A narrow stairway beside the entrance to the main dining room leads from the entry foyer through a rustic hallway to the six guest rooms, all with full baths and four with fireplaces. Most choice is the front corner room with a four-poster bed ensconced in a niche, stenciling, hooked rugs and TV, and a tub with a jacuzzi in the large bathroom. Particularly popular in summer is a small room in the rear with queensize bed and a private balcony facing the woods. The other rooms, outfitted in country style, are somewhat more plain.

The only public sitting area is in the front bar. Continental breakfast is served in the formal dining room (see Dining Spots), where friendly German chef-innkeeper Walter Hayn has achieved a good reputation.

Doubles, $75 to $95.

The Williams Inn, Junction of Routes 7 and 2, Williamstown 01267. (413) 458-9371 or (800) 828-0133.

After the old Williams Inn was taken over by Williams College, the Treadway built a replacement (supposedly "on-the-green at Williams College," though not by our definition). Not a typical country inn, this is a Colonial-modern hotel/motel. A pianist was playing in the almost-empty cocktail lounge and a gaggle of giggling girls was being shepherded through the lobby for a swimming/birthday party the Friday afternoon we stopped in.

The 100 air-conditioned rooms and "junior suites" on three floors come with full baths, color TVs, oversize beds and early American furnishings. Facilities include a spacious and comfortable lobby, indoor pool, a whirlpool and sauna, elevators, lounge and a restaurant serving three meals a day.

The large and formal dining room with ten big brass chandeliers and high-back, leather-seat chairs is in vivid shades of raspberry with black trim and beige table-cloths. The extensive dinner menu (entrées $13.95 to $19.95) includes such continental choices as chicken dijonnaise, roast duck bigarade and veal oscar.

The buffet tables for the much-acclaimed Sunday brunch ($15.95, served from 11:30

to 2:30) take up the entire lobby. With choices from baked eggs in ham, belgian waffles and cheese blintzes to swordfish Louisianne and leg of lamb, no one leaves hungry. Doubles, $100 to $145; junior suites, $160 to $190.

Dining Spots

The Orchards, 222 Adams Road, Williamstown. (413) 458-9611.

Upholstered reproduction Queen Anne chairs, rose and green carpeting, forest green walls and well-spaced tables set with soft mauve linen, ribbed glassware, flowered German china, silver baskets for the rolls and antique teapots – what could be more elegant than the L-shaped, two-part dining room at the Orchards? We enjoyed a Saturday lunch, settled in comfy high-backed rose velveteen chairs in an airy, two-story greenhouse-like area at one end, looking onto the courtyard. It was the next best thing to dining outside under striped umbrellas (it was too cool that day).

The inn's linen bill must be outrageous, based on the layers cautiously arranged by the teenaged busboy (attired in formal maroon jacket and topsiders) as he changed the cloths. Each table bore intricate covered dishes for sugar and saccharin, a pepper grinder and a crystal salt shaker.

Poppyseed rolls were served as we sipped the Maçon white house wine, a not particularly generous glass for $4. Sandwiches, salads, sandwiches and entrées are priced from $5.75 for a "grilled sirloin burger" to $8.75 for broiled rainbow trout with chive beurre blanc or sautéed tenderloin tips with mushroom bordelaise sauce on a bed of buttered noodles. Swordfish soup with vegetables was an interesting starter, as was the excellent chilled apple curry soup. The chicken salad with papaya slices, apples and pecans was a winner, and a beef bourguignonne special was fine.

The changing dinner menu is respected by area chefs because of its reach. Entrées ($18.25 to $21.95) could include Atlantic salmon in leek champagne sauce, veal piccata with shiitake mushrooms, roasted rack of lamb with mint-infused demi-glace and grilled tournedos of beef madagascar.

Start with hardwood smoked salmon on pumpernickel toast or a strudel of sundried tomatoes, Vermont goat cheese and shiitake mushrooms (6.50 to $8.50). Finish with a good-looking apple tart with crumb crust, chocolate roulade or that chocolate decadence from the pastry cart.

Lunch daily, noon to 2; dinner, 6 to 9; Sunday brunch, 8 to 11.

The Mill on the Floss, Route 7, New Ashford. (413) 458-9123.

Genial Maurice Champagne, originally from Montreal, is the chef-owner at this established and well-regarded restaurant. He loves to socialize, and one reason he designed the open, blue and white tiled kitchen was so that patrons could come up and talk with him as he cooked. The dark brown wood building, pleasantly landscaped, was once a mill. Inside it is cozy, with beamed ceilings, paneled walls, a hutch filled with Quimper pottery, white linens and many hanging copper pots.

Assisted by his daughter Suzanne, Maurice presents classic French fare.

Chef Maurice Champagne in his kitchen.

Among starters are duck pâté with plum wine, escargots, prosciutto and melon, and soups like cold cucumber or black bean. Entrées range from $17 for veal kidneys with mustard sauce to $25.50 for rack of lamb. Sweetbreads in black butter, chicken amandine and sliced tenderloin with garlic sauce are some. The fish of the day could be halibut meunière, poached salmon or grilled swordfish.

For dessert, you might find crème caramel, deep-dish pie and grand marnier soufflé, or try café diablo for two. Wines are quite reasonably priced.

Dinner, Tuesday-Sunday from 5.

Le Country Restaurant, 101 North St. (Route 7), Williamstown. (413) 458-4000.

A warm, country atmosphere and the personalities of chef-owner Raymond Canales, his wife Beverly and son Gregory pervade this long-established restaurant in the continental tradition. "We're sort of rustic," Beverly acknowledged as she showed the main dining room done up in beige and brown, with beamed ceiling, a mix of shaded lamps and candles on the tables, and a franklin stove to ward off the chill in winter. One particularly attractive dining room with high ceiling and sunken area with a fireplace is used for special occasions.

A striking antique piece from Brittany is decked out with wines, glasses and grapes; it's the sister to one behind the bar. "We want people to enjoy wines, so we don't have much of a markup," Beverly explained as we noted some extraordinary bargains (carafes for $10, chardonnays in the teens and nothing much over $30).

The extensive menu is supplemented by nightly specials, prime rib and veal curry the night we were there. Entrées are priced from $13.95 for sautéed chicken livers with herb sauce and mushrooms to $21 for broiled lamb chops. They include chicken prepared four ways, and such classics as duckling bigarade, veal marsala, coquilles St. Jacques and tournedos bordelaise. Southern pecan pie and baba au rhum are featured desserts.

Many of the appetizers and desserts are available at lunch, along with sandwiches, salad plates and entrées from $6.95 to $11.95 for items like chicken fricassee on toast, Spanish omelet and shrimp curry.

Lunch, Tuesday-Friday 11:30 to 1:30; dinner, Tuesday-Sunday 5 to 9.

The Cobble Cafe, 27 Spring St., Williamstown. (413) 458-5930.

Three meals a day are offered in this colorful storefront operation by chef Ned Smith, formerly of the Orchards, and his twin brother Sandy, who used to cook in New York and on private yachts. They're partners with local liquor-store owner Gerard Smith, no relation.

Walls hung with contemporary art and a rear wall checkered in black and white are the backdrop for tables dressed in white and teal green.

The prices are modest and the fare interesting. For dinner ($12 to $16.50), how about salmon au poivre on fennel with orange segments, seared tuna with wasabi and pickled ginger, sautéed chicken with mole sauce and roasted poblano pepper, Jamaican jerk chicken with grilled bananas on mesclun greens, or filet mignon flamed with port and shiitake mushrooms?

Appetizers ($3.75 to $6) include soft-shell crab with diablo sauce, pâté du jour and cold poached shrimp on jicama with cilantro-lime vinaigrette. Among homemade desserts are apple crisp, chocolate decadence, linzer torte and cheesecake.

The lunch menu yields interesting salads (smoked trout, grilled tuna, hummus and tabbouleh), sandwiches (the Cobblewich teams grilled eggplant with tomato, goat cheese and basil) and main dishes like chicken quesadilla, chicken gumbo filé in puff pastry and vegetable burrito, $4.50 to $6.

French almond toast, pecan pancakes and breakfast burrito are among the morning offerings, but we'd splurge for eggs Edward (with smoked trout, crème fraîche and chives in puff pastry, $5.95).

Gerard oversees the wine list, offering boutique wines and cordials at affordable prices.

Breakfast, Monday-Saturday 7 to 11:30, Sunday 7 to 1; lunch, Monday-Saturday 11:30 to 3; dinner nightly, 5:30 to 10.

Le Jardin, 777 Cold Spring Road, Williamstown. (413) 458-8032.

The two partitioned dining rooms here are country French and quite elegant, with velvet striped seats, white linens and dark napkins placed sideways, hanging lamps with pierced tin panels, white draperies and plants in every window.

German chef Walter Hayn shares billing for the longest tenure in town with Raymond Canales of Le Country (23 years). His menu is classic French, from the onion soup for $4 to the herring in sour cream and escargots bourguignonne ($8). Dinner entrées are priced from $14 for chicken with artichokes and béarnaise sauce to $20 for filet mignon béarnaise. They run the gamut from frog's legs and sole florentine to Long Island duckling, all nicely prepared and many with fine cream sauces.

Desserts tend to be rich, among them death by chocolate, hot fudge sundae, New York cheesecake and pecan pie.

Dinner nightly, 5 to 9 or 10. Closed Thanksgiving to April.

Savories, 123 Water St., Williamstown. (413) 458-2175.

The old River House made way for Savories, a gourmet takeout store that moved from cramped quarters across the street. Chef-owner Scott Avery, a Culinary Institute of American grad who says he has been apprenticing since he was 12, eventually turned his deli operation here into the handsome, country elegant Hearthside Room and began offering live entertainment many nights in summer in the tavern.

Ever the inventive cook, Scott shines in such changing dinner entrées ($10.95 to $18.95) as broiled swordfish with salsa cruda, baked Idaho trout stuffed with shrimp and asparagus, gingered chicken, veal scaloppine with shiitake mushrooms and port-wine sauce, grilled lamb chops with homemade mint sauce, and grilled New York sirloin steak with blue cheese and bacon. Pasta-lovers go for his penne tossed in a light tomato-vodka cream sauce.

Among starters ($4.95 to $6.95) are blue cheese and ale melt on baguette slices with tomato and bacon, wild mushroom stew on polenta with onions and sundried tomatoes, and smoked trout with cherry chutney and horseradish sauce.

Desserts are a forte of this versatile chef, whose takeout pastry list includes three-berry pie, lemon zingers, double fudge brownies and raspberry squares. "I have 1,500 cakes in my repertoire," says Scott. One is called the "Williams torte" because the lemon cake and blueberry filling represent the college's yellow and purple colors. Another is a chocolate layer cake with chambord mousse filling. His frozen cointreau mousse is enveloped in a meringue swan with a sauce of three berries.

Focaccia pizza, chicken caesar salad and grilled shrimp on bruschetta are samples of the tavern menu.

Dinner, Tuesday-Sunday 5 to 10, tavern from 4.

Robin's, Spring and Lathrop Streets, Williamstown. (413) 458-4489.

A California chef who moved east when her husband joined the Williams College faculty, Robin MacDonald started with a catering business here before opening her dream restaurant in a house at the foot of Spring Street. She is known for innovative

Innovative Mediterranean-style fare is featured at Robin's.

Mediterranean-style fare and recently expanded into the adjacent barber shop for more space.

Although it receives generally good reviews, the place did not meet expectations when we stopped for a Columbus Day lunch. After an interminable wait in the coffee/tableware area that doubled as a holding tank, we finally were seated in one of the two small dining rooms. There was a slice of lemon in the carafe of ice water, a good sign, but the cutlery was so small and wimpy we felt as if we were eating with plastic. We ordered the carrot-ginger soup (which had sold out) and settled for focaccia topped with sausage, tomato and cheese (a pizza-like spread so ample that half went home for lunch the next day) and the smoked Asian chicken salad with sesame soy noodles (a small portion that was niggardly in terms of chicken). Nonetheless, we would return at a slower time to sample more of Robin's lunchtime fare ($7.25 to $8.50), which ranges from an awesome vegetarian chili baked in a loaf of bread and topped with Monterey jack cheese to a duck liver pâté hero (submarine sandwich) with lettuce, tomatoes, caramelized onions and green peppercorn mayonnaise.

Some of the lunch items turn up on the changing dinner menu, which emphasizes locally raised food and organic produce. Main courses run from $16 for roast garlic chicken with balsamic vinegar and fresh herbs to $22.50 for grilled ribeye steak with green peppercorn sauce. The rainbow trout roasted with oranges, lemons and herbs and the lobster ravioli with pesto, cream and tomatoes come highly rated.

Desserts include a dynamite lemon tart, chocolate torte, blueberry shortcake, banana cheesecake and apple-raspberry-almond crumb cake.

Interesting local art adorns the walls, white butcher paper covers the tablecloths and an energetic staff scurries back and forth through the holding tank from kitchen to table. A side deck allows outdoor dining in season beneath three stately white pine trees growing through the floor.

Open daily, 11 to 11; Sunday, 8 to 8; shorter hours in winter.

Hobson's Choice, 159 Water St., Williamstown. (413) 458-9101.

This country-rustic place with paneled walls and beamed ceilings is a favorite of locals. Old tools hang on the walls, Tiffany-type lamps top tables and booths, and there are a few stools at the bar in back of the room. Around the front door are wonderful panes of stained glass with flowers and birds therein.

Chef Dan Campbell, who moved from Montana to join owner Todd Ruthven in the venture, added a Western accent to the cuisine. The dinner menu offers handcut steaks, prime rib, chicken Santa Fe, cajun shrimp, grilled or blackened Norwegian salmon and tuna, from $10 to $17. Or you can make a meal out of chopped sirloin and the salad bar, which is known for its organic produce, for $9.95. Start with shrimp wontons, sautéed mushrooms or fried calamari. Finish with mud pie, grand marnier fudge parfait or apple strudel.

Variations of the dinner menu are available at lunch time, when you can order a chicken Santa Fe sandwich, a green chile cheeseburger, crab salad or soup and salad bar in the $4 to $7 range.

Lunch, Tuesday-Friday 11:30 to 2; dinner, Tuesday-Sunday 5 to 9:30.

Diversions

Williamstown's scenic beauty is apparent on all sides, but less known is the composite of its art and history collections. You get a hint of both on arrival simply by traversing Main Street from the green at Route 7. The hilly street with broad lawns leading to wide-apart historic homes, imposing college buildings and churches is more scenic and tranquil than the main street of any college town we know.

Art and history are best appreciated when viewed close up, away from the crowded settings of the huge museums. As Connoisseur magazine reported, this intimacy is "the great gift" of Williamstown.

Williams College Museum of Art, Main Street, 597-2429. A $4.5 million extension to its original octagonal building in Lawrence Hall makes this museum a sleeper in art circles. Itself a work of art, it contains an 1846 neoclassical rotunda with "ironic" columns that are decorative rather than functional. The eight sides of the rotunda are repeated in soaring newer galleries with skylights, some of their walls hung with spectacular wall art. Once headed by Guggenheim director Thomas Krens, the museum houses fourteen galleries and a staggering 10,000 works, from 3,000-year-old Assyrian stone reliefs to the last self-portrait by Andy Warhol. In an effort to complement the better-known Sterling and Francine Clark Art Institute's strengths in the 19th century, this museum stresses contemporary, 17th- and 18th-century American art and rare Asian art. It features traveling and special exhibitions rivaling those of many a metropolitan museum; Wallworks by Sol LeWitt brightened the three-story entrance atrium at one of our visits. Open Tuesday-Saturday 10 to 5, Sunday 1 to 5. Free.

Nearby is the **Hopkins Observatory,** the oldest working observatory in the United States (1836), offering exhibits on the history of astronomy plus planetarium shows and viewings through college telescopes.

Chapin Library, Stetson Hall, Williams College, 597-2462. Nowhere else are the founding documents of the country – original printings of the Declaration of Independence, the Articles of Confederation, the Bill of Rights and drafts of the Constitution – displayed together in a simple glass case on the second floor of a college hall. This remarkable library contains more than 30,000 rare books, first editions and manuscripts. You might ask to see James Madison's copy of Thomas Paine's *Common Sense.* One floor below is the Williamsiana Collection of town and gown, while the lowest level of Stetson contains the archives of band leader Paul Whiteman, with 3,500 original scores and a complete library of music of the 1920s. Open Monday-Friday, 9 to noon and 1 to 5. Free.

Williamstown Theatre Festival, Adams Memorial Theater, Williams College, 597-

3400. Founded in 1955 (the year of the Clark Art Institute opening), the professional summer festival presents "some of the most ambitious theatre the U.S. has to offer," in the words of the Christian Science Monitor. Such luminaries as Christopher Reeve, Dick Cavett, Edward Herrmann and Marsha Mason return summer after summer to the festival they call home for productions of everything from Chekhov and Ibsen to Tennessee Williams and Broadway tryouts, all the while mingling with the townspeople. The festival uses the theater's main stage, but also includes the smaller Other Stage, emphasizing newer works in the 96-seat Extension added in 1982 to the same building. Leads from the main stage often join the festival's Caberet, which presents late-night revues at area restaurants. Festival performances Tuesday-Saturday, late June through August.

Williams College. Besides the aforementioned highlights, the campus as a whole is worth exploring. Its 50 buildings, predominantly in red brick and gray granite, range through almost every period of American architecture. The lawns and plantings and sense of nature all around contribute to a pleasant walking tour.

Nature. The prime spot – as well as the area's dominant feature – is the **Mount Greylock State Reservation,** a series of seven peaks with a 3,491-foot summit that is the highest in Massachusetts. You can drive, hike or bike to the summit for a spectacular five-state view. Other memorable views are obtained by driving the Taconic Trail through Petersburg Pass and the Mohawk Trail above North Adams. The 2,000-acre **Hopkins Memorial Forest** northwest of the campus is an experimental forest operated by the Williams College Center for Environmental Studies, with nature and cross-country trails, plus the Barn Museum showing old photographs, farm machinery, implements and tools, and the Buxton Gardens, a farm garden designed to have certain flowers in bloom at all times. Williams College also has acquired **Mount Hope Park,** a former estate with extensive gardens and grounds.

Recreation. Golf is the seasonal pastime at the Taconic Golf Club, on the south edge of town and ranked as one of the tops in New England, and at Waubeeka Golf Links in the valley at South Williamstown. In summer, you can swim in the 74-degree waters of Sand Springs Pool and Spa, founded in 1813 and the oldest springs resort still in operation in the country. In winter, there's skiing nearby at Jiminy Peak and Brodie Mountain ski resorts.

Shopping. The college-community stores are generally along Spring Street, which runs south off Main Street opposite the main campus between such campus appendages as museum, science center and sports complex. The **House of Walsh** is an institution for traditional clothing. Try the **Clarksburg Bread Co.** for chunky cheddar cheese bread or an oatmeal-cranberry scone. More than 40 varieties of coffees and 25 of loose teas are available at **Cold Spring Coffee Roasters.** The Library **Antiques** shows dhurrie rugs, English country pine furniture, linens, china and more. It also purveys ice cream, coffee and snacks from an old soda fountain called **2¢ Plain.**

Water Street, a parallel street that blossomed later, has distinctive shops including the **Cottage** gift shop and outdoors equipment at the **Mountain Goat.** We always stop at the **Potter's Wheel,** an outstanding shop with stoneware, porcelain, glass, prints, woods, fibers and jewelry by top craftsmen, and once came out with a nifty little acrylic sheep to hang in our dining-room window.

For foodies, the most interesting shopping of all may be at **The Store at Five Corners,** an 18th-century general store gone decidedly upscale, just south of Williamstown at the junction of Routes 7 and 43. Ex-New Yorkers Stuart Shatken and his wife Andy seek out the unusual as they stock their store with one-of-a-kind items. Expect to find things like Epicurean spices, Mendocino pastas, interesting wines, gifts, Italian biscotti and homemade fudge along with an espresso bar, baked goods from the store's bakery,

Neoclassical white marble temple houses Sterling and Francine Clark Art Institute.

"real NYC bagels," and an assortment of breakfast and lunch items from the deli. There are tables upon which to enjoy, inside or out.

Extra-Special _____

Sterling and Francine Clark Art Institute, 225 South St., Williamstown. (413) 458- 9545.

The most widely known of the town's museums chanced upon its Williamstown location through an old family connection with Williams College and the fact that eccentric collector Sterling Clark, heir to the Singer sewing machine fortune, wanted his treasures housed far from a potential site of nuclear attack. Clark's neoclassical white marble temple opened in 1955 (he and his wife are buried under its front steps) and was expanded in 1973 by a red granite addition housing more galleries and one of the nation's outstanding art research libraries. The Clark's major strength lies in its holdings of French 19th-century paintings, English silver, prints and drawings (the Clark was the single largest source for the Renoir exhibition at Boston's Museum of Fine Arts in 1985-86). Shown mostly in small galleries the size of the rooms in which they once hung, the highly personalized collection of Monets, Turners and Winslow Homers quietly vies for attention with sculptures, porcelain and three centuries worth of silver (Sterling Clark liked good food and the silverware to go with it). All this is amid an austere yet intimate setting of potted plants and vases of dried flowers, furniture and benches for relaxation. Amazingly, it's all free. Open Tuesday-Sunday and Monday holidays, 10 to 5.

Blantyre is a Tudor-style replica of a castle in Scotland.

Lenox, Mass.
The Good (and Cultured) Life

The gentle beauty of the Berkshires has attracted generations of artists, authors and musicians – as well as their patrons who appreciate the good life. At the center of the Berkshires in both location and spirit is Lenox, a small village whose cultural influence far exceeds its size.

In the 19th century, Lenox was home for Nathaniel Hawthorne, Edith Wharton, Henry Ward Beecher and Fannie Kemble. Herman Melville, Henry Adams, Oliver Wendell Holmes, Henry Wadsworth Longfellow, William Cullen Bryant, Daniel Chester French and (later) Norman Rockwell lived and worked nearby.

Such was the allure of this tranquil mountain and lake country that many prominent Americans built palatial homes here. Lenox became "the inland Newport" for such families as Westinghouse, Carnegie, Procter, Morgan and Vanderbilt. Indeed, some of America's 400 summered in Newport and spent the early autumn in the Berkshires.

The artists and the affluent helped make Lenox in the 20th century a center for the arts. Tanglewood, across from Hawthorne's home, is the summer home of the Boston Symphony Orchestra. Edith Wharton's Mount is the stage for Shakespeare & Company. Nearby are the Lenox Arts Center, the Berkshire Theater Festival, Jacob's Pillow Dance Festival and the Aston Magna Festival concerts. Lenox is now the home of the National Music Foundation, whose mission is to build a National Music Center there.

The Lenox area's cultural attractions are well known. Less so are some of its hidden treats: the picturesque Stockbridge Bowl (a lake), the Walker sculpture garden, the

Pleasant Valley wildlife sanctuary, the Church on the Hill, and the mansions along Kemble and Cliffwood streets.

Attractions of a more specialized nature are offered at the Kripalu Center for Yoga and Health and at Canyon Ranch in the Berkshires.

Staying in some of Lenox's inns is like being a house guest in a mansion. Besides lodging in style, visitors may dine at some of New England's fanciest restaurants and enjoy $72 orchestra seats in the Shed at Tanglewood. The budget-conscious can find more reasonable places in which to stay and eat, and, while picnicking on the Tanglewood lawn, can hear the BSO almost as well as those in the Shed.

Except perhaps for the prices, the many charms of Lenox appeal to almost everyone.

Inn Spots

Most Lenox inns require a minimum stay of three nights on summer weekends, and weekend prices usually extend from Thursday through Sunday. Rates quoted here are for weekends in peak season. They may be much lower for weekdays, and vary by the season. Two-night minimums on weekends are often the rule year-round.

Blantyre, 16 Blantyre Road, Box 995, Lenox 01240. (413) 637-3556 or 298-3806 (November-April).

This rambling, Tudor-style brick manor off by itself on 85 private acres was built in 1902 as a summer retreat for a millionaire in the turpentine business. A replica of the Hall of Blantyre in Scotland, it used to be called Blantyre Castle, and was a memorable place for dining in the baronial style. Today, "castle" has been dropped from the name, but the feeling remains in lodging as well as in dining (see Dining Spots).

In 1981, the structure was carefully restored even to the insides of the huge closets by owner Jane Fitzpatrick, whose Red Lion Inn in adjacent Stockbridge has welcomed guests in the old New England tradition for so many years. The result is worthy of a castle, or at the very least an English country-house hotel, says general manager Roderick Anderson with his trace of Scottish accent: a majestic foyer with staircase of black oak, public rooms with high beamed ceilings, rich and intricate carved paneling, crystal chandeliers and fireplaces with hand-carved mantels, and eight elegant suites and guest rooms, five with fireplaces.

The ultra-deluxe Paterson Suite ($585 a night) contains a fireplaced living room with a crystal chandelier, a large bedroom with kingsize bed and two full bathrooms. Victorian-style sofas and chairs make comfortable sitting areas at the foot of the ornate

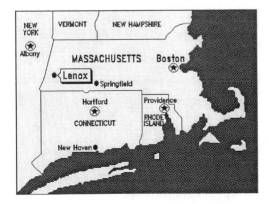

queensize four-poster beds in the Laurel and Cranwell suites. Even the smallest Bouquet and Ribbon rooms are fit for would-be barons and baronesses, if only for a night or two.

A typical bathroom has terrycloth robes and piles of towels, a scale, a wooden valet, heated towel racks, embroidered curtains and at least ten kinds of soaps and assorted toiletries.

Twelve rooms in more contemporary style, several of them

split-level loft suites, are available in the carriage house. They were totally renovated in 1994, down to the handpainted tiles and marble floors of their sparkling bathrooms. All have decks or balconies and wet bars. There also are three cottages, two with kitchenettes and one a simple little affair – a comparative steal at $175 a night.

Four tennis courts (whites required), a swimming pool, jacuzzi, sauna and competition bent-grass croquet lawns are available on the property.

Fruit, cheese and mineral water await guests on arrival. Cocktails and after-dinner coffee and cordials are served in the main foyer and the crystal-chandeliered music room. "Proper evening dress" is required in the house after 6 p.m., Blantyre advises.

A complimentary continental breakfast is served in the breakfast room or on the terrace.

Guests, for whom price is no object, are pampered within an inch of their lives. Blantyre was the first American hotel to win the coveted International Welcome Award from the prestigious Relais & Châteaux association. It also is the top-rated inn and resort in New England in the Zagat hotel survey. Guests don't mince words in the oversize guest book in the entry hall. Many write simply: "Perfection."

Doubles, $245 to $400; suites, $300 to $585. Closed November-April.

Cliffwood Inn, 25 Cliffwood St., Lenox 01240. (413) 637-3330.

A magnificent classic Colonial built in Stanford White style about 1890 by the then-ambassador to France, this is almost a stage set for the furnishings of innkeepers Joy and Scottie Farrelly, acquired during their periods of residence in Paris, Brussels, Italy and Montreal when he was with Ralston Purina Co. Among them are 24 pieces of fine Eldred Wheeler antique reproduction furniture, which are scattered through the house and available for purchase.

The three-story mansion has ten working fireplaces, one of them in the bathroom off a third-floor guest room.

A large foyer gives access to all three main-floor public rooms, each of which has French doors opening to the full-length back porch overlooking a swimming pool and a gazebo. At one end of the house is a living room with twelve-foot-high mirrors and a white marble fireplace. The music room in the center leads to the formal dining room, which has a dark green marble fireplace.

Upstairs are seven air-conditioned guest rooms, all with private baths and six with working fireplaces. Each is named for one of the Farrellys' ancestors (a scrapbook describing the particular one is at the foot of each bed, and it turns out they were an illustrious lot). The Walker-Linton Suite, with a sitting room fashioned from a former

Cliffwood Inn is classic Colonial built about 1890 by an ambassdor to France.

Lenox inns are known for sumptuous dining facilities, like this breakfast room at The Gables.

bedroom, has a step-up four-poster bed. A Victorian loveseat faces the fireplace in the Helen Walker Room, pretty in pink, white and rose. The Nathaniel Foote Room on the third floor comes with a canopied queensize Sheraton field bed and side tables, two wing chairs in front of the fireplace, a plush armchair in the window corner and no fewer than four oriental rugs, one from Saudi Arabia. A gaily painted lunch pail is a decorative accent in one room, and Joy has crafted folk-art boxes for Kleenex in the others. You'll be intrigued by her many ingenious decorating touches.

In the early evening, the Farrellys put out wine and hors d'oeuvre, perhaps salmon mousse, marinated olives and hot artichoke dip. Joy occasionally offers "dinners in a party atmosphere" in the spring.

For what they call a "copious continental breakfast," the Farrellys serve a renowned fruit compote and baked apples with nuts and crème fraîche, homemade yogurt, granola, muffins and cornbread. At our latest visit, they were about to acquire an AGA cooker and were thinking of adding egg dishes. The meal is served in the paneled dining room with tapestried, high-back chairs or on the back porch.

Doubles, $100 to $200. No credit cards. No smoking.

The Gables Inn, 103 Walker St., Lenox 01240. (413) 637-3416.

Edith Wharton made this her home at the turn of the century while she was building her permanent edifice, the Mount. Her upstairs room is one of the most attractive at this restaurant-turned-inn. Ask innkeeper Frank Newton to show you the famous eight-sided library where she once wrote some of her short stories.

The nineteen guest rooms and suites, all with private baths, are full of verve and Victorian warmth. The Jockey Club Suite offers a brass bed in a niche, an ample sitting area with two sofas facing a big-screen TV, and a private entrance from the back-yard pool area. Also in demand are two large second-floor suites built out over a former roof. Both have cathedral ceilings, high windows, swagged draperies, fireplaces and TVs. One, the Teddy Wharton, is masculine in hunter green and mauve. It contains a leather sofa, two wing chairs and a carved bas relief of Shakespeare in the bedstead.

More feminine in pink and teal floral prints is the Edith Wharton Suite with a four-poster bed and Gibson Girl prints on the walls.

We like the Show Business Room, full of signed photos of old stars and a library of showbiz volumes, with which to curl up on the chintz loveseat in front of the fireplace. The Presidents' Room is aptly named, with lots of memorabilia and memoirs, including a long handwritten letter from Michael Dukakis thanking the Newtons for their hospitality after he was stranded here when his car broke down following a Tanglewood concert in 1989.

Frank, a former banker and sometime pianist, writes and produces summertime shows featuring name entertainers at the Lenox Town Hall Theater. His wife Mary conducts quilting seminars and takes in guests down the street in the home they restored in 1992, built by a cousin of Edith Wharton and called **The Summer White House.** Here, Mary "really fusses" as she pampers overnight guests in six spacious bedrooms with private baths and prepares fancy continental breakfasts. "This is our home," she says, "and we treat everyone here as our house guests."

The Newtons first operated the Gables as a restaurant before converting their banquet hall into lodging and making theirs "a special inn." That explains the spectacular breakfast room, with one long table in the center and, along the sides, six round tables for two skirted in pink, green and white. Full breakfasts are served. French toast, pancakes, waffles or eggs are typical fare, supplemented by sour-cream cake, bran muffins and pumpkin, lemon-almond and banana breads.

In the back yard are a tennis court and an enclosed, solar-heated swimming pool with a jacuzzi.

"We like to be hosts and to enjoy our guests," says Frank. That they do very well.

Doubles, $80 to $150; suites, $195. Summer White House, $150 to $165, July and August only.

Garden Gables Inn, 135 Main St., Box 52, Lenox 01240. (413) 637-0193.

What a difference a change of ownership and a few years can make! The woman who had run this triple-gabled house as a homey little inn since 1951 retired in 1988 and sold to Mario and Lynn Mekinda, an energetic couple with two then-teenagers from Toronto. Mario, an engineer who says he loves to tinker and fix things, has done wonders in renovating the main structure and undertaking major expansion projects, including an attached house behind for their family quarters. The returning visitor from a decade ago scarcely would recognize the place.

First, Mario added private baths for each of the eleven original guest rooms. Some rooms remain rather small, but are cozy and clean. All have been pleasantly redecorated by Lynn with attractive comforters and floral wallpapers. All but three now have queensize beds, and a corner room has the first of eight new fireplaces. All rooms are equipped with telephones and small clock-radios.

The most dramatic changes result from new construction. Two new suites have been added above the inn's expanded dining room. They offer hexagonal cathedral ceilings, corner fireplaces, whirlpool baths, kingsize canopy beds, sitting areas and sliding doors onto private balconies. "Everything people ask for we've got in these suites," says Mario. Also popular is a rear bedroom on the main floor containing a kingsize bed with a solid Germanic-looking headboard, a private deck and a large bathroom with jacuzzi.

The latest additions are four deluxe, light and airy units in a new detached front cottage, which continues the gabled-dormer theme of the other buildings. Here you'll find more cathedral ceilings, fireplaces, air-conditioning, cable TV/VCR and queensize Eldred Wheeler canopy beds.

The former innkeeper's gift shop has been transformed into a charming dining room,

Dramatic renovations and expansion have upgraded Garden Gables Inn.

which has been expanded by opening onto a new wraparound screened porch. A buffet breakfast of juice, fruit, cereal, yogurt, homemade pastries and things like hard-boiled eggs, sausages, smoked salmon and quiches is served.

The Mekindas have totally redone the cozy entry parlor and the larger living room, which has a TV/VCR and a Steinway baby grand.

A 72-foot-long swimming pool and prolific gardens also are attractions at this verdant, five-acre oasis set well back from the road in the heart of Lenox.

Doubles, $110 to $165; suites and cottages, $195.

The Birchwood Inn, 7 Hubbard St., Lenox 01240. (413) 637-2600 or (800) 524-1646.

The sophisticated tastes, food and travel magazines, accessories and collections of owners Joan and Dick Toner have upgraded this lovely inn, listed on the National Register and dating to 1767 when it was the site of Lenox's first town meeting. Their purchase was inspired by son Dan, a Cornell hotel graduate who had worked for the Marriott and Sheraton chains. "He got us interested," said Joan, as her husband, an Air Force brigadier general, was looking for something to do in retirement. "We love to travel and to entertain." With Dan helping run the inn, they have time for both.

The Toners have repainted the exterior and restored the gardens of their hilltop property across from Lenox's landmark Church on the Hill. Inside, they have spruced up the ten comfortable guest rooms with designer towels, linens and pillows, joined twin beds to make them kingsize and added oriental decorative accents here and there. All but two rooms have private baths, most quite large since they were fashioned from former maid's quarters. Most bedrooms also are large, one in the front corner containing a canopy queen four-poster bed, two plush chairs and a settee for reading. Some have oriental rugs and fireplaces, three have TV and all contain telephones. Old hat pins stuck into an oversize pin cushion make a striking decorative accent in a rear room. There's a teddy bear's picnic in the window of a third-floor hallway, part of an assortment Joan started collecting for her grandchildren "and then I couldn't bear parting with all of them." Two suites with kitchen facilities are available in a rear carriage house.

Food and travel magazines are displayed in every room from the Toners' complete sets that are stocked in the enormous sunken living room, where walls of books are available for the borrowing. There are two separate seating arrangements here, one in front of the fireplace, as well as window seats along an outside wall. The Toners have hung in the living room a remarkable rendering of Strasbourg, which looks like a painting but turns out to have been done totally in different kinds of wood by Europe's foremost practitioner of wood marquetry. Another cozy parlor with a TV set leads into the large dining room, where Hitchcock chairs are at five tables set with woven cloths and coffee mugs bearing the inn's logo.

Breakfast starts with a buffet of fruit, juice, cereals, homemade breads and muffins. The main course, posted by the week on a blackboard, might be tarte d'Alsace, ham and cheese omelet, eggs benedict or cranberry pancakes. Tea, wine and cheese are served in the afternoon, taken seasonally on a wide front porch outfitted in wicker.

Doubles, $95 to $195. No smoking.

Walker House, 74 Walker St., Lenox 01240. (413) 637-1271 or (800) 235-3098.

It's clear that ex-Californians Peggy and Richard Houdek, who opened this B&B fifteen years ago in the heart of Lenox, like music. A pecan Kimball grand piano in the living room is used for recitals and singalongs, a pump organ is in the front hall and the guest rooms are named for composers, with appropriate memorabilia of the person and the period in each. Dick Houdek was a music critic and Peggy in administration at the San Francisco Opera, which is where they met.

It's clear also that the Houdeks like flowers, which are in profusion everywhere, inside and out, and cats (they have seven live ones and uncounted inanimate replicas in the form of pictures, pillows and the like). We coveted the poster in the dining room picturing three earnest-looking cats with the message, "we don't want you to smoke."

The result is an engaging clutter that shows the public rooms are clearly meant to be used. Ditto for the screened side porch and the wide rear veranda looking onto a landscaped yard and three acres of woods in back.

All eight guest rooms in the house, built in 1804 as the Walker Rockwell House, come with private baths and five with working fireplaces. Some have clawfoot tubs, most have hooked rugs and comforters, and several have canopied beds with high oak headboards. The Verdi room with its wild green and white wallpaper, white iron bedsteads and wicker furniture is in airy contrast to the dark colors and period wallpapers in most of the rooms. The Puccini room downstairs has rose walls, queen iron canopy bed, modern bathroom, fireplace and its own little porch.

Guests watch foreign films, operas, concerts and special events like the Olympics in the inn's Library Video Theater with a stereophonic sound system and a giant 100-inch screen. They also keep a running commentary on local dining experiences in an informative guest book. Tea is offered in the afternoon, and a half liter of wine awaits in each guest room.

Continental breakfast of fresh fruit or baked apples, assorted cereals, muffins and croissants is served in the dining room, where a stuffed tiger, lion, bear and cat are seated at one table, and on warm mornings on the back porch. The welcoming aroma of spices fills the room day and night. More than 100 mugs with all kinds of logos on them are hung on a wall. If you're late for breakfast, Peggy advises guests, your cup may be from Cleveland or Fargo, N.D.

Doubles, $100 to $180.

Brook Farm Inn, 15 Hawthorne St., Lenox 01240. (413) 637-3013 or (800) 285-7638.

This would be just another charming inn, were it not for the former owners' bent for literature and music. "There is poetry here," says the stylish cover of their brochure, and indeed there is.

You'll find it in each of the twelve guest rooms as well as in the front parlor, where there are shelves full of poetry volumes, tape recorders and a collection of poetry tapes. The poetry tradition has continued under new owners Joe and Anne Miller, New

The Birchwood Inn occupies hilltop across from landmark Church on the Hill.

Jersey transplants who had never heard of Lenox – "we must have been living under a rock," quips Anne – until they arrived on an inn-seeking trip, walked in the door of Brook Farm Inn and decided this was the one.

Fortunately, the Millers have taken to poetry, and Anne says her contractor-husband has turned into "quite a reader." As did his predecessor, in the morning he types out a poem of the day to display on the lectern. He does a poetry reading every Saturday at tea time, when guests enjoy his wife's scones, and sponsors a writing seminar every spring. Such is to be expected from an inn that takes its name from the mid-19th-century Brook Farm literary commune in West Roxbury, Mass.

The Millers also have upgraded seven of the inn's twelve guest rooms, starting with those that needed enhancement the most. The results show throughout, from the pretty sand-colored facade with green shutters and cream trim to the new bridal suite, where white sheer fabric is draped around the canopied queen bed and guests enjoy two wing chairs beside the fireplace. That is one of two front rooms that the Millers gutted to redo into their premium lodgings, right down to the enlarged bathrooms and "new everything," in Anne's words. All guest rooms have private baths, handsome furnishings and, of course, good reading lights on the bed headboards. Some include fireplaces, colorful stained-glass windows and skylights.

There is more than intellectual nourishment at Brook Farm. A hearty breakfast could include cheese strata or french toast casserole topped with fruit after preliminaries of sliced fruit, homemade granola and assorted pastries. Each bedroom contains a decanter of sherry from Joe's special blend.

Guests also enjoy a heated swimming pool and lovely gardens in back.

Doubles, $105 to $170. No smoking.

Underledge, 106 Cliffwood St., Lenox 01240. (413) 637-0236.

A large white house with corner turret and solarium atop a hill some distance out Cliffwood Street, known to Lenox residents as *the* street but one often missed by tourists, this estate built in 1900 by two sisters was converted into an inn in 1982 by Marcie Lanoue, her carpenter son Tom and her daughter Cheryl.

All nine air-conditioned guest rooms and suites have private baths and are of such size to warrant their description as "parlor bedrooms." Five bedrooms have fireplaces, and all have sofas and loveseats that make for comfortable relaxing. Marcie did the stenciling that enhances a couple of third-floor rooms, one an enormous bathroom converted from a former bedroom. A second-floor beauty has a kingsize bed, fireplace and a private balcony. We're partial to the large room off the stairway landing to the second floor, with its fireplace framed in oak, two loveseats, a kingsize brass bedstead and a pleasant porch. One summery room on the main floor with a kingsize bed, chintz sofa, fireplace and a large walk-in shower is converted to a breakfast room in winter.

The entry foyer is richly paneled in stained oak. Contemporary off-white sofas surround the fireplace just off the lobby. In the living room are television, stereo, a grand piano and games. A continental breakfast, including muffins made by Cheryl, is served in the solarium in season.

Doubles, $140 to $175.

Applegate Bed & Breakfast, 279 West Park St., RR 1, Box 576, Lee 01238. (413) 243-4451.

Just across the Lenox town line is this sparkling white Georgian Colonial with a pillared porte cochere. It was built by a New York surgeon in the 1920s as a weekend retreat and now is one of the area's more inviting B&Bs. Applegate is set nicely back from the road on six tranquil acres bearing venerable apple trees, towering pines, flower gardens and a beckoning swimming pool. Inside are elegant common rooms, six guest rooms with private baths and an effervescent welcome by Nancy and Rick Cannata, she an airline flight attendant and he a pilot, who decided to alight here in 1990 and convert their large home into a B&B. They plan their flight schedules so at least one of them is always on hand.

Off a grand entry foyer are a fireplaced dining room, where three tables are each set for breakfast for four, and an uncommonly large living room equipped with a grand piano. To the side of the living room is a sun porch, newly enclosed for use as a reading and TV room. Off the dining room is a screened back porch facing the pool and gardens.

Porte cochere at Applegate.

A carved staircase leads to the four main guest rooms, one the master suite with a kingsize poster bed, family photos on the mantel above the working fireplace, a sitting area with a sofabed and two chairs, and a great steam shower. The other rooms are slightly less grand in scale, holding queensize beds. One has Shaker-style pine furniture, another a walnut sleigh bed and a third an antique white iron bed and white and blue wicker furnishings. Two newer rooms are situated in a far wing of the house. One is a sunny corner space swathed in pale lavenders and greens with a tiger-maple four-poster, a sitting area and the best view of the grounds. The other is a smaller room done up in Victorian style with an antique bed and matching marble-topped dresser and a hat rack holding an opera cape and granny hats. A rear carriage house has been renovated into a two-bedroom, condo-style apartment, available for $330 a night, three-night minimum.

Godiva chocolates and decanters of brandy are in each room. The Cannatas offer wine and cheese around 5 p.m. The continental-plus breakfast, including cereal and yogurt, is served amid stemware and antique cups and saucers.

Doubles, $120 to $225. Smoking restricted.

Amadeus House, 15 Cliffwood St., Lenox 01240. (413) 637-4770 or (800) 205-4770.

Music is the theme and in the air at this new B&B, nicely restored in 1993 by classical music buffs John Felton, an ex-Midwestern newspaper reporter and former deputy foreign editor of National Public Radio, and his wife Marty Gottron, a freelance editor. With a renovation crew of fifteen, they breezed through the former seasonal tourist home in ten weeks, repainting every inch inside and out. The result is eight varied accommodations, from the deluxe ground-floor Mozart Room to two small bedrooms that share a bath to a two-bedroom apartment rented by the week.

Some would say the heart of the house is the cozy parlor/music room. It harbors a collection of 500 classical CDs that are played throughout the day, and the walls are hung with musical posters. Others gravitate to the larger dining room with brick wall and cast-iron stove, which opens into a country kitchen. Here is where three tables are set for breakfast – perhaps mushroom quiche, frittata with seasonal vegetables, orange waffles, omelets or honey-baked french toast with honey syrup. The tables are used for games or puzzles at night.

Guests are housed in style in the Mozart Room, with an Eldred Wheeler queensize tiger maple bed, a wicker sitting area facing the wood stove in the fireplace and a private porch. Also popular are the spacious rooms with queensize beds and private baths on the second floor, the Brahms Room in back with a wicker sofa and two rockers, and the Bach in front with an extra twin bed and two rockers. Two mid-size rooms with private baths comprise the "Tanglewood wing." Here, John points out a couple of prized acquisitions: a Japanese Sony record catalog signed by Leonard Bernstein, and a framed album cover signed by Aaron Copland. John bills two small bedrooms sharing a bath in the rear as the best B&B values in Lenox. The third-floor Beethoven Suite offers a full kitchen, two bedrooms with king/twin beds and a small, window-less library/living room in the middle.

Afternoon tea is served on the wraparound porch. Guests also enjoy the flower gardens and a wooded, undeveloped greenbelt in back.

Doubles, $85 to $175. Two-bedroom suite, $800 weekly.

Gateways Inn and Restaurant, 71 Walker St., Lenox 01240. (413) 637-2532.

The landmark white, dark-shuttered mansion, built in 1912 by Harley Procter of Procter & Gamble and said to resemble a cake of Ivory soap, has long been a fixture in Lenox. Renowned chef-innkeeper Gerhard Schmid sold it in 1988 to Queens caterer Vito Perulli, who redecorated the lobby to make it more welcoming.

Architect Stanford White inspired the two leaded windows by the main side entrance and the sweeping central staircase, which upon descending makes you feel as if you're floating into a ballroom. The eight guest rooms with private baths on the second floor are richly furnished in Colonial style with antiques and oriental rugs.

A front corner suite lined with books and containing a couch and two fireplaces was home for Arthur Fiedler during his Boston Pops concerts at Tanglewood. A semi-suite has a pillar in the middle with the bed at an angle, while a third room has heavy furniture carved in Austria. The west corner room harbors an eight-piece bird's-eye maple and black walnut Victorian bedroom set.

A complimentary continental breakfast is served in the dining room, which also houses a restaurant that capitalizes on the reputation of its previous owner.

Recently, Vito converted his home at 174 Main St. into an elegant Victorian B&B called **The Hilltop Inn.** A resident innkeeper oversees five bedrooms and a suite, each with king or queen bed, private bath, fireplace and television. Rates there range from $125 to $295.

Doubles, $165 to $185; Fiedler Suite, $295.

Wheatleigh, Hawthorne Road, Lenox 01240. (413) 637-0610.

People who demand opulence and luxury are partial to this Italian palazzo built in 1893 as a wedding gift for the Countess de Heredia. It's romantic, extravagant, dramatic and ornate.

The imposing (some might say intimidating) entrance of the honey-colored brick building framed in wrought iron leads into a soaring Great Room with a couple of sitting areas, a majestic staircase rising to the second floor, parquet floors and fine art all around. For its centennial year in 1993, owners Susan and Linwood Simon redecorated most of the establishment, "bringing in antiques we've been collecting for years," in Susan's words. Window treatments now match the fancy partial canopies draped above the beds, and bathrooms sport new tiles and fixtures. All seventeen air-conditioned guest rooms are different. Seven are huge, two merely large, two medium and the rest, frankly, small. Nine have fireplaces and some have terraces or balconies. Each comes with a telephone, but no TV.

Susan's aim was to be "true to the period of the house and its architectural style" (it took her five years to find the right pattern of English axminster, for the carpeting in the halls). The period can be austere; some guests think the rooms could use more furnishings and more of a cozy feeling. Having seen all the rooms, we'd urge would-be guests to splurge for the best to avoid disappointment; the small rooms seem claustrophobic in comparison. The exception would be what Wheatleigh considers a last-choice designation called 2NO: a small bedroom with queen bed and a separate sitting room, both quite serviceable for $255 a night. To us it appealed far more than the premium room 2I with, surprise, a crib in one corner and an antique writing desk in another, renting for almost twice the price. Even the best appear dressed for show; we saw no good lights for reading, nor few places one would wish to curl up.

Things were looking up in 1994 under new general manager François Thomas, a suave Parisian who had managed a four-star hotel in Bordeaux. He recognized the negatives of the smallest rooms and planned to improve them. "We can't make them bigger," he conceded, "but we can make them different. Our guests don't want to feel at home – they want a different experience." He vowed to provide caring, four-star service in an establishment that sometimes had come across as aloof.

We'd suggest he start by including breakfast in the deal. Guests paying top dollar don't expect to fork over an extra $8.50 per for continental breakfast or, ordering carefully à la carte, toting up a bill that could easily exceed $40 for two before tax and gratuity.

Of course, big-spending romantics may not care. They have what they want in a large bedroom and a showy, first-class restaurant (see Dining Spots). And outside are the joys of a 22-acre property within walking distance of Tanglewood, a tennis court and a swimming pool hidden away in a sylvan glade.

Doubles, $185 to $495, EP.

Dining Spots

Church Street Cafe, 69 Church St., Lenox. (413) 637-2745.

This is the casual, creative kind of place of which we never tire, the one we keep returning to for a quick but interesting meal whenever we're in Lenox. We're not

alone, for it's generally No. 1 on the list of everyone's favorite eating establishments in town.

Owners Linda Forman and Clayton Hambrick have furnished their small dining rooms and outdoor deck simply but tastefully. On one visit we admired all the amusing paintings of zebras on the walls, part of the changing art exhibits and all for sale. We also like the bar stools painted like black and white cows, udders hanging below, as well as the ficus trees lit with tiny white lights, the white pottery with colorful pink and blue flowers, the flute music playing in the background, and the jaunty outside dining deck. In 1994, the cafe gained more space with the acquisition of the adjacent gallery, where tables for 30 are set amid artworks lit by track lights.

Once Ethel Kennedy's chef, Clayton also

Dining area at Church Street Cafe.

worked in a creole restaurant in Washington and that background shows. Blackened redfish might be a dinner special; Louisiana shrimp and andouille filé gumbo is apt to be a dinner appetizer and a luncheon entrée. Lately, the fare has acquired a Southwest accent, as in an appetizer of Southwestern barbecued duck in a corn pancake with tomatillo salsa and smoked chile cream or a main dish of black bean, smoked corn and green chile quesadilla.

The menu lists six appetizers and about a dozen entrées at dinner. Start with a wild mushroom and roasted garlic sandwich with native greens or a salad of endive, pears, spiced hazelnuts and roasted beets. For entrées ($14.50 to $17.50), consider sautéed Maine crab cakes, pan-seared cod with crispy polenta, roasted pork tenderloin with cider and sage sauce, or cilantro and garlic fettuccine with shrimp, smoked corn, chiles and pumpkin seeds.

Our latest lunch included a super black bean tostada with three salsas and the Church Street salad, a colorful array of goat cheese, chick peas, sprouts, eggs and red pepper, with a zippy dijon vinaigrette dressing on the side and whole wheat sunflower seed rolls, so good that we accepted seconds. Prices are $7.25 to $8.95.

Among desserts, the chilled cranberry soufflé topped with whipped cream, the apple walnut crisp and the chocolate macadamia nut torte are superior.

Lunch, Monday-Saturday 11 to 2; dinner nightly, 5:30 to 9; Sunday brunch in summer and fall. Closed Monday and Tuesday in winter. No smoking.

Blantyre, Route 20 and East St., Lenox. (413) 637-3556.

An English country-house hotel setting is the backdrop for the contemporary French cuisine offered by chef David Lawson, who trained with Albert Roux in London before becoming chef at the acclaimed Old Inn on the Green in nearby New Marlborough.

Here, Blantyre general manager Roderick Anderson gave him free rein to develop changing menus reflecting local ingredients and incorporating his "phenomenal grasp of taste and textures." Prix-fixe dinners of three to five courses for $65 are offered to house guests and the public in the formal dining room and two smaller rooms. The tables are set with different themes, the china and crystal changing frequently as owner Jane Fitzpatrick adds to the collection.

Invited to cook for the James Beard Foundation in New York, David prepared an extravagant New England dinner that culminated in Cape scallops with lobster chunks in phyllo dough and saddle of salt-crusted venison with cèpes, pumpkin gnocchi and wild blueberries. A typical dinner here starts with a "surprise," perhaps foie gras or veal sweetbreads with sauternes and carrot juice. The appetizer could be Maine crab cake with red and yellow pepper sauce or truffled chicken boudin with creamy French lentils and morels; the main course, grilled yellowtail tuna on wilted bitter greens with flageolets and lemon-caviar beurre blanc or roasted tenderloin with mustard crust, morels and root vegetables. Desserts could be a trilogy of three mousses, pumpkin pie with maple-walnut ice cream, pear tarte tatin with warm calvados sauce, cappuccino crème brûlée or cognac parfait with raspberry coulis and pistachio anglaise.

The wine list is exceptionally strong on California chardonnays and cabernets and French regionals, priced up to $220. Most guests take coffee and armagnac in the Music Room, where a harpist and pianist play on weekends.

Lunch on the terrace is à la carte, $8.95 to $22.95.

Lunch, daily except Monday in summer, 12:30 to 2; dinner, Tuesday-Sunday 6 to 9; reservations and jackets required. Closed November-April.

Wheatleigh, Hawthorne Road, Lenox. (413) 637-0610.

New general manager François Thomas from Paris says Americans don't have to fly to France any more for good food. "They have it right here with Peter Platt." François, who arrived on the Lenox scene in 1994 and knows what he's doing, was so impressed with resident chef Peter Platt that he took him to Paris the next spring to demonstrate American cooking – "the first time that's ever happened back there," he said. François, who is adept in the nuances of hotel management, reeled off a number of planned changes in service and atmosphere to make the Wheatleigh experience more approachable. He also scheduled a series of food theme weekends, including one in 1995 featuring truffles for a cool $1,450 a couple.

The food has long been highly rated, thanks to head chef Peter, a Williams College history graduate who's been at Wheatleigh since 1986. He oversees a cooking staff of thirteen, including a Japanese sous chef, a French pastry chef and a Canadian chef who give an international flavor to what Peter describes as "new French classic cuisine."

The chandeliered, high-ceilinged main dining room has been refurbished with Chippendale armchairs imported from England. Round tables are dressed in white linens and adorned with individual vases of exotic flowers. Three tile murals, each weighing 500 pounds, were found in England and put up on the walls; they acquire a luminescent quality in the candlelight.

Dinner here remains as serious as ever. Three five-course tasting menus are prepared each evening – regular ($68), low-fat ($68) and vegetarian ($55). You can pick and choose between them. Or, if the entire table agrees, you can try the dégustation menu to sample a number of preparations for $90. A smaller, à la carte menu ($15.50 to $24) is available seasonally in the Grill Room.

Wheatleigh's kitchen uses exotic ingredients and is said to be labor-intensive. You know why when you see one night's regular offerings: a trio of Maine oysters with golden ossetra caviar, truffle mousseline and mignonette sauce; seared California squab

Wheatleigh and its noted restaurant occupy this Italian palazzo built in 1893.

with Hudson Valley foie gras, French green lentils and savoy cabbage, sautéed Atlantic salmon with ginger fumet and purple-top turnips; roast loin of Texas antelope with wild rice and dried fruit compote, and warm apple tarte tatin with iced sour quenelles.

Owners Susan and Linwood Simon have doubled the size of their wine list, with a number available in half-bottles. "At the high end," says Linwood, "our wines become very reasonable. If you're of a mind to drink Château Lafite, this is the place to do it." François also had in mind adding some wines in the $30 range, a price point conspicuously missing at our last visit.

Dinner nightly, 6 to 9; closed Tuesday in winter. Grill Room, 5 to 9, July and August only.

Cafe Lucia, 90 Church St., Lenox. (413) 637-2640.

Jim Lucie transformed the former Ganesh, which was an art gallery cum cafe, into an expanded cafe with art as a sideline. "We're a restaurant that shows and sells art," explains Jim, who opened up the kitchen so patrons can glimpse the goings-on.

Jim's Italian cuisine is favored by locals, who praise his pasta creations, baked polenta with homemade sausage and Italian codfish stew. The osso buco with diced vegetables and risotto is so good that it draws New Yorkers back annually, and Jim reports he almost had a riot on his hands when he took the linguini and shrimp alla medici off the menu (it was promptly restored, even though he had offered it on specials). Pastas are priced from $11.95 to $17.95 and entrées from $13.95 to $20.95. Lamb stew served over white Tuscan beans with celery, carrots, shallots and escarole appealed at one visit. Another time we were tempted by the mixed grill of pan-seared duck leg and hot Italian sausage, finished with a fig sauce on a bed of braised escarole.

Start with a ragoût of rabbit and wild mushrooms over soft polenta or the antipasto of Monterey chèvre crusted with black peppercorns and parsley, served with roasted garlic, arugula and crostini. Finish with the cold chocolate soufflé cake with almonds and amaretto, frangelico and hazelnut cheesecake, gorgonzola and fresh pears, or a sautéed apple, cinnamon and sour cream pie.

Those desserts, a fine port or brandy and cappuccino can be taken on the flower-bedecked patio on warm summer evenings.

Dinner nightly from 5; closed Sunday and Monday in winter. No smoking.

Zampano's, 579 Pittsfield-Lenox Road, Lenox. (413) 448-8600.

"We can cook" is the slogan under the logo for this hot spot in an inauspicious looking roadhouse. Can they ever.

You can tell just from the salad buffet at one end of the small dining room. Unlike any salad bar we've seen, it puts others to shame. There's a bowl of mixed greens and a few of the predictable toppings, but the rest of the "salad bar" looks like a display case at Dean & DeLuca. A few choices at our visit: marinated artichokes, spiced pears, mixed peppers, barley and kidney beans, paprika potato salad, wild mushrooms and chick peas. This salad bar is enough to make a convert of the salad bar antagonist among us; the other, who frequently picks a trio of salads for lunch, would have a field day with this for a meal anytime. It's $6.50 for lunch, $7.99 for dinner and $4.99 with an entrée. "Eat all you can," says the menu, "but please: only one person per order. Salad buffet is not to be shared beyond tasting!" We liked it so much that we went back for a dessert of fresh fruits and a whole poached pear in cinnamon sauce.

Hefty burgers and sandwiches, veggie pockets and guacamole-sprout sandwiches in pita pockets are among lunch offerings ($2.99 to $3.99). We enjoyed a pasta special called Nantucket Bay parmesano ($5.95), a sensational dish of scallops and fettuccine. The specials "are where we have our fun," says Culinary Institute-trained chef Chris Masiero, who with his brother Matt runs the nearby Guido's Freshmarket Place. For dinner, the blackboard lists such specials ($12.95 to $14.95) as oyster stew, shrimp scampi, scallops with pesto and broccoli, grilled swordfish and steak à la grecque.

Desserts are up to the rest of the fare, perhaps black-raspberry cheesecake, chocolate mousse pie with walnuts, strawberry-rhubarb pie and bread pudding with maple sauce. There's a good, attractively priced beer and wine selection as well.

Decor is country cafe, with booths and tables bearing white and blue checkered cloths and fresh flowers. A trellised outdoor deck nearly doubles the size in summer.

Lunch daily, 11:30 to 4; dinner nightly, from 5.

The Candlelight Inn, 53 Walker St., Lenox. (413) 637-1555.

A new chef has elevated the dining experience at this old-timer, long a Lenox landmark with its large antique wagon on the front lawn. There's an outdoor courtyard for dining in summer. Inside are four pleasant dining rooms, seating a total of 140, that look like what every visitor thinks a restaurant in a New England inn should look like.

Chef Glenn Strickland's menu is a cut above. Expect starters like country pâté with apple-ginger chutney, house-cured gravlax with lemon-dill vinaigrette or pan-fried polenta with parmesan cream and tomato coulis. The spinach salad with roasted red peppers, feta cheese and warm scallion vinaigrette comes highly recommended.

Main courses are priced from $15.95 for braised lamb shank with cannellini beans, garlic and tomato to $21.95 for pan-seared medallions of New Zealand venison with wild rice and black currant sauce. Sautéed shrimp and scallops with dijon-peppercorn sauce, confit of duck with cognac and shallot sauce, and grilled veal chop with shiitake mushrooms in marsala demi-glace are other possibilities.

Lunch daily in summer, noon to 2:30, weekends in off-season; dinner nightly, 6 to 9:30, Sunday from 5. Closed Tuesday in off-season.

Roseborough Grill, 83 Church St., Lenox. (413) 637-2700.

Chef Laura Shack-Willnauer, a former New York caterer and student of James Beard,

Artworks are hung on dining-room walls at Cafe Lucia.

took over the old Cheesecake Charlie's in 1992 and upgraded it into an antiquey, country-style grill and bar. There's seating for 140 in the bar-lounge, in two mauve and hunter green dining rooms, on an awning-covered side yard and on a back porch.

Laura's lunch menu includes such standouts as white bean chili with grilled chicken and fresh tomato salsa, a grilled portobello mushroom sandwich and, for the adventuresome, a roasted garlic plate accompanied with herbed goat cheese, caramelized onions, red bell peppers, niçoise olives and homemade croutons. Prices vary from $4.95 to $8.95.

Dinner ($12.95 to $18.95) brings pastas and main dishes like shrimp scampi, braised lamb shank. roast duckling with black currant sauce and roesti potato pancake, and grilled sirloin with portobello mushroom sauce. Some of the lunch items turn up on the light dinner menu, available only in the off-season.

The dessert of choice is roseberry pie, a house specialty teaming blackberries, blueberries, raspberries and strawberries.

Open daily, 11:30 to 9 or 10.

Dakota, Route 7, Lenox. (413) 499-7900.

Patrons wait for up to two hours on busy weekends to get a table in this restaurant, which seats 250 in a variety of rooms. The focal area contains two enormous salad bars (with a spectacular selection, say local innkeepers), an open grill, a lobster tank, a display case containing slabs of beef, and a table where huge loaves of Buffalo bread are displayed (and cost $10 to take home).

Western grain-fed beef is featured, priced from $12.95 for top sirloin or teriyaki sirloin to $17.95 for prime rib. Wood-grilled chicken, swordfish and shrimp are offered separately or in a variety of combinations from $11.95 to $14.95. The day's specials when we were there included Norwegian salmon with lime coriander butter, wood-grilled yellowtail tuna or rainbow trout, and baked scrod. Light entrées, including bread and salad bar, go for $9.95 to $10.95. It's little wonder that the place is packed.

Dinner nightly, 4 to 10 or 11; Sunday brunch, 10:30 to 2.

Lenox 218, 218 Main St., Lenox. (413) 637-4218.

Even unflappable Lenox residents were agog a few years back with the opening of this strikingly contemporary, New Yorkish restaurant in the old Log Cabin. Vastly expanded, it now contains a state-of-the-art kitchen, an inviting lounge and two airy dining rooms (one the Fireplace Room and one the Sunroom) with soaring cathedral ceilings. Decor is mostly black and white with black lacquered chairs, gray striped wallpaper coordinated with black and gray carpeting with stripes on the diagonal, mod posters and handsome black-rimmed Shaunwald china from Germany.

Peripatetic local restaurateurs Jim and Lynne DeMayo sold their Painted Lady restaurant in Great Barrington not long after opening to concentrate on their largest venture yet. A grand place it is, particularly for the New Yorkish crowd that feels at home here.

Its with-it menu ($14.95 to $21.95) ranges from grilled salmon with roasted red pepper sauce and breast of chicken with almonds, sesame and sunflower seeds to veal saltimbocca and rack of lamb. Jim DeMayo makes the pastas, and desserts like french apple tart, banana cream pie and cappuccino-chocolate custard.

For lunch, there are sandwiches, salads and light entrées. At little round black tables in the bar, with its black and white tiled floor, you can snack on shrimp, oysters and clams, or maybe a taco salad.

Lunch, Monday-Saturday 11:30 to 2:30; dinner nightly, 5 to 10; Sunday brunch, 10:30 to 2:30.

Diversions

Tanglewood, West Street, Lenox, 637-1940. The name is synonymous with music and Lenox. The summer home of the Boston Symphony Orchestra since 1936, the 210-acre estate above the waters of Stockbridge Bowl in the distance is an idyllic spot for concerts and socializing at picnics. The 6,000 reserved seats in the open-air Shed sell for $13.50 to $72; up to 10,000 fans can be accommodated at $11.50 each on the lawn (bring your own chairs, blankets, picnics and wine, or pick something up from the cafeteria). Concerts are at 8:30 Friday and Saturday and 2:30 p.m. Sunday, from the last weekend of June through August. Free open rehearsals for the Sunday concert are scheduled Saturday mornings at 10:30. The new, acoustically spectacular Seiji Ozawa Hall seats 1,200 inside and another 200 on sloping lawns so situated that you can see right onto the stage. It's used for chamber music concerts and student recitals most weeknights in summer and for community events in spring and fall.

Shakespeare & Company, Plunkett Street, Lenox, 637-3353. Edith Wharton's former 50-acre estate above Laurel Lake, the Mount, is the setting for Shakespeare plays presented in repertory Tuesday through Sunday evenings in summer, outdoors in the Mainstage amphitheater and indoors at the 108-seat Stables Theater. Other plays are presented in the intimate Wharton Theater in the drawing room of the Mount. The neo-Georgian home of the novelist is open for tours ($4) Tuesday-Friday 10 to 5, weekends 9:30 to 5 in summer, Thursday-Sunday in fall.

Lenox Town Hall Theater, Walker Street, Lenox. Local innkeeper Richard Houdek headed the committee that refurbished the auditorium of the town hall into a community theater in 1992. Another local innkeeper, Frank Newton, writes and produces a number of shows with name entertainers here.

Pleasant Valley Wildlife Sanctuary, West Road off Route 7 north, Lenox. The

Massachusetts Audubon Society maintains a 1,150-acre nature preserve high up Lenox Mountain next to Yokum Brook. A museum of live and stuffed animals and seven miles of nature trails through forests, meadows and marshes are a pleasant refuge for a few hours. Open daily except Monday year-round.

Shopping. Lenox offers some of the most exclusive shops in the Berkshires. Along Church Street, **Mary Stuart Collections** has wonderful needlework, potpourris and fragrances, children's clothes fit for royalty, heavenly lingerie and fine glass, china and antiques. Neat casual, natural-fiber clothes are at **Glad Rags,** and handsome contemporary crafts at the **Hoadley Gallery. Ormsby's** is an interesting gift, games and accessories shop. **Tanglewool** sells English cashmeres and other handknits, Italian bags, Arche shoes from France, creative jewelry, and imported yarns and knitting patterns; everything here has flair. **Weaver's Fancy** displays lovely weavings, from placemats to pillows to coats. **Mac-Kee-Nac Trading Co.** specializes in Native American clothing, pottery, accessories and jewelry.

On Walker Street you'll find **Talbots** for classic clothes and **Evviva!** for contemporary. At the **Curtis House Shops** on the ground floor of the old Curtis Hotel, which has been converted to apartments, are **The Hand of Man,** an interesting crafts gallery, and **Celtic Origins** with Irish and Scottish imports.

Stop at **Crosby's** for gourmet foods and the makings for wonderful picnics. **Cheesecake Charlie's & Wholesome Harold's** combines cheesecakes and coffees with health foods and a juice bar. Some of the area's best breads and pastries come from **Suchèle Bakers.**

For an ice cream fix, head to **Bev's Homemade Ice Cream,** 26 Housatonic St., where Beverly Mazursky and sons Dan and Jeff make all the wonderful flavors in two machines behind the counter. They're known for their raspberry-chocolate chip, served in a sugar cone. You can order gelatos, frappes, smoothies, sherbet coolers and even a banana split ($5.50). Soups and sandwiches are available except in summer, when their popular Jamaican patties (different kinds of Caribbean breads with such fillings as beef, mixed veggies and broccoli-cheese, $2.50) are the only things that get in the way of their ice cream.

Just north of town, **Brushwood Farms** is a changing collection of shops worth exploring. Across the street, the **Lenox House Country Shops** includes a number of factory outlets.

Extra-Special ───────────────────────

The National Music Center, 70 Kemble St., Lenox, 637-1800 or (800) 872-6874.

Ending a long nationwide search, the National Music Foundation settled on the 63-acre campus of the former Lenox School for Boys as the home for its planned $30 million Music Center. Already open is the 1,200-seat Berkshire Performing Arts Center, once a gymnasium and hockey rink, and now outfitted with rehearsal and recording studios. Foundation chairman Dick Clark told of "the dream that has taken form here in Lenox" at the 1994 inaugural performance launching a series of pop, folk, blues, country and jazz performances by name entertainers. The school library will be converted into a music library and archives, and a dormitory will become a hands-on, interactive museum of American music. Under construction is a retirement residence where professionals from the music, radio and recording community can retire among their peers and provide a core faculty for the center's educational and mentor programs. Up to 200 musicians are expected to live, teach and perform here, adding a year-round dynamic to an already vibrant musical community.

Chatham, Mass.
Serenity Beside the Sea

Of all Cape Cod's towns, we are fondest of Chatham, a sophisticated, sedate and serene enclave of affluence beside the sea. This is the elbow of the Cape, where the hubbub of much of the Cape's south shore yields to treed tranquility before the land veers north to face the open Atlantic and form the dunes of the National Seashore.

Known locally as "The First Stop of the East Wind," Chatham is one of the Cape's oldest towns (settled in 1656) and one of its most residential. Hidden in the trees and along the meandering waterfront are large homes and estates.

Explore a bit and you may see the gorgeous hydrangea walk leading up to a Shore Road mansion. Across from a windmill in a field of yellow wildflowers sparkling against a backdrop of blue ocean, it's the essence of Cape Cod. Or you may follow Mooncusser's Lane and find that the road ends abruptly at the water. Admire the view from the drawbridge on Bridge Street as well as the classic views of the Chatham Light.

Because it's so residential, Chatham has escaped the overt commercialism and tourism of much of the Cape. It does not cater to transients; some inns and motels encourage long stays, and many of the accommodations are in cottages or rented houses.

The summer social scene revolves around private clubs and parties. But almost everyone turns out for the Friday evening band concerts in Kate Gould Park.

Although Main Street, which winds through the center of town, seems filled with pedestrians and shoppers, chances are they're residents or regulars. Perhaps its air of stability and tradition is what makes Chatham so special.

Inn Spots

Wequassett Inn, Pleasant Bay, Chatham 02633. (508) 432-5400 or (800) 225-7125.

Blessed with a fine location above its private beach and peninsula separating Round Cove from Pleasant Bay, this inn reflects its Indian name for "crescent on the water." The new blends quite nicely with the old in a resort compound with structures dating back more than 200 years. Eighteen Cape Cod-style cottages, motel buildings and condo-type facilities totaling 103 rooms are distributed across 22 rolling, beautifully landscaped acres amid colorful flowers of the season and huge old pines.

Large guest rooms and suites are furnished traditionally with cheery colors, pat-

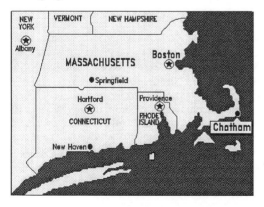

terned fabrics, pine furniture, quilted bedspreads, duck-print wall hangings and needlepoint rugs. We like best the 37 waterview suites, with windows onto the bay and decks for outdoor lounging. Others are partial to the tennis villas, many with cathedral ceilings and private balconies overlooking the woods or courts. Rooms have cable TV, clock radios, mini-refrigerators, phones, air-conditioning and Crabtree & Evelyn toiletries.

Pleasant Bay is backdrop for dining at Wequasset Inn.

Amenities like these helped the Wequassett earn membership in the prestigious Preferred Hotels association of luxury resorts. It was the first New England inn so honored.

At the disposal of guests are five tennis courts with a resident pro, sailboats and canoes, a large swimming pool with a bar where one can order a light lunch, a half-mile-long beach and a small health and fitness center, newly ensconced in what had been a game room. A boat shuttles swimmers to the barrier beach that protects Pleasant Bay. In conjunction with its 50th anniversary year in 1994, the inn opened the Pleasant Bay Espresso Cafe for afternoon coffee and pastries on the lower level of the new, two-tiered veranda off the lounge, a glorious place from which to observe the bay goings-on.

The public may join guests for meals in the historic "square top" Eben Ryder House (see Dining Spots).

Doubles, $215 to $310, EP; suites, $470. Add $88 for MAP, $116 for full AP. Open May-October.

Chatham Bars Inn, Shore Road, Chatham 02633. (508) 945-0096 or (800) 527-4884.

The colorful new landscaping with luxuriant flowers, gas lanterns and brick steps tiered up the hillside toward the main entrance of this venerable inn/resort "make a statement," in the words of its management. So do the beautifully refurbished Victorian foyer and South Parlor, the front veranda awash in wicker, the redecorated dining room and tavern.

Such statements signal the changes since the inn was acquired in late 1993 by Carl Lindner, the Ohio big-business entrepreneur who's lately into hotels. His vision is to restore the hotel to its original grandeur, circa 1914. Our guide, who had been here for twenty years under several owners, was "very excited about the changes at this special place."

He pointed with pride to the sunny new library at the end of the South Parlor, a cozy haven with leather loveseats, oriental rugs and a pressed brass ceiling. "It looks turn of the century," he noted. "But it's not at all domineering or depressing Victorian." He showed three newly renovated side cottages. Variously outfitted with tiled fireplaces, built-in TVs, lighted closets, handpainted cabinets, window seats, oversize beds and even a grandfather's clock, they are the ultimate in taste, comfort and low-key luxury. The desk in one has an old writing box bearing a picture of the old hotel; the base of a lamp in another is laminated with hotel postcards from days gone by. They make a statement of tradition, but also signify change. All the cottages are to be refurbished in similar style over the next five years. Being readied for 1995 at the north end of the main hotel were two master suites that would make these "look paltry," we were advised. One of 1,300 square feet on the second floor has two bedrooms, a parlor and a living room with decks on all sides.

The Chatham Bars complex of an imposing inn and charming oceanfront houses and cottages existed virtually as a private club from its beginnings as a hunting lodge in 1914 until its acquisition by a Boston real-estate developer in 1987. One of the last great oceanfront resorts, it's perched on a bluff with half a mile of shoreline overlooking Pleasant Bay and the barrier beach separating it from the Atlantic. The 152 rooms run the gamut from 50 of the traditional type in the main inn to sumptuous suites in 27 cottages, many of them really houses containing two to eight guest rooms and common living rooms with fireplaces. We enjoyed watching the surf pummeling the now-famous breach in the barrier beach from the balcony off the plush sitting room of our cottage suite, which was suavely decorated in shades of mauve and rose.

For meals, the resort has a stately Main Dining Room in which a new chef blends the creative with the traditional and jackets are requested for dinner, and a more casual Tavern at the Inner Bar. Lunch, continental breakfast with an omelet bar and special events take place at the inviting Beach House Grill at water's edge, where the pool area was about to be enlarged and croquet lawns added. Guests enjoy an adjacent nine-hole golf course, five tennis courts and a sandy beach. Although the theme is under-stated luxury, the resort is distinguished by its mix of accommodations. You can mingle and make merry in the main inn, or get away from it all in a house by the sea.

Doubles, $160 to $375 EP; master suites, $650 and $1,000 EP; cottages for two, $160 to $450 EP.

The Captain's House Inn of Chatham, 369-377 Old Harbor Road (Route 28), Chatham 02633. (508) 945-0127.

There's more than a touch of England amid all the Americana of this elegant and comfortable inn that originated in Captain Hiram Harding's restored 1839 home. The first innkeepers built it into one of the few small AAA four-diamond inns in New England. So when Jan and David McMaster took over in 1993, they had only to "enhance what's here, not change it."

Dave, former CEO of a computer company he founded in California, was looking to continue his predecessors' upgrades, planning to add a couple of jacuzzi tubs, expand the dining porch and build four deluxe suites with fireplaces. Already he had developed new English perennial gardens with a three-tiered fountain pond in a rear corner of the two-acre property.

Jan, a proper Brit from Bournemouth, was injecting her heritage into an inn whose staff already imparted an English accent. For some years, the Captain's House had hired hotel students from the University of Bournemouth in Jan's hometown, a striking coincidence, and the McMasters were happy to continue the tradition. Jan serves an elaborate and true English tea in the afternoon. She also has expanded the breakfast offerings to include eggs, bacon and potato pie with salsa, waffles with strawberries or blueberries, quiches and apple crêpes to supplement the traditional fresh fruit, breads and muffins, all individually served at tables in the sunny breakfast room.

The Captain's House Inn of Chatham occupies residential site north of village.

Set on shaded lawns screened by high hedges in a sedate residential section north of the village and a pleasant ten-minute walk from the water, the Captain's House is refined and tranquil. The entrance hall and living room retain the original pumpkin pine floors and are furnished with antiques, fine rugs and period wallpapers.

All sixteen guest rooms come with private baths and six with fireplaces. The eight in the main Greek Revival house have a variety of furnishings, including four-poster beds with pineapple finials, lacy white fishnet canopies, white eyelet-edged curtains, colorful sheets and comforters, thick oversize towels, braided rugs and soft velvet wing chairs for reading. Special French soaps are provided in the bathrooms.

Five ultra-deluxe rooms, a couple with beamed and peaked ceilings, have been fashioned from a rear carriage house. Also coveted is the Captain's Cottage, where the sumptuous suite looks like a library with dark wood paneling, fine oriental rugs on the wide-plank floor, working fireplace, plush sofa and canopied four-poster bed. A jacuzzi tub has been added here.

There's no television, Dave is quick to note. "We see that as a plus. Our guests are looking for a quiet getaway in an elegant setting."

Doubles, $130 to $225. Closed January to mid-February.

The Bradford Inn and Motel, 26 Cross St., Box 760, Chatham 02633. (508) 945-1030 or (800) 562-4667.

An exceptionally attractive inn evolving from a motel, this venerable establishment is well situated in a residential section just off Chatham's Main Street. For years we had admired its cheery exterior with yellow awnings, as well as the well-kept gardens with flowers of every hue. The interior, we found, is just as nice.

Innkeepers William and Audrey Gray live in the 1860 Captain Elijah Smith House, which also serves as **Champlain's Restaurant** (see Dining Spots), run by their son. Exotic small fish flash colorfully in a couple of aquariums in the lobby. The Garden Room at the rear is where a full complimentary breakfast (guests choose from a large menu) is served. The apricot pancakes are so good that they draw the public as well. In season, many prefer to breakfast outside on the shady new entry patio beside trickling fountains and the small pool, savoring the extravagant roses and watching the birds feed.

Five large rooms are in the Bradford House in front, which we found cozy with the fireplace in our room ablaze on a fall evening, while four are in the Carriage House near the pool. The most deluxe are four with king and queensize canopy beds, fireplaces and thick carpeting in the newly built Jonathan Gray House. Eleven more are in the L-

341

shaped motel building in back. Five have kitchens and some are suites. All are individually decorated and include private baths, cable television, refrigerators, telephones and air-conditioning.

Ever expanding and refining, at our latest visit the Grays had gutted Room 19 in a corner of the motel to produce a two-room suite with ceiling moldings, poster bed, ceramic tub, wet bar and two TV sets. Before that they added the fireplaced Lion's Den game room and lounge, and opened a two-bedroom cottage as the **Captain's Hideway.** They restored the **Mulberry Inn** at 44 Cross St. into an elegant B&B with a fireplaced suite on the main floor and two additional luxurious rooms upstairs.

Doubles, $120 to $189. Mulberry Inn, $159 to $179.

Chatham Wayside Inn, 512 Main St., Box 685, Chatham 02633. (508) 945-5550 or (800) 391-5734.

Dating to 1860, this landmark in-town inn was rescued from foreclosure in 1993 by local businessmen David Oppenheim and Grant Wilson. They operated the restaurant that summer, then closed for a total rehab and reopened in 1994 with a new look, a new entry and layout, and 24 upstairs guest rooms. Ready in 1995 were 32 more guest rooms in a new three-story annex out back, occupying the site of four razed cottages. These parkside units have patios and balconies for front-row seats for the Friday night band concerts in Kate Gould Park.

Rooms in the main inn are nicely furnished with an abundance of chintz, vivid fabrics and Waverly prints. They come in three styles: Colonial, European traditional and country pine. All have king or queensize beds and thick carpeting, five have private balconies or terraces and two claim jacuzzis. TVs are ensconced in highboys or on chests facing the beds, and Lord & Mayfair toiletries await in the bathrooms. A writing desk is tucked into one of the nooks and crannies of a dormered third-floor room. "Everything looks and feels old," general manager Suki Scofield said as she showed us around, "but you can be assured it's new."

Three meals a day are served in the inn's restaurant (see Dining Spots). The shady front courtyard facing the passing Chatham street scene is the place to see and be seen in season.

Doubles, $145 to $325, EP. Three-night minimum in season.

The Cranberry Inn at Chatham, 359 Main St., Chatham 02633. (508) 945-9232 or (800) 332-4667.

Once named the Traveler's Home and later the Monomoy House, this red-frame inn dating from the 1830s is Chatham's oldest inn. It was grandly renovated and expanded by Richard Morris and Peggy DeHan, two busy innkeepers who cut their teeth on smaller Chatham B&Bs that they launched and later sold. The Cranberry was sold in 1994, to our surprise, so they could concentrate on their expanding antiques business.

The new owners are retired Boston hotel developer Jim Bradley and his wife Debbie, who were busy taking the eighteen-room inn "to the next (four-star) level." Rates are significantly higher, and the inn now is open year-round. Jim said they had spent $180,000 on upgrades in their first nine months.

The results are evident in the common rooms. Jim showed proudly the entry/reception room that has been formalized with fine oriental carpets, "significant" art, a baby grand piano (which Jim sometimes plays) and rare tables with board games. The handsome bar/lounge has been glamorized and made more authentic with beamed ceiling, expensive oriental art and old hotel registers found in the attic from a century ago. The redecorated dining room is a picture of elegance in showy navy and cranberry, with fabric-covered wood chairs and a remarkable, conversation-piece dollhouse,

Comfortable home of former town physician is now The Old Harbor Inn.

which Jim points out is a replica of their home in Hingham and was a 25th-anniversary gift from their children. The Bradleys also landscaped the inn, adding English gardens ("done by a British couple") and a new nature trail leading to a cranberry bog, the old Mill Pond and out to the ocean.

Back inside, the beds have been triple-sheeted, the pillows converted to feathers, the towels are now 90 percent cotton Dundee, the TVs are remote-controlled and the windows darkened with vinyl blackout shades. Crystal cranberry glasses are in each room, and the ice buckets are now vinyl-coated in cranberry. The previous owners had doubled the fourteen original guest rooms in size, thanks to an addition on the east end. All have new private baths, telephones and television. They also added four fireplaced suites, each with comfortable sitting areas and a couple with private balconies.

Breakfast is now "grand continental" in the formal dining room. Expect a fruit bowl "with a bit of everything," assorted cereals, cheddar cheese, hard-boiled eggs, broccoli quiche, and fresh cranberry and blueberry muffins, banana nut bread, bagels, croissants and English muffins. Afternoon tea brings scones and croissants with raspberry jam. Complimentary popcorn is served in the bar.

Doubles, $165 to $210.

The Old Harbor Inn, 22 Old Harbor Road, Chatham 02633. (508) 945-4434 or (800) 942-4434.

For a change of pace, consider this newer home built for a physician who delivered half the babies in Chatham, according to innkeepers Sharon and Tom Ferguson. Built in a very different style than the Cape Cod norm, it was nicely expanded in 1995 to retain the residential flavor. All is smashingly decorated and luxuriously comfortable in a contemporary kind of way.

The stage is set in the fireplaced living room, all pink and green with lots of chintz, botanical prints on the walls, area rug and a piano in the corner. To the rear is a new breakfast sun room, white floral with lots of wicker, leading onto an attractive deck.

Upstairs are a new library/sitting room and three guest rooms, all with private baths, strikingly appointed in an English country look and bearing the different names the town was called before it became Chatham. One is all red and white, from the white eyelet comforter to the red towels and a porthole in the bathroom. A second in black and floral-print fabrics has a black iron porcelain queensize bed and a huge bathroom with a rug that matches the border trim. The Laura Ashley honeymoon hideaway is all pink, green and white, with wicker chairs, dhurrie rugs, balloon curtains and a wicker queen bedstead.

Two more guest rooms have private entrances in a wing off the first floor. They are equally light, bright and airy in shades of pink, green and gray, and contain the thick rugs, candy and assorted amenities featured in the rest of the house. In 1995, a second floor was added atop this wing to produce two deluxe guest rooms, each with private bath, fireplace and skylit, vaulted ceiling. Named North Beach and South Beach, they are decorated accordingly. The renovations also turned an eighth bedroom on the main floor, cheery with white frilly covers and pillows on the king bed, into a suite with a small sitting room.

A continental-plus breakfast of fruits, cereals, and homemade breads and muffins is served in the morning. On weekends and in winter, a more substantial breakfast including baked eggs or french toast may be served. Tea is served in the afternoon, and guests have access to a butler's pantry.

Sharon, who plays the baritone horn, was the first woman to join the celebrated Chatham Band. She also learned that she is a 13th-generation descendant of William Nickerson, who founded Chatham in 1657.

Doubles, $115 to $195. No smoking.

The Cyrus Kent House Inn, 63 Cross St., Chatham 02633. (508) 945-9104 or (800) 338-5368.

Restored into one of Chatham's first B&B's in 1985 by Richard Morris, this 1877 sea captain's home was acquired in 1993 by Sharon Swan, who had lived in Chatham for fourteen years, "had watched Richard restoring the place and never dreamed that I'd ever own it." She has kept the place much as he left it when he moved to the Cranberry Inn.

Antiques, original art and fresh flowers from the inn's gardens decorate the seven guest rooms in the main house, all with private baths, queensize four-poster beds, wing chairs, televisions, clock-radios and telephones. Some come with fireplaces and decks. The comforters are coordinated with the window treatments.

The rear carriage house harbors a couple of deluxe suites. One on the main floor with a beamed ceiling and a fireplace in the center is furnished in Shaker country style with a four-poster queen bed. The upstairs suite is larger and more formal with a vaulted ceiling. A palladian window with balloon curtains is the focal point of its elegant living room.

A continental breakfast of fresh fruit compote, granola, yogurt and homemade muffins is served in the dining room at individual tables with lace runners, silver and china. Afternoon tea is offered in the off-season in the spacious living room. Guests also enjoy a front porch.

Doubles, $125 to $145; suites, $165.

Moses Nickerson House, 364 Old Harbor Road, Chatham 02633. (508) 945-5859 or (800) 628-6972.

Located across the street from the Captain's House Inn of Chatham, this elongated, 1839 whaling captain's house is remarkable for its narrow width and extreme depth. The main house is one room wide so rooms have windows on both sides. A new section adds a lovely solarium breakfast room, outfitted with white wrought-iron furniture on a brick floor, and two large new guest rooms.

Elsie and Carl Piccola have decorated with flair, and the delicate, handpainted designs

Elaborate breakfast and afternoon tea are offered at Oceancrest at Chatham.

on the doors are a trademark. The English parlor is pretty in rose and cream with an Aubusson rug and a collection of Sandwich glass. Off the parlor is the front Emily Dickinson Room, which has a handpainted poster bed and a painted armoire amid tons of lace; some of the author's works are on the fireplace mantel. Seven more rooms with private baths and phones are available in one section above the living room, up steep ship's stairs from the dining room or in the newer rear section. Three have fireplaces.

Climb those ship's stairs if you can to see a room with a great window seat full of pillows, a fishnet canopy four-poster bed and a stenciled bathroom. Once here, you may have difficulty leaving – one lanky fellow had to back down the stairs.

A fox in a hunting costume sits on the mantel of the Ralph Lauren room, all dark and masculine with paisley linens on a four-poster bed and a leather chair. It's quite in contrast to the room above, summery in wicker with deep green towels; an old blouse, a pair of high-button shoes and a handbag hanging on a hook above the bed lend a nostalgic touch.

A collection of pewter lines a high shelf in the skylit breakfast room, which looks onto an arbor and a fish pond outside. Here is where the Piccolas serve a continental-plus breakfast, perhaps including pancakes, quiche or scones. At our latest visit, they were looking to add two more guest rooms when they move into the carriage house.

The grounds attract with nice touches like statues, bird feeders and a wooden seagull perched in the crook of an old tree.

Doubles, $119 to $159. Two-night minimum in season. Closed in January. No smoking.

Oceancrest at Chatham, 547 Shore Road, Chatham 02633. (508) 945-3128.
After nine years of running the Inn at Millrace Pond, the seventeen-room inn and restaurant they founded in Hope, N.J., Gloria Barry Carrigan and Richard Gooding retired in 1994 to this handsome white clapboard residence across the street from the ocean. For Gloria it was a homecoming of sorts (she grew up in Beverly on the North Shore). No sooner had they settled in than they started redoing one room a week in preparation for opening a three-room B&B.

The bedrooms, all with private baths, are situated so that no one is over or beside another. Each is named for a naturalist who has had an impact on Cape Cod. Gloria's favorite is the Thornton Burgess Room, where Raggedy Ann dolls rest at the foot of the antique double bed and the author's books line the shelves. A queensize poster bed and an 1837 sea captain's chest are features of the small Henry Beston Room. Most spacious is the main-floor Sargent-Read Room with windows on three sides, two twins joined as a kingsize bed and a TV set available in a closet.

Guests enjoy an upstairs parlor-library as well as the main-floor parlor/music room, where Richard may play the grand piano. Three tables are set for breakfast on the side sun porch overlooking a water garden, complete with two small ponds and a waterfall running between them. Gloria offers a choice of juices, fresh fruit cup served in a champagne glass and a hot main dish, perhaps waffles, pancakes (raspberry or strawberry), scrambled eggs or omelets with salsa. Croissants, muffins or breads accompany. Tea sandwiches and cookies are offered with afternoon beverages.

Gloria planned to create a Cape Cod garden on the large property. Already she had quite a collection of Chatham seashells lining the stairs along the side deck.

Doubles, $125 to $160. Closed January-April.

Dining Spots

Christian's, 443 Main St., Chatham. (508) 945-3362.

For a fine meal, a raw bar, cocktails and dining on an upper deck, or nightly entertainment in the classic English bar, Christian's has been a favorite among locals for more than a decade. It's even more popular now that **Upstairs at Christian's** serves lunch and a casual evening menu.

With the help of his wife Maggie, his brother and his parents, chef Christian Schultz offers the town's most creative dinner menu in the airy, casual porch or the more formal dining room with white linens, beamed ceilings, oriental rugs and latticed dividers.

With drinks comes a complimentary chicken liver pâté served with melba toast. Appetizers ($6.50 to $8) include seafood pancakes studded with corn, lobster and scallops and garnished with caviar; oriental dumplings served with ponzu sauce and a neat-sounding seafood bourbon and basil bisque. We ordered a special of imported and domestic caviars with fried wontons and ginger sour cream, which did not include enough caviar to warrant the $10 tab. On another occasion we liked the crab beurrecks wrapped in phyllo dough and a special called "cockles and such," which happened to be four Monterey oysters in a choron sauce.

Entrées, which change every few weeks, run from $18 for baked codfish topped with a red pepper hollandaise to $26 for rack of lamb crusted with goat cheese, rosemary and pumpernickel. Roast duck with a fresh fruit sauce (once kiwi and raspberry, the next time apple, pear and tarragon) is the house specialty. On various visits, we've enjoyed halibut sauced with asparagus hollandaise, a superb veal and shrimp sauté, the duck with kiwi and raspberries, and pork sautéed with cilantro, deglazed with tequila and served with a green chile corn muffin. These came with interesting vegetables – once green and yellow squash, carrots and rice, another time green beans, cauliflower and turnip puree – plus crusty French bread and a simple salad of hearts of palm with a zesty herb and cheese dressing. The portions are so large that few have room for dessert, though we once splurged for a grand marnier torte topped by a chocolate shell filled with grand marnier.

After dinner, adjourn to **Upstairs at Christian's** for cordials and special coffees. A laid-back, luxurious space with a piano bar, it has a handsome curved oak bar, African mahogany paneling, shelves filled with books, and an interesting mix of eaves and niches with leather sofas and loveseats. When we stopped in, a banjo player, "proud to be a preppy from North Chatham," sang rousing ditties while one of a collection of old movies was shown in "The Critic's Corner."

Airy side porch is setting for creative dinners at Christian's.

It's no wonder that the expanded bistro menu, served here and on the adjacent roof-top deck, is so popular. From a separate kitchen come burgers, gourmet pizzas, salads and entrées priced from $8 for chicken parmesan to $15.50 for filet mignon with béarnaise sauce. After a pedestrian lunch on the canopied deck, however, we think we prefer the downstairs dining experience.

Lunch in summer, 11 to 3; dinner nightly, 5 to 10. Downstairs closed Columbus Day to May except for overflow from upstairs.

The Impudent Oyster, 15 Chatham Bars Ave., Chatham. (508) 945-3545.

With a name like that and an innovative menu, how could this place miss? Always jammed and noisy to the point (for us) of turn-off, patrons crowd together at small glass-covered tables under a cathedral ceiling, with plants in straw baskets balanced overhead on the beams. A huge new mirror on the side wall makes the place seem bigger.

Owner Peter Barnard's international menu, based on local seafood, is an intriguing blend of regional, Chinese, Mexican, Indian, Greek and Italian cuisines, among others. For dinner, we couldn't resist starting with the drunken mussels ($5.95), shelled and served chilled in an intense marinade of tamari, fresh ginger, Szechuan peppercorns and sake, with a side portion of snow peas and red peppers. The Mexican chicken, chile and lime soup, one of the best we've tasted, was spicy and full of interesting flavors. Also delicious were the spinach and mushroom salads with either creamy mustard or anchovy dressings.

Among entrées ($15.50 to $21.50), it was difficult to choose from such imaginative offerings as celestial oysters (poached in champagne, topped with hollandaise and served on pasta), yellowfin tuna marinated in soy sauce and cumin, swordfish au chèvre, scallops San Cristobal with avocado and cilantro or veal avignon (with crabmeat, asparagus and brie). We liked the feta and fennel scrod, a Greek dish touched with ouzo, and the swordfish with sundried tomato and basil sauce. A spicy pinot grigio for $14.50 went well with such assertive fare. A plate of several ice creams made with fresh fruit was a cooling finale.

The menu changes frequently, and is supplemented by nightly specials. It's the kind of cuisine of which we never tire, although we would prefer to have it in a more peaceful setting.

Lunch, Monday-Saturday 11:30 to 3, Sunday noon to 3; dinner, 5:30 to 9:30 or 10.

Wequasset Inn, Pleasant Bay, Chatham. (508) 432-5400.

Among area restaurants, we know of no more majestic water view amid more elegant surroundings than from the restored 18th-century sea captain's mansion that houses the Wequasset Inn's dining room. Floor-to-ceiling windows on three sides is about all the decor you need in the main dining room, recently redone in dusty rose and pink with candles flickering in hurricane lamps and a pianist entertaining in the background. A new, two-tiered deck off the lounge is a great place for lunch, coffee and pastries or cocktails overlooking Pleasant Bay.

Chef Frank McMullen, a Culinary Institute of American grad, is partial to fresh seafood and continental cuisine. For starters ($5.50 to $10.75), we liked his escargots with pine nuts in puff pastry, Thai mussels steamed in lobster broth and curry, and a green salad topped with grilled chicken and wild mushrooms. Among entrées ($18.50 to $22.25), standouts were twin beef tenderloins on a bed of simmered lentils and prosciutto, grilled cornish game hen, gulf shrimp over tri-colored pasta and Norwegian salmon baked on a cedar plank, served on ancho chile beurre blanc. Key lime pie and a strawberry tart were refreshing desserts.

Lunch daily, 11:30 to 2; dinner, 6 to 10. Open May to October.

Champlain's, 26 Cross St., Chatham. (508) 945-1030.

The restaurant at the Bradford Inn has proven so successful that it now occupies three small dining rooms, virtually the entire main floor. The main garden dining room is homey with floral cloths on the tables and white sheer curtains on the windows. Two smaller dining rooms with fireplaces in the front of the house are employed for overflow.

Chef Robert Gray, son of the innkeepers, offers an ambitious menu, supplemented by nightly specials. Start with his acclaimed clam chowder, speckled with bits of bacon and carrot, or an appetizer of lobster cake finished with caviar and nestled on roasted julienne pepper or oysters rockefeller on spinach tagliatelle. There's quite a list of entrées, priced from $14.95 for baked scrod to $24.50 for seafood diablo, the house specialty. Expect such innovations as lobster crumb pie, grilled shrimp kari served on coconut rice and finished with grapefruit and a citrus vinaigrette, seared sea scallops over pasta with boursin cheese and green peppercorn beurre blanc, and New Zealand rack of lamb with a sauté of portobello mushrooms and bermuda onions. Meals come with a choice of caesar or garden salad with a tangy house dressing (so popular that the Grays sell it by the bottle), hot poppyseed rolls with curled butter, garnishes of edible flowers and a palate-cleansing strawberry-cranberry sorbet.

Dessert could be a tart apple-cranberry pie with french vanilla ice cream, meringue glacé or the nutty neopolitan, a concoction of macaroons, amaretto, kahlua and ice cream.

The restaurant is named for explorer Samuel de Champlain, who sailed into Chatham's Stage Harbor in 1606.

Breakfast, 8 to 11, Sunday to noon or 1; dinner, Monday-Saturday from 5:30.

Vining's Bistro, 595 Main St., Chatham. (508) 945-5033.

We've had lobster in myriad forms, but never before wrapped in a flour tortilla with spinach and jalapeño jack cheese, and here called a warm lobster taco. With crème fraîche and homemade two-tomato salsa sparked with cilantro, it quickly became an appetizer fixture on the multi-ethnic menu. That and the warm roasted scallop salad with grilled eggplant and yogurt dressing, served on wilted bok choy, made us vow to return.

The bistro is run by chef-owner Steve Vining, who used to have La Grand Rue in Harwichport. It's upstairs in a newish retail complex called the Galleria, with beamed cathedral ceilings and big windows onto Main Street. Vining's is a casual and friendly place where a large stuffed bear was seated at the bar at our latest visit. Many of the dishes are done on the open grill, using woods like cherry, apple and hickory.

For an autumn dinner, we were tempted by the grilled bouillabaisse as well as grilled salmon with stir-fried watercress, ginger and sesame. Other interesting dinner dishes ($11.95 to $17.95) were the Thai fire pot with chicken, sausage and seafood in a hot and sour lemon grass broth, the seafood splashdown with tamari and ginger over angel-hair pasta, and the North African vegetable curry with eggplant chutney. One of us enjoyed the clam and mussel stew, served with arugula, tomatoes and sausage over fettuccine. The other made a meal of a couple of appetizers, the warm lobster taco (again) and Thai chicken satay, plus a bistro salad with feta cheese and kalamata olives. Portions were huge and the food assertive, prompting a faint-hearted couple of our acquaintance to shun the place as "too spicy." They wouldn't even think of trying the pasta from hell, made with Scotch bonnet peppers and incorporating smoked chicken, hot sausage and banana-guava ketchup.

There's a small and sophisticated little wine list, plus a long list of beers (some imported from Kenya, China and Thailand) to go with. End your meal with maple-pecan bread pudding or chocolate pudding cake.

Dinner nightly, 5:30 to 9 or 10.

The Chatham Squire Restaurant, 483 Main St., Chatham. (508) 945-0945.

Once little more than a bar and still a hangout for summering collegians, the Squire has soared lately with its food, to the point where on recent visits everyone was mentioning it as one of the best in town. It's the place of choice among those who find Vining's Bistro too spicy, although it shares with the bistro a commitment to interesting food, especially the lengthy list of daily specials. The atmosphere is perky, the decor old Cape Cod, with murals of local scenes and the bar decked out with old license plates and sailing flags.

Regulars like to sit at the bar, which faces Main Street, and watch the passing parade as they slurp a hearty fish chowder or peel their own shrimp from Chatham's only raw bar.

At lunch, burgers are served with those yummy Cape Cod potato chips. We enjoyed a thick and clammy clam chowder with a blue cheeseburger, and the day's blue-plate special, a platter of fish cakes and beans, served with cole slaw and brown bread for $4.95. The grasshopper mousse torte ($3) was great for dessert.

Dinner entrées run from $10.95 for baked codfish to $17.95 for grilled sirloin with madeira sauce and mushrooms. Nightly specials might include grilled ocean perch with a cilantro and smoked tomato cream sauce, codfish cheek jambalaya, gulf shrimp sautéed with artichoke hearts and leeks, and roast Long Island duckling with grapefruit and dark rum sauce. Start with the whistling oysters or Cape Codder pâté with sundried cranberries, walnuts and bartlett pears. Finish with coconut cream pie or blueberry cobbler à la mode.

Lunch daily, 11:30 to 5; dinner nightly, 5 to 11; shorter hours in winter.

Campari's, 352 Main St., Chatham. (508) 945-9123.

Chef Bob Chiappetta cooks in an open kitchen in this Italian bistro at the Dolphin of Chatham inn and motel. By day it's the **Bittersweet Cafe,** serving breakfast and spilling outdoors onto a covered patio area that becomes Alfresco's for cocktails in the evening. At night it turns cozy and intimate as patrons gather at tables topped with red-checked cloths amid candles in chianti bottles, hanging plants, an aquarium and two fireplaces. Italian opera music plays as guests sip the bottled San Pellegrino water from Italy.

The kitchen resembles the household kitchen it once was, open to the dining room and imparting tantalizing aromas throughout. The five entrées ($17 to $23) from the short, changing menu come with soup (often a complex Veneto onion soup), salad and pasta. Starters could be crab cakes parmigiana, herb flavored and with a subtle tomato sauce, or calamari sautéed with prosciutto and flamed with vodka. Main courses could include scampi with mussels over cappellini, swordfish siciliana, chicken tuscano, and veal with sundried tomatoes and mushrooms.

Bob's wife Lisa does the baking, perhaps a honey-nut pie. She oversees the short, reasonably priced Italian wine list as well. The couple also own **Carmine's,** a good little pizza, espresso and gelato parlor at 595 Main St. in the Galleria.

Breakfast daily from 8; dinner nightly except Monday, from 6; off-season, Wednesday-Saturday from 6.

Chatham Wayside Inn, 512 Main St., Chatham. (508) 945-5550.

When we first vacationed in Chatham three decades ago, the Wayside seemed the quintessential New England inn – located in the heart of town and containing a lively tavern that was perfect for an after-dinner drink. Now the tavern operation has been scaled back and the restaurant has been upscaled. It's a fairly vast expanse that's seems a bit austere, as often is the case in this "new, meant-to-look-old" genre. Green woven mats and little candles top bare wood tables; the bare floors and formal window treatments convey a sense of history. The side deck remains the place to be in summer.

Three meals a day are served, and the extensive menus cover all the bases. At dinner, main courses run from $9.95 for fish and chips to $21.95 for baked stuffed lobster. Expect such choices as baked stuffed scrod, shrimp scampi, cioppino, lobster pie, roast chicken with walnut-cornbread stuffing and apricot-sage sauce, filet mignon and steak au poivre. Appetizers range from deep-fried chicken tenders to baked stuffed quahogs and shrimp cocktail. Desserts include carrot cake, cheesecake, key lime tart and apple-cranberry crisp.

Breakfast daily, 8 to 11; lunch, 11:30 to 5; dinner, 5 to 10, to 9 in winter.

Pate's, Route 28, Chatham. (508) 945-9777.

This substantial steakhouse that's a panorama of red decor with pinkish lights is not the kind of place we look for when vacationing on the Cape. But it's filled nightly with locals and tourists seeking good steaks and seafood, and has been for 37 years.

The list of appetizers offers the old standbys, from escargots to french onion soup, from clams casino to oysters rockefeller. Entrées run from $13.95 for fried haddock to $18.95 for lamb chops. Many are prepared on the open-hearth grill. Filet mignon, baked stuffed shrimp and prime rib are relative bargains for $17.95, and if you can't decide, settle for surf and turf ($17.95). Tossed or caesar salad and rice or potatoes come with; desserts like cheesecake, brownie à la mode and chocolate parfait are $3.50 to $3.95.

Dinner nightly, 5:30 to 10. Closed Monday in off-season and mid-October to spring.

Diversions

From Chatham's choice location at the elbow of Cape Cod, all the attractions of the Cape are at your beck and call. People who appreciate Chatham tend not to head west toward Hyannis but rather north to Orleans, Wellfleet and the Truros, if they leave Chatham at all.

Beaches. Chatham has more beach area and shoreline than any other Cape Cod

Restored Chatham Wayside Inn attracts both diners and overnight guests.

town, but much of it is privately owned or not easily accessible, and a lot of it suffered a beating in a 1991 storm. Those with boats like the seclusion of the offshore sandbar at the southern tip of the Cape Cod National Seashore, a barrier beach that sheltered Chatham from the open Atlantic until it was breached in an infamous 1987 winter storm. Swimming is available by permit at such town beaches as Harding Beach on Nantucket Sound or the sheltered "Children's Beach" at Oyster Pond. Those who want surf and open ocean head for Orleans and the state beaches to the north.

Monomoy National Wildlife Refuge. Accessible by a short boat trip from Morris Island, this wilderness island stretching south into the Atlantic is a haven for birds – 285 species, at latest count. The 2,500-acre refuge encompasses islands, dunes, saltmarsh, tidal flats, freshwater ponds and seaside thickets that are a natural habitat for nesting gulls, terns, herons and other shore birds. It's also a major stopping point for migratory waterfowl along what ornithologists call the Atlantic Flyway.

Chatham Fish Pier. The fish pier down the slope off Shore Road is popular with sightseers who want to see the real thing. Boats make their run to the fishing grounds ten to one hundred miles into the Atlantic and return with their catch to the pier starting in the early afternoon, depending on tides. Visitors may watch from an observation balcony. Harbor tours also are available here.

Museums. The **Old Atwood House** (1752) on Stage Harbor Road, owned and maintained by the Chatham Historical Society, is one of the town's oldest houses. Upwards of 2,000 antiques are shown in its fourteen display rooms. Among its offerings are seashells, Sandwich glass and the nationally known murals of Alice Stallknecht Wight, "Portrait of a New England Town." Changing exhibits illustrate Chatham life through photos, paintings and artifacts. The museum is open Tuesday-Friday from 1 to 4, mid-June through September; adults, $3. Also open Tuesday-Saturday in summer is the 35-year-old **Railroad Museum,** the former town depot now filled with more than 8,000 models, relics and photos, plus a 1910 caboose. Other historic sites are the **Mayo House** on Main Street, the old **Chatham Grist Mill,** and the **Chatham Light.**

Shopping. Some of Cape Cod's finest shops are located along tree-lined Main Street; more shops seem to open every year and encroach on the residential section to the east. Just stroll along and poke inside any number that appeal. A MacKenzie-Childs table caught our eye at **Lion's Paw** at 403 Main, a branch of the outstanding Nantucket gift shop. Across the street, a red English phone booth at the entry drew us inside **Uniques Ltd.,** three floors of interesting gifts and accessories, from the basement golf room to cedar doormats and a stenciled "Welcome to the Lake" sign. The cotton clothing and gifts, mostly T-shirts and sweat shirts, are attractive at **Habitat Coast,** and the jewelry appealed at the **Dolli Llama.** The **Tale of the Cod** at 450 Main is a ramble of rooms filled with gifts and furniture. Almost across the street is the **Swinging Basket** complex of boutiques. A highlight there is the new **E Komo Mai,** featuring Hawaiian foods, art and gifts. We also liked **Mark August Jewelry,** made locally. **The Artful Hand Gallery** shows especially nice American crafts and contemporary art. **Mark, Fore & Strike** has classic apparel for men and women. Handpainted clothing, especially the shirts decorated with irises, appeal at **Frillz.** We never can resist a stop at **Chatham Cookware** at 524 Main, a fine kitchen store and food shop. Check the linens from France and the colorful pottery from Fitz and Floyd; we especially like the tureens. Take your pineapple scone or your cream of zucchini and almond soup and curried chicken salad to the small outside deck.

The Wayside Inn's new **Gallery/Gift Shop** is a joy to pop into. Owner Helene Wilson, wife of the inn's co-owner, seeks fun and frivolous things. "I'm from New York and look for something different," says she. "If it doesn't make me smile, I don't buy it." The stock in her large shop made us smile from start to finish. Especially intriguing was the lifesize man made of dryer lint with a pocket watch on a chain and a sign saying "please don't touch the grandfather clock — it makes him cranky!" The clock quickly sold for a cool $1,200. Less esoteric but still fun were a table handpainted with bunnies and a rug shaped like a cow.

West of town on Route 28 is **The Cornfield Marketplace,** a special shopping area of interest to those who like culinary excursions. The expanded **Fancy's Farm Market** has the best of vegetables and meat. We like to stop at the **Pampered Palate** to pick up a picnic lunch of sandwiches and salads. It has many specialty foods, too. Also of interest here are **Chatham Natural Foods** and the **House of Birds,** which carries great bird feeders and garden accessories. Upstairs is **Chatham Winery,** with a wide array of fruit wines from cranberry mead to hibiscus flower (the $8 dry blush is issued in a lobster bottle). **Chatham Fish and Lobster** is here as well, so you have all the makings for a picnic or a party at one stop.

Extra-Special

Town Band Concerts. It's hard to imagine in sophisticated Chatham, but upwards of 6,000 people turn out for the Friday evening band concerts, a town tradition every July and August, in Kate Gould Park. Brightly colored balloons bob festively overhead as Whit Tileston, band director since 1946, waves his baton and the band plays on. The 40 instrumentalists, most of them townspeople who rehearse weekly during winter, are joined by the multitudes for rousing singalongs. The natural amphitheater is good both for listening and for watching the children (and often their elders) dance to the music. Before the concerts' 8 p.m. start, St. Christopher's Episcopal Church offers chowder suppers, First United Methodist Church serves lobster roll suppers and the Lions Club runs a hot dog stand in front of the Wayside Inn.

Architecturally rich Nantucket holds treasures like this, now the Jared Coffin House.

Nantucket, Mass.
Island of History and Romance

Stepping onto Steamboat Wharf after a two-and-a-half-hour ferry ride twenty miles into the Atlantic is a bit like stepping onto another land in another time.

"This is the island that time forgot," announces one of Nantucket's visitor guides. "Steeped in tradition, romance, legend and history, she is a refuge from modernity."

Flanked by brick sidewalks, towering shade trees and gas lamps, the cobblestone streets lead you past more fine old sea captains' homes still standing from Nantucket's days as the nation's leading whaling port than most people see in a lifetime. The 400-plus structures from the late 1700s and early 1800s that make up the historic district represent the greatest concentration in America, evoking the town's description as "an architectural jewel."

So much for the island that time forgot. The island's romance draws thousands of well-heeled visitors to a sophisticated side of Nantucket that is uniquely chic and contemporary. More distant than other islands from the mainland and yet readily accessible to the affluent, Nantucket is all the more exclusive.

That's the way island businessman-benefactor Walter Beinecke Jr. planned it when he created the Nantucket Historical Trust in 1957 and later co-founded the Nantucket Conservation Trust. His efforts led to the preservation of 6,100 acres of open space – one-fifth of the island's land total. Through his historic and real-estate interests, the village has been transformed into what the late New England Monthly magazine termed "a perfect oasis – neat, tidy and relentlessly quaint – for upscale vacationers."

It's a bit precious and pricey for some tastes, this town in which whaling fortunes were amassed and which now is predicated on tourism for the elite. (Once you get away from Nantucket village and Siasconset, you'll find the folks on the south beaches and the west side of the island let their hair down). The week our family roughed it, so to speak, in a cottage near the beach at Surfside was far different from the fall weekends starting a decade later when we returned, as so many couples do, for getaways in Nantucket village, 'Sconset or Wauwinet.

Nantucket is perfect for an escape – away from the mainland and into a dream combining Yankee history and the *Preppy Handbook.* You don't have to wear Nantucket pink trousers or dine at Le Chantecleer, although many do. Simply explore the village's treasures, participate in its activities, or relax and watch a select world go by.

Inn Spots

The inn and B&B phenomenon started later on Nantucket and is changing faster than in most areas. The town's traditional boarding and guest houses are being upgraded, and more and more are staying open longer each year. As elsewhere in this book, rates here are quoted for peak season, which generally runs from June through September and the Christmas Stroll. Off-season rates are lower.

The Wauwinet, 120 Wauwinet Road, Box 2580, Nantucket 02554. (508) 228-0145 or (800) 426-8718.

Grandly restored in 1988, this understated "country inn by the sea" is the most elegant on Nantucket and among the most deluxe in New England. Newton (Mass.) developers Stephen and Jill Karp, longtime Nantucket summer home owners, spared no expense in turning the weathered old Wauwinet House into the ultimate in taste and comfort.

The Wauwinet holds a fond place in the memories of the island's gentry, which helps explain the success of its restaurant and the number of sightseers who have oohed and aahed over the intricacies of its transformation since its reopening, and have been coming back ever since. Certainly the location is unmatched – a private, parkland/residential area on a spit of land with the Atlantic surf beyond the dunes across the road in front, the waters at the head of Nantucket Harbor lapping at the lawns in back.

Twenty-four rooms are available in the inn and eleven more rooms and suites are in five cottages across the road. Our Bay View room was not large but was nicely located on a third-floor corner facing the harbor so that we were able to watch spectacular sunsets every night. Fresh and pretty, it had a queensize bed with a striped dust ruffle and lace-trimmed pillows, wicker and upholstered armchairs, and a painted armoire topped with a wooden swan and two hat boxes (one of the inn's decorating signa-

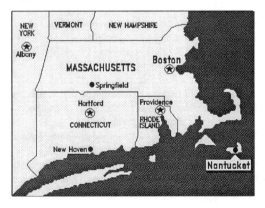

tures). The modern bathroom contained a multitude of thick white towels and a basket of Crabtree & Evelyn amenities. During turndown service, the towels were replenished, mints placed by the bed and the radio turned on.

All the rooms we saw had different, striking stenciled borders (some turning up in the most ingenious places), interesting artworks and sculptures, ceiling fans, and such fillips as clouds

Wicker-furnished back porch looks onto harbor at The Wauwinet.

painted on the ceiling. The deluxe rooms included bigger sitting areas, but many did not seem to be as well located as ours was. Every room holds a TV/VCR, tapes for which may be ordered from a selection of 300, along with a bowl of gourmet popcorn.

The main floor harbors a lovely living room and library done in floral chintz, a back veranda full of wicker that you sink into, a couple of guest rooms, the restaurant and a small, classy lounge. Outside, chairs are lined up strategically on the back lawn, a croquet game is set up, drinks and snacks are available at a small beachside grill, and a resident pro gives lessons on two tennis courts tucked away in the woods. You can swim from a dock or a not particularly inspiring beach along the harbor, or walk a couple of minutes from the hotel through the dunes to the most gorgeous, endless and unoccupied strand we've seen on the Atlantic coast. Sailboats are available.

Friendly service is provided by a staff of 110, an unusually high ratio for the maximum of 80 guests, according to general manager Russell Cleveland, who came to the Wauwinet from the top executive posts at the Williamsburg Inn in Virginia and Salishan Lodge in Oregon. A van is available to transport guests back and forth to town for shopping or to catch the ferryboat. Port and cheese are served house guests every afternoon in the library.

Three meals a day are available in the spacious Topper's (see Dining Spots) and an adjacent patio facing the harbor. A full breakfast is included in the room rate. Guests may order any item from a menu spanning a spectrum from strawberry and rhubarb pancakes to eggwhite omelet with spa cheese and fresh vegetables.

Bedrooms, $290 to $650, B&B; cottages, $490 to $1,300. Four-night minimum in summer. Open mid-May through October.

Jared Coffin House, 29 Broad St., Box 1580, Nantucket 02554. (508) 228-2405 or (800) 248-2405.

One of New England's grand old inns, the famed Jared Coffin House is handsomely furnished with museum-quality pieces. It's also active and busy – like a train station 24 hours a day, some islanders say, in something of an exaggeration.

The public rooms, restaurant, tap room with entertainment and outdoor patio are busy, that is, for this is a center for Nantucket life and a must visit for tourists, if only for a drink or to sample one of the restaurant's brunches or buffets.

The restoration of the island's earliest three-story house was accomplished by Walter Beinecke Jr. and the Nantucket Historical Trust, which acquired it in 1961 for $10,000, renovated and furnished it, and finally sold it in 1975 to innkeepers Phil and Peg Read for more than $750,000 – an example of the gentrification of Nantucket.

The 60 guest rooms are scattered in six buildings, two of which are connected to the main 1845 Jared Coffin House. Three are in houses 30 feet on either side of the main complex. All have private baths and telephones and most have television. Rates include a full breakfast.

Some guests prefer the seven twin and double rooms upstairs in Jared's former home, each furnished with period antiques, artworks and island-woven fabrics. Others covet one of the three large rooms with queensize canopy beds and sitting areas in the 1700s Swain House attached to the main building or, across the street, one of the eighteen queensize canopy rooms in the 1821 Henry Coffin House and the Greek Revival Harrison Gray House.

The public areas are a sight to behold, the living room and library furnished in priceless Chippendale and Sheraton antiques.

Jared's, the inn's large, hotel-style main dining room where jackets are required, features classic American cuisine and changing seasonal menus. Dinner entrées are priced from $16 for broiled sea scallops with garlic and a splash of vermouth to $22 for veal and lobster, sautéed with brandy and mushrooms and served over cappellini. Less formal dinners in the beamed, pine-paneled **Tap Room** downstairs are in the $11.75 to $17.75 range. A "light bite" menu offers things like soups and burgers. Lunch on the patio might be the "Pride of New England," a choice of jumbo frankfurter or deep-fried codfish cake with baked beans, brown bread and cole slaw.

Doubles, $150 to $200.

Centerboard, 8 Chester St., Box 456, Nantucket 02554. (508) 228-9696.

Possibly the most elegant – and certainly the most romantic – of Nantucket's small inns is this winner of a restoration at the edge of the historic district. It's owned by Long Island artist and interior designer Marcia Wasserman, who calls it the fulfillment of a fantasy. She bought the guest house in 1985 and finally reopened it in 1987 after renovations took seven times longer and cost three times more than planned.

There's a big window seat in the living room, outfitted with a TV and stereo, and the floors bear a pickled finish. Adjacent is a casually formal dining room, with cane chairs around a handful of tables, where "the largest continental breakfast you could imagine is served," says resident manager Reggie Reid. A big bowl of fruit (from kiwi to blueberries), granola and cereals, assorted muffins (blueberry-cranberry and mandarin orange-chocolate chip, at our latest visit) and Portuguese breads are the fare.

A two-room suite on the first floor was inspired by a masculine sitting room in an English manor house. It has a library-style living room in dark woods and hunter green, a bedroom with a queensize canopy feather bed with down comforters, and a glamorous bathroom in deep green marble, with a jacuzzi in one section, a large marble-tiled shower in another, and the sink and toilet in still another. The suite has two TVs and plush furnishings, and no fewer than six bouquets of fresh and dried flowers were scattered about when we stayed.

Upstairs, "the theme is romantic – one of Victorian elegance and charm," says Reggie. All with queens or two double beds, private baths, telephones, TVs and refrigerators stocked with soft drinks, the four guest rooms here are bright, airy and decorated in soft pastels. They have ceiling fans, iron and brass bedsteads, lacy pillows, bathrooms with baskets of Gilchrist & Soames toiletries, and even a couple of murals painted by Martha's Vineyard artist Richard Immarrino. A studio apartment in the basement has built-in double beds and a tiny kitchen. All the rooms are air-conditioned.

Doubles, $165; suite, $265. No smoking.

The Sherburne Inn, 10 Gay St., Nantucket 02554. (508) 228-4425.

The first time Pittsburgh corporate types Dale Hamilton III and Susan Gasparich traveled to Nantucket, they took their bicycles off the ferry, pedaled a couple of blocks and decided, "this was the place," in Dale's words. He didn't really have to convince

Balcony view from The Sherburne Inn.

his partner, both of whom had been considering a career change. Thirty days later, in the fall of 1993, they were back on the island negotiating the purchase of the Sherburne (née The House at 10 Gay) Inn. By the spring of 1994, Dale had sold his construction companies in Pennsylvania and the pair were in residence in the structure, which was built as the Atlantic Silk Factory, but has served as a lodging establishment for most of its 160 years.

Dale and Susan continued the renovating and redecorating launched by the previous owner. They offer eight guest rooms, now all with private baths and king or queen beds. Four are on the main floor and four on the second; a beautiful winding staircase connects the two. Interestingly, there's a fireplaced parlor with television on each floor. The bedrooms, bright and cheery, are decorated to the Federal period. They contain canopy and poster beds, oriental rugs and fine artwork. One upstairs in back has a private balcony overlooking the side and rear yards. Another holds a small library and a mini-refrigerator.

Susan bakes blueberry or rhubarb muffins to supplement the natural breads, bagels and English muffins served for continental breakfast. Fresh fruit and juice accompany. The meal is taken in the main-floor parlor, on a deck on one side of the house or in the yard surrounded by gardens and a privet hedge on the other side. Tea and cookies or wine and cheese may be served in the afternoon. The quiet residential setting is a prime attraction.

Doubles, $125 to $160.

Cliff Lodge, 9 Cliff Road, Nantucket 02554. (508) 228-9480.

The eleven rooms and one apartment in this sea captain's home dating to 1771 are more comfortable and have more flair than many in town. And there are all kinds of neat places to sit, inside and out.

Innkeeper Gerrie Miller puts out a breakfast buffet in one of the sitting rooms, or guests can adjourn to the patio or take trays to their rooms. Fresh fruit, granola, cereal, coffeecake, apple crisp and bagels with cream cheese are typical fare. In the afternoons, she offers hot or iced tea and cocktail snacks.

Rooms are notable for spatter-painted floors, Laura Ashley wallpapers, frilly bedding, fresh flowers and antiques. All have private baths, telephones and remote-control TV sets neatly built into the walls or concealed in armoires, and many have kingsize beds and fireplaces. Room 6 yields a view of the ocean, and two others offer harbor views. One single room is available for $65 a night, while the apartment goes for $200.

The five sitting rooms on three floors, a rooftop deck with harbor view, reading porches and a brick patio beside a secluded garden provide plenty of gathering spots for guests.

Doubles, $100 to $160.

Cobblestone Inn, 5 Ash St., Nantucket 02554. (508) 228-1987.

A collection of wooden lighthouses lines the stairs, typical of the thoughtful touches offered at this B&B by Robin Hammer-Yankow, a Chamber of Commerce officer and young mother, and her husband Keith, a local attorney. Their 1725 house along a cobblestoned street is nicely furnished with period pieces.

All of their five guest rooms have private baths and queensize canopy beds, and some have fireplaces. Among the decorative touches are painted Colonial windows and beams, oriental rugs and swag curtains that match the canopies. A sense of history is imparted by tilted doorways, wide-plank floors and narrow closets. The third-floor bedroom, all white and pink with a fancy brass and iron headboard and teal spatter-painted floors, yields a harbor view.

Given its in-town location and the cobblestones on the street outside, we were surprised to find our second-floor room so utterly quiet – at least until the church bells tolled at 7 a.m., as they're prone to do in old New England towns. We arose to prepare for Robin's continental breakfast, served family style at a long table in the dining area behind the living room. Fresh fruit, orange juice, homemade granola, cereals and melt-in-the-mouth pumpkin and zucchini breads provided sustenance for the day ahead.

Guests have room to spread out in the living room with fireplace and cable TV, a sun porch with wicker furniture, and a brick patio overlooking the garden. Robin's childhood Eloise keeps an eye on things from her perch on the ledge of a double dutch door.

Doubles, $100 to $140. No credit cards. No smoking.

Ships Inn, 13 Fair St., Nantucket 02554. (508) 228-0040.

Built in 1831 by whaling captain Obed Starbuck, this house occupies the site where Martha Coffin Mott, the first woman abolitionist, was born in 1793. Nicely restored in 1991 by chef-owner Mark Gottwald and his actress-wife Ellie, it now claims some of Nantucket's most comfortable accommodations as well as a small restaurant of distinction.

Eight of the ten guest rooms have private baths. Named after ships that Starbuck commanded, they contain many of the original furnishings. They have been refurbished with new wallpapers and tiled baths and come with interesting window treatments, Neutrogena toiletries and mini-refrigerators in cabinets beneath the TV sets. Most have reading chairs and half have desks. All but two tiny single rooms that share a bath are more spacious than most Nantucket bedrooms.

Guests enjoy afternoon tea with coffeecake and cookies in the living room. Innkeeper Meghan Moore sets out a continental-plus breakfast of fruit, cereal, scones and muffins.

Chef Mark, who trained at Le Cirque in New York and at Spago in Los Angeles, oversees the restaurant on the lower level (see Dining Spots). The Gottwalds winter with their young children in Vero Beach, Fla., where they opened Ellie's, a new American restaurant on the Intra-Coastal Waterway, in the winter of 1994.

Doubles, $125. Open Memorial Day to Columbus Day.

76 Main Street, 76 Main St., Nantucket 02554. (508) 228-2533.

A costly restoration in 1984 upgraded the old White Eagle Inn into an elegant B&B in an 1883 sea captain's home. It's the only one on central Main Street, a residential section of stately 19th-century mansions.

Front room at 76 Main Street has wing chairs and canopied four-poster bed.

Innkeeper Shirley Peters, who arrived in Nantucket by way of Wellesley, Japan and England, restored the original cherry, oak and walnut floors that had been covered by rugs and papered the walls hidden behind layers of paint. They added private baths for the eleven guest rooms, each furnished with queensize beds, upholstered chairs and antiques.

The large front corner room on the main floor with a canopied four-poster bed and Victorian furnishings is a showplace renting for $135 a night. Besides the other guest rooms on the second and third floors are six family units with TV and refrigerator in a motel-style annex.

Off a grand entry hall are a formal Victorian parlor for reading and the kitchen with dining area, where a continental breakfast of fruits, granola, and homemade muffins and breads is served. Outside are a sheltered courtyard and shady patio with a peach tree in the middle.

Doubles, $115 to $135. No smoking.

Nantucket Landfall, 4 Harbor View Way, Nantucket 02554. (508) 228-0500.

Personal touches such as a scrapbook detailing things to do and restaurant menus are offered by Gail and David More at this B&B located across from the water.

Their old house with a great front porch furnished in white and navy wicker was nicely expanded in 1990 with two larger front rooms on the main floor – one with a kingsize bed and the other with a queen canopy – facing the harbor.

All seven guest rooms have private baths, a couple ingeniously tucked into cubicles "because this is a small house and we had to use every inch," says Gail. She made up for lack of space with interesting decor and colorful comforters. Two second-floor rooms have sitting areas overlooking the harbor, and a downstairs room has its own private patio. The living room contains a fireplace and library. Guests have access to a small kitchen.

The Mores serve a continental-plus breakfast of fresh fruit, local bakery breads and occasionally extras like hard-boiled eggs, pineapple-blueberry cobbler and baked apples.

Doubles, $95 to $160.

Anchor Inn, 66 Centre St., Box 387, Nantucket 02554. (508) 228-0072.

Built by a whaling ship captain, this B&B in the heart of the historic district was the home in the 1950s of the Gilbreths of "Cheaper by the Dozen" fame, who wrote of their experience in the book *Innside Nantucket.* Today it's run very personally by Charles and Ann Balas, active Nantucket promoters who are resident owners and hosts. Retired from their former Nantucket Fine Chocolates store, they still put out chocolates at night in the inn's front parlor.

The interior retains its original random-width floorboards and antique paneling. Eleven guest rooms, named after whaling ships, have private baths, queen or twin beds, and period furnishings. There are the usual Nantucket parlor with a rust-colored corduroy sofa and wing chairs, and a side porch with checked cafe curtains. Here is where Charles's homemade muffins are served for continental breakfast to the accompaniment of classical music.

There's a pleasant patio with lounge furniture in the side pocket-garden.

Doubles, $95 to $145. Closed January-March.

Martin House Inn, 61 Centre St., Box 743, Nantucket 02554. (508) 228-0678.

A broad range of accommodations and prices awaits visitors at this inn, lately transformed by new owners Ceci and Channing Moore "and getting better by the second," in the words of an admiring colleague. This 1803 mariner's home had been a guest house since the 1920s and was rather monastic and short of creature comforts. No more. The Moores, who lived previously in Hong Kong and Wilmington, Del., have tackled their Nantucket project with taste and TLC.

Exceptionally pretty are the large open front foyer and the long front parlor and dining area, with sponged royal blue walls and lovely oriental rugs. The dining-room table is set for breakfast for eight, although some prefer to eat on a tray at one of the wicker chairs on the side veranda. An expanded continental breakfast of two fresh fruits, two cereals, granola, Nantucket breads and homemade muffins is the fare.

The Moores offer thirteen guest rooms, nine with private baths and most with queensize beds. We saw a couple of spacious rooms with canopy beds, fireplaces, cherry dressers and either a loveseat or two plush club chairs. Especially popular is Room 21 with a canopied queen and its own porch. Four rooms on the third floor share baths. One room with two double beds can accommodate four people, and two single rooms are offered at $50 a night.

Doubles, $80 to $150.

Seven Sea Street, 7 Sea St., Nantucket 02554. (508) 228-3577.

This guest house of post and beam construction was built in 1987 on the last vacant lot in town by the Parker family, who also run the Tuckernuck Inn and the Parker Guest House. Son Matthew Parker and his wife Mary oversee this B&B, where guests enter via the dining room. This is where Matthew serves the blueberry and cranberry muffins he bakes for continental breakfast, as well as coffeecake and fresh fruit, nicely presented on Villeroy & Boch china.

The house includes eight guest rooms with queensize fishnet canopy beds, TVs, phones and painted furniture Matthew assembled himself. All contain small refrigerators and modern baths with a vanity outside. Guests have use of a couple of small common rooms on the second floor, the widow's walk deck with a view of the harbor, an indoor hot tub and a pleasant brick patio edged by gardens and hedges.

While Matthew tends to the innkeeping, his wife edits the slick Nantucket Journal magazine, of which he is the co-publisher and business manager.

Doubles, $165. No smoking.

Dining rooms are decorated in Williamsburg style at 21 Federal.

Carlisle House Inn, 26 North Water St., Nantucket 02554. (508) 228-0720.

The fifteen guest rooms in this 1765 house range from a large corner front with fireplace, queensize canopy bed with eyelet cover and rose spread to a small single with pencil-post bed and shower. A third-floor room with strawtop canopy bed and wicker furniture has an inviting, summery air. Nine have private baths, and each has an antique bed with iron or brass headboard or canopied four-poster.

Nowadays in Nantucket, "people want more than a rooming house – they want a place to gather," says owner Peter Conway, who since has opened the deluxe Harbor Light Inn in Marblehead, where he is based. Here he provides an attractive common room with a fireplace, a sun porch with wicker furniture where breakfast is set up buffet style in summer, a Victorian lounge looking onto the garden, and a pleasant back yard.

In the winter, breakfast is served at a huge trestle table by the original kitchen fireplace with its beehive oven and cauldron. Breakfasts include fresh fruits, homemade fruit breads and Portuguese bread.

Doubles, $80 to $150.

Dining Spots

21 Federal, 21 Federal St., Nantucket. (508) 228-2121.

One of Nantucket's larger and higher-profile restaurants (its founding chef opened another restaurant of the same name —now changed — in Washington, D.C.), 21 Federal is on two floors of a sand-colored house with white trim, designated by a brass plaque and elegantly decorated in Williamsburg style. There are six dining rooms of museum-quality, Federal period decor, some with their white-linened tables rather too close together for privacy.

Our latest lunch in a small room next to the convivial bar produced a smashing pasta

($15) – spaghettini with two sauces, one thyme-saffron and one smoked tomato, topped with crabmeat-stuffed shrimp – and a grilled shrimp salad with Greek olives, feta cheese, pine nuts and spinach ($14). Three varieties of breads came with, and a tropical fruit sorbet was a refreshing ending.

Even more memorable was a summer lunch in the courtyard, where white-linened tables create an elegant setting. The pheasant and wild rice soup of the day and a linguini salad with shrimp and pine nuts were out of this world.

Proprietor Chick Walsh and chef Michael Getter change the short dinner menu weekly. Expect main courses ($17 to $28) like crispy salmon with beet sauce, cucumber and tomato; grilled swordfish with corn and chile ragout; spit-roasted chicken with roast garlic, kalamata olives and capers, and charred beef tenderloin with roast shallots and wild rice. The new country grill yields pork, lamb or veal chops or black angus sirloin, each served with green beans and a creamy potato and leek gratin.

For starters ($6 to $14), how about tortilla soup with cilantro and chicken, gravlax with avocado salsa and fried leeks, or foie gras with blackberries, mâche and brioche? Finish with toasted coconut tart, Boston cream pie with cappuccino crème anglaise, or one of the great homemade ice creams and sorbets.

This is Nantucket dining at its best, not as pretentious (though just as pricey) as some and more exciting than many.

Lunch daily, 11:30 to 2:30; dinner, 6 to 9:30. Closed January-March.

Topper's at the Wauwinet, Wauwinet Road, Nantucket. (508) 228-8768.

Named for their dog, whose portrait is in one of the dining rooms, Topper's succeeded beyond its owners' dreams and the kitchen had to be expanded after the initial season. Dining is leisurely in two elegantly appointed, side-by-side rooms with large windows. Upholstered chairs in blue and white are comfortable, tables are well-spaced (or screened from their neighbors), and masses of flowers are all around.

Executive chef Peter Wallace changes his dinner menu weekly. Prices range from $9.50 to $14.50 for appetizers, $24 to $34 for entrées. Among the former, we were impressed with lobster crab cakes with smoked corn and a divine mustard sauce, champagne risotto with sweetbreads and wild mushrooms, and Asian fried quail with sticky rice. The caesar salad ($8.50), a menu fixture, is so delicious that some regulars order it with every meal.

Good main courses are things like roast rack of lamb with potato-fennel brandade and grilled veal chop with wild grape compote, both accompanied by baby vegetables (tiny pattypan squash and carrots about a big as a fingernail) and a wedge of potatoes. Seafood dishes include grilled arctic char with lemon sections and fried capers, lobster with chardonnay beurre blanc and saffron fettuccine, seared tuna with shallot jus and fresh spinach, and grilled swordfish with orange and black sesame seed butter.

Worthy endings might be a refreshing pineapple-papaya sorbet, pecan-praline ice cream and brandysnap horns with devon cream and raspberries. Pastry lovers applaud the drunken chocolate cake with crème anglaise, maple crème caramel and mixed blueberry napoleon on blackberry sauce.

The sparkling Wauwinet Water pours freely from antique cobalt blue bottles, the bread is crusty, salt and pepper are served only on request, and the award-winning wine list is strong in American and French vintages from a selection of more than 500.

The Wauwinet Lady, a 26-passenger water launch, offers complimentary round-trip excursions from town to Topper's for lunch or dinner in season. Lunch features a tasting menu; try several appetizer-size portions such as grilled flatbread with plum tomatoes and goat cheese, wild turkey hash, chiffonade caesar salad and smoked seafood chowder. There's also a three-course, prix-fixe Sunday brunch for $29.

All is elegant for dinner guests at Topper's at the Wauwinet.

Lunch, Monday-Saturday noon to 2; dinner nightly, 6 to 9; Sunday brunch, 10:30 to 2:30. Lounge and bar menu daily, noon to 10. Closed November to mid-May.

The Second Story, 1 South Beach St., Nantucket. (508) 228-3471.

The second floor of a building across from the harbor is all in pink and green, with pink walls, pink and green floral overcloths, and green napkins. Mismatched chairs with cane seats are at tables topped by mums in bud vases and enormous hurricane lamps enclosing candles. An alcove area beside the window onto the harbor is awash with comfy pillows. At night, the place is illuminated entirely by candles, and the setting could not be more glamorous.

The exotic fare served up by chef-proprietor David Toole is a mix of regional cuisines from around the world. The hand-written dinner menu changes frequently and is so completely enticing that one of us could happily graze all the way through. Appetizers ($9 and $10) might be salmon stir-fried with sorrel and mustard and served over fried wantons, bo bun (lamb and rice noodles in a mild Vietnamese shallot and lemon dressing), and grilled oysters with a zesty catalan salsa. We sampled the hot country pâté, a huge slab of goose, duck, chicken and sausage, piping hot and bathed in a creamy green peppercorn sauce. Good monkey bread was hot as could be. The Parducci chardonnay was chilled in a large silver ice bucket, and salt was in a crystal dish.

Entrées ($17 to $24) range from peppered tuna with a horseradish and sundried-tomato vinaigrette to sautéed duckling with sweet and sour grapefruit-shallot sauce. The lobster and black bean enchilada with goat cheese and cilantro sauce, accompanied by guacamole and salsa, is a perennial favorite. The scallops au gratin (with avocado, tomato, garlic and cream) was a portion so ample that we needed neither salad (an extra $4.50) nor appetizer. The Thai shrimp with black bean and coriander sauce was super spicy and left the mouth smoldering long into the night.

For dessert, the amaretto soufflé turned out neither hot nor cold, but more like a mousse with only a hint of amaretto. Better choices might have been grand marnier crème caramel or an Asian napoleon (layers of fried wantons with citrus pastry cream, fruit and a ginger-raspberry sauce.

Dinner nightly except Monday, seatings at 7 and 9:15; Sunday brunch and lunch seasonally. Closed January-March. No smoking.

American Seasons, 80 Centre St., Nantucket. (508) 228-7111.

A simple square room with whimsical decor, eclectic American food and moderate prices make this one of Nantucket's restaurant hits of the 1990s. Chef-owner Everett G. Reid III and his wife Linda made a conscious decision "not to charge Nantucket's awful prices" at their out-of-the-way site. Fifty patrons can be seated in the dining room, which is notable for a colorful wall mural of an Oregon hillside and polyurethaned tables whose tops are handpainted game boards. Twenty-five more can be accommodated on the outdoor patio.

The menu is divided into four sections – Pacific Coast, Wild West, Down South and New England – and you're encouraged to pick and choose among them. One of us made a dinner of three first courses: a bowl of smooth, suave chilled tomato and leek soup with herb brioche croutons and goat cheese, with sprinkles of parsley on the accompanying plate (the remarkable decorative garnishes on the rims make each plate look different). This was followed by corn tortilla flutes with shredded pork and a spicy black bean sauce, heaps of salsa and guacamole. Last was a salad of wild greens, smoked cheddar and crabmeat. The other diner tried the assertive-tasting smoked tomato pasta with grilled sea scallops, fricassee of wild mushrooms and watercress pesto. Entrées were priced from $14 for the New England boiled dinner of cured beef brisket, parsnips and horseradish crème fraîche to $22 for braised venison osso buco with a crispy potato pancake and a sauce of red wine and caramelized onions.

We shared a dessert of raspberry-mango shortcake with raspberry coulis, presented artistically with fresh fruit on a square plate decorated with squiggles of chocolate and crème anglaise.

With one of the reasonably priced bottles from the all-American wine list, we had a memorable meal for what would be considered reasonable mainland prices.

Dinner nightly, 6 to 10. Closed Wednesday in off-season and January-March.

Le Languedoc, 24 Broad St., Nantucket. (508) 228-2552.

Although the Grennan family offer twenty guest rooms in four buildings, their attractive white building with blue shutters across from the Jared Coffin House complex is noted most for its dining.

Downstairs is a cafe with checkered cloths. Upstairs are four small dining rooms with peach walls and white trim, windows covered with peach draperies and valances, and changing art from a local gallery. Windsor chairs are at nicely spaced tables bearing hurricane chimneys with thick candles and vases, each containing one lovely salmon-hued rose.

Among appetizers ($7.75 to $12.50), smoked Nantucket pheasant with cranberry relish was very good and very colorful with red cabbage and slices of apples and oranges on a bed of lettuce. Good warm French bread compensated a bit for the lack of salad (a seasonal salad is $4.50 extra).

Of chef-owner Neal Grennan's entrées ($19.75 to $28.50), one of us sampled noisettes of lamb with artichokes in a rosemary sauce. The other had sautéed sweetbreads and lobster in puff pastry, in a sauce that included shiitake mushrooms, cognac and shallots. Nicely presented on piping hot oval white plates, they were accompanied by snow peas, broccoli, pureed turnips, yellow peppers, sweet potato and peach slices. Other

Second-floor dining room at Le Languedoc is handsome in shades of peach.

interesting choices were fennel-crusted salmon with spaghetti squash and savoy salad, truffled loin of rabbit with sundried cherries and pan-seared veal chop with perigourdine sauce.

For dessert, we passed up strawberry pie and pears poached in a reduction of port to share a dense chocolate hazelnut torte spiked with grand marnier.

You can dine less expensively but well in the cafe, where nothing is priced above $15.50. Lunch is available here and on a canopied sidewalk terrace.

Lunch, 11:30 to 2:30; dinner nightly, 6 to 10. Closed February to mid-April.

Straight Wharf Restaurant, Straight Wharf, Nantucket. (508) 228-4499.

Marian Morash of television and cookbook fame was the original force behind this summery restaurant on the waterfront. She wrote the encyclopedic Victory Garden Cookbook in 1982 with inspiration from her husband Russell, a television producer and weekend gardener, plus Jim Crockett and Julia Child. She left in 1987 to finish a seafood cookbook, but the menu style and spiffy decor remain the same.

Seafood is featured in this popular spot that is the height of chic and priced to match. The complex includes a fish market, a gourmet shop called **Provisions** and a contemporary restaurant, consisting of a large room with soaring, shingled walls topped by billowing banners made by owner Elaine Gifford, a canopied and rib-lit harborfront deck, and a popular bar where appetizers, light entrées and desserts are served.

The menu changes weekly. Appetizers ($7 to $10) could be lobster and fish cakes with tomato-basil beurre blanc, pan-fried shrimp wontons, Malpeque oysters with mignonette sauce and fish soup with rouille. Entrées ($22.50 to $28) run the gamut from grilled tuna with wasabi lime butter and pan-fried salmon with honey-mustard crème fraîche to rack of lamb with roasted garlic. We enjoyed a complimentary bluefish pâté that came with drinks, some first-rate lobster crêpes and a grilled salmon with tarragon-mustard sauce, and the peach Bavarian laden with raspberry sauce. We were not impressed with the vaunted vegetables, which turned out to be plainly cooked broccoli and carrots.

Regulars rave about the bar menu, served from 7 to 10 in the noisy, crowded bar. Here you can order some of the same appetizers and desserts as in the dining room plus five entrées "from the grill" at half the price. Or stop in for espresso and one of the delectable desserts.

Dinner nightly except Monday by reservation, seatings at 6:45 to 9:15. Open mid-June to mid-September. Bar open to mid-October; no reservations.

The Boarding House, 12 Federal St., Nantucket. (508) 228-9622.

The Boarding House provided our first great meal on Nantucket during its inaugural summer of 1973. It since has moved around the corner to considerably larger quarters, and several owners (and chefs) have come and gone. Lately taken over by Seth and Angela Raynor (he a former sous chef at 21 Federal and both veterans of the famed Chanticleer in Siasconset), it's better than ever.

A cathedral-ceilinged Victorian lounge with small faux-marble tables on a flagstone floor opens into a sunken dining room. The latter is striking as can be in rich cream and pink, with a curved banquette at the far end in front of a mural of Vernazzia. The Raynors own the originals but sell lithographs of the exclusive Nantucket series "Streets of Paris," which hang on the walls. Villeroy & Boch china of the Florida pattern graces the nicely spaced tables, which allow for one of Nantucket's more pleasant dining situations.

Equal to the setting is the cooking of Seth, one of 30 chefs chosen to appear on the Great Chefs of the East television series. We were impressed with our latest dinner here: mellow sautéed crab cakes with scallion crème fraîche and grilled quail with crisp fried onion rings and baby mixed greens, among starters from $3.95 to $11, and pan-roasted salmon with Thai curried cream and crispy rice noodles and a spicy Asian seafood stew with lobster, shrimp and scallops, among entrées from $17 to $24.

Accompanying was a powerful Caymus sauvignon blanc ($19) from a well-chosen wine selection with less than the normal Nantucket price markup. Coffee ice cream with chocolate sauce and a dense chocolate-kahlua terrine were worthy endings.

We'd happily return to try more signature dishes, including rare yellowfin tuna with wasabi aioli and soy ginger glaze, grilled lobster tails and grilled tenderloin with wild mushrooms and a creamy potato gratin.

The outdoor terrace is appealing for cocktails and a bistro lunch or supper. We've also found it a felicitous setting for an after-dinner liqueur while watching the late-night strollers pass by.

Lunch daily in season, noon to 2; dinner nightly, 6 to 10. Closed mid-October to mid-November. No smoking.

The Beach Plum Cafe, 11 West Creek Road, Nantucket. (508) 228-8893.

This unpretentious little cafe that started as a bakery on a residential side street at the southern edge of town is a pillar of culinary strength at reasonable prices.

Service is as casual as the decor, but we were rewarded with what CIA-trained chef Jean Dion calls his "upscale food at low-end cost." Two appetizers were exceptional: the ravioli of the evening ($6.50) with feta cheese, sweet peppers and a fabulous sauce of chutney and tomato beurre blanc, and sautéed veal sweetbreads in puff pastry ($8.50). Among entrées ($13.95 to $16.50), we liked the mildly spicy peppered flank steak and the pan-seared loin of lamb with roasted shallot and rosemary sauce. These came with the cafe's trademark potatoes, sliced and baked in olive oil in a convection oven, plus snow peas and fresh corn.

A bottle of the house red wine (Heitz Cellar's Ryan's Red for $14) accompanied. Since this was first a bakery, the desserts are stellar.

For breakfast, try walnut-apple french toast made from baguettes, eggs benedict, Mexican omelets or feather-light buckwheat pancakes with blueberries or cranberries.

Breakfast, Monday-Friday 7 to 10:45, Saturday 7:30 to 1; 61:30, Saturday to 12:30; dinner nightly, 6 to 9:30; lunch in spring and fall, 11:30 to 2; Sunday brunch, 8 to 1.

Ships Inn, 13 Fair St., Nantucket 02554. (508) 228-0040.

Dinners here have received considerable attention since chef-owner Mark Gottwald and his actress-wife Ellie took over. Mark, who trained at Le Cirque in New York and

at Spago in Los Angeles, oversees the cooking duties with a sizable kitchen staff, some of whom accompany the couple in the winter to Florida, where they have opened the acclaimed Ellie's in Vero Beach.

The dining room on the ground level here is attractive with apricot walls over white wainscoting, exposed beams, a white fireplace in the center of the room, candles in the many-paned windows, and white-linened tables dressed with candles and fresh flowers. There also are tables for eating in the adjacent Dory Bar.

Among entrées ($17.50 to $22), you might find seared tuna with tomato-ginger coulis and broccoli rabe, broiled cod with sweet onion confit, crispy salmon with cabernet sauce and celery root puree, lamb osso buco with toasted couscous and steak

Entrance to Ship's Inn.

au poivre with horseradish bordelaise and french fries. Or consider a pasta, perhaps gratin of lobster with tomato compote, potato gnocchi and roasted garlic sauce. Start with fried calamari with ponzu sauce or a sauté of wild mushrooms with creamy polenta. Finish with raspberry sorbet or chocolate-soufflé cake. A well-chosen but pricey wine list starts in the twenties.

Dinner, nightly except Tuesday, 5:30 to 9:15. Closed Columbus Day to Memorial Day.

Diversions

Nantucket's attractions run the gamut from beaches to history to architecture to art and antiques. Except for the beaches, almost everything the visitor needs or wants to do is right in Nantucket village, and easily reached on foot or by bicycle or moped. A number of pamphlets detail interesting walking tours.

Fourteen buildings and exhibits of special interest are maintained by the Nantucket Historical Association, which offers a combination pass to eleven for $8. Among them:

The Whaling Museum, the largest complex and one most visitors pass just after they leave the ferry, is considered the nation's best after the New Bedford Whaling Museum. Originally a candle factory, it contains an original beam press still poised to render whale spermaceti into candles and oil. Rooms are devoted to scrimshaw, whaling equipment and objects brought home by seamen from the South Seas. A whale jaw with teeth, the skeleton of a 43-foot whale and whalecraft shops – a sail loft, cooperage, shipsmith and such – are among the attractions.

Fair Street Museum and Quaker Meeting House. Nantucket's art museum records the lives of early citizens in portraits. An upstairs gallery houses more recent works and special exhibitions. The adjoining Meeting House was built in 1838.

Farther from the center of town are the **Oldest House** (1686), the **Old Mill** (1746) and the **Old Gaol** (1805). Numerous other structures are under Historical Association auspices, but if you simply walk any of the streets fanning out from the center you'll stumble onto your own finds. Don't miss central Main Street, particularly the three handsome Georgian mansions known as **The Three Bricks.**

Walking Tours. The best of several is that led by Roger Young, former town selectman and an energetic semi-retiree, who goes "where the buses don't," through hidden alleys and byways, all the while spinning tales of Nantucket lore. Well worthwhile, the two-hour tours leave daily at 9:30 or 1:30 (the first to make a reservation sets the time); adults, $10.

Art Galleries and Antiques Shops. Besides beaches and good food, it's said that visitors are attracted to Nantucket by all the galleries and antiques shops. They certainly have a wide choice: one brochure is devoted to antiquing on Nantucket, and one of summer's big events is the annual antiques show in early August. Such Nantucket scenes as cobblestoned streets, deserted moors and rose-covered cottages in Siasconset appeal to artists, whose works hang in galleries all along the wharves. **Erica Wilson Needle Works** is a local attraction.

Shopping. Nantucket is a shopper's paradise and, were it not for the cobblestoned streets and salt air, you could as easily picture yourself in Newburyport or New Canaan. Specialty stores with names like **Nobby Clothes** compete with the more traditional like **Murray's Toggery** and **Mitchell's Book Corner,** all across the several square blocks of "downtown" Nantucket. We love the **Lion's Paw,** an exceptional gift shop full of cheerful pottery; check out the animal's tea party. Other standouts are **Zero Main** for suave women's clothing, the **Forager House Collection** of folk art and accessories and **Nantucket Looms** with beautiful, whimsical woven items and a sweater in the window for "only $750." **The Spectrum** is good for arts and crafts. **The Complete Kitchen** is one of the better kitchenware stores we've seen. **Chanticleer to Go** is the in-town gourmet takeout shop where locals and tourists splurge when they can't get out to its namesake restaurant in 'Sconset.

Extra-Special

Nantucket Lightship Baskets. The lightships that protected boats from the treacherous shoal waters off the south and east end of the island in the mid-18th century spawned a cottage industry indigenous to Nantucket. The crews of the South Shoal Lightship turned to basket-weaving to while away their hours on duty. Their duty ended, the seamen continued to make baskets ashore – first primitive and heavy-duty types for carrying laundry or groceries, later more beautiful handbags appealing to visitors. The latter were inspired by the Sayle family, who continue the tradition at their shop on Washington Street Extension. Today, Nantucket's famed baskets come in all shapes and sizes (including 14-karat gold miniatures) and seem to be ubiquitous in the shops and on tanned arms. The handbags have ivory carvings on top and carry hefty price tags. The Four Winds Craft Guild on Straight Wharf claims to have the largest collection.

Edgartown, Mass.
Fall for the Vineyard

One of the best things about visiting an island is the ferry ride over from the mainland. The ringing of ships' bells, the whistle as you depart, the hustle and bustle of getting cars on and off – they all add to the anticipation of what is to come.

Even though the trip to Martha's Vineyard from Wood's Hole takes less than an hour, that's time enough to listen to the buoys clanking, and to watch one shore fade in the distance and another grow closer.

It's time enough also for a transition – to leave mainland cares behind, before arriving at Vineyard Haven or Oak Bluffs and stepping into a different milieu.

The Vineyard is nothing if not varied. Oak Bluffs, where the many-splendored gingerbread cottages present a rainbow of hues, is a Methodist campground, Victorian beach resort and summer home to many affluent African-Americans. At the other end of the island are the Indian-owned restaurants and shops atop windswept Gay Head, its cliffs a mosaic of colors and an Eastern mini-version of the Big Sur. In the interior of West Tisbury and Chilmark, the landscape is such that you might not even think you were on an island.

Then there's Edgartown, as up-to-date as a resort town can be while still reflecting a heritage back to 1642. It's a prosperous seaport village, which boomed during the whaling days of the 19th century and became a yacht-ing center in the 20th century. It's

Daggett House inn backs up to Edgartown Harbor.

been in the news lately during summer visits by President Clinton and his entourage.

Long a retreat for the rich and famous as well as the rich and not-so-famous, Edgartown is best appreciated in the off-season. The crowds are gone, but the charm remains as benign autumn weather lingers at least through Thanksgiving. The beaches are deserted except for strollers. The waters are left for the fishermen and a few hardy sailors and wind-surfers. Cottages and condos are battened down for the winter.

Autumn is the season that islanders and knowing visitors look forward to, particularly in Edgartown, a year-round haven for retirees and escapees from the mainland. Many inns and restaurants remain open most of the year, but prices are reduced. You can be near the ocean in a moderate clime, and immerse yourself in a delightful community.

"Fall for Martha's Vineyard," the magazine ads entice in trying to boost autumn trade. It's hard to imagine how anyone wouldn't.

Inn Spots

Rates at Edgartown inns vary seasonally, and seasons vary from inn to inn. "In-season" is generally from sometime in June to sometime in September or October, "off-season" is usually from November to March or April, and "interim season" covers the periods in between. Rates quoted here, as elsewhere, are for peak season.

The Charlotte Inn, South Summer Street, Edgartown 02539. (508) 627-4751.

You register at a front desk so ornate that it is pictured in the centerfold of the Architectural Digest inn book. At one side of the main floor are a two-room art gallery and across the street a gift shop, both destinations in themselves. Behind is a small, deluxe restaurant in which you dine romantically in an indoor-outdoor garden reminiscent of New Orleans or Europe. You relax beforehand on the side porch running the depth of the Summer House, rejoicing in the fountains and flowers and a scent resembling eucalyptus; the ice for your drinks comes in a green leather bucket. And later you retire in one of 25 guest rooms that are so lavishly and tastefully furnished as to defy expectation.

The Charlotte Inn compound, which Gery (for Gerret) and Paula Conover have developed from a private home he acquired in 1971, is nothing short of a masterpiece. It carries the aura of elegance that's the hallmark of Relais & Châteaux properties. But it's also a very personal place, a reflection of Gery's desire to have an art gallery (he runs a restoration and real estate business as well) and of Paula's flair with flowers, decorating and stitchery. She made many of the pillows and comforters that enhance each guest room.

Rooms are in the main two-story 1860 house, a rear carriage house that Gery built without blueprints in 1980, the 1705 Garden House (so called because of its lovely English garden in back) across the street, the 1840 Summer House next door, and the Coach House Suite.

The much-photographed deluxe suite upstairs in the Carriage House has an English hunting feel to it: a queensize bed with brass bedstead, a mahogany sleigh bed redecorated as a sofa, a working marble fireplace, a beamed cathedral ceiling, thick beige carpeting, walls covered in hunter green or red and green stripes, a TV and stereo hidden away in a chest, and a treasury of bric-a-brac from a gentleman's riding boots to one of the earliest cameras perched on a tripod in the corner. Even more to our liking is the Coach House Suite, bigger and less masculine, outfitted like a well-planned house. The bed is covered with lace, there's a tiny balcony with wicker chairs, and the living room, with its easy chairs and hassocks, is exquisite. The walk-in dressing room/

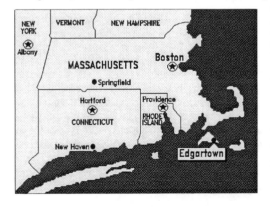

closet is a fantasy of hats, fans and hat boxes. Downstairs is what general manager Carol Reed routinely calls the garage; it would be a museum anywhere else. Here – amid so many museum-quality treasures – it goes relatively unnoticed by all but the Coach House occupants, who have their own museum for the duration upstairs. The suites rent for $395 to $550, and Gery says they're booked almost every night.

After seeing these and a sampling of other opulent rooms, we wondered about ours (the last available and at the other end of the price scale). No. 18 in the Summer House had a private entrance off the wicker-filled side porch (we happened to be its only users on a couple of mild October days and nights). Although relatively small, it was luxuriously comfortable, with a four-poster bed, two wingback chairs and many an-

tiques that are typical throughout. Even the hallways are decorated just so with fine paintings and antiques. Most rooms come with television and telephones.

The compound is a landscaper's dream, full of exotic greenery, vivid flowers, trickling fountains and trellised arbors. Gery laid the spacious courtyard in front of the Coach House Suite brick by brick, and tends to the flowers with old watering cans from one of his many and diverse collections.

Continental breakfast is served in the conservatory dining room and terrace that houses the inn's restaurant, **L'Étoile** (see Dining Spots). Classical music and a splashing fountain are the backdrop for fresh orange juice, tea or coffee and breads (perhaps raisin or cranberry) and muffins (walnut-sour cream, cheese, cranberry and apple) served with raspberry preserves and marmalade. More substantial breakfasts are available at extra cost, a choice of rasp-

Coach House Suite at The Charlotte Inn.

berry waffles or a sour cream and asparagus omelet, preceded by broiled grapefruit, at our visit.

Dinners at L'Étoile, whose space is leased by chef-owner Michael Brisson, are considered the priciest and most elegant on the island. After dinner, you can wander around the art gallery, watch television or play games in the small fireplaced living room of the Garden House, or simply relax on the wicker rockers on the porch of the Summer House, taking in the sights of the illuminated Charlotte Inn complex and the sounds of the fountains and the church bells on the hour.

Doubles, $195 to $425; suites, $395 to $550.

Tuscany Inn, 22 N. Water St., Box 2428, Edgartown 02539. (508) 627-5999.

Gorgeous annuals line the walkway to this showy new inn, all renovated and redecorated from head to toe from its rooming-house days as the old Captain Fisher House. Laura Scheuer, a native of Pisa who was schooled in Florence, and her retired IBM husband, Rusty, moved here from Potomac, Md., to create her vision of an eight-room Tuscan inn on a New England island.

"Everything you see here has been restored," said Rusty, whose wife obviously spared no expense to promote authenticity and style. It took two workmen four months just to strip the stairway and newel posts back to their original chestnut sheen. The first floor of the Italianate Victorian house is devoted to common space as the Scheuers "try to make guests feel at home." They're at home very nicely in the stunning parlor, light and airy with yellow-sponged walls, snow-white sofas and chairs, and splashy art all around. In the clubby library, a table discreetly displays the Scheuers' stack of snapshots of President Clinton playing the saxophone at a reception. The formal dining room holds an impressive collection of blue plates. The remarkable breakfast room reminds Laura of home. It's a work of art, with an archway onto the semi-open commercial kitchen, distressed wood trim, shelves of cookbooks and four tables dressed in blue and white checked cloths and topped with pots of flowers.

Here is where Laura combines her twin passions: interior design (she was a decorator in New York for twenty years) and cooking (she has been seeking zoning approval to operate a small restaurant here someday). Guests are treated to sumptuous fare in the breakfast room or on the side patio beside the cutting gardens. Laura gets the day off to a good start with juices and fruits, homemade breads and one of her specialties: frittatas, buttermilk blueberry pancakes or french toast made from baguettes.

Breakfast room at Tuscany Inn.

Upstairs on two floors are eight guest rooms with private baths, three with marble whirlpool tubs. Lovely in blue and white, the honeymoon room offers a view of the harbor, a kingsize bed with a fabric-covered headboard, two halogen reading lights beside the bed, a couple of wing chairs and Lord & Mayfair toiletries. The tiny La Bohème, its twin beds tucked into the gable, has a semi-open bathtub with hand-held shower beneath a skylight. A loveseat facing the window of the second-floor front room takes full advantage of the harbor view. The curving stairway to the third floor passes a niche where a spotlight illuminates the Japanese-style flower arrangement. With an obvious eye for what goes with what, Laura has decorated the rooms with great taste to showcase acquisitions from the couple's travels.

Besides the interior of the house, guests enjoy a side gazebo on the small wrap-around porch and a back yard that's uncommonly large for a location in the center of town.

Doubles, $185 to $295. Closed January-March.

Point Way Inn, Main Street at Pease's Point Way, Box 128, Edgartown 02539. (508) 627-8633 or (800) 942-9569.

Remodeled from a 150-year-old whaling captain's house, this fifteen-room inn offers a variety of comfortable accommodations and personality galore. Ben and Linda Smith, who landed in Edgartown Harbor in 1979 after a 4,000-mile sailing cruise, spent that winter turning the house into an inn reflecting family interests through and through.

You'll enjoy the pictures of their 38-foot ketch, the Point Way (on which they used to offer cruises off Florida or the Caribbean islands in winter), as well as the memorabilia of the Edgartown Mallet Club, a croquet group that ex-lawyer Ben formed to play on the inn's lawn, all the yachting and golfing trophies, the photos of the Yale Whiffenpoofs of which Ben was a member, and the paintings by his aunt, who was of the Boston School of Impressionists and studied with Monet.

Each of the guest rooms, grouped off various stairways in separate sections of the house, has a private bath and ten contain fireplaces. Canopy and four-poster beds, colorful quilts, wing chairs, wicker or tweedy sofas, a couple of tiny porches and a

Croquet court is ready for play alongside the Point Way Inn.

large deck – it's a delightful mishmash that's comfortable as can be. Each room also bears nice touches like decanters of sherry, stamped envelopes, pin cushions and taffy. Six rooms have french doors opening onto private balconies or terraces. The star of the show is a two-room suite with deck and fireplace.

The cozy living room comes with a fireplace, games, a spectacular 500-piece wood jigsaw puzzle and a well-stocked honor bar. Assorted sailing trophies hold fresh flowers. Flags that Ben used on his boats are under the glass-covered tables in the breakfast room, in which fresh orange juice, cereals, granola, popovers, coffeecake, muffins and breads are served buffet style on dishes and mugs emblazoned with birds.

Tea or lemonade and cookies (oatmeal, just like our mothers used to make, at our last visit) plus clams – if guests have been successful on clamming expeditions – are an afternoon highlight in the ivy-covered outdoor gazebo, which is part of the mallet club. Guests as well as members may play croquet if they wish.

Doubles, $120 to $200; suite, $235.

The Victorian Inn, 24 South Water St., Edgartown 02539. (508) 627-4784.

Masses of impatiens brighten the striking facade of this inn, nicely located across from the famous Pagoda Tree in an area of ship's captain's homes. It's as Victorian as can be, well deserving of its listing in the National Register. It's also generally as luxurious as can be, from its elegantly furnished rooms to the gourmet breakfasts served in the English garden backing up to the Charlotte Inn compound in the rear.

Keen new innkeepers Stephen and Karyn Caliri from Plymouth happened to be staying here when they learned the inn was being sold at auction. They put in the winning bid and set about a five-year upgrading plan, promising the inn would be "pretty spiffy when we're done." To start, they restored the fireplaces in the parlor and breakfast room to working order, redecorated the dining room, and redid three bedrooms and six bathrooms. They were looking to enhance the rest of the fourteen guest rooms, all with private bathrooms (only one with a tub) and some with inviting sitting areas. Karyn's favorite is the large and elegant Room 9 with king poster bed, Empire chest and sofa in the bay window. It and another deluxe room at the rear have porches with deck chairs and loungers overlooking the English garden and the carriage house of the Charlotte Inn. Stephen is partial to the third-floor Room 10, with queen canopy bed, dusty rose carpeting and two balconies, one facing the harbor. He also likes Room 14 with kingsize plantation bed and trundle beneath, white sofa and green armchairs and a deck beyond. Rooms vary considerably in size and appeal, as the range in rates suggests. Deep, rich shades of rose, green and blue are the prevailing colors, and some of the sheets and shower curtains are patterned with roses. Decanters of sherry and bowls of apples are put out in the Victorian parlor, where tea or lemonade are offered in the afternoon.

Karyn and a chef share the cooking chores for the four-course breakfast, which also is available to the public by reservation for $12.50. Fresh fruits, five kinds of juices and a pastry basket filled with assorted muffins (from orange to banana) and croissants start the repast. Main courses could be pumpkin pancakes, eggs benedict, fish cakes topped with poached eggs and creamed spinach, or Mexican eggs with cheese, corn and chiles. In summer, breakfast is served outside at white tables on a delightful brick patio amid the greenery and flowers of the English garden.

Doubles, $110 to $225.

The Shiverick Inn, Pent Lane at Pease's Point Way, Box 640, Edgartown 02539. (508) 627-3797 or (800) 723-4292.

Built in 1840 for the town physician, this mansion was restored in 1984 by Philadelphia descendants of the Shiverick line and opened as the Dr. Shiverick House, a fancy if somewhat austere-feeling inn that suffered under high-powered owners.

Denise and Marty Turmelle took over in 1992 and started warming up an antiques-filled masterpiece that some had found intimidating. Warmth is a hallmark of the lady of the house, an effusive type who goes by the name Denny and calls everybody honey or darling.

The theme, as described in the inn's brochure, is still a "grandly romantic sequence of visual pleasures and physical comforts purposely designed to enchant the senses and enrich the spirit." Inside the oak double-door entry is a high-ceilinged entrance hall with the original mahogany staircase and a remarkable showpiece spool cabinet.

Ahead is a formal parlor/dining room, notable for gorgeous rugs over random-width floorboards restored from a barn in Vermont. A crystal chandelier hangs over the dining table, and porcelain figures line the mantel. Balloon draperies frame the parlor's windows onto a spacious garden room, which has a long sofa along one wall, wrought-iron furniture with ivy-patterned seats, and a long tiled counter (painted with ivy) for breakfast or cocktail service. Beyond is a delightful patio and garden colorful with pink and white flowers, which are also on view from an upstairs porch. A sunny library is made for relaxing.

The inn has ten guest rooms and suites on the first and second floors. Each has a full bath and six have working fireplaces. They are sumptuously furnished with four-poster or canopy beds, a variety of art objects and antiques, oriental rugs, and rich wallpapers and fabrics. The Turmelles have changed two twin-bedded rooms to kings and queens "to go along with the theme of romance."

A continental-plus breakfast starts with fresh fruit, cereal, yogurt and granola. The main event involves three kinds of homemade pastries (at our visit, carrot and banana breads and orange-walnut coffeecake), plus English muffin toasting bread that Denny makes every day. In the afternoon, she offers tea or lemonade, depending on season.

The Turmelles moved here from management jobs in New Hampshire when their three sons left the nest. They occupy the inn's third floor and are hands-on innkeepers.

Doubles, $175 to $225; suites, $250.

Rear cottage adds to lodging accommodations at Jonathan Munroe House

Jonathan Munroe House, 100 Main St., Edgartown 02539. (508) 627-5536.

His family used to run the Darien Inn in Vermont's Northeast Kingdom, so Chip Yerkes comes by his new sideline naturally. A building contractor on the Vineyard, he applied his carpentry talents in 1994 to his unassuming house built in 1840 and created a promising B&B with eight bedrooms and a cottage.

Guests check in at a corner cabinet in the small front parlor. Beyond is a larger, fireplaced dining room, where personable Chip serves a continental-plus breakfast of fresh fruits, baked goods and cereals. The meal may be taken in season on the rear patio.

All bedrooms have private baths. Four with marble fireplaces come with jacuzzi tubs. The rooms are furnished simply but comfortably with king or queen beds and floral comforters with matching curtains.

We were among Chip's first paying guests, and could determine from his rear cottage what treats were in store. Snug and modern, it has a living room with a plush sofa and a wicker chair facing a brick fireplace, an old wood chest for a coffee table, an antique wood desk bearing a diary in which the first guests waxed ecstatic, and a kitchenette with a ceramic sink, microwave, pottery dishes and an antique side-by-side dining table set for two. Paneling enhances the staircase and second-floor landing, where the whirlpool tub is ensconced beside votive candles and sconces for lighting. The queensize bed is situated beneath a vaulted ceiling in the bedroom. The cottage's screened porch may well be the best place in town to enjoy the carillon hymns played nightly from the nearby St. Andrew's Episcopal Church.

Doubles, $150 to $200; cottage, $240.

Edgartown Inn, 56 North Water St., Box 1211, Edgartown 02539. (508) 627-4794.

The plaque on the side of this 1798 whaling captain's residence notes that Daniel Webster, Charles Sumner and Nathaniel Hawthorne once were guests here. The place fairly oozes history and character, so we did not expect to find such comfortable, nicely furnished rooms at prices that represent excellent value.

The twenty rooms in the main inn, the rear garden house and "Le Barn" vary from three simple rooms with sinks in the room and a shared bath to the spacious King's Room with double beds at either end and a fabric loveseat in the center, facing the bow window and the harbor. The large Nathaniel Hawthorne Room, pretty in Williamsburg blue-green trim and floral wallpapers, comes with kingsize bed and two wicker chairs. Quite idyllic with its own balcony is the skylit Dogwood Room, one of two large and quiet rooms in the rear Garden House overlooking the garden courtyard. It has a kingsize wicker bed, pretty floral wallpaper and draperies, and television. Most rooms are carpeted and nicely refurbished by longtime owner Earle Radford, a Kansas City artist who now lives on Chappaquiddick and whose paintings adorn the inn's hallways and small front TV/common room.

Susanne Faraca, innkeeper since 1982, helps serve what the inn quotes as "the best breakfast on the island." If it's the best, heaven help us, but it certainly is colorful and full of character. The meal is served on the rear garden courtyard or in a small, convivial dining room where every inch of wall and shelf space is covered with bric-a-brac. The focal point is Henry, for 49 years the inn's handyman and man Friday, who was outfitted in a bright red uniform with matching bow tie at our visit (he changes his colors daily, we're told). He served us juice, coffee and a plate of carrot cake before taking orders for poached eggs on the inn's famous cheese toast and scrambled eggs with oatmeal toast. The eggs were ordinary and came with three slices of crisp bacon and only one of toast, but the character of the place more than compensated.

Breakfast, open to the public, is $3.75 for continental, $6.50 for full.

Doubles, $70 to $150, EP. Closed November-March.

The Daggett House, 59 North Water St., Edgartown 02539. (508) 627-4600 or (800) 946-3400.

For a waterfront location, this bed-and-breakfast inn with 26 rooms and suites in two houses and a cottage is unsurpassed in Edgartown. The long, narrow rear lawn with flowers, benches and umbrellaed tables slopes down to the water and a private pier next to the Chappaquiddick Ferry landing.

Guest rooms, all with private baths, are in the main 1750 Daggett House with its historic tavern downstairs, the newer (early 1800s) and larger Captain Warren House across Water Street, and the seaside Garden Cottage, which has three double rooms. Generally quite spacious, the rooms are furnished with oversize canopy and four-poster beds, artworks and antiques. Newest are two suites. The Chappaquiddick in the main house offers a bedroom and bath with whirlpool tub downstairs, an enclosed patio with jacuzzi and a spiral staircase leading up to a living room, kitchen area and private deck overlooking the harbor. Television and telephones are offered here and in the Penthouse Suite, formerly the owner's quarters atop the Captain Warren House. It has two bedrooms, two baths, a living room with sofabed and a private jacuzzi atop the widow's walk with a panoramic view of the harbor.

After its location, the next best thing is the historic downstairs tavern room, which dates from the 1660s and above which the house was later built. The island's first tavern, it looks the way an early tavern should look, with its unusual beehive fireplace chimney, dark beams, wide pine hardwood flooring, old tools and bare wood communal tables for six, where conviviality is the norm. A local artist who illustrates summer resident Carly Simon's books painted the stunning Daggett House mural that now graces one wall.

Breakfast – with wonderful toast made from bread from the recipe of the late Lucille Chirgwin, who with her husband Fred owned the inn for 40 years – costs $4.50 to $7.50 (for a fine eggs benedict). Breakfast is available to the public as well, and the ambiance is such that people gladly wait for a table while sipping coffee served on the rear terrace. Dinners also are available for guests and the public, with entrées priced from $14.50 to $19.

Hidden near the fireplace in the tavern room is a secret staircase that provides steep, low-ceilinged access to an upstairs guest room with kingsize bed, gold wallpaper and a view of the harbor.

Off the entrance to the main inn is a small living room with sofas, wing chairs and a television set. Among the fourteen rooms in the Warren House are several efficiencies and suites good for families. The two sons of the Chirgwins have turned over innkeeping duties to a manager.

Doubles, $140 to $195, EP; suites, $230 to $395, EP. Main house open all year; Captain Warren House and Garden Cottage open April to November. Breakfast, daily 7:30 to 11, Sunday 8 to 1; dinner, Wednesday-Sunday 5:30 to 9.

The Governor Bradford Inn, 128 Main St., Edgartown 02539. (508) 627-9510.

Resident innkeepers oversee a mid-19th century house that has been converted into an appealing inn of comfort and style. All sixteen rooms on three floors have private baths, kingsize brass or four-poster beds, and ceiling fans, most have color TV, and some have Queen Anne wing chairs.

Sherry is provided guests in the formal front parlor full of Victorian antiques. Afternoon tea is served in the television room, decorated in colorful gold and navy and oriental rugs. The paneled garden room has white wicker chairs with green corduroy seats and a bar with a refrigerator with ice and setups.

A full breakfast is served in the country-pretty dining room, where bentwood chairs face round tables dressed in pink and white linens and a willowware collection is on display in the Sheraton china cabinet. The specialty of innkeepers Brenda and Ray Raffurty is homemade cinnamon apple rolls, served with creamed eggs, fruit and juice. Stuffed french toast with cream cheese, pineapple, walnuts and homemade raspberry syrup is another favorite.

Doubles, $95 to $210.

Dining Spots

L'Étoile, South Summer Street, Edgartown. (508) 627-5187.

Ensconced at the rear of the Charlotte Inn, this bow-windowed conservatory/dining room is utterly charming. It's handsomely furnished with white bentwood and cane chairs, brick walls, skylights, paintings, lush ferns and a blooming hibiscus tree.

Chef-owner Michael Brisson and his wife, Joan Parzanese, are known for exquisite food and artistic presentation that is altogether worthy of the inn's Relais & Châteaux designation. The 34-year-old chef, who cooked for four years at the acclaimed L'Espalier in Boston, takes special pride in his treatment of game, lamb and native seafood. He also is partial to the understated place settings of white, gold-edged Villeroy & Boch china, the Reed & Barton silverplate and fluted crystal wine glasses at white-linened tables seating 45 inside. Another twenty or so can be accommodated on an outdoor patio beside a trickling fountain.

Dinner is prix-fixe ($56), with some items carrying substantial surcharges. You can tell there's a master in the kitchen from some of the appetizers: a chilled soup of sweet yellow banana peppers and golden tomatoes with cucumber and crabmeat salsa; a country pâté of veal with black truffles, pickled summer vegetables and two mustards, or pastrami-smoked salmon and grilled shrimp on mesclun greens with avocado and belgian endive, caviar croustades, and a roasted white corn and molasses vinaigrette.

A homemade sorbet clears the palate for the main course. Among the six choices could be dover sole fillets on sautéed summer greens and lobster mushrooms with champagne-lemon-saffron sauce, seared Long Island duck breast with a pinot noir and blackberry sauce and a pan-fried quinoa and vegetable croquette, roasted lamb noisettes with goat cheese and toasted walnut-filled baby eggplant, and grilled filet mignon with white truffle and cognac cream sauce, forest mushrooms and white truffle ravioli.

Desserts include chocolate marquis, lemon-lime tart with strawberry coulis, crème courvoisier with peach coulis, or caramelized macadamia ice cream with Bailey's crème anglaise.

The wine list starts with many champagnes, since for most this is special-occasion dining. But it offers a variety of good French and California choices at affordable prices.

Dinner nightly in summer, 6:30 to 9:45; Tuesday-Sunday in off-season, weekends in winter; Sunday brunch, 10:30 to 12:30. Closed January to mid-February.

Savoir Fare, Post Office Square, Edgartown. (508) 627-9864.

What began as basically a gourmet takeout shop has expanded into "a garden of epicurean delights" – a small but full-fledged, inside-outside restaurant known for the best lunches in town. Since 1988, owners Scott and Charlotte Caskey have been serving dinners as well. Chef Scott, who used to cook in Vail, works in an open kitchen at one end of the small restaurant, which is a picture of pristine white from its glass-covered linened tables to the lights on a ficus tree. There's a counter with four chairs, but most of the action is outside at tables on a deck.

For lunch, you order inside from a blackboard menu ($7.50 to $12.50) and the staff brings your choices to the table. We savored a caesar salad topped with grilled chicken, which everyone seemed to be ordering that day, and a small combination plate of curried chicken and pesto-pasta salads, accompanied by good French bread and a glass of the house Spanish wine.

At night, food comes from a short, changing menu of contemporary cuisine. Typical summer fare might begin with appetizers ($7.50 to $10) like Tuscan grilled vegetable antipasti, warm lobster and green bean salad with toasted almonds, and crimini mushroom and seared duck breast salad with risotto cakes. Main dishes ($19 to $24) could be polenta-crusted salmon with braised lentils and barolo sauce, seared sea scallops on sherry shrimp risotto with arugula, a classic veal osso buco, or grilled pork chops with creamy polenta, tomato concasse and chipolata. You want lobster? Try it Caskey style sautéed with potato ravioli, English peas, sweet corn and apple-smoked bacon, an ethereal treat.

Banana cream pie with mascarpone and chocolate ganache, lemon tart with crème anglaise, and tirami su are among the desserts.

Lunch, Monday-Saturday 11:30 to 2:30; dinner nightly, 6 to 10; slightly shorter hours in off-season. Closed mid-October to mid-March.

Lattanzi's, Old Post Office Square, Edgartown. (508) 627-8854.

Our longtime favorite Warriner's restaurant gave way in 1994 to Lattanzi's, the new Italian showplace for chef-owner Albert Lattanzi, who had been chef for years at Andrea's. Here, he lightened up the walls of the elegant library room at Warriner's to produce a Mediterranean look, and topped the white linened tables with white butcher paper for an Italian bistro feeling.

The atmosphere is refined and the food so abundant that some actually complain the portions are much too big. The manager advises that almost everyone takes the leftovers home in a Lattanzi basket, and many phone to say how much they enjoyed it the next day. Albert makes his pastas by hand, cooks his meats on a hardwood grill and buys his seafood from fishermen who come to his back door as soon as they get off the boat.

Conservatory/dining room at L'Étoile.

Deck at Savoir Fare faces Lattanzi's.

The pasta dishes ($16 to $19) are highly rated, especially the penne carbonara with bacon, onions, carrots and cream and the fettuccine picante with anchovies, hot cherry peppers and garlic. Main courses are priced from $18 for grilled chicken with morels and porcini cream or grilled pork tenderloin with apricots, garlic and herbs to $28 for porterhouse steak. The mixed grill with lamb, hot Italian sausage, pork and spicy peach chutney and the grilled lamb ribeye steak appealed the night we were there.

Appetizers here are good but superfluous. Save room instead for a stellar tirami su, the chocolate cannoli, the fresh fruit tarts or, at the very least, a cheese plate. The wine list focuses on Italian vintages.

Dinner nightly, 6 to 9:30; lunch in off-season, noon to 3. No smoking.

Sandcastles, 71 Main St., Edgartown. (508) 627-8446.

The folks from Warriner's – Sam and his son, Steve – moved to the old Martha's restaurant facility in 1993 and reopened it as Sandcastles. They ran both restaurants for a year before deciding to close Warriner's and concentrate on this, a seasonal operation.

The place retains the best of the old Martha's look, particularly the trademark porches along the front and side. The inside is pretty in peach and green, though we find the tables too close for comfort. Those seeking less conviviality and more privacy may be happier upstairs in the bar or a larger dining room. Or, if you can snag a table, on one of the porches overlooking the street scene.

We were the only ones who chose to do so on a coolish October evening when everyone else coming and going asked "aren't you cold?" Indeed not, and we were very well served and fed. The caesar salad and roasted asparagus wrapped with red pepper, chèvre and prosciutto were satisfying starters. For main courses ($16 to $23), one of us tried the mixed grill of chicken, beef tenderloin and smoked Polish sausage and shrimp. The other was enticed to try a special of jalapeño cheddar ravioli with corn and crab sauce and grilled gazpacho vegetables – very unusual, as the waiter had said, and very good. A bottle of our favorite Hogue sauvignon blanc ($18) accompanied. When the dessert recitation (chocolate-almond tart, key lime pie, chambord cheesecake and fruit crisp) didn't include anything particularly cooling, we only had to saunter down the block to Vineyard Scoops for a couple that hit the spot: peach frozen yogurt and ginger ice cream.

The marinated steak salad that we'd eyed on the dinner menu also turns up at lunch, when you could be tempted by a smoked turkey sandwich with boursin and roasted red peppers or a lobster roll ($5.95 to $9). Sandcastles also makes a good stop for breakfast. Corned beef hash with eggs and potatoes, Portuguese sweet bread french toast and a bagel with smoked salmon are in the $5 to $8 range.

Breakfast, daily in summer; lunch, 11:30 to 2:30; dinner, 6 to 10. Shorter hours in off-season and closed late October to May.

Shiretown Inn, 21 North Water St., Edgartown. (508) 627-3353.

In season, the large indoor-outdoor dining room and covered terrace at the rear of the Shiretown Inn is one of the more popular spots in Edgartown. Pink linens and pink and green wallpaper provide a soft backdrop for the garden setting, and many diners like to have drinks in the garden or in Jack's Pub adjacent to the dining room.

Well-spaced tables, soft candlelight and quiet music provide a glamorous backdrop for the widely acclaimed fare of chef Jack Hakes, one of the island's veterans. Seafood is the specialty, and the inn claims the best clam chowder on the island ($4). Other starters include lobster bisque (whose recipe is a well-kept secret), Maryland crab cake with rouille, steamed mussels with basil and baked littlenecks with garlic. Typical entrées ($17.50 to $25.95, except $35 for a three-pound lobster stuffed with crabmeat) are sautéed halibut véronique, chargrilled Menemsha swordfish steak, rack of lamb dijon, veal chop madeira with shiitake ragout, and tournedos sautéed with crabmeat and brandy, served with avocado pâté and béarnaise sauce.

Three kinds of breads in a basket and salads with caesar dressing and pine nuts preceded our entrées of four jumbo shrimp in a rich garlic sauce, accompanied by baby vegetables that were past their prime, and an enormous helping of baked Norwegian salmon in puff pastry.

Fancy ice creams are the dessert specialty, among them the Shiretown wonder: ice cream with hot fudge sauce, crème de menthe and shredded coconut. We decided instead on a slice of tangy key lime pie, smothered with whipped cream, from the pastry cart.

Light fare is offered on a pub menu, priced from $5.95 for a burger to $16.50 for filet mignon with thyme and balsamic vinaigrette.

The weekend brunch for $9.95 is an island tradition.

Dinner nightly except Tuesday, 6 to 9 or 10; Saturday and Sunday brunch, 8 to 1. Open spring to mid-fall. No smoking.

Starbuck's, 131 North Water St., Edgartown. (508) 627-7000.

This is the large, columned dining room of the restored Harbor View Hotel, which observed its centennial in 1991 and set out to make a culinary mark on the island. All is ever-so-elegant, from the fancy wood armchairs with tapestry seats and heavy swagged draperies to the silverware in a shell pattern and the white napkins folded like flowers. Windows on two sides afford ocean views.

The fare reads better than it tastes, at least at one autumn lunch. We sampled quahog and corn chowder, which turned out to be thick but bland and lacking any corn; an appetizer of pistachio-crusted goat cheese with shiso red basil pesto, a niggardly portion for $5.95, and a grilled chicken salad with tomatoes, spiced cilantro and sweet onion vinaigrette ($7.95), the only item with a bit of a kick. The sliced fruit bread that accompanied had so little taste we couldn't determine its flavor.

Blandness can be a problem here, according to local consensus, although you'd never guess it from the menu. Dinner entrées ($15.95 to $24) like grilled yellowfin tuna with roasted onion and corn salsa, seared tenderloin tostada with black beans and

roasted green chiles, and roasted lamb chops with a warmed apple and blackberry conserve spark interest. The format certainly ranges widely, from mix-and-match seafood preparations to a most appealing grazing menu available for lunch, dinner and all day long in **Breezes,** the dark and intimate lounge beside the front porch. Chef Deborah Huntley is a nutritionist who uses organically grown produce and local ingredients.

Specialty desserts include hazelnut crème brûlée, flourless chocolate-amaretto cheesecake, passionfruit curd tart and a special treat called double chocolate and berry phyllo – white and dark chocolate marquise with blackberries and raspberries, baked in phyllo and served with fruit coulis.

The wine list is extensive and interesting, with many offerings priced in the teens.

Lunch, Monday-Saturday noon to 2; dinner nightly, 6 to 9 or 10; Sunday brunch, 8 to 2. Open Wednesday-Sunday in winter.

Harborview tables at Starbuck's.

Chesca's, 38 North Water St., Edgartown. (508) 627-1234.

After a brief, high-profile fling as Isola under auspices of Boston super-chef Todd English and celebrity investors, this establishment calmed down in 1994 under new owners Susan Peltier and Joanne Patterson. Both known locally, they retained the trendy trattoria look with rustic ceiling, low upholstered booths and banquettes, and tables topped with floral overcloths and tall bottles of olive oil. In the back is a long bar; out front, a few tables on an enclosed porch.

Pastas are the specialty, available in any number of combinations from $12.95 to $22.95. We liked the sound of farfalle with scallops, asparagus and pancetta in a spicy tomato cream sauce, and the mixed grill of seafood, chicken and Italian sausage served over linguini. Three or more can indulge in the family pasta dinner, served with house salad, for $10.95 each. There are a handful of "other specialties," from $15.95 for baked scrod to $18.50 for grilled sirloin with vidalia onions and roasted peppers.

Start with baked artichoke hearts, stuffed mushrooms or a hot shrimp, pancetta and gorgonzola dip served with herbed toasts. Finish with chocolate truffle tart, lemon charlotte or apple brown betty with vanilla ice cream.

Most of the dinner appetizers join a variety of sandwiches as the mainstays on the lunch menu.

Breakfast, 8 to 11; lunch, noon to 2:30; dinner, 5 to 10; Sunday brunch, 9 to 1. Closed late October to April.

Truly Scrumptious, 11 South Summer St., Edgartown. (508) 627-3990.

Truly wonderful is this little cafe and gourmet takeout shop that opened in 1994 in a side-street space formerly occupied by a Mad Martha's ice cream shop.

Here's the place for wonderful lunches and snacks from an all-day menu that changes daily. Consider one day's possibilities ($4.50 to $7.25): Thai grilled beef salad with watercress, red cabbage, chiles and cilantro; grilled chicken caesar salad with reggianno parmigiano; Canadian salmon and orzo salad with snap peas, sundried tomatoes and dill, and smoked bluefish pâté with garlic crostini. There are usually half a dozen exotic salads. And always three luscious specials ($5.95 to $7.50), this day panini with roast turkey and brie, focaccia pizzetta with roma tomatoes and calamata olives, and focaccia sandwich with soft-shell crab, watercress and roasted red pepper aioli. Desserts and breakfast pastries are equally interesting.

There are a handful of little round tables upon which to indulge.

Open daily in summer, 8 to 8; spring and fall, 10:30 to 3:30. Closed November to April.

The Square-Rigger Restaurant, Upper Main Street at West Tisbury Road, Edgartown. (508) 627-9968.

The folks who run the immensely popular Home Port seafood restaurant in Menemsha acquired this 1800 house and turned it into a restaurant of deceptively large size, specializing in grilled American foods. The theme is nautical at tables set with woven blue mats and surrounded by captain's chairs.

An open hearth provides a variety of charbroiled entrées ($12.50 to $20), from bluefish and swordfish to sirloin steaks, lamb chops and duck. There are also prime rib, pastas, vegetable stir-fries, lobster and bouillabaisse for those who prefer. For a modest surcharge, you can order a complete dinner including appetizer (anything from quahog chowder to lobster cocktail), salad, beverage and dessert (from parfaits and sorbets to chocolate truffles). No wonder it's a favorite with families.

Dinner nightly from 6.

David Ryans, 11 North Water St., Edgartown. (508) 627-3030.

Named for the two sons of owner Dennis Maxwell, who also owns restaurants in New Hampshire, this is a lively bar and cafe favored by the young set on the main floor. Upstairs is a contemporary room, where one solitary deuce has a view of the harbor across the rooftops and the rest of the tables look out onto the street.

The extensive menu embraces everything from burgers and fajitas to pastas and porterhouse steak with mushroom-sherry cream sauce. Dinner entrées are priced from $13.95 to $21.95. Baked stuffed sole, chicken and shrimp piccata, lobster ravioli, jalapeño chicken with penne pasta, Menemsha seafood pie and Jack Daniels steak are among the choices.

Pricey salads, sandwiches and burgers are featured at lunch.

Open daily from 11:30.

Mad Martha's, 7 North Water St., Edgartown.

One of a group of ice-cream parlors around the island, this offers an amazing variety of flavors (we loved the Bailey's Irish cream overflowing from its crackly cone, $2.25) and concoctions, from walkaway waffle sundae to oreo cookie nookie. The most outrageous is the pig's delight ($18): a dozen scoops of ice cream topped with the usual banana-split trimmings. "Order by saying 'oink,'" advises the sign at the door. Some do.

Diversions

Edgartown is an eminently walkable town and everything (except some of the beaches) is within walking distance. That's fortunate, for in summer the place tends to be wall-to-walk people, bicycles and cars. The shops, restaurants and inns are compressed into a maze of narrow streets leading from or paralleling the harbor. Interspersed with them and along side streets that live up to the description "quaint" are stately large white whaling captain's homes, neatly separated from the brick sidewalks by picket fences and colorful gardens. Here you see and sense the history of a seaport village preserved from the 19th century.

Walk around. Don't miss the churches: The Old Whaling Church, the tall-columned Greek Revival structure that doubles as the Performing Arts Center, the little St. Andrew's Episcopal Church with its beautiful stained-glass windows, a cheery interior and a carillon that tolls quite a concert across town in the late afternoon; the imposing First Federated Church with old box pews and a steeple visible far at sea. Other highlights are the newspaper offices of the revered Vineyard Gazette in a 1764 house across from the Charlotte Inn, the towering Pagoda Tree brought from China as a seedling in a flower pot early in the 19th century and now spreading over South Water Street to shade the Victorian and Harborside inns, the Old Sculpin Art Gallery showing works of various artists, and all the august sea captain's homes of diverse architectural eras along Water and Summer streets in particular.

The Dukes County Historical Society, at School and Cooke streets, is a block-size museum complex worth a visit. The twelve rooms of the 1765 Thomas Cooke House are filled with early island memorabilia. You're apt to see historians at work in the Gale Huntington Library of History, through which you pass to get to the Francis Foster Museum, which has a small maritime and island collection. Outside is a boat shed containing a whaleboat, fire engine and old wagon, plus the original Fresnel lens from the old Gay Head Lighthouse, mounted in a replica of the lighthouse lantern and watch room, and still lighted at night. Open July and August, daily 10 to 4:30; spring and fall, Tuesday-Saturday 10 to 4:30; rest of year, Wednesday-Friday 1 to 4 and Saturday 10 to 4; adults, $5.

Beaches. Katama Beach, the public part of the seemingly endless South Beach along the open shore three miles south of Edgartown, has excellent surf swimming, a tricky undertow, shifting dunes and a protected salt pond inhabited by crabs and scallops. A shuttle bus runs from Edgartown in summer. Non-surf swimming is available at the picturesque Joseph A. Sylvia State Beach, a narrow, two-mile-long strip between Edgartown and Oak Bluffs. Back toward Edgartown is Bend-of-the-Road Beach; its shallow waters are good for children. In town is Lighthouse Beach at Starbuck's Neck, on the harbor at the end of Fuller Street and seldom crowded.

Chappaquiddick Island. Reached by a five-minute ride on the On Time ferry from Edgartown, it has a public beach facing the Edgartown Harbor at Chappy Point, plus the Cape Pogue Wildlife Refuge and Wasque Reservation beaches. These are remote and secluded, three miles from the ferry – best reached by car as bicyclists may find it difficult negotiating some of the sandy roads (but parking is limited). On the way you'll pass the forested Mytoi Trustees Preservation and the Chappaquiddick General Store and gasoline station, surrounded by abandoned cars and the only commercial enterprise of size on Chappaquiddick.

Shopping. Main Street and adjacent streets are crammed with interesting stores. **The Fligors'** (billed as the Vineyard's most delightful store for 35 years) is an intriguing maze of rooms and levels that make it almost a department store; suave gifts, dolls, resort clothing (fabulous handknit sweaters for every holiday imaginable), toys, Christmas shop, a fantastic basement sale room – you name it, Carol and Richard Fligor probably have it. They also offer The Fligor Apartments at 69 North Summer St., 627-4745, four newly renovated and furnished one-room efficiency cottages done in a colorful grape motif – a find for $150 a night.

Tashtego is a one-of-a-kind shop with "a new design for living on Martha's Vineyard" and lovely china, colorful pillows and furniture from antique through contemporary. We liked the speckled Stippleware from California. Sweaters from Australia are featured at **Island Pursuit.** Pick up your foul-weather gear at **Sundog,** which has the correct kind of Vineyard apparel – as does **Very Vineyard,** even more so.

We enjoy popping into the **Vermont Shop,** the idea for which was thought up in one snow-less winter by Robin Burke, who has a ski house there. It has expanded to the point that 40 percent of the merchandise mix comes from elsewhere, but you'll find Woody Jackson cows, Vermont pottery and foods like common crackers and cheeses; we liked the ceramic steamers and came out with an interesting pair of titanium earrings. Nevin Square is a conglomeration of nice shops behind the Colonial Inn. Also of interest are the fine arts at **Vineyard Vignettes** gallery and at **Willoughby's,** the clothing and footwear at **Le Roux,** the clothing, jewelry and folk art at **Chica,** all manner of wonderful wooden things from spoons to birdhouses to a $1,200 rocking house at **Edgartown Wood Shop,** the clothing at **Petunia's** and at **The Great Put-On,** and the antiques and gifts at **Past and Presents.**

The wildly colorful vases in the window lure passersby into **Designs,** which features "handcrafted elegance" by fifteen potters. Exotic jewelry is displayed amid towering plants at **Jambu.** Very different looking sweaters, handpainted terry robes and children's things are featured at **Top Drawer.** More one-of-a-kind items, from hand-woven jackets and vests to paintings and antiques, are shown by Sue Cooper-Street at **The Elegant Crow.** We were struck there by the wonderful furniture, paintings and lamps made from musical instruments by her husband, artist Tom Street.

If you get bushed from all this shopping and walking, rest awhile on the benches atop the Memorial Wharf pavilion off Dock Street, a salubrious vantage point for contemplating the harbor.

Extra-Special

Chicama Vineyards, Stoney Hill Road, West Tisbury. (508) 693-0309.
The wild grapes that gave Martha's Vineyard its name are now being cultivated by

ex-Californians George and Catherine Matheisen and daughter Lynn Hoeft, the winemaker, who makes "the kinds of wines we like to drink," Catherine says. They specialize in dry viniferas, among them a robust red zinfandel, a Summer Island red that's meant to be drunk young, and the first Martha's Vineyard-appellation merlot. Much of the winemaking operation is outside and rather primitive, as you might expect after negotiating Stoney Hill Road, a long mile of bumps and dirt that we'd rename Stoney Hole. Several hundred people make the trek on a busy summer day and relish the shop's choice of wine or herbal vinegars, dressings and jams, all neatly displayed in gift baskets and glass cases lit from behind so the herbs show through. In the fall, the Christmas shop also offers festive foods, wreaths and hot mulled wine. Open daily 11 to 5, Sunday 1 to 5, May-December.

Vinegars on display at Chicama Vineyards.

Newport waterfront is on view from restaurant deck on Bannister's Wharf.

Newport, R.I.
A Many-Splendored Place

For the visitor, there are perhaps five Newports.

One is the harborfront, the busy commercial and entertainment area along the wharves and Thames Street. This is the heart of Newport, the place from which the Tall Ships and America's Cup winners sailed, the area to which the tourists gravitate.

Another Newport is a world apart. It's up on fabled Bellevue Avenue among the mansions from the Gilded Age. Here the Astors, Vanderbilts, Morgans and others of America's 400 built their summer "cottages," palatial showplaces designed by the nation's leading architects. Here near the Casino at the turn of the century was a society summer resort unrivaled for glitter and opulence.

A third Newport is its quaint Point and Historic Hill sections, which date back to the 17th and 18th centuries when Newport was an early maritime center. Here are located more Colonial houses than any other place in the country, and some of the oldest public and religious edifices as well.

A fourth Newport is the windswept, open land around Ocean Drive, where the surf crashes against the rocky shore amid latter-day mansions and contemporary showplaces. This is the New England version of California's Pebble Beach and Seventeen-Mile Drive.

And then there's the rest of Newport, a bustling, Navy-dominated city that sprawls south along Aquidneck Island, away from the ocean and the other Newports.

Join these diverse Newports as history and geography have. The result is New England's international resort, a wondrous mix of water and wealth, of architecture and history, of romance and entertainment.

You can concentrate on one Newport and have more than enough to see and do, or try to savor a bit of them all. But likely as not, you won't get your fill. Newport will merely whet your appetite, its powerful allure beckoning you back.

Inn Spots

Newport has at least 200 inns and B&Bs, more than any other place in the country. They vary widely, and many of the more advertised ones lack the personal touch conveyed by owners who are also in residence as innkeepers. Opened lately are some excellent new inns whose owners lavish TLC on their guests as well as their properties.

Cliffside Inn, 2 Seaview Ave., Newport 02840. (401) 847-1811 or (800) 845-1811.

What a stunner of a place is this lovely old Victorian house with a high Victorian flair. It's being meticulously yet extravagantly upgraded by new owner Winthrop Baker of Wilton, Conn., who has lavished big bucks and great taste in an effort to turn his first East Coast inn into one of the nation's best.

A former Westinghouse broadcasting executive and film producer, he caught the inn bug while building from scratch an oceanfront B&B in Princeton-by-the-Sea, Cal. Here, a block from the ocean, he took over a small B&B that had been built as a summer villa in 1880 by the governor of Maryland. He has redone the inn from top to bottom, adding seven luxury rooms and suites that, he opines, are "clearly room for room the best in Newport."

For starters, he turned the former innkeeper's quarters into the Governor's Suite, which has a huge bed-sitting room clad in dark green and white floral wallpapers and swags. A two-sided fireplace faces both the kingsize bed and the double jacuzzi tub in the bathroom, which comes equipped with an antique steam shower, a rare back-to-back double vanity, thick green robes and, for good measure, a TV and a telephone. Above that is The Attic in which he literally raised the roof for a cathedral ceiling, a skylit bath with jacuzzi, a bedroom with a matching armoire, kingsize bedstead and dressing table from Singapore, and two plush floral chairs. An old favorite, Miss Beatrice's Room, was transformed into a majestic area around a Lincoln-style queen bed, with a mound of pillows along a full-length Victorian window seat across the front and an enormous bathroom of marble, antique paneling and an oval whirlpool bath in the bay window.

The third-floor Turner Suite, elaborately outfitted in white and blue Laura Ashley fabrics, offers a half-tester queensize bed designed for the room, a sitting room with a loveseat and chair in deep green, and a skylit bathroom with jacuzzi. It made the adjacent TV room look drab, so Win turned it and a bedroom into the Seascape Suite, harboring a small parlor with a cast-iron Victorian stove in the fireplace, a queensize bed, a whirlpool bath and more skylights. At our latest visit, Win was fulfilling his vision by constructing the Tower Suite, a two-story "labor of love" complete with a decorative,

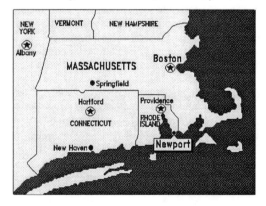

six-sided Victorian tower. The entire lower floor is devoted to the bathroom, including whirlpool tub and bidet. Upstairs is a bed-sitting room beneath an octagonal cathedral ceiling, with fireplace and bay window. Besides representing the most interesting space in the inn, Win says, the tower has an esthetic purpose. "It finishes off the front of the building to complete the Victorian look."

No room in the house has es-

Self-portrait of Beatrice Turner overlooks breakfast table at Cliffside Inn.

caped his touch, whether it be the main-floor Victorian Room with a new whirlpool bath plus a dresser and a queensize four-poster bed bearing a shell headboard that he acquired at a Woolworth estate auction in Connecticut, or the newly enlarged Veranda Room, a great summer room with a bay window off the front porch. Starting with no working fireplaces, the Cliffside now has seven, plus nine whirlpool tubs. All thirteen guest rooms have private baths, air-conditioning and TV sets, many with VCRs, as Win turns the bedrooms of his Victorian inn into places in which to stay – not from which to escape, as too often we find is the case.

There are fine gathering places as well. The large fireplaced parlor is cheerfully redecorated in shades of orange-coral and moss green; the faille draperies are a sight to behold. Classical music and opera play in the background in the afternoon as guests enjoy hot apple cider, lemonade or iced tea, depending on the season, with treats like duck liver pâté, shrimp in puff pastry and brie with crackers. They help themselves to a cabinet stocked with juices, sodas and the like. They also relax on the wide front veranda, which yields glimpses of the ocean down the street.

The guest's every need is fulfilled by a pampering staff headed by resident inn-keeper Stephen Nicolas, a young Johnson & Wales University hospitality graduate whose experienced demeanor belies his youth. The 23-year-old son of a French chef and cookbook author, he prepares not only the afternoon canapés but a memorable breakfast. In our case it began with orange juice, two kinds of muffins and a remark-able (for winter) array of raspberries, blackberries and strawberries to lather upon home-made granola or mix with yogurt. The pièce de résistance was eggs benedict with a subtle hollandaise sauce.

There's food for the soul at Cliffside as well. During the renovations, Win became fascinated by the works of reclusive Newport artist Beatrice Turner, onetime owner of the house. He gathered many of her paintings from hither and yon to mount a fascinating retrospective exhibit that drew wide attention for the inn in 1993. More than 100 images of her art, including a haunting self-portrait above the breakfast credenza, remain on permanent display. They add still another dimension to a luxurious inn of distinction.

Doubles, $145 to $225; suites, $225 to $325. No smoking.

Elm Tree Cottage, 336 Gibbs Ave., Newport 02840. (401) 849-1610 or (800) 882-3356.

Large and lovely common rooms, comfortable and elegant bedrooms, enthusiastic and personable hosts. What more could you ask? You get them all at this extra-special "cottage" not far from the water. In 1990, Priscilla and Tom Malone and their three young daughters took over the cottage, built in 1882 and later owned by Mrs. Crawford Hill, the Pennsylvania Railroad heiress and member of Newport's 400.

With an eye to getting the most mileage for their money, they have furnished the huge house with their own furniture and acquisitions from auctions and estate sales. "Our entire house fit into this living room," Priscilla noted of their move from Long Island. There's an 87-foot sweep from dining room to parlor, which ends at a curved wall of windows overlooking Easton's Pond and First Beach. Chintz sofas and a grand piano welcome guests to a living room that could be pictured in a design magazine. To the side are a morning garden room, great for lounging, and a handsome bar room furnished in wicker. Here the Malones put out snacks for guests who BYOB and sit at the great old bar with 1921 silver dollars embedded in its top and pictures of the former owner's Pekinese and a lion reverse-painted on the mirror behind. Mrs. Hill's grand-niece, who showed up at an open house, told the Malones the background of the mirror.

Three tables in the enormous dining room are where Priscilla serves an elaborate breakfast: perhaps pear-stuffed crêpes, heart-shaped waffles, Portuguese sweet bread french toast, or apple crêpes in the shape of calla lilies. At our autumn visit, breakfast opened with juice and homemade oatmeal (the dish arrived on a saucer decorated with five varieties of dried leaves). The main event was pumpkin waffles. The day's calligraphed menu went home as a souvenir.

We'd happily stay in any of the four large bedrooms or the master suite, four with fireplaces, on the second floor. All have private baths. The suite, all 23 by 37 feet of it, is pretty in salmon and seafoam green. It contains a Louis XV kingsize bed with a crown canopy, two sitting areas (one in front of the fireplace) and a huge bath with a dressing table and Austrian crystal legs on the porcelain washstand. Country French and English linens and antiques dress this and the other four rooms, which pale only modestly in comparison. The new library bedroom on a corner of the main floor, handsome in wine and teal colors, is outfitted in an English hunt theme and comes with a fireplace and TV. Constantly upgrading, the Malones are adding more kingsize crown canopy beds and redid the corner Easton Room in a "city French look" complete with a double soaking tub and coral-colored marble from Turkey.

In all the rooms, bottles of Poland Spring water await guests. The bedding and pillows are so extravagant that it takes Priscilla many minutes to turn down the beds at night and leave mints on the pillows. She has "fluffed up the rooms" with such touches as dried flowers, racks with old hats and individual stained-glass pieces. Tom's background in interior design and Priscilla's in fine arts and woodworking stood them in good stead for the inn's refurbishing as well as for the thriving stained-glass business they run along with innkeeping and child-raising duties.

Doubles, $165 to $325; two-night minimum on weekends. No smoking.

Louis XV kingsize bed with crown canopy is feature of master suite at Elm Tree Cottage.

The Francis Malbone House, 392 Thames St., Newport 02840. (401) 846-0392.

Elegant decor, an abundance of flowering plants and a landscaped back-yard retreat make this a favorite with those who like to be in the thick of things along Lower Thames Street. Five partners acquired the imposing residence in 1990 and converted it into one beautiful inn.

The downstairs common rooms are uncommonly inviting, the burgundy, pale pink and blue striped upholstery on some of the sofas and chairs in two high-ceilinged parlors matching the handsome draperies. In the rear library, the colors are also coordinated with the oriental carpet. All three rooms have fireplaces, and there's a TV/VCR in the library. The biggest fireplace is in the dining room, which served as the kitchen when the house was built in 1760 for a shipping merchant. Innkeeper Will Dewey likes to show the hidden servants' stairway leading to the attic beside the tiled fireplace and the old bread oven in the hearth. At our spring visit, the rooms abounded with a profusion of colorful house plants, from African violets to hydrangeas to an hibiscus that had burst into bloom in a sunny window that morning.

A hallway with a shelf of cobalt blue glass leads to the sunken downstairs suite (built as an office by the physician who once owned the house) with a private entry, a lacy kingsize four-poster bed facing the TV, a sitting area with a sofabed and two chairs, more cobalt blue glass in a corner display cabinet, and a large bath with an oversize marble shower and a new corner jacuzzi for two, with a rubber duck resting on the ledge.

Upstairs off a center hall are eight corner rooms on two floors, all with private baths (two with tubs). The front rooms are bigger and afford harbor views. Each is exquisitely furnished with antique queensize beds covered by monogrammed duvet covers in white. Baskets of Gilchrist & Soames toiletries are in each bathroom and interesting magazines are displayed in the bedrooms.

Innkeeper Will, a culinary graduate of Johnson and Wales in Providence, goes the extra mile to pamper guests. He offers a full breakfast at a long, linen-covered table in the dining room that fairly oozes historic ambiance. A buffet spread of fresh fruit, cereals, muffins, bagels and croissants accompanies such entrées as pear crêpes, belgian waffles, baked french toast with fruit, eggs benedict, a variety of quiches or scrambled eggs with cheese.

Out back is a flagstone courtyard with a fountain and, a real asset for an inn in downtown Newport, a large and shady lawn with colorful gardens. Afternoon cookies and snacks are served here in season.

Doubles, $160 to $195; suite, $295. No smoking.

The Inn at Old Beach, 19 Old Beach Road, Newport 02840. (401) 849-3479.

Unusual touches prevail in this romantic, intimate B&B opened in 1989 by Luke and Cyndi Murray. One is the old anchor embedded in the third-story turret of the home built as the Anchorage in 1879. Another is the ornate wedding bed with lace draped in the center in the Forget-Me-Not bedroom. How about the palladian arch leading into the jacuzzi bathroom off the Ivy Room, handsome in dark green and burgundy with a faux book case along one wall and an antique woodburning fireplace?

The Murrays offer seven guest rooms with private baths. Cyndi says she likes "a lot of different styles." They are reflected in the English country decor in the rooms, named after flowers and full of whimsical touches. In the Rose Room, a pencil-post canopy bed angles from the corner beneath a ceiling beamed in black bamboo. Done up in black and pink, it has a fireplace, a handpainted dresser with hand-carved rose drawer pulls and even the white toilet seat cover is sculpted like a rose. Little antique dresses hang from the walls and rabbits are scattered here and there in the Lily Room. Check out the bishop-sleeve draperies with valances in the first-floor Wisteria Room. Cyndi decorates for the season, especially at Christmas, but the front hall's original stained-glass window representing the four seasons shines at all times.

Ever upgrading, the Murrays added two new rooms with separate entrances in the rear carriage house, part of which they converted into quarters for themselves and their young sons. These have TVs and a more contemporary air. The Sunflower, lovely in

Large back yard is an asset at in-town Francis Malbone House.

Interesting angles dominate exterior of 1879 structure housing The Inn at Old Beach.

pale yellow and wicker furnishings, is done in a sunflower motif, from the lamps on a nightstand to a handpainted shelf.

Guests gather in a small front parlor or a new, larger Victorian living room made available when the Murrays moved out back. Here, two plush chairs and a couch face a glass cocktail table resting on four bunnies. The room holds a rabbit fashioned from moss, a tiled fireplace and a copper bar in the corner.

The Murrays serve continental breakfast at four tables in the dining room or outside on the porch or a brick patio overlooking a pleasant back yard with a gazebo and lily pond. It usually involves juice, fruit and pastries like muffins, croissants and coffeecake.

Doubles, $135 to $145.

The Victorian Ladies, 63 Memorial Blvd., Newport 02840. (401) 849-9960.

All is light and airy in these two Victorian beauties, one behind the other and separated by a lovely brick courtyard with a gazebo, birdbath, wicker furniture and tempered-glass tables, surrounded by colorful flower boxes. Innkeepers Helene and Donald O'Neill gutted and renovated the houses, opening the first of Newport's more comfortable and inviting B&Bs in 1987.

Eleven guest rooms, all with private baths, are decorated in a Victorian theme with a light touch. One of the nicest has a queensize bed and sitting area; it is fresh and feminine with dhurrie rugs and rose carpeting, puffy curtains, down comforters, eyelet ruffles, thick pink and blue towels, potpourri and vials of dried flowers on the doors.

Although Helene had never decorated before, she did a gorgeous job throughout. The small pink and blue parlor has a crystal chandelier and crystal sconces on the mantel; the fireplace was ablaze the chilly October morning we first visited. Balloon curtains adorn the parlor and the adjacent dining room, where an enormous 1740 hutch-sideboard of English pine displays plates and country knickknacks.

In 1991, the O'Neills moved into the rear caretaker's cottage and added two deluxe

391

suites upstairs. Both contain lavender carpeting with which Helene paired a pale yellow color scheme in one suite and red and dark green in the other. One has a wicker loveseat and a corner writing desk. Both have telephones in addition to the television sets common to all rooms.

Don, a contractor, built the gazebo and the courtyard, and his green thumb shows in a profusion of flowers in the surrounding gardens. He's also responsible for the colorful paint job on the main house.

Helene serves up a marvelous breakfast, from all kinds of muffins to grand marnier french toast, eggs benedict, or an egg and spinach casserole. "She loves to cook and keeps expanding her repertoire," says Don. "I'm the dishwasher."

Doubles, $125 to $175.

Rhode Island House, 77 Rhode Island Ave., Newport 02840. (401) 848-7787.

Fountains and gardens out front greet visitors to this elegant B&B, which opened in 1993. The landscaping is the work of John Rich, partner in the endeavor with cooking instructor Michael Dupré. The inside is Michael's province. Trained at La Varenne in Paris, the former private chef for the Auchincloss family offers culinary weekends in winter and serves breakfasts to remember in a dining room with Chinese Chippendale chairs at tables for four.

"I like to experiment," says Michael of his breakfasts, in something of an under-statement. He presents a written menu, which changes daily. The meal starts with a buffet on the sideboard. Fresh orange juice, a medley of fresh fruit, homemade granola, whole-grain cereals, scones, muffins, grapefruit custard, rice pudding and jonnycakes are mere preliminaries to the main event, perhaps a soufflé omelet, grand marnier french toast, fruit crêpes or eggs benedict. These treats originate in a well-designed professional kitchen, where Michael caters and gives cooking lessons, including wintertime "culinary escape weekend" classes in which everyone participates and then sits down to partake of a themed, five-course dinner.

Michael, an avid collector, has furnished the house with taste and flair, in both common rooms and bedrooms. The great hall/foyer is notable for yellow faux-marble walls. Off one side is an airy sun room. In front is a cozy library. On the other side is an inviting living room with a remarkable set of elaborate arched windows.

Upstairs are five guest rooms with queensize beds, chaise lounges and private baths. Four have working fireplaces. The bath in the small Mary Kay Room occupies a sun porch and retains the original pink and gray fixtures. The antique headboard on the bed matches the chest of drawers in the creamy white and floral green front Garden Room, where an ivy motif coordinates curtains, comforters and pillows. The Auchincloss Room is "dainty, lovely and nice – just like her," Michael says of the late Mrs. Auchincloss, his favorite grande dame. It has a full bath with an enormous jacuzzi, as does the rear Hunter Room, masculine in hunter green and complete with lounge chairs on a private balcony overlooking the back yard. All the rooms have large windows and are bright and airy, which is unusual for Victorian houses of the period.

Doubles, $150 to $195. No smoking.

Ivy Lodge, 12 Clay St., Newport 02840. (401) 849-6865.

A striking, three-story entry hall, 33 feet high and paneled in carved oak, awaits visitors to this attractive B&B, tucked away at the end of a residential street behind Bellevue Avenue. Taking a house that had been described by an 1886 newspaper as "one of the prettiest cottages in Newport," innkeepers Maggie and Terry Moy have enhanced some spectacular architectural touches with comfortable furnishings. The paneling is awesome and there's "no plaster in any part of the hall," as the 1886 news-

Pillared Georgian Colonial is home to artists who run Samuel Watson House as B&B.

place, and another with two twin beds and a TV. They share a large bath. A third room with a double bed and two layouts of lace doilies displayed on the lavender walls has its own bath. There's also a single room with shared bath, and a laundry for guests' use.

Jo serves a full breakfast of homemade mini-muffins that she says get crisp on all sides, popovers, omelets and bacon or ham.

Check out the jigsaw puzzle in progress in the TV parlor. It's one of the remarkable handcut wooden puzzles that Bob makes in their studio out back. "Our guests are his captive audience," quips Jo. If they become involved in the puzzle, they're apt to end up out in the studio. There they find dozens of intricate and really challenging puzzles cut on his jigsaw from pictures mounted on plywood. They range from Renoir paintings to Woody Woodpecker cutouts to Kennebunkport maps (one was sent to former President Bush and the Godfreys have framed his thank-you letter), and cost from $10 to $300 – roughly 50 cents a piece. Each puzzle is different, except for Bob's trademark, a piece shaped like a flying gull. There's no picture – just a clever title that may give a clue to the finished puzzle. Jo helps sand the puzzles and is a sign carver in her own right.

Doubles, $60 to $70.

Golden Hill Farm, 389 Wrights Crossing Road, Pomfret Center 06259. (203) 928-3351.

A long, tree-lined driveway leads into the heart of a plantation-like farm complex that now includes a fledgling B&B. The owners are local stockbroker Jim Weiss, a former state legislator, and his wife Nancy, director of development for the University of Connecticut College of Agriculture. They converted a 1790 half Cape, formerly the assistant farm manager's house, into a two-bedroom guest house in 1994.

The ground floor of the building, located 30 feet from their family residence, includes a small living room with beamed ceiling and fireplace, a galley kitchen and a bedroom

425

with queensize poster bed, fireplace and a new bathroom. The upstairs has a second bedroom with twin beds and full bath. Each floor is booked separately, or the entire house can be rented for $125 a night.

The Weisses provide the makings for an ample continental breakfast in the kitchen. Here guests help themselves to fruits, cereals, beverages and baked goods.

The Weisses have hayfields and a few farm animals on their part of an original 600-acre working farm. Nearby are hiking and nature trails in a little-known, 1,000-acre Connecticut Audubon Society sanctuary.

Doubles, $65 and $75.

Dining Spots

The Golden Lamb Buttery, Hillandale Farm, Bush Hill Road, Brooklyn. (203) 774-4423.

For more years than we care to remember, Golden Lamb Buttery has been our most cherished restaurant. We love it for summer lunches, when the surrounding fields and hills look like a Constable painting. We love it for summer evenings, when we have cocktails on a hay wagon driven by a tractor through the fields and listen to Susan Smith Lamb's pure voice as she sings and plays guitar. We love the picnic suppers followed by, perhaps, dancing to an eighteen-piece band playing songs from the '40s and '50s, or maybe a musical done by a local theater company on occasional Wednesday and Thursday nights in summer. And we love fall lunches and dinners ensconced beside the glowing fireplace. We especially love the Elizabethan dinners served in December, when a group of renaissance singers carol through the rooms and pork tenderloin is a festive main course. And everyone loves Jimmie and Bob Booth, the remarkable owners of the farm on which the restaurant stands – she the wonderful chef and he the affable host.

Pond is on view from Golden Lamb Buttery.

You can tell as you enter through the barn, where a 1953 Jaguar convertible is displayed among such eclectic items as a totem pole and a telephone booth, that you are in for an unusual treat. Step out on the back deck and gaze over the picturesque scene as waitresses in long pink gingham skirts show the blackboard menu ($65 prix fixe) and take your order. After you are seated following the hayride, the table is yours for the evening.

Appetizers consist mostly of soups, and Jimmie makes some knockouts. Using herbs from her garden – especially lovage, her favorite – she might concoct country cottage, minestrone mother earth, cabbage soup made with duck stock or, in summer, a cold soup like raspberry puree or cucumber.

There is usually a choice of four entrées, always duck and often salmon, châteaubriand and lamb. These are accompanied by six to eight vegetables, served family style and to us almost the best part of the meal. Marinated mushrooms are always among them and, depending on the season and what's in the garden, you might find celery braised with fennel, carrots with orange rind and raisins, tomatoes with basil and lime juice or a casserole of zucchini and summer squash with mornay sauce. Jimmie cooks without preservatives or salt, and believes strongly in fresh and healthful food. Desserts might include a chocolate roll made with Belgian chocolate, coffee or grand marnier mousse, or butter cake with fresh berries.

This unfoldment takes place in dining rooms in the barn or the attached building with a loft that was once a studio used by writers. The old wood of the walls and raftered ceilings glows with the patina of age, as do the polished wood tables in the flickering candlelight. Colored glass bottles shine in the windows, and the whole place is filled with barny things like decoys, deacons' benches, pillows, bowls of apples and rag rugs. Add classical music or Susan Lamb's folksongs and a bottle from Bob's well-chosen wine list, and you will likely find yourself in the middle of a midsummer night's dream.

For lunch, entrées in the $9.50 to $14 range could include pasta parmesan, seafood crêpes, red salmon quiche, Hillandale hash and Londonderry pork stew. New is a daily special for $13.50, yielding soup, entrée and coffee or wine.

Lunch, Tuesday-Saturday noon to 2:30; dinner, Friday and Saturday, one seating from 7. Closed January-May. No credit cards. Dinner reservations required far in advance.

The Inn at Woodstock Hill, 94 Plaine Hill Road, Woodstock. (203) 928-0528.

This glamorous restaurant spreads across three rooms of an equally glamorous inn. It has earned its spurs over the years under German chef Richard Naumann, partner with innkeeper Sheila Becks.

The setting is elegant, whether in the main inn, a small dining room with banquettes draped in chintz in the carriage house or, beyond, the long, narrow main dining room with windows onto fields and forest. Blue armchairs are at tables set with Villeroy & Boch china and pink napkins stashed in big wine glasses.

For a springtime lunch, we were seated in the small, pretty peach and blue dining room in the carriage house, the armchairs a bit too low (the banquettes are the right height) and the atmosphere a bit too hushed until some more lunchers trickled in. Most of the menu struck us as more appropriate for dinner, with main courses going from $8.50 for chicken dijon to $13.50 for filet mignon "hunter style." The menu listed three tempting sandwiches ($6.50 to $8, for mesquite chicken, beef tips or grilled shrimp), appetizers of the dinner variety, a couple of soups and two salads, one of mixed greens and the other the house version of a chef's salad for $6.50. Chosen to follow an excellent baked french onion soup for $2.80, it turned out to be a rather strange concoction lacking the advertised boiled egg and topped with salami, turkey and cheese. It did come with a super mint-apple dressing, however. One of us ordered the day's pasta off the appetizer list, a fine dish of ravioli stuffed with mushrooms and a sundried tomato sauce that was almost a salsa. Another sampled the chicken sandwich topped with pineapple, ham and melted swiss cheese, served with potato chips and chunks of fruit, too much to finish.

Based on our almost-dinner lunch, we would expect dinner here to be fine. Entrées at night are priced from $15.50 for two chicken dishes through the low to mid-twenties to $28 for surf and turf (filet mignon and broiled lobster). Coquilles St. Jacques, grilled pork tenderloin with a spicy peanut sauce, roast duckling with orange sauce, rack of lamb and veal oscar are other possibilities. Most of the desserts at our visit were chocolate.

Lunch, Monday-Saturday 11 to 2; dinner nightly, 5:30 to 9; Sunday, brunch 11 to 2, dinner 4 to 8.

Vernon Stiles Inn Restaurant, Route 193, Thompson Hill. (203) 923-9571.

Built in 1814, this venerable stagecoach tavern is what an old New England restaurant should look like: a homey place with beamed ceilings, a fire blazing in the pub, a ramble of dining rooms and a great picture of the inn made with what look to be pieces of tiles. The establishment was named for one of its more colorful landlords, who claimed that more stage passengers dined there every day than at any other house in New England.

A winter tradition that is always sold out is the weekly Stew and Story session on Wednesday evenings. Cocktails and a supper of stew (perhaps lamb or beef) precede a fireside story told by local actors or professors in the reading room. The event attracts 40 people a week, and often many are turned away.

Chef-owner Joseph Silbermann oversees an extensive continental menu that is well regarded locally. Dinner entrées ($10.95 to $18.95) run the gamut from broiled scrod, seafood casserole and shrimp provençal to roast duckling with cherry sauce, filet mignon and steak diane. Chicken peking and shoreline veal (sautéed with shrimps, scallops and lobster) add interest, as does the pasta à la Stiles (chicken and shrimp with scallions and pimentos over pine nuts).

Lunch here is good value, from $4.95 for an open-face turkey lorraine sandwich or aegean spinach salad to $6.95 for sautéed tenderloin with garden salad or a lobster roll, both served with steak fries.

Lunch, Wednesday-Friday 11:30 to 2; dinner, nightly except Tuesday 4:30 to 8:30 or 9:30; Sunday, brunch 11 to 2:30, dinner 4 to 8.

The Vine Bistro, 85 Main St., Putnam. (203) 928-1660.

Up-and-coming downtown Putnam gained a good little contemporary American bistro in the autumn of 1994. Lisa Cassettari and Kim Kirker produced a stark white space accented with blond tables (dressed with white linens at night) and large, colorful paintings done by a local artist.

At lunch, things get off to a good start when the ice water is poured with a slice of lemon into oversize brandy glasses. Plates puddled with olive oil, garlic and rosemary arrive for soaking up the good, crusty bread. There is quite a selection of soups, sandwiches and salads, most in the $5.25 to $6.95 range – the last for caesar salad served with Maryland crab cakes and vodka rigatoni, which one of us tried and pronounced successful. Others in our party sampled an appetizer of portobello mushrooms sautéed with spinach, roasted peppers, tomatoes, garlic and olive oil, and a generous sandwich of turkey, swiss and whole berry cranberry sauce. A sensational finale was tangerine sorbet, served in a frozen tangerine on a big white plate squiggled with raspberry puree. Pumpkin cheesecake laced with cognac was another winner.

Much the same fare is available at dinner, minus the sandwiches and plus half a dozen specials ($12.95 to $16.95). Expect treats like vodka rigatoni with jumbo shrimp, broiled salmon with a velvety dill sauce, "chicken d'vine," veal marsala and a signature rack of lamb, each with seven or eight chops.

The owners planned to serve cappuccino and desserts on their side alleyway in season.

Lunch daily, 11 to 3; dinner, Wednesday-Sunday, 5 to 9. Wine and beer license. No smoking.

The Corner Cafe, 88 Main St., Putnam. (203) 963-0105.

The owners of the Arts & Framing Shop sought more traffic and got it, turning a section of their corner store in 1994 into a convivial cafe and espresso bar offering light lunches and desserts.

Barbara Lussier's blackboard menu might yield a tuna or mozzarella salad plate, a

Artworks and floral displays grace interior of The Vine Bistro.

hummus plate or sandwiches like curried egg salad or smoked ham and brie, $4.50 to $5.25. The stars of the show are the soups, perhaps french onion or chicken with wild rice, served with a twist in crusty bread bowls.

The layered mixed berry tart was a standout among the desserts. It and a cup of cappuccino made a delightful afternoon break between antiquing forays. There are small tables upon which to partake, inside or out.

Open Tuesday-Sunday, 9:30 to 5.

Fox Hunt Farms Gourmet & Cafe, 292 Route 169, South Woodstock. (203) 928-0714.

Starting with a gourmet deli par excellence, Linda Colangelo and Laura Crosetti have expanded into a cafe with an espresso bar and an outlying building housing an ice cream and sweet shop. Any number of fancy sandwiches are available in the $4 to $6 range, served on a variety of fresh breads. We've made good lunches of the goat cheese and sundried tomato sandwich, the smooth duck pâté on French bread, a cup of gazpacho with half a honey ham and boursin sandwich on sourdough, and a warm croissant filled with chicken and red peppers. There's seating inside and on a spacious outdoor deck.

New in 1994 was **The Fox's Fancy,** a sweets shop in which the partners were adding an old-fashioned ice cream parlor, featuring gourmet gifts, homemade fudge, chocolates and ice cream. Chocolate candies are served with ice creams, and sundaes may be served over fresh melons.

Open Tuesday-Friday 10 to 7, weekends 10 to 5.

The Vanilla Bean Cafe, Junction of Routes 169, 44 and 97, Pomfret. (203) 928-1562.

"People won't pay more than $6.50 for a meal here," say members of the Jessurun family who opened this lively and expanding cafe in a 150-year-old barn near the campuses of the Rectory and Pomfret schools. So that's what they charge, be it for their oversize sandwiches and quiches, their stews and chilis, their occasional pasta specials or their summertime cookouts on the outdoor patio. The grill fare involves hot dogs, hamburgers and fresh fish caught by one of the family, who is a fisherman. Even tuna steak and lamb kabobs remain under the $6.50 price limit.

Here is a true place, where the turkey sandwich is "not that awful turkey roll," says the blackboard menu, but "the real thing, roasted here at the Bean." Ditto for the albacore tuna sandwich, the house-smoked meats, the spicy lentil or falafel burgers, the award-winning chili ($3.25) and the hearty soups (ham and bean, fish chowder, chicken gumbo). Gumbos, venison or beef stews, quiches and perhaps a special of warm sautéed chicken on a bed of julienned vegetables prove popular for supper.

Diners partake at eight tables beneath an eighteen-foot-high ceiling in one room containing the food counter and an aquarium or in a larger side room with a piano for Friday evening entertainment starting at 8. The entertainment proved so popular that the Bean added a third room beyond with sofas and overstuffed chairs. Beers and wines, espresso and cappuccino are featured.

Open Monday and Tuesday 7 to 3, Wednesday-Sunday 7 or 8 to 8 or 9.

The Tea Room at the Livery, Routes 169 and 171, South Woodstock. (203) 963-0161.

Coffee, luncheon, tea and weekend dinners are offered at this new enterprise, and if that doesn't suffice, try Saturday breakfast. Owner Carol Twardowski-Heap comes with fine credits. She and fellow chef Peter Cooper had turned around the Brown University Faculty Club and then teamed up at the Harvest at Bald Hill, a well-regarded South Woodstock restaurant that closed unexpectedly in 1994.

Here in partnership with her husband, Scott Heap, she serves a variety of delectable fare in a charming, country garden room off to the side of The Livery Shops. Come for coffee and pastry, from lemon dream bars to cappuccino walnut bars to raspberry squares to cinnamon-apple scones. How about lunch ($4.95 to $6.95): perhaps New England clam chowder with salad and half a smoked turkey sandwich, crab cakes and salad or a grilled lamb sandwich with roast potatoes? Traditional tea with assorted sandwiches and baked goods is available for $6.

Weekend dinners yield such treats as scallops scampi over spinach fettuccine, broiled swordfish and chicken basilico, $11.95 to $14.95. Start with sautéed peking ravioli with dipping sauce; finish with a flaky butter horn with ice cream.

Stop by on Saturday for breakfast, from the simple (toasted bagel with cream cheese, $1.25) to the sublime (zucchini tomato and cheese frittata with home fries and toast, $3.75).

Open Monday-Thursday 7 to 3; Friday 7 to 8:30, Saturday 7:30 to 8:30.

Diversions

Heritage Corridor. President Clinton signed the bill designating much of the Quiet Corner a National Heritage Corridor in November 1994. The area's 25 hill and mill towns are cooperating with the National Park Service to promote regional greenways and preserve the rural quality of life from encroaching development. On the annual Walking Weekend each Columbus Day Weekend, experts in their fields guide upwards of 3,000 people on a total of 45 walks, visiting towns, farms, forests, parks and more.

A booklet called "Hill Towns and Mill Villages," prepared by the Association of Northeastern Connecticut Historical Societies, is a helpful adjunct for touring rural

Woodstock, Pomfret, Brooklyn and Canterbury as well as the nearby mill towns of Thompson, Putnam, Killingly and Plainfield. We particularly enjoy "The Street" lined with academic buildings, churches and gracious homes in Pomfret, the Woodstock Hill green with a three-state view available behind Woodstock Academy, and the stunning Thompson Hill common.

Other little treasures are the spireless **Old Trinity Church** in Brooklyn, the oldest Episcopal church now standing in the oldest diocese in the country (open some summer afternoons but used only once a year on All Saints Day); the one-room law office of Daniel Putnam Tyler in Brooklyn, and the brick one-room **Quassett School** in Woodstock. The Brooklyn and Woodstock fairs are among the nation's oldest.

A favorite driving tour follows Scenic Route 169 which slices north-south through the heart of this region. Buildings and land along both sides have been placed on the National Register. The 32-mile stretch is the longest officially designated scenic road in Connecticut and one of the nation's ten most scenic as designated by Scenic America.

Roseland Cottage, Route 169, Woodstock, 928-4074. Roses and the Fourth of July were the twin passions of Woodstock native Henry C. Bowen, a New York merchant and publisher who planted a rose garden outside his summer house, upholstered much of its furniture in pink and named it Roseland Cottage. To his wild pink Gothic Revival mansion trimmed in gingerbread for his famous Independence Day celebrations came the day's luminaries, among them Ulysses S. Grant, Benjamin Harrison, Rutherford B. Hayes and William McKinley. The house, its furnishings and pink parterre garden remain much as they were in the 19th century. In the rear barn is the oldest extant bowling alley in a private residence; balls of varying sizes line the chute. Open Wednesday-Sunday noon to 5 in summer, Friday-Sunday through October. Adults, $4.

Prudence Crandall Museum, Routes 14 and 169, Canterbury, 546-9916. The site of New England's first black female academy has a fascinating history to reveal. Asked to educate their children, Prudence Crandall ran afoul of townspeople when she admitted a black girl in 1833. They withdrew their children, so she ran a boarding school for "young ladies and misses of color" until she was hounded out of town. Now a museum, the house is interesting for its architecture and exhibits on 19th-century Canterbury, blacks and Miss Crandall. Open Wednesday-Sunday 10 to 4:30, mid-February to mid-December. Adults, $2.

For seasonal local color, visit Mervin Whipple's annual **Christmas Wonderland** of 100,000-plus lights, mechanized scenes, outdoor displays and a chapel – surely the biggest extravaganza of its kind. Much of it is gaudy but much is tasteful, including animated figures that once were in window displays in New York department stores. Signs point the way for the 50,000 visitors who come from miles around to see the nightly spectacle each December along Pineville Road in the Ballouville section of Killingly.

Shopping. Until lately, shopping for many has begun and ended in South Woodstock. **Scranton's Shops,** a ramble of rooms in an 1878 blacksmith shop, is full of country wares from more than 70 local artisans. The array is mind-boggling, and we defy anyone to get out without a purchase. Behind Scranton's, gourmet gifts are available at **Fox Hunt Farms** Gourmet & Cafe and its new adjunct, **The Fox's Fancy.**

Nearby, **The Livery Shops** offer more small rooms given over to antiquers and local artisans who show their wares on consignment. At one visit, the impressive, one-of-a-kind items included an amusing picnic dish set with flies and ants painted on, the striking dishes of Majilly Designs, and the watercolors of Tom McCobb, one of which inspired a surprised "hey, that's my house" from our tour guide.

Other shoppers like **Cornucopia Crafts** for baskets, **Brunarhans Designworks** for wood furnishings, the **Woodstock Orchards Apple Barn** and the **Christmas Barn,** all scattered about Woodstock. At the **Irish Crystal Co.** you may find exquisite Tyrone crystal of the same quality as Waterford, says proprietor Celine Swanberg, at much lower prices. From perfume decanters to wine glasses to lamps, it all shimmers in the Woodstock showroom.

A major downtown antiques district has emerged in Putnam. It started in late 1991 when Jere Cohen restored the old C.D. Bugby department store at Main and Front streets into the **Antiques Marketplace,** renting space to 250 dealers on three floors and producing the largest group showroom in Connecticut. More than a dozen antiques stores quickly followed. Word spread that here was the antiques capital of New England, if not the entire Northeast, stocking an incredible array of goods from fine furniture to tag-sale trinkets. Three emporiums in the center of town dominate the scene and draw noted collectors and designers as well as dealers and common folk. On one floor of the 22,000-square-foot marketplace, Jere Cohen shows the largest selection of antique Stickley furniture in New England at his **Mission Oak Shop.** Down the street, young Greg and Michelle Renshaw own the 30,000-square-foot **Putnam Antique Exchange,** featuring architectural antiques, furniture, salvage items and other major pieces in a variety of period rooms. Everything from carved staircases to marble fireplaces is stocked in the **New England Architectural Center,** housed in the basement of the exchange. Old paintings and reproduction frames share space with a new cafe at **Arts and Framing.** British antiques and books, along with such hard-to-find foods as haggis, bridies and salad cream, turn up at **Mrs. Bridges' Pantry.** Poke around town and you'll find your own discoveries.

It's a jungle inside **Logee's Greenhouses,** a must stop for gardeners and plant lovers in Killingly. Begonias, orchids and geraniums are specialties at this century-old family enterprise, but you can find just about anything else that grows.

Extra-Special

Caprilands Herb Farm, Silver Street, Coventry. (203) 742-7244.

Herbalist Adelma Grenier Simmons, an indomitable octogenarian with a twinkle in her eye, presides over 38 theme gardens, herbal lectures and luncheons, an array of shops and her book-writing endeavors at historic Caprilands, a don't-miss attraction in Coventry. Most people book far in advance for the daily luncheons, which start about 11 o'clock with herbal tea in the greenhouse. Following a noon lecture on herbal and seasonal topics by Mrs. Simmons, visitors move to her 18th-century farmhouse for lunch. It includes canapés and a punch that packs a punch, bread, soup, salad and a main course of perhaps shrimp and mushroom casserole, accompanied by a couple of vegetable dishes. Herbs, familiar and exotic, flavor every dish. Dessert and more tea are served afterward in the greenhouse. Then browse through the Bouquet and Basket Shop, the Bookstore, the Herb Shop and the main gift shop as well as the gardens. Grounds and shops are open daily 9 to 6. Herbal luncheon programs by reservation, April-Dec. 24, $18.

NOTE: The telephone area code for this area and most of Connecticut is scheduled to change to 860 as of October 1996.

Oliver Cromwell warship was launched in Revolution from what is now Steamboat Dock.

Essex and Old Lyme, Conn.
River Towns, Arts and Charm

Nearing the sea after lazing 400 miles through four states, the Connecticut River wends and weaves between forested hillsides and sandy shores. Finally it pauses, almost delta-like, in the sheltered coves and harbors of Essex and Old Lyme before emptying into Long Island Sound.

A sand bar blocked the kind of development that has urbanized other rivers where they meet the ocean. Indeed, the Connecticut is the nation's biggest without a major city at its mouth.

It is in this tranquil setting that Essex was settled in 1635, its harbor a haven for shipbuilding in the past and for yachting these days. From Essex the first American warship, the Oliver Cromwell, was launched in time for the Revolution. From Essex, leading yachtsmen sail the Atlantic today.

Touted by the New Yorker magazine as "a mint-condition 18th century town," Essex relives its past in the Connecticut River Museum at Steamboat Dock, in the boatworks and yacht clubs along its harbor, in the lively Tap Room at the Griswold Inn, in the lovely old homes along Main Street and River Road.

Across the river from Essex is Old Lyme, which has less of a river feel but exudes a charm of its own. In a pastoral area that is now part of an historic district, artists gathered at the turn of the century in the mansion of Florence Griswold, daughter of a boat captain. The American Impressionist movement was the result, and the arts are celebrated and flourish here to this day.

Just inland from historic Essex along the Falls River are Centerbrook and Ivoryton. They and Old Lyme provide a setting in which inns and restaurants thrive. Up river are Deep River, Chester, Hadlyme and East Haddam, unspoiled towns steeped in history.

You still have to drive the long way around to get from one side of the river to the other, unless you take the tiny ferry that has been plying between Chester and Hadlyme for 200 years. The Valley Railroad's steam train and riverboat link the towns as in the past, offering visitors scenic ways to see both river and shore.

Inn Spots

Old Lyme Inn, 85 Lyme St., Box 787 B, Old Lyme 06371. (203) 434-2600.

With eight sumptuous guest suites, a 1985 addition transformed what was basically an acclaimed restaurant into a full-service inn of distinction.

The north wing was so tastefully added that the casual passerby in Old Lyme's carefully preserved historic district wouldn't suspect it was newer. On two floors, the rooms are individually decorated in a plush Victorian theme – canopy and four-poster queensize beds with Marblehead mints perched atop their oversize pillows, comfortable sofas or chairs grouped around marble topped-tables, cable TVs and large, gleaming white bathrooms outfitted with Dickinson's Witch Hazel (made in Essex) and herbal shampoos. These rooms are so attractive they make the five smaller rooms in the original 1850s farmhouse pale in comparison.

Innkeeper Diana Field Atwood has furnished guest rooms and public areas alike with choice Empire and Victorian pieces acquired at auctions, tag sales and antiques shows. The mirror over the fireplace in the bar was purchased at an auction for $5 – no one else wanted it, says Diana. The marble mantels in the bar and parlor came from a Wethersfield woman who had saved them as her family's home was being razed. Many of the inn's notable collection of paintings represent the Old Lyme School of artists who were based at the Florence Griswold House across the street.

Guests have use of Sassafras's Library (named for the inn's late cat), which has a marble-topped fireplace and television. The Victorian bar dispenses drinks, shellfish from a raw bar, light snacks, special coffees and dessert pastries. Diana, a self-described "serious fan of professional croquet," urges guests to try their hand on the inn's backyard layout.

Homemade croissants and granola are served for continental breakfast in the Rose Room. Lunch and dinner are available daily in three formal dining rooms (see Dining Spots).

Doubles, $98 to $144. Closed first two weeks of January.

Copper Beech Inn, 46 Main St., Ivoryton 06442. (203) 767-0330.

Long rated highly as a restaurant (see Dining Spots), the Copper Beech has catered to the luxury market in lodging since it opened nine guest rooms in 1986 in a restored carriage house behind an imposing mansion shaded by the oldest copper beech tree in Connecticut.

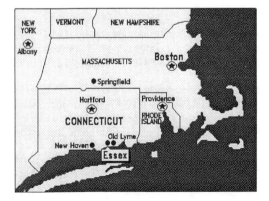

Eldon and Sally Senner from Washington, D.C., he a banker and she an interior decorator, purchased the inn in 1988 and enhanced it with their extensive collection of fine antiques, marine paintings and oriental porcelains. They also restored the

Addition blends into original structure and expands lodging capacity at Old Lyme Inn.

dining experience to levels it had not matched since the restaurant's glory days in the 1970s under founders Jo and Robert McKenzie.

The newer deluxe guest rooms are furnished in "French country chic," with canopy and four-poster beds, comfortable sitting areas and TV sets. Each offers a jacuzzi bathtub and French doors that open onto an outdoor deck or balcony overlooking landscaped gardens. Second-floor rooms feature cathedral ceilings with exposed beams. The Senners keep adding more antiques and have hung their own botanical prints on the walls.

The four period bedrooms in the main inn are attractive as well. Nicely decorated in rich shades of blue, the master suite has a striking floor-to-ceiling fabric canopy enveloping a kingsize bed, a loveseat in front of the fireplace, a chaise lounge across the room and a large table for two in the front dormer window. Another room is bright and cheery with wicker furniture and a brass bed. All the rooms hold good-looking furnishings and antiques, as befits a mansion once occupied by an ivory comb and keyboard manufacturer.

There's a sitting area upstairs in the spacious hall, and a small gallery in which the Senners show fine oriental porcelain by appointment. Guests gather in an elegant, plant-filled Victorian conservatory that wraps around the front and side of the inn. It's a quiet and relaxing refuge year-round. In restoring the gardens around the inn, the Senners have planted thousands of spring bulbs, and are adding terraces of annuals and perennials.

Guests enjoy a continental-plus breakfast buffet in the clubby Copper Beech Room, a handsome dining room with a view of the great tree, blue oriental carpets on the floor and tables spaced well apart. Fresh fruits, cereals, a toaster for raisin bread and English muffins, and at least a couple of French pastries like croissants, brioches and puff pastry turnovers are typical.

Doubles, $105 to $165. No smoking.

Bee and Thistle Inn, 100 Lyme St., Old Lyme 06371. (203) 434-1667 or (800) 622-4946.

Stately trees, gardens all around and a flower-bedecked entrance welcome visitors

Bee and Thistle Inn welcomes guests for dining as well as lodging.

to this cheery yellow inn, set on five acres bordering the Lieutenant River in the historic district of Old Lyme. Built in 1756 with subsequent additions and remodeling, the structure is a delightful ramble of parlors and porches, dining rooms and guest rooms.

It is this scene that attracted Bob and Penny Nelson in 1982. Wishing to leave the corporate life in northern New Jersey, they were looking to buy a traditional New England inn. A broker told them of one they weren't familiar with along the Connecticut shore. "It was only two hours from home so we said we'd go look," Bob Nelson recalls. "We walked in the front door, saw the center entrance hall and graceful staircase and said, 'This is it.'"

With sofas to sink into and fireplaces ablaze, the parlors on either side are inviting. On sunny days, the enclosed porches beyond are great for lingering over breakfast or lunch. The Nelsons, now joined in the operation by son Jeff and daughter Lori, have refurbished most of the inn's public spaces and guest rooms, and upgraded the restaurant (see Dining Spots), which is often cited as the most romantic in Connecticut.

Nine of the eleven guest rooms upstairs come with private baths and all have fresh flowers and period country furnishings. They vary in size from small with twin beds to large with queensize canopy beds and loveseats. Four-poster, fishnet canopy and spool beds are covered with quilts or afghans. Some rooms have wing chairs and ruffled curtains, and one even has a washstand full of flowers. Nooks are full of games and old books are all around. A deck off the bedroom of the prized riverside cottage wraps around a fireplaced reading room, a TV room and a kitchen; continental breakfast is included in its rates.

A winter feature is afternoon tea. Served Monday, Wednesday and Thursday from 3:30 to 5 for $10.95, it's generally booked solid. Scones, tea sandwiches and a dessert of the day accompany the beverages.

Breakfast is available for an extra charge on the sunny dining porches, a great place to start the day. Breakfast in bed may be ordered the night before. The popover filled with scrambled eggs, bacon and cheese ($4.75) draws the public as well as overnighters.

Doubles, $69 to $125, EP; cottage, $195. No smoking.

Riverwind, 209 Main St., Deep River 06417. (203) 526-2014.

Innkeeper Barbara Barlow found a dilapidated 1850 house in 1983 and spent a year restoring it into a B&B, doing most of the work herself. Contractor Bob Bucknall didn't blanch when she told him in 1987 she wanted to build an addition 150 years older than her existing inn. The result is a skillful blend of old and new, from eight guest rooms with private baths to an equal number of common rooms affording space for mingling or privacy, plus a marriage made during construction. You guessed it, the innkeeper married the contractor and they became joint innkeepers.

This is a cozy inn crammed full of antiques and folk art, with a noteworthy collection of pigs in all guises, all over the house. Barbara, who grew up in Smithfield, Va., and whose dad was a hog farmer there, serves up slices of the red, salty Smithfield ham for breakfast every morning to her guests. The hams hang from the ceiling in her kitchen, where cupboards are made of wood from a gristmill in upstate New York and the counter is a 200-year-old piece of hemlock. Guests eat breakfast by candlelight at a table for twelve in the new dining room and at a table in the adjacent room. Coffeecake, real Southern biscuits in the shape of pigs, egg dishes (perhaps sliced hard-boiled eggs with artichoke hearts and mushrooms in a cheese sauce), fresh fruit in summer and hot curried fruit in winter, and her homemade jams and preserves are the fare.

There's a twelve-foot stone cooking fireplace in the "new" 18th-century keeping room. We're always attracted to the original fireplaced parlor loaded with antiques and nifty touches. Quilts, hooked and woven rugs, a set of blocks shaped like houses spelling "welcome," a wonderful lighting fixture of wooden animals holding candles and a piano topped with all kinds of sheet music make for an exceptionally welcoming room. A decanter of sherry is always out for guests. Games in the trophy room include an antique checkerboard, and upstairs is a library with a fireplace. The narrow porch in front, set with white wicker furniture, looks as if it were made for Scarlett O'Hara.

Up steep stairs, lined with old preserve jars filled with dried flowers, are the original guest rooms. The Smithfield Room, all red, white and blue, has bluebirds stenciled around the walls and a high rope maple bed with a chamber pot underneath. A stenciled floor and her grandmother's carved oak hall tree and headboard give Zelda's Suite a decidedly Gatsby flavor. Flowers on the bedroom wallpaper, hearts on the bathroom wallpaper and a heart-filled stained-glass window are featured in the Hearts and Flowers Room. The ultimate is the Champagne and Roses Room with a private balcony, a bathroom with a Japanese steeping tub, a bottle of champagne awaiting on a table between two wing chairs, and a fishnet canopy bed too frilly for words.

Is it any wonder that Barbara bills Riverwind as a place for romance? She knows from experience, and has become a justice of the peace so that she can perform weddings. Her classic Bentley limousine parked out front intensifies the aura.

Doubles, $90 to $155.

Griswold Inn, 36 Main St., Essex 06426. (203) 767-1776.

The Griswold Inn has an historic appeal matched by few inns in this country. There's the requisite tap room containing a steamboat-Gothic bar, potbelly stove and antique popcorn machine – Lucius Beebe called it probably the most handsome barroom in America. Copious meals and an unexcelled hunt breakfast are served in four dining rooms that are a kaleidoscope of Americana. And the floors in some of the guest rooms list to port or starboard, as you might expect of an inn dating to 1776, when it was built as Connecticut's first four-story structure.

Commandeered by the British during the War of 1812, the inn was found to be long on charm but short on facilities. Today, all 26 guest rooms in the main inn, the annex and in houses across the street come with private baths, air-conditioning, telephones and – a new one for us – piped-in classical music that plays from 7 a.m. to 11 p.m., but can be turned off or down at will. This last fillip seems ironic, considering that there's no television other than in a small common lounge in the Hayden House.

Fifteen standard rooms in the inn and annex are unabashedly simple and old-fashioned, though most have been enhanced cosmetically of late. One upstairs front room facing the street has a beamed ceiling and sloping floor, twin beds, marble-topped table and a small bath with shower. A cut above are petite suites, somewhat larger rooms with double beds and pleasant sitting areas. Two luxury suites harboring large sitting rooms with franklin stoves and four-poster beds in the bedrooms were erected above the Steamboat Room during a massive kitchen renovation in 1989. They and four suites across the street in a retail complex known as Griswold Square are the most deluxe, in a comfortable and historic way. Two above the Red Pepper shop each have a bedroom and a sitting room with gas fireplace. The Garden Suite is a two-story house involving a large room upstairs with two double beds and, downstairs, a living room with sofabed, wet bar, dining table and a bathroom. It served as the honeymoon suite until 1994, when the Fenwick Suite opened next door. The Fenwick's main room is equipped with a kingsize bed, a brick fireplace and two wing chairs in opposite corners. An intimate sitting room with sofa and club chair leads to a large bath with clawfoot tub and separate shower. Now, general manager Sarah Grader says, the bridal party tends to reserve the Garden Suite for the wedding preliminaries and the bride and groom book the Fenwick for the wedding night.

A continental breakfast buffet of juice, coffee and danish pastry is put out in the Steamboat Room section of the restaurant.

The "Gris," as it's known to neighbors and travelers from near and far, serves hundreds of meals a day (see Dining Spots), and the Sunday hunt breakfast is an institution. Before and after dinner, the Tap Room is a happy hubbub of banjo players, a singalong pianist and sea chantey singers, depending on the night. You can snack from the raw bar, sample popcorn from the old red machine, hoist a few brews and readily imagine you've been transported 200 years into the past.

Doubles, $90; suites, $95 to $175.

Hidden Meadow, 40 Blood St., Lyme 06371. (203) 434-8360.

When the family homestead gradually emptied as her four daughters went off to college, Karen Brossard opened this country house of a B&B. It's a beauty of a home on four rural acres, dating to 1760. Subsequent additions (some by Broadway actor Henry Hull in the mid-1930s) produced a rambling, pale yellow Colonial Revival with circular driveway, Georgian entry, a number of stone terraces, iron railings and a re-flecting pool.

The Brossards offer three guest rooms with private baths. Each is nicely outfitted with family furnishings and queensize or king/twin beds. Guests enjoy a living room with fireplace and original beehive oven, a library with TV and a fireplaced dining room with a table set for eight ("we sometimes have extra visitors for breakfast," explains Karen, an engaging hostess who enjoys a good party). Breakfast in summer is served on an unusual curved slate porch overlooking the reflecting pool. Beyond are a large swimming pool, a raspberry patch, stables and riding trails. Karen keeps two horses, and used to teach her pony club here three days a week. Now she teaches paddle tennis as the pro at Old Lyme Country Club.

Breakfast is an event. The fare might be baked eggs with brie, basil and heavy cream; orange-flavored french toast with brandy, or gingerbread pancakes with lemon sauce. Fruits, homemade muffins and zucchini bread accompany.

Doubles, $90 to $125.

French restaurant once known as Fine Bouche is now Steve's Centerbrook Cafe.

Dining Spots

Steve's Centerbrook Cafe, 78 Main St., Centerbrook. (203) 767-1277.

What a difference a change in name and concept can make. Master chef Steve Wilkinson found out when he decided in mid-1994 it was time to lighten up the interior of his small French restaurant, Fine Bouche, a culinary beacon in the area for fifteen years. One thing led to another and, next we knew, Fine Bouche was out and Steve's Centerbrook Cafe was in. A major change? Yes – and no. As the owner puts it, "we didn't want to throw out the baby with the bath water."

The interior, even lightened up, still resembles the old Fine Bouche. The menu, although more varied and appearing more affordable, retains some traditional specialties. And, nice touch, fifteen quality wines are available for $15, although the full, 250-selection wine list especially strong in Bordeaux retains the Wine Spectator's award of excellence.

So, for happy diners now packing a place that had begun to languish in terms of numbers, it's the best of both possible worlds. They enjoy Steve's culinary expertise in a casual yet elegant setting.

Steve's is possibly the highest-style cafe you'll find. Pristine in white with peach trim, it seats only 45 at well-spaced tables in four small rooms. The tables are dressed with white linens, fresh flowers and a stash of bread sticks. Steve's wife Eva has brightened up the table settings, mixing Fiestaware with the traditional Villeroy & Boch china. After an admittedly slow start, the staff has quickened the pace enough to turn tables twice on weekend nights to keep up with public demand.

Customers whom Steve had been seeing only for special occasions are now showing up regularly to graze their way through an appealing menu. You could start with the chef's selection of appetizers ($5), which changes daily. Or, on a winter's evening, specify the lentil soup with garlic croutons, the peking duck taco or the veal and pork pâté. Salads and pastas come in small and large sizes. A salad of endive, bosc pear, chèvre and roasted walnuts could be teamed with a butternut squash gnocchi with smoked mozzarella or rigatoni with shrimp, white beans and broccoli.

Main courses are priced from $10.95 for grilled chicken diablo to $19.50 for rack of lamb. Consider the grilled salmon fillet with lime and mango sauce, bouillabaisse, cassoulet, grilled pork loin with spicy savoy cabbage, sautéed duck with caramelized pear and green peppercorn sauce, or sautéed veal medallions with mushroom ragoût.

Save room for dessert, a Wilkinson strong point. Expect a classic marjolaine, a pear and walnut tarte tatin, and crème brûlée (the flavor changes daily). Or chill out on a selection of homemade ice creams (amaretto and crystallized ginger) and sorbets (passion fruit, kiwi and raspberry).

The success of the cafe concept led to the demise of the establishment's traditional wine-tasting dinners and the closing of Sweet Sarah's pâtisserie and takeout shop, the expanded endeavor that had begun in 1979 with Fine Bouche.

Dinner, Tuesday-Sunday 5:30 to 9.

Bee and Thistle Inn, 100 Lyme St., Old Lyme. (203) 434-1667.

Head chef Francis Brooke-Smith, who trained at the Ritz in London, delights in innovative touches and stylish presentations at this highly regarded dining room. Among them are edible flowers for garnishes and fresh herbs he grows hydroponically year-round. He has help in the kitchen now from Jeff Nelson, son of the innkeepers, a Culinary Institute of America grad who trained at the Ritz-Carlton in Boston. They present sophisticated fare that won ten awards, more than any other restaurant, in Connecticut magazine's annual readers' choice poll two years in a row. "Romantic dining" and "best desserts" are their hallmarks.

Dining on the enclosed side porches overlooking the lawns is a treat. Ladderback chairs are at tables with blue and rose cloths or mats. Windows open to let in the breeze. Baskets hang from the ceiling in one, and hanging plants thrive in the other.

Luncheon choices ($8.95 to $13.95) are of the brunch and dinner variety: smoked salmon-stuffed blini, shrimp and mozzarella tart, shepherd's pie, Maryland crab cakes with mango chutney, petite filet mignon and lamb chops. The only salad is goat cheese on warm greens; the only sandwich, homemade sausage with swiss cheese and roasted red peppers on French bread.

Candlelight dinners are served on the porches or in a small rear dining room, where a guitar-playing couple sings love songs on Friday nights and a harpist plays in a corner on Saturdays. Dinner entrées range widely from $18.95 for ragoût of chicken to $26.95 for grilled venison chops with caramelized onions and spaetzle. Peanut trout, crab ravioli, poached salmon, grilled quail, pulled rabbit and linguini, and roasted filet mignon were recent choices, their simple names here failing to do justice to the complexities of their preparation.

Start with the house-cured gravlax on a potato galette, the country pâté with a mustard crème fraîche or warmed goat cheese on a bed of greens among appetizers ($6.95 to $8.95). Finish with apricot bread pudding with brandied caramel sauce, banana flan over mango puree, a silky port chocolate truffle, white chocolate mousse or a fresh fruit sorbet. Bob Nelson put together the wine list with an eye for reasonable prices.

Lunch, daily except Tuesday 11:30 to 2; dinner nightly except Tuesday 6 to 9 or 9:30; Sunday brunch, 11 to 2.

Copper Beech Inn, 46 Main St., Ivoryton. (203) 767-0330.

The level of dining at the Copper Beech has been elevated to its original heights by innkeepers Sally and Eldon Senner. They give credit to their chef, Robert Chiovoloni, a Culinary Institute of America grad who was executive sous chef at the famed Montpelier Room of Washington's Madison Hotel, which the Senners considered the city's best restaurant when they lived in Washington.

The main Georgian Room is elegant indeed, with three chandeliers, wall sconces, subdued floral wallpaper and crisp white napkins standing in twin peaks in the water glasses. The paneled Comstock Room with beamed ceiling looks a bit like the old billiards parlor that it was, lately enhanced by the Senners' paintings. Nearby is a charming little garden dining porch, its four tables for two spaced well apart amid the plants. Windows in the clubby blue Copper Beech Room afford views of the great tree outside. In each dining room, tables are centered by one perfect red rose.

The menu is printed in French with English translations. The ten hors d'oeuvre start at $7.95 for a chard and scallion tart and top off at $25.25 for ossetra caviar with blinis. Lobster paprika and foie gras on a confit of red cabbage appeal to those with high tastes.

Typical of the dozen or so entrées ($22.75 to $25.75) are roulade of salmon, bouillabaisse, veal sweetbreads with a mustard-peppercorn sauce, roasted venison and beef wellington with fresh foie gras wrapped by the inn's own pastry.

Desserts in the $6 range might be marjolaine, tarte tatin, charlotte au chocolat and a trio of tropical sorbets served in a pastry ring with vanilla custard sauce. Finish with one of the liqueured coffees, dessert wines or fine brandies for an occasion to remember.

Dinner, Tuesday-Saturday 5:30 to 8:30 or 9, Sunday 1 to 8. Closed Tuesday in winter. No smoking.

Old Lyme Inn, 85 Lyme St., Old Lyme. (203) 434-2600.

Thrice given a three-star rating by the New York Times and its desserts featured in successive issues of Bon Appétit magazine, the Old Lyme Inn has been a mecca for traveling gourmets since Diana Field Atwood took it over in 1976.

The food is inventive and the setting is formal in three large dining rooms, all regally furbished in gold and blue. Tables in the long, high-ceilinged main dining room are angled in strict formation, a vase with one perfect rose atop each. Beyond are two more dining rooms, one with an intimate windowed alcove containing a table for four.

Chef Stuart London oversees an ambitious menu. Lunch prices run from $6.95 to $9.95. Look for interesting salads (local lamb over romaine leaves, chicken and sweet peppers), a smoked salmon reuben, omelets, pasta and grilled pizza. Our latest visit produced a dish called wild American meatloaf, blending wild boar and buffalo and served with mashed potatoes and mushroom gravy. Earlier, we liked the curried cream of squash soup, a special of Niantic scallops and the sweetbread fritters with tomato coulis.

For dinner, appetizers ($8.25 to $10.75) could be Irish smoked salmon, seafood sausage with a zesty Thai curry sauce, carpaccio with artichoke vinaigrette, pheasant ragoût and terrine of local lamb. Seasonal "interludes" might be a frisée and roquefort salad or a salad of cold poached scallops with grapefruit and red onions.

Entrées ($19.50 to $29.50) include braised swordfish with sorrel cream sauce and caviar, lobster thermidor, sautéed sweetbreads with a creamy prosciutto and pea sauce, broiled venison with johnnycakes and ballotine of Connecticut pheasant with a green peppercorn and port sauce.

The inn's raspberry cheesecake Japonnaise was pictured on the cover of Bon Appétit, and its entries won the Ultimate Chocolate Dessert Award in a Hartford contest three years in a row. We can vouch for a fruit tart with an apricot glaze and kiwi and strawberries on top and a chocolate truffle cake with mandarin-flavored pastry cream topped with a layer of sponge cake soaked in cointreau.

The wine list is choice and pricey. Cafe Diana with chambord and chocolate liqueur is a worthy finale. A light supper menu is available nightly in the grill room, with most items in the $15 range.

Lunch, Monday-Saturday noon to 2; dinner, Monday-Saturday 6 to 9; Sunday, brunch 11 to 3, dinner 4 to 9.

Griswold Inn, 36 Main St., Essex. (203) 767-1776.

Even when its kitchen was closed for nearly a year as a new one was built, the famed "Gris" kept going with an abbreviated menu. You'd expect no less from an institution that since its founding in 1776 had served "precisely 3.1416 times the number of meals which had been cumulatively prepared in all the steamships of the Cunard Line, the dirigibles Graf Zeppelin and Hindenburg, and the Orient Express," as a statement to customers noted.

"Our aim is simply to create New England's finest kitchen here," said innkeeper Bill Winterer. "The old one lasted 213 years and we expect the same performance from the new one."

A meal at the Gris, whether prepared in old kitchen or new, is an experience in Americana. There's much to see in a variety of dining rooms: the important collection of Antonio Jacobsen marine oils in the dark paneled Library, the Currier and Ives steamboat prints in the Covered Bridge Room (actually fashioned from a New Hampshire covered bridge), the riverboat memorabilia in the Steamboat Room, the musket-filled Gun Room with 55 pieces dating to the 15th century. All together, they rank as one of the outstanding marine art collections in America.

The atmosphere is the match for the food, which is country New England, fresh and abundant. "We have no pretenses," says the informative Innkeeper's Log. "Our menu is printed in English. We call fish fish and beef beef." The menu is a mixed bag of seafood, fish and game, priced at night from $16.25 for farm-raised trout with shrimp creole stuffing to $19.95 for grilled salmon, prime rib or sirloin strip steak. Fried oysters, broiled scrod, shrimp and scallop pesto over linguini, spit-roasted duckling with shiitake-blueberry sauce and country veal stew are typical offerings.

Three versions of the inn's patented 1776 sausages are served as a mixed grill with sauerkraut and German potato salad for $16.50 at dinner. They're in even more demand for lunch, when each is $7.25. You also can get eggs benedict or Welsh rarebit, duck salad or yankee pot roast, from $5.50 to $11.95. At our latest lunch, a wicker swan full of packaged crackers helped sustain us as we waited (and waited) for our orders of crostini and shepherd's pie. The oil lamps were lit at noon, the place was hopping and the atmosphere was cheery on a dank November day. That we remember, more than the food.

The ever-popular Sunday hunt breakfast ($12.95) is an enormous buffet of dishes ranging from baby cod and creamed chipped beef to scrambled eggs and a soufflé of grits and cheddar cheese.

Lunch, Monday-Saturday 11:45 to 3; dinner, 5:30 to 9 or 10; Sunday, hunt breakfast 11 to 2:30, dinner 4:30 to 9.

The Black Seal, 29 Main St., Essex. (203) 767-0233

The legendary Tumbledown's Cafe gave way to this casual and appealingly nautical place. All the stuff to look at along the walls of the front tavern and in the rear dining room could distract one from the food, of which there's something for everyone day and night.

Basically the same fare is offered at lunch and dinner, though lunch brings more sandwiches and dinner more entrées. Graze on chili nachos, fire-pot chili, stuffed potato skins, cajun shrimp, Rhode Island clam chowder, California burgers, and cobb and hunter salads anytime for $3.95 to $7.95.

At night, entrées run from $13.95 for mussels marinara, baked scrod dijon or vegetable and shrimp stir-fry to $16.95 for steak au poivre or "Seals Delight" – mussels, clams, scallops, shrimp and calamari in red clam sauce over pasta. Grilled tuna with tomato and capers and whitefish baked in parchment paper with wine, cream and chives

Historic Griswold Inn in Essex, as viewed from Griswold Square complex across street.

were specials at one visit. Desserts include chocolate mousse terrine, pumpkin-praline torte, chocolate-raspberry cake and apple crumb pie.

Lunch, daily 11:30 to 3:30; dinner, 5 to 10 or 11.

Oliver's Taverne, Plains Road (Route 153), Essex. (203) 767-2633.

Named for Essex's first ship, the Oliver Cromwell, this casual spot occupies a breathtakingly high space in a former Hitchcock furniture store. The decor is mostly wood with a massive stone fireplace and a three-story window with large hanging panels of stained glass to catch the light. Ladders, wheels and parts of old car bodies accent the soaring walls. The vast upstairs loft holds a long oak and mahogany bar from Cicero, Ill., at which Al Capone once drank, lounge areas (one with 1950s-den-style sofas and chairs) and a game room with two pool tables.

Huge sandwiches served with french fries, burgers and a few entrées like quiche, crêpes or teriyaki sirloin are in the $4.95 to $8.95 range at lunch. Snacky things like nachos, potato skins, fried calamari, light fare and fajitas are also offered at night, when entrées range from $9.95 for yankee pot roast to $15.95 for sirloin steak. The barbecued pork ribs are praised by those in the know. Bailey's Irish Cream mousse cake and chocolate chip cookie pie are popular desserts.

With a children's menu, the place is popular with families as well as singles.

Lunch, Monday-Saturday 11:30 to 4:30; dinner, 4:30 to 10:30 or 11; late menu until midnight; Sunday brunch, 11:30 to 4.

The Hideaway, Old Lyme Shopping Center, Halls Road, Old Lyme. (203) 434-3335.

A Caribbean-style decor in pink and green, with rattan furnishings and works of local artists on the walls, enhances this aptly named eatery hidden in the rear corner of a small shopping plaza. Etched glass separates the bar from the dining room, a lighted ficus tree grows two stories high, and soaring windows on the main floor and a mezzanine look out unexpectedly across the Lieutenant River marshes. They give a bird's-eye view of three big bird feeders – made in the shape of castles by a physician-friend who gives one annually to owner Carl Lutender on his birthday – which attract lots of takers (and watchers). Ornithologist Roger Tory Peterson, who lives nearby,

443

told Carl he saw a bird he'd never seen before at one of the feeders at lunch just before we were there.

Carl, his wife Lois and son Keith gear their convivial establishment to locals and families. They expanded the bar into the adjacent storefront, where they offer the extensive, all-day menu in a pub setting. The basic fare is described in "from the deli," salads, pastas, "south of the border," vegetarian and healthful dishes and petite entrée categories and priced accordingly. Appetizers are of the nachos, chicken fingers, Buffalo wings and baked brie variety.

Dinner dishes ($12.95 to $14.95) include scampi over rice or linguini, Caribbean scallops, pesto chicken, cajun pork chops, veal oscar and filet mignon with béarnaise sauce.

Open daily, 11 to 9:30 or 10, Sunday to 9.

She Sells Sandwiches, Brewers Dauntless Shipyard, Essex. (203) 767-3288.

The riverfront space once occupied by the acclaimed Gull restaurant has lately become a place for casual fare, served inside or out. Sit at one of the counters facing the windows overlooking the marina, or snag a picnic table on the canopied deck beyond.

Owner Tina Owen's specialty is sandwiches, of course. They range from a three-dimensional peanut butter and jelly ($2.75) to the house club (with liverwurst and Canadian bacon, $5.95). There are also a whole earth pita, a muffuletta and a fishes and loaves grinder on a half loaf of French bread ($6.50). The turkey gobbler and the tuna sandwiches are top sellers. Four kinds of fried egg sandwiches ($2.25 to $2.50) are offered for breakfast, when the specialty turns out to be the rollover, two scrambled eggs rolled in a flour tortilla with the works. Desserts include pies, brownies and cookies.

Open daily, 7:30 to 5. No smoking.

Cappuccino Cafe, 62 Halls Road, Old Lyme. (203) 434-4778.

Owner Maria Beard is pictured at the espresso machine in the colorful mural painted on the wall of her new bake shop and cafe. Sit at little tables along the landscaped sidewalk of the shopping plaza or inside the black and white interior and enjoy what one innkeeper says is the best espresso anywhere, or a cup of cappuccino or cafe latte. The delectable desserts in the display cases tempt, from cheesecakes topped with great big blackberries (this in mid-winter) to tirami su. Breakfast pastries and sandwiches ($4.75 to $5.50) make this an all-hours meeting spot. Maria dedicates a wall of changing artworks to all the artists in Old Lyme.

Open weekdays, 6 a.m. to 11 p.m. or later, Saturday 8 to 1 a.m., Sunday 8 to 8.

Diversions

The Essex Waterfront. As a living and working yachting and shipbuilding town, the Essex waterfront is a center of activity. For yachtsmen, it holds some of the same cachet as Marblehead, Mass., or Oxford, Md.

Connecticut River Museum, Steamboat Dock, 67 Main St., Essex, 767-8269. Restored in 1975 from an 1878 steamboat warehouse, this interesting structure at the foot of Main Street is a living memorial to the Connecticut River Valley in an area from which the first American warship was launched. The main floor has changing exhibits. Upstairs, where windows on three sides afford sweeping views of the river, the permanent shipbuilding exhibit shows a full-size replica of David Bushnell's first submarine, the strange-looking American Turtle, plus a model of a Dutch explorer ship that sailed up the river in 1614, given by the William Winterer family of the Griswold Inn. Open Tuesday-Sunday, 10 to 5. Adults, $4.

The foundation property also includes a small waterfront park with benches and the

1813 Hayden Chandlery, now the Thomas A. Stevens maritime research library. Just to the south off Novelty Lane are the historic Dauntless Club, the Essex Corinthian Yacht Club and the Essex Yacht Club. The historic structures here and elsewhere in town are detailed in a walking map, available at the Connecticut River Museum.

Uptown Essex. Besides the waterfront area, Methodist Hill at the other end of Main Street has a cluster of historic structures. Facing tiny Champlin Square is the imposing white **Pratt House** (circa 1648), restored and operated by the Essex Historical Society to show Essex as it was in yesteryear (open June-Labor Day, weekends 1 to 4, $2). The period gardens in the rear are planted with herbs and flowers typical of the 18th century. The society also operates the adjacent **Hill's Academy Museum** (1833), an early boarding school that now displays historical collections of old Essex. Next door in the academy's former dormitory is the Catholic Church and, next to it, the Baptist Church, one of only two Egyptian Revival structures in this country.

Old Lyme. One of Connecticut's prettiest towns has a long main street lined with gracious homes from the 18th and 19th centuries, including one we think is particularly handsome called Lyme Regis, the English summer resort after which the town was named. Lyme Street, once the home of governors and chief justices, is a National Historic District.

Florence Griswold Museum, 96 Lyme St., Old Lyme, 434-5542. This is the pillared 1817 landmark in which the daughter of a boat captain ran a finishing school for girls and later an artists' retreat, with most of the rooms converted into bedrooms and studios in the barns by the river. Now run as a museum by the Lyme Historical Society, it has unique painted panels in every room, but especially prized is the dining room with panels on all sides given over to the work of the Old Lyme artists, who included Childe Hassam. Across the mantel the artists painted a delightful caricature of themselves for posterity. The arts colony thrived for twenty years and its works are exhibited in the second-floor galleries. Open Tuesday-Saturday 10 to 5 and Sunday 1 to 5, June-October, and Wednesday-Sunday 1 to 5, November-May. Adults, $3.

The **Lyme Art G**allery, next door to the Florence Griswold Museum, is headquarters of the Lyme Art Association, founded in 1902 and the oldest summer art group in the nation. It exhibits six major shows each season (Tuesday-Sunday noon to 4:30, late April to late September). Nearby is the handsome, Federal-style **Lyme Academy of Fine Arts,** with changing exhibits and workshops (Monday-Friday 8:30 to 5, Saturday 9 to 4, Sunday 1 to 4). The works of Lyme's American Impressionists also are hung in the Town Hall, and the public library often has exhibits.

Deep River, just above Essex and reached most rewardingly via the River Road, is a sleepy river town best known for its annual ancient muster of fife and drum corps. Portrayed lately by the New York Times as on the verge of chic between Essex and Chester, its downtown has a couple of good shops – **Celebrations** for neat cards and paper goods, as well as jewelry, children's clothes and toys and wonderful papier-mâché cats, and, next door, **Pasta Unlimited.** Here pasta of all shapes and flavors (we liked the tomato-basil and the black peppercorn) is made in the front window. Goodies like broccoli-almond salad with fusilli pasta, "not your Mom's" macaroni and cheese, and key lime mousse are available for takeout. Try one of the sandwiches in pita ($3.50 to $4.50) and a slice of pumpkin cognac cheesecake for a picnic. North of town is **Riverwind Antiques & Country Shops,** a house full of antiques, gifts and more.

Up river are the delightful town of **Chester,** an up-and-coming area of restaurants and shops; the restored **Goodspeed Opera House** at East Haddam, where lively musicals are staged in a Victorian structure beside the river, and actor William Gillette's eccentric stone **Gillette Castle** on a hilltop above the river at Hadlyme. All are well worth a visit.

Shopping. Most first-timers are impressed by the quality of shopping in Essex, some of it nautically oriented. The **Talbots** store confronting visitors head-on as they enter the downtown section sets the tone. Also fashionable are the **Bermuda Shop** and a colorful newcomer called **Equator.** The **Clipper Ship Bookstore** specializes in nautical volumes. **Fenwick Cottage** purveys wonderful things with which to decorate your garden, as well as great baskets and wreaths. Another concentration of stores is farther down Main Street at Griswold and Essex squares. **Red Balloon** offers precious clothes for precious children. At **Red Pepper,** we saw items we had never seen anywhere else, among them interesting glasses and goblets in all kinds of colors made in Upstate New York, and cat pins by a woman who lives on a farm with seven cats. The shop carries clothing from small designers, almost all made in this country – which is unusual these days. The smell of fresh fudge nearly overpowered at **Sweet Martha's,** where you can find ice cream in 27 flavors; try caramel-almond-praline or a cappuccino frozen yogurt. Next door is **Ken's Coffeehouse,** which grinds twenty kinds of coffees from around the world, sells pastries to go with your cappuccino or latte, and offers live music on weekend nights. Genial owner Peter Charbonnier, who's on hand seemingly around the clock, has fun with the place. He says Ken is "the guy in the coffee cup" on his logo, a fictional genie of sorts. Nearby is **Olive Oyl's** for excellent carryout cuisine and specialty foods. Proprietor Jen Kendall's sandwiches start at $2.25 for peanut butter and jelly and go to $5.95 for the French connection: pâté, brie and mustard on French bread. Or how about the liverachi: liverwurst, swiss, dijon mustard and red onion? Soups, salads, chowder and chili also are available.

In Centerbrook, look for **Seaflour Foods,** a gourmet takeout. Sandwiches (one combines smoked salmon with caper cream cheese, red onion and avocado on pumpernickel) are $3.50 to $4.95. Lunch and picnic menus feature soups like butternut-apple bisque and perhaps taco or apricot and pecan chicken salad, and key lime mousse pie.

In Old Lyme, check out the **Elephant Trunk** for antiques, and **Bowerbird** for funny cards, stocking stuffers and earrings. **The Cooley Gallery** was staging a special exhibit of Lyme painters at our visit. The **Grist Mill** is a natural gourmet store with imported cheeses and pâtés, handmade pastas like lemon-pepper and garlic-parsley, and sauces like Admiral Pierpont's Royal Thai peanut sauce, which packs a punch.

Extra-Special

The Valley Railroad, Exit 3 off Route 9, Essex. (203) 767-0103.

Its whistle tooting and smokestack spewing, the marvelous old steam train runs from the old depot in the Centerbrook section of Essex through woods and meadows to the Connecticut River landing at Deep River. There it connects with a riverboat for an hour's cruise past Gillette Castle to the Goodspeed Opera House and back. The two-hour trip into the past is rewarding for young and old alike. Trips run daily in summer, mainly weekends in spring and fall and at Christmas. Adults, $14 train and riverboat; $8.50 train only. Newly associated with the Valley Railroad is the **North Cove Express,** a dinner train using the same tracks but its own restored dining cars. It offers dinner excursions Friday and Saturday for $29.95, periodic barbershop quartet dinner trips as well as great train robbery and murder mystery excursions. Every Thursday night in summer is the new rail-to-river rendezvous. With dinner on the train and a moonlight cruise followed by dessert on the train, it's considered good value for $39.95.

NOTE: The telephone area code for this area and most of Connecticut is scheduled to change to 860 as of October 1996.

Stanley-Whitman House dating to 1660 is home of Farmington Museum.

Farmington Valley, Conn.
The Best of Both Worlds

A long mountain range separates the Hartford area from its outlying western suburbs. The Talcott Mountain range – "the mountain," as it's called locally – shields the Farmington River valley from the Capital City and creates a place apart.

It is a special place of bucolic landscapes, meandering streams, venerable structures and lingering history. It's the place where their founders established no fewer than five private preparatory schools, where an industrialist's daughter gave her home as a prized museum, and where many executives of corporate Hartford today make their homes.

The "valley," as it's called locally, expands or contracts, depending on who is doing the defining. It always includes historic Farmington, home of the exclusive Miss Porter's School and some of the area's finest estates as well as office parks and corporate headquarters. Here you find a country club occupying one of the prime four corners in the center of town.

It includes Avon, a forested expanse of newer houses that command the region's highest prices. It includes Simsbury, a schizophrenic suburb that has lost more of its obvious 17th-century heritage than has Farmington but has retained more sense of community than Avon. It includes Canton, where suburban sprawl starts yielding to rural wilderness. For these purposes, the valley does not include Granby, Burlington, Harwinton or, for that matter, our hometown of West Hartford, which is the largest town in the Farmington Valley Visitors Association but does not consider itself part of the valley at all.

The valley is a place more for seeing and doing than for contemplation. Hot-air ballooning, hang-gliding, horseback riding and river tubing are the activites of note after tennis and golf. The new International Skating Center of Connecticut adds another dynamic. There are museums to explore, countless shops (from boutiques to art galleries), interesting restaurants, rural byways and, lately, a handful of inns that qualify the valley as an inn spot as well as a special place.

Although this is suburbia, don't expect to see tract houses or many commercial strips. Most of the houses are tucked away on large lots off winding roads in the woods. The shops, except along the main Route 44, are in old houses and new clusters.

Stray from the mainstream, which is easy to do in the valley. You won't believe that a "suburb" is just around the corner, or that Hartford is just over the looming mountain. Partake of suburban and rural pleasures, but know that the diverse offerings of Connecticut's capital city are only a dozen miles away.

"We have the best of both worlds," say leaders of the Farmington Valley Visitors Association. They have much to promote and increasingly receptive takers.

NOTE: The telephone area code for this area and most of Connecticut is scheduled to change to 860 as of October 1996.

Inn Spots

Merrywood Bed & Breakfast, 100 Hartford Road (Route 186), Simsbury. 06070. (203) 651-1785.

Michael Marti, a high-powered Pratt & Whitney manager, and his German-born wife Gerlinde had traveled the world, so they knew exactly what they wanted when they decided to open the valley's first professional, fulltime B&B. They found it in the old Glover estate, a 1939 Colonial Revival brick mansion hidden in five acres of an evergreen forest on the side of Avon Mountain.

After three years of renovations and immersion in Connecticut Culinary Institute classes and an innkeeping seminar, they were ready in October 1994. They offer common areas unusual in both decor and number on the main floor, plus a second floor with three air-conditioned bedrooms and a suite, all with private baths and the creature comforts typical of a deluxe hotel, from sitting areas with TV/VCRs and a collection of old black and white movies to the odd whirlpool tub, sauna and steam shower.

Enter the impressive foyer and find a living room that is, well, unique. The furnishings are all antiques from the Continent, but most startling is the large display on the wall of spread-out Indian ceremonial robes, hats from the Far East and, on the floor beneath, a lineup of at least twenty pairs of children's wooden shoes, mostly Dutch. Gerlinde collects textiles and is a dealer in antiques, and both are displayed liberally throughout the house. Off the living room is a large enclosed sun porch. Behind the living room is a sunny, well-stocked library of particular interest to travelers. Breakfast may be served here or in a formal, somewhat formidable dining room outfitted in ornate Jacobean carved furniture that probably came, Michael thinks, from a church in Germany or

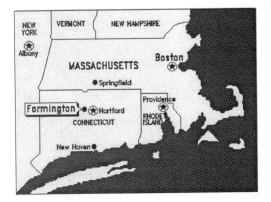

Italy. From a butler's pantry and adjacent kitchen comes the morning's meal, a wide selection from belgian waffles to german pancakes to eggs hussard, the choices checked off by the guest the night before. The Martis serve afternoon tea with finger sandwiches. They also will prepare four-course dinners ($50 for two, including wine), served by candlelight in front of the fireplace in the living room.

Upstairs are the rear Empire

Colonial Revival mansion is now Merrywood Bed & Breakfast.

Room (all American Empire antiques) with kingsize poster bed and the front Victorian Room, frilly and feminine with a queen bed draped from head to ceiling to foot in twenty feet of an antique lace tablecloth, with a wicker loveseat and two chairs nearby. The Continental Suite harbors a small queensize bedroom, an exotic bathroom with a sitdown sauna in a closet and related sauna amenities known to travelers in the Far East, and an enormous living room with two sitting areas, a Louis XV writing desk and, in one section, a full kitchenette used by long-term business guests who stay here. Just when you think you've seen everything, Michael shows the bridal suite, aka the hosts' bedroom. They vacate the room upon demand for honeymooners to enjoy a queen bed amid a jungle of plants under the stars (or sun) in a secluded solarium, plus an enormous bathroom with whirlpool tub, an oversize steam shower with multiple shower heads and a decided Oriental motif.

Light opera or new-age music plays on a sound system throughout the house. Outside is a swimming pool enclosed in a pool house. The Martis bill theirs as "a bed and breakfast adventure." Responsive guests would agree.

Doubles, $85; two-room suite, $130; bridal suite, $185.

Simsbury 1820 House, 731 Hopmeadow St., Simsbury 06070. (203) 658-7658 or (800) 879-1820.

Listed on the National Register of Historic Places, this country manor on a gentle rise above Simsbury's main street was restored by some of Hartford's movers and shakers, among them a corporate leader, a decorator and a restaurateur.

A veranda full of wicker, luncheon tables and baskets of hanging flowers greets guests at the entrance of the imposing gray building, reopened as an inn in 1986. The entry and the public rooms retain the remarkable wainscoting, carved molding and leaded-glass windows of the original structure; all the gilt-framed oil paintings are reproductions. The living room, sun room and dining room are furnished in the manner of a country estate, although they appear quite business-like when used by day for meetings and functions.

Reproduction and English antiques grace the 23 guest rooms and suites on the inn's three floors. King and queensize four-poster beds, wing chairs, chintz curtains, and shades of mauves and blues predominate. Most of the private baths have windows and have been tucked ingeniously into the nooks and crannies with which the house fascinates (one bathroom goes around a corner and is almost bigger than its bedroom). Most rooms have comfortable sitting areas for reading but not for watching television – the TVs are entrenched in front of the beds.

Across the side lawn designed by Frederick Law Olmsted, the Carriage House offers eleven more rooms and suites, some of them on two or three levels and decorated in dark and masculine tones, a couple with an equine theme. Particularly interesting is the "executive suite" with its own garden terrace, a sitting room like a men's club and, up a couple of stairs, a room with a kingsize four-poster bed and an armoire. Beyond is a bathroom with a jacuzzi tub big enough for two, a separate shower, and his and her sinks. "European romance in Southern New England" is how one guest described a stay here.

A continental breakfast of fruits, juices, granola, cereal, homemade muffins and breads is taken in the inn's sun room. Dinner is served nightly in three serene, candlelit rooms downstairs (see Dining Spots).

Doubles, $85 to $130; suite, $140.

The Simsbury Inn, 397 Hopmeadow St., Box 287, Simsbury 06089. (203) 651-5700 or (800) 634-2719.

New in 1988 and stylish as can be, this is really a sleek, gracious hotel with 98 rooms and suites. A fireplace warms the soaring lobby with its parquet floors that lead to the Nutmeg snack bar and gift shop. Upstairs past a stunning antique chandelier is Twigs, a lounge with a semi-circular bar. Guests pass a wine cellar along the hallway to **Evergreens,** the inn's main restaurant (see Dining Spots). An indoor pool opens to the outside in summer and adjoins an exercise room with whirlpool and sauna.

Up the elevators are curving hallways leading to the light and pleasant guest rooms on three floors. Pineapples top the headboards of the beds, each covered with custom-designed pastel spreads. Lace curtains or draperies, antique clocks, remote-control TVs, closets with removable coat hangers and two double beds or one kingsize are standard. Bathrooms have superior lighting, solid brass fixtures, mini-refrigerators, built-in hair dryers and a basket of the inn's own amenities, including a small sewing

B&B guests are welcome at Barney House, suburban mansion turned into conference center.

Historic manor has been converted into Simsbury 1820 House.

kit. Beds are turned down on request and fresh towels are added to the ample supply on hand.

The living room of each suite is attractive in Colonial Williamsburg style with a chintz sofa, an oriental rug over deep blue carpeting, a round table circled by four Queen Anne chairs and a TV with VCR hidden in an armoire. Another TV and a kingsize four-poster on a raised platform are in the adjoining bedroom. Extra touches like electric shoe polishers set the inn apart.

Breakfast is available in the snack bar or dining room.

Doubles, $125 to $139, EP; suites, $175 to $350.

The Barney House, 11 Mountain Spring Road, Farmington 06032. (203) 674-2796.
You can live as the Farmington gentry do in this stately 1832 mansion, situated amid formal gardens on a winding street of secluded estates. It was donated by the family of the head of the Hartford Electric Light Co. to the University of Connecticut Foundation, which turned it into a low-key educational conference center and a B&B of character.

Business magazines and conference accoutrements are evident in the main-floor rooms, among them two dining rooms, a great hall lit by crystal chandeliers, a fireplaced library, and spacious porches framed with wisteria and awash with wicker. They give way on the second and third floors to seven unusually spacious guest rooms with private baths. Only the fact that five have twin beds hints at the conference-center use; two have kingsize beds. The one in the third floor's Yale Room "is for the honey-mooners," our guide pointed out. The smallest room in the house with lots of angles and ells, it's big enough to accommodate a twin bed as well.

Each room is distinguished by high ceilings, tall windows fronted by free-standing plants, well-worn oriental rugs and period furniture. Each has a small TV set and a phone. The rear Farmington Room is especially appealing, with huge closets, an enormous bath with separate shower and tub, and a pink chaise lounge for enjoying the many books. Through the window you can watch the sun set over a pond.

Guests enjoy the grounds, particularly the open side lawn, the formal gardens with a Victorian greenhouse whose lettuce and herbs later turn up in the dining room, and the long, deep swimming pool. They also enjoy a continental breakfast of juice, cereal and a basket of fresh fruits, muffins and breads in the roomy second-floor hall where a sunny window seat is heaped with pillows. A small refrigerator in the third-floor hall contains sodas and tonic water, and a hot pot is at the ready for tea or coffee.

If they're lucky, overnight guests may happen onto a conference and enjoy a fine luncheon buffet or a dinner of highly regarded new American cuisine (prices vary, depending on the fare). Two chefs prepare meals for the conferences and private parties, and overnight guests are welcome to eat by prior arrangement. A typical dinner might be assorted hors d'oeuvre, grilled lobster with saffron mayonnaise and tropical fruit, a salad of greenhouse lettuce, grilled rack of lamb with brandied mushroom sauce and stir-fried vegetables, and a Tuscan rum cake with ice cream.

Doubles, $89.

Avon Old Farms Hotel, Routes 10 and 44, Box 961, Avon 06001. (203) 677-1651 or (800) 836-4000.

What started long ago as an ordinary motel has grown like topsy up and around a hill through two major additions and many levels into first an inn and now a hotel. The Brighenti family have parlayed it into something of a local lodging empire, lately acquiring the financially troubled Simsbury Inn and then the Farmington inn.

The original Avon motel with exterior doorways remains opposite the main entrance and the large, homey lobby where coffee is put out all day near the fireplace. Above the lobby, a second floor curves uphill to become the main floor. Eventually the visitor enters the grand new wing, a soaring spectacle of three marble floors with an open lobby, curving staircases and an elevator.

The 160 rooms and suites have kingsize or two double beds or a queensize bed with pullout sofa. They are distinguished by handsome watercolors of Farmington Valley scenes – more than 400 originals in all – and the current month of the Travelers Insurance Cos. calendars of Currier & Ives etchings framed on the walls.

Rooms increase in size and price as they wind up the hill. Those in the new Georgian-style wing adopt a luxury-hotel style with kingsize pencil-post beds, stenciled borders matching the fabrics, remote-control TVs and bathroom scales. Many yield woodland views. The mini-suites have sofas and three Queen Anne chairs.

There are an exercise room and sauna, and the twenty acres of grounds include a stream and a pool.

Three meals a day are served in the hotel's **Seasons Restaurant** (see Dining Spots), a glass-enclosed dining room overlooking woods and stream. Continental breakfast is included in the rates.

Doubles, $79 to $129; mini-suites, $160.

The Farmington Inn, 827 Farmington Ave., Farmington 06032. (203) 677-2861 or (800) 648-9804.

Totally gutted and refurbished in 1988, the old Farmington Motor Inn was transformed into an inn of taste and value. We barely recognize the place where we stayed during a house-hunting trip over two decades ago.

More than most refurbished motels, this seems like an inn, from its lovely reception area with a fireplace, a couple of comfortable seating groupings and a basket of shiny red apples, to the jaunty second-floor dining area. A continental-plus breakfasts of juice, cereals, muffins and pastries is served here.

Seventy-two rooms and "junior suites" go off interior hallways. Each has a recessed door beneath an overhead spotlight and bears a brass nameplate – "like entering your own home or apartment," as the manager put it. Rooms have king, queen or two double

Gazebo frames view of The Simsbury Inn.

beds and are decorated in country or traditional style. The country involves light pine furniture and overstuffed club chairs. The traditional means dark cherry furniture, teal carpeting and mauve Queen Anne wing chairs. Framed small pieces of handmade quilts adorn the walls. Bathrooms have lucite fixtures, separate vanities and baskets of Dial toiletries.

The TVs are hidden in armoires in the junior suites, far from the bed and at an awkward angle from the sofas in the oversize rooms. With swagged draperies and substantial furnishings in teal and pink decor, the suites for $120 represent good value.

Doubles, $90; suites, $120.

Hartford Marriott Hotel/Farmington, 15 Farm Springs Road, Farmington 06032. (203) 678-1000.

A deluxe suburban hotel, this low-slung structure opened near the end of a forested office park in 1982 and did so well that a three-story wing added 42 more rooms, 34 of them on a concierge level. The 381 rooms are spacious and individually decorated. Many have small balconies. A major redecoration was in the works for all rooms in the original building in 1995.

The setting is pleasant, hidden in the trees off Interstate 84 with roundabout roads upon which to walk or jog, outdoor tennis courts, and indoor and outdoor swimming pools and a jacuzzi. The hotel has all the urban amenities of a staffed health club, a video game room and a lively lounge frequented by suburban singles.

The colorful **Village Green** restaurant serves an ample luncheon buffet ($8.25) as well as a varied menu for lunch and dinner. At night, entrées (served with soup or salad bar) run from $13.50 for shrimp or scallops stir-fry to $15.75 for filet mignon. Broiled swordfish oriental, seafood pasta, Sicilian chicken and prime rib are among the choices. The dinner buffet is $12.95. There's a full deli case, a sit-down bar and tables and booths for 70 in a library-style setting. Late-night snacks, drinks and dancing are offered in the **Proprietors** lounge.

Doubles, $99 to $109.

Dining Spots

Apricots, 1591 Farmington Ave., Farmington. (203) 673-5405.

Outside on the jaunty terrace beside the Farmington River. Inside on the enclosed porch, its windows taking full advantage of the view, its white walls painted whimsically with branches of apricots. Beyond in a more formal dining room of brick and oak. Or downstairs in a cozy pub with exposed pipes painted with more apricots. These are the varied settings offered by one of the Hartford area's more popular restaurants.

The food is usually equal to the setting, thanks to the inspiration of Ann Howard, a Farmington resident first known for her cooking lessons and later the Ann Howard Cookery, from which she and her staff cater some of the best parties in town. In 1982 she reopened an abandoned French restaurant in an old trolley barn sandwiched between Route 4 and the river, calling it Apricots, "a juicy pub."

We know folks who eat dinner at least once a week in the cozy, convivial pub (entrées, $7.50 to $10.95), but we prefer the upstairs porch with its view of the passing river. For lunch, we've enjoyed the spinach and strawberry as well as the cobb salads, the specialty chicken pot pie, a vegetarian focaccia pie with romaine and radish salad, a creamy fettuccine with crab and mushrooms, grilled lime chicken and wonderful mussels ($7.50 to $10.95).

At night, when the dining room turns serene, entrées start at $15.95 for gingered chicken with tian of provençal vegetables and shoestring potatoes. They top off at $28.50 for sesame-crusted rack of lamb with Chinese mustard and bliss potatoes. Seared Atlantic salmon with lentils and wilted greens, grilled five-spice pork tenderloin with sweet potato and cashew hash, and confit of duck with grilled duck sausage and green flageolet beans are seasonal favorites. Start with terrine of venison with fennel slaw, warm goat cheese soufflé with Italian bacon crisps and mesclun greens, or seared nori-crusted tuna with crispy rice noodles and miso dressing ($6.75 to $8). Finish with apricot gelato, tirami su or one of the heavenly cakes – marquis au chocolate, charlotte russe, New York cheesecake with strawberry puree and lemon roulade – for an experience to remember. Or indulge in the Ann Howard ice cream sandwich: chocolate biscuits with almonds and white chocolate chunks held together with praline ice cream and set atop strawberry sauce with a white chocolate lace.

The staff, some of whom have been at Apricots for years, treats customers like the old friends that many of them are.

Lunch, Monday-Saturday 11:30 to 2:30; dinner nightly, 6 to 10; pub from 2:30; Sunday, brunch 11:30 to 2:30, dinner 5:30 to 9.

Max-A-Mia, 70 East Main St., Avon. (203) 677-6299.

A fabulously successful offshoot of Hartford's inspired Max on Main, this suburban hot spot is hot. Hot as in trendy, hot in value and hot in popularity. Folks are lined up day and night and waits of an hour or more are not uncommon.

And why not, when you can dine well and happily on a variety of thin-crusted pizzas called stone pies, assertive pastas (some baked al forno in the wood-fired oven) and a few grills, at nighttime prices from $7.95 to $15.95, with most around $10?

A birthday lunch became quite festive here when four of us sampled the sautéed chicken livers (served elaborately with white beans, roasted shallots, arugula, plum tomatoes, porcini mushrooms and fresh herbs), the sautéed catfish topped with a cucumber salad and served over a roasted plum tomato and lavender coulis, the PLT (prosciutto, arugula, roma tomatoes and fresh mozzarella served on focaccia), and a di Bella Luna stone pie with white clams, sweet roasted peppers, pancetta and parmigiana ($5.95 to $9.95). An order of bruschetta and a $14 bottle of pinot grigio from the all-

Apricot stenciling adorns porch dining room overlooking Farmington River at Apricots.

Italian wine list accompanied. Tirami su, ricotta cheesecake with amarone cherries, chocolate polenta cake with cappuccino sauce and chocolate-hazelnut gelato were better than any birthday cake.

As if the wide-ranging menu weren't enough to draw regulars back, the daily specials here are really special. As it should, the food takes precedence over the decor, which is sleek but simple in yellow and brown with wood trim, track lighting and a mix of tables and booths. A bottle of olive oil and a container of impossibly tall and thin breadsticks are the centerpiece on each. The lively crowd provides the rest of the color. And, we should warn you, this place can be so noisy that you can't hear yourself think.

Open daily, 11:30 to 10 or 11; Sunday, brunch 11 to 2:30, dinner 4 to 9.

Métro bis, 928 Hopmeadow St., Simsbury. (203) 651-1908.
You might think the name for this 60-seat charmer is short for Metropolitan Bistro, which in a sense it is. But it's really a dual meaning, says Kathleen Schwartz, partner with French chef-caterer Claude Martin of the former Métro Kitchen in Granby. Bis is the French word for once again, and this encore to the Granby operaton is furnished in part with subway benches, doors and other paraphernalia from the Paris métro that Claude's family was involved in renovating.

The long, narrow room is ever-so-sophisticated and inviting, with cut lace curtains along the side windows, crystal chandeliers, fascinating art on every available inch of wall space, copper pans, marble-top tables and, beside the entrance, entire regiments of lead soldiers in a glass case. And we like the spirit of the contemporary French fare. At a winter lunch, we sampled an outstanding tomato-pasta-pesto soup of the day, with chunks of nuts floating therein, samplers of exotic salads, and the best crêpes we have ever tasted, the delicate pancakes filled with large shrimp and scallops with a lovely sauce. We also liked the black forest mousse and the cappuccino.

At dinner, you might begin with escargots, carpaccio or a country pâté of veal, pork and ham with a caramelized onion, red wine and cassis confit. Entrées ($14.95 to $18.95) include potato-crusted salmon with browned butter sauce, magret of duck with sundried cherries, roast tenderloin of pork with mustard-sage cream sauce, and tournedos with a stellar marchand de vin sauce. Lighter eaters could order the salade bis with egg, potato, prosciutto and chicken, the Paris pup (a hot dog in a baguette) with fried potatoes, omelette bis and fried potatoes, or even a side order of domestic and wild mushrooms. There are always several interesting specials, and we hear good things about the cocoa dacquoise and the crêpes chantilly with strawberries or chocolate ganache. We can vouch for the ginger tuile flower filled with grand marnier pastry cream, kiwi-strawberry compote and raspberry puree.

A breakfast menu is served on weekends, including many flavors of croissants. Métro french toast made with oatmeal bread, cream cheese and warm fruit sauce sounds wonderful.

Lunch, Tuesday-Friday 11 to 2; breakfast and lunch, weekends 9 to 2; dinner, Tuesday-Saturday 5:30 to 9 or 10, Sunday 5 to 8.

Piccolo Arancio, 819 Farmington Ave., Farmington. (203) 674-1224.

Of all the contemporary Italian restaurants sprouting like topsy, this is one of the more warm and inviting. The owners of Hartford's acclaimed Peppercorns Grill branched out in 1994 with what they'd considered in the first place. Detoured from their original plan for a suburban trattoria when they decided to get their feet wet downtown, brothers Salvatore and Dino Cialfi opened "as authentic-looking a trattoria as you'll ever see in Connecticut," in Dino's words, "because it's like the ones where we lived in Italy."

They converted the ground floor of a former office building next to the Farmington Inn into a couple of dining rooms done up in Mediterranean earth tones, with rich mahogany trim and a ceiling of light blue to give the impression of being outside. A carafe of ice water with a slice of lemon awaits on each table along with copper salt and pepper shakers. A tape of an Italian singer provides background music.

From a wood oven, wood grill and rotisserie in the semi-open kitchen, chef Sal serves what he calls rustic, simple fare. That translates to entrées ($13.95 to $18.95) like roasted red snapper on a bed of sautéed fennel, grilled garlic chicken with egg-plant and peppers, roasted round of veal with rosemary and white wine, osso buco and black angus steak with green peppercorn and cognac sauce. A Tuscan-style pot roast hits the spot on a winter night.

Expect such starters ($4.50 to $6.95) as carpaccio, grilled portobello mushroom and polenta, a couple of bruschettas, oven-roasted clams and the day's antipasti. There are a few robust pizzas ($8.95 to $9.95) and quite a selection of homemade pastas ($13.95 to $16.95). The lasagna might be layered with chicken and broccoli rabe and the ravioli filled with rock shrimp and tossed with shrimp butter sauce.

Crème caramel, chocolate mousse and an ethereal eggless custard are typical desserts.

Lunch, Monday-Friday 11:30 to 2:30; dinner, Monday-Saturday 5 to 10 or 11.

Serge, 236 Simsbury Road (Route 10), Riverdale Farms, Avon. (203) 677-6026.

Valley residents were happy to hear of the return in 1994 of Serge Backes, who took over the once-respected Chanticleer, which had gone downhill in the last couple of years. His former Avon restaurant, Chez Serge, had received plaudits in the 1970s before he left to work in California.

With a Moroccan chef, and partner Paul Manson, formerly an owner of the ac-claimed West Street Grill in Litchfield, Serge has devised a menu that emphasizes the cooking of Provence and the Mediterranean. The cooking style fits right in with the restaurant's original provençal decor, the sunny dining room with stucco walls, bare polished wood tables, rush ladderback chairs (not the most comfortable), wrought-iron chandeliers and sconces, and many plants in the windows. The gigantic and color-ful dinner plates, almost like bowls, are from Great Barrington Pottery in the Berkshires.

At a winter lunch, we tried a zesty Moroccan cauliflower and red pepper soup and

Artworks and old subway bench as banquette line wall at Métro bis.

Tuscan white bean soup with sausage. The crusty French bread was served with both butter and herbed olive oil. Stellar entrées were an eggplant casserole with lentils, black olives, tomatoes, goat cheese crouton and lots of herbs, a veal burger with leek and fennel confit on a toasted baguette, mussels provençal and an artichoke and shrimp rémoulade salad with endive and mushrooms. Lunch is not exactly cheap, with entrées from $8.50 to $12.50, and sandwiches starting at $6.75.

At night, main courses run from $14.50 for free-range chicken with lentil ragoût to $24.50 for a grilled veal chop with wild mushrooms and truffle sauce. Start with the seldom-seen (around here) pistou soup or a ragoût of snails with pernod, fennel and mushrooms. Continue with, perhaps, braised lamb shank with garlic mashed potatoes. End with one of Serge's excellent desserts like chocolate kirsch torte or caramel apple tart.

One caveat; although service at our lunch was competent, we have heard rumblings about horrendously long waits both to be seated and to be served at dinnertime, and about the haughty attitude of the staff. With no advertising, Serge certainly has caught on, perhaps to its disadvantage.

Lunch daily, 11 to 4; dinner from 5. No smoking.

Lily's of the Valley, 142 Hopmeadow St. (Route 10), Simsbury. (203) 651-3676.
Hearts and flowers, romance and nostalgia. Those are the ingredients of this wildly popular restaurant that's packing in standing-room crowds day and night. The red building painted with white hearts represents a dream come true for Barbra and Robert McCarthy, for whom this was "the perfect move."

They started small. On a shoestring budget and with a lot of sweat, the couple put together a tiny bistro in a pink and green Victorian farmhouse in Canton in 1988 and called it Lily's after her late mother. There they seated 45 people at fifteen tables topped with paper mats and votive candles. Bentwood chairs, bare floors and funky old cans and packages – remember Duz? – were the decor. The atmosphere was friendly, and the food ranged from homespun to sublime.

The formula worked. In late 1994, they moved into larger quarters once occupied by Rijsttafel restaurant near the Avon-Simsbury line. Same menu and cooking style. Same hokey decor, from pie tins, signs and license plates on the walls to mismatched Christmas lights strung around the ceiling. Add red and white checkered tablecloths and a cafe/pub with an eat-at bar. If you don't get here by noon, you probably won't get a seat. Ditto for 6 o'clock on busy nights. After running two places for six months, the McCarthys closed the original Lily's in 1995.

Barbra is the mastermind who gilded the new Lily with such affection. Bob, who "pushed and pulled me" to move, is the chef extraordinaire. He cooks impeccably fresh food in a down-home manner (roast loin of pork with pan gravy and mashed potatoes is one popular dish) but with elegant touches. Along with a thick and hearty lentil soup, we sampled escargots in mushroom caps ($5.95) in an ethereal sauce, so good we asked for more bread with which to soak it up. Crab cakes on a bed of roasted corn relish ($6.95) and baked brie en croute ($7.95 for two) might also be on the menu.

The dinner menu lists about a dozen entrées, priced from $12.95 to $18.95. Before them comes a salad of mixed greens topped by shredded carrots with choice of vinaigrette, honey-mustard or a creamy garlic dressing. Our party of three was delighted with a perfectly cooked salmon fillet with pimento-lemon butter sauce, sea scallops sautéed with garlic cream sauce, and linguini with clams, scallops and shrimp. All portions were generous, fresh as could be, and served with good rice pilaf and a side dish of summer squash in a zesty tomato sauce. Roast duckling with honey-raisin-pecan sauce is a perennial favorite here.

Chocolate-banana bread pudding or grilled banana bread are popular desserts. White chocolate apricot cake, Swedish apple cake, chocolate pecan torte and warm ginger-bread are others.

At lunch, Lily's serves hot sandwiches like sautéed breast of chicken with bacon and cheddar on a bun, cold ones like egg salad made with caramelized onions, pastas and salads, in the $4.25 to $6.95 range. For Sunday breakfast, you'll find that grilled banana bread (the recipe from Barbra's mother), and her aunt Sonia's sour cream coffeecake, as well as buttermilk biscuits, omelets, corned beef hash and homefries.

Lunch, Monday-Saturday 11:30 to 2:30; dinner nightly, 5 to 10; cafe menu, 2:30 to 10; Sunday breakfast from 9.

The Grist Mill, Mill Lane, Farmington. (203) 676-8855.

The 1650 grist mill beside the Farmington River was reopened in 1994 as a cafe and restaurant by veteran restaurateur Mario Zacco (of Farmington's late Corner House and New York Restaurant Associates fame). He and his longtime chef, Jean-Pierre Haffrengue, were back in the kitchen for what he called "our last hurrah." The site had been the home of an antiques shop and of our favorite Reading Room restaurant, but had been empty for some years.

Mario kept the decor of the historic building as authentic as possible, with exposed beams and rustic walls, a grist mill wheel in the dining room and mill chains hanging from the ceiling. Mirrors and angles add dimension, and there's a river view from most tables in the 50-seat restaurant. Mario designed a 30-seat cafe in the old Reading Room for people to drop in for cappuccino, late breakfasts and snacks, but the space tends to go begging as the older clientele gravitates to the more dramatic setting of the restaurant.

The kitchen is on full display through big windows to the outside as you enter. Its focal point is a rotisserie turning natural-grain chicken, roasts of beef, pork and lamb, game in season and even roasted lobster. Other main courses on the French/Italian menu ($13.95 to $22.50) include pastas, seafood from saltwater shellfish to fresh trout from the mill's own tank, the chef's casserole of the day, and such "traditions" as

Wraparound windows at The Grist Mill yield views of Farmington River.

dover sole meunière, veal piccata, lamb chops and filet mignon with sauce bercy. Quail, partridge, squab and rabbit are prepared with advance notice.

Expect such starters as house-smoked salmon, pasta alla vodka and a warm salad of belgian endive and mixed greens topped with assorted seafood. Desserts include Italian ice creams that Mario makes himself, crêpes filled with apples and raisins, amaretto cheesecake, fresh fruit tortes and gelati.

Despite contemporary accents, the place tends to be a replay of the Corner House, right down to the pretentious staff.

Lunch, Monday-Saturday 11:30 to 2:30; dinner, 5:30 to 9 or 10, Sunday 11:30 to 8. Cafe open daily from 10. No smoking.

Avon Old Farms Inn, 1 Nod Road, Avon. (203) 677-2818.

The sign inside the old entry identifies this as one of the twenty oldest restaurants in the country. The sign serves a purpose, for the huge new banquet and conference facility, a focal point in back, conveys quite another impression.

Established in 1757, this is strictly a restaurant and function house (a hotel of similar name but separate ownership is across the busy intersection of Route 44 and Route 10). The heart of this endearing place has always been the seven dining rooms that sprawl through a series of additions hugging the old Albany Turnpike in front. The choicest is the Forge Room, far at the end of the old building. A splendid tavern atmosphere is this, with rough dark stone walls, flagstone floors, cozy booths made from old horse stalls, and lots of equestrian accessories hanging from dark beams. Bright red tablecloths and red leather chairs add color to the room, which is one of the most atmospheric around.

The Sunday brunch for $14.95, including two glasses of champagne, has been voted best in the state for fifteen years by Connecticut magazine readers. Set up in the main dining room, the spread is dished out by twenty servers at two long banquet tables, then taken to one of the six other rooms, which have enough nooks and crannies to offer privacy. Up to 700 people may be served at three seatings.

American food in a quintessential Yankee setting is featured at lunch and dinner, when service is personal and each dining room functions almost as its own restaurant. The extensive dinner menu opens with treats like baked onion soup, spinach and watercress salad, shrimp ravioli in a champagne cream sauce, lobster strudel and oysters rockefeller. Veal sentino, a house specialty, combines tender medallions with layers of Danish cheese, asparagus and mushrooms. Other entrées ($18.95 to $26.95) include swordfish orsini, cioppino, sautéed salmon with champagne-ginger sauce and wilted greens, roast duckling with pecan stuffing, prime rib with popover and a mixed grill of veal, tenderloin and lamb chop served on watercress and garden salsa over pasta. It's festive dining, and the English trifle is a masterpiece among desserts.

Lunch, Monday-Saturday noon to 2:30; dinner, Monday-Saturday 5 to 9:30 or 10; Sunday, brunch 10 to 2:30, dinner 5:30 to 8:30.

Seasons Restaurant, Avon Old Farms Hotel, Routes 10 and 44, Avon. (203) 677-6352.

Off an atrium in the hotel's new wing is a glass-enclosed restaurant, lately upgraded from a cafe and becoming known for regional American cuisine. The semi-circular back room looks out onto the trees and changing seasons. It is colorful in pink, green and white with balloon curtains framing the view and green beams on the ceiling. Piano music and monthly art shows provide entertainment.

Chef Glenn Thomas's interesting fare changes with the seasons. At our winter visit, we were tempted by entrées ($16 to $19) like seafood marmite of sweet cockles, shrimp and scallops atop house fettuccine, a scaloppine of Pacific salmon and spinach greens atop puff pastry, a hearty cassoulet, roasted pheasant and twin tournedos of beef with ginger-mustard sauce.

Grilled quail with rosemary polenta and porcini mushrooms, country terrine with cranberry-citrus chutney and a salad of smoked trout and apples with horseradish and field greens make good starters. Among desserts are chocolate mousse cake, citrus genoise, raspberry linzer torte and homemade sorbets.

A special, four-course prix-fixe menu ($30, with three or four choices of appetizer and entrée) represents good value.

There's a three-course, prix-fixe lunch menu ($13.95), as well as a variety of à la carte choices ($6.25 to $8.95) from a smoked turkey BLT on sourdough bread to shrimp tossed with garlic, artichokes and tomatoes on angel-hair pasta.

Lunch, Monday-Friday 11:30 to 2; dinner, Monday-Saturday 5 to 9; Sunday brunch, 11 to 1.

Evergreens, Simsbury Inn, 397 Hopmeadow St., Simsbury. (203) 651-5700.

The elegant main dining room at this inn is a beauty in white and pink, with rich wood pillars, quite an array of brass sconces and chandeliers, windows onto an outdoor dining terrace and a mural of 18th-century Simsbury along the back wall. Tables are set with English bone china, crystal and sterling silver.

Dinners entrées generally run from $16.95 for grilled chicken served on ginger-scallion crêpes or braised lamb shank bouquetière to $23.95 for sautéed veal with portobello mushrooms and smoked bell peppers. The grilled sea bass might come with grilled bermuda onions and a caviar-crème fraîche sauce.

Starters include radicchio-fennel salad, warm salmon cakes, goat cheese and pepper terrine, and wild mushroom ragout. The dessert cart might yield key lime pie, white chocolate mousse and pumpkin cheesecake. Wines come from a cellar visible off the entry hall.

Lunch, Tuesday-Friday 11:30 to 2; dinner, Tuesday-Sunday 5:30 to 9; Sunday brunch buffet, 11 to 1:30.

Simsbury 1820 House, 751 Hopmeadow St., Simsbury. (203) 658-7658.

The dark and intimate lower floor of the Simsbury House provides a refined setting for meals that rise and fall depending on who is chef at the time. Brick archways, forest green walls and carpeting, reproduction Chippendale chairs, hunting prints and green-rimmed china service plates on white linens are the backdrop for three cozy dining rooms and a small bar. A single rose graces each table.

At dinner, we liked the grilled bluepoint oysters served chilled with a splash of pernod, and a rather diminutive trio of smoked fish with lime-horseradish sauce ($7.75 and $8.25 respectively). Pastas and entrées run from $14.95 for grilled chicken over sautéed spinach and prosciutto to $24.95 for grilled veal chop with a roasted vidalia onion coulis or grilled tournedos on a red bell pepper rouile. We can vouch for the roast Long Island duckling sauced with black currants and white port wine and the roasted rack of lamb marinated in tequila, rosemary and thyme. Good, crusty French bread comes with; salads are extra.

Among desserts are crème brûlée, chocolate-orange mousse cake and a signature white chocolate and raspberry

Table for four at Simsbury 1820 House.

ganache tart. The Simsbury 1820 House coffee – with chocolate liqueur, grand marnier, whipped cream and orange zest – is said to be lethal.

Lunch, Monday-Friday 11:30 to 2; dinner nightly, 6 to 9 or 10; Sunday, brunch 11:30 to 2:30, dinner 5:30 to 9.

Diversions

Stanley-Whitman House, 37 High St., Farmington, 677-9222. The most painstakingly accurate restoration said to have been undertaken in a New England house preceded the 1988 reopening of this 1660 structure that houses the Farmington Museum, one of the best examples of a 17th-century frame overhang house in New England. With rare diamond-paned windows, it is furnished with early American pieces, many the gifts of local residents. It offers a fascinating glimpse into the life and conditions enjoyed – or endured – by the early colonists. Open May-October, Wednesday-Sunday noon to 4; Sundays in early spring and late fall, noon to 4. Adults, $3.

Massacoh Plantation, 800 Hopmeadow St., Simsbury, 658-2500. Three centuries of Simsbury history dating to Indian days are recreated in this little complex of buildings most interesting for its reproduction of a 1683 meeting house, nicely hedged and screened from a nondescript shopping plaza. The adjacent 1771 Elisha Phelps House shows the furnishings of an early tavern and canal hotel. The low-key complex also has a 1740 school house, a pastor's cottage, sheds full of Victorian carriages and, surprise, the Arlene McDaniel gallery of contemporary art and sculpture. Open May-October, Sunday-Friday 1 to 4; Phelps House also open November-April, weekdays 1 to 4. Adults, $5.

Farmington Valley Arts Center, Avon Park North, Route 44, Avon, 678-1867. A park-like setting of century-old factory buildings contains a complex of studios for twenty artists, who open at their whim but often can be seen at work on weekends. The Fisher Gallery Shop is open all year, Tuesday-Saturday 10 to 4. The Center's annual Christmas show and sale is a great place to pick up holiday gifts.

Heublein Tower, Talcott Notch State Park, Route 185, Simsbury. The landmark, 165-foot-high tower built as a summer home by the Gilbert Heublein family (of Heublein liquor fame) atop Talcott Mountain is open as an observation tower and small museum. The four-state view from the top is especially smashing during fall foliage, but worth the 1.2-mile climb from the parking lot at any time. Along the ridge you may see members of the Connecticut Hang Gliding Association soaring from the cliffside trail that's considered one of the best gliding spots anywhere. Open free, April 15 to Labor Day, Thursday-Sunday 10 to 5; Labor Day to mid-November, daily 10 to 5.

Hot-Air Ballooning. For reasons best known to those involved, the same mountain and valley that are so good for hang-gliding are also favorable for balloonists. No fewer than six outfits now float over the area in season, presenting a colorful spectacle at dawn and sometimes at dusk. The hour's ride is quite an event, which must explain the price ($175 to $200 per person). KAT Balloons Inc. leaves from the "balloon farm" at 40 Meadow Lane, Farmington, and Airventures leaves from Simsbury Farms or Weatogue. Reservations are required long in advance.

International Skating Center of Connecticut, 1375 Hopmeadow St., Simsbury, 651-5400. Olympic champions Oksana Baiul and Viktor Petrenko are among those in residence at this eye-popping new center, which emerged quickly from concept to reality in 1994. Two side-by-side indoor rinks are busy day and night with Olympic training sessions, hockey games, skating lessons and public skating hours (mostly on weekends). Also here are a skate shop, the Sk8ters Cafe and even a video arcade featuring hockey games.

The **Farmington River** is popular with canoeists and bird-watchers. Hikers can walk along sections of its banks in Farmington, Avon and Simsbury. Water-skiers may be seen jumping in the Collinsville section of Canton. The latest activity is tubing. Young and old alike enjoy riding double-inflatable tubes down the river from Satan's Kingdom State Recreation Area in New Hartford to Canton. Tubes may be rented at Satan's Kingdom for $9 a ride.

Shopping. This sophisticated suburban area provides a variety of shopping opportunities, from the upscale stores (Lord & Taylor, Brooks Brothers, Abercrombie's and, soon, Nordstrom) at **Westfarms Mall** on the Farmington-West Hartford border to free-standing shops throughout the valley.

Farmington center offers the **Ann Howard Cookery** for sensational breads and maybe a corned beef and swiss croissant to take out for a picnic along the river. Adjacent is **Granite Lake Pottery,** showing good-looking crafts.

An historic atmosphere pervades the site and shops of Old Avon Village along Route 44. Browsers like the setting and such stores as the **Player Piano Emporium, Little Silver Shop, The Grapevine** for jewelry and **Blumen Laden** for floral arrangements. Gifts and garden things are offered at **Ribbons & Roses,** while **Country at Heart** stocks rag rugs, handpainted pottery and lots of dolls.

The shops get tonier as Old Avon Village melds into the new Shops at River Park. You'll find every pattern you could imagine at **The China Shop** and every with-it children's outfit at **Little Darlings.** A branch of **The Secret Garden of Martha's Vineyard** carries gifts, paper goods and toiletries. **The Pampered Bath** speaks for itself.

Nearby is Avon's Riverdale Farms, which advertises "today's shopping amid yesterday's charms." Some buildings have been converted from barns from a 19th-

Fine Colonial Revival country house is home of prized Hill-Stead Museum.

century dairy farm, while others are newly built (the latest looks barn-like from the outside but plants cascade down a two-story atrium inside its handsome interior). The tenant mix changes but among the new and old are **Neuchatel Chocolates, E.L. Wilde** (furnishings and accessories), **Plain Folk** (early New England country items), **Montage** (casual clothing and accessories), and **Baldenza Company Store** for silk separates at factory prices.

Situated along Route 44 just west of the Route 10 intersection are branches of **Talbots** and **Country Curtains** plus **The Dovetail,** local specialist in handcrafted 18th-century furnishings. Route 44 in western Avon and Canton is lined with shopping plazas and stores of varying interest to visitors.

The Simsburytown Shops are the most interesting in Simsbury. **The Work Shoppe** offers gifts and accessories of timeless tradition (though we thought their bird "lunch stations" were hardly traditional). **Finula's** stocks women's sportswear and **La Grande Pantrie,** cheeses, specialty foods and kitchen accessories.

Extra-Special

Hill-Stead Museum, 35 Mountain Road, Farmington. (203) 677-4787.

This cultural treasure is important on three fronts: art, architecture and furnishings. The 29-room white clapboard house with rambling wings and a Mount Vernon facade is considered one of the finest Colonial Revival country houses in America. Willed as a museum by its designer and last occupant, architect Theodate Pope Riddle, it's a pleasantly personal masterpiece of a mansion that remains as she left it. Hung on its walls is the matchless collection of one of the earliest American collectors of Impressionist paintings before they became fashionable – what Henry James in 1907 called "wondrous examples of Manet, of Degas, of Claude Monet, of Whistler." The furnishings include remarkable mementos of an early 20th-century family, from Corinthian pottery and Chinese porcelain to a first edition of Samuel Johnson's *Dictionary* and a handwritten letter from Franklin D. Roosevelt. As you are guided on an hour-long tour, it is "as if the owners, having to be away for the afternoon, nevertheless invited you to stop for a time to delight in their house and collection," as a museum guide puts it. The property's elaborate sunken gardens, designed by landscape architect Beatrix Farrand, have been reconstructed to their pre-1925 state. Open Tuesday-Sunday 10 to 4, winter 11 to 3. Adults, $6.

Lake Waramaug provides backdrop for wines at Hopkins Vineyard.

Litchfield-Lake Waramaug
Connecticut's Colonial Country

Nestled in the hills of Northwest Connecticut, picturesque Lake Waramaug boasts an alpine setting that appeals enough to an Austrian innkeeper to call it home. Nearby is Litchfield, the quintessential Colonial Connecticut town preserved not as a restoration in the tradition of Williamsburg, with which it has been compared, but as a living museum community.

The lake and the town, though ten miles apart, are linked by a mystique of timeless isolation. They represent the heart of the Litchfield Hills, a chic yet sedate area of prep schools and foxhunts, of church spires and town greens. The landed gentry who call this never-never land home are joined by celebrity New Yorkers who savor its low-key lifestyle.

Hills rise sharply above the boomerang-shaped Lake Waramaug. Its sylvan shoreline is flanked by a state park, substantial summer homes, and four country inns. With little commercialism, it's enveloped in a country feeling, away from it all.

Litchfield, a small county seat whose importance long has transcended its borders, is perched atop the crest of a ridge. Its beautiful North and South streets are lined with gracious homes and history (George Washington slept here, Harriet Beecher Stowe was born here, Ethan Allen lived here, the nation's first law school and its first academy for girls were founded here). The village is so preserved and prized that only in recent years has it attracted inns and restaurants and the kind of shops that affluence breed.

Between the hills and lakes are fine natural and low-key attractions – Connecticut's largest nature sanctuary, a world-famous garden center, two farm wineries, state parks and forests. Connecticut's entire Northwest Corner has much to commend it, but there's no more choice a slice than Litchfield and Lake Waramaug.

NOTE: The telephone area code for this area and most of Connecticut is scheduled to change to 860 as of October 1996.

Inn Spots

Mayflower Inn, Route 47, Box 1288, Washington 06793. (203) 868-9466.

It's long been hidden away on 28 hilly, wooded acres overlooking the campus of The Gunnery, the private school that used to own and operate it. But a $15 million renovation and expansion has cast this venerable inn into the limelight as one of the premier English-style country hotels in America.

"Stately" is the word to describe the entire place as styled in 1992 by New York owners Robert and Adriana Mnuchin and steered since by general manager John Trevenen. The Mnuchins – he a Goldman Sachs whiz for 30 years and she a retailer and born-to-shop collector – have a weekend home here and, with an obsession for detail, dedicated themselves to putting the up-and-down Mayflower Inn of the past on the up path forever.

No expense was spared in producing 25 guest rooms and suites that are the ultimate in good taste. A staff of 85 adds to the feeling of pampered luxury. Fifteen rooms are upstairs on the second and third floors of the expanded main inn. Ten more are in two guest houses astride a hill beside a magnificent tiered rose garden leading up to a heated swimming pool and a tennis court.

Fine British, French and American antiques and accessories, prized artworks and elegant touches of whimsy – like four old trunks stashed in a corner of the second-floor hallway – dignify public and private rooms alike. Opening off the lobby, an intimate parlor with plush leather sofa and chairs leads into the ever-so-British gentleman's library. It possesses one of the largest collections of mystery novels in Connecticut, Playbills from the 1930s and the complete works of Wharton and James, plus a curved bay window looking across the side veranda to manicured lawns. Across the back of the inn are three dining rooms (see Dining Spots), and along one side is an English-style bar. Downstairs is a state-of-the-art fitness center that would do many a private club proud. The outlying Teahouse is a tranquil, Adirondack-style lodge that's the ultimate meeting facility. Opposite the front desk is a gift shop offering small antiques, Italian leather goods, cashmere sweaters, jewelry and such of appeal to Adriana's New York set (the first guests to book a suite were Mike Nichols and Diane

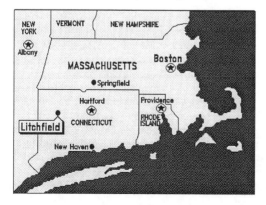

Sawyer, who were at the inn for Stephen Sondheim's birthday party).

Suite or no, each guest room is a sight to behold and some are almost breathtakingly glamorous. Room 24 offers a kingsize canopy four-poster feather bed awash in pillows, embroidered Frette linens, a feather duvet and a chenille throw. An angled loveseat faces the fireplace, and oversize wicker rockers await on the balcony. Books and magazines are spread out on the coffee table, the armoire contains a TV and there's a walk-in closet. The paneled bathroom, bigger than most bedrooms, has marble floors, a double vanity opposite a glistening tub, a separate toilet area and a walk-in shower big enough for an army. Even all that didn't prepare us for a second-floor corner suite with a large living room straight out of Country Life magazine, a dining-conference room, a lavatory, a bedroom with a kingsize canopied four-poster and a second bathroom, plus a porch overlooking the sylvan scene. And so it goes, room after room of great comfort and élan – each full of surprises and "everything with a story behind it," according to our guide. Fancy toiletries and fresh orchids and nosegays of roses (Adriana's favorite flowers) are much in evidence. The rear balconies and decks off the rooms in the guest houses face the woods and are particularly private.

The outside is equally magnificent, from the acres of lawns shimmering in emerald green to the exotic specimen trees strategically placed all around. The 28 acres of horticultural Eden include terraced Shakespeare, rose and cutting gardens. The Mnuchins had a hiking trail blazed to the top of the big hill they renamed Mayflower Mountain, where a ring of stones is now "Meditation Circle."

Breakfast, available from a full menu, is a pricey extravagance that's likely to add $25 to $40 more to an overnight bill for two. The oversize Limoges breakfast cups were custom-designed for the Mayflower based on what the Mnuchins enjoyed during whirlwind travels to Europe as they planned their inn.

From the beguiling botanical and canine prints in the hallways to the weeping Alaskan blue atlas cedar and boxwood gardens outside, the place is a treasure for those who appreciate the finest.

In 1995, the Mayflower became the first Connecticut property to become associated with the Paris-based Relais & Châteaux hotel group. It also recorded a stunning 80 percent annual occupancy rate. Said manager Trevenen, with a trace of his Australian heritage: "We've reached the niche where we want to be."

Doubles, $225 to $350, EP; suites, $295 to $495, EP. Two-night minimum on weekends.

The Boulders Inn, Route 45, New Preston 06777. (203) 868-0541 or (800) 552-6853.

Its setting just across the road from Lake Waramaug, its handsome and comfortable living room, its deluxe guest houses and carriage house, and its fine kitchen make this an appealing inn. Built as a private home in 1895, it has been a small inn since about 1950. Kees and Ulla Adema of Fairfield, he a ship's broker from Holland and she born in Germany, took it over in 1988 as a retirement venture. "We were thinking of a three-room B&B," recalls Ulla. "Instead, we bought an inn with a restaurant and now we seem to be running a restaurant with an inn."

The food operation (see Dining Spots) keeps them busy, but the Ademas have made fine improvements to the four guest rooms and two suites in the inn as well as the eight more contemporary rooms in four outlying duplex guest houses. They also added a rear carriage house with three choice, carpeted guest rooms with plush chintz seating in front of stone fireplaces.

Rooms upstairs in the main house come with thick carpeting, comfortable sofas or chairs, and king or queensize beds, most covered with handsome quilts. Period antiques, American folk art and Ulla's intricate cut-paper lampshades are the norm. Three rooms facing the lake offer large, cushioned window seats to take in the view, and a corner suite has its own balcony. All come with private baths, as do the eight rooms in the duplexes scattered along the hillside behind the inn. Renovated and upgraded in 1994 with four-poster beds, air-conditioning and fireplaces, guest houses have new decks in front and back facing woods and lake, and four have whirlpool tubs. The fireplaces

Library at Mayflower Inn is dressed in finest British style.

and whirlpools make them especially popular with the New Yorkers who comprise the bulk of the Boulders clientele.

Back in the inn, a basement game room offers ping-pong and skittles, and a library has been added to a small den with a color TV. The paneled living room, its picture windows overlooking the lake (binoculars are provided), is a lovely mix of antiques and groupings of sofas and wing chairs in reds, blues and chintz. In one corner are book shelves and a stereo with many tapes. A Russian samovar may dispense tea in winter months, and guests also enjoy cocktails here.

In summer, swimming, sailing and canoeing are favorite pastimes. If you feel lazy, just sit in the beach house's wicker swing and watch the changing moods of the lake.

A full breakfast is served by the windows in the six-sided Lake Dining Room. A help-yourself cold buffet is set up with fresh fruit and juices, cereals and coffee cake. Eggs any style, omelets, french toast and pecan, apple or blueberry pancakes with bacon, sausage or ham can be ordered and are accompanied by English muffins or homemade whole wheat toast.

Doubles, $200 to $250, B&B; $250 to $300, MAP. Three-night minimum on summer weekends.

Toll Gate Hill, Route 202, Litchfield 06759. (203) 567-4545 or (800) 445-3903.

The rural 1745 landmark home near the Torrington town line in which Captain William Bull once took in travelers on the Hartford-Albany stage route was handsomely restored and reopened as a small inn and a good restaurant in 1983. Inviting it is, situated back from the road in a stand of trees, its red frame exterior dimly illuminated at night and appearing to the traveler much as it must have more than two centuries ago.

Such was the demand for the six original rooms that innkeeper Fritz Zivic opened four more rooms and suites in the adjacent "school house" in 1986. A new building with ten more rooms and suites and a much-needed lobby/reception area opened toward the rear of the property in 1990.

Although the main inn with the restaurant is listed on the National Register of Historic Places, the most choice guest rooms are those in the outbuildings. They're splashily decorated with comfort in mind, and an emphasis on coordinated Hinson and Schumacher fabrics, bright colors, queensize canopy beds, and upholstered chairs and loveseats. Fireplaces are attractions in three rooms and five suites; the latter also have minibars stocked with a split of wine and Perrier. The bathrooms are outfitted with Gucci colognes. The bedspreads are coordinated to match the shower curtains, and in the soaring two-story lobby, the paisley print on the walls is repeated in the chairs and curtains. Balconies overlooking the woods off rooms in the new building hold chairs and a small table.

The nicest rooms in the main inn are three larger ones on the second floor, each with a working fireplace. A small parlor for house guests is located on the second-floor landing next to the ballroom.

A continental breakfast of fresh juice and homemade breads and rolls is served on trays in the guest rooms or in the restaurant (see Dining Spots).

Doubles, $110 to $140; suites, $175.

Hopkins Inn, 22 Hopkins Road, New Preston 06777. (203) 868-7295.

This landmark yellow inn astride a hill above Lake Waramaug is known far and wide for its European cuisine (see Dining Spots), and we often recommend it when asked where to take visitors for lunch in the country. Its reputation was built by Swiss-born innkeepers and has been continued since the late 1970s by Austrian Franz Schober and his wife Beth.

Built in 1847 as a summer guest house, the Federal structure with several additions was converted from a boarding house into an inn in 1945, and the guest rooms have been considerably enhanced by the Schobers. Warmed only by small heating units (thus used only from late March through December), the eleven guest rooms and an apartment on the second and third floors have been sparingly but comfortably furnished with brass or wood bedsteads, thick carpeting, floral wallpapers, chests of drawers and the odd loveseat or rocker. Nine rooms have private baths.

Guests share a couple of small main-floor parlors with restaurant patrons, and may use the inn's private beach on the lake. There's no better vantage point for lake-watching than the expansive outdoor dining terrace, shaded by a giant horse chestnut tree and distinguished by striking copper and wrought-iron chandeliers and lanterns. Breakfast is available for house guests.

Doubles, $57 to $67, EP. Closed January to late March.

The Inn on Lake Waramaug, 107 North Shore Road, New Preston 06777. (203) 868-0563 or (800) 525-3466.

From private home to village inn to boarding house for summer guests, this has grown since the 19th century into a year-round destination resort with an indoor pool and whirlpool, sauna, game room, meals in two dining rooms or at lakeside, a beach and 23 guest rooms, five in the main inn and the rest in redecorated guest houses below.

This is a place for people who like activity. A succession of innkeepers has kept things busy with lake excursions on the inn's 30-passenger Showboat in summer, events from frog-jumping contests to raft races to Scottish bagpipe festivals to handbell choir concerts, and many package plans for individual guests, groups and conferences. White lawn chairs are lined up in rows around the grounds, the better for watching all the goings-on.

After taking over from the defunct Baron Group in late 1994, new owner Nancy Conant of West Hartford was in residence and providing a more personal brand of hospitality than had been dispensed in the recent past. All guest rooms have cable

Landmark 19th-century hilltop structure above Lake Waramaug houses Hopkins Inn.

television and air-conditioning; there are fireplaces in sixteen, and many have canopy beds, maple furniture and upholstered chairs. The top of the line are the eight master bedrooms with working fireplaces and water views.

Three meals a day are served in peak season in the inn's dining rooms, on the terrace or at the boathouse beside the lake. A new gallery, converted from a former TV room, features works of local artists.

Doubles, $209 to $229, MAP. Two-night minimum on weekends.

Litchfield Inn, Route 202, Litchfield 06759. (203) 567-4503 or (800) 499-3444.

Set back from the road west of the village on a vast expanse of lawn in need of more landscaping, local entrepreneur James Irwin's Litchfield Inn is a relatively new (1982) white Colonial-style inn with modern accoutrements, 30 guest rooms and a couple of suites, a banquet facility and plans for 70 more rooms, a function hall and a swimming pool/health club. More seedlings, a pond and a fountain were in evidence at our latest visit, and a new look was ahead for the dining room.

Furnished with early American reproduction pieces, the rooms are air-conditioned and include a single double bed or two double beds, modern baths, color TV and telephones, and some have wet bars. Commanding top dollar are eight "theme rooms," ranging from the Sherlock Holmes to the Western Room to the Lady Agnew Suite. The Lace Room, all white and lacy with canopy bed and swagged draperies, is billed for honeymooners. The Presidential Quarters commemorates past presidents with mounted coin displays and wall hangings.

New life was injected into the dining operation by food and beverage manager Zeus Goldberg, a former New York restaurateur and now a Litchfield resident. At our visit, he was in the midst of upgrading the dining-room decor (elegant in white with lacquered oxblood-red upholstered chairs) and was about to launch a "regional/eclectic" menu. Chef Steve Miko moved from Santa Fe with a desire to mate his Southwestern cooking background with his New England roots. His opening dinner menu included such entrées ($15 to $20) as poached ginger salmon served on an Asian snow pea slaw, lobster napoleon with sherried tomato and red bell pepper coulis, and grilled veal chop on a bed of leeks and lentils with orange-cranberry relish. The adjacent tavern also was in for an upgrade, as Zeus sought to make the inn "an all-occasion place" for locals as well as travelers.

Doubles, $100 to $150. Lunch daily, noon to 3; dinner, 5:30 to 9:30 or 10.

Dining Spots

West Street Grill, 43 West St., Litchfield. (203) 567-3885.

The food here is the subject of raves from food reviewers and the perfect foil for the trendoids who make this their own at lunch and dinner seven days a week. The two rooms were full the winter Saturday we first lunched here, and the host rattled off the names of half a dozen celebrities who had reserved for that evening.

An instant hit since its opening in 1990, the grill is the kind of place weekending New Yorkers love. It's sleek in black and white, with a row of low booths up the middle, tables and mirrors on either side, and a back room with stunning trompe-l'oeil curtains on the walls. The only color comes from the changing fine art on a side brick wall and from the power clientele.

The kitchen has maintained its culinary high through a succession of talented chefs, thanks to owner James O'Shea's magic touch. Our first lunch here began with a rich butternut squash and pumpkin bisque and the signature grilled peasant bread with parmesan aioli ($4.95). Main dishes were an appetizer of grilled country bread with a brandade of white beans and marinated artichokes ($5.50) and a special of grilled smoked pork tenderloin with spicy Christmas limas ($8.95). Among the highly touted desserts, we succumbed to an ethereal crème brûlée and an intense key lime tart that was really tart. With two generous glasses of wine ($3.75 each), the total lunch bill for two came to a rather New Yorkish $50.

Memorable as it was, lunch was nothing compared with a special tasting dinner showcasing the summer menu (starters, $7.95 to $10.95; pastas and main courses, $14.95 to $23.95). That extravaganza began with beet-green soup, grilled peasant bread with roasted tomato and goat cheese, corn cakes with crème fraîche and chives, roasted-beet and goat-cheese napoleons with a composed salad, and nori-wrapped salmon with marinated daikon, cucumbers and seaweed. A passion fruit sorbet followed. By then we felt that we had already dined well, but no, on came the entrées: tasting portions – which we shared back and forth – of pan-seared halibut with a beet pappardelle, spicy shrimp cake with ragoût of black beans and corn, grilled ginger chicken with polenta and ginger chips, and grilled leg of lamb with a ragoût of lentils, spicy curried vegetables and fried greens, including flat-leaf spinach. A little bit here, a little there, and next we knew emerged a parade of desserts: a plum tart in a pastry so tender as not to be believed, a frozen passion fruit soufflé, a hazelnut torte with caramel ice cream and a sampling of sorbets (raspberry, white peach and blackberry).

Both meals testified amply to West Street's incredible culinary prowess.

Lunch daily, 11:30 to 2:30 or 3, weekends to 4; dinner, 5:30 to 9 or 10.

Doc's, Flirtation Avenue at Route 45, New Preston. (203) 868-9415.

Who could help but like a place with a name like this? An address at Flirtation Avenue, across from Lake Waramaug? A roadside stand gone upscale – well, a little bit?

This is where Adam Riess, a Californian fresh out of the University of Pennsylvania, opened an Italian cafe, pizzeria and bakery in 1989 to immediate success. The rustic dining room contains 30 chairs painted pea green, spartan tables bearing butcher paper,

Wall of boulders at Boulders Inn.   **Mirrored dining room at West Street Grill.**

votive candles and big bottles of extra-virgin olive oil (plus metal containers that the menu notes contain salt, not cheese), and a handful of posters and plants for accents.

Chef Riad Aamar, who cooked in Italy, and his energetic young kitchen staff of six have enhanced and expanded the computerized menu, which is printed daily. New-wave flatbread pizzas are the specialty, in small and large sizes, about $7.50 and $18.50 respectively. Try the cipollina (caramelized onions, gorgonzola and fresh rosemary) or the olivetta (bel paese, olives, sundried tomatoes, mozzarella and oregano). Praise is lavished on the puglia breads and pastas ($10.75 to $13.75), perhaps handmade fettuccine with smoked trout, tomato, garlic and olive oil or farfalle with garlic, basil, tomato sauce and goat cheese.

Share a pizza or grilled bruschetta to start, or try the grilled portobello mushrooms, sea scallops sautéed with shallots and saffron or a salad of asparagus, roasted peppers, shiitake mushrooms and ricotta ($5.75 to $8.75). This is exciting grazing fare, which is why weekenders rank the pintsize place right up there with the West Street Grill. Entrées at our latest visit, for those of a mind, were priced from $14.25 for roasted chicken with Italian sausage and garlic to $18.25 for roasted rack of lamb with white beans and herbs. Desserts could be pecan spice cake with poached pear and vanilla-caramel sauce, marble cheesecake with chocolate biscotti crust and fudge sauce, or peach-blueberry streusel pie.

The name? Adam was thinking of naming it Adamo's, but ended up naming it for his grandfather, a physician who has summered on the lake for 40 years.

Lunch in summer, Saturday and Sunday noon to 2:30; dinner, Wednesday-Sunday 5 to 10. No credit cards. BYOB.

Bee Brook, 20 Bee Brook Road (Route 47), Washington Depot. (203) 868-6633.

Blessed with a fancy renovation, a chef from the West Street Grill, an expansive canopied deck and a new flagstone terrace beneath a spreading maple tree beside the rushing Bee Brook, how could this place miss? It opened in 1994 in space formerly occupied by Jonathan's and Today's. Bee Brook promised to be the best yet, thanks to the considerable investment of longtime Greenwich Village restaurateur Richard McDermott and local partner Carol Sirowich. They literally raised the roof to form a two-story-high arched ceiling in the center of the dining room, containing a soaring fieldstone fireplace. They painted the wainscoting and walls a pale cream color, dressed the tables with cream-colored linens, and tiled the floor in the bar.

The whole scene, indoors and out, is a nifty setting for the innovative fare of chef Matthew Fahrner. "The chef likes Asian spices," said our waitress as she served a terrace full of weekend lunchers. Chewy peasant bread arrived first with a carafe of olive oil containing a sprig of thyme. This whetted our appetite for a hefty bowl of lobster bisque, its color heightened by a smidgen of saffron; a salad of smoked salmon with marinated fennel ($7.50) and a stellar linguini with sundried tomatoes, broccoli rabe, basil and garlic ($8.95). With a bottle of Covey Run Johannesburg riesling ($12.50), we were ready to while away the afternoon, but people were still waiting for tables. A pear and dried cherry crisp with vanilla ice cream sent us happily on our way. The house breads and desserts are for sale in the retail bakery downstairs.

We'd return any time for lunch ($7.50 to $10.95), perhaps a cod cake sandwich with Asian greens and garlic sauce or sesame-crusted salmon with spicy pickled sausage. And certainly for dinner ($13.95 to $19.95), when the offerings might be pan-seared calamari with roasted chiles and curry, served with ginger broth and basmati rice, or grilled marinated leg of lamb with flageolet bean succotash. Start with grilled quail served with barley salad, persimmon and chili sauce. Finish with orange-infused crème brûlée or maple-walnut tart with ginger anglaise. Your meal should prove to be as memorable as the setting.

A couple of private balconies for two overlooking the terrace are located off the dining room. Shielded by prolific flowers in window boxes, they're the place for romantics to see and not be seen.

Open daily, 11 to 10.

Mayflower Inn, Route 47, Washington. (203) 868-9466.

The three dining rooms along the back of the house are as stately as the rest of this grandly refurbished inn. As you would expect, the kitchen is equal to the task. Chef John Farnsworth was lured home to his native Connecticut from RockResorts' Lodge at Keole in Hawaii after being named one of America's top ten chefs in 1991 by Food and Wine magazine. His staff here includes five colleagues from the Culinary Institute of America, of which he was a member of the first two-year class to graduate following its move from New Haven to Hyde Park, N.Y.

The dining rooms are appointed in English country-house style with upholstered high-back chairs at tables covered with white linens over dark green patterned skirts that match the draperies. Tapestries and wrought-iron furniture decorate the garden room. The bar room is English-looking in hunter green.

The chef's new-age crab cake suspends flakes of crabmeat in delicate scallop mousse, with none of the traditional crumb binding. His signature rabbit ballotine is folded around a delicate loin and roasted to a turn. One winter night's menu also listed grilled diver sea scallops on a carrot risotto with fava beans and chervil and grilled veal chop with garlic-cheese potatoes and stone-ground mustard sauce, among dinner entrées ($15.50 to $27). Starters were as simple as a mixed green salad with chardonnay vinaigrette ($5.75) and as complex as grapevine smoked salmon with potato caper salad and potato crackers ($11.25).

Desserts are to die for, from caramel roasted pears served over a warm semolina terrine to warm peach pound cake with homemade peach ice cream. Two pages of fine wines are available by the glass from a wine list honored by the Wine Spectator.

Fireplace is focal point of arched dining room at Bee Brook.

Some of the dinner appetizers and pastas turn up on the lunch menu, when main dishes are priced from $7.75 for a toasted ham and cheese sandwich with french fries to $9.25 for chicken salad with melon and pancetta.

Lunch daily, noon to 2; dinner nightly, 6 to 9. Bar menu daily, 11:30 to 3 and 5 to midnight.

The Boulders Inn, Route 45, New Preston. (203) 868-0541.

Boulders are a good part of the decor at this inn, jutting out from the walls of the intimate inner dining room as well as in part of the smashing six-sided addition, where, through large wraparound windows, almost every diner has a view of Lake Waramaug across the road. Three levels of a spacious outside deck/terrace are the delightful setting for cocktails and dinner during the warmer months.

Inside, chandeliers with pierced lampshades made by innkeeper Ulla Adema hang from the ceilings. Other light is provided by hurricane lamps on tables covered with white cloths over forest green.

The scene is rustically elegant, and the food quite sophisticated. House guests on the MAP plan have full choice (no surcharges) from the same à la carte menu that draws the knowing public from near and far.

One recent night's main courses ($18 to $22.50) included rosemary-seared red snapper with warm tomato and cucumber salad, grilled Atlantic salmon stuffed with leeks on a bed of spinach, sautéed pork loin with corn crêpes and roasted pepper relish, and grilled prime sirloin with roasted shallot and bacon bordelaise.

Among appetizers ($6 to $8) were shrimp and scallop risotto with truffle oil and fresh herbs, grilled vegetable and goat cheese terrine with tomato-basil coulis, and fresh asparagus salad with prosciutto and sherry vinaigrette. Desserts were blueberry shortcake with buttermilk biscuits and crème fraîche, a seasonal apricot tart and an ethereal cheesecake with candied ginger crust.

Dinner nightly except Tuesday in summer, 6 to 9, Sunday from 4; Thursday-Sunday in winter.

Toll Gate Hill, Route 202, Litchfield. (203) 567-4545.

Innkeeper Fritz Zivic, who founded the late Black Dog Tavern steakhouse chain in the Hartford area in the 1960s, features a changing menu of what he calls "light, unencumbered food" in two small, charming dining areas on the inn's main floor and upstairs in a ballroom complete with a fiddler's loft for piano and other musical entertainment.

The original dining rooms took on a new look in 1994, when tall booths were added to the old tavern with its dark wood and wide-plank floors. The more formal room, dressed with peach linens and Villeroy & Boch china, was enhanced by wall murals of 18th-century Litchfield painted by a local artist.

The menu changes seasonally. Dinner entrées start at $18 for roasted cod with horseradish crust and lemon-scallion butter or pan-seared free-range chicken infused with opal basil oil and caramelized sweet onions. Prices top off at $24 for walnut-crusted rack of lamb, pan-seared veal rib chop with coriander roasted tomato jus and the inn's specialty shellfish pie, about which we've heard raves. Other favorites are poached salmon with garlic and sundried tomato sauce and New York strip steak with roasted garlic.

For appetizers ($5 to $8), look for a signature deep-fried onion florette, cut to open like a blossom and served with a Russian dressing and blue cheese sour cream, or fresh salmon and crab cakes with smoked tomato-chive mayonnaise. Dessert could be chocolate-walnut grappa cake, crème brûlée, and homemade bread pudding with nugget caramel sauce and spicy apple chutney. Much the same style of fare is available at lunch, $7 to $11.

Corner table at Toll Gate Hill.

The wine list is choice and reasonably priced, the soups are creative and our summer dinners a few years ago of shrimp in beer batter and sautéed sea scallops with sweet butter and braised leeks were outstanding.

Lunch daily, noon to 3; dinner, 5:30 to 9:30 or 10:30; Sunday brunch, 11:30 to 3:30. Closed Tuesday in winter.

Hopkins Inn, Hopkins Road, New Preston. (203) 368-7295.

On a warm summer day or evening, few dining spots are more inviting than the large outdoor terrace under the giant horse chestnut tree at the entrance to the Hopkins Inn. With the waters of Lake Waramaug shimmering below and a bottle of wine from the Hopkins Vineyard next door, you could imagine yourself in the Alps. No wonder Austrian chef-owner Franz Schober feels right at home.

Dining inside this 1847 Federal structure, a visual time warp, is endearing as well. Two dining rooms stretch around the lakeview side of the inn; the overflow goes to a paneled Colonial-style taproom up a few stairs. One dining room is Victorian, while the other is rustic with barnsiding and ships' figureheads on the walls.

The menu reflects the Austrian and Swiss dishes of the chef's heritage. You might start with pâté maison, eggs à la russe, escargots or bundnerteller ($3.75 to $6.25). Dinner entrées are $15.75 to $18.75 for specialties like wiener schnitzel and sweetbreads that we remember fondly from years past. Chicken cordon bleu, loin lamb chops and filet mignon with béarnaise sauce appeal to traditional palates and, keeping up with the times, there's a vegetable platter for $16.75. In spring, you can get shad roe; Beth Schrober says her husband's roast pheasant with red cabbage and spaetzle is especially popular in fall. How about veal piccata or backhendl with lingonberries, both under $16? Vegetables are special, especially unusual things like braised romaine lettuce.

Regulars cherish the frozen grand marnier soufflé glacé and strawberries romanoff, among such choices as frozen éclair, crème caramel, pear hélène and kahlua parfait, all $3.25 to $4.25. The wine list offers twenty cabernet sauvignons from $15 to $80 as well as several Swiss and Austrian whites and an incredible list of bordeaux and burgundies. Finish with a flourish with cappuccino or liqueured coffees.

The luncheon menu offers many of the same specialties at lower prices. Entrées like lamb curry and sirloin steak are in the $7 to $9.50 range. It's not surprising the place is so popular.

Lunch, Tuesday-Saturday noon to 2; dinner, 6 to 9 or 10, Sunday 12:30 to 8:30; closed Monday. No lunch in April, November and December. Closed January to late March.

Thé Cafe, Route 45, New Preston. (203) 868-1787.

An old stove is at the entrance to this intimate place whose name plays on the French word for tea. Folks spill out from the grotto-like, 30-seat interior beneath the Rigamarole Shop onto tables on the porch and even the asphalt. Decor is casual with rough fieldstone walls, track lighting, a floor of black and white painted squares, and bentwood chairs at white formica tables. A case at the front displays pastries and breads to go, and a sideboard at the back is laden with the day's desserts, from cookies to pumpkin tart to lemon-cranberry cake.

This is a place for an interesting, albeit intimate (because the tables are so close together) meal. Belgian waffles, omelets and brioche french toast are featured for breakfast. The day's lunch offerings ($6.75 to $9.75) might include nifty pizzas, a BLT on toasted brioche, a chippewa salmon sandwich on Indian skillet bread with watercress mayonnaise, penne arrabiata and burgers on focaccia buns. The cafe misto salad combines roasted eggplant, red peppers, imported olives, wild greens, feta cheese, caramelized onions and sauce verte and comes with grilled bread.

Some of the lunch treats show up at dinner as appetizers. Main dishes ($10.95 to $17.95) could be pan-seared tuna with ginger and sesame, garlic shrimp with tropical salsa, penne with salmon or angel-hair pasta with shrimp, shiitake mushrooms, garlic and basil.

This is a popular spot for afternoon tea with a dessert from the sideboard display.

Breakfast, 9 to 11:30; lunch, 11:30 to 4; tea, 4 to 5; dinner, 6 to 9:30. Closed Tuesday; hours vary seasonally. No credit cards. BYOB.

Grappa, 26 Commons Drive (off Route 202), Litchfield Commons, Litchfield. (203) 567-1616.

This Italian offshoot of the West Street Grill opened in 1994 in the former Wickets restaurant at the rear of a shopping complex. Here all is convivial and intimate (make that very) with rich wood tables cheek-by-jowl in two dining areas and a solarium. Mirrors are positioned to make the place look bigger. It manages to seat 96 inside and 44 more outside on a courtyard in season.

Warm, warm, warm is the sunny southern exposure in the solarium, partially shaded by billowing curtain-type affairs on the ceiling. That and the adjacent 650-degree wood-burning oven, with walls of brick and a floor of lava from Mount St. Helen's, must produce quite an air-conditioning bill (or perhaps save on heating in winter). From the oven, which is open to the bar area, come exotic thin-crust pizzas ($8.95 to $13.95), a dozen or more versions from paella to roasted shrimp.

The kitchen also is strong on novel starters ($4.95 to $7.95). At our winter visit they included potato and watercress soup, warm polenta casserole with gorgonzola and rosemary, grilled calamari with arugula and balsamic-mustard vinaigrette, and crisp fish and potato balls with an olive oil and lemon emulsion. There are a few pastas and entrées of the day, priced from $9.95 to $13.95. Expect things like spaghettini with rock shrimp and capers, baked salmon on a bed of spinach with pine nuts and lemon-fennel potatoes, and Tuscan veal stew with crimini mushrooms, madeira and ditali pasta.

Predictable desserts include white chocolate cheesecake, apple turnover and tirami su. At our 1995 visit, co-owner Charles Kafferman was about to install an ice-cream machine for frozen drinks and sundaes to attract the family trade. He planned to open for lunch, starting on weekends in spring and daily in summer.

Lunch daily in season, 11:30 to 3; dinner nightly except Monday, 5 to 10 or 11, Sunday 4 to 9.

The Inn on Lake Waramaug, North Shore Road, New Preston. (203) 868-0563.

Dining here is in a large, pleasant room with brass chandeliers and sconces, swagged draperies and Hitchcock chairs and in an adjacent, more airy room. Both are appointed in white and hunter green.

For dinner, entrées are priced from $15.95 for chicken and herbed spinach risotto cake with wild mushroom ragoût to $19.50 for a dish called veal pastrami, sliced thin and served over tomato-basil linguini. Mediterranean-style seafood stew, grilled Norwegian salmon glazed with sundried tomatoes and black olive pesto, grilled lamb loin with a lingonberry compote and roasted chestnut port sauce, and medallions of venison with black pepper-plum sauce are seasonal possibilities. Appetizers ($4.95 to $6.95) could be peppered smoked salmon, seafood ravioli and venison sausage. The wine list was honored by the Wine Spectator in 1994.

Hamburgers for lunch are barbecued in summer at the inn's Boathouse, where a short menu yields things like ribs, salads and poached salmon in the $5 to $9 range.

Lunch in season, Monday-Friday noon to 2:15; dinner, Monday-Saturday 6 to 9; Sunday, brunch 11:30 to 1:30, dinner 4:30 to 7:30.

La Tienda Cafe, Sports Village, Route 202, Litchfield. (203) 567-8778.

A green neon cactus beckons in the window of this two-room Mexican cafe with a bar in the rear. Glass tops the cloths of wide, bright stripes and a cactus in a small pot may be on each table. Colorful prints and rugs adorn the walls.

Crispy homemade tortilla chips and a fairly hot salsa are served. We found a lunch of Mexican pizza ($5.95) almost more than one could handle: a flour tortilla topped with ground beef, cheese, lettuce, tomato, chiles, guacamole and sour cream. One half had hot peppers, the other mild. An order of burritos ($7.95), one stuffed with cheese and one with chicken, was also delicious and hearty.

Both lunch and dinner menus include "north of the border" dishes, but who would come here for a BLT or strip steak? Black bean soup, flautas, Arizona-style nachos (topped with ground beef) and seafood quesadilla are some of the starters ($3.95 to $8.50) and there's even a Mexican egg roll. Dinners include Mexican rice and refried beans or salad, and run from $7.95 for folded tacos to $14.25 for seafood chimichanga. Everything may be ordered mild, medium or hot. Lime pie is the favored desert, but flan and sopaipilla also are popular.

Lunch, Tuesday-Saturday 11:30 to 2:30; dinner, Monday-Saturday 4:30 to 9 or 10, Sunday noon to 9.

Spinell's Litchfield Food Company, On the Green, Litchfield. (203) 567-3113.

Rick Spinell, pastry chef at New York's famed River Cafe, answered a for-sale ad "for that expensive takeout place in Litchfield" and ended up owning it. He thought running a specialty-foods shop, bakery and deli with a handful of tables would be easier than a full restaurant, but found that he had to become jack of so many trades that he's rarely in the kitchen. While he's out front, several chefs and bakers work behind scenes to prepare baked goods from scratch, delectable salads and soups of the day (perhaps tomato-bean-rosemary and mushroom-brie-onion). Rick lowered the prices charged by his high-profile predecessors and added breakfast items every day but Wednesday. He planned to build a brick oven in which to bake wood-fired breads, and hoped someday to have time to resume his dessert forte. Meanwhile, savor treats like foccacia sandwich with sundried tomatoes, goat cheese, roasted peppers, oil and vinegar ($6.95).

Open daily, 8 a.m. to 7 p.m., Sunday to 6.

Black Bear Coffee Roasters, 239 New Milford Tpke. (Route 202), Marbledale. (203) 868-1446.

Just a mile west of New Preston and supplier to many area restaurants is this new coffee roasting shop, bakery, lunch spot and gift shop run by Kate and Jeff Oetjen. In a little white house, with tables and chairs spread out on the wide lawn in back, you may savor the aromas of exotic coffee beans, blended and roasted to order, at hefty prices ($8.50 for a pound of Sumatra Mandheling). You could lunch on grilled eggplant, peppers, zucchini and goat cheese in a citrus soy marinade, or have a bowl of Octoberfest stew incorporating different German wursts with vegetables and rice. Soups might be tomato-fennel puree or arugula, garlic and potato. Of course there are lattes, cappuccino royales, and all the other fancy coffees, as well as bagels, muffins, cookies, pastries and even oatmeal and granola for breakfast. Eat in, on French cafe chairs, or take out. The gifts have a tea or coffee theme – we liked a needlepoint footstool that said "Tea for Two." On Saturday nights in summer there might be live music.

Open Tuesday-Thursday 8 to 5, Friday to 6, Saturday and Sunday 10 to 5.

Diversions

Lakes and Parks. Lake Waramaug State Park at the west end of the lake is a wonderfully scenic site, its picnic tables scattered well apart along the tree-lined shore, right beside the water. The lake's Indian name means "good fishing place;" it's also good for swimming and boating, and blessedly uncrowded. On the north and east sides of the lake are the forested Above All and Mount Bushnell state parks. Not far from Lake Waramaug on the road to Litchfield (Route 202) is **Mount Tom State Park.** It has a 60-acre spring-fed pond for swimming and again picnic tables are poised at shore's edge. A mile-long trail rises to a tower atop Mount Tom.

White Memorial Foundation and Conservation Center, Route 202, Litchfield, 567-0875. Just west of Litchfield are 4,000 acres of nature sanctuary bordering Bantam Lake. Thirty-five miles of woodland and marsh trails are popular with hikers, horseback riders and cross-country skiers. This is a great place for observing wildlife, birds and plants in a variety of habitats. The Conservation Center in a 19th-century mansion contains a natural history museum with good collections of Indian artifacts, butterflies, live and stuffed animals, and an excellent nature library and gift shop. Grounds open free year-round; museum, Tuesday-Sunday, $1.50.

White Flower Farm, Route 63, Litchfield, 567-8789. This institution three miles south of Litchfield is a don't-miss spot for anyone with a green thumb. In fact, people come from across the country to see the place made famous by its catalog, wittily written by the owner under the pen name of Amos Pettingill. Eight acres of exotic display gardens are at peak bloom in late spring; twenty acres of growing fields reach their height in late summer. Greenhouses with indoor plants, including spectacular giant tuberous begonias, are pretty all the time. Shop and grounds open daily, mid-April to late October.

Litchfield Historic Sites. The Litchfield Historic District is clustered along the long, wide green and out North and South streets (Route 63). The seasonal information center on the green has maps for walking tours, which are the best way to experience Litchfield. Note the bank and the jail with

a common wall at North and West streets. Along North Street are Sheldon's Tavern, where George Washington slept, plus the birthplace of Harriet Beecher Stowe and the Pierce Academy, the first academy for girls. South Street is a broad, half-mile-long avenue where two U.S. senators, six Congressmen, three governors and five chief justices have lived. Here too is the **Tapping Reeve House and Law School** (1773), the first law school in the country. The house with its handsome furnishings and the tiny school with handwritten ledgers of students long gone are open Tuesday-Saturday 11 to 5 and Sunday 1 to 5, May-October, $2. The **Litchfield Historical Society Museum** has four galleries of early American paintings, decorative arts, furniture and local history exhibits. Open Tuesday-Saturday 11 to 5, Sunday 1 to 4, April-October, $2.

Litchfield Congregational Church.

Wineries. Two of New England's premier wineries occupy hilltop sites overlooking the beauty of Litchfield and Lake Waramaug. **Haight Vineyard,** Connecticut's first farm winery just east of Litchfield, occupies an English Tudor-style building with a large tasting room and gift shop across Chestnut Hill Road from its original barn. Guided winery tours on the hour and a fifteen-minute vineyard walk are among the attractions. You can pick up a bottle of award-winning covertside white or chardonnay plus a pink T-shirt ("Never bite the foot that stomps your grapes"), wine accessories and such. Open Monday-Saturday 10:30 to 5, Sunday noon to 5.

Hopkins Vineyard, Hopkins Road, New Preston. A hillside location with a good view of Lake Waramaug marks this family operation run by Bill and Judy Hopkins, dairy farmers turned winemakers. The rustic red barn provides a quick, self-guided tour from an upstairs vantage point, an attractive showroom and tasting area, and the fine Hayloft Gallery showing works of local artists. The gift shop sells wine-related items like baskets, grapevine wreaths and stemware, even handmade linen towels. The winery's cat may be snoozing near the wood stove, upon which a pot of mulled wine simmers on chilly days. On nice days, you can sip a superior seyval blanc or an estate chardonnay in a small picnic area overlooking the lake. Open daily 10 to 5, May-December; Friday-Sunday rest of year.

Shopping. Good shops have sprung up in the center of Litchfield and its western environs. Enter the ever-so-suave **Mason Gift Shop,** just off the common, to smell the Arkansas potpourri called Scent of Spring and to check out some delightful gifts. **The**

Litchfield Exchange, where practically everything is handmade, including lovely clothes for children, **Wildlife Landing** (a nature lover's gift store, from figurines and jewelry to bird feeders) and the **Kitchenworks** are worth visiting in the courtyard around the corner. On the green is **Workshop Inc.,** a boutique with updated women's apparel and accessories; downstairs is a gallery of home furnishings, from wicker furniture to pillows and dhurries to two-tone china and unusual placemats. **Barnidge & McEnroe,** a good book store, has an espresso bar up front. **Hayseed** stocks a great selection of cards along with jewelry, sweaters and clothes.

Litchfield Commons, a cluster of shops in an attractive grouping around a brick walk, is worth a stop as you traverse Route 202 west of town. Beyond is **House in the Country Ltd.,** where new homeowners can furnish their digs.

New Preston, a mountain hamlet just down the hillside from Lake Waramaug, is experiencing a flurry of shop openings. We never can leave **J. Seitz & Co.** without wishing we could make a purchase. In a converted garage overlooking a waterfall, Joanna Seitz shows clothing, antiques and accessories from around the world, with a decided emphasis on the American Southwest. The coats made of old Pendleton Indian blankets for $425 are unique, as are the baby jackets made of Southwest blankets ($125) and the handpainted furniture. Decorative housewares and antiques are shown at **Rigmarole.** Other shops worth browsing are **Timothy Mawson Bookseller,** specializing in gardening, landscape architecture and English country life; **Room with a View** for antiques and decorative objects; **Jonathan Peters** for fine linens and lacy things; **The Trumpeter** for antiques and autographs, and **Black Swan Antiques.**

Just south of Route 202 in tiny **Washington Depot,** stop at **Gracious Living** for gifts and jewelry and **Finula's** for women's sportswear. At the **Tulip Tree Collection** you'll find Canadian antiques, porcelain, terra cotta, painted boxes and baskets and the like. **Nimble Fingers** stocks wonderful yarns and handmade sweaters. **Hickory Stick Bookshop,** which also has a large room full of stationery and gifts, is super for browsing.

Extra-Special _____

The Pantry, Titus Road, Washington Depot. (203) 868-0258.

One of our favorite places for lunch and shopping is this upscale gourmet shop lovingly run by Michael and Nancy Ackerman. A counter displays and a blackboard lists the day's offerings from an extensive repertoire, and you can get anything to take out as well. The fare is innovative, with especially good soups, salads, sandwiches and desserts. Our latest spring visit brought forth soups like celery-leek and curried cauliflower. Among entrées ($7.50 to $8.95) were fresh tuna and swordfish niçoise with tarragon carrots, torta rustica, salmon cakes with mixed green salad and a vegetarian chili with watercress cabbage slaw. Continental breakfast is served from 10 to 11:30; a huge sticky bun and cappuccino would make a good break from nipping around Washington Depot's shops. In summer, poached salmon is a favorite, more salads are offered, and soups like gazpacho teem with fresh vegetables. For dessert, chocolate indulgence, mayan torte and pecan tart with ginger ice cream are worth the calories. Tables, decorated perhaps with lilies in flat bowls, are set amidst high-tech shelves on which are just about every exotic chutney, mustard, vinegar, extra-virgin olive oil and the like that you could imagine, as well as kitchenware and tableware, baskets and pottery. Open Tuesday-Saturday 10 to 5:30, lunch from 11:30 to 3:30, tea from 3:30 to 5.

NOTE: The telephone area code for this area and most of Connecticut is scheduled to change to 860 as of October 1996.

Index

481